JN007857

CONTENTS

英検®とは？

文部科学省後援　実用英語技能検定（通称：英検®）は，英語の4技能「読む・聞く・話す・書く」を総合的に測定する試験です。1963年に第1回検定が実施されて以来，日本社会の国際化に伴ってその社会的評価が高まり，現在では，学校・自治体などの団体を対象とした英語力判定テスト「英検IBA®」，子どもを対象としたリスニングテスト「英検Jr.®」を合わせると，年間約420万人が受験しています。大学入試や高校入試，就職試験でも，英語力を測るものさしとして活用されており，入試においての活用校も年々増えています。アメリカ，オーストラリアを中心に，海外でも英検®は，数多くの大学・大学院などの教育機関で，留学時の語学力証明資格として認められています（英検®を語学力証明として認定している海外の教育機関は英検®ウェブサイトに掲載されています）。

本書の使い方

本書は，2021年度第3回から2023年度第2回まで過去6回分の試験問題を掲載した，過去問題集です。**6回分すべてのリスニング問題CDがついています**ので，過去6回の本試験と同じ練習を行うことができます。また，リスニング問題の小問ごとにトラック番号を設定していますので，自分の弱点を知ること，そしてその弱点を強化するためにくり返し問題を聞くことができます。

また本書では，**出題されやすい「文法事項」と「イディオム・口語表現」**を，効率的に学習できるよう分類ごとにまとめてあります。過去問題と併せて活用していただければ幸いです。

英検®では，能力を公正に測定するという試験の性格上，各回・各年度ほぼ同レベルの問題が出されます。したがって，試験の傾向はある程度限定されたパターンをとることになりますので，過去の試験問題をくり返し解き，本試験へと備えてください。

本書を利用される皆様が，一日も早く栄冠を勝ちとられますよう，心より祈念いたします。

本書は，原則として2024年１月15日現在の情報に基づいて編集しています。

まずはここから

受験ガイド

2024年度　試験日程(本会場)

二次試験は２日間設定されています。

第１回	申込期間	2024年3月15日～5月5日（書店は4月19日締切）		
	試験日程	一次試験	2024年6月2日(日)	
		二次試験	A日程	2024年7月7日(日)
			B日程	2024年7月14日(日)
第２回	申込期間	2024年7月1日～9月6日（書店は8月30日締切）		
	試験日程	一次試験	2024年10月6日(日)	
		二次試験	A日程	2024年11月10日(日)
			B日程	2024年11月17日(日)
第３回	申込期間	2024年11月1日～12月13日（書店は12月6日締切）		
	試験日程	一次試験	2025年1月26日(日)	
		二次試験	A日程	2025年3月2日(日)
			B日程	2025年3月9日(日)

※二次試験日程は年齢によって決まります。詳しくは英検®ウェブサイトでご確認ください。
※クレジットカード決済の場合，申込締切は上記の日付の３日後になります。

申込方法

① 個人申込
・特約書店・・・検定料を払い込み，「書店払込証書」と「願書」を必着日までに協会へ郵送。
・インターネット・・・英検® ウェブサイト（https://www.eiken.or.jp/eiken/）から申込。
・コンビニ申込・・・ローソン・ミニストップ「Loppi」，セブン-イレブン・ファミリーマート「マルチコピー機」などの情報端末機から申し込み。

問い合わせ先　公益財団法人 日本英語検定協会
TEL 03-3266-8311　英検® サービスセンター（個人受付）
（平日9:30～17:00　土・日・祝日を除く）

② 団体申込
団体申込に関しましては各団体の責任者の指示に従ってお申し込みください。

成績表

成績表には合否結果のほかに，英検バンド，英検CSEスコアも表示されます。

●**英検バンド**　一次試験，二次試験の合格スコアを起点として，自分がいる位置を＋，－で示したものです。例えば，英検バンドの値が＋1ならばぎりぎりで合格，－1ならば，もう少しのところで合格だったということがわかります。

●**英検CSEスコア**　欧米で広く導入されている，語学能力のレベルを示すCEFR（Common European Framework of Reference for Languages）に関連づけて作られた，リーディング，リスニング，ライティング，スピーキングの4技能を評価する尺度です。英検®のテスト結果の，4技能それぞれのレベルと総合のレベルがスコアとして出されます。

一次試験免除等

一次試験に合格し，二次試験を棄権または不合格になった人に対して，一次試験免除制度があります。申込時に申請をすれば，一次試験合格から1年間は一次試験が免除されます。検定料は，一次試験を受ける場合と同様にかかります。

※検定料，試験時間については英検®ウェブサイトでご確認ください。

英検S-CBTについて

実用英語技能検定準1級，2級，準2級，3級で，新方式英検S-CBTが毎月実施されています。従来型の英検®，英検S-CBTのどちらの方式でも，合格すれば同じ資格が得られます。英検S-CBTの合格証書・証明書とも，従来型の英検®と全く同じものとなります。

◎英検S-CBTの試験実施方法

●コンピューターで4技能（リーディング，ライティング，リスニング，スピーキング）すべてを1日で受験することになります。
●通常の英検®と同じ検定試験で，問題構成・レベルも通常の英検®と同じです。
●英検S-CBTはスピーキングテスト（通常の英検®の二次試験），リスニングテスト，リーディングテスト，ライティングテストの順に試験が行われます。
●リーディングテスト，ライティングテスト，リスニングテストのCSEスコアに基づいて一次試験の合否が判定されますが，一次試験の合否にかかわらず，すべての受験者が4技能を受験し，4技能のCSEスコアを取得することになります。一次試験合格者のみスピーキングテストのCSEスコアに基づき二次試験の合否が判定されます。
●試験はパソコン上で行われるため，Windowsパソコンの基本的な操作（マウスクリック，キーボード入力）ができる必要があります。ただし，ライティングテストはキーボード入力か筆記のいずれかの解答方法を申込時に選択します。

※従来型の試験で二次試験不合格の場合，一次試験免除申請をして英検S-CBTでスピーキングテストのみを受験することができます。
※英検S-CBTで一次試験に合格，二次試験不合格となった場合は，一次試験免除資格が与えられます。次回以降に，一次試験免除申請をして，従来型の英検®を申し込むことができます。

英検S-CBT受験ガイド

◎試験実施月

※原則として毎週土曜日・日曜日，一部会場においては平日・祝日も実施されます。詳しくは英検®ウェブサイトをご参照ください。

第1回…4月，5月，6月，7月
第2回…8月，9月，10月，11月
第3回…12月，翌年1月，2月，3月

◎**持参するもの**

●英検S-CBT受験票，身分証明書。身分証明書として認められるのは，学生証・生徒手帳・健康保険証・運転免許証・パスポート・社員証・住民基本台帳カード・マイナンバーカード・在留カード・健康保険証のコピー（年少者のみ）です。

◎**申し込み**

●申し込みは先着順です。個人申込のみで団体申込は受け付けていません。

●申し込み時に指定した会場で受験します。会場ごとに定員があり，定員になり次第締め切られます。

●英検S-CBT受験票は申込サイトからダウンロードします。

※検定料，試験時間については英検®ウェブサイトでご確認ください。

英検S-CBTスピーキングテストについて

●英検S-CBTのスピーキングテストとは，通常の英検®の二次試験で行われる面接試験のことです。

●英検S-CBTではコンピューターの映像を通して面接委員とやり取りし，録音形式で試験が行われます。

●試験の内容やレベルは通常の英検®二次試験と同じです。二次試験の試験内容については11，19ページをご参照ください。

●英検S-CBTの，特にスピーキングテストではヘッドセットやマイクの使い方，音量の調整にある程度慣れておく必要があります。

英検S-CBTはパソコン上で行われるため，試験当日の流れ，受験方法の面で通常の英検®と異なるところもあります。特に，最初にスピーキングテストが行われる点は大きな違いです。通常の英検®の二次試験と同じと言っても，面接委員と直接対面するか，画面を通して対面するかという違い，パソコンの操作があるかないかという違いは決して小さなことではありません。試験当日の流れ，受験方法の面で通常の英検®と異なるところについては，受験前に必ず英検®ウェブサイトでしっかり確認して，落ち着いてスピーキングテストに臨めるようにしましょう。

要チェック!!

準1級受験の注意点

解答用紙の記入についての注意

筆記試験，リスニングテストともに，別紙の解答用紙にマークシート方式で解答します。解答にあたっては，次の点に留意してください。

1 解答用紙には，はじめに氏名，生年月日などを記入します。生年月日はマーク欄をぬりつぶす指示もありますので，忘れずにマークしてください。

不正確な記入は答案が無効になることもあるので注意してください。

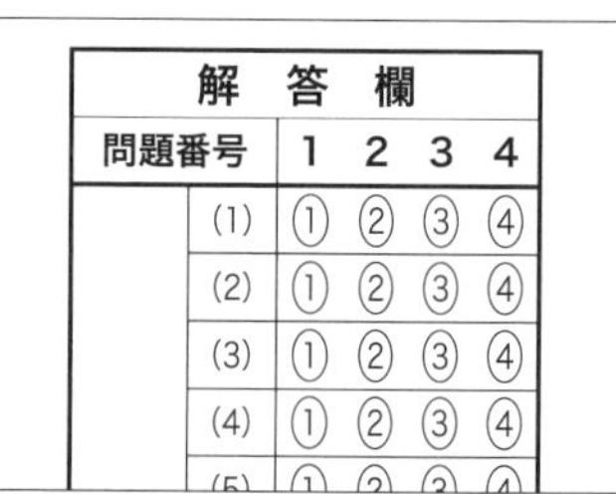

2 マークはHBの黒鉛筆またはシャープペンシルを使って「マーク例」に示された以上の濃さで正確にぬりつぶします。

解答の訂正は，プラスチックの消しゴムで完全に消してから行ってください。

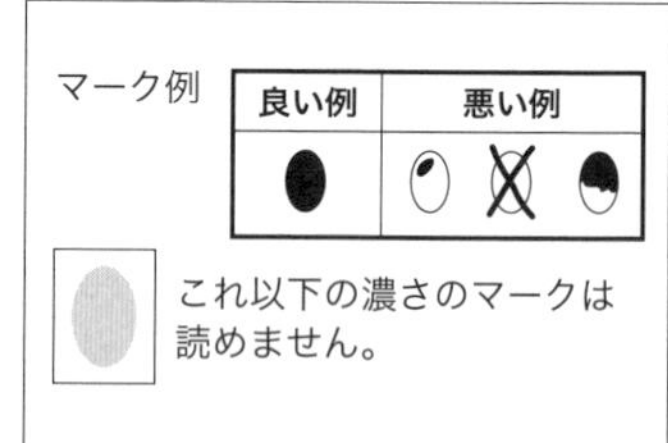

3 解答用紙を汚したり折り曲げたりすることは厳禁です。また，所定の欄以外は絶対に記入しないでください。

準1級のめやすと試験の形式

◉準1級のめやす

準1級のレベルは大学中級程度で，**社会生活で求められる英語を理解し，使用できることが求められます。**

〈審査領域〉

読む……**社会性の高い分野の文章を理解することができる。**

聞く……**社会性の高い内容を理解することができる。**

話す……**社会性の高い話題についてやりとりすることができる。**

書く……**社会性の高い話題についてまとまりのある文章を書くことができる。**

◉準1級試験の内容と形式

一次試験ではまずはじめに筆記試験が行われ，その後にリスニングテストが行われます。二次試験は英語での面接試験で，一次試験の合格者のみを対象とし，一次試験実施後およそ30日後に行われます。

一次試験・筆記（33問・90分）

筆記試験は，４つの大問で構成されており，問題数は33問です（2024年度第１回検定から）。この33問の問題を90分かけて解きます。

2024年度第1回の検定から，問題構成・内容は以下の通りです。

大問	内容	問題数
1	**短文または会話文の穴うめ問題** 短文または1往復の会話文を読み，文中の空所に適切な語句を補う。	18問
2	**長文の穴うめ問題** 説明文，評論文などを読み，パッセージの空所に，文脈に合う適切な語句を補う。	6問
3	**長文の内容に関する問題** 説明文，評論文などを読み，これらの英文の内容に関する質問に答える。	7問
4	**英語の文章の要約を英語で記述する問題** 200語程度の文章の要約を60～70語程度で書く。 **与えられたトピックに対し，意見とその根拠を英文で論述する問題** あるトピックに関する質問に対して，自分の意見とその理由を書く。	2問 （記述式）

一次試験・リスニング（29問・約30分）

リスニングテストは，第1部～第3部で構成されており，問題数は29問です。この29問の問題を約30分かけて解きます。

大問	内容	問題数
1	**会話の内容に関する質問** 会話文を聞き，会話の内容に関する質問に答える。	12問
2	**英文の内容に関する質問** 説明文を聞き，その内容に関する質問に答える。	12問
3	**Real-Life形式の放送内容に関する質問** 自分自身が置かれている状況や場面を読んだうえでアナウンスなどを聞き，その内容に関する質問に答える。	5問

《一次試験で用いられた主な場面と題材》

場面………家庭，学校，職場，地域（各種店舗・公共施設を含む），電話，アナウンス，講義など。

題材………社会生活一般，芸術，文化，歴史，教育，科学，自然・環境，医療，テクノロジー，ビジネス，政治など。

二次試験・面接（約８分）

二次試験は，約８分の受験者対面接委員の１対１の面接です。**面接室への入室から退室までのすべて**が採点の対象になり，**応答内容，発音，語い，文法，語法，情報量，積極的にコミュニケーションを図ろうとする意欲や態度**などで評価されます。

◉二次試験の流れ

① 面接室に入室します。面接委員にあいさつをするとよいでしょう（Good morning./Good afternoon.）。

② 着席するよう指示されます。着席後，名前と受験する級の確認などを含めて簡単な質問をされるほか，面接委員と日常的な会話を行います。

③ 英語で指示が書かれた４コマのイラストつきカードが１枚渡されます。カードを黙読し，イラスト内容のナレーションを考える時間が１分与えられます。

④ その後，カードの指示文に従ってナレーションを始めるよう指示が出されます。ナレーションの言い出し部分は「問題カード」に印刷されていますから，必ずその言い出し部分を使って，ナレーションを始めます。ナレーションの時間は２分間です。それ以上続く場合は，途中でも中止させられます。

⑤ その後，４つの質問が出題されます。最初の質問の後でカードを伏せるよう指示（Please turn over the card. など）が出たら，すみやかに伏せてください。
●質問１……イラストに関連した質問。
●質問２，３…カードのトピックに関連した質問。
●質問４……カードのトピックにやや関連した，社会性のある内容についての質問。質問の前に，話題を導入する文が示されます（2024年度第１回の検定より）。

《二次試験で用いられた主な話題》
在宅勤務，レストランでの喫煙，チャイルドシート，住民運動，キャッチセールス，護身術など。

これでバッチリ!!

準1級の傾向と対策

英検®は出題パターンがある程度決まっています。2024年度第1回の検定からライティングテストの形式と筆記試験の問題数が一部変更されますが，全体として大きな違いはありませんので，過去の問題を何度も解いて傾向をつかみましょう。慣れてきたら，本番を想定した時間配分で解いてみると効果的です。

一次試験・筆記テスト

1 短文または会話文の穴うめ問題

★出題傾向

短文または会話文の（　　）の中に適する単語または語句を4つの選択肢から選び，英文を完成させる。単語→イディオムの出題順がほぼ定着している。
※2024年度第1回の検定から，問題数が25問から18問になりました。

対 策

- **単語とイディオムの知識が問われる。**
- **単語で出題されるのは，名詞，動詞，形容詞などの基本的な品詞がほとんどである。**
- **イディオムでは句動詞（break into，stand byなど）が中心。**

2 長文の穴うめ問題

★出題傾向

・説明文，評論文の空所にあてはまるものを，複数の語句からなる選択肢から選ぶ。大問が2題あり，それぞれに空所が3箇所ずつある。選択肢はそれぞれ4つ。

●長文の体裁

3段落構成の説明文，評論文。語数は250語～300語程度。

●長文のテーマ

過去2年間で出題されたテーマは，最近の題材を中心として，自然科学，環境，社会情勢・問題，医療に関するものがほとんどである。

対 策

- (　　) 前後の文脈を正確に把握し，論理的展開と矛盾しない答えを選ぶ能力が要求される。
- (　　) の前後にある語句との文法的なつながり，時制には特に注意が必要。
- 2大問中，1～2問は空所に適する接続語句を選ぶ問題なので，空所前後の関係を読み取る能力に加え，接続語句の知識が必要。
- イディオムや決まった形の表現の知識も必要である。

3 長文の内容に関する問題

★出題傾向

説明文，評論文の内容についての質問に対する解答を選ぶものと，内容を表す文を完成させるのに適する英語を選ぶものがある。大問が2題あり，最初の大問は小問3題，2つめの大問は小問4題。選択肢はそれぞれ4つである。
※2024年度第1回の検定から，大問数が3題から2題になりました。

●長文の体裁

3～5段落構成の説明文，評論文。2024年度第1回の検定からは，400語程度と520語程度の2題になることが予想される。

●長文のテーマ

最近の題材を中心として，自然科学，科学技術，環境，社会情勢・問題，文化，法律，医療，教育などをテーマとした英文が出題されている。

対 策

- タイトルと第1段落冒頭から，その英文で論じられている主題をつかむ。
- 設問は，段落の順番つまり論旨展開の流れにそって用意されるのがふつうである。これを逆に利用し，「質問文→対応する段落」の順番で読んでいけば，短時間で段落ごとの論点を見つけることができる。
- 各段落や英文全体の論点をつかむうえで重要なポイントとなるのは，①代名詞や代動詞表現（do，do it，do thisなど），②接続語句，③同じ内容の言い換え，④対照表現など。
- 選択肢の英文は本文そのままではなく，同じ意味の語句で言い換えられたり，簡潔に表現されたりしていることが多い。

4 ライティングテスト

★出題傾向

※2024年度第1回の検定から，文章の要約を書く問題が追加されました。

●要約問題

200語程度の文章の内容を60～70語程度の英語で要約する。その際，できる限り自分の言葉で書くという条件がある。

●意見論述問題

与えられたトピックについて120語～150語でエッセイを書く。その際，①与えられているPOINTSから2つを選んで自分の考えを支持する内容(理由,例など)を盛り込む，②「導入→本文→結論」という構成にする，という条件がある。

質問文では，Should A ～「Aは～するべきか」，Agree or disagree「賛成か，反対か」などで始まる英文の中で具体的なトピックが示される。

自分の考えを支持する英文の観点となるPOINTSが4つ示される。

●テーマ

要約問題，意見論述問題ともに，注目度の高い，社会的な問題に関するトピックが予測される。

対 策

- 主語，動詞の一致などの基本的なことを含め，文法的に正しい英文を書く。
- 理由を述べる文では，becauseなど，「理由」であることをはっきりさせる語句を使う。
- 語数の過不足に注意する。
- 意見論述問題では，質問内容を正しくつかむ。
- 意見論述問題では，与えられているPOINTSから必ず2つを選ぶ。

★ライティングテストの採点に関する観点と注意点

ライティングテストの採点にあたっての観点と解答作成時の注意点は以下のとおりである。

●採点の観点

1．内容

要約問題：与えられた英文の内容が正しく書かれているか

要約文を書くので，与えられた英文の内容と異なることを書いたり，自分の考えや感情などを盛り込まないようにする。

意見論述問題：課題で求められている内容(意見とその理由)が含まれているかどうか

自分の意見とその理由をはっきりさせ，意見を支える論拠や説明を説得力のあるものにする。単に「安いから」や「便利だから」といったことだけではなく，安くなったり便利になったりすることで生じる具体的な利点を挙げる。

2．構成

要約問題：与えられた英文の構成に沿っているか

与えられた英文の段落構成と同じ構成,流れでまとめる。英文が「テーマの提示」→「テーマとなるもののプラス面」→「テーマとなるもののマイナス面」という流れであれば，それと同じ流れで要約文を構成する。

意見論述問題：英文の構成や流れがわかりやすく論理的であるか

伝える情報を羅列するのではなく，順番や流れを論理的にする。展開を示す接続語句を正しく使って，自分の意見とその理由，英文全体の構成をわかりやすくする。

3．語い　課題に相応しい語いを正しく使えているか

なるべく多様な語いや表現を使い，同じ語いや表現の繰り返しを避ける。

4．文法　文構造のバリエーションやそれらを正しく使えているか

多様な文のパターンを使い，同じような構文の繰り返しを避ける。

●意見論述問題解答作成時の注意点

英検®ウェブサイトでは,「カジュアルな服装を許容する会社が増えるかどうか」というTOPICを例に挙げて,解答作成にあたっての下記の注意点が公開されている。それぞれの詳細と具体例をウェブサイトで確認しておこう。

1．TOPICに示された問いに答えていない

TOPICに示された問いの答えになっていない場合や，全く関係のないTOPICについて書かれていると判断された場合は，上記のすべての観点で0点と採点されることがある。

2．英語ではない単語を使った解答

英語以外の単語を使う必要がある場合は，その言語を理解できない人にもわかるように説明を加える。そうした説明がない場合は減点の対象となる。

3．意見と矛盾する理由や説明がある

自分が述べた意見に矛盾する内容の理由や説明を書いてある。

4．理由に対する説明や補足がない

理由について，具体的な例や説明がなく，説得力に欠ける。

5．関係のない内容が含まれている

TOPICに示された問いに無関係の内容や，他の部分と矛盾する内容が書かれている。

一次試験・リスニングテスト

対 策（全リスニング問題共通）

英文はすべて1回しか読まれない。全体で約30分，合計29題のリスニングでは，集中力をいかに持続させるかも聞き取りの重要なポイントとなる。また，指示文はすべて英語で読まれるので，あらかじめ試験形式を把握しておくことが必要。

【第1部】会話の内容に関する質問

★出題傾向

70語～100語程度の会話（電話での会話も含む）を聞き，その内容に関する質問の答えを4つの選択肢から選ぶ。

●放送されるもの

会話→質問文。

対 策

- 放送文が始まる前に，問題用紙の選択肢に目を通しておき，会話の場面や質問の内容（場所，状況，時間，人物の行動など）を予想する。
- 会話の内容はさまざまで，家庭や職場などでの代表的なシチュエーションが次々と登場する。放送文ごとに素早く頭を切り換えることが大切。
- 放送文の一部が聞き取れなくても，全体として状況がつかめれば，消去法で選択肢を絞り込み，正解に到達できることが多い。
- 会話文中に現れる質問文，命令文，依頼文などには特に注意。
- 会話文中に難しい固有名詞が現れることもあるが，聞き取れなくても，少なくともそれが人名なのか地名なのかという段階で理解することが大切。

【第２部】文の内容に関する質問

★出題傾向

２段落から成る130語～150語の文章を聞き，その内容に関する質問の答えを４つの選択肢から選ぶ。１つの文章につき，質問が２つあり，１つの段落について１問ずつ用意されている。

●放送されるもの

英文→質問文。

対 策

- 第１部同様，放送文が始まる前に選択肢に目を通しておくと，聞き取りのポイントを絞ることができる。
- 英文の種類は，基本的に毎回すべて説明文である。テーマは自然科学，科学技術，環境，社会情勢・問題，文化，医療など。
- 説明文なので，第１文からテーマがわかることが多い。
- 逆接のbutやhoweverが出てきた直後の内容や，因果関係を述べている箇所は，特に注意して聞き取るようにする。質問で尋ねてくる確率が高い。
- 難しい固有名詞が出てくることが多いので，正確に聞き取れなくても，それが人名なのか地名なのかという段階で理解できるようにする。
- 西暦や数量を表す数字は質問に絡んでくる場合が多い。

【第３部】Real-Life形式の放送内容に関する質問

★出題傾向

自分自身が置かれている状況を読んだうえでアナウンスなどを聞き，その内容に関する質問の答えを４つの選択肢から選ぶ。

●読むもの・放送されるもの

読むもの：問題用紙に，自分が置かれている状況を示すSituationと質問，答えの選択肢４つが書かれている。Situationは家庭，職場，旅行先，店など，実生活に則した場面でのさまざまな状況。放送の前に，Situationと質問を読む時間が10秒与えられる。

放送されるもの：それぞれのSituationでのアナウンス，店員の発言，家族・友人・同僚などからの電話など。

対策

- Situationの内容をよく読んで，自分が置かれている状況を理解する。未経験の状況である場合もあるので，想像力を働かせる必要もある。
- 選択肢は，名詞句，不定詞で始まるもの，動詞の原形で始まるものなど，それぞれの問題で同じ形になっている場合がほとんどなので，Situationと質問から放送される内容と聞き取りのポイントを予想する。
- 質問はwhatまたはwhichで始まるものがほとんどで，自分がとるべき行動を問うものなので，自分がするべきことを予想することで聞き取りのポイントもつかみやすくなる。
- 解答者自身がするべきことを問われるので，放送文中からわかる周囲の状況のほかに，指示や依頼を述べている箇所には特に注意が必要。

二次試験・面接

★出題傾向

問題カードには英文の指示と４コマのイラストが印刷されている。面接試験は，以下のような流れで行われる。

①面接委員と簡単な日常会話を行う
②英文を黙読し，イラスト内容を説明するナレーションを考える（１分間）
③カードの指示文に従ってナレーションを行う（２分間）
④イラストの４コマ目に関する質問（No. 1）
⑤カードのトピックに関連する質問（No. 2，3）
⑥カードのトピックにやや関連した，社会性のある内容に関する質問（No. 4）
※2024年度第１回の検定から，No. ４の質問の前に話題が示されます。

対策

- **答えの正確さ（発音・語い・文法など）のほか，情報量や表現方法（意欲や態度を含む）も評価対象となる。入退室時の挨拶，ナレーションの前の面接委員との会話も含めて，十分な声量で自信を持って受け答えしよう。**
- **面接委員が尋ねる質問は，問題カードに書かれていないので，その質問内容を正確に聞き取ることが重要となる。**
- **ナレーションに続く４つの質問は，いずれも解答者の意見を問うもので，イラストの内容を正しく理解し，質問に対して短時間で答えを出す必要がある。質問は社会全般に関わるものなので，日頃から社会で起こっている事柄や社会情勢に関心を持ち，自分の基本的な考えをまとめておくことが重要。できるだけ面接委員と視線を合わせながら答える姿勢も大切。**
- **No. １ではイラスト４コマ目を見て，もし自分がイラストの人物だったらどう考えるかを問われる。最初の黙読の段階で自分の基本的な意見を決めておき，答えるときはそのように考える理由も加えるべきである。**
- **No. 2と3は原則として，カードのトピックに関する意見や考え方に同意するかしないかを問う質問だが，ここでも根拠となることや具体例などを加え，意見としてまとまりのある英文で答えることが重要である。同意する / しない→理由・根拠→結論という流れで答えるとよい。**
- **No. 4はカードのトピックをさらに広い視点で捉えたうえでの質問。まずは質問の前に提供される話題を正しく理解することが重要。No. 2，3同様に理論的に意見をまとめよう。**

まとめて復習

準1級でよく出る文法

準1級レベルの文法

ここでは，準１級の文法問題や英文読解に必要な文法事項の基本を確認します。効率的に学習することができるよう，設問形式別にまとめてあります。

※付属の赤シートで答えを隠して取り組みましょう。

●語句選択補充問題 ――（　）に適するものを選びましょう。

1 高速道路を運転するのは避けた方が良い。混雑しているだろう。
We should avoid （ ③ ） on the expressway. It will be crowded.
① to drive　② drive　③ driving　④ to driving

解説 avoidは動名詞を目的語にとる。

2 その男は多くの人々に店から逃げて行くところを見られた。
The man was （ ① ） away from the shop by many people.
① seen running　② seeing to run　③ seen run　④ seeing running

解説 知覚動詞seeを受動態で使った文。

3 あなたがここに着くころには，私たちは夕食を終えているだろう。
We will （ ④ ） dinner by the time you arrive here.
① be eaten　② be eating　③ be finished　④ have finished

解説 未来完了の文。

4 私は空港に着くとすぐに母に電話をかけた。
（ ② ） at the airport, I called my mother.
① In arriving　② Upon arriving　③ With arriving　④ Arriving

解説 〈upon＋動名詞〉「～するとすぐに」。

5 劇場でおじに会うとはまったく思わなかった。
（ ④ ） I would meet my uncle at the theater.
① Had not I thought　② Not I had thought
③ Never I had thought　④ Never had I thought

解説 倒置の文。

6 この問題について，信頼できる人なら誰にでも相談した方がよい。
You should consult （ ② ） about this problem.
① whoever to trust　② whomever you trust
③ whoever trusted　④ whomever to be trusted

解説 目的格の複合関係代名詞。

事項

7　彼女がもう少し早く起きていれば始発電車に乗れただろうに。
If she (　②　) up a little earlier, she (　②　) the first train.
①　had gotten, could caught　②　had gotten, could have caught
③　got, had caught　④　got, could have caught

解説 仮定法過去完了の文。

8　締め切りが近づいているので，今夜は眠る時間がほとんどない。
(　①　) the deadline (　①　), I have little time to sleep tonight.
①　With, approaching　②　With, approach
③　On, approaching　④　On, approached

解説 付帯状況を表すwith。

9　あなたと同じように，私もテレビドラマには興味がない。
I'm not interested in TV dramas (　④　) than you are.
①　no more　②　much less　③　no less　④　any more

解説 not ～ any more than ...「～でないのは…でないのと同じ」。

10　私が帰宅するまでに部屋は掃除されていなかった。
The room (　②　) by the time I got home.
①　was not been cleaned　②　had not been cleaned
③　has not cleaned　④　had never got cleaning

解説 受動態の過去完了。

11　マイクはどんな仕事に就けばよいのかわからないで困っています。あなたが彼の父親だとしたら，彼にどうするように助言しますか。
Mike is at a loss as to what career to pursue. (　③　) that you were his father, what (　③　) you advise him to do?
①　If, will　②　If, would
③　Suppose, would　④　Suppose, will

解説 仮定法過去の文。Suppose that ～＝If ～

12　私は父の故郷について聞かれて何も言うことができなかった。
I could not say anything (　②　) about the hometown of my father.
①　when questioning　②　when questioned
③　though I questioned　④　though questioning

解説 接続詞の後の〈S＋V〉(I was) が省略された文。

●語句補充問題 ——（　　）に適する語を入れましょう。

1 私はパスポートを更新してもらう必要がある。

I need to get my passport (**renewed**).

解説 〈get＋O＋過去分詞〉「Oを～してもらう」。

2 この夏は数週間雨が降らず，多くの植物が枯れる原因となった。

We had no rain for several weeks this summer, (**causing**) many plants to die.

解説 結果を表す分詞構文。

3 彼女には息子が2人いて，その1人はプロ野球チームの一員だ。

She has two sons, (**one**) (**of**) (**whom**) is a member of a professional baseball team.

解説 非制限用法の関係代名詞。

4 旅行に行くのに朝早く家を出たので，私たちは予想していたよりも多くの場所を訪れることができた。

(**Having**) (**left**) home for the trip early in the morning, we were able to visit more places than we had expected.

解説 完了形の分詞構文。

5 父は，私が高校を卒業したら留学することを許してくれた。

My father allowed (**me**) (**to**) (**study**) abroad after I graduated from high school.

解説 〈allow＋O＋to *do*〉「Oが～するのを許可する」。

6 誰が来ようともドアを開けてはいけない。

Don't open the door (**whoever**) (**comes**).

解説 主格の複合関係代名詞。

7 私はあなたが駅に着くまで20分くらい待っていた。

I (**had**) (**been**) (**waiting**) for you for about 20 minutes when you arrived at the station.

解説 過去完了進行形。

8 息子は熱がある。だから釣りには行かせないよ。

My son has a fever. That's (**why**) I won't let him go fishing.

解説 That's why ～「そういうわけで～，だから～」。

9 私はそのレストランに行くといつもスパゲッティーを食べる。

I eat spaghetti at that restaurant (**whenever**) (**I**) (**go**) there.

解説 whenever「～するときはいつでも」。

10 そのアメリカ人の歌手が流ちょうな日本語でスピーチをして，私たちは大いに驚いた。

The American singer made a speech in fluent Japanese, (**which**) surprised us very much.

解説 非制限用法の関係代名詞。

11 子供たちを起こさないように静かに部屋に入ってね。

Go into the room quietly (**so**) (**that**) you might not wake the children.

解説 目的を表すso that。

12 もう一度パリへ行ったら，私は3回そこに行ったことになる。

If I go to Paris again, I (**will**) (**have**) (**been**) there three times.

解説 未来完了の文。

13 姉はたとえ勉強で忙しくても，私を車で駅まで連れて行ってくれた。

My sister drove me to the station, (**even**) (**though**) she was busy with her studies.

解説 even thoughの後には事実が続く。

14 調査に基づくと，この村の人口はこの10年間で30パーセント減少した。

(**Based**) (**on**) research, the population of this village has decreased 30 percent over the past ten years.

解説 過去分詞で始まる分詞構文。

15 この規則が適用されない例外的なケースがいくつかある。

There are some exceptional cases (**in**) (**which**) this rule does not apply.

解説 〈前置詞＋関係代名詞〉。

16 その国の言葉についてほとんど理解していなかったけれども，少女は何とかそこの人々とうまくやっていくことができた。

(**Though**) (**understanding**) little about the language of the country, the girl managed to get along with the people there.

解説 接続詞を伴う分詞構文。

17 たとえ彼にお金がたくさんあったとしても，彼は生き方を変えないだろう。

(**Even**) (**if**) he had a lot of money, he would not change his life-style.

解説 仮定法過去の文。even ifの後には事実に反する内容が続く。

18 幹線道路でひどい自動車事故が起こったことが明らかになった。
(**It**) became clear (**that**) a terrible car accident had happened on the highway.

解説 that以下を受ける形式主語のit。

19 もう試験は終わったのだから，休暇の計画でも立てよう。
(**Now**) (**that**) the exam is over, I'll plan my vacation.

解説 now that「(今は) ～なのだから」。

20 とても寒かったが，ボランティアたちは朝早く災害現場へ出て行った。
(**It**) (**being**) very cold, the volunteers went out to the disaster site early in the morning.

解説 独立分詞構文。

21 彼と話して初めて，彼がいかに知的であるかがわかった。
(**Not**) (**until**) I talked with him (**did**) I realize how intelligent he was.

解説 倒置の文。

22 天気予報を調べておくんだった。
I (**should**) (**have**) checked the weather forecast.

解説 〈should have＋過去分詞〉後悔を表す。

●語句整序問題 ――（　）内の語句を正しく並べかえましょう。

※(　)の中では，文のはじめにくる語も小文字になっています。

1 火事のせいで森の半分が消滅した。
The fire (to / half / disappear / the forest / caused / of).

解答 caused half of the forest to disappear **解説** 〈cause＋O＋to *do*〉「Oに～させる［Oが～する原因となる］」。

2 どうしてあなたはあんな失礼な振る舞いができるの？
(you / rude / behave / in / could / a / how / such) way?

解答 How could you behave in such a rude **解説** 反語表現の文。

3 彼は月に50冊も本を読む。
He (books / less / month / than / reads / fifty / no / a).

解答 reads no less than fifty books a month **解説** no less than ～「～ほども多くの」。

4 電車の遅延のせいで，そこに着くには本来の３倍の時間がかかるだろう。
(times / as / take / there / long / to / will / three / as / it / get) it should because of the train delay.

解答 It will take three times as long to get there as **解説** It takes ～「(時間が) ～かかる」。～ times as ... as ―「―の～倍…」。

5 私たちが乗る飛行機は嵐のために遅れると予測されている。

Our plane (delayed / of / is / to / because / expected / be) the storm.

解答 is expected to be delayed because of **解説** **〈expect＋O＋to *do*〉「Oが～すると予期［期待］する」を受動態で使った文。**

6 この庭園では多くの種類の花が栽培されているのを見ることができる。

We can (kinds / grown / many / of / flowers / see / being) in this garden.

解答 see many kinds of flowers being grown **解説** **〈see＋O＋現在分詞〉「Oが～しているのを見る」。being grownは受け身の形。**

7 あなたの支援がなかったら，この計画は失敗していただろう。

(support / not / it / your / had / for / been), this project would have failed.

解答 Had it not been for your support **解説** **仮定法過去完了の倒置文。**

8 湖にはほとんど水が残っていなかったので，村の人々は雨乞いをした。

(left / being / the lake / little / there / in / water), people in the village prayed for rain.

解答 There being little water left in the lake **解説** **There is ～構文の分詞構文。**

9 私は犬が小川を泳いで渡るのを見た。

I (across / small / swim / a dog / river / saw / a).

解答 saw a dog swim across a small river **解説** **〈see＋O＋動詞の原形〉「Oが～するのを見る」。**

10 あなたのいなくなった猫はどのような見た目なのか教えてください。

Please tell (cat / like / what / me / missing / looks / your).

解答 me what your missing cat looks like **解説** **間接疑問文。**

11 ジョンはアジアの国々へ旅行することを考えていたが，彼の父親の病気のために旅行することができなくなった。

John was thinking of traveling to some Asian countries, but (for / made / his / travel / illness / impossible / it / him / father's / to).

解答 his father's illness made it impossible for him to travel **解説** **無生物主語の文。itは形式的な目的語。**

12 私は両親に，その大学に入学するには相当な努力が必要だと言われた。

I was told by my parents that (of / would / to / accepted / take / a lot / it / effort / be) by that college.

解答 it would take a lot of effort to be accepted **解説** **itは形式主語。**

13 あなたが私の立場だったらどうしているだろうか。

(doing / were / be / if / you / what / would / in / you) my place?

解答 What would you be doing if you were in **解説** **仮定法過去の文。**

まとめて復習

準1級でよく出るイディ

準1級レベルのイディオム

ここでは，準1級でよく出るイディオムを集めました。効率的に学習できるよう，文の中での使い方を覚えられる例文形式で紹介しています。

日本文の意味を表す英文になるように，（　　）に適する英語を入れましょう。

※付属の赤シートで答えを隠して取り組みましょう。

名詞を含むイディオム

1. We (**took**) (**advantage**) (**of**) the good weather to enjoy cycling.
私たちは好天気を利用してサイクリングを楽しんだ。

2. The reconstruction of the castle will (**give**) the local economy a (**boost**).
その城の再建は地元経済に活気を与えるだろう。

3. Buying daily necessities (**in**) (**bulk**) allows you a bit of savings.
日用品をまとめ買いすれば，ちょっとしたお金の節約につながる。

4. Using a spell-checking tool saves you a (**bundle**) (**of**) time.
スペルチェックの機能を使えば，多くの［大幅に］時間を節約できる。

5. The hurricane did devastating (**damage**) (**to**) the coastal areas.
そのハリケーンは沿岸地域に壊滅的な被害をもたらした。

6. These days, many families are struggling to (**make**) (**ends**) (**meet**).
最近では，多くの家庭が家計をやりくりするのに四苦八苦している。

7. Sarah was brought (**face**) (**to**) (**face**) with the horrors of war.
サラは戦争の恐ろしさに直面した。

8. Larry will (**land**) (**on**) his (**feet**) whatever happens to him.
何事が起ころうとも，ラリーはきっとうまく切り抜けるだろう。

9. Kate didn't want to (**make**) a (**fuss**) over nothing.
ケイトはつまらないことで騒ぎ立てたくなかった。

10. You should (**have**) (**a**) (**go**) at fishing in mountain streams.
ぜひ渓流釣りをやってみるべきだよ。

11. Skipping meals to lose weight (**does**) (**harm**) to your health.
減量のために食事を抜くことは健康に悪影響を及ぼす。

12. You need something to take your (**mind**) (**off**) work.
あなたには何か仕事を忘れさせてくれるものが必要ですよ。

13. These days, many companies allow workers to (**take**) a (**nap**).
最近では，多くの会社が社員に昼寝をすることを許可している。

14. That noise really gets (**on**) my (**nerves**).
あの騒音は本当に神経に障る。

15. We're running out of time, so you should (**stick**) (**to**) the point.
時間がないので，問題点からそれないようにお願いします。

16. Social unrest sometimes (**gives**) (**rise**) to riots.
社会不安は時として暴動を引き起こす。

17. Running every day is one of the best ways to get (**in**) (**shape**).
毎日ジョギングすることは体を鍛えるのに最も良い方法の1つだ。

18. George always takes (**sides**) (**with**) his sister.
ジョージはいつも妹の味方をする［肩を持つ］。

19. The police officer (**lost**) (**sight**) of the suspect in the crowd.
警官は人混みの中で容疑者を見失った。

20. The airliner came to a (**full**) (**stop**) at the gate.
旅客機はゲートのところで完全に停止した。

21. Our boss often (**loses**) his (**temper**) over trivial things.
私たちの上司はよくささいなことでカッとなる)。

22. The drought (**took**) a heavy (**toll**) on crops.
干ばつで農作物に大きな被害が出た。

23. Please get (**in**) (**touch**) (**with**) us right away if you have a problem.
問題があれば，すぐに私たちに連絡してください。

24. Peter keeps (**in**) (**touch**) with his family by phone.
ピーターは電話で家族と絶えず連絡を取り合っている。

25. Terry walks every morning (**with**) a (**view**) to improving his health.
テリーは健康を増進する目的で毎朝散歩している。

動詞を含むイディオム①

1. Coffee (**accounts**) (**for**) more than 10% of the country's export revenue.
コーヒーはその国の輸出収入の10パーセント以上を占めている。

2. The total development cost (**added**) (**up**) to 50 million dollars.
開発費の総額は5,000万ドルに上った。

3. Many people (**associate**) Canada (**with**) maple syrup.
多くの人々はカナダと聞くとメープルシロップを連想する。

4. The party leader refused to (**back**) (**down**) his comments on the refugee issue.
その党首は難民問題に関する彼の発言を撤回するのを拒んだ。

5. We should (**back**) (**off**) and let Andy make his own decision.
私たちは口出し［干渉］をやめて，アンディに自分で決めさせるべきだよ。

6. Anne is a bit nervous before an important game. Just (**bear**) (**with**) her.
アンは大事な試合の前で少し緊張しているの。大目に見てあげてちょうだい。

7. Negotiations between the two countries (**broke**) (**down**).
その２国間の交渉は決裂した。

8. A fire (**broke**) (**out**) downtown and destroyed several stores.
繁華街で火災が起きて，いくつかの店が焼けた。

9. The bribery scandal may (**bring**) (**down**) the minister.
その贈収賄事件は大臣をその座から引きずり下ろすかもしれない。

10. The idea of outsourcing some work was (**brought**) (**up**) at the meeting.
会議では作業の一部を外注する案が提出された。

11. I know you're busy, but be careful not to (**burn**) (**out**).
忙しいのはわかるが，くれぐれも燃え尽きないように注意してね。

12. A bomb disposal team was (**called**) (**in**) to deal with a suspicious package.
不審な荷物を処理するために爆弾処理班が呼ばれた。

13. The fireworks were (**called**) (**off**) because of rain.
雨のため，花火大会は中止になった。

14. Don't get (**carried**) (**away**) and spend too much money.
あまり調子に乗ってお金を使いすぎないようにね。

15. Mike didn't (**catch**) (**on**) to what was going on.
マイクには何が起きているのか理解（することが）できなかった。

16. John had to work hard to (**catch**) (**up**) on his studies.
ジョンは勉強の遅れを取り戻すのに必死に勉強しなければならなかった。

17. Let's (**check**) (**out**) the lowest price of the camera on the Internet.
そのカメラの最安値をネットで調べよう。

18. Bill and Judy (**chipped**) (**in**) to buy their father a tie.
ビルとジュディーはお金を出し合って父親にネクタイを買ってあげた。

19. How's your history report (**coming**) (**along**)?
歴史のレポートの進み具合はどう？

20. Sarah (**came**) (**down**) with the flu the day before her trip.
サラは旅行に行く前日にインフルエンザにかかってしまった。

21. The new printer (**comes**) (**in**) three colors —— white, red, and black.
この新しいプリンターは白，赤，黒の３色がそろっている。

22. Lucy (**came**) (**into**) a large amount of money after her grandmother died.
祖母が亡くなったあと，ルーシーは莫大なお金を相続した。

23. All we can do now is wait and see how things (**come**) (**out**).
今私たちにできるのは事態がどうなるか見守ることだけだ。

24. Why don't you (**come**) (**over**) to my house this afternoon?
今日の午後，僕の家に（遊びに）来ませんか？

25. Eating high-calorie fast food every day (**contributes**) (**to**) obesity.
高カロリーのファースフードを毎日食べることは肥満の原因となる。

26. Ralph is someone you can (**count**) (**on**) in time of need.
ラルフはいざという時に頼りにできる人だ。

27. Alan (**covered**) (**for**) Helen while she was on vacation.
ヘレンが休暇をとっている間，アランが彼女の代わりを務めた。

28. Energy-saving air conditioners will help (**cut**) (**back**) on electricity bills.
省エネ型のエアコンは電気代を節約する助けとなるでしょう。

動詞を含むイディオム②

1. I just can't afford to (**dish**) (**out**) $2,000 for replacing computers.
コンピュータの買い換えに２千ドルも出費する余裕はない。

2. You should not (**drag**) your children (**into**) adult affairs.
子供たちを大人の事情に巻き込むべきではない。

3. The sales meeting (**dragged**) (**on**) for hours.
営業会議は何時間も延々と続いた。

4. His presentation was good, but he (**dragged**) it (**out**) a bit too long.
彼の発表はよかったが，彼は少し長々と引っ張りすぎた。

5. Jack didn't want to get (**drawn**) (**into**) their arguments, so he kept silent.
ジャックは彼らの議論に巻き込まれたくなかったので，黙っていた。

6. Abel (**drew**) (**on**) his knowledge of the law to write the courtroom mystery.
アベルは法律に関する知識を活用して，その法廷ミステリーを書いた。

7. As the financial resources (**dried**) (**up**), the project failed halfway.
財源が枯渇したため，その計画は途中で行き詰まった。

8. Adam has some savings in the bank to (**fall**) (**back**) on in an emergency.
アダムはいざという時に当てにできる預金が銀行に少しある。

9. Sam almost (**fell**) (**for**) the salesperson's smooth talk.
サムはもう少しでセールスマンのうまい話に引っかかるところだった。

10. The responsibility for caring for his aging parents (**fell**) (**on**) his shoulders.
年老いた両親の介護の責任が彼の肩にのしかかった。

11. The construction plan (**fell**) (**through**) due to local objection.
その建設計画は地元住民の反対で失敗に終わった。

12. Brian tried to (**figure**) (**out**) what's wrong with his microwave.
ブライアンは彼の電子レンジのどこが悪いのか突き止めようとした。

13. Could you (**fill**) (**in**) for me at the meeting this afternoon?
今日の午後の会議，私の代わりに出ていただけますか。

14. You just need to (**fill**) (**out**) this application form to register.
登録するにはこの申し込み用紙に記入するだけでよいのです。

15. The restaurant (**fills**) (**up**) quickly after six every evening.
そのレストランは毎晩６時を過ぎるとすぐに一杯になる。

16. Now many manufacturers are (**focusing**) (**on**) reducing the cost.
今や多くのメーカーはコスト削減に集中している。

17. Thomas finally got (**around**) (**to**) rearranging his room last weekend.
先週末になってトーマスはようやく部屋の模様替えをする時間がとれた。

18. Alice tried to (**get**) (**at**) the truth about the case.
アリスはその事件の真相を突き止めようとした。

19. Nobody will (**get**) (**away**) with such a serious crime.
このような重大な犯罪を犯して逃げおおせる者などだれもいない。

20. I don't think I can (**get**) (**by**) without using the Internet.
インターネットを使わずにやっていけるとは思えません。

21. The roof of the warehouse (**gave**) (**in**) under the weight of the snow.
倉庫の屋根は雪の重みで壊れた。

22. The factory management finally (**gave**) (**in**) (**to**) the workers' demand.
工場の経営者側はついに労働者たちの要求に屈した。

23. Nuclear waste continues to (**give**) (**off**) harmful radiation.
放射性廃棄物は人体に有害な放射線を放出し続ける。

24. I guess we have to (**go**) (**along**) with the president's decision.
私たちは社長の決定に従うしかなさそうだ。

25. I think I'll (**go**) (**for**) this tuna salad sandwiches.
私はこのツナサラダサンドイッチにしようと思います。

26. (**Go**) (**over**) your report once again before you hand it in.
提出する前にもう一度レポートを見直しなさい。

27. Ron's family (**went**) (**through**) several hurricanes over the last two years.
ロンの家族はこの２年間に数回のハリケーンを経験した。

28. The committee (**hammered**) (**out**) a solution to the issue.
委員会はその問題に対する解決策を打ち出した。

29. Mary took a shower before (**heading**) (**off**) to work.
メアリーは仕事に出かける前にシャワーを浴びた。

動詞を含むイディオム③

1. Katie struggled to (**hold**) (**back**) her tears.
ケイティーは必死に涙をこらえようとした。

2. Randy (**held**) (**off**) making a decision on the matter.
ランディはその件に関して決断するのを先延ばしにした。

3. The boy managed to (**hold**) (**on**) without food for three days.
その少年は３日間食べ物なしで何とか持ちこたえた。

4. Their food supplies won't (**hold**) (**out**) for another week.
彼らの食料はあと１週間はもたないだろう。

5. Frank (**jumped**) (**at**) the opportunity to try the product out for free.
フランクは無料でその製品を試すことができる機会に飛びついた。

6. Paul had difficulties (**keeping**) (**up**) at school.
ポールは学校で勉強についていくのが難しかった。

7. It is not easy for us to (**keep**) (**up**) (**with**) world affairs.
私たちにとって世界情勢に遅れずについて行くことは簡単なことではない。

8. They (**kicked**) (**off**) the celebration event with a parade.
その祝賀イベントはパレードで始まった。

9. The old apartment house is going to be (**knocked**) (**down**).
その古いアパートは取り壊されることになっている。

10. The school (**laid**) (**down**) strict rules about the use of smartphone.
その学校はスマートフォンの使用に関する厳しい規則を定めた。

11. The factory was forced to (**lay**) (**off**) hundreds of workers.
その工場では何百人もの従業員を解雇する事態に追い込まれた。

12. You said you could meet the deadline. Don't (**let**) me (**down**).
締め切りには間に合うと言ったじゃないか。がっかりさせないでくれよ。

13. If we (**let**) (**up**) now, all our efforts could come to nothing.
ここで気を抜いたら，私たちの努力はすべて水の泡になるでしょう。

14. Alan stopped trying to (**live**) (**up**) to his parents' expectations.
アランは両親の期待に応えようと努力することをやめた。

15. Sarah is (**looking**) (**into**) doing some volunteer work on her days off.
サラは休みの日にボランティアの仕事をすることを検討している。

16. The sign reads, "(**Look**) out (**for**) falling rocks."
その標識には「落石に注意せよ」と書かれている。

17. Some consumers feel the economy is (**looking**) (**up**).
経済が上向いていると感じている消費者もいる。

18. You'll (**make**) (**it**) on time for the train if you take a taxi.
タクシーを使えば列車に間に合いますよ。

19. Bill simply couldn't (**make**) (**out**) what his boss said.
ビルは上司の言うことを全く理解することができなかった。

20. Keith is struggling to (**make**) (**up**) (**for**) lost time.
キースは時間の遅れを取り戻そうと必死になっている。

21. The art exhibition didn't (**measure**) (**up**) to her expectations.
その美術展は彼女の期待に沿うものではなかった。

22. The company (**passed**) (**off**) imported beef as domestic beef.
その会社は輸入牛肉を国産とごまかした。

23. Tom looked dissatisfied because he got (**passed**) (**over**) for a promotion.
トムは昇進が見送られて憮然とした表情だった。

24. I can't believe Brian (**passed**) (**up**) such a good offer.
ブライアンがあのような良いオファーを見送ったなんて信じられない。

25. The group (**pushed**) (**for**) a ban on smoking in public places.
そのグループは公共の場所での喫煙禁止を強く求めた。

26. They (**put**) (**forward**) a plan for promoting e-learning in public schools.
彼らは公立学校におけるeラーニング奨励の計画を提出した。

27. The police have not (**ruled**) (**out**) the possibility of terrorism.
警察はテロの可能性を排除していない。

28. I want to (**take**) (**in**) a musical during my stay in New York.
ニューヨーク滞在中にミュージカルを見に行きたい。

29. The restaurant was full, so the staff had to (**turn**) (**away**) customers.
レストランは満席だったので，係員は客の入店を断らねばならなかった。

30. Engineers have (**worked**) (**out**) some issues with the new airliner.
技術者たちはその新型の旅客機のいくつかの問題点を解決した。

形容詞を含むイディオム

1. Russia is (**abundant**) (**in**) natural resources.
ロシアは天然資源が豊富である。

2. Julia is (**apt**) (**to**) believe easily what the mass media tells.
ジュリアはマスコミの言うことを簡単に信じる傾向がある。

3. They are (**committed**) (**to**) fighting against poverty in developing countries.
彼らは開発途上国における貧困との戦いに献身的に取り組んでいる。

4. Many people are (**concerned**) (**about**) the safety of food.
多くの人々は食品の安全を心配している。

5. The results of the experiment are (**consistent**) (**with**) our hypothesis.
実験結果は私たちの仮説と一致している。

6. All exchange students are (**exempt**) (**from**) paying tuition fees.
交換留学生は授業料の支払いを免除される。

7. The Christmas event is (**geared**) (**toward**) children.
そのクリスマスのイベントは子供が対象である。

8. The company (**went**) (**bankrupt**) due to massive debt.
その会社は巨額の負債を抱えて倒産した。

9. We're (**grateful**) (**for**) your most generous support in the past.
私たちはあなたのこれまでの絶大なるご支援に感謝いたします。

10. Many people are (**ignorant**) (**of**) the beauty of nature on the island.
多くの人々はその島の自然の美しさを知らない。

11. The falling unemployment rate is (**indicative**) (**of**) an improving economy.
失業率の減少は経済が回復に向かっていることを示している。

12. The Internet is (**indispensable**) (**to**) our daily life.
インターネットは私たちの日常生活に欠かせない。

13. The boy is (**liable**) (**to**) respiratory diseases.
その男の子は呼吸器系の病気にかかりやすい。

14. Miyuki is (**particular**) (**about**) her food.
ミユキは食べ物の好みがうるさい。

15. Oliver was (**reluctant**) (**to**) talk about his past.
オリバーは自分の過去について話すのを嫌がった。

前置詞を含むイディオム

1. The engineer worked (around) the (clock) to fix the problem.
その技師はその問題を解決するために24時間ぶっ通しで働いた。

2. We must make this event a success (at) (all) (costs).
私たちはなんとしてもこのイベントを成功させなければならない。

3. You must hand in your report by October 14th (at) the (latest).
レポートは遅くとも10月14日までに提出しなければなりません。

4. In many cases, invasive species are introduced (by) (accident).
多くの場合，侵入生物種は偶然持ち込まれる。

5. Fred didn't turn up for the meetings three times (in) a (row).
フレッドは3回連続してミーティングに姿を見せなかった。

6. Most local residents are (in) (favor) (of) the construction of the railroad.
地域住民の大部分はその鉄道の建設に賛成している。

7. (In) (terms) (of) service quality, the hotel was excellent.
サービスの質に関してはそのホテルは申し分なかった。

8. The pamphlet shows us what to do (in) the (event) (of) an earthquake.
この小冊子は地震の際に私たちがどうすべきかを教えてくれる。

9. The twin sisters looked after their puppy (in) (turn).
その双子の姉妹は自分たちの子犬を交替で世話した。

10. Keith tried (in) (vain) to track down his old friend.
キースは古い友人を見つけ出そうとしたがだめだった。

11. The popularity of the rock band is (on) the (rise) around the world.
そのロックバンドは世界中で人気が上昇中だ。

12. Scott turned down the offer (on) the (spot).
スコットはその場でその申し出を断った。

13. Many plant and animal species are (on) the (verge) (of) extinction.
多くの植物種や動物種が絶滅の危機に瀕している。

準1級レベルの口語表現

リスニング問題のPart 1と3，また筆記の大問1では，日常生活やビジネスシーンで使われる決まり文句，口語表現が多数出てくるのが特徴です。場面ごとに頻出の英文をチェックしておきましょう。

日本文の意味を表す英文になるように，(　　)に適する英語を入れましょう。

※付属の赤シートで答えを隠して取り組みましょう。

あいさつ

1. Oh, it's Bruce! (**Long**) (**time**) no (**see**). How's life?
—— (**Looking**) up. I got a promotion to the sales manager last month.
まあ，ブルースじゃないの。久しぶりね。調子はどう？
—— 上向いてきているよ。先月営業部長に昇進したんだ。

2. Thanks for calling Iris Bookstore. (**How**) may I help (**you**)?
—— Hello, I'm calling about my order I made ten days ago.
アイリス書店にお電話をいただき，ありがとうございます。ご用件を承ります。
—— もしもし，10日前に注文した品物のことでお電話したのですが。

3. I'll check your order status and call you back later.
—— I'd really (**appreciate**) that.
お客様のご注文の状況を調べて，後ほどこちらからお電話いたします。
—— それは非常に助かります。

4. (**How**) are you (**feeling**) this morning, Kate? Is your cold any better?
—— (**Much**) (**better**) than yesterday, thanks.
ケイト，今朝の気分はどうだい？　風邪は少しはよくなった？
—— 昨日よりはずっと気分がいいわ。ありがとう。

5. (**It**) was great (**to**) see you, Sophie.
—— You (**too**)*. See you again, Randy.
ソフィー，お会いできてうれしかったよ。
—— 私もよ。また会いましょう，ランディ。

＊ You too. = It was great to see you, too.

許可を求める・依頼する

6. Would you (**mind**) (**my[me]**) smoking here?
—— No, (**not**) at (**all**). /
I'd rather (**you**) (**didn't**).
ここでたばこを吸ってもいいですか。
—— かまいませんよ。/ 吸わないでくださるとうれしいです。

7. Mr. Hawkins, would you (**mind**) sparing a few minutes?
—— Sure. What is it? /
I'm sorry, but I'm (**tied**) (**up**) at the moment.
ホーキンスさん，少しお時間をいただけますでしょうか。
—— いいとも。なんだい？/ 申し訳ないが，今手が離せないんだ。

8. I have a (**favor**) to (**ask**), honey. Could you pick me up at the station?
—— No (**problem**). I'll be there in fifteen minutes.
あなた，お願いがあるの。駅まで車で迎えに来てくれないかしら。
—— いいよ。15分でそちらへ行くから。

9. Ms. Ellen, I was (**wondering**) (**if**) you (**could**) give me advice. —— I'm always ready to help you. (**What's**) up?
エレン先生，アドバイスをいただけませんでしょうか。
—— いつでも力になるわよ。どうしたの？

勧誘・提案する

10. Would you (**care**) for some hot drinks?
—— Yes, I'd (**like**) some tea.
何か温かい飲み物はいかがですか。—— はい，紅茶をいただきます。

11. If you're free this afternoon, why (**not**) go shopping with me?
—— In this rain? I'd (**rather**) stay at home and read a book.
今日の午後暇なら，一緒に買い物に行かない？
—— こんな雨の中をかい？　僕は家にいて本を読む方がいいや。

12. How (**about**) (**letting**) Bill organize the event? I think he's suited for that kind of job. —— Maybe you're (**right**).
そのイベント，ビルに企画を任せたらどうかしら。そういう仕事に彼は適任だと思うわ。—— 君の言う通りかもしれない。

13. Why (**don't**) (**we**) order some pizza tonight?
—— I'm (**for**) that. I'm too exhausted to make dinner.
今夜はピザを取らないか？
—— 賛成よ。くたくたで夕食を作る気力もないわ。

14. I (**was**) (**wondering**) (**if**) you'd like to join our party next Sunday.
—— That's sweet (**of**) (**you**), but I'm booked that day.
今度の日曜日，私たちのパーティーにいらっしゃいませんか。
—— ご親切にありがとうございます。でも，その日は別の約束があるのです。

15. Why (**don't**) (**you**) try to sell your unwanted items through an online auction?
—— Oh, I didn't think of that. It may be worth a try.
不要品をネットオークションで売ってみたらどう？
—— それは考えてもいなかったよ。試してみる価値はあるかもね。

意見・感想を求める

16. How (**was**) the new theme park? —— We (**found**) it highly amusing! It has loads of attractions for kids.
新しいテーマパークはどうだった？ —— とてもおもしろかったよ。子供向けのアトラクションがたくさんあってね。

17. How are you (**getting**) (**along**) (**with**) your dorm roommate?
—— Yes, he's a very friendly guy. He's a little messy, though.
寮のルームメイトとはうまくやっているの？
—— うん，とても気さくなやつだよ。ちょっと散らかし屋だけどね。

相手をほめる・評価する・励ます

18. I've just been promoted to sales manager.
—— (**Congratulations**)! This calls for a celebration.
たった今，営業部長に昇進が決まったの。
—— おめでとう！　これはお祝いをしなくちゃね。

19. Mr. Robert, I've just finished all the documents for tomorrow's meeting.
—— You (**made**) (**it**), Emily!
ロバートさん，ちょうど明日の会議のための資料を全部作り終えました。
—— やったじゃないか，エミリー。

20. I don't think we can finish this job by five, Peter.
—— (**Hang**) (**in**) there, Mary. We're almost done.
この仕事，５時までに終えられそうにないわ，ピーター。
—— がんばれ，メアリー。もうほとんど終わりかけているじゃないか。

申し出る・勧める・忠告する

21. Please (**feel**) (**free**) (**to**) call me when you're in trouble.
—— That's very kind of you. I'll be (**counting**) on you.
困ったときは，どうぞ遠慮なく電話してください。
—— ご親切にどうもありがとう。頼りにしています。

22. Please don't (**hesitate**) (**to**) contact us if you have any questions.
質問があるときはどうぞご遠慮なくご連絡ください。

健康（病気・けが・薬）

23. It sounds like your cough is (**hanging**) (**on**). Are you OK? —— I think my asthma is (**acting**) (**up**). I'm going to see a doctor tomorrow.
君の咳，なかなか止まらないみたいだね。大丈夫かい？
—— ぜんそくがまたひどくなっているみたいなの。明日医者に診てもらうわ。

24. My mother broke her leg last week, and she's (**in**) the (**hospital**). —— Oh, (**that's**) too (**bad**). I hope she'll recover soon.
先週母が足の骨を折って，入院しているのです。
—— それはお気の毒ですね。早く治るといいですね。

相づち・つなぎ言葉（談話標識）

25. What a coincidence, running into you at the art gallery!
—— (**Actually**), my sister's paintings are displayed here.
画廊であなたに会うなんて偶然ね！
—— 実は姉の描いた絵がここに展示されているんだ。

26. Don't you like sweets, Kana? —— (**On**) the (**contrary**). I love them, but I'm on a diet now.
カナ，君は甘い物が好きじゃないの？
—— とんでもないわ。大好きよ。でも，今ダイエット中なの。

27. Can I ask you to work overtime today, Anne?
—— No (**way**)! I have an appointment today. Ask someone else.
今日残業をお願いできるかな，アン。
—— お断りします［絶対に嫌です］。今日は用事があるのです。ほかの人に頼んでください。

準1級

2023年度 第2回

一次試験 2023.10.8実施

二次試験 A日程 2023.11.5実施
B日程 2023.11.12実施
C日程 2023.11.23実施

一次試験・筆記(90分)
pp.42～57

一次試験・リスニング(約31分)
pp.58～63
CD青-1～26

二次試験・面接(約8分)
pp.64～67

※解答一覧は別冊p.3
※解答と解説は別冊pp.4～46

※別冊の巻末についている解答用マークシートを使いましょう。

合格基準スコア

- 一次試験…1792
  (満点2250／リーディング750, リスニング750, ライティング750)
- 二次試験…512(満点750／スピーキング750)

◉一次試験・筆記

1 *To complete each item, choose the best word or phrase from among the four choices. Then, on your answer sheet, find the number of the question and mark your answer.*

(1) Layla found the workouts in the advanced class too (　　　), so she decided to change to an easier class.

1 subtle　**2** contrary　**3** strenuous　**4** cautious

(2) The tax accountant asked the woman to (　　　) all her financial records over the past year. He needed to see them before he could begin preparing her tax forms.

1 punctuate　**2** compile　**3** bleach　**4** obsess

(3) Emilio discovered a small leak in one of the water pipes in his house. To be safe, he turned off the (　　　) to stop the water until he knew exactly what the problem was.

1 depot　**2** canal　**3** valve　**4** panel

(4) ***A:*** How long have you and Linda been (　　　), Bill?
B: Oh, we've known each other for at least 10 years, maybe longer.

1 acquainted　**2** discharged　**3** emphasized　**4** subdued

(5) Our local community center usually has one main room, but when necessary, we can close the (　　　) and create two smaller rooms.

1 estimation　**2** partition　**3** assumption　**4** notion

(6) Tyler's father suggested that he get some foreign (　　　) from his local bank before his vacation because changing money abroad is often more expensive.

1 tactic　**2** bait　**3** currency　**4** menace

(7) Thanks to the country's ( ) natural resources, it is able to earn a great deal of money through exports such as metals, coal, and natural gas.

1 unjust **2** insubstantial **3** elastic **4** abundant

(8) At first, Enzo listed all six of his previous jobs on his résumé. He had to remove two of them, however, in order to ( ) the document into one page.

1 dispute **2** mumble **3** mistrust **4** condense

(9) In most countries, foreigners working without a proper visa are ( ) if they are discovered. However, sending them home can cost a lot of money.

1 mended **2** deported **3** perceived **4** distributed

(10) Tim is worried that he is spending too much time using his smartphone. He feels a strong ( ) to check his e-mail every few minutes.

1 suspension **2** extension **3** seclusion **4** compulsion

(11) ***A:*** Did you make a New Year's ( ) this year, Serena?
B: Yes, I decided to start eating healthy snacks instead of sweets between meals. It's been difficult to keep away from the chocolate and candy, though.

1 astonishment **2** resolution **3** vulnerability **4** repression

(12) Miranda noticed that the amount of money in her savings account was ( ), so she decided to start spending less every month.

1 grazing **2** dwindling **3** browsing **4** rebounding

(13) The girl was scared of high places, so she ( ) her father's hand. She held it tightly as they looked out the window from the top of the tower.

1 harassed **2** breached **3** drained **4** gripped

(14) Akiko could not help but be (   ) when she saw her colleagues having a quiet conversation. She moved closer to them to hear what they were talking about.

1 obedient **2** flexible **3** sinful **4** nosy

(15) Due to the snowstorm, the climbers were unable to reach the mountain's (   ). They had to turn around just a few hundred meters from the top.

1 subsidy **2** mirage **3** summit **4** crutch

(16) When Jonathan started at his company, he was often (   ) all day. However, after a few months, he took on more tasks and now has little free time.

1 idle **2** agile **3** sane **4** needy

(17) ***A:*** Guess what? I've got an interview for that job as a TV announcer!
B: That's great, but don't be too (   ) just yet. There'll be a lot of competition for that position.

1 courteous **2** optimistic **3** suspicious **4** flustered

(18) During her commute, Josie found the noise from the earphones of the train passenger next to her so (   ) that she decided to move to another seat.

1 bothersome **2** compelling **3** flattering **4** daring

(19) ***A:*** I couldn't believe how crowded this year's summer parade was.
B: I know! There were so many (   ) in the streets I could barely move.

1 patriots **2** spectators **3** mimics **4** executives

(20) Joseph was not sure if he could afford a taxi home from work, but after checking his wallet, he found that he had (   ) money for the ride.

1 ample **2** regal **3** vain **4** crafty

(21) ( ) involvement has been shown to enhance student performance in school. One example is helping children with schoolwork at home.

1 Obsolete **2** Numb **3** Parental **4** Infamous

(22) Over the past few decades, many species have nearly been ( ) by pollution. However, recent conservation efforts are helping some of them to recover.

1 wiped out **2** broken up **3** fixed up **4** turned down

(23) Dave was happy when his neighbor gave him a basket of fresh vegetables, but when he got home, he realized he did not know how to ( ) cooking them.

1 go about **2** pull out **3** take in **4** bring down

(24) ***A:*** Our company allows employees to wear comfortable clothes, as long as they don't look too unprofessional.

B: That's new for me. Wearing casual clothes was ( ) at my last job.

1 frowned upon **2** carried on
3 entered into **4** crossed off

(25) The regional manager visited the small branch office last week and ( ) a few meetings to observe how things were going there.

1 went back on **2** sat in on
3 spoke down to **4** looked up to

2 *Read each passage and choose the best word or phrase from among the four choices for each blank. Then, on your answer sheet, find the number of the question and mark your answer.*

The Documentary Boom

In recent years, the growth of TV streaming services has created a huge new market for documentaries. The number of documentaries being made has skyrocketed, providing welcome new opportunities for filmmakers, but there are also negative aspects. One issue is that many filmmakers feel they are (***26***). Some documentaries have attracted huge audiences and brought tremendous financial returns, so companies that operate streaming services have become more generous with their production budgets. With so much money involved, the intense pressure often makes filmmakers feel as though they have no choice but to alter the stories they tell to give them greater commercial appeal.

This has led to concerns regarding the (***27***) documentaries. While documentaries used to be considered a form of investigative journalism, there has been a noticeable shift in their subject matter. As the popularity of genres such as true crime has increased, the line between factual information and entertainment has become blurred. Documentaries, which were once devoted to informing viewers and raising awareness of problems in society, are too frequently becoming sensationalist entertainment designed primarily to shock or excite viewers.

Another worrying trend for filmmakers is the rise of celebrity documentaries. In the past, filmmakers generally followed the journalistic tradition of not paying ordinary subjects of documentaries for fear that doing so would encourage people to exaggerate or tell outright lies. Famous people, such as musicians, however, are now paid millions of dollars for their stories—often because such stars are guaranteed to attract viewers. (***28***), noncelebrities are also starting to demand compensation, which is creating a moral dilemma for filmmakers.

(26)
1 still being ignored
2 not being paid enough
3 losing control over content
4 in need of large budgets

(27)
1 way people interpret
2 people who appear in
3 growing costs of creating
4 decreasing social value of

(28)
1 Above all
2 Understandably
3 In contrast
4 Nevertheless

Anting

The field of ethology involves studying animals in their natural habitats to understand their behavior. Drawing conclusions about the reasons behind what animals do, however, is not always easy. Certain birds, for example, display a behavior called "anting." This usually involves a bird picking up some ants with its beak and rubbing them on its feathers. (***29***), birds have even been observed sitting on anthills with their wings spread out and allowing ants to crawl all over their bodies. Despite extensive observation, ethologists remain unsure why birds engage in this behavior.

One popular theory is that (***30***). Ants naturally produce a substance called formic acid that protects them against bacteria and fungi, and which is also toxic to other insects. If this substance is rubbed onto a bird's feathers, it could help inhibit disease and deter harmful pests. While birds commonly use ants, some have been seen picking up certain beetles and millipedes instead. The fact that these organisms also produce chemicals that keep harmful pests away provides support for this theory.

Another proposed idea is that rubbing ants on a bird's feathers (***31***). In an experiment, scientists discovered that some birds were more likely to consume ants that had their formic acid removed by the scientists than ants that retained the chemical. The formic acid is stored in a sac located next to an ant's nutrient-rich abdomen. Anting, some scientists suspect, may cause ants to release their formic acid without birds having to try to remove the sacs with their beaks—a process that could damage the area of ants that makes them such an appealing snack.

(29)
1 In other words
2 For one thing
3 Similarly
4 Consequently

(30)
1 the ants eat organisms that harm the birds
2 the behavior contributes to birds' health
3 the behavior helps control ant populations
4 the birds are trying to attract other insects

(31)
1 helps remove damaged feathers
2 transfers nutrients to the ants
3 increases the bird's appetite
4 prepares the ants to be eaten

3

Read each passage and choose the best answer from among the four choices for each question. Then, on your answer sheet, find the number of the question and mark your answer.

The Development of Colleges in the United States

Selling land is a common way to increase wealth, but for rural landowners in the United States during the nineteenth century, this was not always easy. Rural populations at the time were small, so landowners needed ways to attract buyers. One method was to keep prices low, but landowners also turned to another strategy: building colleges. Doing this made the land in their area more desirable, as colleges were centers of culture and learning. Colleges were built at an incredibly rapid pace, and by 1880, there were five times more colleges in the United States than there were in Europe.

With the exception of a few older, elite institutions, most US colleges only had a small number of students and instructors. Rather than being scholars, the faculty members were often religious men representing the different branches of Christianity that existed in the United States at the time. Administrators knew this would help to attract students from those religious organizations. Gaining admission to colleges was generally not difficult as long as students could pay the tuition, which, as a result of fierce competition to recruit students, was kept low. Unfortunately, low student numbers meant that many colleges were forced to close down, and those that survived could only continue operating through constant fundraising.

Demand for higher education, however, continued to increase along with the US population in the twentieth century. As the remaining colleges had well-established infrastructures, including land, buildings, and libraries, they were in a good position to accommodate this demand. Furthermore, they generally offered high-quality education and good sports and leisure facilities because one way they had survived was by being sensitive to students' needs. Another way the colleges ensured their futures was by maintaining close ties with their graduates, from whom they would receive generous donations. All of these factors have helped the US college system to transform itself into one of the most successful in the world.

(32) Why were so many colleges built in the United States in the nineteenth century?

1 Increasing levels of wealth in rural areas led to more families wanting their children to receive a college education.

2 Wealthy landowners built colleges as a way to improve their public image and ensure that they would be remembered after their death.

3 Europeans living in the United States wanted colleges that would provide the same level of education that was available in their home countries.

4 Building colleges was a way for people who owned land in rural areas to increase the value of their land and attract more buyers.

(33) What is true regarding many faculty members at US colleges in the nineteenth century?

1 They quit after a short time because of the poor conditions they were forced to work under.

2 Their salaries were usually paid by religious organizations rather than by the colleges themselves.

3 There was a high degree of competition among them to gain the best positions at the colleges.

4 Their religious backgrounds tended to be an effective way to get students to enroll at their colleges.

(34) One reason US colleges succeeded in the twentieth century was that they

1 formed partnerships with local sports teams to increase the quality of their physical education programs.

2 were able to increase their financial security by creating lasting relationships with their former students.

3 decreased the competition with other colleges by focusing on recruiting students mostly from their local areas.

4 kept their costs down by using facilities already available in the community instead of building their own.

Machine or Human?

In 2004, NASA's exploration rover Opportunity landed on Mars. The golf-cart-sized rover, which was nicknamed "Oppy," was sent to survey the planet and capture images of its surface. Oppy's mission was supposed to last 90 days, but the rover continued to beam pictures and data back to Earth for the next 15 years. During that time, it captured the public's imagination. In fact, people became so attached to Oppy that when it ceased to function, they sent messages of condolence over social media similar to those intended for a deceased person.

The act of giving human traits to nonhuman things, which is known as anthropomorphism, is something humans do naturally, even at a young age. It is not unusual, for example, for people of all ages to form emotional attachments to objects such as toys, cars, and homes. Even the engineers, who frequently referred to Oppy as "she" or thought of it as a child, were not immune to this tendency. One effect of projecting human qualities onto a nonliving object seems to be that this makes people feel protective of it and brings out concern for its well-being. NASA appears to have utilized this phenomenon to its advantage by deliberately making Oppy seem more human, designing it with eyelike camera lenses in a headlike structure that extended from its body. Prior to the Opportunity mission, well-publicized failures had weakened public confidence in NASA, and the agency's funding had been reduced. It has been suggested that giving Oppy human characteristics was an effective strategy to win over the public and perhaps even attract additional funding for NASA's mission.

While thinking of Oppy as a human may seem harmless, there can be unfortunate consequences to anthropomorphizing objects. Assuming AI works in the same way as the human brain, for example, may lead to unrealistic expectations of its capabilities, causing it to be used in situations where it is unable to provide significant benefits. Anthropomorphism can also make people apprehensive of nightmare scenarios, such as AI and machines rising up in rebellion against humans. This idea of machines as a threat arises from the misunderstanding that they reason in the same way as humans do. It appears, however, that people cannot help themselves from anthropomorphizing. As journalist

Scott Simon writes, "if you spend a lot of time with a mechanism—talk to it, wait to hear from it and worry about it—even scientists begin to see personality in machinery."

(35) What do we learn about people's reactions to Oppy?

1 People immediately supported Oppy because they were interested in any new discoveries about Mars.

2 People found it difficult to relate to Oppy because little effort had been made to inform them about the significance of its mission.

3 People soon lost interest in Oppy's mission because the information Oppy sent back to Earth was too technical for nonscientists to understand.

4 People felt such an emotional connection to Oppy that they expressed sympathy for it when it stopped operating.

(36) According to the second paragraph, it seems likely that making Oppy appear more human was

1 a strategy designed to increase overall support for NASA's activities and to help it receive more money.

2 based on experiments in which children showed an increased interest in robots that looked like humans.

3 done because psychologists suggested that the strategy would make the engineers work harder to complete it on time.

4 the result of government pressure on NASA to make its designs more likely to be used in toys.

(37) According to the passage, what is a potential problem with anthropomorphism?

1 It can make people rely on machines to perform tasks that would be cheaper for humans to do themselves.

2 It can make people mistakenly assume that AI and machines do not need any guidance to perform tasks correctly.

3 The belief that AI and machines act in a similar way to humans can cause people to misunderstand what they are able to do.

4 The relationships scientists form with AI can cause them to prioritize its development over the needs of humans.

The Marian Reforms

Around the end of the second century BC, the Roman Republic faced the threat of an invasion by tribal peoples from Western Europe and experienced a series of humiliating defeats in Africa. Realizing that the Roman army was no longer able to meet the needs of the rapidly expanding republic, the Roman leader Gaius Marius set about implementing sweeping reforms. These became known as the Marian reforms, and they transformed the Roman army into a nearly unstoppable military machine that was arguably the most effective fighting force in ancient times. Traditionally, enlistment of soldiers into the Roman army had been on a temporary basis, which necessitated constant recruitment and inevitably led to new recruits often having no previous fighting experience. Furthermore, property ownership was required for entry into the army, and increasing poverty within the Roman Republic severely reduced the pool of potential recruits who could meet this requirement.

The Marian reforms consisted of several measures, including the removal of both property requirements and the need for recruits to prepare their own weapons and armor. This allowed even the poorest citizens to enlist and led to better-equipped soldiers because the army could standardize and improve the weapons and armor used. Soldiers in the army became known as "legionaries," and they were trained in military strategy. Perhaps most importantly, the reforms provided a crucial incentive for enlistment—any soldier who served for 16 years was compensated with a plot of farmland and full Roman citizenship. The rapid expansion of the Roman Republic meant there were many noncitizen inhabitants who lived in poverty and for whom an opportunity to escape their situation was hugely appealing.

The Roman army's better-trained and more highly motivated soldiers led to it achieving significant military triumphs that contributed to Rome's expansion. The land that former legionaries received was generally in newly conquered provinces, so these veterans were instrumental in spreading Roman culture. Their presence also made it easier to overcome local resistance to Roman rule and facilitated the process of integration into the Roman Republic. The mere presence of the veterans brought greater security to new territories, since they could assist in preventing rebellions and resisting invasions.

While the Marian reforms greatly improved the Roman army, they also had an unexpected impact on Roman society that eventually led to the downfall of the republic. When the army was composed mostly of wealthy citizens enlisted on an as-needed basis, it had little influence on Roman politics. Following the Marian reforms, however, legionaries in the army became highly disciplined and developed an intense loyalty to their generals. In consequence, generals found it difficult to resist the temptation to use the forces under their command to gain political influence for themselves rather than to ensure the protection and expansion of the Roman Republic. This resulted in civil wars, and eventually, Julius Caesar successfully used the army to overthrow the elected government and declare himself the Roman leader. This marked the end of the relatively democratic Roman Republic and paved the way for the creation of a dictatorship ruled by all-powerful emperors.

(38) What was one reason for the Marian reforms?

1 Financial problems within the Roman Republic meant a Roman leader had no choice but to reduce funding for the military.

2 As the number of soldiers in the army increased, it became more difficult to transport them to Western Europe and Africa to defend the Roman Republic.

3 Complaints arose among soldiers because they were forced to stay in the army for many years and received low pay for their service.

4 A Roman leader was concerned that the army did not have the manpower or skills required to allow the Roman Republic to achieve its military goals.

(39) What was an important change that occurred because of the Marian reforms?

1 A rule was introduced stating that only Roman citizens could join the Roman army, leading to more people trying to get Roman citizenship.

2 Serving in the Roman army became more attractive because it was a way for people living in the Roman Republic to improve their lives.

3 The Roman army struggled to find enough recruits because it would only accept men who already had military experience.

4 The number of years that soldiers were required to spend in the Roman army was reduced, which lowered the average age of soldiers.

(40) According to the third paragraph, after the Roman army took over new territories,

1 the number of soldiers sent to those areas would be greatly increased to allow the army to attack neighboring regions and continue the expansion of the Roman Republic.

2 local people were invited to Rome's capital to learn the Roman language and culture so that they could quickly become accustomed to Roman society.

3 ex-soldiers were given land there, which made it much easier to control the local people and ensure that the areas could be defended from various threats.

4 the areas were often lost again quite quickly because it was impossible for the army to prevent the many rebellions that occurred.

(41) What effect did the Marian reforms have on Roman society?

1 The army was used as a political tool, creating a system in which a Roman leader gained his position by military power rather than by being chosen by the people.

2 The wealth and social standing of people who refused to serve in the army decreased, while former legionaries often obtained high government positions.

3 The Roman army became so large that the cost of maintaining it became a major cause of the fall of the Roman Republic.

4 The lack of discipline among the legionaries led to tension between Roman citizens and the army, which eventually resulted in civil wars.

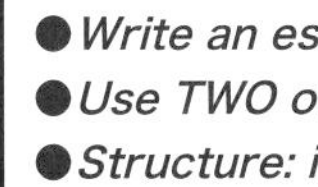

● *Write an essay on the given TOPIC.*
● *Use TWO of the POINTS below to support your answer.*
● *Structure: introduction, main body, and conclusion*
● *Suggested length: 120-150 words*
● *Write your essay in the space provided on Side B of your answer sheet. Any writing outside the space will not be graded.*

TOPIC

Should companies be required to produce goods that are easy to recycle?

POINTS

● *Company profits*
● *Customer demand*
● *Pollution*
● *Product quality*

◉一次試験・Listening Test

There are three parts to this listening test.

Part 1	Dialogues:	1 question each	Multiple-choice
Part 2	Passages:	2 questions each	Multiple-choice
Part 3	Real-Life:	1 question each	Multiple-choice

※ Listen carefully to the instructions.

Part 1

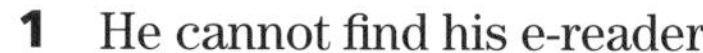

No. 1

1 He cannot find his e-reader.
2 He does not want to buy e-books.
3 He has broken his e-reader.
4 He finds it hard to download e-books.

No. 2

1 Take private yoga classes.
2 Find a different activity.
3 Continue with his current class.
4 Join another yoga group.

No. 3

1 She has some new ideas for the division.
2 She knows little about publishing.
3 She was an excellent student.
4 She wants to increase staff salaries.

No. 4

1 She wants to help a family in need.
2 They no longer fit her well.
3 There is an event at her school.
4 She does not have storage space for them.

No. 5

1 It will help reduce his workload.
2 It will mean more work with independent agents.
3 It will make his company more successful.
4 It will lead to many staff being fired.

No. 6

1 They will become less expensive in the future.
2 They would not save the couple money.
3 They need to be replaced after a few years.
4 They do not have many environmental benefits.

No. 7

1 Miki has not completed her translation work.
2 The deadline is likely to change.
3 The client has made a number of mistakes.
4 Miki often does not work carefully enough.

No. 8

1 He found many online complaints.
2 The cost of the cruise has increased.
3 He cannot get time off from work.
4 He is unable to book another cruise.

No. 9

1 It has a lot of unique characters.
2 The show's writing has improved greatly.
3 The plot was hard to predict.
4 It may not be renewed for another season.

No. 10

1 He is busier than Yasuhiro.
2 He does not get along with Genevieve.
3 He often makes poor decisions.
4 He may not have enough experience.

No. 11

1 Her lectures tend to be long.
2 She gives too much homework.
3 Her political views are extreme.
4 She does not grade fairly.

No. 12

1 Search for solutions online.
2 Get help from a professional.
3 Ask their neighbors for advice.
4 Move to a quieter neighborhood.

Part 2

(A)

No. 13

1 To improve the quality of their crops.
2 To give thanks for the food they grew.
3 To pray they could leave the desert.
4 To celebrate their time in Egypt.

No. 14

1 They have desert images on the walls.
2 They are covered to keep them cool.
3 Meals must be cooked in them.
4 People can see the sky from inside them.

(B)

No. 15

1 Vultures help stop them from affecting humans.
2 Vultures often spread them to other animals.
3 They can be deadly to vultures.
4 They survive in vultures' stomachs.

No. 16

1 Vultures' feeding habits help to reduce its effects.
2 It has increased vulture populations worldwide.
3 Vultures' food sources have changed because of it.
4 It has forced vultures to find new habitats.

(C)

No. 17

1 Workers often think they do not deserve praise.
2 Random praise can improve performance.
3 Too much praise can hurt performance.
4 Most bosses do not give enough praise.

No. 18

1 They tend to react negatively to praise.
2 They worry too much about their work.
3 They may benefit from having a growth mindset.
4 They affect the mindsets of workers around them.

(D)

No. 19

1 They believed an invasion would not happen.
2 They worried that the art would be destroyed.
3 They thought Canada was likely to be invaded.
4 They feared Germans would be able to steal the art.

No. 20

1 The importance of art during wartime.
2 A way to create larger mines.
3 The effects of low temperatures on paintings.
4 Ways of keeping art in good condition.

(E)

No. 21

1 To help warn about an attack.
2 To check the location of British soldiers.
3 To gather supplies for American troops.
4 To lead her father away from danger.

No. 22

1 There is evidence a different woman rode that night.
2 There are no records of an attack by the British army.
3 It was not officially documented.
4 A history book claims it did not happen.

(F)

No. 23

1 They had to relocate to more-populated areas.
2 They had to close due to unhappy customers.
3 They were not receiving enough snow.
4 They were opposed to using artificial snow.

No. 24

1 The use of artificial snow has hurt its business.
2 It makes use of the wind to help it operate.
3 It provides snow to other ski resorts in its local area.
4 Its slopes are at unusually high altitudes.

Part 3

(G)

No. 25

Situation: You are staying at a hotel. It is 6:30 p.m. now, and you want to have dinner at a nearby restaurant around 7:00 p.m. The concierge tells you the following.

Question: Which restaurant should you choose?

1 Kingsley's.
2 Shrimp Lover.
3 Randy's.
4 Boca.

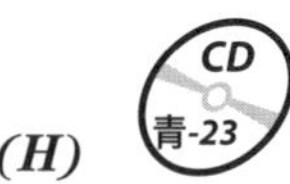

(H)

No. 26

Situation: You have decided to sell half of your collection of 500 music CDs. You call a shop that buys and sells used CDs and hear the following recorded message.

Question: What should you do?

1 Start the sales procedure online.
2 Begin packing your CDs into boxes.
3 Download a form from the website.
4 Make an appointment for an assessment.

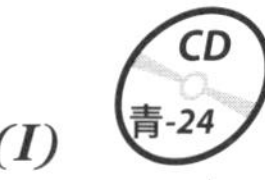

(I)
No. 27

Situation: You are a college student. You want to learn about ancient Greeks and Romans and do not like group work. You are listening to an academic adviser's explanation.

Question: Which class should you take?

1 History 103.
2 Philosophy 105.
3 History 202.
4 Latin 102.

(J)
No. 28

Situation: The tablet computer you bought for your daughter two weeks ago has broken. It has a one-year warranty. You call the product manufacturer and hear the following recorded message.

Question: What should you do?

1 Press 1.
2 Press 2.
3 Press 3.
4 Press 4.

(K)
No. 29

Situation: You and your seven-year-old son are at a science museum. You want to take a tour. You must leave the museum in 45 minutes. You hear the following announcement.

Question: Which tour should you choose?

1 Spark of Genius.
2 The Age of Dinos.
3 Deep into the Sea.
4 Museum after Dark.

◉二次試験・**面接**

※本書では出題例として２種類のカードを掲載していますが，本番では１枚のみ渡されます。
※面接委員の質問など，二次試験に関する音声はCDに収録されていません。

受験者用問題　カード　A

You have **one minute** to prepare.

This is a story about a couple who liked traveling.
You have **two minutes** to narrate the story.

Your story should begin with the following sentence:
One day, a couple was talking at a café.

No.1 Please look at the fourth picture. If you were the woman, what would you be thinking?

Now, Mr. / Ms. _____, please turn over the card and put it down.

No.2 Will Japan continue to be a popular tourist destination in the future?

No.3 Do you think employees in the service industry are treated well enough by their employers?

No.4 Is people's quality of life these days better than it was in the past?

受験者用問題　カード　B

You have **one minute** to prepare.

This is a story about a couple whose son liked sports.
You have **two minutes** to narrate the story.

Your story should begin with the following sentence:
One day, a family was at home.

No.1 Please look at the fourth picture. If you were the father, what would you be thinking?

Now, Mr. / Ms. _____, please turn over the card and put it down.

No.2 Should playing video games be considered a sport?

No.3 Do you think parents should discuss important family issues with their children?

No.4 Should the government provide more university scholarships for students?

準1級

2023年度 第1回

一次試験　2023.6.4実施

二次試験　A日程 2023.7.2実施
B日程 2023.7.9実施
C日程 2023.7.16実施

一次試験・筆記（90分）
pp.70～85

一次試験・リスニング（約32分）
pp.86～91
CD青-27～52

二次試験・面接（約8分）
pp.92～95

※解答一覧は別冊p.47
※解答と解説は別冊pp.48～90

※別冊の巻末についている解答用マークシートを使いましょう。

合格基準スコア

- 一次試験…1792
（満点2250／リーディング750，リスニング750，ライティング750）
- 二次試験…512（満点750／スピーキング750）

一次試験・筆記

1 *To complete each item, choose the best word or phrase from among the four choices. Then, on your answer sheet, find the number of the question and mark your answer.*

(1) At first, Mick was (　　　) by the idea of going to live abroad by himself. Once he did it, however, it was less difficult than he had feared.

1 pacified　**2** restored　**3** daunted　**4** tackled

(2) Students are advised to pace their studying throughout the semester instead of (　　　) right before their exams.

1 cramming　**2** detaining　**3** swelling　**4** embracing

(3) The two candidates' tempers (　　　) during the presidential debate. They angrily attacked each other's positions on issues throughout the night.

1 flared　**2** digested　**3** professed　**4** tumbled

(4) Many banks required government (　　　) to stay in business after the stock market crash. The help mostly came in the form of large loans.

1 intervention　**2** appreciation
3 accumulation　**4** starvation

(5) Police must follow strict (　　　) at a crime scene to make sure the evidence is not damaged or altered in any way.

1 tributes　**2** protocols　**3** reservoirs　**4** portions

(6) The umpire (　　　) the two players for fighting. They were not allowed to play in the rest of the game.

1 slaughtered　**2** administered
3 ejected　**4** conceived

(7) Cats are known to be protective of their ( ). They often attack other animals that they think could be a threat to their kittens.

1 prey **2** offspring **3** rituals **4** remains

(8) Fans of Greenville United were disappointed when the team's poor performance throughout the season led to its ( ) from the A-League to the B-League.

1 demotion **2** craving **3** aggravation **4** hassle

(9) Bibi loves hiking and playing sports, so she needs clothes that do not wear out too quickly. When she goes shopping, she generally buys clothing that is ( ).

1 swift **2** aloof **3** shallow **4** durable

(10) Consumers should not ( ) any personal information to callers claiming to be from the bank, as such calls are sometimes from criminals.

1 sway **2** detest
3 contemplate **4** disclose

(11) Because the tennis champion is unfriendly to other players and claims he is the greatest player who has ever lived, he is often criticized for his ( ).

1 commodity **2** arrogance **3** neutrality **4** specimen

(12) Many readers found the author's novels ( ). He was known for writing long, confusing sentences that had no clear meaning.

1 genuine **2** impending
3 subdued **4** incomprehensible

(13) "Class, I want you all to listen very ( )," the teacher said. "Much of what I will say is not in the textbook but will be on the test."

1 attentively **2** consecutively
3 wearily **4** eloquently

(14) The school is known for being at the (　　　) of education. Its teachers use the newest teaching methods and the latest technology in the classroom.

1 forefront　**2** lapse　**3** doctrine　**4** myth

(15) The mayor used (　　　) language in his speech because he thought it was extremely important that the citizens support his plan for public transportation.

1 forceful　**2** merciful　**3** futile　**4** tranquil

(16) When the pop singer died, she left her favorite charity a (　　　) of over $10 million. "We are so grateful for her generosity," said a charity spokesperson.

1 rhyme　**2** justice　**3** legacy　**4** majority

(17) As they approached the top of the mountain, some of the hikers began to feel sick because of the low oxygen levels at the high (　　　).

1 apparatus　**2** equation　**3** altitude　**4** mileage

(18) Ted lives on a (　　　) income. He makes just enough to afford a small apartment, pay his bills, and occasionally go out for dinner.

1 blissful　**2** modest　**3** showy　**4** sturdy

(19) The carpenter was careful to choose a (　　　) piece of wood for the table. There would be problems if it did not have the same thickness throughout.

1 reckless　**2** gaping　**3** dreary　**4** uniform

(20) Although Pieter was a private, quiet man who rarely showed his (　　　) for his children, they knew that he truly loved them.

1 affection　**2** circulation　**3** oppression　**4** coalition

(21) Anton heard a strange ( ) coming from his speakers, so he checked to make sure all the cables were properly connected.

1 buzz **2** peck **3** thorn **4** core

(22) Late last night, a man was caught trying to ( ) a convenience store. The police forced him to drop his weapon and arrested him.

1 shrug off **2** sit out **3** run against **4** hold up

(23) Jill had always loved France, so when there was a chance to work in her company's Paris office, she ( ) it. In fact, she was the first to apply.

1 plowed through **2** pulled on
3 threw off **4** jumped at

(24) ***A:*** How's the class you signed up for going to ( ) with your work schedule?

B: It's online, and I can study at my own pace. I can read the material when I get home from work, so it should be fine.

1 get over **2** fit in **3** hold onto **4** take after

(25) Before moving to her new section, Betty will ( ) all of her current projects to the person who will be doing her job from now on.

1 beef up **2** bank on **3** hand over **4** slip by

2 *Read each passage and choose the best word or phrase from among the four choices for each blank. Then, on your answer sheet, find the number of the question and mark your answer.*

Beyond Small Talk

Research indicates that the relationships people have can influence their well-being. Positive relationships not only lead to increased happiness but also have a beneficial effect on physical health. So far, most studies have focused on relationships with people we are close to, such as family members or friends. This makes sense, as when we have a problem or want to share our thoughts and opinions, we are most likely to talk to such people. (*26*), some recent studies have explored how we interact with strangers, and the results were rather surprising.

In one study, subjects were paired up with someone they had never met before, and each pair was asked to come up with a light discussion topic, such as the weather, and a more substantial one, such as their personal goals. At the beginning of the study, most subjects thought they would enjoy casual conversations more. After each conversation, the subjects were asked to rate it based on enjoyment and feeling of connection with their partners. The results showed that the (*27*). That is, most subjects reported having a more positive experience overall after discussing serious topics.

The study's results suggest that people would benefit from interacting on a deeper level with strangers. In fact, the subjects in the study generally expressed a desire to have meaningful conversations with people they did not know more often in their lives. However, they also thought that (*28*). The researchers believe that this assumption is incorrect, and that, for the most part, strangers are also interested in going beyond casual conversation.

(26)
1 In exchange
2 For instance
3 In contrast
4 In short

(27)
1 topics had made the subjects nervous
2 subjects' ratings did not always match
3 topic choices had been too varied
4 subjects' expectations had been wrong

(28)
1 communicating clearly would be difficult
2 other people did not share this desire
3 their family members would not approve
4 their privacy should come first

The Thing

After spending nearly a decade on a museum shelf in Chile, a mysterious fossil known as "The Thing" has finally been identified. Researchers now believe it is a 66-million-year-old soft-shelled egg and that it probably contained a mosasaur, a large aquatic reptile that existed around the same time as dinosaurs. Previous fossil evidence had suggested that mosasaurs (***29***). The researchers' findings challenge this idea, however, and the researchers say the fossil's size and the fact that it was discovered in an area where mosasaur fossils have been found support their conclusion.

Although the researchers are excited to have identified The Thing, it has opened a new debate. One theory suggests mosasaurs would have laid their eggs in open water, with the young hatching almost immediately. (***30***), some scientists believe the mosasaurs would have laid their eggs on the beach and buried them, much like some modern reptiles do. Further research, it is hoped, will reveal which of these is correct.

Another group of researchers from the United States has shed additional light on the eggs of prehistoric creatures after taking a closer look at previously discovered fossils of baby dinosaurs. It was believed that dinosaurs produced hard-shelled eggs, but the fossils on which this assumption was based represent a limited number of dinosaur species. Through their analysis, the US researchers discovered evidence that suggests the eggs of early dinosaurs were, in fact, soft-shelled. If true, this could explain why (***31***). Since softer materials break down easily, they are much less likely to be preserved in the fossil record.

(29) **1** were likely hunted by dinosaurs
2 relied on eggs for food
3 did not lay eggs
4 may not have existed with dinosaurs

(30) **1** Likewise
2 On the other hand
3 As a result
4 For example

(31) **1** few dinosaur eggs have been found
2 there are not more dinosaur species
3 some dinosaurs were unable to produce eggs
4 dinosaur babies often did not survive

3 *Read each passage and choose the best answer from among the four choices for each question. Then, on your answer sheet, find the number of the question and mark your answer.*

The Chicken of Tomorrow

Before the 1940s, most chickens in the United States were raised on family farms, and the main emphasis was on egg production rather than obtaining meat. Poverty and food shortages were common at that time, so people wanted to maintain a regular source of protein without sacrificing their chickens. Additionally, there were a tremendous variety of chickens being raised, as farmers generally chose a breed based on how well it was adapted to the local conditions—whether it was suited to a dry or a humid climate, for example.

After World War II, however, the growing availability of meat such as pork and beef meant eggs could not compete as a source of protein. The US Department of Agriculture therefore set up an event called the Chicken of Tomorrow contest to find a type of chicken that could be raised economically and produced more meat. The overall winner, which was a combination of different breeds, grew faster and larger than other types, and it could adapt to various climates. Inspired by the contest, breeding companies began creating complicated mixtures of chicken varieties to guarantee a consistent supply of birds with these same desirable features. Since producing such genetic combinations was difficult, most farmers had no choice but to purchase young chickens from those companies rather than breeding them by themselves—a development that completely changed the industry.

The contest helped popularize the consumption of chicken meat, but this trend also had a dark side. It became more economical to raise massive numbers of chickens in large facilities where they were confined in small cages. Not only did this force numerous small farms out of business, but it also created conditions for the birds that, according to animal rights activists, caused the chickens stress and led to higher levels of sickness. While the contest made chicken a regular food item, some people questioned whether it was worth it.

(32) What is one thing that we learn about the US chicken industry before the 1940s?

1 The type of chicken raised on each farm usually depended on the climate in the area where the farm was located.

2 Each farm would raise more than one type of chicken in case there was a sudden change in environmental conditions.

3 Chickens were generally only eaten by very poor people or at times when there were food shortages.

4 Because there were so many chicken farms across the country, many of the eggs produced ended up being wasted.

(33) The US Department of Agriculture organized the Chicken of Tomorrow contest because

1 other types of meat, such as pork and beef, were becoming more expensive, so the American people wanted a cheaper alternative.

2 most chicken farms were focused on egg production, which led to a need to create a chicken that was more suitable for producing meat.

3 a large number of chicken farms in America went out of business, which severely decreased the availability of chicken meat.

4 the American people were tired of eating the same type of eggs for so long, so producers wanted a different type of chicken.

(34) What is one way that the contest affected the chicken industry?

1 Farmers learned that it was relatively easy to combine several types of chickens, which encouraged them to breed new varieties.

2 Although the number of small chicken farms increased across America, many of these were often poorly run and had cheap facilities.

3 It started a move toward keeping chickens in conditions that increased the birds' suffering and made them less healthy.

4 Farmers realized that improving their farming methods could help them to raise chickens that produced more and better-tasting meat.

Discipline in American Schools

For decades, methods of discipline used in American schools have been based on the theories of psychologist B. F. Skinner, who believed that systems of reward and punishment were the most effective methods of improving people's behavior. Commonly, students who break rules are given punishments, such as being prohibited from attending classes for a day or more or being made to stay in class after the school day ends. These are designed to teach the students to follow teachers' instructions and respect classmates. Recent psychological studies, however, have determined that as effective as punishment may be in bringing peace to the classroom temporarily, it can intensify the very behavior it is intended to correct when used continually over an extended period of time.

Many experts now believe that in order for children to learn to behave appropriately, it is essential that they develop self-control. When students are punished to make them obey the rules, they are being forced to adopt good behavior through external pressure. Self-control, on the other hand, comes from internal motivation, self-confidence, and the ability to be tolerant of others, and using punishment as a substitute for these things can actually delay or prevent their development. Similarly, the use of rewards such as stickers leads to students merely attempting to please the teacher rather than understanding the importance of gaining knowledge and social skills that will help them throughout their lives.

In recent years, an increasing amount of research has been backing up these ideas. A region of the brain known as the prefrontal cortex helps us to concentrate on tasks and is responsible for self-discipline and allowing us to consider the consequences of our actions. Research suggests that the prefrontal cortex may be less developed in students with behavioral problems. Fortunately, though, there is evidence that repeated experiences can alter the brain's structure, which suggests that it is also possible to influence the development of the prefrontal cortex. Child-behavior expert Ross Greene believes that when educators change their attitudes so that they actually listen to students' feelings about their bad behavior and encourage them to come up with solutions to the issues they face, this can have a physical effect on the prefrontal cortex. Greene has designed a highly successful program that has greatly reduced behavioral problems at many schools, and as a result of the extensive media coverage his ideas have received in recent years, they are being adopted by more and more educators.

(35) What has psychological research shown about the use of punishment in schools?

1 It is only likely to be effective when it is used together with rewards in order to reduce its negative effects.

2 Though it may succeed in producing better behavior in the short term, it can actually be harmful in the long term.

3 There are various new types of punishment that are far more effective than physical punishment.

4 Using some form of punishment is necessary for forcing students to obey teachers and respect their classmates.

(36) According to the passage, what is one effect the use of rewards has on students?

1 It can teach them the advantages of hard work and make them better at focusing on their academic goals.

2 It causes them to want material things and makes them less aware of the need to behave in ways that are pleasing to other people.

3 It can prevent them from developing important skills that would be beneficial to them later in life.

4 It helps them to realize the importance of deciding their own goals rather than just doing what their teachers tell them to do.

(37) What does Ross Greene believe about children's brains?

1 Helping children solve their own problems can promote the development of the part of the brain that controls behavior.

2 Since the brains of younger children function in a different way to those of older children, different methods of dealing with behavioral issues are necessary.

3 The region of the brain known as the prefrontal cortex may be less important in controlling children's behavior than some scientists believe it is.

4 Bad behavior does not only have a negative effect on children's academic performance but also permanently prevents the normal development of their brains.

Robert the Bruce and the Declaration of Arbroath

In 1286, the sudden death of King Alexander III of Scotland resulted in a power struggle among various nobles that nearly brought the country to civil war. To settle the matter, England's King Edward I was asked to select a new ruler from among the rivals. Edward, who himself had ambitions to ultimately rule Scotland, agreed only on the condition that the new leader pledged loyalty to him. He chose a noble named John Balliol as the new king, but resentment soon grew as England repeatedly exerted its authority over Scotland's affairs. The turning point came when Edward attempted to force Scotland to provide military assistance in England's conflict with France. When Balliol allied his nation with France instead, Edward invaded Scotland, defeated Balliol, and took the throne.

This was the situation faced by the Scottish noble Robert the Bruce as he attempted to free Scotland from English rule. Robert, whose father had been one of Balliol's rivals for the throne, gained political dominance and led a rebellion that drove English forces from Scotland. Robert was crowned king of Scotland in 1306, and although he enjoyed tremendous support domestically, he had angered the Pope, the leader of the Roman Catholic Church. Not only had he ignored the church's requests that he make peace with England, but he had also taken the life of his closest rival to the throne in a place of worship before being crowned king.

Scotland's leadership knew that the country would remain internationally isolated and vulnerable without the church's recognition. International acceptance of Scotland's independence would be especially important if the country were to exist in the shadow of a mighty nation like England, which still failed to officially acknowledge Robert as Scotland's king despite having retreated. In 1320, Scotland's most powerful nobles therefore gathered to create a document known today as the Declaration of Arbroath. It proclaimed Scotland's independence and requested the Pope recognize Robert as the country's ruler. The response the nobles received later in the year, however, indicated that the declaration initially had not been effective. The Pope not only refused Scotland's request but also failed to confirm its self-proclaimed independence, although he did urge England to pursue a peaceful resolution in its dealings with the nation. A few years later, however, the declaration's influence contributed to the Pope recognizing Robert and his kingdom after a peace treaty finally freed Scotland from England's threat.

Today, the Declaration of Arbroath is one of the most celebrated documents in Scottish history. Some historians even argue it inspired the US Declaration of Independence, although proof of this is lacking. Scholars generally agree, however, that what makes the Declaration of Arbroath so historic is the assertion that the king may rule only with the approval of the Scottish people; specifically, the nobles used the document to boldly insist on their right to remove any ruler who betrayed them. In this sense, the document was a pioneering example of a contract between a country's ruler and its people, in which the ruler was responsible for ensuring the people could live in a free society.

(38) What happened following the death of King Alexander III of Scotland?

1 Scotland was able to trick King Edward I into choosing John Balliol even though it was not in Edward's interest to do so.

2 King Edward I began to question the loyalty of the Scottish nobles who had not supported John Balliol's attempt to become king.

3 King Edward I attempted to use the situation to his advantage in order to increase his power over Scotland.

4 Scotland felt so threatened by France's military power that diplomatic relations between the countries worsened.

(39) What problem did Robert the Bruce face after he became king of Scotland?

1 Although he was a great military leader, his lack of political skills led him to negotiate a poor agreement with England.

2 The disagreements he had with his rivals about religion caused many Scottish people to stop supporting him.

3 The religious differences between Scotland and England made it likely that Scotland would be attacked again.

4 Because of the things he had done to gain power, Scotland could not get the support it needed to be safe from England.

(40) In the year the Declaration of Arbroath was written,

1 it became clear that the Pope considered it a priority to recognize Scotland's independence as a nation.

2 the Pope attempted to encourage peace between England and Scotland despite not acknowledging either Robert or his country.

3 the promise of peace between England and Scotland was endangered by Scotland's attempt to get help from the Pope.

4 Scotland was able to achieve enough international recognition to get the Pope to admit that Robert was the country's true king.

(41) What is one common interpretation of the Declaration of Arbroath?

1 It demonstrates that Robert was actually a much better leader than people had originally thought him to be.

2 It brought a new way of looking at the duty that a country's ruler had to the people he or she was governing.

3 It reveals that there was much more conflict between Scottish rulers and nobles at the time than scholars once believed.

4 It suggested that a beneficial system of government was not possible with a king or queen ruling a country.

4	● *Write an essay on the given TOPIC.* ● *Use TWO of the POINTS below to support your answer.* ● *Structure: introduction, main body, and conclusion* ● *Suggested length: 120-150 words* ● *Write your essay in the space provided on Side B of your answer sheet. Any writing outside the space will not be graded.*

TOPIC

Should businesses provide more online services?

POINTS

- *Convenience*
- *Cost*
- *Jobs*
- *The environment*

◉一次試験・Listening Test

There are three parts to this listening test.

Part 1	**Dialogues:**	1 question each	Multiple-choice
Part 2	**Passages:**	2 questions each	Multiple-choice
Part 3	**Real-Life:**	1 question each	Multiple-choice

※ Listen carefully to the instructions.

Part 1

No. 1

1 Visit her brother in the hospital.
2 Submit her assignment.
3 Ask her brother for help.
4 Choose a new assignment topic.

No. 2

1 Too much money is spent on education.
2 The budget is likely to be decreased soon.
3 The government is wasting money.
4 The media is unfair to the government.

No. 3

1 The man will become much busier.
2 The woman will need to attend more meetings.
3 The woman dislikes the people on the fourth floor.
4 The man did not want his new position.

No. 4

1 To give her a massage.
2 To pick up some food.
3 To give her a gift certificate.
4 To do some housework.

No. 5

1 Ask the shop to replace the printer.
2 Get the old printer fixed.
3 Try to get money back from the shop.
4 Visit the shop to check other models.

No. 6

1 His client canceled the deal.
2 The contract needed to be revised.
3 The lawyer made a serious mistake.
4 He arrived late for an important meeting.

No. 7

1 His boss does not trust him.
2 He has very tight deadlines.
3 He lacks the skills required.
4 His boss is not well organized.

No. 8

1 Get a new sofa right away.
2 Buy a sofa online.
3 Look for a sofa on sale.
4 Repair their current sofa.

No. 9

1 Checking the weather news.
2 Taking a trip to their cabin this weekend.
3 Preparing emergency supplies.
4 Going out for ice cream.

No. 10

1 She lacks enthusiasm for her job.
2 She is going to be dismissed.
3 She is unpopular with the clients.
4 She needs to improve her computer skills.

No. 11

1 The man should try to sell them for a profit.
2 They should be hung in an art gallery.
3 The man should find out what they are worth.
4 They should be displayed properly.

No. 12

1 He forgot to fill the water bottles.
2 He did not tell her the water would be turned off.
3 He lost the notices about the water pipe inspection.
4 He damaged the water pipes.

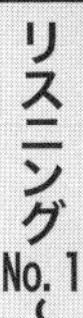

Part 2

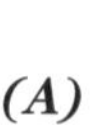

(A)

No. 13

1 When each of the crops is planted is important.
2 They only grow in a small region of North America.
3 They have difficulty competing with weeds.
4 There needs to be space between the plants.

No. 14

1 Use more-modern growing techniques.
2 Find new plants that can be grown in the desert.
3 Teach others how to grow the Three Sisters.
4 Recover forgotten growing methods.

(B)

No. 15

1 They do not give enough thought to their children's safety.
2 They are often forced to set strict rules for their children.
3 They should spend more time with their children.
4 They are giving their children a variety of experiences.

No. 16

1 Set times when streets are closed to cars.
2 Remove parking lots from playgrounds.
3 Build new roads outside the center of cities.
4 Make cars safer by changing their design.

(C)

No. 17

1 They explain how the rain forest formed.
2 They show what early humans looked like.
3 They include creatures that have died out.
4 They were used in religious ceremonies.

No. 18

1 They do not need to be preserved.
2 They were probably made by Europeans.
3 They used to be much more detailed.
4 They are not thousands of years old.

(D)

No. 19

1 It was based on a popular movie.
2 It gave away many luxury items.
3 It had weekly comedy competitions.
4 It led many people to buy TV sets.

No. 20

1 Starting a charity to support Black performers.
2 Fighting racism in the TV industry.
3 The unique advertisements he produced.
4 His amazing dancing ability.

(E)

No. 21

1 It occurs more often when people are younger.
2 Previous research on it had involved mainly male subjects.
3 It became more common after the nineteenth century.
4 People often mistake it for other feelings.

No. 22

1 Exploring large public locations.
2 Viewing spaces that had exactly the same furniture.
3 Performing the same activity in different spaces.
4 Entering a space with a familiar layout.

(F)

No. 23

1 They traveled faster than other arrows.
2 They were effective against armor.
3 They were the longest type of arrow.
4 They were commonly made with steel.

No. 24

1 He forced men to practice using longbows.
2 He was an expert at shooting a longbow.
3 He was badly injured in a longbow attack.
4 He sold longbows to foreign armies.

Part 3

CD 青-48

(G)

No. 25

Situation: You need a bag to use during your upcoming business trip. You will also go hiking using the bag on your days off. A shop employee tells you the following.

Question: Which bag should you buy?

1 The Western.
2 The Dangerfield.
3 The Spartan.
4 The Winfield.

CD 青-49

(H)

No. 26

Situation: You need to park your car near the airport for 16 days. You want the best price but are worried about your car being damaged. A friend tells you about options.

Question: Which parking lot should you use?

1 SKM Budget Parking.
2 The Vanier Plaza Hotel.
3 Nelson Street Skypark.
4 The Econolodge.

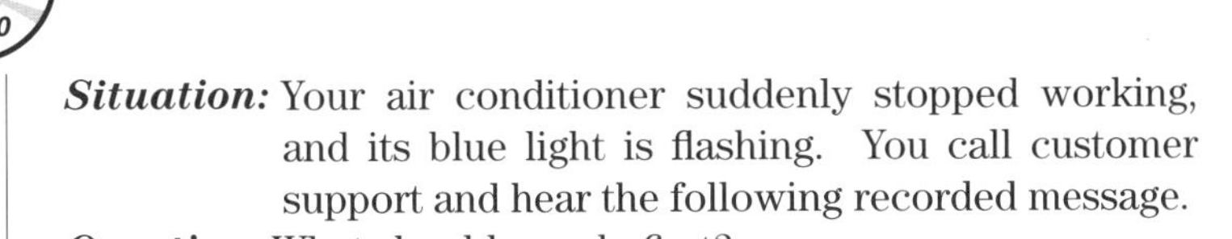

(I)

No. 27

Situation: Your air conditioner suddenly stopped working, and its blue light is flashing. You call customer support and hear the following recorded message.

Question: What should you do first?

1 Remove the air conditioner filter.
2 Open up the air conditioner panel.
3 Disconnect the air conditioner.
4 Arrange a service appointment.

(J)

No. 28

Situation: You want to order a back issue of a monthly science magazine. You are interested in genetics. You call the magazine publisher and are told the following.

Question: Which issue should you order?

1 The July issue.
2 The August issue.
3 The October issue.
4 The November issue.

(K)

No. 29

Situation: You bought five cans of Bentham Foods tuna fish at the supermarket on May 30. You hear the following announcement on TV. You have not eaten any of the tuna.

Question: What should you do?

1 Take the cans to the store you bought them at.
2 Call the Bentham Foods recall hotline.
3 Arrange to have the cans picked up.
4 Visit the Bentham Foods website for instructions.

◉二次試験・面接

※本書では出題例として２種類のカードを掲載していますが，本番では１枚のみ渡されます。
※面接委員の質問など，二次試験に関する音声はCDに収録されていません。

受験者用問題　カード　A

You have **one minute** to prepare.

This is a story about a university student who lived with his family.
You have **two minutes** to narrate the story.

Your story should begin with the following sentence:
One day, a university student was watching TV with his mother and grandfather.

No. 1 Please look at the fourth picture. If you were the university student, what would you be thinking?

Now, Mr. / Ms. _____, please turn over the card and put it down.

No. 2 Do you think parents should be stricter with their children?

No. 3 Can people trust the news that they see on TV these days?

No. 4 Will more people choose to work past retirement age in the future?

受験者用問題　カード　B

You have **one minute** to prepare.

This is a story about a woman who worked at a dentist's office.
You have **two minutes** to narrate the story.

Your story should begin with the following sentence:
One day, a woman was working at the reception desk of a dentist's office.

No.1 Please look at the fourth picture. If you were the woman, what would you be thinking?

Now, Mr. / Ms. _____, please turn over the card and put it down.

No. 2 Do you think it is harder to raise children now than it was in the past?

No. 3 Do you think companies focus too much on making their products cheaper?

No. 4 Will the government be able to meet the needs of Japan's aging society?

準1級

2022年度 第3回

一次試験 2023.1.22実施

二次試験 A日程 2023.2.19実施
B日程 2023.2.26実施
C日程 2023.3.5実施

一次試験・筆記(90分)
pp.98〜113

一次試験・リスニング(約31分)
pp.114〜119
CD赤-1〜26

二次試験・面接(約8分)
pp.120〜123

※解答一覧は別冊p.91
※解答と解説は別冊pp.92〜134

※別冊の巻末についている解答用マークシートを使いましょう。

合格基準スコア

- **一次試験**……1792
(満点2250/リーディング750,リスニング750,ライティング750)
- **二次試験**……512(満点750/スピーキング750)

◉一次試験・筆記

To complete each item, choose the best word or phrase from among the four choices. Then, on your answer sheet, find the number of the question and mark your answer.

(1) Fernando has been (　　　) to the success of the company, so everyone is worried about what will happen after he quits next month.

1 desperate　**2** philosophical
3 inadequate　**4** instrumental

(2) Some people feel the film was (　　　). Although it did not win any awards, there are those who believe it was a great work of art.

1 overtaken　**2** overridden　**3** underfed　**4** underrated

(3) More than 50 million people (　　　) during World War II. That is more deaths than in any other war in history.

1 worshiped　**2** perished　**3** haunted　**4** jeered

(4) Walt's restaurant serves dishes that were traditionally eaten by poor people in the countryside. He says (　　　) were skilled at creating delicious meals from cheap ingredients.

1 correspondents　**2** janitors
3 captives　**4** peasants

(5) The discovery of a serious (　　　) in the design plans for the new building caused the construction to be delayed by several months.

1 clog　**2** boom　**3** flaw　**4** dump

(6) When it came time to deliver her presentation, Rachel found herself (　　　) with fear. She simply stood in front of everyone, unable to speak.

1 trimmed　**2** teased　**3** paralyzed　**4** acquired

(7) Despite the fact that the two countries had once fought each other in a war, they now enjoy an (　　　) relationship and are, in fact, allies.

1 alleged　**2** amicable　**3** abusive　**4** adhesive

(8) Tina's new goal is to get healthy. In addition to including more vegetables in her diet, she has decided to (　　　) an exercise program into her daily routine.

1 commemorate　**2** alienate
3 liberate　**4** incorporate

(9) Some historians believe the (　　　) of dogs occurred over 10,000 years ago. They have been kept as pets and used to work on farms ever since.

1 elevation　**2** domestication
3 deception　**4** verification

(10) Oscar is well-known for his friendly personality and good manners. Every morning, he (　　　) greets everyone in the office as he walks toward his desk.

1 scarcely　**2** courteously　**3** tediously　**4** obnoxiously

(11) The plan for a new library was put on hold because of a lack of funds. A few years later, however, the plan was (　　　), and construction work started.

1 deprived　**2** revived　**3** obstructed　**4** agitated

(12) Maggie's grandmother has recently become very (　　　). She now needs help to walk and cannot climb stairs by herself.

1 poetic　**2** savage　**3** frail　**4** rash

(13) The novelist likes to work in (　　　). She says she can only write well when she is in her country house, which is located in an area with no people around.

1 solitude　**2** corruption　**3** excess　**4** consent

(14) Archaeologists found many ( ), including pieces of jewelry and pottery, while digging at the ancient burial ground. These will be given to the local history museum.

1 setbacks **2** artifacts **3** pledges **4** salutes

(15) With faster Internet connections and better computers, more information can be ( ) at high speed than ever before.

1 transmitted **2** rejoiced **3** nauseated **4** offended

(16) Maria criticized her brother and called him ( ) after she learned that he had lost all of his money gambling.

1 pathetic **2** analytical **3** dedicated **4** ceaseless

(17) The architect was famous for designing buildings in a ( ) style. He wanted his designs to reflect current social and cultural trends.

1 preceding **2** simultaneous

3 plentiful **4** contemporary

(18) A lack of media ( ) left the town uninformed about the chemical leak. The media only started reporting about the incident once the leak was out of control.

1 enrollment **2** coverage **3** assortment **4** leverage

(19) After years of spending more money than taxes brought in, the government now has a ( ) of trillions of dollars.

1 fatigue **2** petition **3** deficit **4** conspiracy

(20) The artist made a living by ( ) detailed figures out of stone. In order to cut such a hard substance, she used a number of special tools.

1 carving **2** luring **3** soothing **4** ranking

(21) Ruth watched from the bench as her team ran up and down the court. Unfortunately, a shoulder injury had forced her to ( ) from the game.

1 withdraw **2** bypass **3** upgrade **4** overload

(22) Jocelyn could see the storm ( ) from the west. The skies began to darken, and the wind gradually grew stronger.

1 rolling in **2** adding up
3 holding out **4** passing down

(23) The company suffered from five years of decreasing sales until it finally ( ). It closed its doors forever last week.

1 dialed up **2** went under
3 came along **4** pulled through

(24) The print on the contract was so small that Gus needed a magnifying glass to ( ) the words.

1 make out **2** tune up **3** draw up **4** blow out

(25) The cat was ( ) her newborn kittens. She became nervous whenever anyone stepped too close to them.

1 packing up **2** looking into
3 watching over **4** showing up

2

Read each passage and choose the best word or phrase from among the four choices for each blank. Then, on your answer sheet, find the number of the question and mark your answer.

California Chinatown

In the late nineteenth century, Chinese immigrants to the United States faced significant discrimination from White Americans when looking for employment and accommodation. (***26***), they tended to live in neighborhoods known as Chinatowns, where there were better opportunities to find jobs and housing. One of the largest Chinatowns was in the city of San Jose, California, but because it was destroyed in a fire in 1887, little has been known about the lives of its inhabitants.

It was long assumed that the food items supplied to San Jose's Chinatown originated in Hong Kong and China. Recently, however, archaeologists' analysis of fish bones at a former trash pit has provided evidence that (***27***). These particular bones stood out because they belonged to a species known as the giant snakehead. Since the fish is native not to China or Hong Kong but rather to Southeast Asian nations, archaeologists believe it was transported to Hong Kong after being caught elsewhere, then shipped to the United States for consumption.

While the discovery offers insight into the complexity of the trade networks that supplied San Jose's Chinatown, other discoveries at the site have revealed information about the lifestyles of the neighborhood's immigrant residents. For example, it seems residents (***28***). While the presence of cow remains suggests residents had adopted the Western habit of eating beef, pig bones were the most common type of animal remains archaeologists discovered. As pork was a staple of the diets in their home country, the bones indicate the custom of raising and consuming pigs continued among the immigrants.

(26)
1 Consequently
2 Despite this
3 Similarly
4 In contrast

(27)
1 has led to more mystery
2 many foods were of poor quality
3 this was not always the case
4 not all shipments arrived safely

(28)
1 were more divided than previously thought
2 often sent packages to China
3 struggled to obtain enough food
4 maintained some of their food traditions

Plant Plan

Most flowering plants rely on insects for pollination. When an insect makes contact with a flower, it gets pollen on its body. Then, when the insect moves around on the plant or visits another plant of the same species, this pollen comes into contact with the female part of that plant. This pollination process allows plant reproduction to occur. (***29***), the plants usually provide something the insect needs, such as a meal of nectar.

Flowering plants succeed in attracting pollinating insects in various ways. For example, some plants draw the attention of flies with the use of brightly colored petals. Researchers recently found that one plant, *Aristolochia microstoma*, attracts flies by smelling like the dead beetles that some flies lay eggs in. But the plant does more than simply (***30***). It temporarily traps them within its flowers; as a fly moves around inside, the pollen on its body spreads onto the plant. The plant also ensures its own pollen gets onto the fly's body so that the insect can pollinate another plant after being released.

The researchers found the plant actually releases the same chemical that gives dead beetles their smell. Because this chemical is rarely found in plants, the researchers believe the plant has evolved specifically to target flies that use dead beetles as egg-laying sites. They also say that (***31***). This comes from the fact that the plant's flowers are located among dead leaves and rocks on the ground—exactly where the flies usually search for dead beetles.

(29)
1 Rather
2 In short
3 Nonetheless
4 In exchange

(30)
1 collect dead insects
2 hide its smell from insects
3 trick the flies with its smell
4 provide a safe place for flies

(31)
1 there is further support for this theory
2 the chemical has another purpose
3 the plant is an important food source
4 many insects see the plant as a danger

3	*Read each passage and choose the best answer from among the four choices for each question. Then, on your answer sheet, find the number of the question and mark your answer.*

Fences and Ecosystems

Fences help to divide property and provide security, among other things. They can also affect ecosystems. A study in the journal *BioScience* concluded that fences create both "winners" and "losers" among animal species in the regions in which they are placed. According to the study, generalist species—those that can consume a variety of foods and can survive in multiple habitats—have little problem with physical boundaries. On the other hand, specialist species, which require unique conditions to survive, suffer from being cut off from a particular food source or geographical area. Because specialist species outnumber generalist species, the study found that for every winner, there are multiple losers.

The impact of fences is not limited to ecosystems. In the mid-twentieth century, Botswana in Southern Africa erected fences to address international regulations designed to prevent the spread of a disease affecting cattle. While the fences have helped protect cattle, they have prevented the seasonal movements of animals such as wildebeests and blocked their access to water. The resulting decline in wildebeest populations threatens not only the ecosystem but also the region's wildlife tourism. The government's continued reliance on fences has led to concerns that limiting animal migration will hurt wildlife tourism, which is valuable to Botswana's economy.

The negative ecological effects of fences can be limited by making changes to them to allow certain animals through. Nevertheless, the study's authors believe a more fundamental change is necessary. Eliminating all fences, they say, is not a realistic option; instead, fence planning should be carried out with an eye on the big picture. For example, fences are often constructed to obtain short-term results and then removed, but researchers have found that months—or even years—later, some animals continue to behave as if the fences are still there. Consideration should therefore be given to all aspects of fence design and location to ensure a minimal impact on ecosystems.

(32) The study introduced in the first paragraph showed that

1 fences that cross through more than one type of habitat benefit animals more than those built within a single habitat.

2 although fences create many problems, they have less of an effect on the ability of animal populations to survive than previously thought.

3 fences are effective at protecting some species from other harmful species that tend to use up the resources many animals need to survive.

4 although fences are not harmful to some species, they can have serious negative effects on a large number of animals.

(33) What is true with regard to the fences that were built in Botswana?

1 The changes that they caused in the migration patterns of animals resulted in the spread of disease among cattle.

2 They could be responsible for indirectly affecting an industry that is important to the country's economy.

3 They are considered necessary in order to increase the safety of tourists who visit the country to see wildlife.

4 The success they have had in reducing disease-spreading species has benefited ecosystems in unexpected ways.

(34) What is one reason that careful planning is necessary when constructing fences?

1 Changing the design of a fence after it has been built can actually cause more problems than building a new one.

2 It is possible that fences will continue to have an effect on animals in an area even after the fences have been removed.

3 Putting up multiple fences in a given area without a clear plan beforehand has not stopped animals from entering dangerous areas.

4 The number of animal species that make use of fences to protect themselves from predators has increased.

The Soccer War

In July 1969, there was a short yet intense war between the Central American countries of El Salvador and Honduras following a series of World Cup qualifying soccer matches they played against each other. Although the conflict is often called the "Soccer War," its causes went far beyond sports.

Honduras is much larger than El Salvador but is far less densely populated. Since the late 1800s, land in El Salvador had been controlled primarily by elite families, which meant there was little space for ordinary farmers. By the 1960s, around 300,000 Salvadorans had entered Honduras illegally to obtain cheap land or jobs. The Honduran government blamed the immigrants for its economic stresses and removed them from their lands, forcing them out of the country. Wealthy Salvadorans feared the negative economic effects of so many immigrants returning home and threatened to overthrow the Salvadoran president if military action was not taken against Honduras. This, combined with border disputes that had existed for many years, brought relations between the countries to a low point.

Tensions were raised further by the media of both countries, which made up or exaggerated stories that fueled their bitterness toward one another. The Salvadoran press accused the Honduran government of cruel and illegal treatment of Salvadoran immigrants, while the Honduran press reported that those same immigrants were committing serious crimes. Such reports were made at the request of the countries' governments: in El Salvador, the goal was to convince the public that military force against its neighbor was necessary, while in Honduras, the government wanted to gain public support for its decision to force Salvadoran immigrants out of the country.

The World Cup qualifying matches were happening at the same time as the migrant situation was intensifying. On the day of the last match, El Salvador accused Honduras of violence against Salvadorans and cut off relations, and within weeks, El Salvador's military attacked Honduras, beginning the war. Historians note that the term Soccer War was misleading. At the time, the United States was part of an alliance with Central American nations, but it chose to stay out of the war. In fact, according to an American diplomat, the inaccurate belief that a sporting event was behind the conflict led the US government to overlook its seriousness. Issues such as land ownership, which were the true origin of the conflict, remained unresolved. This led to continued political and social instability and, ultimately, a civil war in El Salvador in the following decades.

(35) According to the second paragraph, in what way were Salvadoran immigrants to Honduras a cause of the "Soccer War"?

1 El Salvador's president believed the removal of the immigrants from their homes in Honduras was a sign that Honduras was going to attack.

2 The Honduran government began sending poor Hondurans to seek land in El Salvador, causing upset Salvadoran farmers to move to Honduras in response.

3 Rich Salvadorans pressured their government to make war against Honduras after the immigrants were forced out of their homes.

4 The immigrants' constant movement back and forth between the countries created trouble for Honduran border officials.

(36) In the time before the start of the Soccer War, the media in each country

1 attempted to pressure both governments to ensure that the Salvadoran immigrants received better treatment.

2 were prevented by their governments from reporting on illegal acts that were being committed against citizens.

3 put so much emphasis on the soccer rivalry that they failed to report more-important news about illegal acts.

4 were asked by their governments to make up untrue or misleading news stories that made the other country look bad.

(37) What does the author of the passage suggest in the final paragraph?

1 American diplomats still continue to worry that fighting will break out between Honduras and El Salvador again.

2 The terrible effects of the Soccer War made Honduras and El Salvador realize that their actions leading up to the war were wrong.

3 A mistaken belief about the Soccer War meant that its real causes were not recognized, resulting in another conflict.

4 The US government's policies caused many Central American nations to cut off relations, making the conflict in the region worse.

Competing against Braille

Although Braille is the standard writing system for blind people today, this alphabet of raised dots representing letters was not always the only system. Another system, Boston Line Type, was created in the 1830s by Samuel Gridley Howe, a sighted instructor at a US school for blind people. Howe's system utilized the letters in the standard English alphabet used by sighted people, but they were raised so they could be felt by the fingers. Blind students, however, found it more challenging to distinguish one letter from another than they did with Braille. Nevertheless, Howe believed that the fact that reading materials could be shared by both blind and sighted readers outweighed this disadvantage. His system, he argued, would allow blind people to better integrate into society; he thought Braille encouraged isolation because it was unfamiliar to most sighted people.

It gradually became clear that a system using dots was not only easier for most blind people to read but also more practical, as the dots made writing relatively simple. Writing with Boston Line Type required a special printing press, but Braille required only simple, portable tools, and it could also be typed on a typewriter. Still, despite students' overwhelming preference for Braille, Boston Line Type remained in official use in schools for the blind because it allowed sighted instructors to teach without having to learn new sets of symbols. Even when Boston Line Type lost popularity, other systems continued to be introduced, leading to what became known as the "War of the Dots," a situation in which various writing systems competed to become the standard.

One of these, called New York Point, was similar to Braille in that it consisted of raised dots. Its main advantage was that typing it required only one hand. Braille, though, could more efficiently and clearly display capital letters and certain forms of punctuation. There were other candidates as well, and debates about which was superior soon became bitter. Blind people, meanwhile, were severely inconvenienced; books they could read were already in short supply, and the competing systems further limited their options, as learning a new system required great time and effort. At one national convention, a speaker reportedly summed up their frustrations by jokingly suggesting a violent response to the next person who invents a new system of printing for the blind.

The War of the Dots continued into the 1900s, with various groups battling for funding and recognition. In the end, the blind activist Helen Keller was extremely influential in ending the debate. She stated that New York Point's weaknesses in regard to capitalization and punctuation were extremely serious and that reading it was hard on her fingers. Braille won out, and other systems gradually disappeared. Although the War of the Dots interfered with blind people's education for a time, it had a silver lining: the intense battle stimulated the development of various technologies, such as new typewriters, that greatly enhanced blind people's literacy rates and ability to participate in modern society.

(38) What did Samuel Gridley Howe believe about Boston Line Type?

1 The time it saved blind people in reading made up for the fact that it took much longer to write than Braille.

2 The fact that it combined raised dots with other features made it easier for blind people to use it when communicating with one another.

3 Although it was difficult for students to learn, the fact that it could be read more quickly than Braille was a major advantage.

4 It was worth adopting because of the role it could play in helping blind people to better fit in with people who are able to see.

(39) In the second paragraph, what does the author of the passage suggest about Boston Line Type?

1 Its continued use was not in the best interests of blind people, whose opinions about which system should be used were seemingly not taken into account.

2 Teachers at schools for the blind convinced students not to use it because they thought systems with fewer dots would be easier for students to read.

3 Despite it causing the "War of the Dots," its popularity among students was a key factor in the development of other tools for blind people.

4 It was only successfully used in writing by students in schools for the blind after the introduction of the typewriter.

(40) The suggestion by the speaker at the national convention implies that blind people

1 felt that neither Braille nor the New York Point system could possibly meet the needs of blind readers.

2 were unhappy that the debates over which system to use were indirectly preventing them from accessing reading materials.

3 did not like that they were being forced to use a writing system that had not been developed by a blind person.

4 were starting to think that other types of education had become much more important than learning to read books.

(41) What conclusion does the author of the passage make about the War of the Dots?

1 It was so serious that it is still having a negative influence on the research and development of technology for the blind today.

2 It would have caused fewer bad feelings if Helen Keller had not decided that she should become involved in it.

3 It had some positive effects in the long term because the competition led to improvements in the lives of blind people.

4 It could have been avoided if people in those days had been more accepting of technologies like the typewriter.

4

- *Write an essay on the given TOPIC.*
- *Use TWO of the POINTS below to support your answer.*
- *Structure: introduction, main body, and conclusion*
- *Suggested length: 120-150 words*
- *Write your essay in the space provided on Side B of your answer sheet. Any writing outside the space will not be graded.*

TOPIC

Agree or disagree: The government should do more to promote reusable products

POINTS

- *Costs*
- *Effect on businesses*
- *Garbage*
- *Safety*

◉一次試験・Listening Test

There are three parts to this listening test.

Part 1	**Dialogues:**	1 question each	Multiple-choice
Part 2	**Passages:**	2 questions each	Multiple-choice
Part 3	**Real-Life:**	1 question each	Multiple-choice

※ Listen carefully to the instructions.

Part 1

No. 1

1 Get the man to fill in for the receptionist.
2 Ask the man to fire the receptionist.
3 Do the receptionist's job herself.
4 Warn the receptionist about being late.

No. 2

1 He has to improve his class performance.
2 He cannot change his work schedule.
3 He will quit his part-time job.
4 He does not go to science class.

No. 3

1 He cannot pay his children's college fees.
2 He lives too far from his company.
3 He believes he is being underpaid.
4 He feels unable to leave his current job.

No. 4

1 She is frequently given new goals.
2 She is not paid enough for overtime work.
3 Her vacation request was denied.
4 Her report received negative feedback.

No. 5

1 She should complete her master's degree next year.
2 She should get some work experience.
3 She can rely on his help for one year.
4 She should save some money first.

No. 6

1 Review the website more carefully.
2 Choose the same plan as the man.
3 Request a meeting with personnel.
4 Look for another insurance plan.

No. 7

1 He got stuck in heavy traffic.
2 He had trouble with his car.
3 He slept for too long.
4 He got lost on the highway.

No. 8

1 Jason's teachers should make more effort.
2 Jason should transfer to a private school.
3 Jason's homework load has increased.
4 Jason should be sent to a tutor.

No. 9

1 The man should return to his previous position.
2 She will change her position soon.
3 The man should spend more time at home.
4 She would like to travel for work more.

No. 10

1 The station renovations are behind schedule.
2 Her train was more crowded than usual.
3 She had trouble changing trains.
4 The station she always uses was closed.

No. 11

1 To keep her mind active.
2 To improve her job skills.
3 To take her mind off work.
4 To get ideas for her fiction writing.

No. 12

1 He is an experienced mountain climber.
2 He has not gotten much exercise recently.
3 He wants to take a challenging trail.
4 He dislikes riding in cable cars.

Part 2

(A)

No. 13

1 To improve her failing health.
2 To show off her cycling technique.
3 To challenge a gender stereotype.
4 To test a new kind of bicycle.

No. 14

1 She helped companies to advertise their products.
2 She made and sold women's clothing.
3 She founded a spring water company.
4 She took jobs that were usually done by men.

(B)

No. 15

1 The images reminded them of Germany.
2 The images were made by professional artists.
3 The images were believed to bring good luck.
4 The images were painted on strips of fabric.

No. 16

1 More people have begun sewing as a hobby.
2 Tourism has increased in some areas.
3 Competition among farms has increased.
4 More barns have been built on farms.

(C)

No. 17

1 It lasted a little under a century.
2 It led to new discoveries about weather patterns.
3 It had the largest effect on people near volcanoes.
4 It had a global impact on farming.

No. 18

1 Europeans in North America started building large cities.
2 Forests expanded across the Americas.
3 The growing global population increased pollution.
4 Disease killed off many trees across Europe.

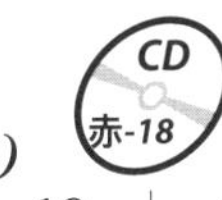

(D)

No. 19

1 The increase in noise caused by growing cities.
2 People's attempts to catch them.
3 The brightness of urban areas.
4 Growing competition with other insects.

No. 20

1 Locate fireflies that are not producing light.
2 Help them to get more funding for research.
3 Use a different type of light around their homes.
4 Make reports on any fireflies they see.

(E)

No. 21

1 To study dogs' understanding of words.
2 To study dogs' responses to different voices.
3 To study various ways of training dogs.
4 To study how dogs react to their owners' emotions.

No. 22

1 It was consistent with their owners' reports.
2 It varied depending on the breed of the dog.
3 It was opposite to that of human brains.
4 It increased in response to familiar commands.

(F)

No. 23

1 They help people to keep warm in winter.
2 They are useful for storing some vegetables.
3 Their name comes from their shape.
4 They are used to grow vegetables all year round.

No. 24

1 They help to support the local economy.
2 They provide a model for surrounding villages.
3 They help the fishing industry to survive.
4 They were found to contain valuable minerals.

Part 3

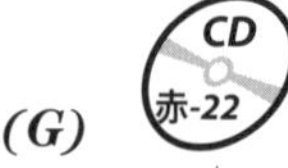

(G)

No. 25

Situation: You have just landed at the airport. You need to get downtown as soon as possible. You are told the following at the information desk.

Question: How should you go downtown?

1 By bus.
2 By subway.
3 By taxi.
4 By light-rail.

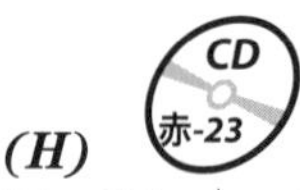

(H)

No. 26

Situation: You speak some Italian but want to brush up before your vacation in Italy in three months. You are free on Mondays and Thursdays. A language-school representative tells you the following.

Question: Which course should you choose?

1 Martina's.
2 Giovanni's.
3 Teresa's.
4 Alfredo's.

(I)

No. 27

Situation: You have just arrived at a shopping mall to buy a new business suit. You want to save as much money as you can. You hear the following announcement.

Question: Which floor should you go to first?

1 The first floor.
2 The second floor.
3 The third floor.
4 The fourth floor.

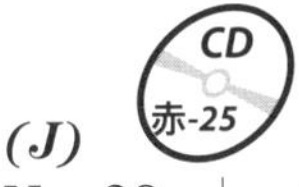

(J)

No. 28

Situation: You and your family are at a theme park. Your children are very interested in animals and nature. You hear the following announcement.

Question: Which attraction should you go to?

1 Lizard Encounter.
2 Discovery Drive.
3 Into the Sky.
4 Dream Fields.

(K)

No. 29

Situation: You want your son to learn a new skill. He already takes swimming lessons after school on Wednesdays. A school administrator makes the following announcement.

Question: Who should you speak to?

1 Mr. Gilbert.
2 Ms. DeLuca.
3 Mr. Roth.
4 Ms. Santos.

◉二次試験・面接

※本書では出題例として2種類のカードを掲載していますが，本番では1枚のみ渡されます。
※面接委員の質問など，二次試験に関する音声はCDに収録されていません。

受験者用問題　カード　A

You have **one minute** to prepare.

This is a story about a president of a small company.
You have **two minutes** to narrate the story.

Your story should begin with the following sentence:
One day, a company president was walking around the office.

No.1 Please look at the fourth picture. If you were the company president, what would you be thinking?

Now, Mr. / Ms. _____, please turn over the card and put it down.

No. 2 Do you think that salary is the most important factor when choosing a career?

No. 3 Are people's opinions too easily influenced by the media?

No. 4 Should the government do more to protect workers' rights?

受験者用問題　カード　B

You have **one minute** to prepare.

This is a story about a girl who wanted to learn to skateboard.
You have **two minutes** to narrate the story.

Your story should begin with the following sentence:
One day, a girl was walking home from school.

No.1 Please look at the fourth picture. If you were the girl, what would you be thinking?

Now, Mr. / Ms. _____, please turn over the card and put it down.

No. 2 Is it important for parents to participate in their children's school life?

No. 3 Is playing sports a good way for young people to develop a strong character?

No. 4 Do you think international events such as the Olympics can improve relations between nations?

準1級

2022年度 第2回

一次試験 2022.10.9実施

二次試験 A日程 2022.11.6実施
B日程 2022.11.13実施
C日程 2022.11.23実施

一次試験・筆記(90分)
pp.126～141

一次試験・リスニング(約31分)
pp.142～147
CD赤-27～52

二次試験・面接(約8分)
pp.148～151

※解答一覧は別冊p.135
※解答と解説は別冊pp.136～178

※別冊の巻末についている解答用マークシートを使いましょう。

合格基準スコア

- 一次試験……1792
(満点2250／リーディング750, リスニング750, ライティング750)
- 二次試験……512(満点750／スピーキング750)

◉一次試験・筆記

1

To complete each item, choose the best word or phrase from among the four choices. Then, on your answer sheet, find the number of the question and mark your answer.

(1) ***A:*** Mom, can you make hamburgers for dinner tonight?
B: Yes, but I'll have to take the meat out of the freezer and let it (　　) first.

1 reckon　**2** thaw　**3** stray　**4** shatter

(2) Jocelyn always reminded her son not to tell lies. She believed it was important to (　　) a strong sense of honesty in him.

1 remodel　**2** stumble　**3** overlap　**4** instill

(3) Zara was very angry with her boyfriend, but she forgave him after hearing his (　　) apology. She was sure that he really was sorry.

1 detectable　**2** earnest　**3** cumulative　**4** underlying

(4) At first, the Smiths enjoyed their backyard swimming pool, but keeping it clean became such a (　　) that they left it covered most of the time.

1 bureau　**2** nuisance　**3** sequel　**4** metaphor

(5) Throughout the course of history, many great thinkers were at first (　　) for their ideas before eventually being taken seriously.

1 saturated　**2** flattered　**3** ingested　**4** ridiculed

(6) At first, the little girl felt (　　) in front of the large audience at the speech contest, but after about a minute she began to feel more confident.

1 mortal　**2** bashful　**3** pious　**4** concise

(7) Typewriters are a (　　　) of the past. They remind us how far technology has advanced since they were common in offices and homes.

1 jumble　**2** relic　**3** fraud　**4** treaty

(8) When the man approached the tiger's cage, the huge animal (　　　) deeply. The man stepped back in fear at the terrifying sound.

1 sparkled　**2** leered　**3** disproved　**4** growled

(9) Police officers must promise to (　　　) the law. This includes, of course, following the law themselves.

1 gravitate　**2** detach　**3** uphold　**4** eradicate

(10) All employees have a (　　　) medical checkup every year. Companies are required by law to make sure all their workers do it.

1 gloomy　**2** compulsory　**3** reminiscent　**4** muddled

(11) Biology students must learn how cell (　　　) works, as this process of a single cell splitting into two is commonly found in nature.

1 division　**2** appliance　**3** imposition　**4** longitude

(12) After the two companies (　　　), several senior employees became unnecessary and lost their jobs.

1 merged　**2** posed　**3** conformed　**4** flocked

(13) In order to avoid becoming (　　　) while exercising, one should always drink enough water. The longer the workout, the more water is necessary.

1 dehydrated　**2** eternal　**3** punctuated　**4** cautious

(14) Ken was always well behaved at home, so his mother was shocked when his teacher said he was one of the most (　　) students in his class.

1 momentary **2** miniature **3** disobedient **4** invincible

(15) The police questioned (　　) at the scene of the crime, hoping someone who had been nearby had seen what happened.

1 bystanders **2** reformers **3** mourners **4** pioneers

(16) Several generals attempted to (　　) the country's prime minister. However, they were unsuccessful, and he remains in power.

1 irrigate **2** harmonize **3** outpace **4** overthrow

(17) Caleb finished a draft of his proposal, so he asked his manager to (　　) it. Unfortunately, she thought it still needed a lot of improvement.

1 scrub **2** enchant **3** prune **4** evaluate

(18) American presidents Thomas Jefferson and John Adams exchanged letters with each other for over 50 years. This (　　) is an important part of American history.

1 matrimony **2** federation
3 horizon **4** correspondence

(19) During the riot, the town was in a state of (　　). People were out in the streets fighting and breaking windows, and many stores were robbed.

1 disclosure **2** admittance **3** attainment **4** anarchy

(20) The flowers of some plants are actually (　　) and can be used to make salads both more delicious and more visually attractive.

1 stationary **2** candid **3** edible **4** hideous

(21) No one was surprised when the famous scientist made many mistakes during his speech. He is ( ) for his poor speaking skills.
1 treacherous **2** momentous **3** flirtatious **4** notorious

(22) All of Brad's hard work and long hours ( ) when his boss gave him a promotion last month.
1 paid off **2** wrote back **3** chopped up **4** made over

(23) Since the CEO's speech was so vague, it took Gina a while to ( ) to the fact that the company was in serious financial trouble.
1 fill in **2** duck out **3** catch on **4** give up

(24) Each member of the team has a job to do for the new project, but the responsibility for coordinating all of their efforts ( ) the manager.
1 falls on **2** squares with **3** drops by **4** stacks up

(25) The employee tried to ( ) his theft from the company by destroying files and other evidence that proved his guilt.
1 tuck away **2** latch onto **3** cover up **4** doze off

2	*Read each passage and choose the best word or phrase from among the four choices for each blank. Then, on your answer sheet, find the number of the question and mark your answer.*

Nabta Playa's Stone Circle

Many prehistoric societies constructed stone circles. These were created for various reasons, such as tracking the sun's movement. The oldest such circle known to scientists can be found at Nabta Playa in Egypt. At around 7,000 years old, this circle predates England's Stonehenge—probably the world's best-known prehistoric stone circle—by more than 1,000 years. Nabta Playa's climate is extremely dry today, but this was not always the case. (***26***), heavy seasonal rainfall during the period when the circle was built led to the formation of temporary lakes, and these attracted cattle-grazing tribes to the area.

Nabta Playa's first settlers arrived around 10,000 years ago. Archaeologists have uncovered evidence that these settlers created a system of deep wells that gave them access to water year-round, and that they arranged their homes in straight rows and equipped them with storage spaces. They also practiced a religion that focused on the worship of cattle, which were central to their lives. These discoveries are evidence that the settlers (***27***).

Research findings show that some of the circle's stones would have lined up with the sun on the longest day of the year around 7,000 years ago. This suggests the circle was used as a calendar. One astrophysicist, however, believes the circle (***28***). He points out that the positions of other stones match those of stars in the constellation Orion at the time the circle was built. Because of this, he proposes that the circle was an astrological map showing the positions of stars in the night sky.

(26)
1 On the other hand
2 In fact
3 Despite this
4 Similarly

(27)
1 questioned religious ideas
2 lost interest in raising cattle
3 experienced serious internal conflicts
4 developed a sophisticated society

(28)
1 also had another purpose
2 was created much earlier
3 was originally built elsewhere
4 caused people to avoid the area

The Good Roads Movement

Beginning in the late nineteenth century, the Good Roads Movement transformed America's landscape, helping to create the nation's system of roads and highways. This movement (***29***). While most people today assume that the road system was first developed in response to the needs of automobile drivers, this is a myth. Actually, the demand started mainly with cyclists. The invention of the modern bicycle led to a cycling craze in the 1890s, and millions of Americans wanted better, safer roads to cycle on.

Cyclists began pressuring local governments to improve the quality of roads, which were often poorly maintained and dangerous. At first, the movement was resisted by farmers, who did not want their tax dollars to be spent supporting the leisure activities of cyclists from cities. Gradually, however, farmers (***30***). One reason for this was an influential pamphlet called *The Gospel of Good Roads: A Letter to the American Farmer*. It convinced many farmers by emphasizing the benefits of roads, such as making it easier for them to transport their crops to markets.

As automobiles became common, the movement quickly gained momentum. (***31***), the invention of the Ford Model T in the early 1900s led to many new drivers, who were also eager for better roads. Millions of these affordable cars were sold, and the increase in drivers put pressure on governments to build more roads and improve the quality of existing ones.

(29) **1** was started by car manufacturers
2 had a surprising origin
3 created disagreement among drivers
4 angered many cyclists

(30) **1** increased their protests
2 started using different roads
3 began to change their minds
4 turned against cyclists

(31) **1** By contrast
2 In particular
3 Nonetheless
4 Therefore

3	*Read each passage and choose the best answer from among the four choices for each question. Then, on your answer sheet, find the number of the question and mark your answer.*

Recognizing Faces

Humans are generally very good at recognizing faces and quickly interpreting their expressions. This is achieved by having specific areas of the brain that specialize in processing facial features. The development of this ability makes sense in terms of evolution, since early humans would have needed to judge, for example, whether those around them were angry and therefore potentially dangerous. One unintended consequence, however, is that people often think they see faces on objects in their environment. People perceive these so-called false faces on a variety of objects, from clouds and tree trunks to pieces of food and electric sockets.

Researchers in Australia recently performed a study to learn more about how the brain processes false faces. Previous studies have revealed that for real faces, people's judgment of what emotion a face is expressing is affected by the faces they have just seen. Seeing a series of happy faces, for example, tends to make people assess the face they next see as expressing happiness. In the Australian study, the researchers showed participants a series of false faces that expressed a particular emotion. They found that, as with real faces, the participants' judgments of the emotions expressed by the false faces were affected by the ones they had just been shown. Based on this finding, the researchers concluded that the brain processes false faces in a way similar to how it processes real ones.

The researchers also noted that any object with features that even loosely resemble the layout of a human face—two eyes and a nose above a mouth—can trigger the brain to assess those features for emotional expression. In other words, the brain's criteria for recognizing a face are general rather than specific. The researchers say this is one reason the brain can assess facial expressions so quickly.

(32) In the first paragraph, why does the author of the passage mention objects such as clouds?

1 To support the idea that people's surroundings can affect how well they are able to judge the emotions of others.

2 To describe how people who cannot identify faces also have trouble identifying certain other objects.

3 To help explain that our reactions to everyday objects in our environment are controlled by different areas of the brain.

4 To provide examples of everyday things on which people imagine they can see faces.

(33) Previous studies have shown that

1 people's judgments about what emotions real faces are expressing are influenced by other real faces they have seen immediately before.

2 people attach emotional meaning to false faces more quickly than they do to real faces.

3 people tend to judge the emotions expressed by false faces as happier and more positive than those expressed by real faces.

4 people take longer to distinguish false faces when the faces are not expressing any emotions.

(34) What do the researchers in Australia say about the brain's ability to assess the emotions expressed by faces?

1 The ability will likely disappear over time as it no longer provides an advantage to humans in terms of survival.

2 The fact that the brain uses loose criteria to identify faces allows people to quickly judge the emotions faces express.

3 The brain is only able to accurately identify the emotions faces express if those faces have very specific features.

4 The evolution of this ability occurred even though it created disadvantages as well as benefits for humans in the past.

Durians and Giant Fruit Bats

The football-sized durian fruit is well known for its unpleasant smell and creamy, sweet flesh. Known as the "king of fruits," durians are believed to have originated in Borneo, but they are now cultivated more widely, with over half of all durians consumed worldwide being grown in Thailand. Durians have long been popular throughout Southeast Asia, but their popularity is now spreading to other parts of the world. There are hundreds of kinds of durians, but the Musang King variety, which is grown almost exclusively in Malaysia, is one of the most highly valued. Durians contain high levels of vitamins, so they are often promoted for their health benefits, which has led to rising exports. In fact, experts predict there will be a 50 percent increase in shipments from Malaysia to China alone during the next decade. In order to take advantage of this situation, many Malaysian farmers have stopped producing crops such as palm oil in favor of producing durians.

Durian trees are not easy to grow, however. They require regular watering and feeding with fertilizer, and they are highly sensitive to temperature. Furthermore, they do not naturally grow in groves, but rather thrive when grown among other trees and shrubs, so growing them in an orchard as a single crop presents a challenge. Ensuring sufficient pollination of the flowers for the trees to produce a good harvest of fruit is a further difficulty for farmers. One characteristic of durian trees is that their flowers only release pollen at night, so insects such as honeybees that feed during the day do not pollinate them. Animals that are active at night take over the role of pollination, but only about 25 percent of a durian tree's flowers ever get pollinated naturally. Because of this, many farmers resort to the labor-intensive practice of pollinating by hand.

Studies have shown that giant fruit bats are the main natural pollinators of durian flowers. However, these bats are chased away or killed by many farmers, who simply see them as pests because they cause damage and reduce profits by feeding on the fruit. The bats are also threatened as a result of being hunted and sold as food, since there is a belief in some Southeast Asian cultures that eating the bats' meat helps to cure breathing problems. Without educating people about the benefits of giant fruit bats, the bats' numbers may decline further, which could have serious consequences for durian farming.

(35) According to the first paragraph, what is true about durian production?

1 Durians are now mainly grown in Malaysia because there is no longer enough land available to cultivate them in other Southeast Asian countries.

2 Although durians have been selling well in places where they were traditionally grown, they have yet to gain popularity in other countries.

3 Premium varieties of durians have been criticized by consumers because they have no more nutritional value than cheaper varieties.

4 Because of the increasing demand for durians, Malaysian farmers are switching from growing other crops to growing durians.

(36) One factor that durian farmers need to consider is that

1 although durian trees can be grown in almost any warm climate, they do best in areas where there are few other plants growing.

2 the tendency of durian trees to push out other plants is causing a sharp decline in the number of native plants.

3 durian trees should be grown in a location where they can be easily found by honeybees and other daytime pollinators.

4 if durian trees are left alone to be pollinated naturally, the trees are unlikely to produce a large amount of fruit.

(37) What is one thing the author of the passage says regarding giant fruit bats?

1 Durian production might suffer if awareness is not raised about the important role giant fruit bats play in durian flower pollination.

2 Many people in Southeast Asia have become ill as a result of eating bat meat that was sold illegally at some markets.

3 Some durian farmers deliberately attract giant fruit bats to their orchards so that they can catch them and sell their meat.

4 There has been a significant drop in natural pollinators of durian flowers because many giant fruit bats have died from breathing problems.

The Long Range Desert Group

During World War II, the British fought against Germany and Italy in the deserts of North Africa. Desert warfare was characterized by small battles between troops that were widely spread out, and there was a need to move quickly and at night to avoid both detection and the dangerous daytime heat. The area's vast size and sandy terrain made transporting supplies difficult, and the lack of water severely limited operations.

However, for one British army officer, Major Ralph Bagnold, these harsh conditions presented a strategic opportunity. Having spent years exploring the North African desert before the war, Bagnold knew the terrain well, and he was convinced that a small, highly mobile motorized unit that could observe and track enemy forces would be invaluable. At first, British commanders rejected his proposal to form such a unit, believing airplanes were better suited for such long-range intelligence gathering. Bagnold insisted, however, that gathering information on the ground would be advantageous, and his persistence led to the formation of the Long Range Desert Group (LRDG), with Bagnold as commander, in June 1940.

The LRDG was an unconventional unit from the outset. Usual distinctions between ranks did not apply; officers and regular soldiers were on first-name terms, and they were all expected to perform the same tasks. Rather than seeking men who would fight bravely on the battlefield, Bagnold wanted individuals with great stamina, resourcefulness, and mental toughness—men who could, for example, remain motivated and alert for extended periods despite limited access to drinking water. With specialized trucks adapted to desert conditions, the LRDG's patrols were equipped to operate independently for around three weeks and over a range of more than 1,600 kilometers. All necessary items, such as fuel, ammunition, and food, were carried by the unit, so careful supply planning was extremely important.

The LRDG's work mainly involved traveling deep behind enemy lines to observe their movements. The unit had access to a range of weaponry, and while the men were primarily trained to gather intelligence, they also planted mines and launched attacks against enemy airfields and fuel depots. When the Special Air Service (SAS)— a British army unit formed in 1941 to conduct raids behind enemy lines— suffered heavy casualties after parachuting into enemy territory on its first mission, the LRDG was tasked with bringing back the survivors. The rescue mission was a success, and because of its men's extensive knowledge of the desert, the LRDG was given the responsibility of bringing the SAS to and from all future targets by land, providing both transportation and navigation. This almost certainly helped the SAS accomplish its raids with greater success and fewer casualties.

The LRDG's greatest achievement came in 1943, when the unit found a route that enabled British forces to get around heavily defended enemy lines without being detected, allowing them to attack at weaker points in the defenses. This was a crucial turning point in the campaign in North Africa and contributed greatly to the British victory there. The LRDG went on to make significant contributions to the war effort in Europe until 1945.

(38) Major Ralph Bagnold was able to convince British army commanders that

1 their soldiers were having limited success on missions in the desert because they were not being supplied with the right resources.

2 the airplanes being used to fly over enemy territory and make observations in the desert were in need of major improvements.

3 he could lead a unit of men on missions in the desert despite the fact that he had little experience in such an environment.

4 using a ground-based unit to gather information about enemy activities in the desert would be an effective strategy.

(39) What is true regarding the Long Range Desert Group (LRDG)?

1 The characteristics of the men chosen for it and the way it operated were different from those of traditional military units.

2 Because of its limited budget, it had to manage with fewer resources and older weapons than other units.

3 There were a large number of men in its patrols, so the officers had to have special training in management techniques.

4 The success of its missions was heavily dependent on the group having supplies sent to it behind enemy lines on a regular basis.

(40) Which of the following best describes the relationship between the LRDG and the Special Air Service (SAS)?

1 The two units were combined so that land and air raids could be performed at the same time.

2 The similar nature of their operations led to competition between the two units and their unwillingness to assist each other.

3 The LRDG used its knowledge of the desert to help the SAS improve both the effectiveness and safety of its missions.

4 The involvement of the SAS in LRDG missions made it more difficult for the LRDG to stay behind enemy lines for long periods of time.

(41) According to the author of the passage, what happened in 1943?

1 A mistake made by the LRDG allowed enemy forces to strengthen their hold on territory that the British hoped to gain.

2 The transfer of the LRDG to Europe meant the SAS had no choice but to attack enemy forces in a heavily defended area without LRDG support.

3 The activities of the LRDG made it possible for the British army to gain a significant advantage that led to it defeating enemy forces in the area.

4 British commanders decided the LRDG would be better put to use defending British-held territory than observing enemy activities.

- *Write an essay on the given TOPIC.*
- *Use TWO of the POINTS below to support your answer.*
- *Structure: introduction, main body, and conclusion*
- *Suggested length: 120-150 words*
- *Write your essay in the space provided on Side B of your answer sheet. Any writing outside the space will not be graded.*

TOPIC

Should people trust information on the Internet?

POINTS

- *Learning*
- *News*
- *Online shopping*
- *Social media*

◉一次試験・Listening Test

There are three parts to this listening test.

Part 1	Dialogues:	1 question each	Multiple-choice
Part 2	Passages:	2 questions each	Multiple-choice
Part 3	Real-Life:	1 question each	Multiple-choice

※ Listen carefully to the instructions.

Part 1

No. 1

1 Get a blood test today.
2 Try to eat less for breakfast.
3 Go to lunch with Noah.
4 Have a medical checkup next week.

No. 2

1 She needs to take more time off.
2 She should be less concerned about money.
3 She is not ready for so much responsibility.
4 She deserves more pay.

No. 3

1 He needs to undergo further tests.
2 He will not be able to play in the game.
3 He needs to find a different form of exercise.
4 He has to stay at the hospital.

No. 4

1 Contact the new employee.
2 Speak to the manager.
3 Work the shift herself.
4 Change shifts with him.

No. 5

1 Contact the hotel about Internet access.
2 Confirm the meeting schedule.
3 Finish preparing the presentation.
4 Buy a ticket for the flight.

No. 6

1 Take a taxi home.
2 Order more wine.
3 Catch the last train home.
4 Walk to the closest bus stop.

No. 7

1 Pick up the children from school.
2 Cook dinner for his family.
3 Buy the ingredients for tonight's dinner.
4 Order food from a new restaurant.

No. 8

1 He has to pay an unexpected fee.
2 He canceled his insurance policy.
3 He is late for a meeting.
4 The company cannot find his policy number.

No. 9

1 The man should not change his major.
2 A career in communications might suit the man better.
3 Graphic design is a good choice for the man.
4 The man is not doing well in class.

No. 10

1 Find another online chat tool.
2 Prepare a request for a software upgrade.
3 Get more people to join online meetings.
4 Ask to increase the company's budget.

No. 11

1 Go to the plant.
2 Study Spanish.
3 Meet with Barbara.
4 Look for an interpreter.

No. 12

1 Radio for an ambulance.
2 Move the woman's car for her.
3 Give the woman a parking ticket.
4 Wait in his police car.

Part 2

(A)

No. 13

1 It could not fly high enough.
2 It was too small and light.
3 It could only fly short distances.
4 It used a rare kind of fuel.

No. 14

1 It was tougher than other planes.
2 It had a new kind of weapon.
3 It could land very quickly.
4 It could drop bombs accurately.

(B)

No. 15

1 Water supplies decreased.
2 The air became less polluted.
3 Many people had to leave the island.
4 The number of trees increased.

No. 16

1 How to classify the new ecosystem.
2 What to use the water supply for.
3 Whether native plants should be protected.
4 Where agriculture should be allowed.

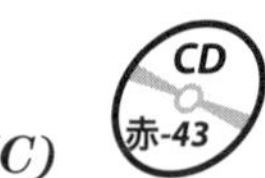

(C)

No. 17

1 She carried her camera everywhere.
2 She made friends with emergency workers.
3 She lent her camera to the children she took care of.
4 She went to many places as a tourist.

No. 18

1 She became famous early in her career.
2 She mainly took photos at auctions.
3 She held very large exhibitions.
4 She did not show people her photos.

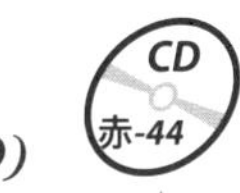

(D)

No. 19

1 It does not require the use of fresh water.
2 It can only be done in certain climates.
3 It produces a large amount of gas.
4 It uses less meat than it did in the past.

No. 20

1 The machines it uses are very expensive.
2 It is damaging to wide areas of land.
3 It releases chemicals into nearby farmland.
4 It is frequently dangerous for workers.

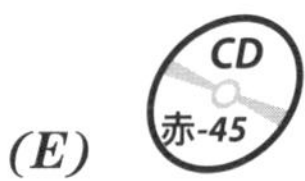

(E)

No. 21

1 Young people's changing interests.
2 Young people's increasing need for exercise.
3 Young people's economic situation.
4 Young people's passion for nature.

No. 22

1 They are unlikely to survive long.
2 They do not do well outside of cities.
3 They rarely employ local people.
4 They take up too much space.

(F)

No. 23

1 Alligators have efficient jaws.
2 Alligators are related to dinosaurs.
3 Alligators have muscles in unusual places.
4 Alligators evolved at the same time as *T. rex.*

No. 24

1 To help with food digestion.
2 To sense other animals.
3 To create new blood vessels.
4 To control their body temperature.

Part 3

CD 赤-48

(G)

No. 25

Situation: You are on a plane that has just landed, and you need to catch your connecting flight. A flight attendant is making an announcement.

Question: What should you do first after getting off the plane?

1 Collect your luggage.
2 Take a bus to another terminal.
3 Find a gate agent.
4 Get a new boarding pass printed.

CD 赤-49

(H)

No. 26

Situation: You want to buy some stick-type incense to burn to help you relax. A store clerk tells you the following.

Question: Which incense brand should you buy?

1 Bouquet Himalaya.
2 Magnolia's Sanctuary.
3 Akebono.
4 Shirley's Gift.

(I)

No. 27

Situation: It is Monday, and you receive a voice mail from a representative at your new Internet provider. You have to work this Thursday from noon to 8 p.m.

Question: What should you do?

1 Reschedule for this weekend.
2 Reschedule for a weekday next week.
3 Reschedule for this Thursday morning.
4 Reschedule for this Friday after 6 p.m.

(J)

No. 28

Situation: You are applying to a college to study psychology. An admissions officer is talking to you about your application.

Question: What should you do?

1 Pay your application fee.
2 Go to a campus event next week.
3 Get a letter of recommendation.
4 Submit your high school records.

(K)

No. 29

Situation: You are on a trip abroad and want to take a free local tour. You get carsick easily. You are told the following at your hotel's information desk.

Question: Which tour is the best for you?

1 The one from 1 p.m.
2 The one from 2:30 p.m.
3 The one from 3 p.m.
4 The one from 5 p.m.

◉二次試験・面接

※本書では出題例として2種類のカードを掲載していますが，本番では1枚のみ渡されます。
※面接委員の質問など，二次試験に関する音声はCDに収録されていません。

受験者用問題　カード　A

You have **one minute** to prepare.

This is a story about a couple that wanted to save money.
You have **two minutes** to narrate the story.

Your story should begin with the following sentence:
One day, a woman was talking with her husband.

No. 1 Please look at the fourth picture. If you were the woman, what would you be thinking?

Now, Mr. / Ms. _____, please turn over the card and put it down.

No. 2 Do you think it is better to buy a home than to rent a place to live?

No. 3 Should Japan increase the amount of green space in its cities?

No. 4 Do people these days maintain a good balance between their private lives and their careers?

受験者用問題　カード　B

You have **one minute** to prepare.

This is a story about a couple who lived near the ocean.
You have **two minutes** to narrate the story.

Your story should begin with the following sentence:
One day, a couple was taking a walk by the beach.

No. 1 Please look at the fourth picture. If you were the husband, what would you be thinking?

Now, Mr. / Ms. _____, please turn over the card and put it down.

No. 2 Do you think Japanese people should express their political opinions more?

No. 3 Do you think companies should do more to help society?

No. 4 Is it possible for the actions of individuals to help reduce global warming?

準1級

2022年度 第1回

一次試験 2022.6.5実施

二次試験 A日程 2022.7.3実施
B日程 2022.7.10実施
C日程 2022.7.17実施

一次試験・筆記(90分)
pp.154～169

一次試験・リスニング(約30分)
pp.170～175
CD緑-1～26

二次試験・面接(約8分)
pp.176～179

※解答一覧は別冊p.179
※解答と解説は別冊pp.180～222

※別冊の巻末についている解答用マークシートを使いましょう。

合格基準スコア

- 一次試験……1792
(満点2250／リーディング750, リスニング750, ライティング750)
- 二次試験……512(満点750／スピーキング750)

◉一次試験・筆記

1

To complete each item, choose the best word or phrase from among the four choices. Then, on your answer sheet, find the number of the question and mark your answer.

(1) After considering the case, the judge decided to show ( ) and only gave the man a warning. She said that he was clearly very sorry for his crime.

1 disgrace **2** closure **3** mercy **4** seclusion

(2) Lisa looks exactly like her twin sister, but she has a completely different ( ). She is very calm and rarely gets angry, unlike her sister.

1 temperament **2** accumulation
3 veneer **4** glossary

(3) ***A:*** Annabel, don't just ( ) your shoulders when I ask you if you've finished your homework. Give me a clear answer.
B: Sorry, Mom. I'm almost done with it.

1 echo **2** bow **3** dump **4** shrug

(4) When there is a big business convention in town, it is almost impossible to find a hotel with a ( ). Most hotels quickly get fully booked.

1 sprain **2** segment **3** transition **4** vacancy

(5) The detective ( ) the gang member for hours, but he would not say who had helped him commit the crime. Eventually, the detective stopped trying to get information from him.

1 discharged **2** converted **3** interrogated **4** affiliated

(6) To treat an injured ankle, doctors recommend ( ). This can be done by wrapping a bandage tightly around the injury.

1 depression **2** progression **3** compression **4** suspicion

(7) ***A:*** It suddenly started raining heavily on my way home, and I got completely wet.

B: You should have (　　　) my advice and taken an umbrella with you.

1 molded　**2** heeded　**3** twisted　**4** yielded

(8) As a way of attracting more (　　　) customers, the perfume company began advertising its products in magazines read mainly by wealthy people.

1 theatrical　**2** brutal　**3** frantic　**4** affluent

(9) The teacher said that, apart from a few (　　　) errors, the student's essay was perfect. He gave it the highest score possible.

1 trivial　**2** conclusive　**3** palatial　**4** offensive

(10) The injured soccer player watched (　　　) as his replacement played in the final game. He had really wanted to continue playing.

1 substantially　**2** previously

3 enviously　**4** relevantly

(11) The new hotel in front of Abraham's apartment building is not tall enough to (　　　) his view of the mountains beyond the city. He can still see them clearly.

1 obstruct　**2** delegate　**3** entangle　**4** boost

(12) Having spilled red wine on the white carpet, Martha tried to remove the (　　　) with soap and water. However, she could not remove it completely.

1 stain　**2** slit　**3** bump　**4** blaze

(13) The war continued for a year, but neither side could (　　　). With victory seemingly impossible, the two countries agreed to stop fighting.

1 devise　**2** prevail　**3** evolve　**4** reconstruct

(14) The leader used the political instability in his country as a ( ) for introducing strict new laws aimed at preventing any opposition to his rule.

1 trance **2** downfall **3** rampage **4** pretext

(15) The suspect continued to ( ) his innocence to the police. He told them repeatedly he had been nowhere near the place where the crime had occurred.

1 conceal **2** counter **3** expire **4** assert

(16) Good writers make every effort to ( ) mistakes from their work, but occasionally they miss some errors and have to make corrections later.

1 eliminate **2** expend **3** stabilize **4** oppress

(17) After the kidnappers returned the child to its parents in exchange for a large ( ), they tried to escape with the money. Police soon caught them, however, and returned the money to the couple.

1 ransom **2** applause **3** monopoly **4** prank

(18) Gaspar applied to go to a ( ) university. Unfortunately, his grades were not good enough, so he had to go to a lesser-known one.

1 prestigious **2** spontaneous
3 cordial **4** petty

(19) The spies ( ) themselves as army officers in an attempt to enter the military base without being noticed.

1 chronicled **2** disguised **3** rendered **4** revitalized

(20) Timothy is a very ( ) employee. He is reliable and eager to help, and he always shows loyalty to his company and coworkers.

1 grotesque **2** defiant **3** devoted **4** feeble

(21) To help Paul lose weight, his doctor recommended that he (　　　) his diet. Specifically, she suggested that he eat fewer fatty foods and more fiber.

1 modify　**2** pluck　**3** exclaim　**4** distill

(22) ***A:*** I've been so busy at work, and now I have to (　　　) training our newest employee.

B: That's too much. You should ask your boss if someone else can do it instead.

1 turn over　**2** contend with

3 prop up　**4** count off

(23) The young boy tried to blame his dog for the broken vase. However, his mother did not (　　　) the lie and sent him to his room.

1 fall for　**2** hang on　**3** see out　**4** flag down

(24) In his speech, the CEO (　　　) his plan for the company's development over the next five years. He hoped this would help guide everyone's work as the company grew.

1 mapped out　**2** leaped in　**3** racked up　**4** spaced out

(25) Last year, Harold spent all his money buying shares in various companies. He was (　　　) the stock market performing well over the next few years.

1 casting away　**2** putting down

3 stepping up　**4** betting on

2 *Read each passage and choose the best word or phrase from among the four choices for each blank. Then, on your answer sheet, find the number of the question and mark your answer.*

The Peter Principle

A theory known as the Peter Principle may explain why there are many people in managerial positions who (*26*). According to the theory, employees who perform well in lower-level positions will eventually rise to positions they are not prepared for. The reason for this is that employees generally get promoted based on how well they perform in their current positions. Although this kind of promotion policy may seem logical, failing to fully consider employees' strengths and weaknesses results in them eventually reaching positions for which their abilities are unsuited.

One study examined the careers of salespeople who were promoted to managerial positions. As expected, the study found that the best salespeople were the most likely to receive promotions, but it also found that they performed the worst in managerial roles. The study showed that promoting employees based solely on current performance (*27*). Not only do companies end up with poor managers but they also lose their best workers in lower-level positions.

The researchers who carried out the study say that one problem is that companies make the mistake of simply assuming that high-performing employees will naturally be good managers. In most companies, new employees receive specialized training in how to do their jobs. (*28*), new managers are often given little or no training. This seems to suggest that one way to lessen the effects of the Peter Principle is to provide proper training for new managers.

(26)
1 earn lower-than-average salaries
2 love their jobs
3 have worked for several companies
4 perform poorly

(27)
1 has two disadvantages
2 cannot be avoided
3 is a gamble worth taking
4 prevents creative thinking

(28)
1 Of course
2 On the other hand
3 What is more
4 For a similar reason

Nearsightedness

Nearsightedness has been increasing around the world at a rapid rate. People with this condition can see objects that are close to them clearly, but objects that are far away appear blurry. Many people blame this trend on the use of digital screens. They claim that using devices such as computers and smartphones leads to eyestrain, and that blue light, which is produced by digital screens, damages light-sensitive cells in the back of the eye. However, there is no clear evidence that digital screens (***29***).

In fact, the rise in nearsightedness began before digital screens became widely used. Some research suggests that the real issue is that people (***30***). This results in a lack of exposure to natural light. Nearsightedness is caused by the stretching of the lens in the eye, which reduces its ability to focus light. However, the release of dopamine, a chemical produced by the brain, can prevent this from occurring, and exposure to natural light leads to greater dopamine production.

Some experts say that being outdoors for about three hours a day can help prevent nearsightedness. For many people, however, doing this is impossible due to school and work schedules. (***31***), it may be more practical for people to change the kind of lighting they use in their homes. There is already lighting available that provides some of the benefits of natural light, and it is hoped that research will provide more alternatives in the future.

(29)
1 have long-term effects on eyesight
2 can help solve the problem
3 can be used on all devices
4 will improve in the future

(30)
1 sit too close to their screens
2 rely too much on vision
3 spend too much time indoors
4 fail to do enough physical exercise

(31)
1 In the same way
2 For example
3 Despite this
4 Instead

3	*Read each passage and choose the best answer from among the four choices for each question. Then, on your answer sheet, find the number of the question and mark your answer.*

Honey Fungus

The largest living organism on Earth is not a whale or other large animal. Rather, it belongs to the group of organisms which includes mushrooms and toadstools. It is a type of fungus commonly known as honey fungus, and its rootlike filaments spread underground throughout a huge area of forest in the US state of Oregon. DNA testing has confirmed that all the honey fungus in the area is from the same organism, and, based on its annual rate of growth, scientists estimate it could be over 8,000 years old. They also calculate that it would weigh around 35,000 tons if it were all gathered together.

As impressive as this honey fungus is, it poses a problem for many trees in the forest. The fungus infects the trees and absorbs nutrients from their roots and trunks, often eventually killing them. Unfortunately, affected trees are usually difficult to spot, as the fungus hides under their bark, and its filaments are only visible if the bark is removed. In the late fall, the fruiting bodies of the fungus appear on the outside of the trees, but only for a few weeks before winter. Although the trees attempt to resist the fungus, they usually lose the battle in the end because the fungus damages their roots, preventing water and nutrients from reaching their upper parts.

Full removal of the honey fungus in Oregon has been considered, but it would prove to be too costly and time-consuming. Another solution currently being researched is the planting of tree species that can resist the fungus. Some experts have suggested, however, that a change of perspective may be necessary. Rather than viewing the effects of the honey fungus in a negative light, people should consider it an example of nature taking its course. Dead trees will ultimately be recycled back into the soil, benefiting the area's ecosystem.

(32) According to the passage, what is one thing that is true about the honey fungus in Oregon?

1 It is a combination of different mushroom species that started to grow together over time.
2 It grew slowly at first, but it has been expanding more rapidly in the last thousand years.
3 It shares the nutrients it collects with the trees and other types of plant life that it grows on.
4 It is a single organism that has spread throughout a wide area by growing and feeding on trees.

(33) Honey fungus is difficult to find because

1 the mushrooms it produces change color depending on the type of tree that it grows on.
2 it is generally not visible, except when it produces fruiting bodies for a short time each year.
3 not only does it grow underground, but it also has an appearance that is like that of tree roots.
4 it is only able to survive in areas that have the specific weather conditions it needs to grow.

(34) What do some experts think?

1 People should regard the honey fungus's effects on trees as a natural and beneficial process.
2 The only practical way to deal with the honey fungus is to invest more time and money in attempts to remove it.
3 Trees that have been infected by the honey fungus can be used to prevent it from spreading further.
4 The honey fungus can be harvested to provide people with an excellent source of nutrients.

Intentional Communities

For hundreds of years, people have formed self-sustaining communities, often referred to as intentional communities, which are characterized by shared ideals, collective ownership, and common use of property. The first known intentional community was established in the sixth century BC by a Greek philosopher. Over the following centuries, a number of such communities were created by religious groups wishing to live outside mainstream society. Some of these, such as Christian monasteries and the collective farms called kibbutzim in Israel, remained successful for generations, while others lasted only a few years.

In the twentieth century, philosophical idealism, as seen in the back-to-the-land movement of the 1960s and 1970s, also motivated people to form intentional communities. By the early 1970s, it has been estimated that there were thousands of such communities in the United States alone, though many of those later disbanded. The Foundation for Intentional Communities now lists fewer than 800 communities in the United States and just under 250 in the rest of the world. Intentional communities that failed generally faced a similar challenge. Some people who came to stay were committed to ideals of shared work, growing their own food, and living collectively, but others were less serious. A cofounder of one community recalled, "We had an impractical but noble vision that was constantly undermined by people who came just to play."

Not all intentional communities are destined to fall apart, however. The ongoing success of Damanhur, a spiritual and artistic collective near Turin, Italy, is attributed to open communication and a practical approach. Damanhur organizes its members into family-like groups of 15 to 20 people. The community has found that creating intimacy becomes difficult if a "family" has more than 25 people. In contrast, when there are too few people in the "family," there is not enough collective knowledge to allow for effective decision-making. Damanhur's ideals, which are outlined in its constitution, are upheld by elected leaders, and tensions in the community are handled by holding playful mock battles where people fight with paint-filled toy guns.

It seems that all successful intentional communities share a common trait: the ability to constantly think ahead. As one Damanhur member put it, "You should change things when they work—not when they don't work." This strategy of making changes before problems occur has worked well for Damanhur and other successful communities, which suggests it is an effective way for intentional communities to fulfill the needs of their members in the long term.

(35) A common issue faced by intentional communities that failed was that

1 a majority of the community was in favor of someone joining, but a small number of individuals opposed it.

2 people joined the community with genuine interest, but they lacked the skills or knowledge to contribute effectively.

3 some members worked hard to follow the community's ideals, while others took a more casual approach to communal living.

4 the community set out to complete an ambitious project, but it could not complete it because of a lack of knowledge and financial resources.

(36) What is true of the social structure at Damanhur?

1 "Families" are free to create their own rules and do not necessarily have to follow the rules contained in the community's constitution.

2 The number of people in a "family" is controlled to create the best conditions for resolving group issues and maintaining good relationships.

3 The mock battles that are intended to solve disagreements sometimes become serious and result in some members leaving their "families."

4 The community contains "families" of different sizes so that members can choose whether to live in a large or a small group setting.

(37) According to the passage, how is Damanhur similar to other successful intentional communities?

1 Members of the community are allowed to exchange their responsibilities from time to time to prevent them from becoming exhausted.

2 The type of work the community does to earn income changes periodically so that members can learn new skills.

3 Members of the community take turns carrying out maintenance on the buildings and equipment that are owned collectively.

4 The community continually finds ways to satisfy the needs of its members rather than simply reacting to problems when they arise.

The British in India

Established in 1600, the British-owned East India Company was one of the world's largest corporations for more than two centuries. By trading overseas with various countries, such as India and China, it was able to import luxury items from these countries into Britain. The British government received a portion of the company's vast profits, so it was more than willing to provide political support. Due to its size, power, and resources, which included a private army of hundreds of thousands of Indian soldiers, the company pressured India into accepting trade contracts that, in general, were only of benefit to the company. After winning a battle against a local ruler in the 1750s, the company seized control of one of the wealthiest provinces in India. As a result, the East India Company was no longer solely acting as a business but also as a political institution, and it began forcing Indian citizens to pay it taxes.

The East India Company gained a reputation among the countries it did business with for being untrustworthy. It also started to lose popularity within the British Parliament because the company's dishonest trading habits damaged foreign relations with China. Then, in the 1850s, angered by the way they were being treated, a group of soldiers in the East India Company's army rebelled. They marched to Delhi to restore the Indian emperor to power, and their actions caused rebellion against the British to spread to other parts of India. The rebellion was eventually brought under control after about two years, but it triggered the end of the East India Company. The British government, which blamed the East India Company for allowing the rebellion to happen, took control of India, and an era of direct British rule began. The British closed down the East India Company, removed the Indian emperor from power, and proceeded to rule India for almost a century.

While some claim that India benefited from British rule, typically using the construction of railways as an example, many historians argue that the country was negatively affected. In an effort to reinforce notions that British culture was superior, Indians were educated to have the same opinions, morals, and social preferences as the British.

The British also implemented a policy known as "divide and rule," which turned Indians from different religious backgrounds against each other. The British government used this strategy to maintain its control over India, as members of these religions had joined forces during the earlier rebellion. However, nationalist feelings among Indians increased from the early 1900s, and India eventually gained its independence in the late 1940s.

Although the East India Company stopped operating more than a century ago, it has had a lasting influence. Some experts say it pioneered the concept of multinational corporations and ultimately led to the economic system of capitalism that is widespread today. Moreover, the connection between the British government and the East India Company set a precedent for using political power to help achieve business objectives.

(38) What was one result of India doing business with the East India Company?

1 India could afford to increase the size of its military because it was able to make trade deals with other countries.

2 India had little choice but to agree to business agreements that were unfavorable to it.

3 The Indian government needed to raise taxes in order to pay for losses from failed trade contracts.

4 The Indian government's relationship with China became worse, which almost resulted in a break in trade between the two countries.

(39) What led to the British government taking control of India?

1 The British government held the East India Company responsible for an uprising that occurred.

2 The Indian people voted for British rule after losing confidence in the Indian emperor's ability to rule the country effectively.

3 The Indian people asked for the help of the British in preventing a war between India and China.

4 The Indian emperor decided to join forces with the British as a political strategy to maintain control of India.

(40) One effect that British rule had on India was that

1 Indians were able to take part in the process of building a government that reflected their economic and social needs.

2 schools made an effort to educate their students to have an awareness of both Indian and British cultures.

3 divisions were created between different groups of Indians to prevent them from challenging British rule.

4 many of the railroads and other transportation systems built by the Indian government were destroyed.

(41) What does the author of the passage say about the East India Company?

1 The company prevented the British government from achieving its aim of expanding its rule to other countries in Asia.

2 While the company may have been successful during its time, its business model would not be effective in today's economy.

3 Although the company no longer exists, it has had a large impact on the present-day global economic landscape.

4 If the company had never been established, another one would likely have ended up having similar political and economic influence.

- *Write an essay on the given TOPIC.*
- *Use TWO of the POINTS below to support your answer.*
- *Structure: introduction, main body, and conclusion*
- *Suggested length: 120-150 words*
- *Write your essay in the space provided on Side B of your answer sheet. Any writing outside the space will not be graded.*

TOPIC

Should people's salaries be based on their job performance?

POINTS

- *Age*
- *Company profits*
- *Motivation*
- *Skills*

◉一次試験・Listening Test

There are three parts to this listening test.

CD 緑-1

Part 1	**Dialogues:**	1 question each	Multiple-choice
Part 2	**Passages:**	2 questions each	Multiple-choice
Part 3	**Real-Life:**	1 question each	Multiple-choice

※ Listen carefully to the instructions.

Part 1

No. 1

1 He no longer drives to work.
2 His car is being repaired.
3 He cannot afford to buy gas.
4 His new bicycle was stolen.

No. 2

1 He wants to move out.
2 He likes to have parties.
3 He is not very open.
4 He is very messy.

No. 3

1 The other candidates were more qualified.
2 He forgot to call the manager yesterday.
3 The manager did not like him.
4 He missed the interview.

No. 4

1 The woman needs to pass it to graduate.
2 It does not match the woman's goals.
3 It is too advanced for the woman.
4 Passing it could help the woman find a job.

No. 5

1 The woman should take a break from school.
2 Working as a server is physically demanding.
3 Restaurant workers do not make much money.
4 Students should not get part-time jobs.

No. 6

1 Buy a gift from the list.
2 Decline the wedding invitation.
3 Speak to Carla and Antonio.
4 Return the silver dining set.

No. 7

1 It has large portions.
2 It is a short drive from home.
3 It is cheaper than other places.
4 It has a good reputation.

No. 8

1 Spend time hiking.
2 Go fishing at a lake.
3 Take a ski trip.
4 Go sightseeing.

No. 9

1 Some customers complained about it.
2 One of the posts needs to be revised.
3 Kenneth should not edit the latest post.
4 It should be updated more frequently.

No. 10

1 Her wallet is missing.
2 Her train pass expired.
3 She missed her train.
4 She wasted her money.

No. 11

1 She did not like the pianist's playing.
2 She arrived at the concert late.
3 She could not focus on the concert.
4 She was unable to find her ticket.

No. 12

1 Call him back in the evening.
2 Give him new delivery instructions.
3 Change her delivery option online.
4 Tell him what time she will be home.

Part 2

(A)

No. 13

1 Water levels have decreased in many of them.
2 Laws to protect them need to be stricter.
3 Countries sharing them usually have the same usage rights.
4 They often make it difficult to protect borders.

No. 14

1 To suggest a solution to a border problem.
2 To suggest that poor nations need rivers for electricity.
3 To show that dams are often too costly.
4 To show how river usage rights can be complicated.

CD 緑-16

(B)

No. 15

1 It could be used as a poison.
2 It was tested on snakes.
3 It was difficult to make.
4 It was the first medical drug.

No. 16

1 It took many days to make.
2 Only small amounts could be made daily.
3 Production was very loosely regulated.
4 People there could watch it being made.

CD 緑-17

(C)

No. 17

1 They hunted only spirit bears with black fur.
2 They tried to keep spirit bears a secret.
3 They thought spirit bears were dangerous.
4 They believed spirit bears protected them.

No. 18

1 It is easier for them to catch food.
2 They are less sensitive to the sun.
3 It is harder for hunters to find them.
4 Their habitats are all well-protected.

(D)

No. 19
1 They generate power near where the power is used.
2 They are preferred by small businesses.
3 They do not use solar energy.
4 They are very expensive to maintain.

No. 20
1 Governments generally oppose its development.
2 Energy companies usually do not profit from it.
3 It can negatively affect property values.
4 It often pollutes community water sources.

(E)

No. 21
1 Caring for them costs too much money.
2 They are too difficult to capture.
3 They suffer from serious diseases.
4 They rarely live long after being caught.

No. 22
1 Zoos need to learn how to breed them.
2 Governments must make sure laws are followed.
3 They must be moved to new habitats.
4 Protecting them in the wild is not possible.

(F)

No. 23
1 They are more numerous than is typical.
2 They are similar to those of a distant area.
3 They are the largest in the region.
4 They include images of Europeans.

No. 24
1 To indicate certain times of the year.
2 To warn enemies to stay away.
3 To show the way to another settlement.
4 To provide a source of light.

Part 3

(G)

No. 25

Situation: You want to feed your parrot, Toby, but cannot find his pet food. You check your cell phone and find a voice mail from your wife.

Question: Where should you go to find Toby's food?

1 To the kitchen.
2 To the living room.
3 To the front door.
4 To the garage.

(H)

No. 26

Situation: You want to read a book written by the author Greta Bakken. You want to read her most popular book. A bookstore clerk tells you the following.

Question: Which book should you buy?

1 *The Moon in Budapest.*
2 *Along That Tree-Lined Road.*
3 *Mixed Metaphors.*
4 *Trishaws.*

(I)

No. 27

Situation: Your company's president is making an announcement about a change in office procedures. You want to take time off next week.

Question: What should you do?

1 Speak to your manager.
2 Submit a request on the new website.
3 E-mail the members of your department.
4 Contact ABC Resource Systems.

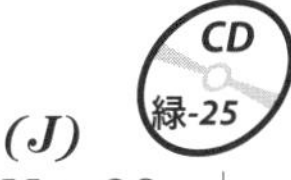

(J)

No. 28

Situation: Your professor is showing your class a course website. You want to get extra credit to improve your grade.

Question: What should you do?

1 Submit an extra research paper through the website.
2 Complete additional reading assignments.
3 Create an online resource for the class.
4 Sign up for a lecture via the news section.

(K)

No. 29

Situation: You are a writer for a newspaper. You arrive home at 8:30 p.m. and hear the following voice mail from your editor. You need two more days to finish your column.

Question: What should you do?

1 Send the file to Bill.
2 Send the file to Paula.
3 Call Bill's office phone.
4 Call Bill on his smartphone.

◉二次試験・面接

※本書では出題例として２種類のカードを掲載していますが，本番では１枚のみ渡されます。
※面接委員の質問など，二次試験に関する音声はCDに収録されていません。

受験者用問題　カード　A

You have **one minute** to prepare.

This is a story about a mayor who wanted to help her town.
You have **two minutes** to narrate the story.

Your story should begin with the following sentence:
One day, a mayor was having a meeting.

No. 1 Please look at the fourth picture. If you were the mayor, what would you be thinking?

Now, Mr. / Ms. _____, please turn over the card and put it down.

No. 2 Do you think people should spend more time outdoors to learn about nature?

No. 3 Should companies provide workers with more vacation days?

No. 4 Should the government do more to protect endangered animals?

受験者用問題　カード　B

You have **one minute** to prepare.

This is a story about a woman who wanted to advance her career.
You have **two minutes** to narrate the story.

Your story should begin with the following sentence:
One day, a woman was talking with her company's CEO in the office.

No. 1 Please look at the fourth picture. If you were the woman, what would you be thinking?

Now, Mr. / Ms. ______, please turn over the card and put it down.

No. 2 Are parents too protective of their children these days?

No. 3 Does the fast pace of modern life have a negative effect on people?

No. 4 Do you think the birth rate in Japan will stop decreasing in the future?

準1級

2021年度 第3回

一次試験 2022.1.23実施

二次試験 A日程 2022.2.20実施
B日程 2022.2.27実施
C日程 2022.3.6実施

一次試験・筆記(90分)
pp.182～197

一次試験・リスニング(約30分)
pp.198～203
CD緑-27～52

二次試験・面接(約8分)
pp.204～207

※解答一覧は別冊p.223
※解答と解説は別冊pp.224～266

※別冊の巻末についている解答用マークシートを使いましょう。

合格基準スコア

- 一次試験……1792
(満点2250／リーディング750，リスニング750，ライティング750)
- 二次試験……512(満点750／スピーキング750)

◉一次試験・**筆記**

1

To complete each item, choose the best word or phrase from among the four choices. Then, on your answer sheet, find the number of the question and mark your answer.

(1) Roberto was a true ( ), so he immediately volunteered to join the army when his country was attacked by its neighbor.

1 villain **2** patriot **3** spectator **4** beggar

(2) "Let's take a break now," said the chairperson. "We'll ( ) the meeting in about 15 minutes to talk about the next item on the agenda."

1 parody **2** resume **3** impede **4** erect

(3) The first time Dan tried skiing, he found it difficult, but on each ( ) ski trip, he got better. Now he is an expert skier.

1 sufficient **2** arrogant **3** subsequent **4** prominent

(4) The professor is an expert in his field but his ( ) behavior is a source of embarrassment to his colleagues. "He's always doing or saying strange things," said one.

1 secular **2** eccentric **3** vigilant **4** apparent

(5) Because the vegetable stand was unable to ( ) that the vegetables it sold were organic, Eddie refused to buy them. It was his strict policy to eat only organic foods.

1 diverge **2** certify **3** evade **4** glorify

(6) As a school guidance counselor, Ms. Pereira specializes in helping students find their ( ). She believes people should have careers that fit their personality and skills.

1 boredom **2** vocation **3** insult **4** publicity

(7) The marathon runner was so thirsty after the race that she drank a large sports drink in just a few ( ) and then quickly asked for another one.

1 herds **2** lumps **3** gulps **4** sacks

(8) The sleeping baby was ( ) by the loud music coming from her brother's room. She woke up crying, and it took a long time before she fell asleep again.

1 startled **2** improvised **3** prolonged **4** tolerated

(9) ***A:*** I've been living in this apartment for a year now, and the ( ) is about to end. I have to decide if I should stay or move.

B: If your rent will be the same, I recommend renewing your contract and staying.

1 token **2** lease **3** vicinity **4** dialect

(10) The presidential candidate blamed the ( ) economy on the current president. He promised he would improve it if he were elected.

1 bulky **2** functional **3** ethnic **4** sluggish

(11) ***A:*** Annie, how have you been? Did you enjoy your trip to Italy last year?

B: I did, Pablo. Actually, I loved it so much that I've been ( ) moving there. I'd have to wait until my son graduates from high school, though.

1 contemplating **2** emphasizing
3 vandalizing **4** illustrating

(12) All the senators said they supported the new law, so it was no surprise when they voted for it ( ).

1 unanimously **2** abnormally **3** mockingly **4** savagely

(13) ***A:*** Did you go to Professor Markham's lecture?

B: I did, but it was so boring I could only ( ) it for 15 minutes. After that, I left and went to a café.

1 execute **2** discern **3** endure **4** relay

(14) Houses built in cold regions can be surprisingly (　　　) during the winter. Fireplaces, wood furniture, and nice carpets give the homes a warm, comfortable feeling.

1 rigid　　**2** rash　　**3** cozy　　**4** clumsy

(15) Mrs. Wilson was angry when her son broke the window, but she was more disappointed that he tried to (　　　) her by telling her that someone else had done it.

1 pinpoint　　**2** suppress　　**3** reroute　　**4** deceive

(16) After Wanda was late for the third time in one month, her manager had a long talk with her about the importance of (　　　).

1 congestion　　**2** drainage　　**3** optimism　　**4** punctuality

(17) The young author decided not to follow (　　　) storytelling rules and wrote his novel in a unique style.

1 vulnerable　　**2** clueless　　**3** conventional　　**4** phonetic

(18) The items in the box were packaged carefully because they were (　　　), but some of them were still damaged when they were being delivered.

1 coarse　　**2** fragile　　**3** immovable　　**4** glossy

(19) The queen (　　　) her adviser to the palace, but she became extremely angry when he took a long time to arrive.

1 summoned　　**2** hammered　　**3** mingled　　**4** trembled

(20) The general knew his troops were losing the battle, so he ordered them to (　　　). Once they were safely away from the battlefield, he worked on a new plan to defeat the enemy.

1 entrust　　**2** discard　　**3** strangle　　**4** retreat

(21) After Bill began university, he quickly realized that he did not have the ( ) to study advanced math, so he changed his major to geography.

1 capacity **2** novelty **3** bait **4** chunk

(22) The police officer was shocked when his partner suggested they ( ) a suspect in order to force him to admit he had stolen money. Using violence in this way was not allowed.

1 rough up **2** give out **3** break up **4** take over

(23) Julius was lucky to see a rare eagle on his first day of bird-watching. However, 20 years ( ) before he saw another one.

1 held out **2** went by **3** laid off **4** cut off

(24) ***A:*** Are you going to cancel your weekend beach trip? There's a typhoon coming.

B: We haven't ( ) going yet. It depends on which direction the typhoon moves in.

1 ruled out **2** stood down
3 dragged into **4** scooped up

(25) Jun always saved as much money as possible so he would have something to ( ) if he lost his job.

1 look up to **2** fall back on
3 come down with **4** do away with

2	*Read each passage and choose the best word or phrase from among the four choices for each blank. Then, on your answer sheet, find the number of the question and mark your answer.*

Donor Premiums

In recent years, it has become common for charities to give donor premiums—small gifts such as coffee mugs—to people who donate money to them. Many charities offer them, and it is widely believed that people give more when they receive donor premiums. However, researchers say that donor premiums tend to (***26***). Most people initially give money because they want to make the world a better place or help those who are less fortunate. When they receive gifts, though, people can start to become motivated by selfishness and desire. In fact, they may become less likely to donate in the future.

There may, however, be ways to avoid this problem. Research has shown that telling people they will receive gifts after making donations is not the best way to ensure they will contribute in the future. In one study, donors responded better to receiving gifts when they did not expect them. (***27***), future donations from such people increased by up to 75 percent. On the other hand, donors who knew that they would receive a gift after their donation did not value the gift highly, regardless of what it was.

Donor premiums may also have indirect benefits. Experts say gifts can (***28***). Items such as fancy shopping bags with charity logos, for example, signal that a donor is part of an exclusive group. Such gifts not only keep donors satisfied but also increase the general public's awareness of charities.

(26) 1 use up charities' resources
2 change donors' attitudes
3 encourage people to donate more
4 improve the public's image of charities

(27) 1 Instead
2 Nevertheless
3 In contrast
4 Furthermore

(28) 1 help promote charities
2 easily be copied
3 have undesirable effects
4 cause confusion among donors

Government Policy and Road Safety

Traffic-related deaths have declined in the United States due to the introduction of safety measures such as seat belts. Many critics of government policy claim, however, that fatalities could be further reduced with stricter government regulation. In fact, some say current government policies regarding speed limits may (***29***). This is because speed limits are often set using the "operating speed method." With this method, speed limits are decided based on the speeds at which vehicles that use the road actually travel, and little attention is paid to road features that could increase danger. Unfortunately, this means limits are sometimes set at unsafe levels.

Critics also point out that the United States is behind other nations when it comes to vehicle-safety regulations. In the United States, safety regulations are (***30***). Although some vehicles have become larger and their shape has changed, laws have not changed to reflect the increased danger they pose to pedestrians. Critics say that regulating only the safety of vehicle occupants is irresponsible, and that pedestrian deaths have increased even though there are simple measures that could be taken to help prevent them.

One measure for improving road safety is the use of cameras at traffic signals to detect drivers who fail to stop for red lights. Many such cameras were installed in the 1990s and have been shown to save lives. (***31***), the number of such cameras has declined in recent years. One reason for this is that there is often public opposition to them due to privacy concerns.

(29)
1 further support this trend
2 reduce seat-belt use
3 encourage dangerous driving
4 provide an alternative solution

(30)
1 designed to protect those inside vehicles
2 opposed by many drivers
3 actually being decreased
4 stricter for large vehicles

(31)
1 For instance
2 Likewise
3 Despite this
4 Consequently

3 *Read each passage and choose the best answer from among the four choices for each question. Then, on your answer sheet, find the number of the question and mark your answer.*

Caligula

The Roman emperor Caligula, also known as the "mad emperor," became so infamous that it is difficult to separate fact from legend regarding his life. During his reign, Caligula suffered what has been described as a "brain fever." It has often been said that this illness caused him to go insane, a claim that is supported by his seemingly irrational behavior following his illness. Today, however, some historians argue that his actions may have been a deliberate part of a clever, and horribly violent, political strategy.

After his illness, Caligula began torturing and putting to death huge numbers of citizens for even minor offenses. He also claimed to be a living god. These actions may suggest mental instability, but another explanation is that they were intended to secure his position. While Caligula was ill, plans were made to replace him, since he had not been expected to survive, and he likely felt betrayed and threatened as a result. Similarly, while claiming to be a god certainly sounds like a symptom of insanity, many Roman emperors were considered to become gods upon dying, and Caligula may have made the claim to discourage his enemies from assassinating him.

The story of how Caligula supposedly tried to appoint his horse Incitatus to a powerful government position is also sometimes given as evidence of his mental illness. However, Caligula is said to have frequently humiliated members of the Roman Senate, making them do things such as wearing uncomfortable clothing and running in front of his chariot. Elevating his horse to a position higher than theirs would have been another way to make the Senate members feel worthless. Eventually, though, Caligula's behavior went too far, and he was murdered. Efforts were made to erase him from history, leaving few reliable sources for modern historians to study. As a result, it may never be known whether he truly was the mad emperor.

(32) Some modern historians argue that

1 Caligula's seemingly crazy actions may actually have been part of a carefully thought-out plan.

2 the "brain fever" that Caligula suffered was more serious than it was originally believed to be.

3 Caligula should not be judged based on the period when he was suffering from a mental illness.

4 many of the violent acts that Caligula is reported to have carried out were performed by other Roman emperors.

(33) What may have been one result of Caligula's illness?

1 The fact that he almost died caused him to stop being interested in anything except gods and religion.

2 He felt that he could no longer trust anyone, leading him to change the way he governed.

3 Roman citizens thought he was still likely to die, so he attempted to show them that the gods would protect him.

4 He began to doubt old beliefs about Roman emperors, which led to serious conflicts with other members of the government.

(34) According to the passage, how did Caligula feel about the members of the Roman Senate?

1 He felt the people should respect them more, since they would do anything to protect him from his enemies.

2 He wanted to show his power over them, so he often found ways to make them feel they had no value.

3 He disliked them because he felt that they were physically weak and had poor fashion sense.

4 He was grateful for their support, so he held events such as chariot races in order to honor them.

The Friends of Eddie Coyle

In 1970, American writer George V. Higgins published his first novel, *The Friends of Eddie Coyle*. This crime novel was inspired by the time Higgins spent working as a lawyer, during which he examined hours of police surveillance tapes and transcripts in connection with the cases he was involved in. What he heard and read was the everyday speech of ordinary criminals, which sounded nothing like the scripted lines of TV crime dramas at the time. Higgins learned how real criminals spoke, and their unique, often messy patterns of language provided the basis for *The Friends of Eddie Coyle*. The novel's gritty realism was far removed from the polished crime stories that dominated the bestseller lists at the time. Higgins neither glamorized the lives of his criminal characters nor portrayed the police or federal agents in a heroic light.

One aspect that distinguishes *The Friends of Eddie Coyle* from other crime novels is that it is written almost entirely in dialogue. Given the crime genre's reliance on carefully plotted stories that build suspense, this was a highly original approach. Important events are not described directly, instead being introduced through conversations between characters in the novel. Thus, readers are given the sense that they are secretly listening in on Eddie Coyle and his criminal associates. Even action scenes are depicted in dialogue, and where narration is necessary, Higgins writes sparingly, providing only as much information as is required for readers to follow the plot. The focus is primarily on the characters, the world they inhabit, and the codes of conduct they follow.

Although Higgins's first novel was an immediate hit, not all readers liked the author's writing style, which he also used in his following books. Many complained that his later novels lacked clear plots and contained too little action. Yet Higgins remained committed to his belief that the most engaging way to tell a story is through the conversations of its characters, as this compels the reader to pay close attention to what is being said. Despite writing many novels, Higgins was never able to replicate the success of his debut work. Toward the end of his life, he became disappointed and frustrated by the lack of attention and appreciation his books received. Nevertheless, *The Friends of Eddie Coyle* is now considered by many to be one of the greatest crime novels ever written.

(35) According to the passage, George V. Higgins wrote *The Friends of Eddie Coyle*

1 because he believed that the novel would become a bestseller and enable him to quit the law profession to write full time.

2 after becoming frustrated about the lack of awareness among ordinary Americans regarding the extent of criminal activity in the United States.

3 because he wanted to show readers how hard lawyers worked in order to protect the victims of crime.

4 after being inspired by what he found during the investigations he carried out while he was a lawyer.

(36) In the second paragraph, what do we learn about *The Friends of Eddie Coyle*?

1 Higgins wanted to produce a novel which proved that the traditional rules of crime fiction still held true in modern times.

2 The novel is unusual because Higgins tells the story through interactions between the characters rather than by describing specific events in detail.

3 Higgins relied heavily on dialogue throughout the novel because he lacked the confidence to write long passages of narration.

4 Although the novel provides an authentic description of the criminal world, Higgins did not consider it to be a true crime novel.

(37) Which of the following statements would the author of the passage most likely agree with?

1 Despite the possibility that Higgins could have attracted a wider readership by altering his writing style, he remained true to his creative vision.

2 The first book Higgins produced was poorly written, but the quality of his work steadily increased in the years that followed.

3 It is inevitable that writers of crime novels will never gain the same level of prestige and acclaim as writers of other genres.

4 It is unrealistic for writers of crime novels to expect their work to appeal to readers decades after it was first published.

Mummy Brown

Thousands of years ago, ancient Egyptians began practicing mummification—the process of drying out the bodies of the dead, treating them with various substances, and wrapping them to preserve them. It was believed this helped the dead person's spirit enter the afterlife. Beginning in the twelfth century, however, many ancient mummies met a strange fate, as a market arose in Europe for medicines made using parts of mummies. People assumed the mummies' black color was because they had been treated with bitumen—a black, petroleum-based substance that occurs naturally in the Middle East and was used by ancient societies to treat illnesses. However, while ancient Egyptians did sometimes preserve mummies by coating them with bitumen, this method had not been used on many of the mummies that were taken to Europe. Furthermore, an incorrect translation of Arabic texts resulted in the mistaken belief that the bitumen used to treat mummies actually entered their bodies.

By the eighteenth century, advances in medical knowledge had led Europeans to stop using mummy-based medicines. Nevertheless, the European public's fascination with mummies reached new heights when French leader Napoleon Bonaparte led a military campaign in Egypt, which also included a major scientific expedition that resulted in significant archaeological discoveries and the documentation of ancient artifacts. Wealthy tourists even visited Egypt to obtain ancient artifacts for their private collections. In fact, the unwrapping and displaying of mummies at private parties became a popular activity. Mummies were also used in various other ways, such as being turned into crop fertilizer and fuel for railway engines.

One particularly unusual use of mummies was as a pigment for creating brown paint. Made using ground-up mummies, the pigment, which came to be known as mummy brown, was used as early as the sixteenth century, though demand for it grew around the time of Napoleon's Egyptian campaign. Its color was praised by some European artists, who used it in artworks that can be seen in museums today. Still, the pigment had more critics than fans. Many artists complained about its poor drying ability and other negative qualities.

Moreover, painting with a pigment made from deceased people increasingly came to be thought of as disrespectful—one well-known British painter who used mummy brown immediately buried his tube of the paint in the ground when he learned that real mummies had been used to produce it.

Even artists who had no objection to mummy brown could not always be certain its origin was genuine, as parts of dead animals were sometimes sold as mummy parts. Also, the fact that different manufacturers used different parts of mummies to produce the pigment meant there was little consistency among the various versions on the market. Additionally, the mummification process itself, including the substances used to preserve the bodies, underwent changes over time. These same factors make it almost impossible for researchers today to detect the presence of mummy brown in specific paintings. Given the pigment's controversial origins, however, perhaps art lovers would be shocked if they discovered that it was used in any of the paintings they admire.

(38) According to the author of the passage, why were ancient Egyptian mummies used to make medicines in Europe?

1 Disease was widespread in Europe at the time, so Europeans were willing to try anything to create effective medicines.

2 Because the mummies had not turned black in spite of their age, Europeans assumed they could provide health benefits.

3 Europeans mistakenly believed that a substance which was thought to have medical benefits was present in all mummies.

4 The fact that the mummies had religious significance to ancient Egyptians caused Europeans to believe they had special powers.

(39) What is one thing we learn about Napoleon Bonaparte's military campaign in Egypt?

1 A number of leaders saw it as a reason to also invade Egypt, which led to the destruction of many ancient artifacts.

2 It revealed information about ancient Egyptian culture that led Europeans to change their opinion of medicines made from mummies.

3 It was opposed by wealthy Europeans, who thought it would result in their collections of ancient artifacts being destroyed.

4 It led to an increased interest in mummies and inspired Europeans to use them for a number of purposes.

(40) The author of the passage mentions the British painter in order to

1 provide an example of how the use of mummy brown was opposed by some people because it showed a lack of respect for the dead.

2 explain why mummy brown remained popular among well-known artists in spite of its poor technical performance.

3 give support for the theory that mummy brown was superior to other paint pigments because of its unique ingredients.

4 describe one reason why some artists developed a positive view of mummy brown after initially refusing to use it.

(41) What is one thing that makes it difficult to determine whether a painting contains mummy brown?

1 The substances that were added to the pigment to improve its color destroyed any biological evidence that tests could have detected.

2 The way that ancient Egyptians prepared mummies changed, so the contents of the pigment were not consistent.

3 Artists mixed the pigment with other types of paint before applying it to paintings, so it would only be present in very small amounts.

4 The art industry has tried to prevent researchers from conducting tests on paintings because of concerns that the results could affect their value.

- *Write an essay on the given TOPIC.*
- *Use TWO of the POINTS below to support your answer.*
- *Structure: introduction, main body, and conclusion*
- *Suggested length: 120-150 words*
- *Write your essay in the space provided on Side B of your answer sheet. Any writing outside the space will not be graded.*

TOPIC

Should people stop using goods that are made from animals?

POINTS

- *Animal rights*
- *Endangered species*
- *Product quality*
- *Tradition*

◉一次試験・Listening Test

There are three parts to this listening test.

Part 1	Dialogues:	1 question each	Multiple-choice
Part 2	Passages:	2 questions each	Multiple-choice
Part 3	Real-Life:	1 question each	Multiple-choice

※ Listen carefully to the instructions.

Part 1

No. 1

1 His recent test scores.
2 Having to drop the class.
3 Finding a job.
4 Staying awake in class.

No. 2

1 The man could lose his job.
2 The man forgot his mother's birthday.
3 The man did not reply to her e-mail.
4 The man is not liked by the CEO.

No. 3

1 They take turns driving.
2 They were in a serious accident.
3 They work in a car repair shop.
4 Neither of them can drive next week.

No. 4

1 He cannot use his credit card.
2 He forgot to contact his card issuer.
3 He is short of cash today.
4 He lost his debit card.

No. 5

1 He is not suited to the call-center job.
2 He is learning the wrong interview techniques.
3 He should go to the interview he has been offered.
4 He should prioritize finding his dream job.

No. 6

1 Have the man take some tests.
2 Encourage the man to exercise more.
3 Give the man advice about work-related stress.
4 Recommend the man to a specialist.

No. 7

1 He will take his vacation later in the year.
2 He will meet with the personnel manager.
3 He will do what his manager asks him to do.
4 He will ask the woman to help him.

No. 8

1 It needs brighter colors.
2 It fits the company's image.
3 It is too similar to the current one.
4 It needs to be redesigned.

No. 9

1 He has not read Alice's book yet.
2 He cannot attend Alice's party.
3 He is no longer friends with Alice.
4 He was disappointed with Alice's book.

No. 10

1 Make sure she catches an earlier train.
2 Use a different train line.
3 Ride her bicycle to the office.
4 Go into the office on weekends.

No. 11

1 Garbage collection has become less frequent.
2 Garbage bags will become more expensive.
3 Local taxes are likely to rise soon.
4 The newspaper delivery schedule has changed.

No. 12

1 Try using some earplugs.
2 Have Ranjit talk to her neighbors.
3 Complain about her landlord.
4 Write a message to her neighbors.

Part 2

(A)

No. 13

1 There are too many food choices available.
2 Schools often prepare uninteresting food.
3 They copy their parents' eating habits.
4 They have a desire to lose weight.

No. 14

1 Getting children to help make their own meals.
2 Encouraging children to play more sports.
3 Sometimes letting children eat unhealthy foods.
4 Rewarding children for eating vegetables.

CD 緑-42

(B)

No. 15

1 Ching Shih's pirates gained a number of ships.
2 Many pirate commanders were captured.
3 Most of the pirates were killed.
4 Ching Shih agreed to help the Chinese navy.

No. 16

1 She left China to escape punishment.
2 She gave away her wealth.
3 She formed a new pirate organization.
4 She agreed to stop her pirate operations.

(C)

No. 17

1 Their numbers increase at certain times.
2 They are being hunted by humans.
3 Their habitats have become smaller recently.
4 They have been eating fewer snowshoe hares.

No. 18

1 They only travel when looking for food.
2 They sometimes travel long distances.
3 They live much longer than other wildcats.
4 They always return to their original territories.

(D)

No. 19

1 Modern burial places are based on their design.
2 They were used for religious purposes.
3 They were only used by non-Christians.
4 The entrances were only found recently.

No. 20

1 Women used to be priests long ago.
2 The tunnels were not used as churches.
3 Few early Christians were women.
4 Priests used to create paintings.

(E)

No. 21

1 They often have successful family members.
2 They often have low levels of stress.
3 They may miss chances to enjoy simple pleasures.
4 They may make people around them happy.

No. 22

1 They do not need family support to stay happy.
2 Their incomes are not likely to be high.
3 Their positive moods make them more active.
4 They are more intelligent than unhappy people.

(F)

No. 23

1 They are becoming better at fighting disease.
2 Their numbers are lower than they once were.
3 Many of them are not harvested for food.
4 The waters they live in are becoming cleaner.

No. 24

1 Native American harvesting practices helped oysters grow.
2 Native American harvesting methods included dredging.
3 Native Americans still harvest oysters.
4 Native Americans only harvested young oysters.

Part 3

(G)

No. 25

Situation: You are about to take a tour bus around a town in Italy. You want to join the guided walking tour. You hear the following announcement.

Question: Which bus stop should you get off at?

1 Stop 4.
2 Stop 7.
3 Stop 9.
4 Stop 13.

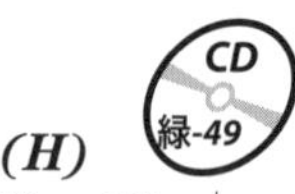

(H)

No. 26

Situation: You are abroad on a working-holiday program. You call the immigration office about renewing your visa and are told the following.

Question: What should you do first?

1 Fill out an application online.
2 Request salary statements from your employer.
3 Show evidence of your savings.
4 Obtain a medical examination certificate.

(I)

No. 27

Situation: You are a supermarket manager. You want to reduce losses caused by theft. A security analyst tells you the following.

Question: What should you do first?

1. Give some staff members more training.
2. Install more security cameras.
3. Review customer receipts at the exit.
4. Clearly mark prices for fruit.

(J)

No. 28

Situation: You want a new washing machine. You currently own a Duplanne washing machine. You visit an electronics store in July and hear the following announcement.

Question: What should you do to save the most money?

1. Download the store's smartphone app.
2. Apply for the cash-back deal.
3. Exchange your washing machine this month.
4. Buy a new Duplanne washing machine in August.

(K)

No. 29

Situation: You see a suit you want in a local store, but it does not have one in your size. You do not want to travel out of town. A clerk tells you the following.

Question: What should you do?

1. Wait until the store gets some new stock.
2. Have the clerk check the other store.
3. Order the suit from the online store.
4. Have the suit delivered to your home.

◉二次試験・面接

※本書では出題例として2種類のカードを掲載していますが，本番では1枚のみ渡されます。
※面接委員の質問など，二次試験に関する音声はCDに収録されていません。

受験者用問題　カード　A

You have **one minute** to prepare.

This is a story about a couple that wanted to be involved with their community.
You have **two minutes** to narrate the story.

Your story should begin with the following sentence:
One day, a husband and wife were going on a walk together.

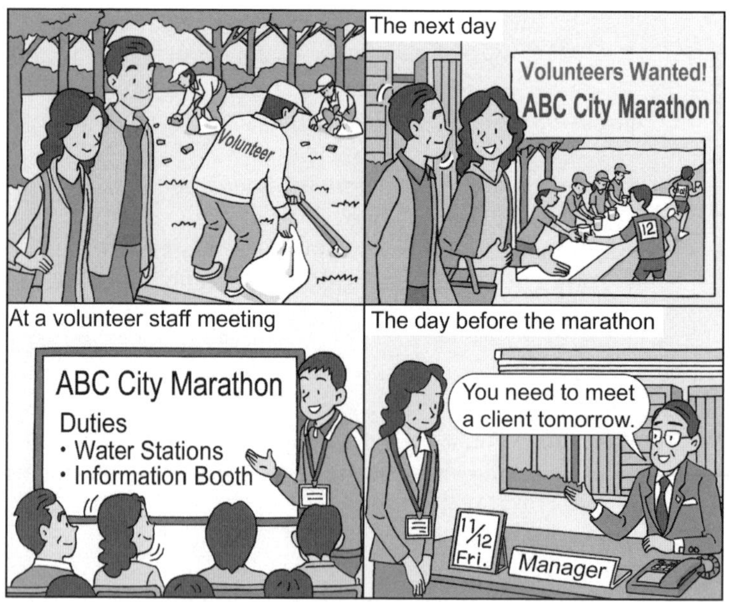

No. 1 Please look at the fourth picture. If you were the wife, what would you be thinking?

Now, Mr. / Ms. _____, please turn over the card and put it down.

No. 2 Do you think parents should participate in school events such as sports festivals?

No. 3 Do public libraries still play an important role in communities?

No. 4 Should more companies offer their employees flexible work schedules?

受験者用問題　カード　B

You have **one minute** to prepare.

This is a story about a woman who wanted to go on a trip.
You have **two minutes** to narrate the story.

Your story should begin with the following sentence:
One day, a woman was talking with her friend.

No. 1 Please look at the fourth picture. If you were the woman, what would you be thinking?

Now, Mr. / Ms. _____, please turn over the card and put it down.

No. 2 Do you think it is good for university students to have part-time jobs?

No. 3 Do you think it is safe to give personal information to online businesses?

No. 4 Should the government do more to increase the employment rate in Japan?

CD作成協力●ELEC録音スタジオ　本文デザイン●松倉浩・鈴木友佳
編集協力●一校舎　企画編集●成美堂出版編集部

本書に関する正誤等の最新情報は，下記のアドレスで確認することができます。
https://www.seibidoshuppan.co.jp/support/

上記URLに記載されていない箇所で正誤についてお気づきの場合は，書名・発行日・質問事項・ページ数・氏名・郵便番号・住所・FAX番号を明記の上，**郵送**または**FAX**で**成美堂出版**までお問い合わせください。

※**電話でのお問い合わせはお受けできません。**

※本書の正誤に関するご質問以外にはお答えできません。また受験指導などは行っておりません。

※ご質問の到着確認後，10日前後に回答を普通郵便またはFAXで発送いたします。
ご質問の受付期限は，2024年度の各試験日の10日前到着分までとさせていただきます。ご了承ください。

・本書の付属CDは，CDプレーヤーでの再生を保証する規格品です。
・CDプレーヤーで音声が正常に再生されるCDから、パソコンやiPodなどのデジタルオーディオプレーヤーに取り込む際にトラブルが生じた場合は、まず、そのソフトまたはプレーヤーの製作元にご相談ください。
・本書の付属CDには，タイトルなどの文字情報はいっさい含まれておりません。CDをパソコンに読み込んだ際，異なった年版や書籍の文字情報が表示されることがありますが，それは弊社の管理下にはないデータが取り込まれたためです。必ず音声をご確認ください。

このコンテンツは，公益財団法人 日本英語検定協会の承認や推奨，その他の検討を受けたものではありません。

英検®準1級過去6回問題集 '24年度版

2024年 3 月10日発行

編　者　成美堂出版編集部

発行者　深見公子

発行所　成美堂出版
〒162-8445　東京都新宿区新小川町1-7
電話(03)5206-8151　FAX(03)5206-8159

印　刷　株式会社フクイン

ISBN978-4-415-23808-1
落丁･乱丁などの不良本はお取り替えします
定価はカバーに表示してあります

文部科学省後援

’24 年度版

英検®準1級 過去6回問題集

英検®は、公益財団法人 日本英語検定協会の登録商標です。

別冊
解答・解説
矢印の方向に引くと切り離せます。

成美堂出版

CONTENTS

※別冊は，付属の赤シートで答えを隠してご利用下さい。

●合格基準スコア●

一次試験 …………………………………………………… 1792

（満点2250／リーディング750, リスニング750, ライティング750）

二次試験 …………………………………………………… 512

（満点750／スピーキング750）

本書で使用する記号	
S＝主語	V＝動詞
O＝目的語	C＝補語

to *do* / *do*ing＝斜体のdoは動詞の原形を表す

空所を表す(　)以外の(　)＝省略可能・補足説明

[　]＝言い換え可能

2023年度 第2回

一次試験・筆記　解答・解説　pp.4～20
一次試験・リスニング　解答・解説　pp.20～40
二次試験・面接　解答・解説　pp.40～46

筆記 解答欄

問題番号		1	2	3	4
1	(1)	①	②	❸	④
	(2)	①	❷	③	④
	(3)	①	②	❸	④
	(4)	❶	②	③	④
	(5)	①	❷	③	④
	(6)	①	②	❸	④
	(7)	①	②	③	❹
	(8)	①	②	③	❹
	(9)	①	❷	③	④
	(10)	①	②	③	❹
	(11)	①	❷	③	④
	(12)	①	❷	③	④
	(13)	①	②	③	❹
	(14)	①	②	③	❹
	(15)	①	②	❸	④
	(16)	❶	②	③	④
	(17)	①	❷	③	④
	(18)	❶	②	③	④
	(19)	①	❷	③	④
	(20)	❶	②	③	④
	(21)	①	②	❸	④
	(22)	❶	②	③	④
	(23)	❶	②	③	④
	(24)	❶	②	③	④
	(25)	①	❷	③	④

問題番号		1	2	3	4
2	(26)	①	②	❸	④
	(27)	①	②	③	❹
	(28)	①	❷	③	④
	(29)	①	②	❸	④
	(30)	①	❷	③	④
	(31)	①	②	③	❹

問題番号		1	2	3	4
3	(32)	①	②	③	❹
	(33)	①	②	③	❹
	(34)	①	❷	③	④
	(35)	①	②	③	❹
	(36)	❶	②	③	④
	(37)	①	②	❸	④
	(38)	①	②	③	❹
	(39)	①	❷	③	④
	(40)	①	②	❸	④
	(41)	❶	②	③	④

4の解答例はp.19をご覧ください。

リスニング 解答欄

問題番号			1	2	3	4
Part 1		No.1	①	②	③	❹
		No.2	①	②	❸	④
		No.3	❶	②	③	④
		No.4	❶	②	③	④
		No.5	①	②	❸	④
		No.6	①	❷	③	④
		No.7	①	②	③	❹
		No.8	❶	②	③	④
		No.9	①	②	❸	④
		No.10	①	②	③	❹
		No.11	①	②	③	❹
		No.12	①	❷	③	④
Part 2	A	No.13	①	❷	③	④
		No.14	①	②	③	❹
	B	No.15	❶	②	③	④
		No.16	❶	②	③	④
	C	No.17	①	❷	③	④
		No.18	①	②	❸	④
	D	No.19	①	❷	③	④
		No.20	①	②	③	❹
	E	No.21	❶	②	③	④
		No.22	①	②	❸	④
	F	No.23	①	②	❸	④
		No.24	①	❷	③	④
Part 3	G	No.25	①	②	❸	④
	H	No.26	①	②	③	❹
	I	No.27	①	②	❸	④
	J	No.28	①	❷	③	④
	K	No.29	①	❷	③	④

1 一次試験・筆記
(問題編pp.42～45)

指示文の訳 各英文を完成させるのに最も適切な単語または語句を4つの選択肢の中から選び，その番号を解答用紙の所定欄にマークしなさい。

(1) 正解 3

訳 レイラは上級クラスのトレーニングはあまりに激しすぎるとわかったので，もっと楽なクラスに変更することに決めた。

解説 空所直前にtoo「あまりにも」とあるので，空所にはthe workouts in the advanced class「上級クラスのトレーニング」の様子を表す形容詞が入る。文後半のshe decided to change to an easier class「もっと楽なクラスに変更することに決めた」から，上級クラスは難しいと考えられるので，**3のstrenuous**「努力を要する，激しい」が適切。subtle「微妙な」，contrary「反対の」，cautious「用心深い」。

(2) 正解 2

訳 税理士はその女性にこの1年間のすべての財務記録をまとめるように要求した。彼は彼女の納税申告用紙を準備し始める前に，それらを見る必要があった。

解説 第1文のThe tax accountant「税理士」，第2文のtax forms「納税申告用紙」などから，納税に関する記述とわかる。空所直後にall her financial records over the past year「この1年間のすべての財務記録」とあるので，**2のcompile**「～を編纂する，まとめる」を入れると文脈に合う。punctuate「～に句読点を付ける」，bleach「～を漂白する」，obsess「(～のことが) 頭から離れない」。

(3) 正解 3

訳 エミリオは自宅の水道管の1つが少し漏れているのを発見した。念のため，何が問題か正確にわかるまで，彼はバルブを閉めて水を止めた。

解説 第1文にa small leak in one of the water pipes「水道管の1つが少し漏れている」とあり，空所の前にturned off「～を止めた」とあるので，**3のvalve**「バルブ」を入れると状況に合う。depot「駅，発着所，倉庫」，canal「運河」，panel「パネル」。

(4) 正解 1

訳 A：あなたとリンダは知り合ってどれくらいになるのですか，ビル。 B：ああ，少なくとも10年は，たぶんもっと長くお互いを知っているよ。

解説 Bがwe've known each other for at least 10 years「少なくとも10年は，お互いを知っているよ」と答えているので，Aは「知り合ってどれくらいになるか」を尋ねたと考えられる。したがって，**1のacquainted**が正解。acquaintは「～を知り合いにさせる」という意味の動詞で，受動態be acquaintedで「知り合いである」という意味を表す。discharge「～を解放する」，emphasize「～を強調する」，subdue「～を征服する，鎮圧する」。

※2024年度第1回から，試験形式の変更に伴い大問1の問題数は18問になります。

(5)　正解　2

訳　私たちの地元の公民館は普段は主要な部屋が1つあるが，必要なときには，間仕切りを閉じて2つの小さな部屋を作ることができる。

解説　空所の前にclose「～を閉じる」とあり，空所にはその目的語が入る。空所の後にcreate two smaller rooms「2つの小さな部屋を作る」とあり，大きなひと部屋を区切って使うこともあるということなので，**2のpartition**「間仕切り」が適切。estimation「評価，見積もり」，assumption「仮定，想定」，notion「観念，意見」。

(6)　正解　3

訳　タイラーの父は，休暇の前に地元の銀行で外貨をいくらか手に入れてはどうかと提案した。というのも，外国で両替するのはもっと高いことが多いからだ。

解説　空所後のbefore his vacation「休暇の前に」，文後半のchanging money abroad is often more expensive「外国で両替するのはもっと高いことが多い」から，外貨両替が話題とわかる。したがって，**3のcurrency**「通貨」が正解。tactic「作戦」，bait「えさ」，menace「脅威」。

(7)　正解　4

訳　豊富な天然資源のおかげで，その国は金属や石炭，天然ガスなどの輸出を通じて多額のお金を稼ぐことができる。

解説　空所直後にnatural resources「資源」，文後半にit (＝the country) is able to earn a great deal of money through exports such as metals, coal, and natural gas「その国は金属や石炭，天然ガスなどの輸出を通じて多額のお金を稼ぐことができる」とあるので，天然資源が豊富だと考えられる。したがって，**4のabundant**「豊富な」が適切。unjust「不当な」，insubstantial「実体のない」，elastic「弾性のある」。

(8)　正解　4

訳　最初，エンツォは履歴書に以前の仕事を6つ全部記載した。けれども，書類を1ページに短縮するために，そのうちの2つを省かなければならなかった。

解説　第2文にHe had to remove two of them (＝six of his previous jobs)「そのうちの2つを省かなければならなかった」とあるので，履歴書が1ページを超えないように短くしたのだとわかる。したがって，**4のcondense**「～を短縮する，圧縮する」が正解。dispute「～に反論する，～を議論する」，mumble「～をつぶやく」，mistrust「～を信用しない」。

(9)　正解　2

訳　たいていの国では，適切なビザなしで働く外国人は見つかると強制送還される。けれども，彼らを故国に送り返すのは多額のお金がかかることがある。

解説　第2文にsending them home can cost a lot of money「彼らを故国に送り返すのは多額のお金がかかることがある」とあり，themはforeigners working without a proper visa「適切なビザなしで働く外国人」を指す。**deport**で「～を強制送還する，国外退去させる」という意味を表すので，**2のdeported**を入れると状況に合う。mend

「～を修繕する」, perceive「～を知覚する，理解する」, distribute「～を分配する」。

(10) 正解　4

訳 ティムはスマートフォンの使用に時間を使いすぎていることを気にしている。彼はEメールを数分おきに確認したいという強い衝動に駆られる。

解説 第1文のhe (＝Tim) is spending too much time using his smartphone「スマートフォンの使用に時間を使いすぎている」, 第2文のcheck his e-mail every few minutes「Eメールを数分おきに確認する」から，スマートフォンを見たくてたまらない様子がうかがえる。**4のcompulsion**「衝動」を入れると，a strong compulsion「強い衝動」となり，文意が通る。suspension「一時停止」, extension「拡張，延長」, seclusion「隔絶，隠遁」。

(11) 正解　2

訳 A：今年は新年の決意はしたの，セリーナ？　B：ええ，間食は甘いものでなく健康にいいものを食べ始めることにしたの。でも，チョコレートやキャンディを避けるのは難しいわ。

解説 Aの質問に対し，BがYes, I decided to start eating healthy snacks ...「ええ，…健康にいいものを食べ始めることにしたの」と自分の決意を答えている。**New Year's resolution**で「新年の決意」という意味を表すので，**2のresolution**「決意，解決」が正解。astonishment「驚き」, vulnerability「弱さ，脆弱性」, repression「鎮圧，抑圧」。

(12) 正解　2

訳 ミランダは預金口座の金額がだんだん減っていることに気づいたので，毎月出費を減らし始めることに決めた。

解説 文後半にshe decided to start spending less「出費を減らし始めることに決めた」とあるので，預金の額が少ないと考えられる。**dwindle**で「だんだん減少する」という意味を表すので，**2のdwindling**が適切。graze「草を食べる」, browse「拾い読みをする，閲覧する」, rebound「跳ね返る」。

(13) 正解　4

訳 その女の子は高い場所が怖かったので，父親の手を握った。彼女は塔のてっぺんから窓の外を見ながら，手をしっかりとつかんでいた。

解説 第2文のShe held it tightlyのitは，空所直後のher father's handを指すので，空所にはholdの同義語が入ると考える。**grip**で「～を握る」という意味なので，**4のgripped**が正解。harass「～を困らせる」, breach「～を破る」, drain「～を排出させる」。

(14) 正解　4

訳 アキコは同僚たちがひそひそ話をしているのを見たとき，詮索せずにはいられなかった。彼女は，彼らが何を話しているのかを聞くために近づいていった。

解説 第2文にto hear what they were talking about「彼らが何を話しているのかを聞くために」とあるので，アキコは同僚たちのひそひそ話の内容を知りたかったとわかる。したがって，**4のnosy**「詮索好きな，知りたがって」が適切。obedient「従順な」,

flexible「柔軟な」，sinful「罪深い」。

(15) 正解 **3**

訳 吹雪のため，登山者たちは山頂にたどり着けなかった。彼らは頂上からほんの数百メートルで引き返さなければならなかった。

解説 第2文They (＝the climbers) had to turn around just a few hundred meters from the top.「彼らは頂上からほんの数百メートルで引き返さなければならなかった」から，登山者たちは登頂できなかったとわかる。したがって，**3のsummit**「頂上」が正解。subsidy「補助金，助成金」，mirage「蜃気楼，幻想」，crutch「松葉杖，支え」。

(16) 正解 **1**

訳 ジョナサンが会社で働き始めたとき，1日中仕事をしないことがよくあった。けれども数か月後には，彼はもっと作業を引き受けるようになり，今は暇な時間がほとんどない。

解説 第2文のhe took on more tasks and now has little free time「彼はもっと作業を引き受けるようになり，今は暇な時間がほとんどない」から，働き始めた当初は任せてもらえる仕事が少なかったと考えられる。したがって，空所には**1のidle**「仕事がない，動いていない」を入れると状況に合う。agile「機敏な」，sane「正気の」，needy「困窮した」。

(17) 正解 **2**

訳 A：ねえ，聞いて。テレビ局のアナウンサーとしてのあの仕事の面接を受けることになったんだ！　B：それはすごいけど，まだ楽観しすぎてはいけないよ。その職を得るための競争は激しいだろうから。

解説 Bが空所の後でThere'll be a lot of competition for that position.「その職を得るための競争は激しいだろうから」と言っていることから，簡単に仕事に就けるとは思っていないとわかり，そのことをAに助言している。空所を含む文はdon'tで始まる否定の命令文なので，空所には**2のoptimistic**「楽観的な」を入れると文脈に合う。courteous「礼儀正しい」，suspicious「疑い深い，怪しい」，flustered「うろたえた」。

(18) 正解 **1**

訳 通勤中に，ジョージーは隣にいる電車の乗客のイヤホンからの音がとてもうるさいと思ったので，別の席に移ることにした。

解説 空所を挟んでso ～ that ...「とても～なので…だ，…なほど～だ」が使われている。thatの後にshe decided to move to another seat「別の席に移ることにした」とあるので，騒音が我慢できなかったと考えられる。したがって，**1のbothersome**「うるさい，わずらわしい」が正解。compelling「やむにやまれぬ，説得力のある」，flattering「お世辞の，喜ばせる」，daring「大胆な，向こう見ずな」。

(19) 正解 **2**

訳 A：今年の夏のパレードがとても混んでいて信じられなかった。　B：そうだよね！通りにすごくたくさんの観客がいて，ほとんど動けないほどだったよ。

解説 Aの発言I couldn't believe how crowded this year's summer parade was.「今年の夏のパレードがとても混んでいて信じられなかった」から，パレードを見物する人たちで混雑していたとわかる。空所には，**2のspectators**「観客」を入れると状況に合う。patriot「愛国者」，mimic「物まね芸人，人まねをする動物」，executive「幹部，重役」。

(20) 正解 1

訳 ジョセフは仕事から家まで帰るのにタクシーに乗る余裕があるかどうかわからなかったが，財布を確認すると，乗車するお金を十二分に持っていることに気づいた。

解説 文前半にwas not sure if he could afford a taxi home from work「仕事から家まで帰るのにタクシーに乗る余裕があるかどうかわからなかった」とあり，butが続くので，後半はそれとは逆の内容となる。したがって，**1のample**「豊富な，十二分の」が正解。regal「威厳ある，堂々とした」，vain「無駄な，虚栄心の強い」，crafty「ずるい」。

(21) 正解 3

訳 両親が関わると生徒の学校の成績が上がることが明らかになった。その一例が，家で子供たちの学校の勉強を手助けすることだ。

解説 空所直後のinvolvement「関わり」に注目。第２文にhelping children with schoolwork at home「家で子供たちの学校の勉強を手助けすること」とあり，手助けをする，つまり関わるのは親だと考えられる。したがって，**3のParental**「親の」が適切。obsolete「すたれた，時代遅れの」，numb「麻痺した，呆然とした」，infamous「悪名高い」。

(22) 正解 1

訳 この数十年，汚染により多くの種が危うく絶滅するところだった。しかしながら，最近の保護活動はそれらの一部が回復するのに役立っている。

解説 第２文が逆接を表すHowever「しかしながら」で始まってconservation efforts「保護活動」によって種の一部が回復してきていることが述べられている。空所に**wipe out ～**「～を絶滅させる」を受動態にした**1**を入れると第２文と対照的な内容になり，２つの文のつながりが自然になる。break up ～「～をばらばらにする」，fix up ～「～を手配する」，turn down ～「～を断る」。

(23) 正解 1

訳 デイブは近所の人がかご１杯の新鮮な野菜をくれてうれしかったが，家に帰ると，どうやってその料理に取りかかったらいいのかわからないことに気づいた。

解説 文後半はbutで始まるので，「野菜をもらってうれしかった」とは対照的な内容となる。空所直前にhe did not know how to「どうやって～したらいいのかわからなかった」，直後にcooking them(＝a basket of fresh vegetables)「それらを料理すること」とあるので，空所には**1のgo about**「～に取りかかる」を入れると文脈に合う。pull out ～「～を引っぱり出す」，take in ～「～を取り入れる」，bring down ～「～を下げる，倒す」。

(24) 正解 1

訳 A：当社はあまりにも職業にふさわしくない外見でない限り，従業員が快適な服装をすることを許可しています。 B：それは初めてです。前職ではカジュアルな服装をするとひんしゅくを買いました。

解説 Aの発言に対するBの反応から，Bはこれまで仕事ではきちんとした服装をしていたと考えられる。空所直後にat my last job「前職では」とあるので，前職ではカジュアルな服装がどう思われていたかを表す語句を選ぶ。**frown upon 〜**で「〜にまゆをひそめる，〜がひんしゅくを買う」という意味を表すので，**1のfrowned upon**が正解。carry on 〜「〜を続ける」, enter into 〜「〜に入る，〜を始める」, cross off 〜「〜を線を引いて消す」。

(25) 正解 2

訳 地域担当部長が先週，小さな支店を訪れ，そこがどんな様子かを見るためにいくつかの会議に同席した。

解説 空所直後にa few meetings「いくつかの会議」とあり，空所に入る句動詞の目的語となっている。**sit in on 〜**で「〜を傍聴する，〜に同席する」という意味を表すので，空所には**2のsat in on**を入れると状況に合う。go back on 〜「(約束など) を破る」, speak down to 〜「〜に見下して話す」, look up to 〜「〜を見上げる，尊敬する」。

2 一次試験・筆記

ドキュメンタリーブーム（問題編pp.46〜47）
蟻浴（問題編pp.48〜49）

指示文の訳 それぞれの文章を読んで，各空所に入れるのに最も適切な語句を４つの選択肢の中から選び，その番号を解答用紙の所定欄にマークしなさい。

ドキュメンタリーブーム

Key to Reading 第１段落：導入（ドキュメンタリーブームの負の側面）→第２段落：本論①（懸念すべき傾向１）→第３段落：本論②（懸念すべき傾向２）という３段落構成の説明文。それぞれの段落のトピックセンテンスを意識し，最近のドキュメンタリーの状況と問題点について，論理的に読み進めていく。

訳

近年，テレビストリーミングサービスの成長により，ドキュメンタリーの巨大な新市場が生まれた。制作されるドキュメンタリーの数は急増しており，映像作家にとってはありがたい，新たな機会を与えているが，負の側面もある。問題の１つは，多くの映像作家がコンテンツをコントロールできなくなりつつあると感じていることである。一部のドキュメンタリーは多くの視聴者を魅了し，莫大な経済的利益をもたらしたため，ストリーミングサービスを運営する企業は，制作予算を惜しまなくなった。多額の資金が絡むため，映像作家は強いプレッシャーから，商業的魅力を高めるためにストーリーを変更せざるを得ないように感じてしまうことがしばしばある。

これにより，ドキュメンタリーの社会的価値の低下が懸念されるようになった。ドキュメンタリーはかつて，調査報道の一つとみなされていたが，その素材には顕著な変化が見られる。実犯罪などのジャンルの人気が高まるにつれ，事実情報とエンターテインメントの境界線があいまいになってきているのだ。かつては視聴者に情報を提供し，社会問題に対する意識を高めることに専念していたドキュメンタリーが，主に視聴者に衝撃を与えたり，楽しませたりすることを目的とした，煽情的なエンターテインメントになることが，日常茶飯事となっている。

映像作家にとってもう１つの懸念すべき傾向は，有名人のドキュメンタリーの台頭である。これまで映像作家は一般に，人々が誇張したり，あからさまな嘘をついたりすることを恐れて，平凡なドキュメンタリーの被写体に対しては料金を支払わないという，ジャーナリズムの伝統に従っていた。しかし今，ミュージシャンなどの有名人は，往々にして視聴者を魅了することが保証されているため，彼らのストーリーに対して，数百万ドルの報酬が支払われている。当然のことながら，有名人以外の人々も見返りを要求し始めており，それが映像作家にとって道徳的なジレンマを生み出している。

(26) 正解 **3**

選択肢の訳 **1** 依然として無視されている **2** 十分な報酬が支払われていない **3** コンテンツをコントロールできなくなりつつある **4** 多額の予算が必要である

解説 空所の直後の２文に注目する。companies that operate streaming services have become more generous with their production budgets「ストリーミングサービスを運営する企業は，制作予算を惜しまなくなった」とあり，このことをプレッシャーに感じた映像作家が, feel as though they have no choice but to alter the stories「ストーリーを変更せざるを得ないように感じてしまう」。つまり，本来あるべき姿から外れたものを制作してしまうということ。よって，**3の losing control over content**「コンテンツをコントロールできなくなりつつある」を入れると意味がとおる。lose control overは「～のコントロールを失う，～を制御できなくなる」の意味。

(27) 正解 **4**

選択肢の訳 **1** 人々の解釈の仕方 **2** 登場人物たち **3** 制作コストの増加 **4** 社会的価値の低下

解説 第２段落の最終文より，かつてのドキュメンタリーは，informing viewers and raising awareness of problems in society「視聴者に情報を提供し，社会問題に対する意識を高める」ものであったが，最近は，sensationalist entertainment designed primarily to shock or excite viewers「視聴者に衝撃を与えたり，楽しませたりすることを目的とした，煽情的なエンターテインメント」になりつつあることが分かる。つまり，近年のドキュメンタリーの懸念材料は，**4の decreasing social value of (documentaries)**「（ドキュメンタリー）の社会的価値の低下」。

(28) 正解 **2**

選択肢の訳 **1** 何よりも **2** 当然のことながら **3** その一方 **4** それにもかかわらず

解説 空所を含む文の１文前と空所を含む文の主語が，Famous people, such as musicians「ミュージシャンなどの有名人」とnoncelebrities「有名人以外」と逆の立場の２者であることに注目。前者についてはare now paid millions of dollars for their stories「今，彼らのストーリーに対して，数百万ドルの報酬が支払われている」，後者についてはare also starting to demand compensation「見返りを要求し始めている」とあり，有名人以外も有名人と同様の報酬を求めていることから，**2の Understandably**「当然のことながら」を入れると意味がとおる。

蟻浴（ぎよく）

Key to Reading 第１段落：導入（鳥の蟻浴とは）→第２段落：本論①（鳥の蟻浴の理由１）→第３段落：本論②（鳥の蟻浴の理由２）という３段落構成の説明文である。鳥の蟻浴について，なぜ鳥がそのような行動をするのかを，蟻の特性と絡めて読み進めよう。

訳

動物行動学分野とは，動物の行動を理解するために自然の生息地で動物を研究することである。しかし，動物の行動の背後にある理由について結論を導くことは，必ずしも簡単ではない。例えば，ある鳥は「蟻浴」と呼ばれる行動を見せる。これは通常，鳥がアリをくちばしでつまみ上げ，羽にこすりつけることを指す。同様に，鳥が翼を広げてアリ塚に止まり，アリに体中を這い回らせている様子も観察されている。広範囲を観察したにもかかわらず，動物行動学者は鳥がなぜこのような行動をするのか，未だ確信が持てずにいる。

よく知られている理論の１つは，その行動が鳥の健康に寄与しているというものである。アリは，細菌や真菌から身を守ってくれ，そして他の昆虫にとっては有毒でもある，蟻酸と呼ばれる物質を自然に生成する。この物質を鳥の羽にこすりつければ，病気を抑制し，有害な害虫を寄せ付けないようにできるだろう。鳥は一般的にアリを用いるが，代わりに特定の甲虫やヤスデを用いる鳥も見られる。これらの生物も有害な害虫を遠ざける化学物質を生成するという事実が，この理論を裏付けている。

別に浮上した説としては，鳥の羽にアリをこすりつけることで，アリを食べられる状態に準備するというものがある。科学者らは実験で，一部の鳥は，化学物質を持つアリよりも，科学者が蟻酸を除去したアリを食べる可能性が高いことを発見した。蟻酸は栄養豊富なアリの腹の隣にある袋に蓄えられている。一部の科学者は，鳥は蟻浴により，くちばしでこの袋を取り除こうとしなくても，アリに蟻酸を放出させることができるのだろうと考えている。だがこのプロセスは，アリを魅力的なおやつにする部分を，損なってしまう可能性がある。

(29) 正解 3

選択肢の訳 **1** 言いかえれば **2** 一つの理由には **3** 同様に **4** その結果として

解説 空所を含む文の１つ前の文に，蟻浴について，a bird picking up some ants with its beak and rubbing them on its feathers「鳥がアリをくちばしでつまみ上げ，羽にこすりつける」とある。一方，空所を含む文は，birds … sitting on anthills with their wings spread out and allowing ants to crawl all over their bodies「鳥が翼を広げてアリ塚に止まり，アリに体中を這い回らせている」とあり，これも蟻浴についての追加説明であると推測できることから，**3** の Similarly「同様に」を入れると意味がとおる。

(30) 正解 2

選択肢の訳 **1** アリが鳥に害を及ぼす生物を食べる **2** その行動が鳥の健康に寄与している **3** その行動がアリの数を操作する **4** 鳥が他の昆虫を引き寄せようとしている

解説 空所を含む文の直後の２文を参照。蟻酸についての説明のあと，If this substance is rubbed onto a bird's feathers, it could help inhibit disease and deter harmful pests.「この物質を鳥の羽にこすりつければ，病気を抑制し，有害な害虫を寄せ付けないようにできるだろう」とあることから，**2**の**the behavior contributes to birds' health**「その行動が鳥の健康に寄与している」を入れると意味が通る。

(31) 正解 4

選択肢の訳 **1** 傷んだ羽を取り除くのに役立つ **2** 栄養素をアリに移す **3** 鳥の食欲を増進する **4** アリを食べられる状態に準備する

解説 空所を含む文の直後に科学者が行った実験の結果として，scientists discovered that some birds were more likely to consume ants that had their formic acid removed by the scientists than ants that retained the chemical.「一部の鳥は，化学物質を持つアリよりも，科学者が蟻酸を除去したアリを食べる可能性が高いことを発見した」とある。第２段落より，蟻酸には毒があることから，これが除去されたアリを好んで食べるということは，鳥が蟻浴をすることで，蟻酸を取り除いていると推測できる。よって，**4**の**prepares the ants to be eaten**「アリを食べられる状態に準備する（＝鳥がアリを食べられる状態にする)」が正解。

3 一次試験・筆記

指示文の訳 それぞれの文章を読んで，各質問に対する最も適切な答えを４つの選択肢の中から選び，その番号を解答用紙の所定欄にマークしなさい。

アメリカにおける大学の発展

Key to Reading 第１段落：導入＋本論①（アメリカにおける大学建設の始まり）→第２段落：本論②（大学の生き残り競争）→第３段落：本論③＋結論（アメリカの大学制度が20世紀に成功することができた背景）という３段落構成の説明文。アメリカの大学制度がどのような過程を経て世界で最も成功した例の１つになったかを考えながら読み進めよう。

訳

土地を売ることは富を増やす一般的な方法であるが，19世紀のアメリカの地方の地主にとって，これは必ずしも簡単なことではなかった。当時，地方の人口は少なかったため，地主には買い手を引き付ける方法が必要であった。１つの方法は価格を低く抑えることだったが，地主たちは大学の建設という別の戦略にも目を向けた。大学は文化と学習の中心であるため，これを行うことで，彼らの地域の土地はより望ましいものになった。大学は信じられないほど速いペースで建設され，1880年までにアメリカの大学の数は，ヨーロッパの５倍に達した。

いくつかの古い優良校を除き，アメリカのほとんどの大学には少数の学生と講師しかいなかった。教員は学者というよりも，当時アメリカに存在していたキリスト教の様々な支部を代表する宗教家であることが多かった。大学経営者は，これがそれらの宗教団体からの学生を引き付けるのに役立つことを知っていた。学生が授業料を支払うことができれば，大学入学資格を得ることは一般に難しくなかったが，学生を獲得するための熾烈な競争の結果，授業料は低く抑えられていた。残念ながら，学生数が少ないことにより多くの大学が閉校を余儀なくされ，存続できた大学は継続的な資金集めによってのみ，運営を続ける

※2024年度第１回から，試験形式の変更に伴い大問３の１問目(32)～(34)が削除されます。

ことができた。

しかし，20世紀のアメリカの人口増加に伴い，高等教育の需要は増加し続けた。残った大学には土地，建物，図書館などのインフラが整っていたため，この需要に応えるのに有利な立場にあった。さらに，学生のニーズに敏感であることが存続の１つの手段であったため，それらの大学はほとんどの場合，質の高い教育，優れたスポーツ・レジャー施設を提供した。大学が将来を確かなものにするもう一つの手段は，卒業生との緊密な関係を維持し，気前のよい寄付金を受け取ることだった。これらすべての要因により，アメリカの大学制度は世界で最も成功した例の１つに転換を遂げることができた。

(32) 正解 4

質問の訳 19世紀，アメリカに非常に多くの大学が建てられたのはなぜか。

選択肢の訳 **1** 地方の富のレベルが高まったことにより，子供たちに大学教育を受けさせたいと考える家庭が増えた。 **2** 裕福な地主が，世間のイメージを良くし，死後も確実に記憶されるための手段として，大学を建設した。 **3** アメリカに住むヨーロッパ人が，母国で受けられるのと同じレベルの教育を提供する大学を望んでいた。
4 大学の建設は，地方に土地を所有する人々にとって，土地の価値を高め，より多くの買い手を引きつけるための１つの手段だった。

解説 第１段落では，アメリカでどのようにして大学の数が増えていったかについて述べている。地主が土地の買い手を見つける手段の１つとして，第３文で大学建設を挙げており，続く第４文にその結果として，Doing this made the land in their area more desirable, as colleges were centers of culture and learning.「大学は文化と学習の中心であるため，これを行うことで，彼らの地域の土地はより望ましいものになった」とある。この内容をまとめた選択肢**4**が正解。

(33) 正解 4

質問の訳 19世紀のアメリカの大学の多くの教員について正しいことはどれか。

選択肢の訳 **1** 彼らは劣悪な条件で働かされたため，短期間で辞めた。 **2** 彼らの給与は通常，大学自体ではなく宗教団体から支払われていた。 **3** 大学で最高の地位を獲得するために，彼らの間で激しい競争があった。 **4** 彼らの宗教的背景は，学生を大学に入学させる効果的な手段となる傾向があった。

解説 19世紀のアメリカの大学教員については，第２段落第２文にreligious men representing the different branches of Christianity「キリスト教の様々な支部を代表する宗教家」であることが多かったとあり，次の文に，そのことがそれらの宗教団体からの学生を引き付けるのに役立っていたとある。これらの内容をまとめた選択肢**4**が正解。

(34) 正解 2

質問の訳 アメリカの大学が20世紀に成功を収めた理由の１つは，それらが～

選択肢の訳 **1** 体育プログラムの質を高めるために，地元のスポーツチームと提携したことである。 **2** 元学生との永続的な関係を築くことで，財政面での安全性を高めることができたからである。 **3** 主に地元地域から学生を募集することに重点を置くことで，他の大学との競争を減らしたことである。 **4** 独自の施設を建設するのではなく，地域に既にあった施設を利用することで，コストを抑えたことである。

解説 大学存続の手段については，第３段落第３文にbeing sensitive to students' needs「学生のニーズに敏感であること」，第４文にmaintaining close ties with their graduates, from whom they would receive generous donations「卒業生との緊密な関係を維持し，気前のよい寄付金を受け取ること」とある。この後者の内容と一致する選択肢**2**が正解。

機械か人間か？

Key to Reading 第１段落：導入（火星探査車オッピーの人気）→第２段落：本論①（オッピーの擬人化とNASAの思惑）→第３段落：本論②＋結論（物体の擬人化の危険性）という３段落構成の説明文。なぜ人間は物体を擬人化したがるのか，またそれによりどのような影響が及び得るかを考えながら読み進めよう。

訳

2004年，NASAの探査車オポチュニティが火星に着陸した。「オッピー」という愛称が付けられたゴルフカートほどの大きさの探査車は，惑星を調査し，その表面の画像を撮影するために送られた。オッピーのミッションは90日間続くことになっていたが，探査車はその後15年間にわたり，画像とデータを地球に送信し続けた。その間，それは大衆の興味をかき立てた。実際，人々はオッピーに非常に愛着を持ち，オッピーが動かなくなると，亡くなった人に宛てたものと同様の哀悼のメッセージを，ソーシャルメディアに送信した。

人間以外の物に人間の特性を与える行為は，擬人化として知られており，人間が幼い頃から自然に行っていることである。例えば，おもちゃ，車，家などの物体に愛着心を抱くことは，あらゆる年齢の人々にとって珍しいことではない。オッピーのことを「彼女」と呼んだり，子供のように思ったりするエンジニアたちも，この傾向には無縁ではなかった。人間性を無生物に投影することの効果の１つは，人々がそれを守らないといけない気持ちになり，その幸福に関心を向けさせることのようだ。NASAは，オッピーを意図的により人間らしく見せ，体から伸びた頭のような構造の中に目のようなカメラレンズを備えたデザインにすることで，この現象を有利に利用したようだ。オポチュニティミッション以前は，大々的に報道された失敗により，NASAに対する国民の信頼が低下し，NASAの資金も削減されていた。オッピーに人間の特徴を与えることは，大衆を味方にし，恐らくNASAのミッションのための追加の資金を呼び込むための効果的な戦略であったことが示唆されている。

オッピーを人間として考えることは無害に見えるかもしれないが，物体を擬人化すると不幸な結果を招く可能性がある。例えば，AIが人間の脳と同じように機能すると仮定すると，その機能に対する非現実的な期待が生じ，大きなメリットを提供できない状況でAIが使用される可能性がある。擬人化は，AIや機械が人間に対して反乱を起こすなど，悪夢のようなシナリオを人々に危惧させる可能性もある。機械が脅威であるというこの考えは，機械が人間と同じように論理的に考えるという誤解から生じている。しかし，どうやら人間は擬人化せずにはいられないようだ。ジャーナリストのスコット・サイモンは，「機械に多くの時間を費やして，機械に話しかけたり，機械からの連絡を待ったり，機械のことを心配し始めると，科学者でさえ，機械に個性を見出してしまう」と著している。

(35) 正解 4

質問の訳 オッピーに対する人々の反応について分かることは何か。

選択肢の訳 **1** 火星に関する新しい発見に興味があったため，人々はすぐにオッピーを応援した。　2　オッピーのミッションの重要性を知らせる努力がほとんど行われていなかったため，人々はオッピーに親しみを感じるのが難しいと感じた。　3　オッピーが地球に送り返した情報は専門的すぎて科学者ではない人々には理解できなかったため，人々はすぐにオッピーのミッションへの興味を失った。　4　人々は オッピーに非常に感情的なつながりを感じていたため，オッピーが稼働しなくなったときは哀悼の意を表した。

解説 第1段落最終文に people became so attached to Oppy that when it ceased to function, they sent messages of condolence over social media similar to those intended for a deceased person「人々はオッピーに非常に愛着を持ち，オッピーが動かなくなると，亡くなった人に宛てたものと同様の哀悼のメッセージを，ソーシャルメディアに送信した」とある。この内容をまとめた選択肢**4**が正解。選択肢は，sent messages of condolenceをexpressed sympathyと表している。

(36)　正解　1

質問の訳 第2段落によると，オッピーをより人間らしく見せたのは，～ようだ。

選択肢の訳 1　NASAの活動に対する全面的な支援を増やし，より多くの資金を獲得できるようにするための戦略だった。　2　子供たちが人間に似たロボットにより大きな関心を示したという実験に基づいていた。　3　心理学者が，この戦略により，エンジニアがそれを期限内に完了させるためにより懸命に働くようになるだろうと示唆したために行われた。　4　政府がNASAに，そのデザインをおもちゃに使用しやすいものにするよう，圧力をかけた結果であった。

解説 第2段落最後から2文目より，NASAは当時資金を削減されていた。次の文に，It has been suggested that giving Oppy human characteristics was an effective strategy to win over the public and perhaps even attract additional funding for NASA's mission.「オッピーに人間の特徴を与えることは，大衆を味方にし，恐らくNASAのミッションのための追加の資金を呼び込むための効果的な戦略であったことが示唆されている」とあることから，このことが，オッピーが擬人化された理由であると分かる。これらの内容を言い換えた選択肢**1**が正解。

(37)　正解　3

質問の訳 この文章によると，擬人化にはどのような潜在的な問題があるか。

選択肢の訳 1　人間が自分でやった方がコストがかからない仕事を，機械に頼るようになる可能性がある。　2　AIや機械が仕事を正しく遂行するのに何の指導も必要ないと，人々が誤解する可能性がある。　3　AIや機械が人間と同じように動作するという考えは，人々に彼らが何ができるかを誤解させる可能性がある。　4　科学者がAIと築いている関係により，人間のニーズよりもAIの進歩が優先される可能性がある。

解説 擬人化の問題については，第3段落第2文以降を参照。第2文にAssuming AI works in the same way as the human brain, for example, may lead to unrealistic expectations of its capabilities, causing it to be used in situations where it is unable to provide significant benefits.「例えば，AIが人間の脳と同じように機能すると仮定すると，その機能に対する非現実的な期待が生じ，大きなメリットを提供できない状況でAIが使用される可能性がある」とある。つまり，AIの実際の機能と人間の期待の間に差が生じるということ。これをcause people to misunderstand what they are able to do「人々に彼らが何ができるかを誤解させる」と言い換えた**3**が正解。

マリウスの改革

Key to Reading 第１段落：導入（マリウスの改革が始まるまで）→第２段落：本論①（貧困市民の入隊）→第３段落：本論②（退役軍人の役割）→第４段落：本論③（マリウスの改革の負の影響と共和国の崩壊）という４段落構成の説明文。設問に先に目を通し，読み取るべきポイントを押さえてから，本文を読み進めよう。

訳

紀元前２世紀の終わり頃，ローマ共和国は西ヨーロッパからの部族民による侵略の脅威に直面し，アフリカで一連の屈辱的な敗北を経験した。急速に拡大する共和国のニーズにローマ軍がもはや対応できないことを認識したローマの指導者ガイウス・マリウスは，全面的な改革の実施に乗り出した。これらはマリウスの改革として知られるようになり，ローマ軍を，恐らく古代において最も有能な戦闘部隊であろう，その勢いをほとんど止められないほどの軍事機構に変えた。慣例的に，ローマ軍への兵士の入隊は期限付きで，継続的な募集が必要となったため，必然的に，往々にして戦闘経験のない新兵が多くなった。さらに，軍隊に入るには資産を所有している必要があり，ローマ共和国内の貧困の増加により，この要件を満たすことができる潜在的な新兵の数が大幅に減少した。

マリウスの改革は，資産を所有しているという必要条件と新兵が自分で武器や防具を準備するという必要条件の両方を撤廃することを含む，複数の方策から成っていた。これにより，最貧市民でも入隊することが可能になり，軍は使用する武器や防具を統一および改善できたため，より装備の整った兵士をそろえることができた。軍隊の兵士は「軍団兵」として知られるようになり，軍事戦略の訓練を受けた。恐らく最も重要なことは，この改革により，入隊の決定的な動機が与えられたことである。というのは，16年間務めた兵士には，農地と完全なローマ市民権が報酬として与えられたのだった。ローマ共和国の急速な拡大は，貧困の中で暮らしている非市民の住民が多く存在し，彼らにとってその状況から逃れる機会が非常に魅力的なものだったことを意味していた。

ローマ軍は，より良く訓練され，より高いモチベーションを持った兵士によって重要な軍事的勝利を収め，ローマの拡大に貢献した。元軍団兵が受け取った土地は通常，新たに征服された属州にあったため，これらの退役軍人はローマ文化の普及に貢献した。彼らの存在はまた，ローマの支配に対する地元の抵抗に打ち勝つことを容易にし，ローマ共和国への統合プロセスを円滑に進めることになった。退役軍人がいるだけで，反乱を防ぎ侵略に抵抗することができたため，新しい領土にはさらなる安全がもたらされた。

マリウスの改革はローマ軍を大きく改善したが，同時にローマ社会に予期せぬ影響を与え，最終的には共和国の崩壊を招くことになった。軍隊が必要に応じて徴兵された裕福な市民で大部分を構成されていた頃，軍隊はローマの政治にはほとんど影響を与えなかった。しかし，マリウスの改革の後，軍の軍団兵は非常に統制され，将軍に対する強い忠誠心が育まれた。その結果，将軍たちは，ローマ共和国の安全と拡大を確実にするためというよりはむしろ，自らの政治的影響力を得るために指揮下の軍隊を利用したいという誘惑に抵抗することが困難であると自覚することになった。これが内乱につながり，最終的にジュリアス・シーザーは軍隊を使って選挙で選ばれた政府を打倒し，自らをローマの指導者と宣言することに成功した。これにより比較的民主的なローマ共和政は終わりを告げ，全権を有する皇帝が統治する，専制国家創設への道が開かれた。

(38) 正解 4

質問の訳 マリウスの改革の理由の１つは何か。

選択肢の訳 **1** ローマ共和国内の財政問題は，ローマの指導者が軍への資金を削減するより他に選択の余地がないことを意味した。 **2** 軍隊の兵士の数が増加するにつれて，ローマ共和国を守るために彼らを西ヨーロッパやアフリカに輸送することがより困難になった。 **3** 兵士たちが長年軍隊に留まることを強いられ，軍務に対して低賃金しか受け取らなかったため，兵士たちの間で不満が生じた。 **4** ローマの指導者が，ローマ共和国が軍事目標を達成するために必要な人員や技術が軍隊にないことを懸念した。

解説 第１段落第２文から，ローマ軍が急速に拡大するローマ共和国のニーズに対応できなくなっていたためにマリウスが軍の改革を行ったことがわかる。改革前の軍の状況について第４，５文で，当時のローマ軍への兵士の入隊は期限付きで，継続的に兵士が募集されていたため，new recruits often having no previous fighting experience「戦闘経験のない新兵」が多くなったこと，軍隊に入るには資産を所有している必要があったため，the pool of potential recruits who could meet this requirement「この要件を満たすことができる潜在的な新兵の数」が大幅に減少したことが述べられている。つまり，ローマ軍は人員と技術（manpower or skills）不足に陥っていたと言えるので**4**が正解。

(39) 正解 2

質問の訳 マリウスの改革によって起こった重要な変化は何か。

選択肢の訳 **1** ローマ市民のみがローマ軍に参加できるという規則が導入され，ローマ市民権を取得しようとする人が増加した。 **2** ローマ軍に従事することは，ローマ共和国に住む人々にとって生活を向上させる手段であったため，より魅力的なものとなった。 **3** ローマ軍は既に軍事経験のある男性のみを受け入れたため，十分な新兵を見つけるのに苦労した。 **4** 兵士がローマ軍で過ごすことを求められる年数が短縮され，兵士の平均年齢が下がった。

解説 第２段落第１文で，マリウスの改革によって，the removal of both property requirements and the need for recruits to prepare their own weapons and armor「資産を所有しているという必要条件と新兵が自分で武器や防具を準備するという必要条件の両方が撤廃」されたことが述べられている。また第４文に，これによりa crucial incentive for enlistment「入隊の決定的な動機」が与えられたと述べられている。続く最終文のThe rapid expansion of the Roman Republic meant there were many noncitizen inhabitants who lived in poverty and for whom an opportunity to escape their situation was hugely appealing.「ローマ共和国の急速な拡大は，貧困の中で暮らしている非市民の住民が多く存在し，彼らにとってその状況から逃れる機会が非常に魅力的なものだったことを意味していた」より，これらの内容を１文で表した選択肢**2**が正解。

(40) 正解 3

質問の訳 第３段落によると，ローマ軍が新たな領土を占領した後，〜

選択肢の訳 **1** 軍隊が近隣地域を攻撃し，ローマ共和国の拡大を継続できるよう，それらの地域に送られる兵士の数が大幅に増やされた。 **2** 地方の人々はローマ社会にすぐに慣れることができるよう，ローマの言語と文化を学ぶためにローマの首都に招待された。　**3**　元兵士にそこの土地が与えられ，そのおかげで地元の人々を支配し，その地域をさまざまな脅威から確実に守ることがはるかに容易になった。　**4**　発生した多くの反乱を軍隊が防ぐことができなかったため，その地域はしばしばあっという間に再び失われることになった。

解説 第3段落第2文より，元軍団兵には通常，新たに征服された属州の土地が与えられた。彼らについて，3文目にTheir presence also made it easier to overcome local resistance to Roman rule and facilitated the process of integration into the Roman Republic.「彼らの存在はまた，ローマの支配に対する地元の抵抗に打ち勝つことを容易にし，ローマ共和国への統合プロセスを円滑に進めることになった」，最終文にThe mere presence of the veterans brought greater security to new territories, since they could assist in preventing rebellions and resisting invasions.「退役軍人がいるだけで，反乱を防ぎ侵略に抵抗することができたため，新しい領土にはさらなる安全がもたらされた」とあることから，この内容とほぼ一致する選択肢**3**が正解。本文中のformer legionaries「元軍団兵」，veterans「退役軍人」を選択肢ではex-soldiers「元兵士」と言い換えている。

(41)　正解　1

質問の訳 マリウスの改革はローマ社会にどのような影響を与えたか。

選択肢の訳 **1**　軍隊が政治的手段として利用され，ローマの指導者が市民に選ばれるのではなく軍事力によってその地位を獲得するシステムが生み出された。　**2**　軍隊に従事することを拒否した人々の富と社会的地位は減少した一方で，元軍団兵はしばしば政府の高い官職に就いた。　**3**　ローマ軍が非常に大きくなったため，その維持にかかる費用がローマ共和国崩壊の主な原因となった。　**4**　軍団兵の規律の欠如がローマ市民と軍との間に緊張を生み，最終的には内戦につながった。

解説 第4段落第1文より，マリウスの改革は，had an unexpected impact on Roman society that eventually led to the downfall of the republic.「ローマ社会に予期せぬ影響を与え，最終的には共和国の崩壊を招くことになった」。この具体的な内容を第2文～第5文で述べている。強い忠誠心を持つ軍団兵を有する将軍は，ローマ共和国のためではなく，use the forces under their command to gain political influence for themselves「自らの政治的影響力を得るために指揮下の軍隊を利用する」ことを選択するようになり，結果的に内乱を招き，ジュリアス・シーザーが統治する，専制国家が始まることになった。この内容と一致する選択肢**1**が正解。

4　一次試験・英作文

(問題編p.57)

指示文の訳 ●次のトピックについてエッセイを書きなさい。
●答えの裏付けに，以下に挙げたポイントのうちの2つを使いなさい。
●構成：導入，本論，結論
●長さ：120～150語

※2024年度第1回から，大問4に文章の要約を書く問題が加わります。

●エッセイは解答用紙のB面に用意されたスペースに書きなさい。
スペースの外側に書かれた内容は，採点の対象とはなりません。

トピックの訳 企業には，リサイクルしやすい商品の製造が求められるべきか。

ポイントの訳 ●企業の利益 ●顧客の需要 ●公害 ●商品の品質

解答例

Companies should be required to produce goods that are easy to recycle. This opinion is based on the following reasons: customer demand and pollution.

First, goods that are simple to recycle significantly reduce pollution. They not only lower the carbon footprint of factories but also lead to fewer products thrown away in landfills, where they often release harmful gases. Therefore, producing such goods is a key part of companies' environmental responsibility.

Second, customer demand for sustainable products has been growing rapidly. Consumers are increasingly aware of the impact of their purchasing decisions, and many are actively seeking out eco-friendly products. If companies do not produce goods that are easily recyclable, they will fail to fulfill the needs of this growing market of environmentally conscious consumers.

In conclusion, producing goods that can be easily recycled should be required for companies, as this helps meet new consumer demands and protect the environment.

解答例の訳

企業には，リサイクルしやすい商品の製造が求められるべきだ。この意見は次の理由に基づいている。すなわち，顧客の需要および公害だ。

第一に，リサイクルしやすい商品は公害を著しく減少させる。それらは工場のカーボンフットプリントを下げるのみならず，しばしば有毒ガスの放出元である埋め立て地に処分される商品数の減少につながる。そのため，そのような商品の製造は，企業の環境責任の重要な要素である。

第二に，持続可能な商品に対する顧客の需要は急増し続けている。消費者は，自身の購買決定がもたらす影響をますます意識するようになってきており，大勢の者が環境に優しい商品を積極的に探し出している。企業は容易にリサイクル可能な商品を製造しなければ，成長しつつある環境意識の高い消費者の購買層の需要を満たすことができないだろう。

結論として，容易にリサイクル可能な商品の製造は企業に求められるべきだ，というのもこのことは，新しい消費者の需要に応えることと環境保護の助けとなるからだ。

解説 TOPIC文で示されている意見について，「求められるべきである／求められるべきではない」のどちらかの立場に立って，自分の意見とその根拠をエッセイの形でまとめる形式。エッセイをまとめる際には，POINTSとして示されたキーワードのうち２つを選んで使用する必要がある。これらのキーワードに挙げられている語句については，例えば，Customer demand「顧客の需要」はwhat customers demand「顧客が求めること」などと，必要に応じて形を変えて表現しても良い。

段落構成に関する，導入（introduction）→本論（main body）→結論（conclusion）という基本的な指定は必ず守ること。解答例のように本論を２つに分ける場合は，論点の重複がないように，それぞれの段落を別の視点からまとめる。その際，各段落の論点が明確になるように，談話標識（discourse markers）を使うと論理的にまとまりのある文章となり，効果的である。また，結論をまとめるときは，第1段落の単純な繰り返しにならないよう，表現を若干でも工夫することが好ましい。

TOPIC文 「企業には，リサイクルしやすい商品の製造が求められるべきか」という質問についての意見を求める内容。

語句 be required to ～「～することが求められる」/ goods「商品」

第1段落（導入） エッセイの冒頭で，TOPIC文のテーマを正しく理解していることと，自分が「企業には，リサイクルしやすい商品の製造が求められるべきか」という質問について，「求められるべきである／求められるべきではない」のどちらの立場に立っているかを明示する。解答例は，疑問文のTOPIC文を平叙文に直し，自分が前者の立場であることを明確に示している。また，POINTSの中からCustomer demandとPollution「公害」の2つを取り上げていることも，コロン（:）を用いて簡潔に示している。

語句 be based on ～「～に基づいている」/ following「次の」

第2段落（本論①） 第2段落では，順序を表す談話標識であるFirst「第一に」から始め，第1段落で示した観点の一つである「公害」について述べている。また，第3文では，Therefore「そのため」という談話標識を用いて，リサイクルしやすい商品が環境に優しいゆえに，そのような商品の製造が企業の環境責任の重要な要素であると示している。

語句 significantly「著しく」/ lower「～を低下させる」/ carbon footprint「カーボンフットプリント（商品やサービスの原材料調達から廃棄・リサイクルに至るまでの全工程を通じてもたらされる温室効果ガスの量を二酸化炭素排出量に換算して表示すること）」/ lead to ～「～につながる」/ landfill「埋め立て地」/ release「～を放出する」/ responsibility「責任」

第3段落（本論②） 第3段落では，第1段落で示したもう一つの観点である「顧客の需要」について意見を展開している。この段落では，順序を表すSecond「第二に」から始め，第2文では，第1文で示した持続可能な商品に対する顧客の需要についての補足説明を加えた上で，続く第3文では，企業はリサイクルしやすい商品を製造しなければ，その需要を満たすことができないだろうと述べている。

語句 sustainable「持続可能な」/ be aware of ～「～を意識している」/ increasingly「ますます」/ actively「積極的に」/ eco-friendly「環境に優しい」/ fulfill「～を満たす」/ -conscious「～意識の高い」/ consumer「消費者」

第4段落（結論） 最終段落では，In conclusion「結論として」という談話標識から文を始めて，自分がTOPIC文の質問に対しYesの立場であること，および第2・3段落で述べた意見を，第1～3段落とは多少表現を変えて再度提示し，文章を締め括っている。

語句 meet「～を満たす」/ protect「～を保護する」

Part 1 一次試験・リスニング

（問題編pp.58～59）

指示文の訳 準1級の試験のリスニングテストが始まります。指示を注意して聞いてください。テスト中に質問をすることは許されていません。

このテストは３つのパートに分かれています。これら３つのパートの質問は全て選択肢の中から正解を選ぶ問題です。それぞれの質問について，問題冊子に書かれている４つの選択肢の中から最も適切な答えを選び，解答用紙の該当箇所にその答えをマークしなさい。このリスニングテストの全てのパートで，メモを取ってもかまいません。

それでは，これからPart　１の指示を行います。このパートではNo. １からNo.12まで12の会話が放送されます。それぞれの会話に続いて，質問が１つ流れます。各質問に対して，最も適切な答えを選んで解答用紙にマークする時間が10秒あります。会話と質問は１度しか読まれません。それでは，準１級のリスニングテストを始めます。

No.1　正解　4

放送文 ***A:*** Why are you reading that paperback book, Dad? I just gave you an e-reader for your birthday! ***B:*** I already finished the book you downloaded for me. ***A:*** There's more where that came from. And there are a lot of free e-books on the Internet. ***B:*** Yeah, I know. But downloading them is the problem. ***A:*** I'm always happy to help, Dad. ***B:*** That would be great. And while you're at it, can you show me how to make the letters bigger on the reader? ***A:*** Of course.
Question: What is the man's problem?

訳 A：なんで紙の本を読んでるの，お父さん？　誕生日に電子書籍リーダーをプレゼントしたばかりなのに！　B：お前がダウンロードしてくれた本はもう読み終わったんだよ。　A：ダウンロード元のサイトには，まだまだあるよ。それにインターネットには無料の電子書籍もたくさんあるし。　B：そうだね。でもダウンロードするのが問題なんだ。　A：いつでも喜んで（ダウンロードを）手伝うよ，お父さん。　B：それはありがたいね。ついでに，リーダーで文字を大きくする方法も教えてくれる？　A：もちろん。

質問の訳 男性の問題は何か。

選択肢の訳 **1**　電子書籍リーダーが見つからない。　**2**　電子書籍を買いたくない。
3　電子書籍リーダーを壊してしまった。　**4**　電子書籍をダウンロードするのが難しい。

解説 1往復目のやりとりから，A（＝娘）がB（＝父親）に電子書籍リーダーをプレゼントしたが，Bが電子書籍ではなく紙の本を読んでいる場面。Bが紙の本を読んでいる理由を「お前（＝A）がダウンロードしてくれた本はもう読み終わった」と述べたのに対し，Aが「インターネットには無料の電子書籍がたくさんある」と述べると，Bは「ダウンロードするのが問題なんだ」と述べている。よって，Bはインターネットから電子書籍をダウンロードすることに問題を抱えていることがわかるので，problemをhardと言い換えた**4**が正解。

No.2　正解　3

放送文 ***A:*** It's nice to see you coming to yoga class more regularly, José. ***B:*** Yeah, I've been getting into it a little more lately. Still, the poses don't seem to get any easier. ***A:*** Be patient with yourself; change happens gradually. ***B:*** Sometimes I feel embarrassed because the other students are so much more flexible. ***A:*** Don't worry about comparing yourself with anyone. Yoga is a holistic mind-and-body practice, not a competition. ***B:*** I'll try to keep that in mind next time I fall over in class.

Question: What will the man probably do?

訳 A：あなたがヨガクラスにより頻繁に来てくれるようになってうれしいです，ホセ。 B：はい，最近前より少しはまってきています。でも，ポーズがなかなか簡単にとれないんですけどね。 A：自分に忍耐強くなって。変化は徐々に起こるものです。 B：他の生徒のほうがずっと柔軟性があるので，ぼくはときどき恥ずかしくなります。 A：他人と比べて気にするのはやめて。ヨガは心と体の統合的な実践であって，競争ではありません。 B：今度授業中に転んだら，そのことを心に留めておくようにします。

質問の訳 男性はおそらくどうするか。

選択肢の訳 **1** ヨガの個人レッスンを受ける。 **2** 別の活動を見つける。 **3** 今のクラスを続ける。 **4** 別のヨガグループに参加する。

解説 1～2往復目のやりとりから，A（＝女性）とB（＝José）が，ヨガクラスで話している場面。1往復目でBは「ポーズがなかなか簡単にとれない」と述べ，2往復目でもBは「他の生徒のほうがずっと柔軟性があるので，ぼくはときどき恥ずかしくなります」と述べており，ヨガがうまくできなくて悩んでいるとわかる。これに対しAが「自分に忍耐強くなって」（2往復目），「他人と比べて気にするのはやめて」（3往復目）とアドバイスすると，Bは「今度授業中に転んだら，そのことを心に留めておくようにします」と前向きな発言をしている。Bは今のクラスを続けていくつもりであることがわかるので，next timeを**continue**に，またin classを**his current class**に言い換えた**3**が正解。

No.3 正解 1

放送文 ***A:*** Have you met the new boss? ***B:*** I have. We discovered we're from the same hometown. We even went to the same high school, though she was a few years ahead of me. ***A:*** Small world! What did you think of her? ***B:*** She's very knowledgeable about the publishing business. She has some interesting plans, and that's what our division needs. ***A:*** Well, that's exciting. We need a supportive leader.

Question: What is one thing we learn about the new boss?

訳 A：新しい上司に会った？ B：会ったよ。地元が同じだってわかったんだ。高校も同じだったんだよ，彼女は私より数年上だけどね。 A：世間は狭いね！ 彼女のことをどう思った？ B：彼女は出版ビジネスにとても詳しいの。興味深い計画を持っていて，それは私たちの部署に必要なことなんだ。 A：そうか，それはワクワクするね。ぼくたちには支えてくれるリーダーが必要だもんね。

質問の訳 新しい上司についてわかることの１つは何か。

選択肢の訳 **1** 部署に対しての新しいアイデアを持っている。 **2** 出版についてほとんど知らない。 **3** 優秀な学生だった。 **4** スタッフの給料を上げたいと思っている。

解説 1往復目のやりとりから，A（＝男性）とB（＝女性）が，新しい上司について話している場面。2往復目でBが「（新しい上司は）興味深い計画を持っていて，それは私たちの部署に必要なことなんだ」と述べているので，新しい上司は，Bの部署に対しての新しいアイデアを持っていることがわかる。よって，interesting plansを**new ideas**に，またour division needsを**for the division**に言い換えた**1**が正解。

No.4 正解 1

放送文 ***A:*** Why are all of your clothes piled up on the bed? ***B:*** I'm sorting through them to see which items I want to donate. ***A:*** Didn't you do that about a month ago for a school fund-raiser? It's not like your size has changed since then. ***B:*** No, but the community center is gathering clothes for a family who just had a house fire. They lost everything. ***A:*** That's terrible. Do they need men's clothes? I could part with a few items myself.
Question: Why is the woman giving away her clothes?

訳 A：どうして君の洋服が全部ベッドの上に山積みになっているの？ B：寄付したいものを探すために整理しているの。 A：１か月くらい前にも，学校の募金活動のためにやってなかった？ あれから君の体形が変わったわけでもあるまいし。 B：体形が変わったわけじゃないけど，家が火事になった家族のために公民館で服を集めているのよ。その人たちは何もかも失くしてしまったの。 A：それは大変だね。男性用の服は必要かな？ ぼくも少し分けてあげられるよ。

質問の訳 なぜ女性は自分の服を手放すのか。

選択肢の訳 **1** 困っている家族を助けたいと思っている。 **2** 彼女に合わなくなった。 **3** 学校で行事がある。 **4** 収納場所がない。

解説 1往復目のやりとりから，B（＝女性）が，寄付するものを探すために自分の服を整理している場面。2往復目でBは「家が火事になった家族のために公民館で服を集めているのよ。その人たちは何もかも失くしてしまったの」と述べているので，Bが火事ですべてを失い困っている家族を助けるために，自分の服を寄付したいと考えていることがわかる。よって，donateを**help**に，またlost everythingを**in need**と表した**1**が正解。

No.5 正解 3

放送文 ***A:*** Did you see the latest newsletter? It seems our merger with Evan's Real Estate is now official. ***B:*** I'm dreading moving our offices, but I admit it makes sense. ***A:*** I agree. We've been working with their agents for years. This will just reduce our operating expenses and strengthen our market position. ***B:*** Yeah. But I've heard that some of our staff have decided to leave to work on their own. ***A:*** I think the merger is just convenient timing for them. They've wanted to become independent for a while. ***B:*** Well, I'll still be sad to see them go.
Question: What is one thing the man says about the merger?

訳 A：最新のニュースレターを見た？ ぼくたちとエヴァンズ不動産との合併が正式に決まったようだよ。 B：オフィスを移転するのは大変そうだけど，合併は理にかなっているわ。 A：同感だよ。ぼくたちは何年も彼らの代理店と仕事をしてきた。これで営業経費も削減できるし，市場での地位も強化できる。 B：そうね。でも，スタッフの何人かは独立を決めたそうよ。 A：合併が彼らにとって都合のいいタイミングだっただけだと思うよ。彼らは以前から独立を望んでいたからね。 B：まあ，それでも彼らがいなくなるのは寂しいけどね。

質問の訳 合併について男性が言っていることの１つは何か。

選択肢の訳 **1** 仕事量を減らす助けになる。 **2** 自営の代理店との仕事が増える。

3　会社のさらなる成功につながる。　**4**　多くのスタッフが解雇されることになる。

解説　1往復目のやりとりから，A（＝男性）とB（＝女性）が，自分たちの勤務する会社とエヴァンズ不動産との合併について話している場面。1往復目でBが「合併は理にかなっている」と述べると，Aも「同感だよ」，「これで営業経費も削減できるし，市場での地位も強化できる」と述べているので，Aは合併が自社のさらなる成功につながると考えていることがわかる。よって，reduce our operating expenses and strengthen our market positionを**more successful**に言い換えた**3**が正解。

No.6　正解　2

放送文　***A:*** What do you think about installing solar panels on our roof? The initial costs are a little high, but we'd save a lot on energy bills. ***B:*** Well, panels are becoming more efficient, and they're eco-friendly. But I don't think they'd be a good match for us. ***A:*** Why not? ***B:*** It would take something like 15 years to make our money back on the investment, but we won't be living in this house that long. ***A:*** But wouldn't solar panels make the place worth more when we sell it? ***B:*** Not by much. By then, our panels would be outdated.
Question: What does the man say about solar panels?

訳　A：うちの屋根にソーラーパネルを設置するのはどう？　初期費用はちょっと高いけど，光熱費はかなり節約できるわ。　B：そうだね，パネルの効率はよくなっているし，環境にも優しいよね。でも，うちには合わないと思うな。　A：どうして合わないの？　B：投資の元を取るには15年くらいかかるだろうけど，この家にはそんなに長く住まないだろうし。　A：でも，ソーラーパネルがあれば，売るときに価値が上がるんじゃないかしら？　B：それほどの差はないよ。その頃にはパネルは古くなっているだろうし。

質問の訳　男性はソーラーパネルについてどう言っているか。

選択肢の訳　**1**　将来はより安くなるだろう。　**2**　夫婦のお金の節約にはならないだろう。　**3**　数年で買い換える必要がある。　**4**　環境上の利点はあまりない。

解説　1往復目のやりとりから，A（＝妻）とB（＝夫）が，自分の家の屋根にソーラーパネルを設置することについて話している場面。1往復目でBは「うちには合わないと思うな」と述べ，2往復目でも「投資の元を取るには15年くらいかかるだろうけど，この家にはそんなに長く住まない」と述べている。また，3往復目でAがソーラーパネルがあれば，売るときに価値が上がると述べたことに対しても，「それほどの差はないよ」と述べている。よって，Bはソーラーパネルを設置してもお金の節約にはならないだろうと考えていることがわかるので，don't think they'd be a good match for usを**not save the couple money**と言い換えた**2**が正解。

No.7　正解　4

放送文　***A:*** Could you have a look at this translation, Jared? ***B:*** Sure. Is it the one that Miki did for LTR Chemicals? ***A:*** Yes. Please give it extra attention because they're very particular about accuracy. We can't afford to lose them as a client. ***B:*** OK. Is the deadline urgent? ***A:*** No, we're ahead of schedule and still have a few days until it's due. Miki has a tendency to rush to get things back to me quickly, even though I ask her to take her time. ***B:*** OK, I'll give it a thorough check.

Question: What does the woman imply?

訳 A：この翻訳を見てもらえますか，ジャレッド？　B：ええ。ミキがLTRケミカルズのために翻訳したものですか。　A：はい。彼らは正確さにとてもこだわるので，特に注意して見てください。クライアントとして失うわけにはいきませんから。　B：わかりました。期限は急ぎですか。　A：いえ，予定より早く進行していて，まだ期限まで数日あります。ミキは，私がゆっくりやってくださいと言っても，よく急いで返そうとするんですよ。　B：わかりました，しっかりチェックします。

質問の訳 女性は何を言いたいのか。

選択肢の訳 **1**　ミキはまだ翻訳を終えていない。　**2**　期限が変更になる可能性がある。　**3**　クライアントがたくさんミスを犯している。　**4**　ミキはしばしば十分に注意深く仕事をしない。

解説 1往復目のやりとりから，A（＝女性）がB（＝Jared）に，ミキが翻訳した書類のチェックを依頼している場面。2往復目でAが「彼ら（＝LTRケミカルズ）は正確さにとてもこだわるので，特に注意して見てください」と述べ，さらに「（LTRケミカルズを）クライアントとして失うわけにはいきませんから」と述べているので，チェックをする翻訳が重要なクライアントに関するもので，特に正確性が重視されるものであることがわかる。このような状況の中で，3往復目でAはミキについて，「私が（重要な書類なのでミスしないように）ゆっくりやってくださいと言っても，よく急いで返そうとするんですよ」と述べている。よって，Aはミキはしばしば十分に注意深く仕事をしないと考えていることがわかるので，rush to get things back to me quicklyを**not work carefully enough**と言い換えた**4**が正解。

No.8 正解　1

放送文 ***A:*** Honey, the travel agent just called. He said the cruise is nearly sold out, so we have to decide soon. ***B:*** Actually, I've been having second thoughts. I was looking at reviews on several websites, and there seem to be a lot of dissatisfied customers. ***A:*** Really? A few of the ones I saw were very positive. Well, we don't have to go. I just think you should get some kind of reward for working so hard lately. ***B:*** How about increasing our budget a bit and booking a cruise with a better reputation? ***A:*** OK. I'll talk to the agent.

Question: Why is the man worried about their holiday?

訳 A：あなた，旅行代理店から電話があったの。クルーズはほぼ完売だから，早く決めないといけないって。　B：実は，ちょっと考え直したんだ。いくつかのウェブサイトで口コミを見ていたんだけど，不満を持っているお客さんが多いみたいなんだ。　A：そうなの？　私が見た中にはとても好意的なものもいくつかあったよ。まあ，無理に行く必要はないよね。ただ，あなたは最近すごく頑張っているんだから，何かご褒美があってもいいと思うんだけど。　B：予算を少し増やして，もっと評判のいいクルーズを予約するのはどうかな？　A：わかった，代理店に相談してみるね。

質問の訳 なぜ男性は休暇のことを心配しているのか。

選択肢の訳 **1**　ネットで多くの苦情を見つけた。　**2**　クルーズの料金が上がった。　**3**　仕事の休みが取れない。　**4**　別のクルーズを予約することができない。

解説 1往復目のやりとりから，A（＝女性）とB（＝男性）が，旅行代理店を通してのクルーズの申し込みについて話している場面。1往復目で,「クルーズはほぼ完売だから,早く決めないといけない」と旅行代理店に言われたと述べたAに対し,Bは「実は,ちょっと考え直したんだ」と述べたあと,「いくつかのウェブサイトで口コミを見ていたんだけど,不満を持っているお客さんが多いみたいなんだ」と述べている。よって,Bがそのクルーズについてネットで多くの苦情を見つけたことがわかるので,reviews on several websitesやa lot of dissatisfied customersを**many online complaints**と言い換えた**1**が正解。

No.9 正解 3

放送文 ***A:*** Did you watch the season finale of *Shield Force* last night? ***B:*** Of course! I thought that was the best episode of the entire season. ***A:*** What did you think of the scene where Agent Martinez was revealed to be the traitor? ***B:*** That was such a shocker. I was so sure it was going to be Agent Turner, but the way they explained it made perfect sense. ***A:*** Totally. The writing on that show is just fantastic. ***B:*** I can't wait to see what happens next season.
Question: What do the speakers imply about *Shield Force*?

訳 A：昨夜の『シールド・フォース』のシーズン最終回を見た？　B：もちろん！　シーズン通して最高の回だったと思ったわ。　A：マルティネス捜査官が裏切り者であることが明らかになったシーンはどう思った？　B：あれは衝撃的だった。私はてっきりターナー捜査官が裏切り者だと思ってたんだけど，彼らの説明で完璧に納得したわ。　A：その通りだね。あの番組の脚本は本当に素晴らしい。　B：次のシーズンが待ちきれないね。

質問の訳 話者たちは『シールド・フォース』について何を言いたいか。

選択肢の訳 **1**　個性的なキャラクターが多い。　**2**　番組の脚本が非常に良くなった。　**3**　筋の予測が難しかった。　**4**　もう次のシーズンは更新されないかもしれない。

解説 1往復目のやりとりから,A（＝男性）とB（＝女性）が,昨夜の『シールド・フォース』のシーズン最終回について話している場面。2往復目で，マルティネス捜査官が裏切り者であることが明らかになったシーンの感想をAからたずねられたBは,「あれは衝撃的だった。私はてっきりターナー捜査官が裏切り者だと思ってた」と自分の予想と筋が違っていたことが衝撃だったと述べ，Aも「その通りだね」と同意している。よって，AもBも筋の予測が難しかったと考えていることがわかるので，I was so sure it was going to be Agent Turner, but …を**hard to predict**と言い換えた**3**が正解。

No.10 正解 4

放送文 ***A:*** I've been thinking about assigning Mark to manage the new software project. ***B:*** Do you think he can handle it? I know he's bright, but he's only been with the firm for 18 months. ***A:*** Well, I was originally considering Genevieve, but she's really got her hands full these days. That leaves either Mark or Yasuhiro. ***B:*** In that case, I guess we have no choice but to give it to Mark. The last time we put Yasuhiro in charge of a project, things quickly went off the rails.
Question: What does the woman imply about Mark?

訳 A：マークに新しいソフトウェアプロジェクトの管理を任せようと思っているんだ。B：彼がそれをこなせると思う？　優秀なのは知っているけど，まだ入社してたった18

か月よ。　A：当初はジュヌビエーブを考えていたんだけど，彼女は最近，ほんとに手一杯なんだ。そうなるとマークかヤスヒロのどちらかなんだよね。　B：それなら，マークに任せるしかないわね。前回，ヤスヒロにプロジェクトを担当させたときは，すぐに計画が狂ってしまったもんね。

質問の訳　女性はマークについて何を言いたいか。

選択肢の訳　**1**　ヤスヒロより忙しい。　**2**　ジュヌビエーブと仲が悪い。　**3**　しばしば判断を誤る。　**4**　経験が足りないかもしれない。

解説　1～2往復目のやりとりから，A（＝男性）とB（＝女性）が，新しいソフトウェアプロジェクトの管理を誰に任せるかについて話している場面。1往復目でAから，マークに管理を任せようと思っていると言われたBは，「(マークが）優秀なのは知っているけど」と言ったあと，「まだ入社してたった18か月よ」と述べている。よって，Bは，マークはまだ経験が足りないかもしれないと考えていることがわかるので，only been with the firm for 18 months を **may not have enough experience** と言い換えた**4**が正解。

No.11　正解　4

放送文　***A:*** Hey, did you take Professor Ritter's Politics 302 class last semester? ***B:*** Yeah. Some of the lectures were interesting, but I wouldn't really recommend it. ***A:*** Oh. I heard it involves a lot of reading. Was that the problem? ***B:*** Actually, the workload seemed reasonable to me. My issue was that when she was marking papers, Professor Ritter seemed to favor students who share her political views. ***A:*** Oh, really? ***B:*** If I were you, I'd sign up for Professor Tamura's or Professor Wilson's class instead.

Question: What is the man's opinion of Professor Ritter?

訳　A：ねえ，前学期にリッター教授の政治学302の授業を取った？　B：うん。講義のいくつかは興味深かったけど，あまりお勧めできないね。　A：ああ，読む量が多いって聞いたわ。それが問題だったの？　B：実際，作業量はぼくには妥当に思えたよ。問題は，論文を採点するときに，リッター教授が自分と同じ政治的見解を持つ学生を優遇しているように見えたことなんだ。　A：まあ，そうなの？　B：ぼくが君だったら，代わりにタムラ教授かウィルソン教授のクラスに申し込むな。

質問の訳　男性のリッター教授に対する意見は何か。

選択肢の訳　**1**　講義が長くなりがちだ。　**2**　宿題が多すぎる。　**3**　政治的見解が極端だ。　**4**　公平な採点をしない。

解説　1往復目のやりとりから，A（＝女性）とB（＝男性）が，リッター教授の政治学302の授業を取るべきかについて話している場面。2往復目でBは「問題は，論文を採点するときに，リッター教授が自分と同じ政治的見解を持つ学生を優遇しているように見えたことなんだ」と述べているので，Bはリッター教授が公平な採点をしないと考えていることがわかる。よって，favor students who share her political views を **not grade fairly** と言い換えた**4**が正解。

No.12　正解　2

放送文　***A:*** We need to do something about the dogs. Their barking is becoming a real problem. ***B:*** I don't know. Most dogs bark at strangers, no?

A: Yes, but ours bark every time someone goes past the house. We'll get complaints from the neighbors if this keeps up. ***B:*** Well, we've already tried every training method we could find online. I'm not sure what else we can do. ***A:*** I think we should hire a proper dog trainer. I know it'll be expensive, but it'll be worth it for some peace and quiet. ***B:*** I guess you're right.
Question: What will the man and woman probably do?

訳 A：犬たちのことをどうにかする必要があるわ。鳴き声が本当に問題になってきているの。　B：わからないな。たいていの犬は知らない人に吠えるんじゃないの？　A：そうなんだけど，うちの犬たちは誰かが家の前を通るたびに吠えるのよ。このままだと近所から苦情が来るわ。　B：まあ，ネットで見つけたしつけの方法はもう全部試したし。他に何ができるかわからないな。　A：ちゃんとしたドッグトレーナーを雇うべきだと思うわ。高くつくだろうけど，静かで穏やかな時間を過ごすためには，それだけの価値はあるわよ。　B：君の言うとおりだろうね。

質問の訳 男性と女性はおそらくどうするか。

選択肢の訳 **1**　ネットで解決策を探す。　**2**　プロに助けてもらう。　**3**　近所の人にアドバイスを求める。　**4**　より静かな近隣に引っ越す。

解説 1往復目のやりとりから，A（＝女性）とB（＝男性）が，飼い犬の鳴き声の問題について話している場面。3往復目でAが「ちゃんとしたドッグトレーナーを雇うべきだと思うわ。高くつくだろうけど～それだけの価値はあるわよ」と述べると，Bも「君の言うとおりだろうね」と述べているので，男性と女性はお金を払ってプロのドッグトレーナーに依頼しようと考えていることがわかる。よって，hire a proper dog trainerを**get help from a professional**と言い換えた**2**が正解。

Part 2 一次試験・リスニング
（問題編pp.60～61）

指示文の訳 それでは，これからPart 2の指示を行います。このパートでは(A)から(F)までの6つの文章が放送されます。それぞれの文章に続いて，No.13からNo.24まで質問が2つずつ流れます。それぞれの質問に対して，最も適切な答えを選んで解答用紙にマークする時間が10秒あります。文章と質問は1度しか読まれません。それでは始めます。

(A)

放送文 *Sukkoth*

Sukkoth is a religious holiday celebrated by Jewish people around the world. It originated thousands of years ago as a harvest festival. During the festival, people demonstrated their appreciation to their god for the year's crops. Later, the holiday became connected with the time immediately after the ancient Jewish people had escaped from slavery in Egypt. According to tradition, the Jewish people wandered in the desert and had to live in fragile shelters called sukkahs that protected them from the heat of the sun.
Today, Jewish people celebrate the holiday by building a sukkah in their

backyards or on balconies. Sukkahs generally have three walls, and the roof is made with leaves and has openings so that the stars are visible above. During the festival's seven days, people consume their meals in the sukkah, and if they live in a warm climate, they sleep in it as well.

Questions ***No.13*** Why did people originally celebrate Sukkoth?

No.14 What is one thing we learn about modern sukkah buildings?

訳 仮庵(かりいお)の祭り

仮庵の祭りは，世界中のユダヤ人が祝う宗教的な祭日である。何千年も前に収穫祭として始まった。祭りの間，人々はその年の作物に対する感謝を神に示した。その後，この祝日は，古代ユダヤの人々がエジプトの奴隷状態から脱出した直後のときと結び付けられるようになった。伝統によれば，ユダヤの民は砂漠をさまよい，太陽の熱から身を守るスッカーと呼ばれる壊れやすいシェルターで暮らさなければならなかったという。

今日，ユダヤ人は自宅の裏庭やバルコニーにスッカーを建ててこの祭日を祝う。スッカーには一般的に３面の壁があり，屋根は葉で作られ，星が上に見えるように開口部がある。祭りの７日間，人々はスッカーの中で食事をとり，温暖な気候に住んでいる場合はスッカーの中で眠りもする。

No.13 正解 2

質問の訳 もともと人々はなぜ仮庵の祭りを祝ったのか。

選択肢の訳 **1** 作物の品質を向上させるため。 **2** 自分たちが栽培した食べ物に感謝するため。 **3** 砂漠を出られるように祈るため。 **4** エジプトでの時間を祝うため。

解説 仮庵の祭りのもともとの目的について，第１段落第２文で「何千年も前に収穫祭として始まった」と述べた上で，次の文で「祭りの間，人々はその年の作物に対する感謝を神に示した」と述べられている。よって，もともとは人々が収穫した食べ物に感謝するために仮庵の祭りを祝ったことがわかるので，demonstrated their appreciationを**give thanks**と，またthe year's cropsを**the food they grew**と言い換えた**2**が正解。

No.14 正解 4

質問の訳 現代のスッカーの建物についてわかることの１つは何か。

選択肢の訳 **1** 壁に砂漠の絵が描かれている。 **2** 涼しくするために覆われている。 **3** 食事はその中で調理されなければならない。 **4** 中から空が見える。

解説 現代のスッカーの建物について，第２段落第２文で「(今日の) スッカーには一般的に３面の壁があり～星が上に見えるように開口部がある」と述べられている。よって，現代のスッカーの建物では，開口部を通して中から空が見えることがわかるので，the stars are visibleを**see the sky**と言い換えた**4**が正解。

(B)

放送文 *Vultures*

Vultures are birds well-known for their diet, which consists of the remains of dead animals. This association has given many people a negative impression of the birds, but we in fact owe much gratitude to vultures. By eating dead animals, the birds prevent disease-causing germs from entering the environment, including water sources. And because the strong acid in their stomachs is so good at killing germs, vultures are unlikely to pass on diseases to humans.

The bodies of dead animals do more than spread disease—they also release CO_2 and other greenhouse gases as they decay on the ground. When vultures feed, they prevent this from happening. However, in many parts of the world today, vulture populations have declined significantly, resulting in millions of tons of extra greenhouse-gas emissions entering the atmosphere. Ensuring vulture populations remain healthy is therefore an important step in combating climate change.

Questions ***No.15*** What does the speaker say about disease-causing germs?

No.16 What is suggested about climate change?

訳 ハゲワシ

ハゲワシは動物の死骸を食べることでよく知られている鳥である。そのため，ハゲワシに対してネガティブな印象を持つ人も多いが，実は私たちはハゲワシに多くの恩恵を受けている。動物の死骸を食べることで，ハゲワシは病気を引き起こす菌が水源などの環境に侵入するのを防いでいる。また，ハゲワシの胃の中の強酸は病原菌を殺すのに非常に適しているため，ハゲワシが人間に病気をうつすことはまずない。

動物の死体は病気を蔓延させるだけでなく，地上で腐敗する際に二酸化炭素やその他の温室効果ガスを放出する。ハゲワシが餌を食べることで，これの発生を防ぐことができる。しかし現在，世界の多くの地域でハゲワシの個体数が著しく減少しており，その結果，大気中に何百万トンもの温室効果ガスが余分に排出されている。したがって，ハゲワシの個体数を健全な状態に保つことは，気候変動と闘うための重要な一歩なのである。

No.15 正解 1

質問の訳 病原菌について，話者は何と言っているか。

選択肢の訳 **1** ハゲワシは人間への感染を食い止める。 **2** ハゲワシはしばしばそれらを他の動物に感染させる。 **3** ハゲワシにとって致命的な場合もある。 **4** ハゲワシの胃の中で生き残る。

解説 病原菌について，第1段落第3文で「動物の死骸を食べることで，ハゲワシは病気を引き起こす菌が水源などの環境に侵入するのを防いでいる」と述べたうえで，次の文で「ハゲワシの胃の中の強酸は病原菌を殺すのに非常に適しているため，ハゲワシが人間に病気をうつすことはまずない」と述べられている。よって，ハゲワシが病原菌の人間への感染を食い止めるために役立っていることがわかるので，preventをstopと，またpass on diseases toをaffectingと言い換えた**1**が正解。

No.16 正解 1

質問の訳 気候変動についてどのようなことが示唆されているか。

選択肢の訳 **1** ハゲワシの食習慣は気候変動の影響を軽減するのに役立っている。 **2** 気候変動の結果，世界中でハゲワシの個体数が増加した。 **3** 気候変動のためにハゲワシの食料源が変化した。 **4** 気候変動のためにハゲワシは新しい生息地を見つけざるを得なくなった。

解説 気候変動について，第2段落第1文で「動物の死体は～地上で腐敗する際に二酸

化炭素やその他の温室効果ガスを放出する」と述べた上で，次の文で「ハゲワシが餌を食べることで，これの発生を防ぐことができる」と述べられている。また，第２段落最終文でも「ハゲワシの個体数を健全な状態に保つことは，気候変動と闘うための重要な一歩」と述べている。よって，ハゲワシが動物の死体を食べることが気候変動の影響を軽減するのに役立っていることがわかるので，when vultures feedを**vultures' feeding habits**と，またprevent this from happeningを**reduce its effects**と言い換えた**1**が正解。

(C)

放送文 *Praising Employees*

Everyone knows that praise is important for motivating employees and increasing their satisfaction. Surprisingly, however, according to researchers, praise can improve employee performance even when the employee does not earn the praise. When researchers gave praise to random workers, the quality of the workers' output increased dramatically compared to those who were not praised.

Another study suggests that some kinds of praise are more effective than others. The study identifies two kinds of mindsets. Those with a so-called fixed mindset think they are born with a certain level of ability and that they are unlikely to get better at things. On the other hand, those with a so-called growth mindset feel that they have the capability to acquire new skills and talents. It seems that praising effort rather than results may have a positive effect because it encourages a growth mindset in unhappy employees who would otherwise be frustrated with their jobs.

Questions ***No.17*** What is one thing research found about praising employees?
No.18 What does the speaker suggest about unhappy employees?

訳 従業員を褒める

褒めることが従業員のやる気を引き出し，満足度を高めるために重要であることは誰もが知っている。しかし意外なことに，研究者によれば，たとえ従業員が褒められるようなことをしていなくても，褒めることで従業員のパフォーマンスが向上することがある。研究者が無作為に労働者を褒めたところ，褒められなかった労働者に比べて，労働者の成果の質が劇的に向上したのだ。

別の研究では，ある種の褒め方は他の褒め方よりも効果があることが示唆されている。この研究では，２種類のマインドセットを特定している。いわゆる固定マインドセットを持つ人は，自分の能力は生まれつき決まっており，物事をよりうまくこなす可能性は低いと考える。一方，いわゆる成長マインドセットを持つ人は，自分には新しいスキルや才能を身につける能力があると感じている。結果よりも努力を褒めることは，そうでなければ仕事に不満を抱くであろう不幸な従業員の成長マインドセットを促すので，プラスの効果があるのかもしれない。

No.17 正解 **2**

質問の訳 従業員を褒めることについて，研究によって発見されたことの１つは何か。

選択肢の訳 **1** 労働者はしばしば，自分は褒められるに値しないと考える。 **2** 無作為に褒めることで，パフォーマンスが向上することがある。 **3** 褒めすぎはパフォーマンスを低下させることがある。 **4** ほとんどの上司は，十分に褒めていない。

解説 従業員を褒めることについて，第1段落最終文で「研究者が無作為に労働者を褒めたところ，褒められなかった労働者に比べて，（褒められた）労働者の成果の質が劇的に向上した」と述べられている。よって，無作為に褒めることでもパフォーマンスが向上することがあることがわかるので，gave praise to random workersをrandom praiseと，またoutput increasedをimprove performanceと言い換えた**2**が正解。

No.18 正解 3

質問の訳 不幸な従業員について，話者は何を示唆しているか。

選択肢の訳 **1** 褒められると否定的に反応する傾向がある。 **2** 仕事を心配しすぎている。 **3** 成長マインドセットを持つことが有益かもしれない。 **4** 周りの労働者のマインドセットに影響を与える。

解説 不幸な従業員について，第2段落最終文で「結果よりも努力を褒めることは，そうでなければ仕事に不満を抱くであろう不幸な従業員の成長マインドセットを促すので，プラスの効果があるかもしれない」と述べられている。よって，不幸な従業員にとって，成長マインドセットを持つことが有益かもしれないことがわかるので，have a positive effectをbenefitと，またencouragesをhavingと言い換えた**3**が正解。

(D)

放送文 *Manod Mine*

During World War II, there was great fear that Britain would be invaded by Nazi Germany. In this environment, it was decided that paintings from the National Gallery in London should be moved somewhere safer. At first, it was suggested that they be shipped to Canada, but British leaders worried about the threat from the German submarines that were sinking thousands of ships. Eventually, the art treasures were stored in an old mine in a remote area of Wales called Manod.

Transporting the art was extremely difficult as many of the works were large and had to be moved carefully through the small mine entrance. Furthermore, there was great concern that moisture and cold temperatures would damage the paintings, so special air-conditioned structures were built in the mine to contain them. Thanks to the project at Manod, the paintings survived the war, and much was learned about preserving art.

Questions ***No.19*** Why did British leaders reject the original plan?

No.20 What was learned from the experience at Manod?

訳 マノッド鉱山

第二次世界大戦中，イギリスはナチス・ドイツに侵略されることをとても恐れていた。そんな中，ロンドンのナショナル・ギャラリーの絵画をより安全な場所に移すことが決定された。当初はカナダへの移送が提案されたが，イギリスの指導者たちは，何千隻もの船を沈めていたドイツの潜水艦の脅威を危惧した。結局，美術品はマノッドと呼ばれるウェールズの辺境にある古い鉱山に保管されることになった。

美術品の多くは大きく，小さな坑道の入口から慎重に移動させなければならなかったため，運搬は困難を極めた。さらに，湿気や寒さによって絵画が傷んでしまうことが強く懸念されたため，作品を保管するための特別な空調設備が鉱山内に建設された。マノッドでのプロジェクトのおかげで，絵画は戦争を生き延び，芸術の保存について多くの知見が得られた。

No.19 正解 **2**

質問の訳 なぜイギリスの指導者たちは当初の計画を拒否したのか。

選択肢の訳 **1** 侵略は起きないと信じていた。 **2** 美術品が破壊されることを心配していた。 **3** カナダが侵略される可能性が高いと考えた。 **4** ドイツ人が美術品を盗むことを恐れた。

解説 当初の計画とそれに対するイギリスの指導者たちの反応について，第1段落第3文で「当初はカナダへの移送が提案されたが，イギリスの指導者たちは，何千隻もの船を沈めていたドイツの潜水艦の脅威を危惧した」と述べられている。よって，イギリスの指導者たちは，美術品をカナダに移送する船がドイツの潜水艦によって沈められ，美術品が破壊されることを心配していたことがわかるので，the threatを**the art would be destroyed**と言い換えた**2**が正解。

No.20 正解 **4**

質問の訳 マノッドでの経験から何が学ばれたか。

選択肢の訳 **1** 戦時中の美術品の重要性。 **2** より大きな鉱山を作る方法。
3 低温が絵画に与える影響。 **4** 美術品を良好な状態に保つ方法。

解説 マノッドでの経験から学ばれたことについて，第2段落最終文で「マノッドでのプロジェクトのおかげで，～芸術の保存について多くの知見が得られた」と述べられている。よって，マノッドで美術品を保管した経験から，美術品を良好な状態に保つ方法について多くの知見が得られたことがわかるので，preserving artを**keeping art in good condition**と言い換えた**4**が正解。

(E)

放送文 *The Midnight Ride of Sybil Ludington*

On the night of April 26, 1777, during the American Revolution, a messenger arrived at American commander Henry Ludington's house. The messenger warned of a coming British attack, but Ludington's soldiers were scattered around the region. The commander's daughter, Sybil, bravely volunteered to alert them. Though just 16 years old, Sybil rode on horseback for over 65 kilometers in stormy weather. Thanks to her night ride, the troops assembled and drove away the British. After the war, however, Sybil was forgotten for many years.

Some historians question whether Sybil's ride ever really happened. While documents show that the British attack occurred, there are no official records of Sybil's journey. It appeared in a history book published in the 1800s, but the book failed to give sources to confirm it. Nevertheless, the story has been widely accepted, and Sybil has become a symbol of the role of women in the American Revolution.

Questions ***No.21*** What was the purpose of Sybil Ludington's ride?

No.22 What is one reason some historians doubt Sybil's ride?

訳 シビル・ルディントンの真夜中の騎行

アメリカ独立革命中の1777年4月26日の夜，アメリカ軍司令官ヘンリー・ルディントンの家に使者がやってきた。使者はイギリス軍の攻撃が迫っていることを警告したが，ルディントンの兵士たちは各地に散らばっていた。司令官の娘シビルは，勇敢にも兵士たちに警告するために志願した。シビルはまだ16歳だったが，荒天の中，65キロ以上の距離を馬で駆け抜けた。彼女の夜間騎行のおかげで軍隊は集結し，イギリス軍を追い払った。しかし，戦後，シビルは長い間忘れ去られていた。

歴史家の中には，シビルの騎行が本当にあったことなのか疑問視する者もいる。英国の攻撃があったことは文献に残っているが，シビルの旅についての公式記録はない。1800年代に出版された歴史書にも登場するが，その本にはそれを確認する資料が記載されていない。それにもかかわらず，この物語は広く受け入れられ，シビルはアメリカ独立革命における女性の役割の象徴となっている。

No.21 正解 1

質問の訳 シビル・ルディントンの騎行の目的は何だったか。

選択肢の訳 **1** 攻撃を警告するのに役立てるため。 **2** イギリス兵の位置を確認するため。 **3** アメリカ軍のための補給物資を集めるため。 **4** 父親を危険から遠ざけるため。

解説 シビル・ルディントンの騎行の目的について，第１段落第３文で「司令官の娘シビルは，勇敢にも兵士たちに（イギリス軍の攻撃が迫っていることを）警告するために志願した」と述べられ，次の文で「シビルはまだ16歳だったが，荒天の中，65キロ以上の距離を馬で駆け抜けた」と述べられている。よって，シビル・ルディントンが兵士たちにイギリス軍の攻撃が迫っていることを警告するために騎行したことがわかるので，alertをwarnと言い換えた**1**が正解。

No.22 正解 3

質問の訳 歴史家がシビルの騎行を疑う理由の１つは何か。

選択肢の訳 **1** その夜，別の女性が騎行した証拠がある。 **2** イギリス軍による攻撃の記録がない。 **3** 公式には記録されていなかった。 **4** ある歴史書がそれは起こらなかったと主張している。

解説 歴史家がシビルの騎行を疑う理由について，第２段落第２文で「英国の攻撃があったことは文献に残っているが，シビルの旅についての公式記録はない」と述べられ，次の文でも「1800年代に出版された歴史書にも登場するが，その本にはそれを確認する資料が記載されていない」と述べられている。よって，シビルの騎行が，公式には記録されていなかったことがわかるので，no official recordsをnot officially documentedと言い換えた**3**が正解。

(F)

放送文 *Banff Sunshine Village*

During the economic boom of the 1950s in the US and Canada, interest in recreational activities increased dramatically. One activity that grew in popularity was skiing. However, many ski resorts found that they needed more snow on their mountains to meet customer demand. Machines were developed to create snow artificially using water and compressed air, enabling ski resorts to operate even without a lot of natural snowfall.

However, snowmaking requires significant energy consumption as well as water from reservoirs and lakes. A Canadian ski resort known as Banff Sunshine Village relies instead on a method called snow farming. The resort takes advantage of the area's windy conditions by putting up fences at high altitudes to catch snow that blows in from surrounding mountains. Later, the snow is transported down to slopes that need it. This allows the resort to maximize snow cover in an environmentally sustainable and energy-efficient way.

Questions No.23 What does the speaker say about many ski resorts in the 1950s?

No.24 What is true about Banff Sunshine Village?

訳 バンフ・サンシャイン・ヴィレッジ

1950年代のアメリカやカナダでの好景気の間，レクリエーション活動への関心が飛躍的に高まった。その中で人気が高まった活動の１つがスキーだった。しかし，多くのスキーリゾートは，顧客の需要に応えるためには，山にもっと多くの雪が必要であると認識していた。水と圧縮空気を使って人工的に雪を作る機械が開発され，天然の雪があまり降らなくてもスキーリゾートが営業できるようになった。

しかしながら，造雪には多大なエネルギー消費と貯水池や湖からの水を必要とする。カナダのバンフ・サンシャイン・ヴィレッジというスキーリゾートは，その代わりにスノー・ファーミングと呼ばれる方法を採用している。このリゾートは，周辺の山々から吹き込む雪を受け止めるフェンスを高所に設置することで，この地域の風が強いという条件を利用している。その後，雪を必要とするゲレンデまで雪が運ばれる。これにより，このリゾートは環境的に持続可能でエネルギー効率に優れた方法で，積雪量を最大化することを可能にしている。

No.23 正解 3

質問の訳 1950年代の多くのスキーリゾートについて，話者は何と言っているか。

選択肢の訳 **1** より人口の多い地域に移転しなければならなかった。 **2** 顧客の不評により閉鎖せざるを得なかった。 **3** 十分な積雪がなかった。 **4** 人工雪の使用に反対していた。

解説 1950年代の多くのスキーリゾートについて，第１段落第１～２文で，1950年代のアメリカやカナダでスキーの人気が高まったと述べたうえで，次の文で「多くのスキーリゾートは，顧客の需要に応えるためには，山にもっと多くの雪が必要であると認識していた」と述べられている。よって，1950年代の多くのスキーリゾートには十分な積雪がなかったことがわかるので，needed more snowを**not receiving enough snow**と言い換えた**3**が正解。

No.24 正解 **2**

質問の訳 何がバンフ・サンシャイン・ヴィレッジについて正しいか。

選択肢の訳 **1** 人工雪の使用により，経営が悪化した。 **2** 運営のために風を利用している。 **3** 地域の他のスキー場に雪を提供している。 **4** ゲレンデの標高が異常に高い。

解説 バンフ・サンシャイン・ヴィレッジについて，第2段落第3文で「このリゾート（＝バンフ・サンシャイン・ヴィレッジ）は～この地域の風が強いという条件を利用している」と述べられている。よって，バンフ・サンシャイン・ヴィレッジが運営のために風を利用していることがわかるので，takes advantage ofをmakes use ofと言い換えた**2**が正解。

Part 3 一次試験・リスニング
(問題編pp.62～63)

指示文の訳 それでは最後に，Part 3の指示を行います。このパートでは(G)から(K)までの5つの文章が放送されます。英文は実生活における状況を述べたもので，効果音を含むものもあります。それぞれの文章には，No.25からNo.29まで，質問が1問ずつ用意されています。それぞれの文章が流れる前に，問題冊子に書かれている状況の説明と質問を読む時間が10秒あります。文章を聞いた後に，最も適切な答えを選んで解答用紙にマークする時間が10秒あります。文章は1度しか読まれません。それでは始めます。

No.25 正解 **3**

放送文 *(G)* You have 10 seconds to read the situation and Question No.25.

We're near the harbor, so there are a lot of good seafood options. Kingsley's is a very popular lobster restaurant and bar, but it doesn't open until eight. Shrimp Lover is a seafood restaurant that just opened one month ago. It's about 45 minutes away by train. Randy's is a unique Mexican restaurant just a block away. They only have counter seats, but I'm sure you can be seated right away, even at dinner time. Then, there's Boca here in the hotel, but it's very difficult to get a table if you haven't booked at least a day in advance.

Now mark your answer on your answer sheet.

訳 *(G)* 状況と質問25を読む時間が10秒あります。

港の近くですから，おいしいシーフードのお店がたくさんございます。キングスレイズは大人気のロブスターレストラン＆バーですが，8時オープンです。シュリンプ・ラバーは1か月前にオープンしたばかりのシーフードレストランです。電車で45分ほどの距離です。ランディーズはすぐ近くのブロックにあるユニークなメキシカンレストランです。カウンター席しかありませんが，ディナータイムでもすぐに席に座れると思います。それから，このホテル内にはボカがございますが，少なくとも前日までにご予約いただけませんとテーブルを確保するのは非常に困難です。

それでは，解答用紙に答えをマークしなさい。

状況の訳 あなたはホテルに滞在している。今，午後6時30分で，近くのレストランで午後7時ごろに夕食をとりたいと思っている。コンシェルジュは次のように言った。

質問の訳 あなたはどのレストランを選ぶべきか。

選択肢の訳 **1** キングスレイズ。 **2** シュリンプ・ラバー。 **3** ランディーズ。 **4** ボカ。

解説 Situationからわかるのは，①今，午後6時30分であること，②「あなた」は近くのレストランで午後7時ごろに夕食をとりたいと思っていること。キングスレイズは，第2文で「8時オープンです」とあり，午後7時ごろに夕食をとることができないので不適。シュリンプ・ラバーは，第4文で「電車で45分ほどの距離」とあり，「近くのレストラン」とは言えず，また早くても午後7時15分ごろに着くので，②の条件を満たさず不適。ランディーズは，第5文に「すぐ近くのブロックにある」とあるので「近くのレストラン」という条件を満たし，第6文に「ディナータイムでもすぐに席に座れる」とあるので，「午後7時ごろに夕食をとりたい」という条件も満たすので，**3**が正解。

No.26 正解 **4**

放送文 *(H)* You have 10 seconds to read the situation and Question No.26.

Welcome to CD Masters. This holiday season, don't miss out on our "CD Surprise" boxes with 30 random CDs inside. Additionally, to sell up to 99 CDs, any registered member can log into their account on our website and start the sales procedure. If you don't have an account, you can register today just by filling out the form on our website. If you would prefer to register over the phone, press 1. If you are looking to sell 100 or more CDs at once, press 2. A representative will speak with you to schedule a home visit to assess your CD collection.

Now mark your answer on your answer sheet.

訳 *(H)* 状況と質問26を読む時間が10秒あります。

CDマスターズへようこそ。このホリデーシーズンでは，30枚のCDがランダムに入った「CDサプライズ」ボックスをお見逃しなく。また，最大99枚のCDをお売りになるために，登録メンバーであればどなたでも当ウェブサイトのアカウントにログインし，売却手続きを開始することができます。アカウントをお持ちでない方は，当ウェブサイトのフォームにご入力いただくだけで，今すぐご登録いただけます。電話での登録をご希望の場合は，1を押してください。一度に100枚以上のCDをお売りになりたい場合は，2を押してください。担当者がお客様とお話しし，あなたのCD コレクションを査定するためのご自宅への訪問のスケジュールをお立ていたします。

それでは，解答用紙に答えをマークしなさい。

状況の訳 あなたは，500枚の音楽CDコレクションの半分を売却することを決めた。あなたは中古CDを売買している店に電話し，次のような録音メッセージを聞いた。

質問の訳 あなたは何をすべきか。

選択肢の訳 **1** オンラインで売却手続きを始める。 **2** CDを箱に詰め始める。 **3** ウェブサイトから用紙をダウンロードする。 **4** （買い取り）査定の予約をする。

解説 Situationからわかるのは，「あなた」は500枚の音楽CDコレクションの半分，すなわち250枚のCDを売却するつもりであること。録音メッセージでは，最後から2文目で「一度に100枚以上のCDをお売りになりたい場合は，2を押してください」と述べたあと，次の文で「あなたのCD コレクションを査定するためのご自宅への訪問のスケジュールをお立ていたします」と述べている。よって，「あなた」がすべきことは，（買い取り）査定の予約をすることなので，to scheduleを**make an appointment**と，to assessを**for an assessment**と，それぞれ言い換えた**4**が正解。

No.27 正解 3

放送文 *(I)* You have 10 seconds to read the situation and Question No.27.

In History 103, students can learn about European history in the eighteenth and nineteenth centuries. This class has no group projects, and there is an option available to take it online. Next, Philosophy 105 is for those who want to grasp the gist of Western philosophy, including that of ancient Greece and Rome. Students are expected to take part in spirited team debates in each class. History 202 is a lecture-based class and is non-interactive. It focuses primarily on ancient Egyptian, Greek, and Roman history. Finally, Latin 102 focuses exclusively on ancient Rome. In that class, you'll learn Latin by reading ancient Roman plays.

Now mark your answer on your answer sheet.

訳 *(I)* 状況と質問27を読む時間が10秒あります。

歴史103では，18世紀から19世紀にかけてのヨーロッパの歴史について学ぶことができます。このクラスにはグループ・プロジェクトはなく，オンラインで履修するオプションもあります。次に哲学105は，古代ギリシャやローマを含む西洋哲学の要点を把握したい人のためのクラスです。学生は各クラスで，チーム対抗の活発なディベートに参加することが求められます。歴史202は講義中心のクラスで，双方向性はありません。主に古代エジプト，ギリシャ，ローマの歴史に焦点を当てています。最後に，ラテン語102は古代ローマに特化しています。このクラスでは，古代ローマの戯曲を読みながらラテン語を学びます。

それでは，解答用紙に答えをマークしなさい。

状況の訳 あなたは大学生である。あなたは古代ギリシャとローマについて学びたいが，グループワークは好きではない。あなたは指導教官の説明を聞いている。

質問の訳 あなたはどのクラスを取るべきか。

選択肢の訳 **1** 歴史103。 **2** 哲学105。 **3** 歴史202。 **4** ラテン語 102。

解説 Situationからわかるのは，①「あなた」は古代ギリシャとローマについて学びたいことと，②「あなた」はグループワークが好きではないこと。歴史103は，指導教官の説明の第1文に「18世紀から19世紀にかけてのヨーロッパの歴史について学ぶ」とあり，①の条件を満たさず不適。哲学105は，第4文に「学生は各クラスで，チーム対抗の活発なディベートに参加する」とあり，②の条件を満たさず不適。歴史202は，第5文に「講義中心のクラスで，双方向性はありません」とあり②の条件を満たす。また，第6文に「主に古代エジプト，ギリシャ，ローマの歴史に焦点」とあり①の条件も満たす。よって，**3**が正解。

No.28 正解 2

放送文 *(J)* You have 10 seconds to read the situation and Question No.28.

Thank you for calling the TSS Electronics help desk. For corporate customers who have questions regarding the details of their contracts, press 1.

For technical support or to request a replacement for any of our products currently under warranty, press 2. To arrange for a repair or check the repair status of a product outside of warranty, press 3. For information about the different tablet models and data plans that we provide, press 4. For all other inquiries, please remain on the line until a representative becomes available.

Now mark your answer on your answer sheet.

訳 *(J)* 状況と質問28を読む時間が10秒あります。

TSSエレクトロニクスヘルプデスクにお電話いただきありがとうございます。法人のお客様で，ご契約内容に関するお問い合わせは，１を押してください。保証期間内の製品に関する技術サポートや交換のご依頼は，２を押してください。保証期間外の製品の修理手配や修理状況の確認は，３を押してください。さまざまなタブレット機種やデータプランに関するお問い合わせは，４を押してください。その他のお問い合わせは，担当者がご案内するまでそのままお待ちください。

それでは，解答用紙に答えをマークしなさい。

状況の訳 あなたが２週間前に娘に買ったタブレット・コンピュータが壊れた。１年の保証期間がある。あなたは製品メーカーに電話し，次のような録音メッセージを聞いた。

質問の訳 あなたは何をすべきか。

選択肢の訳 **1**　１を押す。　**2**　２を押す。　**3**　３を押す。　**4**　４を押す。

解説 Situationからわかるのは，①壊れたタブレット・コンピュータは「あなた」が２週間前に買ったものであることと，②タブレット・コンピュータの保証期間は１年であること。②から保証期間は１年であり，①から壊れたタブレット・コンピュータは「あなた」が２週間前に買ったものなので，そのタブレット・コンピュータは保証期間内であることがわかる。録音メッセージでは，保証期間内の製品について，第３文で「保証期間内の製品に関する技術サポートや交換のご依頼は，２を押してください」と述べている。よって，「あなた」がすべきことは，２を押すことなので**2**が正解。

No.29　正解　2

放送文 *(K)* You have 10 seconds to read the situation and Question No.29.

Several tours will be starting shortly. First, Spark of Genius is an hour-long tour about electricity that includes an exciting 30-minute 3D movie. We also have The Age of Dinos, which is a tour that explores the fascinating period when dinosaurs ruled the earth. It takes half an hour. Deep into the Sea is a 40-minute tour that looks at amazing deep-sea creatures. It can be a little scary, so this tour is not recommended for children under the age of 10. Finally, don't forget you can make reservations for our Museum after Dark overnight tour to experience an unforgettable night among our amazing exhibits.

Now mark your answer on your answer sheet.

訳 *(K)* 状況と質問29を読む時間が10秒あります。

まもなくいくつかのツアーが始まります。まず，「スパーク・オブ・ジーニアス」は，30分のエキサイティングな3D映画を含む電気に関する１時間のツアーです。「ジ・エイジ・オブ・ダイノズ」もございます，このツアーは，恐竜が地球を支配していた魅力的な時代を探るツアーです。所要時間は30分です。「ディープ・イントゥー・ザ・シー」は，

驚くべき深海生物に迫る40分のツアーです。少し怖いかもしれませんので，このツアーは10歳未満のお子様にはお勧めできません。最後に，当館の素晴らしい展示品の中での忘れえぬ夜をご体験いただくために，「ミュージアム・アフター・ダーク」のオーバーナイトツアーのご予約をお忘れなく。

それでは，解答用紙に答えをマークしなさい。

状況の訳 あなたと7歳の息子は科学博物館にいる。あなたはツアーに参加したい。あなたはあと45分で博物館を出なければならない。あなたは次のアナウンスを聞いた。

質問の訳 あなたはどのツアーを選ぶべきか。

選択肢の訳 **1** 「スパーク・オブ・ジーニアス」。 **2** 「ジ・エイジ・オブ・ダイノズ」。 **3** 「ディープ・イントゥー・ザ・シー」。 **4** 「ミュージアム・アフター・ダーク」。

解説 Situationからわかるのは，①「あなた」は7歳の息子と科学博物館にいること，②「あなた」はツアーに参加したいこと，③「あなた」はあと45分で博物館を出なければならないこと。「スパーク・オブ・ジーニアス」についてアナウンスでは，第2文に「電気に関する1時間のツアー」とあり，③の条件を満たさず不適。「ジ・エイジ・オブ・ダイノズ」は，第4文に「所要時間は30分」とあり，すべての条件を満たすので，**2**が正解。

カードA 二次試験・面接
（問題編pp.64～65）

指示文の訳 1分間，準備する時間があります。

これは，旅行好きな夫婦についての話です。

ストーリーのナレーションを行うのに与えられる時間は2分間です。

ストーリーは以下の文で始めてください。

ある日，夫婦はカフェで話をしていました。

ナレーションの解答例 **One day, a couple was talking at a café.** The man was telling the woman that he was able to take a week off for summer vacation, and she looked excited. That weekend, the couple was at home making plans for the holiday. The woman was showing him a “Guided Group Tours” brochure, but the man had no interest in it and told her that he would plan their trip himself. A few weeks later, the couple was visiting a tourist site with a traditional tower. There were many tourists. The man was looking at a popular restaurant on his phone and suggested that they go there next. One hour later, the couple arrived at the restaurant. A tour group had arrived before them and was going inside the restaurant. A waiter from the restaurant apologized and told them that the restaurant was fully booked.

解答例の訳 **ある日，夫婦はカフェで話をしていました。**男性は女性に，夏休みに1週間の休暇を取ることができると伝えており，彼女はうきうきしている様子でした。その週末，夫婦は自宅で休暇の予定を立てていました。女性は彼に，「ガイド付き団体ツアー」のパンフレットを見せていましたが，男性はそれには関心がなく，自分たちの旅行を自分で計画すると彼女に伝えました。数週間後，夫婦は伝統的な塔のある観光スポットを訪れていました。大勢の観光客がいました。男性は携帯電話で有名なレストランを見ていて，次にそこへ行こうと提案しました。１時間後，夫婦はそのレストランに到着しました。ツアーの一行は彼らよりも先に到着していて，レストランの店内に入っていました。レストランのウエイターが謝罪し，レストランは全席予約済みだと彼らに伝えました。

解説 ナレーションは，４コマのイラストの進行に沿ってまとめていく。２～４コマ目の左上方にある時間の経過を表す語句は，各コマの描写の冒頭部分で必ず使うこと。また，吹き出し内の文字情報も適宜ナレーションに盛り込むことになるが，せりふに関しては間接話法を使う場合，主語や（助）動詞などを適切な形に変える必要がある点に注意する。他，パンフレットに書かれた文字など，イラスト内の情報も適切な形でストーリーに取り入れること。なお，動詞の時制は，過去形および過去進行形を基本に時間の経過がわかるよう描写するが，解答例のように過去完了形を使うことで，状況をより良く描写できる場合もあることも念頭に置いておきたい。

①１コマ目：夫婦がカフェで話をしている場面。男性の吹き出しにSummer Vacation「夏休み」とあり，その直下に描かれているカレンダーの３日から９日までの日付が一つの大きな赤丸で囲まれていることから，男性が１週間の夏休み休暇を取ることが可能だと女性に伝えている場面だと判断できる。また，女性の心躍っているような表情もナレーションに盛り込むと良い。

②２コマ目：That weekendで始める。夫婦が自宅で休暇の予定を立てている場面。女性がGuided Group Tours「ガイド付き団体ツアー」と書かれたパンフレットを男性に見せているが，男性のI'll plan our trip.「自分たちの旅行は自分で計画するよ」というせりふや表情・仕草から，男性はそのツアーには関心がないのだと考えられる。解答例ではこの男性のせりふを，… told her that he would plan their tripと間接話法で表現し，文末に再帰代名詞himselfを置くことで，内容をより明確に描写している。

③３コマ目：A few weeks laterで始める。夫婦が，伝統的な塔のある観光スポットを訪れている場面。男性が手に持っているスマートフォンの画面に，３つの評価星と共にRestaurant「レストラン」と書かれており，彼がLet's go here next.「次はここへ行こう」と提案している。解答例ではこの様子を，suggest that ～「～ということを提案する」を用いて間接話法で表現しているが，このようにsuggest that ～を使う場合は，that節中の動詞は原形または〈should＋動詞の原形〉とすべき点に注意。また，せりふ中のhereをthereに置き換える必要もある。なお，解答例同様，夫婦の他にも大勢の人々が訪れている点もナレーションに盛り込むと効果的だろう。奥に小さめに描かれているツアーガイドやバスについて描写するのも良い。

④４コマ目：One hour laterで始める。夫婦がレストランに到着した場面。レストラン関係者と思われる人物の吹き出しにWe're fully booked.「全席ご予約でいっぱいです」とあり，謝罪している様子から，夫婦はいざレストランを訪れたものの中に入れない状況なのだとわかる。一方で，レストランの入り口付近には，ツアーガイドと思われる人物，および店内に入って行く複数の人々が描かれている。解答例ではこの様子を，過去完了形を用いてA tour group had arrived before themと表現している。

質問の訳 No. 1　４番目の絵を見てください。あなたがその女性なら，どのようなことを考えているでしょうか。

では～さん（受験者の氏名），カードを裏返して置いてください。

No. 2　日本は今後も，人気の観光地であり続けるでしょうか。

No. 3　サービス業の従業員は，雇い主から十分な高待遇を受けていると思いますか。
No. 4　今日の人々の生活の質は昔よりも良いでしょうか。

No.1 **解答例** I'd be thinking, "I had a feeling something like this would happen. Tour agencies reserve popular restaurants in advance. I should have insisted that we take the group tour."

解答例の訳 「このようなことが起こるような気がしていた。ツアー旅行代理店なら，事前に人気のレストランを予約するものだ。団体ツアーへの参加を主張すべきだった」と私は思っているでしょう。

解説 解答例では，質問の仮定法過去形に合わせて，直接話法で**I'd be thinking, "～."**の形で答えている。4コマ目で描かれているような人気レストランに入店できない状況をsomething like this「このようなこと」と表現し，その類いのことが起こる気がしていたと述べた後，ツアー旅行代理店なら人気レストランを事前予約するものだと言い，最後は後悔を表す〈should have＋過去分詞〉「～すべきだった」を用いて，団体ツアーへの参加を主張すべきだったと悔やんでいる。あるいは，引用符内の2文目以降をHowever, there should be other good eating places around here. All we have to do now is look for them online and try another one.「でも，この辺りには他にも良い飲食店があるはずだ。私たちが今すべきなのは，それらをオンラインで探して，別の所に行ってみることだけだ」などと，その人気レストランへの入店は諦めつつも前向きな内容にするのも良いだろう。

No.2 **解答例** Absolutely. Japan is known all over the world for its safety, hospitality, and good food. Thanks to social media, that information will continue to spread. The number of international visitors continues to increase yearly.

解答例の訳 もちろんです。日本は治安，もてなし，おいしい食べ物で，世界中で知られています。ソーシャルメディアのおかげで，その情報は広がり続けるでしょう。海外からの観光客の数は毎年，増え続けています。

解説 解答例では，Absolutely「もちろんです」と，自分がYesの立場にあることを強調してから，日本が世界的に知られている3点（治安，もてなし，おいしい食べ物）を具体的に挙げ，ソーシャルメディアのおかげでそれらの長所が拡散され続けるだろうと予測している。そして，4文目では，海外から日本への観光客の数が増加傾向にあるという事実を述べ，解答を締め括っている。あるいは，同じYesの立場でありながら，解答例の2文目をThese days, many people in the world associate Japan with unique culture such as anime and manga.「今日，日本といえばアニメや漫画といった独特な文化を連想する人は大勢います」などと，解答例とは別の長所を挙げながら答えても良いだろう。

No.3 **解答例** No.It's common for employees in the service industry to quit their jobs after a short period. This indicates they aren't satisfied with their working conditions. It's the employers' responsibility to keep their employees happy.

解答例の訳 いいえ。サービス業の従業員が短期間で仕事を辞めてしまうのは珍しいことではありません。このことは，彼らがその労働環境に満足していないということを示しています。自社の従業員を満足させ続けるのが雇い主の責務です。

解説 解答例では，Noの立場から，サービス業における従業員の短期間の離職がありふれたものである点に言及し，2文目ではこの内容をThisで指し，このことが労働環境への彼らの不満足を物語っていると論を展開している。そして，3文目で，自社の従業員を満足させ続けねばならないという雇い主側の責務について述べ，解答を締め括っている。あるいは，YesともNoとも断定しない立場から，It depends. Certainly, there are many employees in the service industry who are forced to work under poor working conditions, and this problem should be resolved immediately. But I know there are some workers in the same industry who are treated well and satisfied with their working conditions.「ケースバイケースです。確かに，サービス業界には，劣悪な労働環境で働くことを余儀なくされている従業員が大勢いて，この問題は直ちに解決されるべきです。しかし，同じ業界でも高待遇を受けていて労働環境に満足している働き手がいるということも私は知っています」なども良いだろう。

No.4 **解答例** Definitely. Advancements in technology have made people's lives more comfortable and convenient. For example, household appliances have reduced people's workload at home, so they have more time to do things they enjoy.

解答例の訳 絶対にそうです。テクノロジーの進歩は，人々の生活をより快適に，かつ便利にしてきました。例えば，家電製品は自宅での人々の負担を減らしてきたので，彼らは自分が楽しめることをする時間をより多く持てています。

解説 解答例ではまず，Definitely「絶対にそうです」と自分がYesの立場にあることを強調した後，テクノロジーの進歩が快適さと便利さという点で人々の生活の質を向上させてきたことを述べ，3文目ではその具体例として，家電製品によって人々が享受している負担減というメリットに言及している。他にも，3文目を，One example is the Internet, and it is so convenient that no one can imagine the world without it.「その一例はインターネットで，それはあまりにも便利なので，私たちはそれなしの世界を想像することができません」と，別のテクノロジーの具体例を挙げながら意見を述べても良いだろう。

カードB 二次試験・面接

(問題編pp.66～67)

指示文の訳 1分間，準備する時間があります。

これは，息子がスポーツ好きの夫婦についての話です。

ストーリーのナレーションを行うのに与えられる時間は2分間です。

ストーリーは以下の文で始めてください。

ある日，一家は自宅にいました。

ナレーションの解答例 One day, a family was at home. The mother had been scolding their son, and the father came to see what was happening. The son seemed to have broken a vase by kicking a soccer ball in the house. He was crying as the mother explained to the father that their son's behavior was terrible. That weekend, the couple was out walking and saw a sign for a soccer school for kids in front of the ABC Culture Center. This gave the father an idea. A few months later, the son was proudly showing a trophy and a certificate for "best player" to his parents. They looked proud of him. At a parent-teacher meeting, the father and son were called in by the elementary school teacher. She was showing them the son's report card and said that he only did well in P.E. The son looked embarrassed.

訳 ある日，一家は自宅にいました。母親が息子を叱っていて，父親は何が起こっているかを確認しに来ました。息子は，家の中でサッカーボールを蹴ったことによって花瓶を割ってしまったようでした。母親が父親に，息子の素行がひどいと説明している間，彼は泣いていました。その週末，夫婦は外を歩いていて，ABCカルチャーセンターの正面にある，子ども向けサッカースクールの看板を目にしました。これが，父親にあるアイデアを与えました。数か月後，息子は誇らしげにトロフィーと「最優秀選手」の賞状を両親に見せていました。彼らは彼のことを誇らしく思っている様子でした。保護者面談で，父親と息子は小学校教員に呼び寄せられていました。彼女は彼らに息子の成績通知表を見せていて，彼は体育しか成績が良くないと述べました。息子はばつが悪そうでした。

解説 ナレーションは，４コマのイラストの進行に沿ってまとめていく。２～４コマ目の左上方にある時間の経過や場所を表す語句は，各コマの描写の冒頭部分で必ず使うこと。吹き出し内のせりふは，間接話法または直接話法を使ってストーリーに盛り込むが，間接話法を使う場合，主語や動詞などを適切な形に変える点に注意する。また，建物や看板のイラストの文字情報や，賞状の吹き出し内にある文字情報も適切な形でストーリーに盛り込む。動詞の時制は，過去形および過去進行形を基本に，時間の経過がわかるように描写する。

①１コマ目：泣く息子の前で，母親が彼の素行について父親に伝えている場面。泣いている息子のそばに割れた花瓶とサッカーボールが描かれており，困り顔の母親がHis behavior is terrible.「彼の素行がひどい」と父親に伝えている様子から，息子は家の中でボール遊びをしている最中に花瓶を割ってしまったのだと推察できる。解答例では，母親のせりふを間接話法で，… explained to the father thatに続けて盛り込んでおり，Hisをtheir son'sに，isをwasにそれぞれ正しく置き換えている。なお，父親はドアのそばでドアノブを回していることから，様子を確認しに部屋に入って来たところだと判断できる。

②２コマ目：That weekendで始める。両親がABCカルチャーセンターのそばを歩いている場面。カルチャーセンターの看板にSoccer School for Kids「子ども向けサッカースクール」とあり，これを見ている父親の吹き出し内に豆電球が描かれている点に着目。この様子から，父親は看板を見て何かの着想を得たのだと分かる。解答例では看板についての描写をした後に，This gave the father an idea.「これが，父親にあるアイデアを与えました」と，Thisを用いて簡潔にこの様子を表現している。

③３コマ目：A few months laterで始める。息子が両親に賞状を見せている場面。テーブルにトロフィーが置かれている点，および賞状の吹き出し内にBEST PLAYER「最優秀選手」とある点，息子が誇らしげな様子である点などから，彼は，２コマ目で描かれているサッカースクールに通い出し，そこで賞状を獲得したのだと推察可能。なお，解答例

のように，両親もうれしそうな表情を浮かべている点もナレーションに取り入れると良い。

④4コマ目：At a parent-teacher meetingで始める。学校の面談で息子，父親，教師が話をしている場面。教師が通知表のようなものを見せながら，He only does well in P.E.「彼は体育しか成績が良くありません」と困った表情を浮かべながら話している点に着目し，この様子を簡潔に描写する。息子がうつむきながらばつの悪そうな表情をしている点もナレーションに盛り込むことで，状況がより伝わるナレーションになるだろう。

質問の訳 No. 1　4番目の絵を見てください。あなたがその父親なら，どのようなことを考えているでしょうか。

では～さん（受験者の氏名），カードを裏返して置いてください。

No. 2　テレビゲームのプレーはスポーツと見なされるべきでしょうか。

No. 3　親は我が子と，重要な家庭内問題について話し合うべきですか。

No. 4　政府は学生に，もっと大学の奨学金を与えるべきでしょうか。

No.1 **解答例** I'd be thinking, "My son is still young and full of energy. There's nothing wrong with only doing well in P.E. for now. Eventually, he'll settle down and start doing better in other subjects."

解答例の訳 「息子はまだ幼くて，元気いっぱいだ。当分は，体育の成績しか良くなくても何も問題はない。ゆくゆくは，彼は腰を据えて他の教科の成績を上げ始めるだろう」と私は思っているでしょう。

解説 質問の仮定法過去形に合わせて，直接話法で**I'd be thinking, "～."** のように始めると良い。解答例では，息子の幼さとあふれる活力に言及し，差し当たりは体育の成績しか良くなくても問題がないと述べた後，最終的には体育以外の教科の成績が向上するだろうという希望的観測を伝えている。あるいは，解答例とは異なる観点から，I'd be thinking, "I should have made my son interested not only in sports but also in other things. But it is not too late even now, and we can take this opportunity to lead him to be engaged in other things such as English conversation, music, books, art, etc."「『息子には，スポーツに対してだけでなく他のことにも興味を抱かせるべきだった。でも，今からでもまだ遅くはないし，私たちはこれを機に，彼が英会話や音楽，本，美術といった他のことにも携わるよう仕向けることができる』と私は考えているでしょう」などとしても良いだろう。

No.2 **解答例** Definitely not. Sports are characterized by physical exercise that makes your body fit. Most video games involve just sitting. In fact, I think playing video games for a long time can be harmful to one's physical health.

解答例の訳 絶対にそうされるべきではありません。スポーツは，自分の体を良いコンディションに保つ身体運動によって特徴付けられます。大半のテレビゲームは座っていることだけを必要とします。実際，長時間に及ぶテレビゲームのプレーは身体的な健康の害になり得ると思います。

解説 解答例では，まずDefinitely not「絶対にそうされるべきではありません」と，自分がNoの立場にあることを強調してから，自分の体を良いコンディションに保つ身体運動こそがスポーツの特徴であり，それとは対照的に大半のテレビゲームは座っていることだけが求められる，と対比的に説明している。そして，In fact「実際」という談話標識に続けて，テレビゲームが身体的な健康の害になり得ると思うと意見を展開している。あるいは，Yesの立場から，These days, e-sports are gaining in popularity. Given this growing trend, in my opinion, we are required to consider e-sports as real sports as well in this day and age. Also, e-sports can provide equal opportunities with physically handicapped people, and I think this is a very good point.「最近では，eスポーツは人気が高まっています。この強まる傾向を考慮に入れると，私の意見では，今の時代，eスポーツも同様に真のスポーツと見なすことが私たちには求められています。また，eスポーツは体に障害のある人々にも平等な機会を提供でき，これはとても良い点だと思います」なども良いだろう。

No.3 **解答例** Yes. Important family decisions usually involve the children. They'll have an opinion on something that will affect their future. Furthermore, discussing issues will strengthen the relationships between family members.

解答例の訳 はい。重要な家庭の決断にはたいてい，子どもも関わっています。彼らは，自分の将来に影響することについての意見を持っていることでしょう。さらに，問題についての話し合いで家族間の関係性は強固なものとなるでしょう。

解説 解答例では，Yesの立場から，重要な家庭の決断というのはたいてい子どもも関わってくるという点を述べ，子どもたちも自分の将来に影響することについての意見を持っているはずだと言っている。そして，追加を表すFurthermore「さらに」を用いて，話し合いを通じて家族間の絆が深まり得る点もメリットとして挙げている。あるいは，４文目を，３文目までと同じ路線で，Therefore, parents should take account of their children's opinions as well as theirs.「そのため，親は，子どもたちの意見を自分たちの意見と同じくらい考慮すべきです」と帰結を表す内容にしても良いだろう。

No.4 **解答例** Yes. Education, including higher education, is a basic human right. Governments should provide equality to their citizens, so they should support more students from all economic backgrounds.

解答例の訳 はい。高等教育を含め，教育は基本的人権です。政府は自国民に平等性を提供すべきなので，彼らはあらゆる経済的背景の学生をもっと支援すべきです。

解説 解答例では，Yesの立場から，教育を受ける権利が基本的人権である点を述べた後，政府というものは人々に平等性を提供すべきなのだから，あらゆる経済的背景の学生をもっと支援すべきだと論を展開している。もしくは，同じYesの立場でありながらも，３文目をGovernments should provide more university scholarships which students do not need to pay them back, since many Japanese people are in financial trouble due to the repayment of scholarships after graduation.「政府は返済の必要がない大学奨学金をもっと支給すべきです，というのも，多くの日本人は卒業後，奨学金の返済のせいで金銭的な困難に陥っているためです」などとしても良いだろう。

2023年度 第1回

筆記 解答欄

問題番号		1	2	3	4
1	(1)	①	②	❸	④
	(2)	❶	②	③	④
	(3)	❶	②	③	④
	(4)	❶	②	③	④
	(5)	①	❷	③	④
	(6)	①	②	❸	④
	(7)	①	❷	③	④
	(8)	❶	②	③	④
	(9)	①	②	③	❹
	(10)	①	②	③	❹
	(11)	①	❷	③	④
	(12)	①	②	③	❹
	(13)	❶	②	③	④
	(14)	❶	②	③	④
	(15)	❶	②	③	④
	(16)	①	②	❸	④
	(17)	①	②	❸	④
	(18)	①	❷	③	④
	(19)	①	②	③	❹
	(20)	❶	②	③	④
	(21)	❶	②	③	④
	(22)	①	②	③	❹
	(23)	①	②	③	❹
	(24)	①	❷	③	④
	(25)	①	②	❸	④

問題番号		1	2	3	4
2	(26)	①	②	❸	④
	(27)	①	②	③	❹
	(28)	①	❷	③	④
	(29)	①	②	❸	④
	(30)	①	❷	③	④
	(31)	❶	②	③	④

問題番号		1	2	3	4
3	(32)	❶	②	③	④
	(33)	①	❷	③	④
	(34)	①	②	❸	④
	(35)	①	❷	③	④
	(36)	①	②	❸	④
	(37)	❶	②	③	④
	(38)	①	②	❸	④
	(39)	①	②	③	❹
	(40)	①	❷	③	④
	(41)	①	❷	③	④

4 の解答例はp.62をご覧ください。

リスニング 解答欄

問題番号			1	2	3	4
Part 1		No.1	①	❷	③	④
		No.2	①	②	❸	④
		No.3	❶	②	③	④
		No.4	①	②	③	❹
		No.5	①	②	❸	④
		No.6	①	❷	③	④
		No.7	①	②	③	❹
		No.8	①	②	❸	④
		No.9	①	②	❸	④
		No.10	❶	②	③	④
		No.11	①	②	③	❹
		No.12	①	❷	③	④
Part 2	A	No.13	❶	②	③	④
		No.14	①	②	③	❹
	B	No.15	①	❷	③	④
		No.16	❶	②	③	④
	C	No.17	①	②	❸	④
		No.18	①	②	③	❹
	D	No.19	①	②	③	❹
		No.20	①	❷	③	④
	E	No.21	❶	②	③	④
		No.22	①	②	③	❹
	F	No.23	①	❷	③	④
		No.24	❶	②	③	④
Part 3	G	No.25	①	❷	③	④
	H	No.26	①	❷	③	④
	I	No.27	①	②	❸	④
	J	No.28	①	②	❸	④
	K	No.29	❶	②	③	④

1 一次試験・筆記
(問題編pp.70〜73)

指示文の訳 各英文を完成させるのに最も適切な単語または語句を４つの選択肢の中から選び，その番号を解答用紙の所定欄にマークしなさい。

(1) 正解 3

訳 最初，ミックは１人で外国で暮らすことになるという考えにおじけづいた。けれども，いったんそうしてしまうと，恐れていたよりも難しくはなかった。

解説 空所直後にby the idea of going to live abroad by himself「１人で外国で暮らすことになるという考えに」とあるので，空所にはそれに対するミックの気持ちを表す語が入る。第２文にit was less difficult than he had feared「恐れていたよりも難しくはなかった」とあるので，「恐れていた」という気持ちを表す，**3のdaunted**「おじけづいた」が適切。pacify「〜を静める」，restore「〜を回復する」，tackle「〜に取り組む」。

(2) 正解 1

訳 生徒たちは試験の直前に詰め込むのではなく，学期を通して一定のペースで勉強するよう勧められている。

解説 空所直前のinstead of「〜ではなく」に着目。文前半にpace their studying throughout the semester「学期を通して一定のペースで勉強する」とあるので，空所にはそれとは対照的な内容が入る。**cram**「詰め込み勉強をする」の動名詞である**1のcramming**が正解。detain「〜を拘留する」，swell「膨らむ」，embrace「〜を抱きしめる」。

(3) 正解 1

訳 大統領選討論会で，その２人の候補者の怒りは燃え上がった。彼らはその夜ずっと，諸問題に対する互いの見解について腹を立てて攻撃し合った。

解説 第２文のangrily attacked each other's positions「互いの見解について腹を立てて攻撃し合った」から，候補者は２人とも怒っていたことがわかる。空所直前にThe two candidates' tempers「その２人の候補者の怒り」とあるので，この状況を表すのに適切な語は，**1のflared**「燃え上がった」。digest「〜を消化する」，profess「公言する」，tumble「転ぶ」。

(4) 正解 1

訳 多くの銀行が株式市場の暴落後に事業を続けるため，政府に介入を要求した。支援は主に多額の融資という形で行われた。

解説 第２文のThe help「支援」は空所に入る語を言い換えている。空所直後にto stay in business after the stock market crash「株式市場の暴落後に事業を続けるため」とあることから，銀行が政府に要求したのは，**1のintervention**「介入」が適切。appreciation「評価，感謝」，accumulation「蓄積」，starvation「飢餓」。

※2024年度第１回から，試験形式の変更に伴い大問１の問題数は18問になります。

(5)　正解　2

訳　警察は犯罪現場において確実に，いかなる形でも証拠が損なわれたり，変えられたりしないようにするため，厳格な手順に従わなければならない。

解説　文後半にto make sure the evidence is not damaged or altered in any way「確実に，いかなる形でも証拠が損なわれたり，変えられたりしないようにするため」とあるので，証拠を扱うには厳格な決まりがあると考えられる。これを表す語としては，**2のprotocols**「手順，慣例」が適切。tribute「賛辞」，reservoir「貯水池」，portion「部分」。

(6)　正解　3

訳　審判はその2人の選手が取っ組み合いをしたため退場させた。彼らはその試合の残りでプレーすることは許されなかった。

解説　第2文They(＝the two players) were not allowed to play in the rest of the game.「彼らはその試合の残りでプレーすることは許されなかった」から，2人は退場させられたとわかる。したがって，**3のejected**「～を退場させた」が正解。slaughter「～を虐殺する」，administer「～を運営する」，conceive「～を思いつく」。

(7)　正解　2

訳　猫は自分の子どもたちを守ることで知られている。彼らは，自分の子猫たちにとって危険な存在となり得ると思ったほかの動物を攻撃することがよくある。

解説　空所直前にbe protective of their「自分の…を守る」とあり，第2文にto their kittens「自分の子猫たちとって」とあることから，空所には「子猫」を表す語が入ると考えられる。したがって，**2のoffspring**「子供たち」が正解。offspringは単数も複数も同じ形ということに注意。prey「獲物」，ritual「儀式」，remain「残りもの，遺体」。

(8)　正解　1

訳　グリーンビル・ユナイテッドのファンたちは，シーズン中のチームの成績不振によりAリーグからBリーグへの降格に至るとがっかりした。

解説　when以下のthe team's poor performance「チームの成績不振」，空所直後のfrom the A-League to the B-League「AリーグからBリーグへの」などから，このチームは上位リーグから下位リーグに降格したとわかる。したがって，**1のdemotion**「降格」が正解。craving「切望」，aggravation「悪化」，hassle「口論，面倒」。

(9)　正解　4

訳　ビビはハイキングやスポーツをすることが大好きなので，あまりすぐに傷まない服が必要である。彼女は買い物に行くとき，たいてい長持ちする服を買う。

解説　空所にはどのような服かを表す形容詞が入る。第1文後半のshe needs clothes that do not wear out too quickly「あまりすぐに傷まない服が必要である」から，**4のdurable**「長持ちする」が正解。swift「迅速な」，aloof「離れた，よそよそしい」，shallow「浅い」。

(10) 正解　4

訳 消費者は銀行からだと名乗って電話をかけてくる人に，いかなる個人情報も明かすべきではない。というのも，このような電話は犯罪者からの場合があるからだ。

解説 文後半にas such calls are sometimes from criminals「というのも，このような電話は犯罪者からの場合があるからだ」とあるので，personal information「個人情報」は伝えないべきだと言いたいことがわかる。したがって，**4のdisclose**「～を明らかにする」が適切。sway「揺れる」，detest「～を嫌悪する」，contemplate「～を熟考する」。

(11) 正解　2

訳 そのテニスの優勝者はほかの選手に思いやりがなく，史上最も偉大な選手だと主張しているので，傲慢さを批判されることがよくある。

解説 文前半にthe tennis champion is unfriendly to other players and claims he is the greatest player who has ever lived「そのテニスの優勝者はほかの選手に思いやりがなく，史上最も偉大な選手だと主張している」とあり，空所にはその性格を表す語が入る。したがって，**2のarrogance**「傲慢さ」が正解。commodity「日用品」，neutrality「中立」，specimen「標本」。

(12) 正解　4

訳 多くの読者がその著者の小説は理解できないと思った。彼は，はっきりとした意味のない長くて紛らわしい文を書くことで知られていた。

解説 第２文にlong, confusing sentences that had no clear meaning「はっきりとした意味のない長くて紛らわしい文」とあり，その著者の小説はわかりにくかったと考えられるので，**4のincomprehensible**「理解できない」が正解。genuine「本物の」，impending「差し迫った」，subdued「控えめな」。

(13) 正解　1

訳 「クラスの皆さん，全員にとても注意深く聞いて欲しいと思います」と先生が言った。「私がこれから言うことの多くは教科書に書いてありませんが，テストに出ますよ。」

解説 先生は第２文で，Much of what I will say is not in the textbook but will be on the test.「私がこれから言うことの多くは教科書に書いてありませんが，テストに出ますよ」と，生徒たちに重要なことを伝えている。**1のattentively**「注意深く」を入れて生徒たちに注意深く聞くように促す内容にすると，状況に合う。consecutively「連続して」，wearily「疲れて，うんざりして」，eloquently「雄弁に」。

(14) 正解　1

訳 その学校は教育の最先端にいることで知られている。そこの先生たちは教室で最新の教授法と最新の科学技術を使っている。

解説 第２文のIts teachers use the newest teaching methods and the latest technology「そこの先生たちは最新の教授法と最新の科学技術を使っている」から，**1のforefront**「最先端」が正解。lapse「過失，経過」，doctrine「教義，主義」，myth「神話」。

(15) 正解 1

訳 その市長は演説で力強い言葉を使ったが，それは公共交通機関に関する彼の案を市民が支持することが極めて重要だと彼が考えたからであった。

解説 文後半にit was extremely important that the citizens support his plan「彼の案を市民が支持することが極めて重要だ」とあるので，市長は演説で自分の案を力説したと考えられる。したがって，**1のforceful**「力強い，説得力のある」が適切。merciful「慈悲深い」，futile「無益な」，tranquil「穏やかな」。

(16) 正解 3

訳 そのポップ歌手が亡くなったとき，彼女はお気に入りの慈善団体に1000万ドルを超える遺産を残した。「私たちは彼女の寛大さにとても感謝します」と慈善団体の広報担当者は述べた。

解説 第1文のWhen the pop singer died「そのポップ歌手が亡くなったとき」，空所直後のof over $10 million「1000万ドルを超える」，第2文のso grateful for her generosity「彼女の寛大さにとても感謝します」などから，歌手は慈善団体に遺産を残したと推測できる。したがって，**3のlegacy**「遺産」が正解。rhyme「韻，押韻詩」，justice「公正，司法」，majority「大多数」。

(17) 正解 3

訳 山頂に近づくにつれて，高地で酸素濃度が低いため，何人かのハイカーたちは気分が悪くなり始めた。

解説 文前半にAs they approached the top of the mountain「山頂に近づくにつれて」とあるので，ハイカーたちは高い山の上を歩いているとわかる。したがって，**3のaltitude**「標高，高地」が正解。apparatus「器具一式，装置」，equation「方程式，均一化」，mileage「総走行マイル数」。

(18) 正解 2

訳 テッドはささやかな収入で暮らしている。彼は小さなアパートに住み，勘定を支払い，時々外食できる程度の稼ぎがなんとかある。

解説 第2文の内容から，テッドの収入は決して多くはないことがわかる。この状況を表すには，**2のmodest**「ささやかな，控えめな」が適切。blissful「至福の」，showy「派手な」，sturdy「頑丈な」。

(19) 正解 4

訳 その大工はテーブルのために均一な材木を注意深く選んだ。全体が同じ厚さでなければ，問題が起こるだろう。

解説 第2文後半にif it did not have the same thickness throughout「全体が同じ厚さでなければ」とあるので，大工が選んだのは全体が同じ厚さの材木だと考えられる。この様子を表すには，**4のuniform**「均一の」が適切。reckless「無謀な」，gaping「大きく開いた」，dreary「わびしい，退屈な」。

(20) 正解　1

訳 ピーターは孤独を好む静かな男性で，子どもたちにめったに愛情を示さなかったが，子どもたちは彼に本当に愛されているとわかっていた。

解説 文後半にthey(＝Pieter's children) knew that he(＝Pieter) truly loved them「子どもたちは彼に本当に愛されているとわかっていた」とあるので，ピーターがめったにしなかったのは愛情表現だと思われる。**1のaffection**「愛情」を入れると文脈に合う。circulation「循環」，oppression「圧迫」，coalition「連立」。

(21) 正解　1

訳 アントンはスピーカーからおかしなブーンという音が出ているのが聞こえたので，すべてのケーブルが適切につながれていることを確かめるために点検した。

解説 空所直前にstrange「おかしな」，直後にcoming from his speakers「スピーカーから…音が出ている」とあるので，**1のbuzz**「ブーンという音」が正解。peck「つつくこと，コツコツという音」，thorn「とげ」，core「芯，中心」。

(22) 正解　4

訳 昨夜遅く，１人の男がコンビニ強盗をしようとしていたところを捕まった。警察は彼に武器を捨てさせ，彼を逮捕した。

解説 第２文The police forced him to drop his weapon and arrested him.「警察は彼に武器を捨てさせ，彼を逮捕した」から，その男は犯罪を行ったことがわかる。したがって，**4のhold up**「～を強奪する，～で強盗する」が正解。shrug off「～を受け流す，～を振り払う」，sit out「～に加わらない」，run against「～に出くわす」。

(23) 正解　4

訳 ジルはずっとフランスが大好きだったので，会社のパリ支社で働くチャンスがあったときはそれに飛びついた。実際，最初に志願したのは彼女だった。

解説 第２文にshe(＝Jill) was the first to apply「最初に志願したのは彼女だった」とあるので，ジルは何としてもパリ支社で働きたかったとわかる。この状況に合うのは，**4のjumped at**「～に飛びついた」。plow through「～をかき分けて進む」，pull on「～を引っぱって着る」，throw off「～を振り捨てる」。

(24) 正解　2

訳 A：仕事の予定に合うようにあなたが登録した講座はどんな調子ですか。　B：オンラインなので，自分のペースで勉強できるんです。仕事から家に戻ってから教材を読むことができるので，うまくいきそうですよ。

解説 AはHow's ～ going?「～の調子はどうですか」とBにたずねている。the class (that) you signed up forで「あなたが登録した講座」という意味。空所直前のtoは「～するために」という意味を表す不定詞の副詞的用法。**fit in with ～**で「～に合わせる」という意味を表し，状況に合うので，**2のfit in**が正解。get over「～を克服する」，hold onto「～にしがみつく」，take after「～に似ている」。

(25) 正解 3

訳 新しい課に移る前に，ベティは現在のプロジェクトをすべて今後その仕事を行う予定の人に引き継ぐだろう。

解説 文頭にBefore moving to her new section「新しい課に移る前に」，空所直後にall of her current projects「現在のプロジェクトをすべて」，さらに後半にto the person who will be doing her job from now on「今後その仕事を行う予定の人に」とあるので，ベティは自分の仕事を別の人に引き継ぐと考えられる。**hand over ～ to ...**で「～を…に引き継ぐ」という意味を表すので，**3のhand over**が正解。beef up「～を増強する」，bank on「～を当てにする」，slip by「いつの間にか過ぎ去る」。

2 一次試験・筆記

世間話を超えて（問題編pp.74～75）
シング（The Thing）（問題編pp.76～77）

指示文の訳 それぞれの文章を読んで，各空所に入れるのに最も適切な語句を４つの選択肢の中から選び，その番号を解答用紙の所定欄にマークしなさい。

世間話を超えて

Key to Reading 第１段落：導入（人間関係が人に与える影響）→第２段落：本論①（見知らぬ人との会話に関する最近の研究）→第３段落：本論②（知らない人との世間話以上の会話が有意義であること）という３段落構成の説明文。研究結果やそこから得られる仮説について，空所の前後関係に注目しながら読み進めよう。

訳

ある研究は，人間関係が人の健康状態に影響を与えると示している。肯定的な人間関係は幸福感を高めるだけでなく，身体的健康にも良い影響を与える。これまでのところ，大半の研究は，家族や友人など身近な人との関係に焦点を当ててきた。これは理にかなっている。というのも，私たちが問題を抱えていたり自分の考えや意見を共有したいと思ったりするとき，そのような人に話す可能性が最も高いからである。対照的に，最近の研究では，私たちが見知らぬ人とどのように接するかを調査しており，その結果はかなり意外なものであった。

ある研究では，被験者を初対面の人とペアにし，各ペアに天気などの軽い話題と，個人的な目標など，より本質的な話題を考え出すように求めた。研究開始時，被験者の大半は，カジュアルな会話の方が楽しいだろうと考えた。各会話の後被験者たちは，楽しさとそれぞれのパートナーとの間に感じるつながりに基づいてその会話を評価するように言われた。その結果，被験者の予想は間違っていたことがわかった。つまりほとんどの被験者は，深刻な話題について話し合った後，全体的により肯定的な経験をしたと報告したのである。

この研究結果は，人は見知らぬ人とのより深いレベルでの交流から恩恵を受けられるだろうということを示唆している。実際，この研究の被験者たちは概して，自分たちの生活において，知らない人ともっと頻繁に有意義な会話を行いたいという願望を示した。しかし彼らは，他の人々はそのような願望を共有しないとも考えていた。研究者たちは，この推測は間違っており，ほとんどの場合，見知らぬ人もまた，世間話以上の話をすることに興味があると考えている。

(26) 正解 3

選択肢の訳 **1** 引き換えに **2** 例えば **3** 対照的に **4** 要するに

解説 第1段落第3文では，従来の研究について，most studies have focused on relationships with people we are close to「大半の研究は，身近な人との関係に焦点を当ててきた」と述べ，これを支持する内容が空所の直前まで続く。空所を含む文は，最近の研究ではhow we interact with strangers「私たちが見知らぬ人とどのように接するか」を調査していると述べている。空所前後で対照的な内容になっているので，**3のIn contrast**「対照的に」が正解。

(27) 正解 4

選択肢の訳 **1** 話題が被験者を緊張させた **2** 被験者の評価は必ずしも一致しなかった **3** 話題の選択肢が多様すぎた **4** 被験者の予想は間違っていた

解説 空所直後の文で，研究結果についてmost subjects reported having a more positive experience overall after discussing serious topics「ほとんどの被験者は，深刻な話題について話し合った後，全体的により肯定的な経験をしたと報告した」と述べている。これは研究開始当初の被験者たちのthey would enjoy casual conversations more「カジュアルな会話の方が楽しいだろう」という予想と正反対なので，被験者の予想は間違っていたということがわかる。**4のsubjects' expectations had been wrong**「被験者の予想は間違っていた」が正解。

(28) 正解 2

選択肢の訳 **1** 明確に伝えることは難しいだろう **2** 他の人々はそのような願望を共有しない **3** 家族は認めてくれないだろう **4** 自分たちのプライバシーが第一であるべきだ

解説 空所直後にThe researchers believe that this assumption is incorrect「研究者たちは，この推測は間違っていると考えている」とあるので，文後半の内容によって否定される選択肢を見つければよい。空所直後の文後半のfor the most part, strangers are also interested in going beyond casual conversation「ほとんどの場合，見知らぬ人もまた，世間話以上の話をすることに興味がある」と反対の内容を表す**2のother people did not share this desire**「他の人々はそのような願望を共有しない」が正解。

シング（The Thing）

Key to Reading 第1段落：導入（長らく謎だった化石シングの正体）→第2段落：本論①（モササウルスがどうやって卵を産むのかについての議論）→第3段落：本論②（恐竜の卵についての新たな知見）という3段落構成の説明文である。モササウルスについて従来考えられていたことと新説，恐竜の卵に関する発見などを整理しながら読み進めよう。

訳

チリの博物館の棚に10年近く放置されていた，「シング」として知られる謎の化石の正体が，ついに突き止められた。現在研究者たちは，それは6600万年前の殻の柔らかい卵であり，中にはおそらく恐竜と同時期に存在した大型の水生爬虫類であるモササウルスがいたのだと考えている。これまでの化石証拠は，モササウルスは卵を産まないことを示唆していた。しかし，研究者たちの発見はこの考えを覆すものであり，彼らが言うには，化石の大きさと，それがモササウルスの化石が発見された地域で見つかったという事実が，その結論を裏付けているとのことだ。

研究者たちは「シング」の正体を明らかにしたことに興奮しているが，この発見によって新たな議論が始まった。ある説では，モササウルスは開けた水域に卵を産み，子どもはほとんどすぐに孵化したとしている。一方，モササウルスは現代の爬虫類がそうであるように，浜辺に卵を産みつけ，それを埋めたと考える科学者もいる。どちらが正しいかは，今後の研究によって明らかになるだろうと期待されている。

アメリカの別の研究者グループが以前発見された恐竜の赤ん坊の化石を詳しく調べた結果，先史時代の生物の卵に新たな光が当てられた。恐竜は硬い殻の卵を産むと考えられていたが，この仮説の根拠となった化石は，限られた恐竜種のものであった。米国の研究者たちは，その分析を通じて，初期の恐竜の卵が実は軟らかい殻であったことを示唆する証拠を発見した。もしこれが本当なら，恐竜の卵がほとんど発見されていない理由を説明できるかもしれない。柔らかい素材は分解されやすいので，化石記録として保存される可能性はかなり低くなるのだ。

(29) 正解 **3**

選択肢の訳 **1** 恐竜に狩られた可能性が高い **2** 食糧を卵に頼っていた **3** 卵を産まなかった **4** 恐竜とともに存在しなかったかもしれない

解説 空所を含む文は「これまでの化石証拠は，モササウルスは（　　）ことを示唆していた」という意味。直後に研究者の発見（＝シングはモササウルスの卵である）はchallenge this idea「この考えを覆す」とあるので，選択肢の中から，シングがモササウルスの卵であることと矛盾するものを選ぶ。**3のdid not lay eggs**「卵を産まなかった」が正解。

(30) 正解 **2**

選択肢の訳 **1** 同様に **2** 一方 **3** 結果として **4** 例えば

解説 空所直前の文は，モササウルスが開けた水域に卵を産み，子どもはほとんどすぐに孵化した（would have laid their eggs in open water, with the young hatching almost immediately）という説を述べている。空所を含む文はmosasaurs would have laid their eggs on the beach and buried them「浜辺に卵を産みつけ，それを埋めた」という説で，空所直前の文とまったく異なるので，**2のOn the other hand**「一方」が正解。

(31) 正解 **1**

選択肢の訳 **1** 恐竜の卵がほとんど発見されていない **2** 恐竜の種類が減った **3** 卵を産めない恐竜もいた **4** 恐竜の赤ちゃんはしばしば生き残れなかった

解説 「もしこれ（＝恐竜の卵の殻が柔らかいこと）が本当なら，（　　）理由を説明できるかもしれない」の空所に当てはまる内容を選ぶ。空所直後でSince softer materials break down easily, they are much less likely to be preserved in the fossil record.「柔らかい素材は分解されやすいので，化石記録として保存される可能性はかなり低くなるのだ」とあることから，**1のfew dinosaur eggs have been found**「恐竜の卵がほとんど発見されていない」が正解。

3	一次試験・筆記	明日の鶏（問題編pp.78～79） アメリカの学校における規律（問題編pp.80～81） ロバート・ザ・ブルースとアーブロース宣言（問題編pp.82～84）

指示文の訳 それぞれの文章を読んで，各質問に対する最も適切な答えを４つの選択肢の中から選び，その番号を解答用紙の所定欄にマークしなさい。

明日の鶏

Key to Reading 第１段落：導入＋本論①（1940年代以前のアメリカの養鶏）→第２段落：本論②（戦後の鶏肉需要と業界の変化）→第３段落：本論③（鶏肉の普及の暗い一面）という３段落構成の説明文。従来の養鶏と，戦後の業態の変化，またその変化がどのように影響したかに注目しながら読み進めよう。

訳

1940年代以前，アメリカの鶏のほとんどは家族経営の農場で飼育されており，肉よりも卵の生産に重点が置かれていた。当時貧困と食糧不足が一般的であったため，人々は鶏を犠牲にすることなく定期的なタンパク源を確保したかったのだ。さらに，農家は一般的にその鶏がどれだけその土地の条件に合っているか――例えば乾燥した気候に適しているのか，それとも湿度の高い気候に適しているのか――に基づいて品種を選んだため，実に多種多様な鶏が飼育されていた。

しかし，第二次世界大戦後，豚肉や牛肉などの食肉が普及したため，卵はタンパク源として太刀打ちできなくなった。そこでアメリカ農務省は，経済的に飼育でき，より多くの肉を生産できる鶏の種類を見つけるために，「明日の鶏」コンテストというイベントを立ち上げた。総合優勝に輝いたのは異なる品種の掛け合わせで，より早く育ち，他の種類よりも大きく，様々な気候に適応することができた。このコンテストに触発され，育種会社は，同じような望ましい特徴を持つ鳥を安定的に供給するため，品種を複雑に混ぜ合わせた鶏を作り始めた。このような遺伝子の組み合わせを作り出すことは困難であったため，ほとんどの農家は，自分で鶏を繁殖させるよりも，そのような会社から若鶏を購入するしかなかった――開発が業界を一変させたのだ。

このコンテストは鶏肉消費の大衆化に貢献したが，この流れには暗い面もあった。大量の鶏を小さなケージに閉じ込めた大規模な施設で飼育する方が経済的になったのだ。その結果，多くの小規模農場が廃業に追い込まれただけでなく，動物愛護活動家たちによれば，鶏のストレスとなり，病気のレベルを高める原因となるような飼育環境を作り出した。このコンテストによって鶏肉は通常の食品となったが，その価値があるのかどうか疑問視する声もあった。

(32)　正解　1

質問の訳 1940年以前のアメリカの鶏肉産業についてわかることの一つは何か。

選択肢の訳 **1** 各農場で飼育される鶏の種類は通常，その農場がある地域の気候に左右された。　**2** 各農場は, 突然の環境変化に備えて複数の種類の鶏を飼育していた。

3 鶏が食べられるのは一般的に, 非常に貧しい人々によってか, 食糧不足の時だけだった。

4 全国に多くの養鶏場があったため，生産された卵の多くは無駄になってしまった。

解説 第１段落第３文後半に，farmers generally chose a breed based on how well

※2024年度第１回から，試験形式の変更に伴い大問３の１問目(32)～(34)が削除されます。

it was adapted to the local conditions「農家は一般的にその鶏がどれだけその土地の条件に合っているかに基づいて品種を選んだ」とある。土地の条件には，直後の例で述べられている通り，気候などを含むので，同じ内容を述べている**1**が正解。

(33) 正解 2

質問の訳 米国農務省が「明日の鶏」コンテストを開催したのは，～からである。

選択肢の訳 **1** 豚肉や牛肉などの他の種類の肉が高価になりつつあり，アメリカ国民がより安価な代替品を求めていた　**2** ほとんどの養鶏場は卵の生産に重点を置いており，食肉生産により適した鶏を作る必要性が生じた　**3** アメリカでは多くの養鶏場が廃業し，深刻な鶏肉不足が起こった　**4** アメリカの人々は，長い間同じ種類の卵を食べ続けることに飽き，生産者が違う種類の鶏肉を欲しがった

解説 第２段落第２文に，The US Department of Agriculture therefore set up an event called the Chicken of Tomorrow contest「そこでアメリカ農務省は，『明日の鶏』コンテストというイベントを立ち上げた」とあるので，理由は直前の第１文にある。the growing availability of meat such as pork and beef meant eggs could not compete as a source of protein「豚肉や牛肉などの食肉が普及したため，卵はタンパク源として太刀打ちできなくなった」，つまり卵ではなく鶏肉を生産する必要があったので，選択肢**2**が正解。

(34) 正解 3

質問の訳 コンテストが鶏肉産業に与えた影響の一つはどのようなものか。

選択肢の訳 **1** 農家が，複数の種類の鶏を組み合わせることが比較的簡単であることを知り，新しい鶏の品種作出の励みとなった　**2** アメリカ全土で小規模な養鶏場の数が増えたが，その多くは経営が行き届かず，施設も安っぽいものだった。　**3** 鶏の苦痛を増やし健康を害するような環境で鶏を飼育する動きが始まった。　**4** 農家は，飼育方法を改善することで，より多く，よりおいしい鶏肉を生産できることに気づいた。

解説 第３段落では鶏肉消費の広まりとともに大規模施設で鶏を飼育するようになったことの弊害について述べている。第３文後半にit also created conditions for the birds that, according to animal rights activists, caused the chickens stress and led to higher levels of sickness「動物愛護活動家たちによれば，鶏のストレスとなり，病気のレベルを高める原因となるような飼育環境を作り出した」とあるので，この内容と一致する選択肢**3**が正解。

アメリカの学校における規律

Key to Reading 第１段落：導入(従来の学校教育の基となっていた報酬と罰のシステム)→第２段落：本論①（報酬と罰で教育を行うことの問題点）→第３段落：本論②＋結論（自己規律に関わる脳の部位の解明と，脳構造を変えられる教育方法）という３段落構成の説明文。従来の教育方法と，最新の研究で明らかになったことをそれぞれ把握しながら，本文を読み進めよう。

訳

何十年もの間，アメリカの学校で使われてきたしつけの方法は，心理学者B･F･スキナーの理論に基づいてきた。スキナーは，報酬と罰のシステムが人々の行動を改善する最も効

果的な方法であると考えていた。一般的に，規則を破った生徒には，１日かそれ以上の間，授業への出席を禁じられたり，終業後も教室に残らされたりするなどの罰が与えられる。これらは，生徒が教師の指示に従いクラスメートを尊重するように教えるためのものである。しかし，懲罰は一時的に教室に平穏をもたらすには効果的かもしれないが，長期にわたって継続的に使われると，罰によって正すつもりの行動そのものを強めてしまう可能性があることが，最近の心理学的研究で明らかになっている。

現在，多くの専門家は，子どもたちが適切な行動をとれるようになるためには，自制心を養うことが不可欠だと考えている。規則を守らせるために罰を与えるということは，外的な圧力によって良い行動を取らせるということである。一方，自制心とは，内的な動機づけや自信，他者へ寛容であることから生まれるものであり，これらの代用として罰を用いることは，その発達を遅らせたり，妨げたりすることになる。同様に，シールのようなご褒美の使用は，生涯にわたり生徒の助けとなる知識や社会的能力の重要性を理解するのではなく，生徒がただ先生を喜ばせようとするだけのことになってしまう。

近年，こうした考えを裏付ける研究が増えている。前頭前皮質として知られる脳の領域は，私たちが課題に集中するのを助け，自己規律を守る役割を担っており，これによって私たちは自分の行動の結果を考えることができる。研究によると，問題行動を起こす生徒は前頭前皮質が発達していない可能性がある。しかし幸いなことに，繰り返し経験することで脳構造は変化することが証明されており，このことは，前頭前皮質の発達に影響を与えることも可能であることを示唆している。児童行動専門家のロス・グリーンは次のように考えている。それは，教育者が態度を改め，生徒の悪い行動をしたときの気持ちに耳を傾け，生徒が直面する問題の解決策を考え出すよう促すと，それが前頭前皮質に物理的な影響を与えることができるということだ。グリーン氏は，多くの学校で問題行動を大幅に減らすことに大成功したプログラムを考案し，そして近年，彼のアイデアがメディアで大々的に取り上げられた結果，ますます多くの教育者に取り入れられている。

(35)　正解　**2**

質問の訳　学校における罰の使用について，心理学的研究は何を示しているか。

選択肢の訳　**1**　罰が効果的である可能性が高いのは，その悪影響を軽減するために，報酬と一緒に使われる場合だけである。　**2**　短期的にはより良い行動をもたらすことに成功するかもしれないが，長期的には有害である。　**3**　体罰よりもはるかに効果的な，さまざまな新しいタイプの罰がある。　**4**　生徒に教師に従わせ，クラスメートを尊重させるためには，何らかの罰を与えることが必要である。

解説　学校における罰について，心理学的研究の内容が示されているのは第１段落最終文。文前半では，as effective as punishment may be in bringing peace to the classroom temporarily「一時的に教室に平穏をもたらすには効果的かもしれない」，後半ではit can intensify the very behavior it is intended to correct when used continually over an extended period of time「長期にわたって継続的に使われると，罰によって正すつもりの行動そのものを強めてしまう」と，短期的効果と長期的効果を対比して述べている。この内容と一致する選択肢**2**が正解。文前半のbringing peace to the classroom temporarilyがproducing better behavior in the short termと，後半の内容がbe harmful in the long termと言いかえられている。

(36) 正解 3

質問の訳 この文章によると，ご褒美の使用が生徒に与える効果の一つは何か。

選択肢の訳 **1** 生徒に努力することの利点を教え，学業上の目標に集中することがうまくなるようにすることができる。 **2** 物質的なものを欲しがるようになり，他者に喜ばれるような行動をとる必要性をあまり意識しなくなる。 **3** 後々の人生に役立つはずの重要なスキルを身につけることを妨げうる。 **4** 教師に言われたことをするだけではなく，自分で目標を決めることの大切さに気づかせる。

解説 第2段落では，罰が生徒の自制心を養う妨げになることを述べた後，ご褒美について最終文でSimilarly, ...「同様に～」と述べており，良くない内容が続くことがわかる。生徒はattempting to please the teacher rather than understanding the importance of gaining knowledge and social skills that will help them throughout their lives「生涯にわたり生徒の助けとなる知識や社会的能力の重要性を理解するのではなく，生徒がただ先生を喜ばせようとするだけのことになってしまう」とあるので，これと同じ内容を表す選択肢**3**が正解。prevent ～ from doing ...「～が…するのを妨げる」

(37) 正解 1

質問の訳 ロス・グリーンは子どもの脳についてどのように考えているか。

選択肢の訳 **1** 子どもが自分で問題を解決するのを助けることで，行動を制御する脳の部分の発達を促すことができる。 **2** 低年齢児の脳は高年齢児の脳とは異なる働きをするので，問題行動を扱う際には異なる方法で対処する必要がある。 **3** 脳の前頭前皮質として知られる部位は，子どもの行動をコントロールする上で，一部の科学者が考えているほど重要ではないかもしれない。 **4** 素行不良は，子どもの学業成績に悪影響を及ぼすだけでなく，子どもの脳の正常な成長を永久に妨げる。

解説 ロス・グリーンが子どもの脳について述べているのは最終段落第5文。教育者が生徒の気持ちに耳を傾け問題の解決策を考え出すよう促すと，this can have a physical effect on the prefrontal cortex「それが前頭前皮質に物理的な影響を与えることができる」とある。前頭前皮質（the prefrontal cortex）は，物事に集中したり自己規律を守る役割を担う脳の部分である。この内容と一致する**1**が正解。

ロバート・ザ・ブルースとアーブロース宣言

Key to Reading 第1段落：導入（ロバート・ザ・ブルース台頭前の背景）→第2段落：本論①（ロバートの即位）→第3段落：本論②（アーブロース宣言ができた経緯とその後）→第4段落：結論（アーブロース宣言の歴史的意味）という4段落構成の説明文。人名や各勢力の立場を整理しながら読み進めよう。

訳

1286年，スコットランド国王アレクサンダー3世の突然の死により，様々な貴族の間で権力闘争が起こり，危うく内戦に発展するところだった。この事態を収拾するため，イングランド王エドワード1世が，ライバルたちの中から新しい統治者を選ぶよう要請された。エドワード自身，最終的にはスコットランドを支配したいという野心を持っていたが，新しい指導者が自分に忠誠を誓うことを唯一の条件として同意した。彼はジョン・バリオールという貴族を新王に選んだが，イングランドがスコットランドの問題に対して何度も権勢を振るったため，やがて恨みが募った。転機となったのは，エドワードが，イングランドとフランスとの紛争において，スコットランドに軍事援助を提供するよう強要しようとしたときだった。バリオールが自国をフランスと同盟させたため，エドワードはスコットランドに侵攻してバリオールを破り，王位を奪った。

これが，スコットランド貴族ロバート・ザ・ブルースがイングランドの支配からスコットランドを解放しようとして直面した状況だった。父が王位を巡る争いでバリオールのかつてのライバルの一人であったロバートは，政治的に優位に立ち，イングランド軍をスコットランドから追い出す反乱を起こした。ロバートは1306年にスコットランド王に即位し，国内では絶大な支持を得たが，ローマ・カトリック教会の指導者であるローマ教皇を怒らせてしまった。彼はイングランドとの和平を求める教会の要請を無視しただけでなく，国王に即位する前に，王位に最も近いライバルの命を礼拝の場で奪ったのだ。

スコットランドの指導者たちは，教会の承認がなければ，この国が国際的に孤立し，脆弱なままであることを知っていた。スコットランド独立の国際的な承認は，スコットランドがイングランド――撤退したにもかかわらず，ロバートをスコットランドの王として正式に承認していない――のような強国の影に隠れて存続するためには特に重要なことだった。そこで1320年，スコットランドの最有力貴族たちが，今日「アーブロース宣言」として知られる文書を作成するために集まった。それはスコットランドの独立を宣言し，ローマ教皇にロバートをスコットランドの統治者として承認するよう要請するものだった。しかし，その年の後半に貴族たちが受け取った反応は，当初は宣言が実効性も持たなかったことを示していた。ローマ教皇はスコットランドの要求を拒否しただけでなく，イングランドにはスコットランドとの関係において平和的解決を追求するよう促したが，スコットランドの自称独立を認めることもしなかった。しかし数年後，和平条約によってスコットランドがついにイングランドの脅威から解放された後，この宣言の影響により，ローマ教皇はロバートとその王国を承認した。

今日，アーブロース宣言はスコットランドの歴史において最も有名な文書の一つである。歴史家の中には，この文書がアメリカの独立宣言に影響を与えたと主張する者さえいるが，その証拠は乏しい。しかし，学者たちの主張はおおむね次の点で一致している。それは，アーブロース宣言を歴史的なものにしているのは，国王はスコットランド国民の承認がなければ統治できないと表明している点である。具体的には，貴族たちはこの文書を用いて，自分たちを裏切る支配者を排除する権利を大胆に主張したのである。この意味で，この文書は一国の統治者と国民との間の契約の先駆的な例であり，その契約において統治者は，国民が自由な社会で暮らせるようにする責任があった。

(38) 正解 3

質問の訳 スコットランド王アレクサンダー３世の死後，何が起こったか。

選択肢の訳 **1** スコットランドはエドワード１世を騙して，エドワードの利益に反していたにもかかわらずジョン・バリオールを選ばせることができた。 **2** エドワード１世は，ジョン・バリオールが王になろうとすることを支持しなかったスコットランド貴族の忠誠心を疑い始めた。 **3** エドワード１世は，スコットランドに対する権力を拡大するために，この状況を自分の有利になるように利用しようとした。 **4** スコットランドはフランスの軍事力にたいへんな脅威を感じ，両国の外交関係は悪化した。

解説 第１段落第１～２文から，アレクサンダー３世の死後，王位を巡る諸侯の争いが起こり，この混乱を収めるためにイングランド王エドワード1世が次の王を決めるように要請されたという状況がわかる。エドワード1世が指名に際し，新しい指導者が彼に忠誠を誓うことを条件（the condition that the new leader pledged loyalty to him）にしたこと，また，第4文後半でresentment soon grew as England repeatedly exerted its authority over Scotland's affairs「イングランドがスコットランドの問題に対して何度も権勢を振るったため，やがて恨みが募った」と述べられていることから，この状況を利用して彼がスコットランドに支配力を広げようとしていたことが読み取れる。この内容と一致する選択肢**3**が正解。

(39) 正解 4

質問の訳 ロバート・ザ・ブルースはスコットランド王になった後，どのような問題に直面したか。

選択肢の訳 **1** 彼は偉大な軍事指導者であったが，政治手腕に欠けていたため，イングランドとの交渉がうまくいかなかった。 **2** 宗教に関してライバルと意見の相違があったため，多くのスコットランド国民は彼を支持しなくなった。 **3** スコットランドとイングランドの宗教的な相違により，スコットランドが再び攻撃される可能性が高くなった。 **4** 彼が権力を得るために行ったことのせいで，スコットランドは，イングランドから安全であるために必要な支持を得ることができなかった。

解説 ロバートが王になったことは第2段落第3文で述べられており，同じ文の後半にalthough he enjoyed tremendous support domestically, he had angered the Pope, the leader of the Roman Catholic Church「国内では絶大な支持を得たが，ローマ・カトリック教会の指導者であるローマ教皇を怒らせてしまった」とある。また，その原因は直後に「イングランドとの和平を求める教会の要請を無視した（ignored the church's requests that he make peace with England)」「国王に即位する前に，王位に最も近いライバルの命を礼拝の場で奪った（he had also taken the life of his closest rival to the throne in a place of worship before being crowned king)」と説明されている。さらに，第3段落第1～2文から，教会から認められることが国際的な承認を得るために重要であることがわかる。これらの内容をまとめた選択肢**4**が正解。

(40) 正解 2

質問の訳 「アーブロース宣言」が書かれた年に，

選択肢の訳 **1** ローマ教皇がスコットランドの国家としての独立を認めることを優先事項と考えていることが明らかになった。 **2** 教皇は，ロバートも彼の国も認めていないにもかかわらず，イングランドとスコットランドの和平を促そうとした。 **3** イングランドとスコットランドの間の和平の約束は，スコットランドが教皇から援助を得ようとしたことによって危うくなった。 **4** スコットランドは，ローマ教皇にロバートが真の国王であることを認めさせるのに十分な国際的認知を得ることができた。

解説 アーブロース宣言について述べられているのは第3段落第3～4文で，1320年にその文書を作成するために集まったとある。直後の第5文で，The response the nobles received later in the year ...「その年の後半に貴族たちが受け取った反応は…」とあるので，この辺りに注目する。第6文に，教皇はスコットランドの要求を拒否し，failed to confirm its self-proclaimed independence, although he did urge England to pursue a peaceful resolution in its dealings with the nation「イングランドにはスコットランドとの関係において平和的解決を追求するよう促したが，スコットランドの自称独立を認めることもしなかった」とある。この内容と一致する選択肢**2**が正解。

(41) 正解 **2**

質問の訳 アーブロース宣言の一般的な解釈の１つは何か。

選択肢の訳 **1** それは，ロバートが当初人々が考えていたよりもはるかに優れた指導者であったことを示すものである。 **2** それは，一国の統治者が統治する人々に対して負っていた義務について，新たな見方をもたらした。 **3** 当時，スコットランドの統治者と貴族の間には，学者たちが考えていたよりもはるかに多くの対立があったことを明らかにしている。 **4** 王や女王が国を治めていたのでは，有益な政治体制が成り立たないことを示唆した。

解説 アーブロース宣言の一般的な解釈は最終段落第３文Scholars generally agree, ... 以降で述べられている。この宣言は，国王が国民の承認なしに国を統治できないと表明した点で歴史的であり，最終文に a pioneering example of a contract between a country's ruler and its people「一国の統治者と国民との間の契約の先駆的な例」とある。この内容と一致する選択肢**2**が正解。

4 一次試験・英作文

（問題編p.85）

指示文の訳 ●次のトピックについてエッセイを書きなさい。
●答えの裏付けに，以下に挙げたポイントのうちの２つを使いなさい。
●構成：導入，本論，結論
●長さ：120～150語
●エッセイは解答用紙のB面に用意されたスペースに書きなさい。
スペースの外側に書かれた内容は，採点の対象とはなりません。

トピックの訳 企業はもっとオンラインサービスを提供すべきですか。

ポイントの訳 ●利便性 ●費用 ●職 ●環境

解答例

In today's fast-paced digital world, I believe businesses should provide more online services. The benefits of doing so are related to convenience and cost.

Firstly, providing more online services leads to increased convenience. For instance, online customer support provides people with the means to contact businesses whenever they have queries. This can be particularly beneficial for busy people or international customers who live in different time zones.

Additionally, online services can be cost-effective for businesses. With the rise of e-commerce, moving to online digital platforms can reduce expenses and streamline operations. Selling products online, for example,

※2024年度第１回から，大問４に文章の要約を書く問題が加わります。

can help businesses cut utility bills. Companies can also reach a wider audience and increase profits without constructing more physical stores.

In conclusion, businesses should provide more online services, as this will not only allow them to enhance customers' experiences but also reduce operating costs.

解答例の訳

今日の急成長中のデジタル世界においては，企業はもっとオンラインサービスを提供すべきだと思う。そうすることによってもたらされるメリットは利便性と費用に関連している。

第一に，より多くのオンラインサービスを提供することは利便性の向上につながる。例えば，オンライン上の顧客サポートは人々に，質問があるときにはいつでも企業に連絡する手段を与える。これは，忙しい人や異なるタイムゾーン下で暮らす外国の顧客にはとりわけ有益であり得る。

さらに，オンラインサービスは企業にとって費用効果が高いものであり得る。電子商取引の増加で，オンライン上のデジタルプラットフォームへの移行は経費の削減と業務の効率化を可能にする。例えば，オンラインでの商品販売は，企業が公共料金を削減するのに役立ち得る。また，企業はより幅広い客に認知してもらうこと，および追加の実店舗を建設することなく収益を増加させることも可能だ。

結論として，企業はもっとオンラインサービスを提供すべきだ，というのもこれにより彼らは顧客体験の向上のみならず事業費の削減も可能になるからだ。

解説 TOPIC文について，「提供すべきである／提供すべきではない」のどちらかの立場に立って，自分の意見とその根拠をエッセイの形でまとめる形式。エッセイをまとめる際には，POINTSとして示されたキーワードのうち２つを選んで使用する必要がある。これらのキーワードに挙げられている語句については必要に応じて形を変えて表現したり類義語で置き換えたりしても良い。

段落構成に関する，導入（introduction）→本論（main body）→結論（conclusion）という基本的な指定は必ず守ること。解答例のように本論を２つに分ける場合は，論点の重複がないように，それぞれの段落を別の視点からまとめる。その際，各段落の論点が明確になるように，談話標識（discourse markers）を使うと論理的にまとまりのある文章となり，効果的である。また，結論をまとめるときは，第１段落の単純な繰り返しにならないよう，表現を若干でも工夫することが好ましい。

TOPIC文 「企業はもっとオンラインサービスを提供すべきですか」という質問について意見を求める内容。

語句 business「企業」/ provide「～を提供する」

第１段落（導入） まずエッセイの冒頭で，TOPIC文のテーマを正しく理解していることと，自分が「提供すべきである／提供すべきではない」のどちらの立場に立っているかを明示する必要がある。解答例では，I believe (that) ～「私は～と思う」を使って，自分が前者の立場にいることを最初に示している。また，POINTSの中からconvenience「利便性」とcost「費用」の２つを取り上げていることも明示している。

語句 fast-paced「急成長の」/ benefit「メリット」/ be related to ～「～に関係している」

第２段落（本論①） 第２段落では，順序を表す談話標識であるFirstly「第一に」から文を始め，第１段落で示した１つ目の観点である「利便性」について説明している。また，第２文では，第１文で言及した利便性向上の具体例を，For instance「例えば」という談話標識を用いて挙げ，第３文ではその恩恵を特に享受できる人々を示している。

語句 lead to ～「～につながる」/ increased「向上した」/ means「手段」/ query「質問」/ particularly「とりわけ」/ beneficial「有益な」/ time zone「タイムゾーン」

第３段落（本論②） 第３段落では，第１段落で示した２つ目の観点である「費用」について意見を展開している。追加を表すAdditionally「さらに」で始め，オンラインサービスが企業にとって費用効果が高いものであり得るという意見を先に示し，オンライン上のデジタルプラットフォームへの移行によって企業が可能となることを，費用の観点から説明している。第３文では削減できる経費の具体例を説明する文脈で，例を表すfor example「例えば」を，第４文では会社にとって可能となる他のことを説明する際に，追加を表すalsoを用いている。

語句 cost-effective「費用効果が高い」/ rise「増加」/ e-commerce「電子商取引」/ expenses「経費」/ streamline「～を能率的にする」/ operation「業務」/ utility bill「公共料金」/ physical store「実店舗」

第４段落（結論） 最終段落では，in conclusion「結論として」という談話標識から文を始めて，企業はもっとオンラインサービスを提供すべきだという結論を再度述べ，第２～３段落でそれぞれ述べた２つの観点を理由に挙げ，文章を締め括っている。

語句 enhance「～を向上させる」/ operating costs「事業費」

Part 1 一次試験・リスニング

（問題編pp.86～87）

指示文の訳 準１級の試験のリスニングテストが始まります。指示を注意して聞いてください。テスト中に質問をすることは許されていません。

このテストは３つのパートに分かれています。これら３つのパートの質問は全て選択肢の中から正解を選ぶ問題です。それぞれの質問について，問題冊子に書かれている４つの選択肢の中から最も適切な答えを選び，解答用紙の該当箇所にその答えをマークしなさい。このリスニングテストの全てのパートで，メモを取ってもかまいません。

それでは，これからPart 1の指示を行います。このパートではNo.1からNo.12まで12の会話が放送されます。それぞれの会話に続いて，質問が１つ流れます。各質問に対して，最も適切な答えを選んで解答用紙にマークする時間が10秒あります。会話と質問は１度しか読まれません。それでは，準１級のリスニングテストを始めます。

No.1 正解 2

放送文 ***A:*** Hi, Professor. Can I talk to you about my assignment? ***B:*** Sure. I was surprised when you didn't turn it in at the start of class. That's never happened before. ***A:*** My brother was in an accident, and I was at the hospital with him. ***B:*** I'm sorry to hear that. Is he OK? ***A:*** Yes, he's home now, but I didn't have time to get my assignment done. ***B:*** Well, I can let you turn it in tomorrow. How would that be? ***A:*** Great. Thank you!

Question: What will the woman probably do tomorrow?

訳 A：こんにちは，教授。課題のことで相談してもいいですか。 B：もちろんです。

あなたが授業の最初に課題を提出しなかったので，驚きました。こんなこと初めてでしたから。　A：兄が事故にあって，一緒に病院にいたんです。　B：それはお気の毒に。お兄さんは大丈夫なの？　A：ええ, 今は家にいるんですが, 課題を終わらせる時間がなくて。　B：じゃあ，明日提出ということにしてあげましょう。どうですか？　A：よかった。ありがとうございます！

質問の訳 女性は明日おそらく何をするか。

選択肢の訳 **1** 入院中の兄を見舞う。 **2** 課題を提出する。 **3** 兄に助けを求める。 **4** 新しい課題のトピックを選ぶ。

解説 1往復目のやりとりから，A（＝女性）が授業の課題を提出できなかったことについて，B（＝教授）に相談している場面。2，3往復目で，Aが「兄が事故にあって，一緒に病院にいたんです」,「課題を終わらせる時間がなくて」と，課題を提出できなかった理由をBに述べると，Bは「明日提出ということにしてあげましょう」と期限を延ばす提案をしている。これを受けてAは「よかった。ありがとうございます！」と述べているので，Aは明日課題を提出するだろうことがわかる。よって, turn itを**submit her assignment**と言い換えた**2**が正解。

No.2 正解 3

放送文 ***A:*** I can't believe the government wants to raise taxes again. ***B:*** They say it's necessary to pay for the new education plan. ***A:*** Well, it seems like there are a lot of areas in the budget that could be reduced instead. Spending on highways, for one. ***B:*** That's for sure. I read a news report just yesterday saying that few drivers are using the new highways, even though they cost billions.
A: Right. I'd write a letter to the government if I thought it'd do any good.
Question: What do these people think?

訳 A：政府がまた増税しようとしているなんて信じられないわ。　B：新教育プランのために必要なんだって。　A：あのね, その代わりに減らせる予算はたくさんあるはずよ。幹線道路への支出とかね。　B：確かにそうだね。昨日読んだニュースでは，新しい幹線道路は何十億もかかったのに, ドライバーはほとんど使っていないと言っていたよ。　A：そのとおりね。少しでもよくなるんだったら，政府に手紙でも書くんだけど。

質問の訳 この人たちはどう考えているか。

選択肢の訳 **1** 教育費がかかりすぎる。 **2** 予算はすぐに減らされそうだ。 **3** 政府は無駄遣いをしている。 **4** メディアは政府に対して不公平だ。

解説 1往復目のやりとりから，A(＝女性)とB(＝男性)が，政府の増税について話している場面。2往復目でAが「その（＝新教育プランにかかる費用の）代わりに減らせる予算はたくさんあるはずよ。幹線道路への支出とかね」と述べると，Bも「確かにそうだね」と同意し,「新しい幹線道路は何十億もかかったのに，ドライバーはほとんど使っていないと言っていたよ」と述べているので，2人とも幹線道路への支出など，政府が無駄遣いをしていると考えていることがわかる。よって，there are a lot of areas in the budget that could be reduced insteadを**wasting money**と言い換えた**3**が正解。

No.3 正解 **1**

放送文 ***A:*** Thanks for inviting me to lunch. ***B:*** Sure. I wanted to celebrate your promotion. It's too bad I won't see you as often, though, since you'll be moving to the fourth floor. ***A:*** Well, we'll still have meetings together. And maybe we could have a weekly lunch or something. ***B:*** Great idea. But you'll probably be eating at your desk a lot more often. ***A:*** That's true. I guess my workload is going to be pretty heavy. ***B:*** Yes, at least until you get used to your new position.

Question: What is one thing we learn from the conversation?

訳 A：ランチに誘ってくれてありがとう。 B：どういたしまして。あなたの昇進を祝いたかったんだ。でも，あなたが4階に異動になるから，あまり頻繁に会えなくなるのは残念だけどね。 A：まあ，それでもミーティングは一緒だし。それに，週に一度ランチでもどう？ B：いいね。でも，デスクで食べることが多くなるんじゃない？ A：そうだね。仕事の量がかなり多くなりそうだし。 B：そうだよね，少なくとも新しい役職に慣れるまではね。

質問の訳 この会話からわかることの1つは何か。

選択肢の訳 **1** 男性はずっと忙しくなるだろう。 **2** 女性はより多くの会議に出席する必要があるだろう。 **3** 女性は4階の人たちが嫌いだ。 **4** 男性は新しい役職に就きたくなかった。

解説 1往復目のやりとりから，B（＝女性）が，A（＝男性）の昇進を祝ってAをランチに誘った場面。2往復目で，Aが「(今後は）週に一度ランチでもどう？」とBに提案すると，Bは「いいね」と答えたあとで，「でも，(仕事が忙しくて）デスクで食べることが多くなるんじゃない？」と述べ，それに対しAも「そうだね。仕事の量がかなり多くなりそうだし」と述べている。よって，男性の仕事が今後かなり忙しくなるだろうことがわかるので，my workload is going to be pretty heavyを**become much busier**と言い換えた**1**が正解。

No.4 正解 **4**

放送文 ***A:*** I'm going next door to see Carol. I'll be back in an hour. ***B:*** Sure. By the way, how is she doing after her surgery? ***A:*** She's doing much better, but she still has trouble moving around. Today, I'm going to do a little cleaning and prepare some food for her that she can just heat up. ***B:*** I'm sure she appreciates your help. ***A:*** I think she does. The other day, she got me a gift certificate to a spa so I can get a massage.

Question: Why is the woman visiting her neighbor?

訳 A：隣のキャロルに会いに行ってくるね。1時間で戻るよ。 B：わかった。ところで彼女の手術後の様子はどうなの？ A：だいぶ良くなっているけど，まだ動き回るのが大変みたい。今日は少し掃除をして，温めるだけでできる食事を用意してあげようと思っているんだ。 B：彼女はきっと君の助けに感謝していると思うよ。 A：そうだと思うよ。この間，マッサージが受けられるスパのギフト券を買ってくれたの。

質問の訳 なぜ女性は隣人を訪ねるのか。

選択肢の訳 **1** 彼女にマッサージをしてあげるため。 **2** 食べ物を買うため。

3 彼女に商品券をあげるため。 **4** 家事をするため。

解説 1往復目でB（＝男性）が「彼女（＝隣人のキャロル）の手術後の様子はどうなの？」とたずねると，A（＝女性）は「だいぶ良くなっているけど，まだ動き回るのが大変みたい」と述べたあと，「今日は少し掃除をして，温めるだけでできる食事を用意してあげようと思っているんだ」と述べている。よって，Aが手術後のキャロルを気づかって，キャロルの家事を手伝ってあげている状況であることがわかるので，do a little cleaning and prepare some food for her that she can just heat upを**do some housework**と言い換えた**4**が正解。

No.5 正解 **3**

放送文 ***A:*** Alan, the printer is giving me that error message again. ***B:*** Are you sure the paper is the right size? ***A:*** Of course. I've checked it several times. ***B:*** This is ridiculous. We just bought that printer two weeks ago. I'll call the computer shop and ask them to replace it. ***A:*** I think we should try to get a refund instead. I've seen reviews saying this brand's printers frequently need to be repaired. ***B:*** OK, I'll look into it. We can use our old one until we decide which model we want to buy.

Question: What will the man probably do first?

訳 A：アラン，プリンターがまたエラーメッセージを出しているんだけど。 B：用紙のサイズが合ってるか確認した？ A：もちろん。何度も確認したわ。 B：馬鹿げているよ。そのプリンターは2週間前に買ったばかりなのに。コンピューターショップに電話して交換してもらうよ。 A：返金してもらったほうがいいんじゃない？ このブランドのプリンターは頻繁に修理が必要だというレビューを見たことがあるのよ。 B：わかった，調べてみるよ。どの機種を買うか決めるまで，古い機種を使えばいいんだし。

質問の訳 男性はおそらくまず何をするか。

選択肢の訳 **1** プリンターを交換してくれるように店に依頼する。 **2** 古いプリンターを修理してもらう。 **3** 店から返金してもらうようにする。 **4** 店に行って他の機種を確認する。

解説 1～2往復目のやりとりから，たびたびエラーメッセージが出て，2週間前に買ったばかりのプリンターの調子がよくない状況であることがわかる。2往復目でB（＝Alan）が「コンピューターショップに電話して交換してもらうよ」と述べたのに対し，A（＝女性）が「返金してもらったほうがいいんじゃない？」と提案すると，Bは「わかった」と同意し，「(返金してもらうにはどうすればいいか)調べてみるよ」と述べている。よって，男性はプリンターを返品して店から返金してもらうことを考えていることがわかるので，get a refundを**get money back from the shop**と言い換えた**3**が正解。

No.6 正解 **2**

放送文 ***A:*** How was your business trip to Tokyo last week? ***B:*** It was a disaster. ***A:*** What happened? Did the client back out of the deal? ***B:*** No, but their lawyer objected to the wording of the contract, and there was a big delay while we modified the text. Then, before we could finalize the deal, we had an emergency at headquarters, and I had to return immediately. ***A:*** That's awful.

B: Yes. I'm going to have to go back to Tokyo in a couple of weeks.
Question: What was one problem the man had during his trip?

訳 A：先週の東京出張はどうだった？　B：最悪だったよ。　A：何があったの？クライアントが契約から手を引いたとか？　B：そうじゃないけど，先方の弁護士が契約書の文言に異議を唱えて，文章を修正している間に，大幅な遅れが生じちゃったんだ。その後，契約をまとめる前に本社で緊急事態が発生しちゃって，ぼくはすぐに戻らなければならなかったんだ。　A：それは大変だったね。　B：うん。2週間後に，また東京に戻らなければならないんだ。

質問の訳 男性が出張中に困ったことの1つは何だったか。

選択肢の訳 **1**　クライアントが契約をキャンセルした。　**2**　契約書を修正する必要があった。　**3**　弁護士は重大なミスを犯した。　**4**　彼は重要な会議に遅刻した。

解説 1往復目でB（＝男性）が「（東京出張は）最悪だったよ」と述べたのに対し，2往復目でA（＝女性）が「何があったの？」とたずねている。これに対してBは「先方の弁護士が契約書の文言に異議を唱えて，文章を修正している間に，大幅な遅れが生じちゃったんだ」と述べ，さらに「契約をまとめる前に本社で緊急事態が発生しちゃって，ぼくはすぐに戻らなければならなかったんだ」とも述べている。よって，Bは東京出張中に，契約書の修正を迫られたが，契約前に本社に戻らなければならない状況になり困ったことがわかるので，modified the textを**to be revised**と言い換えた**2**が正解。

No.7　正解　**4**

放送文 ***A:*** Hi, Nick. How's your new job going? ***B:*** Well, it's taking me a while to adjust. ***A:*** Are your responsibilities very different from your last job? ***B:*** No, but my boss is. She always says she's going to do things but then forgets about them! I'm constantly having to remind her about deadlines. ***A:*** That sounds frustrating. ***B:*** It sure is. Still, at least she isn't bothering me about my work. ***A:*** I guess things could be worse.
Question: What does the man say about his new job?

訳 A：こんにちは，ニック。新しい仕事はどう？　B：そうだな，慣れるのに少し時間がかかっているかな。　A：前の仕事とは責務が大きく違うの？　B：いや，でも上司が違うんだ。彼女はいつもやるって言うんだけど，それを忘れちゃうんだ！　ぼくはいつも彼女に期限の念押しをしなければならないんだ。　A：それはイライラしそうだね。　B：そうなんだよ。それでも，少なくとも彼女はぼくの仕事のことで煩わせることはないんだけどね。　A：状況がさらに悪化する可能性もあると思うよ。

質問の訳 男性は新しい仕事について何と言っているか。

選択肢の訳 **1**　上司が彼を信用していない。　**2**　締め切りが非常に厳しい。　**3**　必要なスキルが不足している。　**4**　上司がきちんとしていない。

解説 1往復目のやりとりから，B（＝Nick）の新しい仕事についての会話。2往復目でA（＝女性）から，「（新しい仕事は）前の仕事とは責務が大きく違うの？」とたずねられたBは，「いや，でも上司が違うんだ」と答えたあと，「彼女（＝新しい上司）はいつもやるって言うんだけど，それを忘れちゃうんだ！」と述べ，さらに「ぼくはいつも彼女に期限の念押しをしなければならないんだ」とも述べている。よって，Bは，上司がやるべきことや期限をよく忘れたりして，きちんとしていないことにイライラしていることがわかるので，forgets about themを**not well organized**と言い換えた**4**が正解。

No.8 正解 3

放送文 ***A:*** I'm thinking we should replace the sofa soon. It's getting pretty worn out. ***B:*** Do you want to check out that new furniture store down the road? ***A:*** Nah, I was thinking of just getting one online. That's usually much cheaper. ***B:*** Really? I'd rather we try a sofa out before actually buying it. ***A:*** I suppose you're right. Our budget isn't very large, though, so we'll probably have to put off the purchase until the store offers some discounts. ***B:*** Let's look around some other stores, too. They might have some good deals on.

Question: What will the couple probably do?

訳 A：そろそろソファーを買い換えた方がいいんじゃないかと思っているんだ。だいぶくたびれてきたし。 B：道路沿いにある新しい家具屋さんに行ってみる？ A：いや，ネットで買おうと思っているんだ。たいていは，そのほうがずっと安いよ。 B：そうなの？ 実際に買う前にソファーを試してみたいな。 A：君の言うとおりだね。とはいえ，予算はそれほど多くないから，お店が値引きしてくれるまで買うのは見送ることになりそうだね。 B：他の店もいくつか見てみようよ。掘り出し物があるかもしれないよ。

質問の訳 夫婦はおそらくどうするか。

選択肢の訳 **1** すぐに新しいソファーを手に入れる。 **2** ネットでソファーを購入する。 **3** セール中のソファーを探す。 **4** 今使っているソファーを修理する。

解説 1往復目のA(＝男性)の発言から，ソファーの買い替えについて話している場面とわかる。1往復目でB(＝女性)が道路沿いにある新しい家具屋に行くことを提案すると，Aは「いや，ネットで買おうと思っているんだ」と述べている。しかし，Bが「実際に買う前にソファーを試してみたいな」と言うと，Aも「君の言うとおりだね」と同意し，「お店が値引きしてくれるまで買うのは見送ることになりそうだね」と述べている。さらに，Bも「他の店もいくつか見てみようよ。掘り出し物があるかもしれないよ」と述べているので，夫婦は値引きされたソファーを探すつもりであることがわかるので，some discountsを**on sale**と言い換えた**3**が正解。

No.9 正解 3

放送文 ***A:*** It's so warm today! Hard to believe it's February. I could even go for some ice cream. ***B:*** Today is lovely, but the weather report says we may get a big snowstorm this weekend. ***A:*** Are you kidding? That would be a temperature drop of nearly 20 degrees. ***B:*** We'd better check how much food and water we have and go to the grocery store if necessary. ***A:*** Good idea. After getting snowed in at our cabin last year, I want to make sure we're stocked up just in case.

Question: What does the man suggest?

訳 A：今日はすごく暖かいね！ 2月とは思えない。アイスクリームでも食べに行きたいくらいよ。 B：今日はいい天気だけど，天気予報によると週末は大雪になるかもしれないみたいだよ。 A：冗談でしょう？ 気温が20度近く下がることになるわ。 B：食べ物と水の量を確認して，必要なら食料品店に行っておいたほうがいいね。 A：いい考えね。去年は山小屋で雪に見舞われたから，念のため備蓄はしておきたいわね。

質問の訳 男性は何を提案しているか。

選択肢の訳 **1** 天気予報をチェックする。 **2** 週末に山小屋に行く。 **3** 緊急のための物資を準備する。 **4** アイスクリームを食べに行く。

解説 1往復目でB（＝男性）は「天気予報によると週末は大雪になるかもしれないみたいだよ」と述べ，2往復目では「(大雪に備えて）食べ物と水の量を確認して，必要なら食料品店に行っておいたほうがいいね」と提案している。よって，check how much food and water we have and go to the grocery store if necessaryを**preparing emergency supplies**と言い換えた**3**が正解。

No.10 正解 1

放送文 ***A:*** Good morning, Ms. Redfield. I just got a call from Irene. She says she needs to take a half day off this morning. ***B:*** Again? That's the second time this week. ***A:*** Yes. I'm a bit worried. She's also been late quite a few times in the last couple of months. ***B:*** She's quite skilled with computers, though, and the clients seem very satisfied with her. I *am* concerned about her motivation, however. It might be best to have a talk with her, in case she's considering leaving the company. ***A:*** I'll set up a meeting.

Question: What does the woman imply about Irene?

訳 A：おはようございます，レッドフィールドさん。アイリーンから電話がありました。今朝は半休を取りたいそうです。 B：またですか？ 今週2回目ですよ。 A：はい。ちょっと心配しています。ここ数か月，彼女は何度も遅刻しているし。 B：彼女はコンピューターの扱いにはかなり長けているし，クライアントもとても満足しているようですけどね。ただ，彼女のモチベーションが心配ですね。万が一退職を考えているようなら，一度話をしたほうがいいかもしれませんね。 A：面談の機会を設けます。

質問の訳 女性はアイリーンについて何をほのめかしているか。

選択肢の訳 **1** 仕事への熱意を欠いている。 **2** 解雇されるだろう。 **3** クライアントに不評だ。 **4** コンピューターのスキルを向上させる必要がある。

解説 1～2往復目のやりとりから，A（＝男性）とB（＝Ms. Redfield）が，アイリーンの勤務態度について懸念を抱いている場面。1往復目でBは「また（半休）ですか？今週2回目ですよ」と述べ，Aが「ここ数か月，彼女は何度も遅刻している」と述べると，Bは「彼女のモチベーションが心配ですね」と述べている。よって，Bは，遅刻や半休を繰り返すアイリーンは仕事への熱意を欠いていると感じていることがわかるので，concerned about her motivationを**lacks enthusiasm for her job**と言い換えた**1**が正解。

No.11 正解 4

放送文 ***A:*** Hey, Jack! How was your trip to the Yucatán? ***B:*** Great. Check out these paintings I picked up. ***A:*** Wow! They're gorgeous! Did you find them at a local gallery? ***B:*** No, I got them from artists at local markets, and they were unbelievably cheap. ***A:*** Well, you should get better frames for them before you put them on the wall. ***B:*** Actually, I looked into that today. They cost 10 times what the paintings did, so I'm hesitant. ***A:*** I really think they deserve better than these cheap frames, don't you?

Question: What does the woman say about the paintings?

訳 A：あら，ジャック！　ユカタンへの旅はどうだった？　B：すばらしかったよ。ぼくが買ったこの絵を見て。　A：わあ！　とってもすてきね！　地元のギャラリーで見つけたの？　B：いいや，地元のマーケットでアーティストから買ったんだけど，信じられないくらい安かったよ。　A：ええと，壁に飾る前に，もっといい額縁を買ったほうがいいと思うわ。　B：実は今日，それを調べてみたんだ。額縁は絵の10倍もするから，ちょっと躊躇してるんだ。　A：こんな安っぽい額縁より，もっといい額縁で飾ったほうが絶対いいと思うわ。

質問の訳 女性はその絵について何と言っているか。

選択肢の訳 **1**　男性は絵を売って利益を得ようとするべきだ。　**2**　絵は画廊に飾られるべきだ。　**3**　男性は絵の価値を知るべきだ。　**4**　絵は適切に展示されるべきだ。

解説 1往復目のやりとりから，B（＝Jack）が旅行で買った絵をA（＝女性）に見せている場面だとわかる。2往復目でAは「わあ！　とってもすてきね！」と述べ，3往復目では「壁に飾る前に，もっといい額縁を買ったほうがいいと思うわ」，さらに4往復目でも「こんな安っぽい額縁より，もっといい額縁で飾ったほうが絶対いいと思うわ」と述べている。よって，Aは，その絵はとても美しく，その美しさにふさわしい額縁で展示すべきだとBに伝えていることがわかるので，should get better frames for themやdeserve better than these cheap framesを**displayed properly**と言い換えた**4**が正解。

No.12　正解　2

放送文 ***A:*** Hey, Joseph? There's no water coming from the faucet. ***B:*** Oh, right, they're inspecting the pipes down the street. ***A:*** What? That's news to me. ***B:*** Sorry, I forgot to tell you. There won't be any water until 7 p.m. We got a couple of notices about it while you were out of town. ***A:*** Why didn't you tell me earlier? I wanted to wash some clothes tonight for work tomorrow. ***B:*** I'm sorry. I did prepare some bottles of water, so we have enough for cooking and drinking.
A: That's something, at least.

Question: Why does the man apologize to the woman?

訳 A：ねえ，ジョセフ？　蛇口から水が出ないんだけど。　B：そうなんだよ，通りの水道管を点検してるんだ。　A：え？　それは初耳だよ。　B：ごめん，言うの忘れてた。午後7時まで水は出ないんだ。君が留守の間に何度か水道管点検についてのお知らせがあったんだ。　A：どうしてもっと早く言ってくれなかったの？　明日の仕事のために，今夜服を洗濯したかったのに。　B：ごめん。水のボトルを何本か用意したから，料理をしたり飲んだりするのには十分な水はあるんだ。　A：ともかく，それは良かったわ。

質問の訳 なぜ男性は女性に謝るのか。

選択肢の訳 **1**　水筒に水を入れるのを忘れた。　**2**　水が止まることを彼女に言わなかった。　**3**　水道管点検のお知らせをなくしてしまった。　**4**　水道管を傷つけた。

解説 1往復目でB（＝Joseph）から，通りの水道管の点検で断水していることを聞いたA（＝女性）は，「え？　それは初耳だよ」と述べ，それに対してBが「ごめん，言うの忘れてた。午後7時まで水は出ないんだ。君が留守の間に何度か水道管点検についてのお知らせがあったんだ」と謝っている。よって，Bは水道管点検で断水になるのをAに言い忘れていたことを謝っていることがわかるので，forgot to tell youを**did not tell her**と，また

there won't be any water を **the water would be turned off** と言い換えた **2** が正解。

CD 青-40 ～ CD 青-46

Part 2 一次試験・リスニング
(問題編pp.88～89)

指示文の訳 それでは，これからPart 2の指示を行います。このパートでは(A)から(F)までの６つの文章が放送されます。それぞれの文章に続いて，No.13からNo.24まで質問が２つずつ流れます。それぞれの質問に対して，最も適切な答えを選んで解答用紙にマークする時間が10秒あります。文章と質問は１度しか読まれません。それでは始めます。

(A)

放送文 *The Three Sisters*

For centuries, Native Americans all over North America grew corn, beans, and squash, which were often called the Three Sisters. The Three Sisters were planted together because of the strong benefits that the combination brings. When beans are grown with corn, the corn provides support for the beans as they climb up to get more sunlight. Additionally, squash keeps weeds away, and beans increase the amount of the beneficial chemical nitrogen in the soil. To make the combination work, however, planting each crop at the time when it will most help the others is essential.

In the distant past, Native American farmers were even able to grow the Three Sisters in the desert areas of the American southwest, but, unfortunately, most of this knowledge has been lost. Some Native Americans are currently working to rediscover the techniques that would allow them to grow the vegetables in very dry conditions.

Questions ***No.13*** What is one thing that we learn about growing the Three Sisters?

No.14 What are some Native Americans trying to do now?

訳 スリー・シスターズ

何世紀にもわたり，北米中のネイティブ・アメリカンたちは，トウモロコシ，マメ，カボチャを栽培していたが，それらはしばしばスリー・シスターズと呼ばれていた。スリー・シスターズが一緒に植えられたのは，この組み合わせがもたらす強いメリットのためである。トウモロコシと一緒に豆を栽培すると，トウモロコシは，マメがより多くの日光を浴びるためによじ登る際の支えとなる。さらに，カボチャは雑草を寄せ付けず，マメは土壌中の有益な化学物質である窒素の量を増やす。ただし，この組み合わせをうまく機能させるには，それぞれの作物が他の作物に最も役立つ時期に植えることが不可欠である。

遠い昔，ネイティブ・アメリカンの農民たちは，アメリカ南西部の砂漠地帯でスリー・シスターズを栽培することさえできていたが，残念なことに，この知識はほとんど失われてしまった。現在，一部のネイティブ・アメリカンたちが，非常に乾燥した条件下でも野菜を栽培できるであろうその技術を再発見しようと努力している。

No.13 正解 1

質問の訳 スリー・シスターズの栽培についてわかることの1つは何か。

選択肢の訳 **1** それぞれの作物がいつ植えられるかが重要だ。 **2** 北アメリカのごく限られた地域でしか育たない。 **3** 雑草に打ち勝つのが難しい。 **4** 植物と植物の間にスペースが必要だ。

解説 スリー・シスターズの栽培について，第1段落第2文で「スリー・シスターズが一緒に植えられたのは，この組み合わせがもたらす強いメリットのためである」と述べたうえで，第1段落最終文で「ただし，この組み合わせをうまく機能させるには，それぞれの作物が他の作物に最も役立つ時期に植えることが不可欠である」と述べられている。よって，スリー・シスターズのそれぞれの作物が植えられる時期が重要であることがわかるので，planting each crop at the time when it will most help the othersをWhen each of the crops is plantedと，またessentialをimportantと言い換えた**1**が正解。

No.14 正解 4

質問の訳 今，一部のネイティブ・アメリカンの人々は何をやろうとしているか。

選択肢の訳 **1** より近代的な栽培技術を用いる。 **2** 砂漠で栽培できる新しい植物を見つける。 **3** スリー・シスターズの育て方を他の人に教える。 **4** 忘れられた栽培方法を回復する。

解説 今，一部のネイティブ・アメリカンの人々がやろうとしていることについて，第2段落最終文で「現在，一部のネイティブ・アメリカンたちが，非常に乾燥した条件下でも野菜を栽培できるであろうその技術を再発見しようと努力している」と述べられている。よって，rediscoverをrecoverと，またthe techniques that would allow them to grow the vegetables in very dry conditionsをgrowing methodsと言い換えた**4**が正解。

(B)

放送文 *Children in Cities*

In previous generations, children generally had more freedom to explore their surroundings. These days, parents commonly prohibit children from taking walks, crossing streets, or even playing at playgrounds unsupervised. Author Tim Gill argues children today would benefit from being allowed to do things on their own. However, he acknowledges that since modern cities have become increasingly dangerous places, it is difficult for parents to avoid setting strict rules for children.

Gill believes design is the key to making cities child friendly. Cities are currently designed to allow people to travel easily by car, but cars are one of the greatest threats to children's safety. Rather than simply building more playground spaces, Gill wants to make cities safer for children to move through. While completely rebuilding cities is not realistic in the short term, Gill suggests that easier measures such as turning streets into car-free zones for a short time each week could have immediate benefits.

Questions ***No.15*** What does Tim Gill imply about modern parents?

No.16 What is one thing Gill suggests that cities do?

訳 都市の子どもたち

以前の世代では，子どもたちはたいていはもっと自由に周囲を探検していた。最近では，親は子どもたちに，散歩したり通りを渡ったり，監視のない遊び場で遊んだりすることさえ禁じている。著述家のティム・ギルは，現代の子どもたちは，自分で何かをすることを許された方が有益だと主張する。しかしながら彼は，現代の都市はますます危険な場所になっているため，親が子どもたちに厳しいルールを設けないようにするのは難しいとも認めている。

ギルは，デザインこそが子どもに優しい都市を作るカギだと考えている。現在，都市は人々が車で簡単に移動できるように設計されているが，車は子どもたちの安全にとって最大の脅威のひとつである。ギルは，単に遊び場を増やすのではなく，子どもたちがより安全に移動できる都市にしたいと考えている。都市を完全に再構築することは短期的には現実的ではないが，毎週短時間，道路を自動車乗り入れ禁止区域にするなどの簡単な対策で，すぐに効果が得られるとギルは提案している。

No.15 正解 **2**

質問の訳 現代の親について，ティム・ギルは何を暗示しているか。

選択肢の訳 **1** 子どもの安全を十分に考えていない。 **2** しばしば子どもに厳しいルールを設けることを強いられる。 **3** 子どもと過ごす時間をもっと増やすべきだ。 **4** 子どもにいろいろな経験をさせている。

解説 現代の親に関するティム・ギルの考えについて，第1段落第3文では「ティム・ギルは，現代の子どもたちは，自分で何かをすることを許された方が有益だと主張する」と述べられている一方，次の文では「彼（＝ティム・ギル）は～親が子どもたちに厳しいルールを設けないようにするのは難しいとも認めている」と述べられている。よって，ティム・ギルは，やむを得ないながらも，親が子どもに厳しいルールを設けている現状があると考えていることがわかるので，setting strict rules for childrenを**set strict rules for their children**と表した**2**が正解。

No.16 正解 **1**

質問の訳 ギルが都市に提案していることの1つは何か。

選択肢の訳 **1** 通りが自動車通行禁止になる時間を設定する。 **2** 遊び場から駐車場をなくす。 **3** 都市の中心部の外側に新しい道路を作る。 **4** デザインを変えて車をより安全にする。

解説 ギルが都市に提案していることについて，第2段落最終文で「毎週短時間，道路を自動車乗り入れ禁止区域にするなどの簡単な対策で，すぐに効果が得られるとギルは提案している」と述べられている。ギルは，通りが自動車通行禁止になる時間を設定することを提案していることがわかるので，turning streets into car-free zones for a short timeを**set times when streets are closed to cars**と言い換えた**1**が正解。

(C)

放送文 *Art in the Amazon*

An enormous collection of primitive paintings discovered in the Amazon jungle is causing debate among scientists. Thousands of images have been discovered on rock walls, and the team of researchers who discovered them believe that they include representations of extinct creatures that disappeared after the Ice Age ended. If so, the artists may have been the first humans ever to reach the Amazon region, arriving before it was covered in rain forest. Many of the larger animals appear to be surrounded by men with their hands raised in the air, and it is suspected the animals were being worshipped.

Other scientists, however, have expressed doubts regarding the age of the paintings. Since the images are extremely well-preserved, these critics believe it is likely they were painted centuries rather than millennia ago. Furthermore, since the images lack detail, the scientists argue that they might represent creatures brought to the Americas by Europeans.

Questions No.17 What does the team of researchers believe about the paintings?

No.18 What do some other scientists think about the paintings?

訳 アマゾンのアート

アマゾンのジャングルで発見された原始絵画の膨大なコレクションが，科学者たちの間で議論を呼んでいる。岩壁に描かれた何千枚もの絵が発見され，発見者の研究チームは，それらには氷河期が終わった後に姿を消した絶滅生物の絵が含まれていると考えている。もしそうだとすれば，それを描いた画家たちは，熱帯雨林に覆われる前にアマゾン地域に到達した最初の人類だったのかもしれない。大きな動物の多くは，両手を上げた男性たちに囲まれているように見え，動物が崇拝されていたのではないかと推測されている。

しかし，他の科学者たちは，その絵の年代について疑問を呈している。これらの絵は非常に保存状態が良いので，批評家たちは，数千年前ではなく数世紀前に描かれた可能性が高いと考えているのだ。さらに，この絵は細部まで描かれていないため，科学者たちは，ヨーロッパ人がアメリカ大陸に持ち込んだ生物を表しているのではないかと主張している。

No.17 正解 3

質問の訳 研究者のチームはこの絵についてどう考えているか。

選択肢の訳 **1** 熱帯雨林がどのように形成されたかを説明している。 **2** 初期の人類がどのような姿をしていたかを示している。 **3** 絶滅した生物を含んでいる。 **4** 宗教的な儀式に使われた。

解説 研究者のチームのこの絵に関する考えについて，第１段落第２文では「岩壁に描かれた何千枚もの絵が発見され，発見者の研究チームは，それらには氷河期が終わった後に姿を消した絶滅生物の絵が含まれていると考えている」と述べられている。よって，extinct creatures that disappearedを**creatures that have died out**と言い換えた**3**が正解。

No.18 正解 4

質問の訳 他の科学者たちはこの絵についてどう考えているか。

選択肢の訳 **1** 保存する必要はない。 **2** おそらくヨーロッパ人によって作られた。 **3** 昔はもっと細かく描かれていた。 **4** 何千年も前のものではない。

解説 他の科学者たちのこの絵に関する考えについて，第２段落第１文で「他の科学者

たちは，その絵の年代について疑問を呈している」と述べられ，次の文でも「数千年前ではなく数世紀前に描かれた可能性が高いと考えている」と述べられている。よって doubts regarding the age of the paintingsを**not thousands of years old**と言い換えた**4**が正解。

(D)

放送文 *Milton Berle*

Milton Berle was one of America's most famous comedians. He was successful on stage and in films, and in the 1940s, he began hosting one of the world's first television programs. Berle's variety show was known for its silly comedy and wide range of guest performers. Televisions were rare luxury items when it began, but the program was such an incredible hit that it became a driving reason behind the huge increase in TV ownership.

As well as his pioneering work as an entertainer, Berle also fought for civil rights, famously helping to break down barriers against Black performers appearing on TV. When an advertiser tried to prevent a Black dance group from appearing on his show, Berle refused to perform until the advertiser gave in and the dancers were allowed on. Berle also set a record for appearing in more charity performances than any other performer.

Questions No.19 What is one thing that we learn about Milton Berle's TV show?

No.20 What is one thing Berle was known for?

訳 ミルトン・バール

ミルトン・バールはアメリカで最も有名なコメディアンの一人だった。舞台や映画で成功を収め，1940年代には，世界最初のテレビ番組の1つの司会を始めた。バールのバラエティ番組は，おバカなコメディと幅広いゲスト出演者で知られていた。番組が始まった当時，テレビは稀少な高級品だったが，この番組は驚異的なヒットを記録し，テレビの所有者が激増する原動力となった。

エンターテイナーとしての先駆的な仕事だけでなく，バールは公民権運動のためにも闘い，黒人のパフォーマーがテレビに出演するのを阻む障壁を取り除くのに貢献したことでも有名である。ある広告主が，黒人ダンスグループが彼のショーに出演するのを阻止しようとしたとき，広告主が折れてダンサーたちの出演が認められるまで，バールは出演を拒否した。バールはまた，どのパフォーマーよりも多くのチャリティー・パフォーマンスに出演した記録も作った。

No.19 正解 **4**

質問の訳 ミルトン・バールのテレビ番組についてわかることの1つは何か。

選択肢の訳 **1** 人気のある映画が原作だった。 **2** たくさんの豪華商品をプレゼントした。 **3** 毎週お笑いコンテストがあった。 **4** 多くの人がテレビを買うきっかけになった。

解説 ミルトン・バールのテレビ番組について，第1段落最終文で「番組が始まった当時，テレビは稀少な高級品だったが，この番組は驚異的なヒットを記録し，テレビの所有者が激増する原動力となった」と述べられており，ミルトン・バールのテレビ番組を見るために，当時は稀少な高級品だったテレビを多くの人々が買うようになったことがわかる。よって，became a driving reason behind the huge increase in TV ownershipを**led many people to buy TV sets**と言い換えた**4**が正解。

No.20 正解 2

質問の訳 バールが有名だったことの1つは何か。

選択肢の訳 **1** 黒人パフォーマーを支援するチャリティーを始めたこと。 **2** テレビ業界における人種差別と闘ったこと。 **3** 彼が制作したユニークな広告。 **4** 素晴らしいダンスの技能。

解説 バールが有名だったことについて，第2段落第1文では「バールは公民権運動のためにも闘い，黒人のパフォーマーがテレビに出演するのを阻む障壁を取り除くのに貢献したことでも有名である」と述べられ，次の文でも，黒人ダンスグループの出演を広告主が阻止しようとしたとき，そのグループの出演が認められるまで，バールが出演を拒否したことが述べられている。よって，break down barriers against Black performers appearing on TVを**fighting racism in the TV industry**と言い換えた**2**が正解。

(E)

放送文 *Déjà Vu*

The term "déjà vu" refers to a person's feeling that they have already experienced the situation they are currently in. While causes for déjà vu have been proposed since the nineteenth century, little research was done on it until the 2000s, when the scientist Alan Brown studied the phenomenon. He found that people experience it less as they age and that it is usually triggered by a location or setting.

More recently, researchers used virtual reality to study déjà vu. They had subjects enter virtual environments, such as bowling alleys or subway stations. Some of these spaces were laid out similarly—for example, pieces of furniture with similar shapes but different appearances were arranged in the same positions. The researchers found subjects were more likely to feel déjà vu when entering new spaces that were organized like spaces they had previously entered. Still, they say this is likely just one of many factors that cause déjà vu.

Questions ***No.21*** What was one of Alan Brown's findings about déjà vu?

No.22 In the virtual reality study, what led some subjects to experience déjà vu?

訳 デジャヴ

デジャヴとは，現在自分が置かれている状況をすでに経験したことがあると感じることを指す。デジャヴの原因は19世紀から提唱されているが，2000年代に科学者のアラン・ブラウンがこの現象を研究するまで，ほとんど研究されていなかった。ブラウンは，年齢を重ねるにつれてデジャヴを体験することが減少すること，そしてデジャヴは通常，場所や設定によって引き起こされることを発見した。

最近では，研究者たちがバーチャル・リアリティーを使ってデジャヴを研究した。彼らは，被験者にボーリング場や地下鉄の駅などのバーチャルな環境に入ってもらった。これらの

スペースのいくつかは，例えば，形は似ているが見た目は異なる家具が同じ位置に配置されているなど，同じようにレイアウトされていた。研究者たちは，被験者が以前入ったことのある空間と同じように構成された新しい空間に入るとデジャヴを感じやすいことを発見した。しかし，研究者たちは，これはデジャヴを引き起こす多くの要因のひとつに過ぎない可能性が高いと言っている。

No.21 正解 1

質問の訳 アラン・ブラウンのデジャヴについての発見の１つは何だったか。

選択肢の訳 **1** 若い人にほどよく起こる。 **2** 以前の研究では，主に男性を被験者としていた。 **3** 19世紀以降により多く見られるようになった。 **4** 人々はしばしば他の感情と間違える。

解説 アラン・ブラウンのデジャヴについての発見について，第１段落第３文では「ブラウンは，年齢を重ねるにつれてデジャヴを体験することが減少すること～を発見した」と述べられており，ブラウンは，年を取るほどデジャヴを体験することが減少し，逆に，若い人ほどよくデジャヴを体験することを発見したことがわかる。よって，experience it less as they ageを**occurs more often when people are younger**と言い換えた**1**が正解。

No.22 正解 4

質問の訳 バーチャル・リアリティーの研究で，一部の被験者にデジャヴを体験させたものは何だったか。

選択肢の訳 **1** 大きな公共の場所を探索すること。 **2** 全く同じ家具が置かれた空間を見ること。 **3** 異なる空間で同じ行動をすること。 **4** 見慣れたレイアウトの空間に入ること。

解説 バーチャル・リアリティーの研究について，第２段落第４文では「研究者たちは，被験者が以前入ったことのある空間と同じように構成された新しい空間に入るとデジャヴを感じやすいことを発見した」と述べられており，被験者が見慣れたレイアウトの空間に入るとデジャヴを体験しやすいことがわかる。よって，new spaces that were organized like spaces they had previously enteredを**a space with a familiar layout**と言い換えた**4**が正解。

(F)

放送文 *The English Longbow*

During medieval times, one of the deadliest weapons used by English armies was the longbow. About two meters in length, this powerful weapon allowed an archer to fire extremely rapidly, shooting up to six arrows per minute. A variety of arrows were used, such as the bodkin and the broadhead. The bodkin arrow was the most common, and its narrow tip could pass through most kinds of armor. The larger broadheads, on the other hand, caused more-devastating wounds to lightly armored enemies.

Though highly effective, the longbow required years of practice to master. Since it was an essential tool for English armies, King Henry VIII even passed a law requiring that all healthy males train regularly in its use. Examinations of the skeletons of longbowmen have found that this training actually altered them physically. Bones in their arms became thickened, and their spines became twisted through constant use of the bow.

Questions ***No.23*** What is one thing that we learn about bodkin arrows?

No.24 What does the speaker say about King Henry VIII?

訳 イングランドの長弓

中世の時代，イングランド軍が使用した最も致命的な武器のひとつが長弓だった。長さ約2メートルのこの強力な武器は，1分間に最大6本の矢を放つという極めて速い射撃を可能にした。ボドキンやブロードヘッドなど，さまざまな矢が使われた。ボドキン矢は最も一般的で，先端が細く，ほとんどの鎧を貫くことができた。一方，大型のブロードヘッドは，軽装甲の敵に致命的な傷を負わせた。

長弓は非常に効果的ではあったが，使いこなすには長年の練習が必要だった。イングランド軍にとって必要不可欠な道具であったため，ヘンリー8世は，健康な男子は全員，長弓の使い方を定期的に訓練することを義務づける法律まで制定した。長弓使いの骨格を調べたところ，この訓練が彼らに実際に肉体的な変化をもたらしたことがわかった。腕の骨は太くなり，背骨は弓を使い続けることでねじれたのだった。

No.23 正解 2

質問の訳 ボドキン矢についてわかることの1つは何か。

選択肢の訳 **1** 他の矢よりも速く飛ぶ。 **2** 鎧に有効だった。 **3** 最も長いタイプの矢だった。 **4** 一般的に鋼鉄で作られていた。

解説 ボドキン矢について，第1段落第4文では「先端が細く，ほとんどの鎧を貫くことができた」と述べられており，ボドキン矢が鎧に有効だったことがわかる。よって，could pass through most kinds of armorを**effective against armor**と言い換えた**2**が正解。

No.24 正解 1

質問の訳 話者はヘンリー8世について何と言っているか。

選択肢の訳 **1** 男性たちに長弓を使う練習をさせた。 **2** 長弓を射る名人だった。 **3** 長弓の攻撃で大怪我をした。 **4** 外国の軍隊に長弓を売った。

解説 ヘンリー8世について，話者は第2段落第2文で「ヘンリー8世は，健康な男子は全員，長弓の使い方を定期的に訓練することを義務づける法律まで制定した」と述べており，ヘンリー8世が男性たちに長弓を使う練習をさせたことがわかる。よって，passed a law requiring that all healthy males train regularly in its useを**forced men to practice using longbows**と言い換えた**1**が正解。

CD 青-47 〜 CD 青-52

Part 3 一次試験・リスニング

(問題編pp.90〜91)

指示文の訳 それでは最後に，Part 3の指示を行います。このパートでは(G)から(K)までの5つの文章が放送されます。英文は実生活における状況を述べたもので，効果音を含むものもあります。それぞれの文章には，No.25からNo.29まで，質問が１問ずつ用意されています。それぞれの文章が流れる前に，問題冊子に書かれている状況の説明と質問を読む時間が10秒あります。文章を聞いた後に，最も適切な答えを選んで解答用紙にマークする時間が10秒あります。文章は１度しか読まれません。それでは始めます。

No.25 正解 **2**

放送文 *(G)* You have 10 seconds to read the situation and Question No.25.

OK, the Western is an all-leather backpack. It converts to a briefcase, so it's great for business environments. It's a bit heavy, though, so I wouldn't use it on long walks. The Dangerfield is a waxed canvas backpack that's water-resistant, so it's great for outdoor activities. It's also handsome enough for the office. The Spartan is also made of waxed canvas. It's very functional but a bit too sporty for professional contexts. The Winfield is a similar bag, but it's made of water-resistant leather. The thin strap can make it uncomfortable to carry for extended periods of time, though.

Now mark your answer on your answer sheet.

訳 *(G)* 状況と質問25を読む時間が10秒あります。

はい，ウエスタンはオールレザーのバックパックです。ブリーフケースに変形するので，ビジネスシーンに最適です。でもちょっと重いので，長く歩くときには使いません。デインジャーフィールドはワックス加工されたキャンバス地のバックパックで，防水加工が施されているので，アウトドアに最適です。見栄えがするデザインなので，オフィスでもお使いになれます。スパルタンもワックス加工されたキャンバス地でできています。とても機能的ですが，仕事用には少しスポーティーすぎます。ウィンフィールドも似たようなバッグですが，こちらは防水レザー製です。ストラップが細いので，長時間の持ち運びには不向きかもしれませんが。

それでは，解答用紙に答えをマークしなさい。

状況の訳 あなたは今度の出張で使うバッグが必要だ。また，休日にはそのバッグを使ってハイキングに行くつもりだ。店員はあなたに次のように言っている。

質問の訳 あなたはどのバッグを買うべきか。

選択肢の訳 **1** ウエスタン。 **2** デインジャーフィールド。 **3** スパルタン。 **4** ウィンフィールド。

解説 Situationからわかるのは，①「あなた」は今度の出張で使うバッグを必要としていることと，②「あなた」は休日にはそのバッグを使ってハイキングに行くつもりだということ。店員は，第２文でウエスタンについて「ビジネスシーンに最適です」と述べているので，出張に使うことができ①には合致する。しかし次の文で「ちょっと重いので，長く歩くときには使いません」と述べており，ハイキングには向かないので②には合致しない。店員は，第４文でデインジャーフィールドについて「防水加工が施されているので，アウトドアに最適です」と述べているので②に合致し，さらに次の文で「見栄えがするデザインなので，オフィスでもお使いになれます」と述べているので，①にも合致する。よって，**2**が正解。店員は，第７文でスパルタンについて「仕事用には少しスポーティーすぎます」と述べているので，①に合致せず不適切。店員は，最終文でウィンフィールドについて「長時間の持ち運びには不向き」と述べているので，②に合致せず不適切。

No.26 正解 **2**

放送文 *(H)* You have 10 seconds to read the situation and Question No.26.

Nearest to the airport are SKM Budget Parking and the Vanier Plaza Hotel. They both offer covered parking lots that feature security patrols. SKM Budget Parking is the better deal at $13 per day. It only offers short-term parking, though, for up to a week max. If your trip is longer than that, you could pay a $17 rate at the Vanier Plaza Hotel. If an open, non-patrolled parking lot is acceptable, then Nelson Street Skypark offers parking for $9 per day. Another option would be the Econolodge, which is $19 per day. It's indoors and quite safe, though it's a little far.

Now mark your answer on your answer sheet.

訳 *(H)* 状況と質問26を読む時間が10秒あります。

空港に最も近いのは，SKMバジェット・パーキングとバニエ・プラザ・ホテルだよ。どちらも屋根付き駐車場で，警備員が巡回している。SKMバジェット・パーキングの方が1日13ドルとお得だ。ただし，そこは最長1週間までの短期駐車場しかないけど。それ以上の旅行なら，バニエ・プラザ・ホテルで17ドル払うこともできる。警備員の巡回のない露天駐車場でもいいなら，ネルソン・ストリート・スカイパークが1日9ドルで駐車場を提供している。もうひとつの選択肢はエコノロッジで，1日19ドル。少し遠いけど，屋内でかなり安全だよ。

それでは，解答用紙に答えをマークしなさい。

状況の訳 あなたは空港の近くに16日間駐車する必要がある。最安値ですませたいが，車が傷つくのが心配だ。友人が（駐車場の）選択肢についてあなたに教えてくれている。

質問の訳 あなたはどの駐車場を利用すべきか。

選択肢の訳 **1** SKMバジェット・パーキング。 **2** バニエ・プラザ・ホテル。
3 ネルソン・ストリート・スカイパーク。 **4** エコノロッジ。

解説 Situationからわかるのは，①「あなた」は空港の近くに駐車する必要があることと，②駐車期間は16日間であること，③「あなた」は最安値ですませたいが，車が傷つくのを心配していること。友人は，SKMバジェット・パーキングとバニエ・プラザ・ホテルについて「空港に最も近い」「どちらも屋根付き駐車場で，警備員が巡回している」と述べているので，①と，③の「車が傷つくのが心配」という要請には合致する。しかし，SKMバジェット・パーキングについては，第4文で「最長1週間までの短期駐車場しかない」と述べており，②に合致しないので不適切。バニエ・プラザ・ホテルについては「それ以上の旅行なら，バニエ・プラザ・ホテルで17ドル払うこともできる」と述べているので，②の「16日間」という要請にも合致する。バニエ・プラザ・ホテルの料金は17ドルで，9ドルのネルソン・ストリート・スカイパークより高いが，ネルソン・ストリート・スカイパークは「警備員の巡回のない露天駐車場」なので，③の「車が傷つくのが心配」という要請に合致せず不適切。よって，**2**が正解。エコノロッジは「少し遠い」と言っているので，①と合致せず，また，安全ではあるが「最安値」とは言えないので③とも合致しない。

No.27 正解 **3**

放送文 *(I)* You have 10 seconds to read the situation and Question No.27.

Please look at the display. If the green light is blinking, this means it needs to be cleaned. To do this, simply remove the filter and clean it carefully. You can find a tutorial video on our website. If the blue light is flashing, the air conditioner may be overheating. In such a case, you can speed up cooling by leaving the panel open. Be sure to unplug the air conditioner before touching the unit. If this does not solve the problem, and you would like to schedule a service call by a technician, press 1.

Now mark your answer on your answer sheet.

訳 *(I)* 状況と質問27を読む時間が10秒あります。

表示を見てください。緑色のランプが点滅している場合は，クリーニングが必要なことを意味します。クリーニングするには，フィルターを取り外し丁寧に洗浄してください。当社のウェブサイトでチュートリアルビデオをご覧いただけます。青いランプが点滅している場合は，エアコンがオーバーヒートしている可能性があります。このような場合は，パネルを開けたままにしておくと冷却を早めることができます。エアコンに触る前に必ずコンセントを抜いてください。それでも問題が解決せず，技術者による修理サービスをご希望の場合は，1を押してください。

それでは，解答用紙に答えをマークしなさい。

状況の訳 エアコンが突然動かなくなり，青いランプが点滅している。カスタマーサポートに電話すると次のような録音メッセージが流れてきた。

質問の訳 あなたはまず何をすべきか。

選択肢の訳 **1** エアコンのフィルターを外す。 **2** エアコンのパネルを開ける。
3 エアコンの電源を切る。 **4** サービスの予約をする。

解説 Situationからわかるのは，①エアコンが突然動かなくなったことと，②青いランプが点滅していること。録音メッセージでは，第5文で「青いランプが点滅している場合は，エアコンがオーバーヒートしている可能性があります」と述べられ，第6文で「パネルを開けたままにしておくと冷却を早めることができます」と述べている。ただし，続く第7文では「エアコンに触る前に必ずコンセントを抜いてください」と述べているので，「あなた」がパネルを開ける前にまずすべきこととしては，unplugを**disconnect**と言い換えた**3**が正解。

No.28 正解 3

放送文 *(J)* You have 10 seconds to read the situation and Question No.28.

I understand you've only read the September issue. I'll explain the others briefly. The July issue has an overview of the latest advancements in physics, centering on last year's breakthrough in the field of particle physics. The next issue focuses on recent genetic discoveries and various ongoing experiments with DNA and RNA, but unfortunately, this one is out of print. The October issue is also centered around research in genetics, especially its potential medical applications. Finally, if you'd like to deepen your understanding of modern geology, the November issue would be perfect. It thoroughly explains the current mainstream theories on volcano formation.

Now mark your answer on your answer sheet.

訳 *(J)* 状況と質問28を読む時間が10秒あります。

お客様は9月号しか読んでいらっしゃらないのですね。他の号について簡単にご説明申し上げます。7月号は，素粒子物理学の分野における昨年の飛躍的な前進を中心に，物理学における最新の進歩を概観しています。その次の号は，最近の遺伝子の発見と，DNAやRNAを使った現在進行中の様々な実験を中心としていますが，あいにくこちらは絶版です。10月号も遺伝学の研究，特に医療への応用の可能性に焦点を当てています。最後に，現代地質学についての理解を深めたいのであれば，11月号が最適です。火山形成に関する現在主流の理論を徹底的に解説しています。

それでは，解答用紙に答えをマークしなさい。

状況の訳 あなたは月刊科学雑誌のバックナンバーを注文したい。あなたは遺伝学に興味がある。あなたが雑誌社に電話すると，次のように言われた。

質問の訳 あなたはどの号を注文すべきか。

選択肢の訳 **1** 7月号。 **2** 8月号。 **3** 10月号。 **4** 11月号。

解説 Situationからわかるのは，①「あなた」は月刊科学雑誌のバックナンバーを注文したいことと，②「あなた」は遺伝学に興味があること。第3文で7月号は「物理学における最新の進歩を概観」と述べられており，②に合致せず不適切。続く第4文で「その次の号（＝7月号の次の号）は～絶版です」と述べられているので8月号は注文できないから①に合致せず不適切。10月号については，第5文で「遺伝学の研究～に焦点を当てています」と述べられているので，①，②ともに合致しており，**3**が正解。なお，最後から2文目から，11月号は現代地質学についてなので，②に合致せず不適切。

No.29 正解 1

放送文 *(K)* You have 10 seconds to read the situation and Question No.29.

Bentham Foods is recalling all cans of its tuna sold from May 15 to July 1 because of suspected health risks. Customers who have consumed tuna from these cans are advised to call our recall hotline. For unopened cans, if you have one or more cases of 24 cans, please visit our website for instructions on how to arrange a pickup and a full refund. Customers with less than one case may exchange the cans or return them for a full refund at the store where they were purchased. The cans don't pose any risk while unopened, but please avoid consuming tuna from any cans bought during the affected dates.

Now mark your answer on your answer sheet.

訳 *(K)* 状況と質問29を読む時間が10秒あります。

ベンサム・フーズでは，健康被害の疑いがあるとして，5月15日から7月1日までに販売されたツナ缶の全量を回収いたします。これらの缶詰のツナをお召し上がりになったお客様は，リコール・ホットラインまでご連絡ください。未開封の缶詰については，24缶入りのケースを1ケース以上お持ちのお客様は，弊社ウェブサイトにて引き取りと全額返金のご手配の方法をご確認ください。1ケース未満の缶詰をお持ちのお客様は，購入された店舗にて，缶詰の交換または返品による全額の払い戻しを承ります。未開封であれば危険はありませんが，対象期間中に購入された缶詰のツナの摂取はお控えください。

それでは，解答用紙に答えをマークしなさい。

状況の訳 あなたは5月30日にスーパーマーケットでベンサム・フーズのツナ缶を5缶買った。あなたはテレビで次のようなアナウンスを聞いた。あなたはそのツナをまったく

食べていない。

質問の訳 あなたは何をすべきか。

選択肢の訳 **1** 缶詰を買った店に持っていく。 **2** ベンサム・フーズのリコール・ホットラインに電話する。 **3** 缶を引き取ってもらう手配をする。 **4** ベンサム・フーズのウェブサイトにアクセスし手順を確認する。

解説 Situationからわかるのは，①「あなた」は5月30日にスーパーマーケットでベンサム・フーズのツナ缶を5缶買ったことと，②「あなた」はそのツナをまったく食べていないこと。アナウンスの第4文では「1ケース（＝第3文から24缶）未満の缶詰をお持ちのお客様は，購入された店舗にて，缶詰の交換または返品による全額の払い戻しを承ります」と述べているので，「あなた」がすべきことは，缶詰を買った店に持っていくことであり，**1**が正解。

カードA 二次試験・面接

（問題編pp.92〜93）

指示文の訳 1分間，準備する時間があります。
これは，家族と一緒に暮らしていた大学生についての話です。
ストーリーのナレーションを行うのに与えられる時間は2分間です。
ストーリーは以下の文で始めてください。
ある日，大学生は母親と祖父と一緒にテレビを見ていました。

ナレーションの解答例 **One day, a university student was watching TV with his mother and grandfather.** The TV program was explaining that many elderly drivers were involved in traffic accidents. The grandfather looked concerned by this news and said that he should stop driving. The other family members agreed. The next week, the student was walking outside of ABC Driving School. He was holding a registration form for the school as he had decided to get a driver's license. A few months later, the grandfather and the mother were sitting at home. The student was proudly holding his driver's license and said to his grandfather that now he could drive him anytime. The grandfather seemed delighted to hear this. That weekend, the grandfather was looking at his calendar. He seemed pleased to have made many plans. The mother told her son that his grandfather had plans every weekend.

解答例の訳 **ある日，大学生は母親と祖父と一緒にテレビを見ていました。**テレビ番組では，大勢の高齢ドライバーが交通事故に巻き込まれていると説明していました。祖父はこのニュースを見て心配になった様子で，自分は運転するのをやめるべきだと言いました。他の家族は賛成しました。翌週，大学生はABC自動車教習所の外を歩いていました。彼は運転免許証の取得を決心していたため，教習所の登録用紙を手に持っていました。数か月後，祖父と母は家で腰掛けていました。大学生は得意げに自分の運転免許証を手に持ちながら，祖父にいつでも彼を車で送ることができると言いました。祖父はこれを聞いてとてもうれしそうでした。その週末，祖父はカレンダーを見ていました。彼はたくさんの予定を入れていて満足げでした。母は息子に，祖父には毎週予定が入っていると伝えました。

解説 ナレーションは，4コマのイラストの進行に沿ってまとめていく。2～4コマ目の左上方にある時間の経過を表す語句は，各コマの描写の冒頭部分で必ず使うこと。また，吹き出し内のせりふは，間接話法または直接話法を使ってストーリーに盛り込むが，間接話法を使う場合，主語や動詞などを適切な形に変える必要がある点に注意。他，テレビ画面，用紙，建物，カレンダーなどに書かれた文字など，イラスト内の情報は適切な形でストーリーに取り入れること。なお，動詞の時制は，過去形および過去進行形を基本に，時間の経過がわかるよう描写する。

①1コマ目：大学生が家族とテレビを見ている場面。テレビ画面にAccidents Involving Elderly Drivers「高齢ドライバーを巻き込む事故」と映っており，その下には右肩上がりのグラフが配置されていることから，番組では交通事故に遭う高齢ドライバーの数が上昇している状況を伝えているのだと考えられる。また，I should stop driving.「自分は運転をやめるべきだ」と発言している祖父に対し，大学生と母親はうなずいているので，彼らは祖父の考えに賛意を示しているのだとわかる。なお，祖父はテレビを見ながら心配そうな表情をしているので，解答例ではこの点もlook「～に見える」を用いて盛り込んでいる。

②2コマ目：The next weekで始める。大学生が自動車教習所の外を歩いている場面。大学生が両手で持っている用紙にはRegistration Form「登録用紙」と，向かっている建物にはABC Driving School「ABC教習所」と書かれていることから，彼は運転免許証の取得のために教習所に通う決断をしたのだと判断できる。

③3コマ目：A few months laterで始める。大学生が家族に運転免許証を見せている場面。運転免許証を携えた大学生が明るい表情をしながらI can drive you anytime.「いつでも車で送ってあげられる」と言っていることから，運転免許証の取得を知らせているシーンだと推測できるので，解答例のようにproudly「得意げに」などの語句を使って，学生の気持ちを描写すると効果的だろう。また，解答例では大学生の発言内容を間接話法で盛り込んでいる。なお，祖父も明るい表情を浮かべているので，祖父も大学生の知らせと発言内容に対し喜んでいるのだとわかる。

④4コマ目：That weekendで始める。カレンダーの前に3人で立っている場面。カレンダーのSat.「土曜日」とSun.「日曜日」に漏れなくゴルフと釣りのイラストが描かれている点，および母親のHe has plans every weekend.「彼は毎週末に予定が入っている」という発言内容に着目して，状況を読み取る。母親の発言内容だけでなく，満足げにカレンダーを眺めている祖父の様子もナレーションに取り入れると良い。

質問の訳 No.1　4番目の絵を見てください。あなたがその大学生なら，どのようなことを考えているでしょうか。

では～さん（受験者の氏名），カードを裏返して置いてください。

No.2　親は自分の子どもにもっと厳しくあるべきだと思いますか。

No.3　近頃テレビで見るニュースを人は信用できるでしょうか。

No.4　将来的には，定年を過ぎても働くことを選択する人々が増えるでしょうか。

No.1 **解答例** I'd be thinking that I'll need to talk to my grandfather about his plans. I want to help him get around and enjoy himself, but I also need to be able to make my own plans on the weekends sometimes.

解答例の訳 祖父と，彼の予定について話をする必要があるだろうと私は思っているでしょう。彼がいろいろな場所へ行って楽しむのを手伝いたいとは思っていますが，私も時々は，週末に自分自身の予定を立てることができるようになっておく必要があります。

解説 解答例では，質問の仮定法過去形に合わせて，間接話法で**I'd be thinking that ～.**の形で答えている。祖父の予定について彼と話をする必要性について述べ，彼の移動と楽しみの助けとなりたい旨を示しながらも，自分もたまには週末に予定を立てることができるようになる必要があると締めくくっている。あるいは，regret「～を後悔する」を用いて，I'd be thinking that I regret not telling him that I also wanted to make my own plans on the weekends sometimes. Enjoying my life is important, so I'll tell my feelings to him soon. I'm sure he'll understand.「自分も時々は週末に予定を入れたいと思っているということを彼に伝えなかったのを後悔していると私は思っているでしょう。自分の人生を楽しむのは大切なことなので，近々，彼に自分の気持ちを伝えようと思います。きっと，彼ならわかってくれるでしょう」などと，悔やみながらも，話をすれば祖父は理解を示してくれるだろうという内容にしても良いだろう。

No.2 **解答例** I don't think so. Children need to have some freedom in their lives. Having too many rules prevents children from expressing themselves. Also, children need to learn how to make their own decisions.

解答例の訳 そうは思いません。子どもは自分たちの人生においていくらかの自由を享受する必要があります。ルールの抱え過ぎは子どもが自己表現する妨げとなります。また，子どもは自分たち自身の決断を下す方法を学ぶ必要もあります。

解説 解答例では，Noの立場から，子どもが人生において自由を享受する必要があると主張してから，ルールが多過ぎると自己表現ができなくなると補足している。そして，追加を表すAlsoを用いて，自分で決断を下す方法を学ぶ必要性もあると付け足している。あるいは，Yesの立場で，I think so. Parents should be stricter with their children, and directly teach them what is right and wrong. But needless to say, parents also need to be stricter with themselves so they can be a good example for their children.「そう思います。親は子どもにもっと厳しくして，何が良くて何が悪いかを彼らに直接教えるべきです。しかし，言うまでもありませんが，子どもたちにとっての良き模範となれるよう，親も同様に自分自身により厳しくする必要があります」などとしても良いだろう。

No.3 **解答例** I don't think so. There is tough competition between TV stations to get more viewers. This means that they often exaggerate news stories. Unfortunately, this is also true for many newspapers and news websites these days.

解答例の訳 そうは思いません。より多くの視聴者を獲得しようというテレビ局同士の間の激しい競争があります。この結果，彼らはニュースを誇張することがよくあります。残念ながら，これは近頃の多くの新聞やニュースウェブサイトにも当てはまります。

解説 解答例では，Noの立場から，視聴者数を稼ぐテレビ局同士の間の競争に言及し，この結果としてニュースの誇張がしばしばあると伝えている。さらに，テレビのみならず新聞やインターネット上のサイトでもこの傾向があると補足している。あるいは，YesともNoとも断定しない切り口で，It depends. Some TV programs exaggerate their news stories and cannot be trusted, but others deliver high-quality ones to us. The most important thing is to be critical of information we get, think for ourselves, and judge a particular news story is trustworthy or not.「ケースバイケースです。ニュースを誇張していて信頼できないテレビ番組もありますが，高品質なものを私たちに届けてくれる番組もあります。最も大切なのは，手にする情報に批判的になって，自分の頭で考え，特定のニュースが信頼できるものか否かを判断することです」などでも良いだろう。

No.4 **解答例** Yes. People will receive less money from the national pension system in the future, so they'll have to continue working for several years. Otherwise, they'll be unable to live comfortably after they retire.

解答例の訳 はい。人々は将来，国民年金制度からもらえるお金が減ると思われるので，彼らは数年間働き続ける必要があるでしょう。さもなければ，彼らは退職後，安楽に暮らすことができなくなります。

解説 解答例では，Yesの立場から，将来的には国民年金制度の受給額が減少するという見込みに言及した後，そのために労働を継続する必要が生じるだろうという意見を伝えている。そして，数年間働き続けなければ快適に過ごせなくなるということを，副詞Otherwise「さもなければ」を用いて表現している。あるいは，同じYesでありながらも別の視点から，Yes. At present, many elderly people still continue to work after retiring. This is partly because they need to make a living, but I think some of them chose to keep on working because they wanted to derive satisfaction from work. In this day and age when each individual pursues his or her own happiness, the trend will grow.「はい。現在，多くの高齢者が依然として退職後も働き続けています。これは部分的には生計を立てる必要があるからですが，労働から満足感を得たいという理由で働き続けることを選択した人もいると思います。個人が自分の幸福を追求する現代においては，この傾向は高まるでしょう」などと答えても良いだろう。

カードB 二次試験・面接

（問題編pp.94～95）

指示文の訳 1分間，準備する時間があります。

これは，歯科医院で働いていた女性についての話です。

ストーリーのナレーションを行うのに与えられる時間は2分間です。

ストーリーは以下の文で始めてください。

ある日，女性は歯科医院の受付で働いていました。

ナレーションの解答例 One day, a woman was working at the reception desk of a dentist's office. There were many patients in the waiting room, including children. The children looked very unhappy to be at the dentist and were crying. The woman was concerned to see this. A few days later, the woman was speaking with the dentist. She suggested that the dentist's office should provide toys for children to play with while they wait. The dentist thought it would be a good idea and agreed. The next week, there was a play area with some toys in the waiting room. Some children were playing with the toys, and they looked happy to be at the dentist. The woman was glad to see this. Later that day, the woman was looking at the toys with the dentist. The toys seemed to be badly damaged, and the dentist said that they already needed new toys.

訳 **ある日，女性は歯科医院の受付で働いていました。**待合室には子どもたちを含めて大勢の患者がいました。子どもたちは歯医者にいることがとても嫌な様子で，泣いていました。女性はこれを見て心配しました。数日後，女性は歯科医と話をしていました。彼女は，歯科医院が子どもたちに，待っている間に遊べるおもちゃを提供してはどうかと提案しました。歯科医はそれが良い考えだと思い，賛成しました。翌週，待合室には複数のおもちゃがある遊び場が用意されていました。複数の子どもがおもちゃで遊んでいて，彼らは歯医者にいることに満足している様子でした。女性はこれを見て喜ばしく思いました。その日の後で，女性は歯科医とおもちゃを見ていました。おもちゃはひどく損傷しているようで，歯科医は，自分たちには新しいおもちゃがすでに必要だと言いました。

解説 ナレーションは，４コマのイラストの進行に沿ってまとめていく。２～４コマ目の左上方にある時間の経過を表す語句は，各コマの描写の冒頭部分で必ず使うこと。吹き出し内のせりふは，間接話法または直接話法を使ってストーリーに盛り込むが，間接話法を使う場合，主語や動詞などを適切な形に変える点に注意。動詞の時制は，過去形および過去進行形を基本に，時間の経過がわかるように物語を展開していく。他，登場人物の仕草や表情，吹き出し内のイラストなどに着目しながら状況を読み取り，簡潔に描写するよう心掛けると良い。

①１コマ目：女性が歯科医院の受付で働いている場面。待合室には複数の人々がおり，そのうちの２人の子どもが泣いている。彼らは歯医者に足を運んでいることが嫌なのだと推測でき，この光景を見ている女性の表情が曇っていることから，女性は現状に懸念を抱いているのだと判断できる。他，開かれている奥のドアのそばにいる歯科医や，泣いている子どもに困っている様子の保護者についてふれても良いだろう。

②２コマ目：A few days laterで始める。女性が歯科医と話をしている場面。女性の吹き出し内におもちゃのイラストが描かれており，歯科医がうなずいている様子である。このことから，女性は歯科医に子ども向けのおもちゃを用意することを提案しており，歯科医はこの考えに賛意を示しているのだとわかる。解答例のように，suggest that ～「～を提案する」を使う場合，that節内は〈(should)＋動詞の原形〉にする点に注意しよう。

③３コマ目：The next weekで始める。再び，女性が歯科医院の受付で働いている場面。今回は受付の脇に子ども向けの遊び場が用意されており，そこでは子どもがおもちゃで遊んでいる。また，歯科医の元に向かう子どもも，ぬいぐるみを持っている。１コマ目とは対照的に，描かれているどの人物も困った顔をしておらず，明るい表情を浮かべている点に着目。受付の女性も，自分のアイデアが功を奏していることに満足げな様子である。

④４コマ目：Later that dayで始める。女性と歯科医が遊び場付近で話をしている場面。遊び場にあるおもちゃは２～３コマ目のものと比べるとかなり損傷している様子で，歯科医がWe already need new toys.「私たちにはすでに新しいおもちゃが必要です」と言っていることから，おもちゃは子どもたちが遊んだことで壊れてしまったのだと推測できる。

なお，解答例では歯科医の発言を間接話法でナレーションに盛り込んでいる。

質問の訳 No.1　4番目の絵を見てください。あなたがその女性なら，どのようなことを考えているでしょうか。

では～さん（受験者の氏名），カードを裏返して置いてください。

No.2　今は過去に比べて子育てが難しいと思いますか。

No.3　会社は商品をより安価にすることに力を注ぎ過ぎていると思いますか。

No.4　政府は日本の高齢化社会のニーズを満たすことができるでしょうか。

No.1 **解答例**　I'd be thinking that we should buy more durable toys this time.　Many children play with the toys every day, so it's not surprising that the first ones got damaged quickly.

解答例の訳　今度はもっと耐久性のあるおもちゃを買うべきだと私は思っているでしょう。大勢の子どもが毎日おもちゃで遊ぶので，最初のものがすぐに損傷してしまうのは驚くべきことではありません。

解説　解答例では，質問の仮定法過去形に合わせて，間接話法で**I'd be thinking that ～.**の形で答えている。次回はより耐久性の高いおもちゃを買う必要があると述べた後，日々大勢の子どもがおもちゃで遊ぶために，最初に購入した分のおもちゃがすぐに損傷してしまうのは驚くには当たらないと伝えている。あるいは，I'd be thinking that we need to tell our patients that toys should be treated with care.　Putting up a notice or something might be a good idea.　At any rate, since this is our first attempt, we should try to improve the situation gradually by trial and error.「患者たちに，おもちゃは大事に扱うべきだと伝える必要があると私は思っているでしょう。掲示か何かを出したりすることがいいアイデアかもしれません。とにかく，これは私たちにとっての初の試みなので，試行錯誤で状況を少しずつ改善するよう努めるべきです」などとしても良いだろう。

No.2 **解答例**　I don't think so.　Technology makes it easy for parents to keep their children safe, as parents can use smartphones to contact their children easily or check their locations.　Also, there's a lot of free advice for parents available online.

解答例の訳　そうは思いません。テクノロジーのおかげで親は子どもたちの安全を保ちやすくなっています，というのも親は子どもたちと簡単に連絡を取ったり彼らがいる場所を確認したりするのにスマートフォンを使用できるからです。また，オンライン上では親向けの無料の助言がたくさん閲覧できます。

解説　解答例では，Noの立場から，テクノロジーのおかげで親が子どもたちの安全を確保するのが容易になっていると述べてから，その理由について，スマートフォンで簡単に連絡が取れたり場所を確認できたりすると伝えている。そして，追加を表すAlso「また」を用いて，ネット上で親向けの助言が多数無料で閲覧可能であるというメリットについても言及している。あるいは，Yesの立場から，Due to the development of technology and the rapid spread of the Internet, children today are exposed to many new risks such as fake news, an invasion of privacy, and cyberbullying.　Eliminating these risks is difficult, so the current situation definitely makes it difficult for parents to raise children.「テクノロジーの発展とインターネットの急速な普及のせいで，今日の子どもたちはフェイクニュースやプライバシーの侵害，ネット上でのいじめといった多数の新たなリスクにさらされています。これらのリスクを取り除くのは困難なので，現状は間違いなく，親が子育てをするのを難しくしています」などとしても良いだろう。

No.3 **解答例** Not at all. These days, saving money is the first priority for most people. That means people will prefer to buy cheaper products, and companies that make cheap products will survive in the long run.

解答例の訳 そうは全く思いません。近頃では，貯金をすることが大半の人にとっての最優先事項です。その結果，人はより安い商品を購入したいと思うようになるでしょうし，安価な商品を作る企業は長い目で見れば生き残るでしょう。

解説 解答例ではまず，Not at all.「そうは全く思いません」と，自分がNoの立場であることを強調している。続けて，貯金が多くの人々にとっての最優先事項であるという現状に言及し，その結果として，消費者はより安い商品を購入したいと思うようになり，安価な商品を作る企業は長期的に見れば存続するだろうと予測している。あるいは，解答例とは逆にYesの立場から，Yes. In my opinion, some companies are going all out to produce inexpensive products, and consequently, there are many products in the market that are poor in quality. As consumers, we need to make an appeal to companies, and remind them that quality can be important than quantity.「はい。私の意見では，安価な製品の生産に注力し過ぎている企業もあり，その結果，質がおろそかになっているたくさんの製品が市場に出回っています。消費者として，私たちは企業に訴えかけ，彼らに質の方が量よりも大事であり得るということを念押しする必要があります」などとしても良いだろう。

No.4 **解答例** Yes. Recently, there have been major advancements in medical technology. This includes robots that can take care of elderly patients. Also, the government is working to increase the number of medical facilities.

解答例の訳 はい。最近は，医療技術において大きな前進が見られます。これには，高齢患者の介護をすることができるロボットが含まれます。また，政府は医療施設の数を増やすことに尽力しています。

解説 解答例では，Yesの立場から，政府が日本の高齢化社会のニーズを満たすことができる根拠として，高齢者を介護することが可能なロボットを含めた最近の医療技術の進歩に言及した後，政府が医療施設の数を増やしてもいると述べている。あるいは，Noの立場から，Since the number of elderly people is expected to increase as the days go by, the cost to meet all their needs will be too enormous for the government in the future. Therefore, we may not be able to rely too much on the government's support, and we may be required to support people around us by ourselves.「高齢者の数は歳月が経つにつれて増加する見込みなので，彼らのニーズを漏れなく満たす費用は，将来の政府にとってあまりにも莫大なものとなるでしょう。そのため，私たちは政府の援助に頼り過ぎることができないかもしれず，自分たち自身で身の回りの人々を支えることが求められるかもしれません」でも良いだろう。

2022年度 第3回

筆記 解答欄

問題番号		1	2	3	4
1	(1)	①	②	③	❹
	(2)	①	②	③	❹
	(3)	①	❷	③	④
	(4)	①	②	③	❹
	(5)	①	②	❸	④
	(6)	①	②	❸	④
	(7)	①	❷	③	④
	(8)	①	②	③	❹
	(9)	①	❷	③	④
	(10)	①	❷	③	④
	(11)	①	❷	③	④
	(12)	①	②	❸	④
	(13)	❶	②	③	④
	(14)	①	❷	③	④
	(15)	❶	②	③	④
	(16)	❶	②	③	④
	(17)	①	②	③	❹
	(18)	①	❷	③	④
	(19)	①	②	❸	④
	(20)	❶	②	③	④
	(21)	❶	②	③	④
	(22)	❶	②	③	④
	(23)	①	❷	③	④
	(24)	❶	②	③	④
	(25)	①	②	❸	④

問題番号		1	2	3	4
2	(26)	❶	②	③	④
	(27)	①	②	❸	④
	(28)	①	②	③	❹
	(29)	①	②	③	❹
	(30)	①	②	❸	④
	(31)	❶	②	③	④

問題番号		1	2	3	4
3	(32)	①	②	③	❹
	(33)	①	❷	③	④
	(34)	①	❷	③	④
	(35)	①	②	❸	④
	(36)	①	②	③	❹
	(37)	①	②	❸	④
	(38)	①	②	③	❹
	(39)	❶	②	③	④
	(40)	①	❷	③	④
	(41)	①	②	❸	④

4 の解答例は p.107をご覧ください。

リスニング 解答欄

問題番号			1	2	3	4
Part 1		No.1	①	②	③	❹
		No.2	❶	②	③	④
		No.3	①	②	③	❹
		No.4	❶	②	③	④
		No.5	①	❷	③	④
		No.6	①	②	❸	④
		No.7	①	②	❸	④
		No.8	❶	②	③	④
		No.9	①	②	③	❹
		No.10	①	②	❸	④
		No.11	❶	②	③	④
		No.12	①	❷	③	④
Part 2	A	No.13	①	②	❸	④
		No.14	❶	②	③	④
	B	No.15	①	②	❸	④
		No.16	①	❷	③	④
	C	No.17	①	②	③	❹
		No.18	①	❷	③	④
	D	No.19	①	②	❸	④
		No.20	①	②	③	❹
	E	No.21	❶	②	③	④
		No.22	①	②	❸	④
	F	No.23	①	❷	③	④
		No.24	❶	②	③	④
Part 3	G	No.25	①	❷	③	④
	H	No.26	①	②	③	❹
	I	No.27	①	②	③	❹
	J	No.28	①	❷	③	④
	K	No.29	❶	②	③	④

1　一次試験・筆記
（問題編pp.98〜101）

指示文の訳　各英文を完成させるのに最も適切な単語または語句を４つの選択肢の中から選び，その番号を解答用紙の所定欄にマークしなさい。

(1)　正解　4

訳　フェルナンドは会社の成功にとって重要だったので，来月彼が退社した後に何が起きるか皆心配している。

解説　空所後のto the success of the company「会社の成功にとって」と組み合わせるのにふさわしい選択肢は**4**。**be instrumental to** ～で「にとって重要な」の意味になる。これを入れると，文後半の「来月彼が退社した後に何が起きるか皆心配している」という内容とも合う。desperate「必死の」，philosophical「哲学の，思慮深い」，inadequate「不適当な」。

(2)　正解　4

訳　一部の人たちは，その映画が過小評価されていたと感じている。それは何の賞も受賞しなかったが，それがすばらしい芸術作品だったと信じる人々がいる。

解説　空所後の文にit did not win any awards「何の賞も受賞しなかった」けれどもa great work of art「すばらしい芸術作品」だったと信じる人がいるとある。**4**を入れてthe film was **underrated**「その映画は過小評価されていた」とすると文脈に合う。overtake「～を追い越す」，override「～をくつがえす」，underfeed「～食料を十分与えない」。

(3)　正解　2

訳　第二次世界大戦中に5,000万人を超える人々が亡くなった。それは歴史上，他のどの戦争よりも多くの死亡事例である。

解説　More than 50 million people「5,000万人を超える人々」にduring World War II「第二次世界大戦中に」起きたこととしてふさわしい動詞は**2のperish(ed)**「(戦争や事故などで)死ぬ」。これを入れると次の文のdeaths「死，死亡事例」とも合う。worship「～を崇拝する」，haunt「(幽霊などが) ～に出没する」，jeer「あざける，ひやかす」。

(4)　正解　4

訳　ウォルトのレストランでは伝統的に田園地方の貧しい人々によって食されていた料理を出している。彼は，小作農家の人々は安価な食材からおいしい食事を作るのが上手だったと言う。

解説　選択肢には職業や身分を表す名詞が並んでいる。この中で，第1文のpoor people in the countryside「田園地方の貧しい人々」を表すのにふさわしいのは**4のpeasants**「小作農家の人」である。correspondent「(新聞などの) 特派員」，janitor「管理人，用務員」，captive「捕虜，人質」。

※2024年度第１回から，試験形式の変更に伴い大問１の問題数は18問になります。

(5) 正解 3

訳 新しい建物の設計計画における重大な不備の発見により，建設が数か月遅れることとなった。

解説 a serious (　　) in the design plans「設計計画における重大な（　　）」の空所に入れて意味が通るのは，**3のflaw**「不備，欠点」のみである。この文の主語は空所を含むThe discovery ... buildingで，〈S＋cause＋O＋to do〉「SがOに～させる（原因となる），Sにより（結果的に）Oが～することとなる」という構文になっている。clog「邪魔なもの，故障」，boom「好況，流行」，dump「ごみ捨て場」。

(6) 正解 3

訳 自分のプレゼンテーションをするときになって，レイチェルは自分が不安で動けなくなっていることに気づいた。彼女は話すことができず，皆の前でただ立っていた。

解説 〈find＋oneself＋形容する語〉で「自分が（知らないうちに）～（の状態）になっていることに気づく」という表現になる。選択肢には過去分詞が並んでおり，過去分詞が形容詞的にherselfを形容することになる。空所直後にwith fear「不安で」があること，presentation「プレゼンテーション」というシチュエーションであることから，正解は**3のparalyzed**「麻痺した，動けなくなった」。trim「～を刈り込む」，tease「～をからかう」，acquire「～を獲得する」。

(7) 正解 2

訳 その2か国はかつて戦争で互いに戦ったことがあるという事実にもかかわらず現在は友好的な関係を享受していて，実のところ，同盟国である。

解説 〈the fact that＋S＋V〉で「SがVするという事実」の意味。2か国が戦争したという事実の前にDespite「～にもかかわらず」があるので，空所に**2**を入れてan **amicable** relationship「友好的な関係」とすると自然な流れになる。最後のallies「同盟国」はこの関係を言いかえたものである。alleged「申し立てられた」，abusive「無礼な，暴力的な」，adhesive「粘着性の」。

(8) 正解 4

訳 ティナの新たな目標は健康になることだ。食事にもっと多くの野菜を含めることに加えて，彼女は日課に運動プログラムを組み入れることを決めた。

解説 第1文のto get healthy「健康になる」という目標を達成するための具体例が第2文に書かれている。解答のカギとなるのは，空所後のinto her daily routine「日課に」。空所に**4のincorporate**を入れて，incorporate ～ into ...「…に～を組み入れる」の形にすると文意が通る。commemorate「～を記念する」，alienate「～を疎外する」，liberate「～を解放する」。

(9) 正解 2

訳 一部の歴史家は，犬の飼育は1万年以上前に起こったと考えている。その後ずっと犬はペットとして飼われ，農場で働いていたものだった。

解説 選択肢の中でthe (　　) of dogs「犬の（　　）」の空所に入れて意味が通るのは

2のdomestication「飼育」のみである。なお，the **domestication** of dogs occurred はdogs were domesticatedとしてもほぼ同じ意味になる。elevation「昇進，高度」，deception「だますこと」，verification「証明」。

(10) 正解 2

訳 オスカーは友好的な性格と優しい物腰で知られている。彼は毎朝，自分の机に向かって歩いて行くとき，職場の全員にていねいに挨拶する。

解説 空所直前のheは第1文の主語Oscarをさす。第1文で語られている彼の性格friendly personality and good manners「友好的な性格と優しい物腰」に合うようにするためには，空所に**2**を入れて**courteously** greets everyone「全員にていねいに挨拶する」とすると文の流れに合う。scarcely「ほとんど〜ない」，tediously「うんざりするほど」，obnoxiously「不愉快に」。

(11) 正解 2

訳 新しい図書館の計画は資金不足のために延期されていた。しかし数年後，その計画は復活し，建設工事が始まった。

解説 第1文に新しい図書館の計画がwas put on hold「延期された」とある。第2文に逆接を示す副詞howeverがあるので，続くthe plan was (　　)の空所には延期と反する意味を表す**2のrevived**を入れて「その計画は復活した」とする。そうすると，続くconstruction work started「建設工事が始まった」とも合う。deprive「〜を奪う」，obstruct「〜を妨げる」，agitate「〜（群衆など）を扇動する」。

(12) 正解 3

訳 マギーの祖母は最近とても虚弱になった。彼女は今や歩くのに介助を必要としていて，1人では階段を上ることができない。

解説 空所のある文は現在完了形を用いたSVCの形で，Maggie's grandmother＝very (　　)の関係になる。第2文にneeds help to walk「歩くのに介助を必要としている」，cannot climb stairs by herself「1人では階段を上ることができない」とあるので，マギーの祖母の状態を表すのに適切な選択肢は**3のfrail**「虚弱な」。poetic「詩的な」，savage「獰猛な」，rash「性急な」。

(13) 正解 1

訳 その小説家は1人で仕事をするのが好きだ。周囲に人が誰もいない地域にある田舎の家にいるときだけよく書けると彼女は言う。

解説 第2文のSheは第1文のThe novelistを指す。第2文に，彼女はan area with no people around「周囲に人が誰もいない地域」にある田舎の家にいるときだけよく書けると述べられている。likes to work in (　　)の空所に**1**を入れてin **solitude**「1人で，孤独に」とすると文の流れに合う。corruption「不正行為，堕落」，excess「超過，逸脱」，consent「合意」。

(14) 正解 2

訳 考古学者らは，古代の埋葬地を発掘している際，宝飾品や陶磁器類の破片を含む数多くの人工遺物を発見した。それらは地元の歴史博物館に寄贈される予定だ。

解説 空所後のincluding pieces of jewelry and pottery「宝飾品や陶磁器類の破片を含む」は空所を説明しているので，**2のartifacts**「人工遺物」を入れると文の流れに合う。**artifacts**は，文頭のArchaeologists「考古学者ら」が発見するものとしてもふさわしい。setback「つまずき，後退」，pledge「誓約，公約」，salute「敬礼」。

(15) 正解 1

訳 より高速なインターネット接続とより高機能なコンピュータにより，従来に増して多くの情報が高速で送信されることが可能だ。

解説 助動詞を用いた受け身の文。more information can be ( ) at high speed「より多くの情報が高速で( )ことが可能だ」の空所に入れて意味が通るのは**1のtransmitted**「～が送信される」のみである。rejoice「～を大いに喜ばせる」，nauseate「～に吐き気をもよおさせる」，offend「～の感情を害する」。

(16) 正解 1

訳 マリアは兄がギャンブルで全財産を失ったと知った後で彼を批判して，彼を救いようがないと考えた。

解説 〈call＋人＋形容詞［名詞］〉で「(人) を～だと考える，みなす」という意味になる。空所後の，had lost all of his money gambling「ギャンブルで全財産を失った」人物を形容するのにふさわしい選択肢は**1のpathetic**「救いようがない，哀れな」。analytical「分析的な」，dedicated「ひたむきな」，ceaseless「絶え間ない」。

(17) 正解 4

訳 その建築家は現代風に建物を設計することで有名だった。彼は自分のデザインが現在の社会的，文化的な動向を反映することを求めた。

解説 in a ( ) styleは「～風に，～な様式で」の意味。第２文のreflect current social and cultural trends「現在の社会的，文化的な動向を反映する」と合うようにするには，**4のcontemporary**「現代の，同時代の」を入れるとよい。preceding「先立つ，前の」，simultaneous「同時に起こる」，plentiful「豊富な」。

(18) 正解 2

訳 メディアの報道不足により，化学物質の流出に関してその町に情報が届かないままになった。メディアは流出が制御不能になってようやくその事故に関する報道を開始した。

解説 〈leave＋O＋形容する語〉で「Oを～のままにする」という表現なので，left the town uninformedは直訳すると「その町を情報が届かないままにした」という意味。これの主語がA lack of media ( )「メディアの( )不足」なので，**2のcoverage**「報道」が正解となる。enrollment「入学，申込」，assortment「詰め合わせ（た物）」，leverage「てこ」。

(19) 正解 3

訳 入ってくる税金よりも多くの資金を何年も使い続けた末，政府は現在数兆ドルの赤字を抱えている。

解説 空所前後の部分だけを見て答えられる問題。a (　　) of trillions of dollars「数兆ドルの（　　)」の空所に入れて意味が通る選択肢は**3のdeficit**「赤字」だけである。これを入れれば，文前半の「入ってくる税金よりも多くの資金を何年も使い続けた」とも合う。fatigue「疲労」，petition「歎願（書)」，conspiracy「共謀」。

(20) 正解　1

訳 その芸術家は，石からきめ細かい彫像を彫ることで生計を立てていた。そのような固い物質を彫るために，彼女はたくさんの特別な道具を使った。

解説 make a living by doingで「～することで生計を立てる」という表現。(　　) detailed figures out of stone「石からきめ細かい彫像を（　　）こと」の空所に入れて意味が通るのは**1のcarving**「～を彫刻すること，彫ること」である。lure「～を誘いこむ，誘惑する」，soothe「～をなだめる」，rank「～を位置づける」。

(21) 正解　1

訳 ルースは自分のチームがコートを行ったり来たりして走っているとき，ベンチから見ていた。残念ながら，肩のけがのせいで彼女は試合の出場辞退を余儀なくされていた。

解説 〈S＋forces＋人＋to do〉で「Sが（人）に～することを強要する，Sのせいで（人）が～することを余儀なくされる」という意味になる。a shoulder injury「肩のけが」のせいで余儀なくされることとしてふさわしいのは，**withdraw** from the game「試合の出場を辞退する」こと。正解は**1**。bypass「～を迂回する」, upgrade「～をアップグレードする」，overload「～に（荷物を）積みすぎる」。

(22) 正解　1

訳 ジョセリンは西から嵐が押し寄せてきているのを見ることができた。空は暗くなりはじめ，風が徐々に強くなった。

解説 see ～ doingで「～が…しているのを見る」という意味になる。第２文に「空は暗くなりはじめ，風が徐々に強くなった」とあるので，the storm (　　) from the west「西から嵐が（　　)」の空所には**1のrolling in**「押し寄せてきている」を入れると文意が通る。add up「合計する」, hold out「(最後まで）辛抱する」, pass down「(次世代に）伝える」。

(23) 正解　2

訳 その会社は最終的に倒産するまで５年間，売り上げ低下に苦しんだ。同社は先週，恒久的に廃業した。

解説 第１文前半にsuffered from five years of decreasing sales「５年間，売り上げ低下に苦しんだ」とある。その結果finally「最終的に」起こることとして適切な選択肢は**2のwent under**「倒産した」。なお第２文に出てくるclosed its doorsも「(会社が）廃業した，倒産した」という意味を表す。dial up「～に電話回線で接続する」，come along「やってくる」，pull through「(危機などを）乗り越える」。

(24) 正解 1

訳 その契約書の文字があまりに小さかったので，ガスは言葉を判読するために拡大鏡を必要とした。

解説 文字があまりに小さかったのでneeded a magnifying glass to (　　) the words「言葉を (　　) ために拡大鏡を必要とした」とある。空所には**1のmake out**「判読する」を入れるのが適切。tune up「(楽器を) 調律する」，draw up「(文書などを) 作成する」，blow out「吹き消す，吹き飛ばす」。

(25) 正解 3

訳 その猫は生まれたばかりの子猫たちの世話をしていた。彼女は誰かが彼らに近づきすぎるたびに神経質になった。

解説 The cat was (　　) her newborn kittens「その猫は生まれたばかりの子猫たち (　　)」の空所には**3**を入れると文意が通る。**watch(ing) over**は「～を見守る，～の世話をする」の意味の句動詞。pack up「荷造りする」，look into ～「～を調査する」，show up「姿を現す」。

2 一次試験・筆記

カリフォルニア・チャイナタウン（問題編pp.102～103）
植物の計画（問題編pp.104～105）

指示文の訳 それぞれの文章を読んで，各空所に入れるのに最も適切な語句を４つの選択肢の中から選び，その番号を解答用紙の所定欄にマークしなさい。

カリフォルニア・チャイナタウン

Key to Reading 第１段落：導入（チャイナタウンができた経緯）→第２段落：本論①（サンノゼのチャイナタウンに関する従来の仮説と，最近の新説）→第３段落：本論②（その他の発見から得られた，住民の生活様式に関する洞察）という３段落構成の説明文。遺跡等の分析結果とそこから考えられる仮説を中心に読み進めよう。

訳

19世紀後半，米国に移住した中国人は，仕事や住居を探す際，アメリカ白人からのたいへんな差別に直面した。その結果，彼らは，チャイナタウンとして知られる近隣の地域に集まって住む傾向ができたが，そこでは仕事や住居を見つけるためのより良い機会があった。最大のチャイナタウンのひとつは，カリフォルニア州サンノゼ市にあったが，1887年の火災で焼失してしまったため，住民の生活についてはほとんど知られていない。

長い間，サンノゼのチャイナタウンに供給された食品は，香港や中国からもたらされたものだと考えられてきた。しかし最近，かつてのごみ捨て場にあった魚の骨を考古学者が分析したところ，必ずしもこれが事実であるとは限らないという証拠が得られた。これらの特定の骨が際立っていたのは，ジャイアント・スネークヘッドとして知られる種のものだったからだ。この魚の原産地は中国でも香港でもなく，むしろ東南アジア諸国であるため，考古学者たちは，魚はどこか他の場所で捕らえられた後香港に運ばれ，それから米国で消費するために輸送されたと考えている。

この発見がサンノゼのチャイナタウンに供給を行っていた貿易網の複雑さに関する洞察を提供する一方で，この遺跡での他の発見によって，近隣の移住民の生活様式に関する情報が明らかになった。例えば，住民は，彼らの食の伝統をいくらか維持していたと思われる。牛の遺骨の存在は，住民が牛肉を食べる西洋の習慣を取り入れていたことを示唆しているが，考古学者が発見した動物の遺骨の中で最も多かったのは，豚の骨であった。豚肉は，彼らの本国では主食であったため，この骨は豚の飼育と消費の習慣が移住民の間で続いていたことを示している。

(26) 正解　1

選択肢の訳　**1**　その結果　**2**　このことにもかかわらず　**3**　同様に　**4**　対照的に

解説　空所を含む文の1文前で，Chinese immigrants to the United States faced significant discrimination from White Americans when looking for employment and accommodation「米国に移住した中国人は，仕事や住居を探す際，アメリカ白人からのたいへんな差別に直面した」と述べている。ここから，(　　), they tended to live in neighborhoods known as Chinatowns「(　　), 彼らはチャイナタウンとして知られる近隣の地域に集まって住む傾向ができた」と述べていることから，**1のConsequently**「その結果」が正解。

(27) 正解　3

選択肢の訳　**1**　さらなる謎に導く　**2**　食物の多くは低品質であった　**3**　必ずしもこれが事実であるとは限らない　**4**　すべての積み荷が安全に到着したわけではない

解説　空所を含む文の1文前でIt was long assumed that the food items supplied to San Jose's Chinatown originated in Hong Kong and China.「長い間，サンノゼのチャイナタウンに供給された食品は，香港や中国からもたらされたものだと考えられてきた」と述べている。その後に，空所を含む文がRecently, however, ... と始まることから，従来の仮説を否定する内容が続くことがわかる。**3のthis was not always the case**「必ずしもこれが事実であるとは限らない」が正解。

(28) 正解　4

選択肢の訳　**1**　これまでに考えられていたよりも分裂していた　**2**　しばしば中国へ荷物を送っていた　**3**　十分な食料を得るために苦労していた　**4**　食の伝統をいくらか維持していた

解説　空所後の2文で，pig bones were the most common type of animal remains archaeologists discovered「考古学者が発見した動物の遺骨の中で最も多かったのは，豚の骨であった」，the bones indicate the custom of raising and consuming pigs continued among the immigrants「この骨は豚の飼育と消費の習慣が移住民の間で続いていたことを示している」と述べていることから，**4のmaintained some of their food traditions**「食の伝統をいくらか維持していた」が正解。

植物の計画

Key to Reading　第1段落：導入（開花植物の，昆虫を介した生殖活動）→第2段落：本論①（アリストロキア・ミクロストマがハエを利用して授粉を行う過程）→第3段落：本論②（アリストロキア・ミクロストマに関するさらなる発見と新説）という3段落構成の説明文である。開花植物について既にわかっていること，アリストロキア・ミクロストマに関する発見とそこからの新説を整理しながら読み進めよう。

訳

開花植物の大半は，授粉を昆虫に頼っている。昆虫が花に接触すると，その体に花粉がつく。そして，その昆虫が植物の上を移動したり，同種の別の植物のところへ行ったりすると，この花粉はその植物の雌の部分に接触する。この授粉プロセスにより，植物は生殖することができる。引き換えに，植物は通常，花の蜜など，昆虫が必要とするものを提供する。

開花植物は，様々な方法で花粉媒介昆虫を引き付けることに成功している。例えば，鮮やかな色の花びらでハエの注意を引く植物もある。研究者たちは最近，アリストロキア・ミクロストマという植物が，ハエが卵を産み付ける，甲虫の死骸のような臭いを放つことでハエを引き寄せることを発見した。しかしこの植物は，ただその臭いでハエを騙すだけではない。ハエを一時的に花の中に閉じ込めてしまうのだ。ハエが花の中を動き回ると，その体についている花粉が植物上に広がる。また，その植物は，ハエが放たれた後も別の植物に授粉できるように，自身の花粉をハエの体に確実に付着させる。

研究者たちは，この植物が実際に，死んだ甲虫が放つ臭いと同じ化学物質を放出していることを発見した。この化学物質は植物にはほとんど存在しないため，研究者たちは，この植物は，死んだ甲虫を産卵場所として利用するハエを標的にするために特別に進化したと考えている。また彼らは，この説のさらなる裏付けがあるとも言っている。それは，その植物の花が枯れ葉や地面の岩の間——まさにハエが通常甲虫の死骸を探す場所——にあるという事実である。

(29) 正解 4

選択肢の訳 **1** むしろ **2** 要するに **3** それにもかかわらず **4** 引き換えに

解説 空所直前までの内容と，空所を含む文の関係を考える。空所直前までの内容は，昆虫を利用した植物の生殖方法であり，これは植物の利益になることである。空所を含む文はthe plants usually provide something the insect needs, such as a meal of nectar「植物は通常，花の蜜など，昆虫が必要とするものを提供する」と述べていることから，**4のIn exchange**「引き換えに」が正解。

(30) 正解 3

選択肢の訳 **1** 虫の死骸を集める **2** 虫から臭いを隠す **3** その臭いでハエを騙す **4** ハエに安全な場所を提供する

解説 「しかしこの植物は，ただ（　　）だけではない」の空所に当てはまる内容を選ぶので，空所を含む文の直前を参照する。attracts flies by smelling like the dead beetles that some flies lay eggs in「ハエが卵を産み付ける，甲虫の死骸のような臭いを放つことでハエを引き寄せる」と述べているので，**3のtrick the flies with its smell**「その臭いでハエを騙す」が正解。空所後は，ただ臭いで騙すだけでなく何をするかの内容を述べていることに注意。

(31) 正解 1

選択肢の訳 **1** この説のさらなる裏付けがある **2** 化学物質には別の目的がある

3 植物は重要な食料源である　**4** 多くの昆虫は植物を危険視している

解説 「また彼らは，(　　) とも言っている」の空所に当てはまる内容を選ぶ。空所を含む文の直前でthe researchers believe the plant has evolved specifically to target flies that use dead beetles as egg-laying sites「研究者たちは，この植物は，死んだ甲虫を産卵場所として利用するハエを標的にするために特別に進化したと考えている」と述べている。空所後のthe plant's flowers are located among dead leaves and rocks on the ground──exactly where the flies usually search for dead beetles「その植物の花が枯れ葉や地面の岩の間──まさにハエが通常甲虫の死骸を探す場所──にある」は，その説を裏付ける内容なので，**1のthere is further support for this theory**「この説のさらなる裏付けがある」が正解。

3 一次試験・筆記

柵と生態系（問題編pp.106～107）
サッカー戦争（問題編pp.108～109）
点字との争い（問題編pp.110～112）

指示文の訳 それぞれの文章を読んで，各質問に対する最も適切な答えを4つの選択肢の中から選び，その番号を解答用紙の所定欄にマークしなさい。

柵と生態系

Key to Reading 第1段落：導入＋本論①（柵が生態系に及ぼす影響）→第2段落：本論②（柵が野生動物観光にも悪影響を与える可能性）→第3段落：本論③（柵の影響を抑えるためにどうするか）という3段落構成の説明文。柵が生態系にどのように影響するのか，またそこからどのような問題が起こるのか，どのような方針でそうした問題の解決策を検討すべきかを読み取ろう。

訳

柵は，敷地を分割し，とりわけ安全を確保するのに役立つ。柵はまた，生態系にも影響を与える。BioScience誌に掲載された研究は，柵は，それが設置された地域の動物種の間に「勝者」と「敗者」を生み出すと結論づけている。この研究によると，ジェネラリスト種―様々な食物を摂取し複数の生息地で生き残ることができる種―は，物理的な境界をほとんど問題にしない。一方，生存のために特殊な条件を必要とするスペシャリスト種は，特定の食物源や地理的領域から切り離されることに苦しむ。スペシャリスト種はジェネラリスト種よりも数が多いため，この研究では，各勝者に対して，複数の敗者が存在することがわかった。

柵の影響は生態系に限ったことではない。20世紀半ば，南部アフリカのボツワナでは，畜牛を侵す病気の拡散を防ぐための国際的な規制に対処するため，柵を設置した。柵は牛の保護に役立っているが，ヌーのような動物の季節的な移動を妨げ，水へのアクセスを妨げている。その結果ヌーの個体数が減少し，生態系だけでなく，この地域の野生動物観光も脅かされている。政府が柵に依存し続けることで，動物の移動が制限され，ボツワナの経済にとって貴重な野生動物観光が損なわれるのではないかと懸念されている。

柵の生態系への悪影響は，柵に変更を加えてある種の動物を通過させることで抑えられる。しかし，この研究を著した人々は，より根本的な改革が必要だと考えている。彼らが言うには，すべての柵を撤廃することは現実的な選択肢ではない。その代わりに，全体像

※2024年度第1回から，試験形式の変更に伴い大問3の1問目(32)～(34)が削除されます。

を見据えたフェンス計画を実行するべきだという。例えば，フェンスはしばしば短期的な結果を得るために建設されて撤去されるが，研究者たちは，数か月後，あるいは数年後でも，柵がまだそこにあるかのように行動する動物がいることを発見している。したがって，柵の設計と設置場所については，生態系への影響を最小限に抑えるために，あらゆる側面から検討する必要がある。

(32) 正解 4

質問の訳 第1段落で紹介した研究は，～ことを示している。

選択肢の訳 **1** 複数種の生息地を横断する柵は，単一種の生息地内に設置された柵よりも，動物にとって有益である **2** 柵は多くの問題を引き起こすが，動物個体群の生存能力に与える影響は，以前考えられていたよりも小さい **3** 柵は，ある種を，多くの動物が生き残るために必要な資源を使い果たす他の有害な種から守るのに有効である **4** 柵は一部の種には害はないが，多くの動物に深刻な悪影響を及ぼす可能性がある。

解説 第1段落では，柵がその地域の生態系に及ぼす影響について述べており，柵を問題としない「勝者」であるジェネラリスト種（generalist species）と，柵によって悪影響を受ける「敗者」であるスペシャリスト種（specialist species）があると説明している。第1段落最終文にBecause specialist species outnumber generalist species, the study found that for every winner, there are multiple losers.「スペシャリスト種はジェネラリスト種よりも数が多いため，この研究では，各勝者に対して，複数の敗者が存在することがわかった」とある。この文とほぼ同じ内容を述べている**4**が正解。

(33) 正解 2

質問の訳 ボツワナに建設された柵について，正しいことは何か。

選択肢の訳 **1** 柵が動物の移動パターンに変化を引き起こした結果，牛の間で病気が蔓延した。 **2** 国の経済にとって重要な産業に間接的な影響を与える可能性がある。 **3** 野生動物を見るためにこの国を訪れる観光客の安全性を高めるために必要であると考えられている。 **4** 病気を蔓延させる種を減らすことに成功したことで，生態系に予想外の恩恵をもたらしている。

解説 第2段落は，ボツワナで畜牛の病気感染防止のために設置された柵の影響についての内容である。第3～4文では，ヌーなどの動物の移動が妨げられ個体数が減少した結果，生態系だけでなく，野生動物観光にも悪影響が出ていると述べている。また，第2段落最終文にThe government's continued reliance on fences has led to concerns that limiting animal migration will hurt wildlife tourism, which is valuable to Botswana's economy.「政府が柵に依存し続けることで，動物の移動が制限され，ボツワナの経済にとって貴重な野生動物観光が損なわれるのではないかと懸念されている」とあり，ボツワナ経済にとって，野生動物観光（wildlife tourism）は重要度の高い産業であるということがわかる。これらの内容をまとめた選択肢**2**が正解。

(34) 正解 2

質問の訳 柵の建設の際に慎重な計画が必要な理由のひとつは何か。

選択肢の訳 **1** 建設後に柵の設計を変更すると，実際には新しい柵を建設するよりも多くの問題を引き起こす可能性がある。 **2** 柵が撤去された後も，その地域の動物に影響を与え続ける可能性がある。　**3**　事前に明確な計画を立てずに，ある地域に複数の柵を設置しても，危険区域への動物の侵入を防ぐことはできない。　**4**　捕食動物から身を守るために柵を利用する動物種が増えた。

解説　第３段落最終文にConsideration should therefore be given to all aspects of fence design and location to ensure a minimal impact on ecosystems.「したがって，柵の設計と設置場所については，生態系への影響を最小限に抑えるために，あらゆる側面から検討する必要がある」とあるので，その前文を参照する。researchers have found that months──or even years──later, some animals continue to behave as if the fences are still there「研究者たちは，数か月後，あるいは数年後でも，柵がまだそこにあるかのように行動する動物がいることを発見している」と述べている。この内容と一致する選択肢**2**が正解。

サッカー戦争

Key to Reading　第１段落：導入(「サッカー戦争」の始まり)→第２，３段落：本論①(「サッカー戦争」の真の背景) →第４段落：本論②＋結論（戦争激化の要因とその後）という４段落構成の説明文。設問に先に目を通し，読み取るべきポイントを押さえてから，本文を読み進めよう。

訳

1969年7月，中米のエルサルバドルとホンジュラスの間で，サッカーのワールドカップ予選での両国の対戦をきっかけに，短期間ながら激しい戦争が起きた。この紛争はしばしば「サッカー戦争」と呼ばれるがその原因はスポーツをはるかに超えたところにあった。

ホンジュラスはエルサルバドルよりはるかに大きいが，人口密度ははるかに低い。1800年代後半から，エルサルバドルの土地は主にエリート一族が支配しており，それは，一般農民のための土地はほとんどないということを意味した。1960年代までに，約30万人のエルサルバドル人が安価な土地や仕事を得るためにホンジュラスに不法入国した。ホンジュラス政府は，経済的ストレスの原因は移民であると非難し，移民を土地から追い出し，国外へ追いやった。エルサルバドルの富裕層は，多くの移民が帰国することによる経済的悪影響を恐れ，ホンジュラスに対して軍事行動を起こさなければ，エルサルバドル大統領を転覆させると脅した。これが長年にわたる国境紛争と相まって，両国の関係は最悪になった。

さらに緊張を高めたのは，両国のメディアで，互いへの恨みを煽るような記事をでっち上げたり，誇張したりした。エルサルバドルのマスコミが，ホンジュラス政府はエルサルバドル人移民を残酷かつ違法に扱っていると非難する一方，ホンジュラスの報道機関は，その同じ移民が重大な罪を犯していると報じた。このような報道は，それぞれの国の政府の要請によって行われた。エルサルバドルの目的は，隣国に対する軍事力の必要性を国民に納得させることであり，一方ホンジュラスでは，政府はエルサルバドル移民国外追放の決定について大衆の支持を得たいと考えていた。

ワールドカップ予選の試合は，移民問題が激化していた頃と同時期に行われていた。最終戦の日，エルサルバドルは，ホンジュラスのエルサルバドル人に対する暴力を非難して国交を断絶し，その後数週間以内にエルサルバドル軍がホンジュラスを攻撃し，戦争が始まった。歴史家は，サッカー戦争という言葉は誤解を招きかねないと指摘する。当時，アメリカは中米諸国と同盟を結んでいたが，戦争には参加しないことを選択した。実際，アメリカの外交官によれば，スポーツイベントが紛争の背景にあるという不正確な思い込みによって，アメリカ政府は紛争の深刻さを見過ごしたという。土地の所有権など，紛争の真の発端となる問題は未解決のままだった。結果として，その後数十年間，政治的，社会的に不安定な状態が続き，最終的には，エルサルバドルで内戦が勃発することとなった。

(35) 正解 **3**

質問の訳 第２段落によると，ホンジュラスへのエルサルバドル人移民はどのような点で「サッカー戦争」の原因となったのか。

選択肢の訳 **1** エルサルバドルの大統領は，移民をホンジュラスの家から追い出すことは，ホンジュラスが攻撃してくる兆候だと考えた。 **2** ホンジュラス政府が，土地を求める貧しいホンジュラス人をエルサルバドルに移住させ始めたため，エルサルバドル農民が腹を立て報復にホンジュラスに移住した。 **3** 移民がホンジュラスから追い出された後，金持ちのエルサルバドル人は，ホンジュラスに対して戦争を起こすよう政府に圧力をかけた。 **4** 両国間を行き来する移民の絶え間ない移動は，ホンジュラスの国境当局を悩ませた。

解説 第２段落第５文に，Wealthy Salvadorans feared the negative economic effects of so many immigrants returning home and threatened to overthrow the Salvadoran president if military action was not taken against Honduras.「エルサルバドルの富裕層は，多くの移民が帰国することによる経済的悪影響を恐れ，ホンジュラスに対して軍事行動を起こさなければ，エルサルバドル大統領を転覆させると脅した」とある。この内容と一致する選択肢**3**が正解。

(36) 正解 **4**

質問の訳 サッカー戦争が始まる前の時期，両国のメディアは，

選択肢の訳 **1** エルサルバドル人移民がより良い待遇を受けられるように両政府に圧力をかけようとした。 **2** 両国の政府によって，市民に対する不法行為を報道することが妨げられた。 **3** サッカーの対立に重点を置くあまり，より重要な違法行為に関するニュースを報道できなかった。 **4** 相手国を悪者にするような事実無根の，あるいは誤解を招くようなニュースをでっち上げるよう自国の政府に要請された。

解説 両国のメディアが行ったこととして，第３段落第１文でmade up or exaggerated stories that fueled their bitterness toward one another「互いへの恨みを煽るような記事をでっち上げたり，誇張したりした」と述べている。また，第３文にSuch reports were made at the request of the countries' governments「このような報道は，それぞれの国の政府の要請によって行われた」とある。これらの内容をまとめた選択肢**4**が正解。

(37) 正解 **3**

質問の訳 この文章の著者は最終段落で何を示唆しているか。

選択肢の訳 **1** アメリカの外交官たちは，ホンジュラスとエルサルバドルとの間で再び戦闘が勃発することを今もなお心配し続けている。 **2** サッカー戦争のひどい影響は，ホンジュラスとエルサルバドルに，戦争に至るまでの自分たちの行動が間違っていたことを認識させた。 **3** サッカー戦争に対する誤った思い込みは，その真の原因が認識されなかったことを意味し，その結果，別の紛争が起こった。 **4**アメリカ政府の政策に

より，多くの中米諸国が国交を断絶し，地域の紛争が悪化した。

解説 最終段落第５，６文で，アメリカが，サッカーが紛争の背景にあると考え，土地の所有権など真の原因を見過ごしたため問題は未解決のままだったと述べている。その結果が最終文のcontinued political and social instability and, ultimately, a civil war in El Salvador in the following decades「その後数十年間，政治的，社会的に不安定な状態が続き，最終的には，エルサルバドルで内戦が勃発」なので，この内容と一致する**3**が正解。

点字との争い

Key to Reading 第１段落：導入＋本論①（ボストン・ライン・タイプという視覚障害者のための筆記方式）→第２段落：本論②（明確になっていく点字との差）→第３段落：本論③（「点の戦争」の実態）→第４段落：結論（点の戦争の終結と恩恵）という４段落構成の説明文。選択肢を検討するときは，本文中の語（句）の言い換えに注意しよう。

訳

点字は今日の視覚障害者にとって標準的な筆記方式であるが，盛り上がった点々が文字を表すこのアルファベットだけが，常に唯一の方式だったわけではない。もうひとつの方式であるボストン・ライン・タイプは，1830年代にサミュエル・グリドリー・ハウという，米国の盲学校の目の見える指導員によって作られた。ハウのシステムは，目の見える人が使う標準的な英語のアルファベットの文字を利用したものだが，指で感じられるように文字が盛り上がっていた。しかし，目の不自由な生徒たちにとって，ある文字を別の文字と区別するのは，点字よりも難しいことだった。それでも，ハウは，目の見えない読者と目の見える読者が教材を共有できるという事実が，このデメリットを上回ると考えた。ハウは，彼のシステムによって，視覚障害者は，よりよく社会に溶け込むことができると主張した。彼は，点字はほとんどの健常者にとってなじみがないため，孤立を助長すると考えていた。

点は比較的簡単に書くことができるため，点字は大半の視覚障害者にとってより読みやすいだけでなく，より実用的であることが徐々に明確になっていった。ボストン・ライン・タイプで書くには特別な印刷機が必要だったが，点字は簡単な携帯用具で済む上に，タイプライターでも打つことができた。それでも，生徒たちが点字を圧倒的に好んだにもかかわらず，ボストン・ライン・タイプは盲学校で公式に使われ続けたが，これは，ボストン・ライン・タイプによって，目の見える教師が新しい記号を覚えることなく教えることができたからである。ボストン・ライン・タイプが人気を失っても，他のシステムが導入され続け，様々な筆記方式が標準となるよう競い合い，「点の戦争」として知られるようになった。

その一つがニューヨーク・ポイントというもので，盛り上がった点で構成されているという点で，点字に似ていた。主な利点は，片手でタイプできることだった。しかし，点字の方が，大文字や特定の句読点をより効率的かつ明瞭に表示することができた。候補は他にもあり，どれが優れているかという議論はすぐに激しくなっていった。一方，目の不自由な人たちは大きな不便を強いられた。読める本の供給は既に不足しており，筆記方式の競合により，彼らの選択肢はさらに狭まった。新しい方式を学ぶには多大な時間と労力が必要だったからだ。ある全国大会では，講演者が，次に視覚障害者向けの印刷方式を新たに発明した者には暴力で応じようと冗談交じりに提案し，彼らの不満を要約したという。

点の戦争は1900年代に入っても続き，様々なグループが資金と認知を巡って争った。

最終的には，盲目の活動家ヘレン・ケラーが，この論争に終止符を打つのに多大な影響を与えた。彼女は，大文字と句読点に関するニューヨーク・ポイントの弱点は極めて深刻で，指で読むのはたいへんだと述べた。点字が勝利し，他のシステムは徐々に姿を消した。点の戦争は一時期，視覚障害者教育の妨げになったが，明るい兆しもあった。この激しい戦いは，新しいタイプライターなどの様々な技術の開発を促し，視覚障害者の識字率や現代社会への参加能力を大幅に向上させたのである。

(38) 正解 **4**

質問の訳 サミュエル・グリドリー・ハウはボストン・ライン・タイプについてどのように考えていたか。

選択肢の訳 **1** 視覚障害者が読むのに時間がかからないという事実は，書くのに点字より多大な時間がかかるという点を補って余りある。 **2** 盛り上がった点と他の特徴の組み合わせにより視覚障害者同士の意思の疎通の際，より使いやすくなった。
3 生徒が習得するのは難しかったが，点字よりも早く読めることは大きな利点だった。
4 視覚障害者が，目の見える人とよりよく調和するために役立つという点で，採用する価値があった。

解説 ボストン・ライン・タイプは盲学校の生徒にとっては読みづらいものであったが，それでもハウがそれを使用した理由が第1段落第5文以降で述べられている。目の見える人と同じ英語のアルファベットを使用するので，reading materials could be shared by both blind and sighted readers「目の見えない読者と目の見える読者が教材を共有できる」ため，ハウは，His system ... would allow blind people to better integrate into society「彼のシステムによって，視覚障害者は，よりよく社会に溶け込むことができる」と考え，これが読みづらさを上回る利点であると主張した。これに一致する選択肢**4**が正解。

(39) 正解 **1**

質問の訳 第2段落で，この文章の著者はボストン・ライン・タイプについて何を示唆しているか。

選択肢の訳 **1** その継続的な使用は，視覚障害者の最善の利益にはならなかった。どの方式を使うべきかについての彼らの意見は考慮されなかったようだ。 **2** 盲学校の教師たちは，点の数が少ない方式の方が生徒にとって読みやすいと考え，それを使わないように生徒たちを説得した。 **3** 「点の戦争」を引き起こしたにもかかわらず，生徒の間で人気があり，その人気が，視覚障害者用の他の道具が開発される重要な要因となった。 **4** タイプライター導入後に初めて，盲学校の生徒がボストン・ライン・タイプの筆記に成功した。

解説 第2段落第1，2文で，視覚障害者にとってはボストン・ライン・タイプよりも点字の方が読みやすく書きやすいということがわかる。生徒たちには点字の方が圧倒的に人気であったが，ボストン・ライン・タイプが学校で使用され続けていたのは，it allowed sighted instructors to teach without having to learn new sets of symbols「目の見える教師が新しい記号を覚えることなく教えることができた」（第3文）からである。視覚障害者自身の意見は考慮されなかったということなので，この内容と一致する選択肢**1**が正解。選択肢では，視覚障害者にとって読み書きが難しいということを，Its continued use was not in the best interests of blind peopleと言い換えている。

(40) 正解 2

質問の訳 全国大会での講演者の提案は，視覚障害者が～ことを示唆している。

選択肢の訳 **1** 点字もニューヨーク・ポイント・システムも，目の不自由な読者のニーズを満たせないと思っていた　**2** どちらの方式を使うべきかという議論が，間接的に視覚障害者の読書へのアクセスを妨げていることに不満を感じていた　**3** 視覚障害者によって開発されていない筆記方式の使用を強制されることを嫌っていた　**4** 本を読むことを学ぶよりも，他の種類の教育の方がはるかに重要になっていると考え始めていた

解説 全国大会の講演者の提案に言及しているのは，第3段落最終文。a speaker reportedly summed up their frustrations by jokingly suggesting a violent response to the next person who invents a new system of printing for the blind「とある講演者が，次に視覚障害者向けの印刷方式を新たに発明した者には暴力で応じようと冗談交じりに提案し，彼らの不満を要約したという」とある。この段落では，ニューヨーク・ポイント・システムをはじめ，様々な筆記方式が標準方式としての候補にあがり議論が激化する一方，視覚障害者自身は筆記方式の競合によってむしろ読書の選択肢が限られ，たいへんな不都合を強いられた（severely inconvenienced）ことが述べられている。この内容と一致する選択肢**2**が正解。prevent ～ from doing ...「～が…するのを妨げる」

(41) 正解 3

質問の訳 この文章の著者は点の戦争についてどのような結論を出しているか。

選択肢の訳 **1** それは非常に深刻なもので，今日でも視覚障害者のための技術の研究や開発に悪影響を及ぼしている。　**2** もしヘレン・ケラーがこの争いへの関与を決断しなければ，悪感情を引き起こすことはそれほどなかっただろう。　**3** 競争が視覚障害者の生活向上につながったため，長期的にはプラスの効果もあった。　**4** 当時の人々がタイプライターのような技術をもっと受け入れていれば，この事態は避けられたかもしれない。

解説 著者の結論は，第4段落最終文で述べられている。激しい競争が，stimulated the development of various technologies, such as new typewriters「新しいタイプライターなどの様々な技術の開発を促し」，greatly enhanced blind people's literacy rates and ability to participate in modern society「視覚障害者の識字率や現代社会への参加能力を大幅に向上させた」とある。この内容と一致する選択肢**3**が正解。

4 一次試験・英作文

（問題編p.113）

指示文の訳 ●次のトピックについてエッセイを書きなさい。
答えの裏付けに，以下に挙げたポイントのうちの2つを使いなさい。
●構成：導入，本論，結論
●長さ：120～150語
●エッセイは解答用紙のB面に用意されたスペースに書きなさい。
スペースの外側に書かれた内容は，採点の対象とはなりません。

※2024年度第1回から，大問4に文章の要約を書く問題が加わります。

トピックの訳 あなたは次の意見に賛成ですか，それとも反対ですか：政府は再利用可能な商品を促進するためにもっと多くのことをすべきだ

ポイントの訳 ●費用 ●事業者への影響 ●ごみ ●安全性

解答例

I agree that the government should do more to promote reusable products, particularly in relation to garbage and costs.

Firstly, increasing the adoption of reusable products will directly impact the amount of garbage that humans produce. Throwing away items after a single use, for example, is a significant factor in the buildup of waste in landfills all over the world. By encouraging greater awareness of reusable products, governments can actively help the environment.

Secondly, reusable products can be cost-effective for both consumers and businesses. People still buy plastic bags at supermarkets, and many restaurants purchase single-use chopsticks. Government promotion of reusable alternatives, however, would save money for shoppers and reduce overhead costs for businesses, which could have a wider positive economic impact.

In conclusion, I feel that promoting reusable products should be a priority for the government because the environmental and cost benefits are too important to ignore.

解答例の訳

私は，特にごみと費用との関連で，政府が再利用可能な商品を促進するためにもっと多くのことをすべきであるということに賛成だ。

第一に，再利用可能な商品の採択を増やすことは，人間が生み出すごみの量に直接的に影響を及ぼすだろう。例えば，一度だけ使った後で商品を処分することは，世界中の埋め立て地における廃棄物の蓄積をもたらす重大な要因となっている。再利用可能な商品に対するより高い意識を奨励することにより，政府は積極的に環境を改善することができる。

第二に，再利用可能な商品は消費者にも事業者にも費用対効果が高まる。人々は依然としてスーパーでレジ袋を購入し，多くのレストランは使い捨ての箸を購入している。しかし，再利用可能な代替品を政府が奨励することは，買い物客にとってはお金の節約に，事業者にとっては一般諸経費の削減になり，これはより広範なプラスの経済効果になり得る。

結論として，私は，環境および費用便益が無視できないほどに重要であるため，再利用可能な商品の促進が政府にとっては優先事項であるべきだと思う。

解説 TOPIC文で示されている意見について，「賛成である／反対である」のどちらかの立場に立って，自分の意見とその根拠をエッセイの形でまとめる形式。エッセイをまとめる際には，POINTSとして示されたキーワードのうち２つを選んで使用する必要がある。これらのキーワードに挙げられている語句については，例えば，Effect on businessesはpositive[negative] impacts on industry「業界へのプラスの〔マイナスの〕影響」などと，必要に応じて形を変えて表現しても良い。

段落構成に関する，導入（introduction）→本論（main body）→結論（conclusion）という基本的な指定は必ず守ること。解答例のように本論を２つに分ける場合は，論点の重複がないように，それぞれの段落を別の視点からまとめる。その際，各段落の論点が明

確になるように，談話標識（discourse markers）を使うと論理的にまとまりのある文章となり，効果的である。また，結論をまとめるときは，第1段落の単純な繰り返しにならないよう，表現を若干でも工夫することが好ましい。

TOPIC文 「政府は再利用可能な商品を促進するためにもっと多くのことをすべきだ」という意見について賛成か反対かを求める内容。

語句 government「政府」/ promote「～を促進する」/ reusable「再利用可能な」

第1段落（導入） まずエッセイの冒頭で，TOPIC文のテーマを正しく理解していることと，自分が「政府は再利用可能な商品を促進するためにもっと多くのことをすべきだ」という意見について，「賛成である／反対である」のどちらの立場に立っているかを明示する必要がある。解答例は，文をI agree that ～「私は～ということに賛成である」から始め，自分が前者の立場にいることを明確に示している。また，POINTSの中からGarbage「ごみ」とCosts「費用」の2つを取り上げていることも，すでにここで示している。

語句 particularly「とりわけ」/ in relation to ～「～に関して」

第2段落（本論①） 第2段落では，順序を表す談話標識であるFirstly「第一に」から始め，第1段落で示した1つ目の観点である「ごみ」について述べている。また，第2文では，人間が生み出すごみの具体例を，for example「例えば」という談話標識を用いて挙げている。

語句 increase「～を増やす」/ adoption「採択」/ directly「直接的に」/ impact「～に影響を与える」/ throw away ～「～を処分する」/ item「商品」/ a single use「1回限りの使用」/ significant「重大な」/ factor「要因」/ buildup「蓄積」/ waste「廃棄物」/ landfill「埋め立て地」/ encourage「～を奨励する」/ awareness「意識」/ actively「積極的に」

第3段落（本論②） 第3段落では，第1段落で示した2つ目の観点である「費用」について意見を展開している。この段落では，順序を表すsecondly「第二に」，逆接を表すhowever「しかし」という2つの談話標識を駆使しながら，再利用可能な商品が消費者側にも事業者側にも費用対効果が高いという点に焦点を当てている。

語句 cost-effective「費用対効果が高い」/ consumer「消費者」/ single-use「使い捨ての」/ promotion「奨励」/ alternative「代替物」/ overhead costs「一般諸経費」

第4段落（結論） 最終段落では，In conclusion「結論として」という談話標識から文を始めて，自分がTOPIC文の意見に賛成の立場であることを，第1段落とは多少表現を変えた上で再度述べ，文章を締め括っている。

語句 priority「優先事項」/ cost benefit「費用便益」/ ignore「～を無視する」

Part 1 一次試験・リスニング

(問題編pp.114～115)

指示文の訳 準1級の試験のリスニングテストが始まります。指示を注意して聞いてください。テスト中に質問をすることは許されていません。

このテストは3つのパートに分かれています。これら3つのパートの質問は全て選択肢の中から正解を選ぶ問題です。それぞれの質問について，問題冊子に書かれている4つの選択肢の中から最も適切な答えを選び，解答用紙の該当箇所にその答えをマークしなさい。

このリスニングテストの全てのパートで，メモを取ってもかまいません。

それでは，これからPart 1の指示を行います。このパートではNo. 1からNo.12まで12の会話が放送されます。それぞれの会話に続いて，質問が1つ流れます。各質問に対して，最も適切な答えを選んで解答用紙にマークする時間が10秒あります。会話と質問は1度しか読まれません。それでは，準1級のリスニングテストを始めます。

No.1 正解 4

放送文 ***A:*** Hi, Ron. Why are you sitting there? Where's the new receptionist? ***B:*** She called to say she'll be late. ***A:*** Again? That's the third time since she started. What's her excuse now? ***B:*** She said her babysitter hasn't turned up yet. ***A:*** I know she has her problems, but it can't go on like this. I'll have to have a talk with her. ***B:*** Please do. I'm tired of filling in.

Question: What is the woman going to do?

訳 A：あら，ロン。どうしてそこに座っているの？ 新しい受付係はどこ？ B：彼女から遅れるって電話がありました。 A：また？ 彼女が入ってから3回目ですよ。今度はどういう言い訳をしてるの？ B：ベビーシッターがまだ来ないそうです。 A：彼女にも事情があるのはわかるけど，このままってわけにはいきませんね。彼女と話してみないといけないみたいね。 B：そうしてください。もう穴埋めはうんざりです。

質問の訳 女性はどうするつもりか。

選択肢の訳 **1** 男性に受付係の穴埋めをしてもらう。 **2** 男性に受付係をクビにするように頼む。 **3** 受付係の仕事を自分でやる。 **4** 遅刻について受付係に警告する。

解説 1往復目でA（＝女性）に「新しい受付係はどこ？」とたずねられたB（＝Ron）は，「彼女（＝新しい受付係）から遅れるって電話がありました」と述べ，3往復目では「もう穴埋めはうんざりです」と述べているので，新しい受付係が出勤せず，代わりにBが受付をしている状況だとわかる。2往復目でAは，「彼女が入ってから3回目（の遅刻）」と述べ，さらに3往復目では「このままってわけにはいきませんね。彼女と話してみないといけないみたいね」と述べ，それに対しBも「そうしてください」と答えている。よって，女性は，新しい受付係に遅刻しないように注意するつもりであることがわかるので，have a talk with herを**warn the receptionist**と言い換えた**4**が正解。

No.2 正解 1

放送文 ***A:*** Tim, I'm concerned about your performance in my science class. ***B:*** Didn't I pass the test yesterday? ***A:*** No, and you've missed several assignments. ***B:*** I'm sorry. I've had to work late every night this month at my part-time job. ***A:*** Well, we need to solve this problem. ***B:*** OK. I'll talk to my boss about cutting back my hours. ***A:*** And how about coming in for extra work before or after school? ***B:*** Thanks, Mrs. Roberts. I'll be here early tomorrow morning.

Question: What conclusion can be made about the student?

訳 A：ティム，理科の授業の成績を心配しています。 B：ぼくは昨日のテストに合格しなかったんですか？ A：ええ，それに宿題も何回かやりませんでしたね。 B：すみません。今月はアルバイトで毎晩遅くまで働かなければなりませんでした。 A：では，その問題を解決する必要がありますね。 B：わかりました。アルバイトの時間を減らす

よう上司に相談してみます。　A：それから，学校の前か放課後に特別な課題をするのはどうかしら？　B：ありがとうございます，ロバーツ先生。明日の朝早くここに来ます。

質問の訳 この生徒についてどのような結論が得られるか。

選択肢の訳 **1** 授業の成績を上げなければならない。　**2** 仕事のスケジュールを変更できない。　**3** アルバイトを辞めるだろう。　**4** 理科の授業に出ない。

解説 A（＝女性：Mrs. Roberts）はB（＝生徒：Tim）に1往復目で「理科の授業の成績を心配しています」，2往復目でNoと言ってティムが昨日のテストに合格しなかったことを伝えて「宿題も何回かやりませんでしたね」，さらに3往復目で「その問題を解決する必要がありますね」と述べている。よって，AがBの成績を心配しており，Bはそれを改善しなければならない状況であることがわかるので，concerned about your performance in my science classを**improve his class performance**と言い換えた**1**が正解。Bは「アルバイトの時間を減らすよう上司に相談してみます」と述べており，アルバイトは続けるつもりなので，**3**は不適切。

No.3 正解 **4**

放送文 ***A:*** Hey, Dave. You look down. What's wrong? ***B:*** Well, mostly, it's just that I'm not enjoying my job. ***A:*** Have you thought about doing something else? ***B:*** Yes, but I haven't been able to find anything that pays as well. With the kids almost in college and the house payments, I can't really just quit. ***A:*** I hear you. Well, I hope things work out for you. ***B:*** Thanks, but right now I'm not very optimistic.

Question: What is the man's problem?

訳 ***A:*** やあ，デイブ。浮かない顔しているね。どうしたの？　B：まあ，ちょっと仕事を楽しめていないってだけのことなんだけどね。　A：他の仕事をしようと思ったことはあるの？　B：あるけど，同じくらい給料のいい仕事が見つからないんだ。子供ももうすぐ大学生になるし，家のローンもあるから，辞めるに辞められないんだ。　A：そうだよね。まあ，いろいろうまくいくといいね。　B：ありがとう，でも今はあんまり楽観できないんだ。

質問の訳 男性の問題は何か。

選択肢の訳 **1** 子供の大学の学費が払えない。　**2** 会社から遠すぎるところに住んでいる。　**3** 十分な給料をもらっていないと思っている。　**4** 今の会社を辞められないと感じている。

解説 1往復目でB（＝Dave）は，「ちょっと仕事を楽しめていないってだけのことなんだけどね」と述べているので，Bが仕事に満足できていない状況であることがわかる。2往復目でA（＝女性）に「他の仕事をしようと思ったことはあるの？」と聞かれると，Bは「同じくらい給料のいい仕事が見つからない」，「子供ももうすぐ大学生になるし，家のローンもあるから，辞めるに辞められないんだ」と述べており，転職も考えたが，今の会社を辞められないと思っていることがわかる。よって，can't really just quitを**unable to leave**と言い換えた**4**が正解。

No.4 正解 **1**

放送文 ***A:*** Morning, Fiona. Coffee? ***B:*** Make it a big one! I was working on a project report until midnight last night. I can't believe I'm here so late every

day. ***A:*** Didn't they warn you about the overtime when you interviewed? ***B:*** Well, they sort of did. What really bothers me, though, is that every time I think I've achieved my targets, my manager changes them. ***A:*** That's corporate life. At least you have summer vacation to look forward to. ***B:*** Yeah. I hope they actually let me take it!
Question: What is the woman's main complaint?

訳 A：おはよう，フィオナ。コーヒー飲む？ B：たっぷりのにして！ 昨夜，夜中までプロジェクトの報告書を書いていたの。毎日こんなに遅くまでここにいるなんて信じられないわ。 A：面接のとき，残業について知らされていなかったの？ B：まあ，言われたけどね。でも本当に困るのは，目標を達成したと思うたびに，上司が目標を変えてくることなのよ。 A：それが会社生活というものだよ。いくらなんでも，楽しみにしてる夏休みはもらえるんでしょ。 B：ええ。本当に取らせてもらえるといいんだけどね！

質問の訳 女性の主な不満は何か。

選択肢の訳 **1** 頻繁に新しい目標を与えられる。 **2** 残業代が十分に支払われない。 **3** 休暇の申請が却下された。 **4** 彼女の報告書が否定的な評価を受けた。

解説 2往復目でB（＝Fiona）は，「でも本当に困るのは，目標を達成したと思うたびに，上司が目標を変えてくることなのよ」と述べているので，Bは上司がたびたび目標を変えてくることに困っている状況であることがわかる。よって，every time … my targets, my manager changes themを**frequently given new goals**と言い換えた**1**が正解。Bは「本当に（夏休みを）取らせてもらえるといいんだけどね！」とは述べているが，休暇の申請が却下されたとは述べていないので**3**は不適切。

No.5 正解 **2**

放送文 ***A:*** Dad, I want to go to grad school straight after university. Maybe I'll do a master's in psychology. ***B:*** That's a big commitment, and it doesn't sound like you have a clear plan. How about working for a few years first? ***A:*** I'm afraid if I don't do this soon, I never will. I'm worried about the cost, though. ***B:*** I've told you I'd help with that. But I really think a year or two in the real world would give you valuable experience. ***A:*** OK. Let me think about it a bit more.
Question: What does the man tell his daughter?

訳 A：お父さん，大学を卒業したらそのまま大学院に行きたいと思っているの。たぶん心理学の修士課程に進むと思う。 B：それは大きな決断だけど，明確なプランがあるわけでもなさそうにも思えるね。まずは数年働いてみたらどうかな？ A：すぐにやらないと，いつまでたってもできないんじゃないかと思っているわ。費用が心配なんだけどね。B：それは協力すると言っただろう。でも本当に，実社会で1，2年経験すれば，貴重な経験ができると思うよ。 A：わかった。もう少し考えさせてね。

質問の訳 男性は娘に何と言っているか。

選択肢の訳 **1** 来年修士号を取得するべきだ。 **2** 仕事の経験を積むべきだ。 **3** 1年間彼の助けを借りることができる。 **4** まずはお金を貯めるべきだ。

解説 1往復目でA（＝娘）が「大学を卒業したらそのまま大学院に行きたいと思っているの」と述べたのに対し，B（＝父親）は「まずは数年働いてみたらどうかな？」と提案し，さらに2往復目でも「実社会で1，2年経験すれば，貴重な経験ができると思うよ」

CD 赤

と述べているので，Bは，娘は大学卒業後にすぐに大学院に行くべきではなく，その前にまずは実社会で数年働いてみるべきだと考えていることがわかる。よって，working for a few yearsやa year or two in the real worldを**get some work experience**と言い換えた**2**が正解。

No.6 正解 3

放送文 ***A:*** Shelly, personnel asked me to remind you the deadline for enrolling in an insurance plan is tomorrow. ***B:*** I know, but I have no idea which one's best for me. ***A:*** They're all described on the company website. Why don't you look there? ***B:*** I have, but it wasn't very helpful. I find all the different options so confusing. ***A:*** Maybe you should have someone in personnel explain the choices again. ***B:*** I guess I have no choice.

Question: What will the woman probably do next?

訳 A：シェリー，人事から，君に保険プランの加入期限が明日までだって確認してほしいって言われたんだけど。　B：わかってるけど，どれが私に一番いいのか全然わからなくて。　A：会社のウェブサイトに全部書いてあるよ。見てみたら？　B：見たけど，あまり役に立たなかったのよ。いろいろな選択肢があってすごく混乱するわ。　A：人事の人にもう一度説明してもらった方がいいんじゃないかな。　B：そうするしかないわね。

質問の訳 女性はおそらく次に何をするか。

選択肢の訳 **1**　ウェブサイトをもっと注意深く見直す。　**2**　男性と同じプランを選ぶ。　**3**　人事担当者との面談を申し込む。　**4**　別の保険プランを探す。

解説 1往復目でA（＝男性）から，保険プランの加入期限が明日までだと言われたB（＝Shelly）は，「どれが私に一番いいのか全然わからなくて」と述べ，2往復目でAに，会社のウェブサイトに全部書いてあると言われてもBは，「見たけど，あまり役に立たなかった～すごく混乱するわ」と述べているので，Bはどの保険プランを選べばいいかわからず困っていることがわかる。Aに，人事の人に説明してもらうことを勧められると，Bは「そうするしかないわね」と答えているので，Bが人事の担当者に説明の面談を申し込むだろうことがわかる。よって，have someone in personnel explainを**request a meeting with personnel**と言い換えた**3**が正解。

No.7 正解 3

放送文 ***A:*** Happy birthday, Kimiko! ***B:*** Farouk, there you are! I was getting worried you wouldn't make it to the party. Did you get lost? ***A:*** Sorry to be so late. No, your house was easy to find. Actually, I felt a little drowsy, so I pulled off the highway for a short nap. The next thing I knew, an hour had passed. ***B:*** Well, I'm just glad you made it here safely. How was the traffic? ***A:*** Not as heavy as I'd feared. Is it all right if I sit down? ***B:*** Of course.

Question: Why did the man arrive late?

訳 A：キミコ，誕生日おめでとう！　B：ファルーク，来てくれたんだ！　パーティーに来られないんじゃないかって心配してたのよ。道に迷ったの？　A：だいぶ遅くなってごめん。いや，君の家はすぐに見つかったよ。実は，少しうとうとしちゃったんで，幹線道路を降りて少し仮眠したんだ。気がついたら1時間経ってたんだ。　B：そうなの，無事に来てくれてよかったわ。渋滞はどうだった？　A：心配していたほどではなかったよ。座ってもいい？　B：もちろん。

質問の訳 男性はなぜ遅れて到着したのか。

選択肢の訳 **1** 大渋滞に巻き込まれた。 **2** 車の調子が悪かった。 **3** 長時間眠りすぎた。 **4** 幹線道路で道に迷った。

解説 1～2往復目からB（＝Kimiko）の誕生日パーティーにA（＝Farouk）が遅れて到着した場面だとわかる。「道に迷ったの？」とBにたずねられたAは「いや，君の家はすぐに見つかったよ」と言ったあと，「幹線道路を降りて少し仮眠したんだ。気がついたら1時間経ってたんだ」と述べているので，Bはうっかり長く仮眠しすぎたことがわかる。よって，I pulled off ～ for a short nap. The next thing I knew, an hour had passedを**slept for too long**と言い換えた**3**が正解。「渋滞はどうだった？」とたずねられたBは「心配していたほどではなかったよ」と述べているので，**1**は不適切。

No.8 正解 1

放送文 ***A:*** Honey, look at Jason's report card. He's still struggling in math. ***B:*** I guess I should start helping him with his homework again. ***A:*** I think it's past that point now. We need to seriously consider getting him a tutor. ***B:*** We're already paying so much for his private schooling. Shouldn't his teachers be doing something about it? ***A:*** I understand your frustration, but I think some one-on-one time in another environment would really help him. ***B:*** I just hate to think of spending even more money right now.

Question: What does the man think?

訳 A：あなた，ジェイソンの成績表を見て。数学にまだ苦労しているみたい。　B：また宿題を手伝ってやり始めた方がいいかな。　A：もうそういう時期は過ぎたと思うの。家庭教師をつけることを真剣に考えないと。　B：ぼくたちはすでに彼の私立学校のためにとても高いお金を払っているんだよ。先生たちが何とかしてくれないのかな？　A：不満はわかるけど，別の環境で1対1の時間を持つことは，かなり彼の助けになると思うのよ。　B：ぼくはただ，今，さらにお金を使うことを考えるのは嫌なんだよ。

質問の訳 男性はどう考えているか。

選択肢の訳 **1** ジェイソンの先生はもっと努力すべきだ。 **2** ジェイソンは私立学校に転校すべきだ。 **3** ジェイソンの宿題の量が増えている。 **4** ジェイソンを家庭教師のもとに行かせるべきだ。

解説 1往復目から，両親が息子のジェイソンの成績表を見て，数学の成績を心配している状況だとわかる。A（＝女性）から家庭教師をつけることを提案されたB（＝男性）は「ぼくたちはすでに彼の私立学校のためにとても高いお金を払っているんだよ。先生たちが何とかしてくれないのかな？」と述べ，3往復目でも「（家庭教師の費用として）さらにお金を使うことを考えるのは嫌なんだよ」と述べているので，男性は家庭教師をつけるのではなく，ジェイソンの学校の先生に息子の成績改善のためにもっと尽力してほしいと思っていることがわかる。よって，Shouldn't his teachers be doing something about it?を**Jason's teachers should make more effort.**と言い換えた**1**が正解。

No.9 正解 4

放送文 ***A:*** Hello, Michael. How are you liking your new position? I hear it's been keeping you on the road quite a bit. ***B:*** Yes, I've spent more time abroad recently than I have at home. ***A:*** I envy you. I'm tired of going to the office every single day. ***B:*** Well, even though I'm traveling, mostly all I get to see is the inside of hotels and factories. ***A:*** I hope you're not regretting changing positions. ***B:*** No, things should settle down soon.

Question: What does the woman imply?

訳 A：こんにちは，マイケル。新しい仕事はどう？ 出張が多いって聞いているわよ。 B：うん，最近は家にいる時間より海外で過ごす時間の方が長いんだ。 A：うらやましいな。毎日毎日，会社に行くのはうんざりよ。 B：まあ，旅行といっても，ほとんどホテルと工場の中しか見ないけどね。 A：転職したことを後悔していないよね。 B：うん，もうすぐ落ち着くと思うんだ。

質問の訳 女性は何を言いたいのか。

選択肢の訳 **1** 男性は前職に戻るべきだ。 **2** 彼女はもうすぐ職位を変えるだろう。 **3** 男性はもっと家で過ごすべきだ。 **4** 彼女は仕事でもっと旅行したい。

解説 1往復目でA（＝女性）から「新しい仕事はどう？」とたずねられたB（＝Michael）が，「最近は家にいる時間より（仕事で）海外で過ごす時間の方が長いんだ」と答えると，Aは「うらやましいな。毎日毎日，会社に行くのはうんざりよ」述べているので，Aは毎日会社に行くだけでなく，Bのようにもっと出張したいと思っていることがわかる。よって，tired of going to the office every single dayを**would like to travel for work more**と言い換えた**4**が正解。

No.10 正解 3

放送文 ***A:*** Morning, Deborah. Hey, are you OK? ***B:*** What? Oh, sorry, Stan. I'm just in a bad mood. ***A:*** What happened? ***B:*** I got confused while transferring at Baxter Station and almost missed my usual train. It's like a maze now because of the construction. ***A:*** They're doing major renovations, right? ***B:*** Yes, and the directions for passengers were unclear. I never thought I'd get lost in the train station I use every morning. ***A:*** How long will the work continue? ***B:*** Until the end of the year. I guess I'll have to get used to it.

Question: Why is the woman in a bad mood?

訳 A：おはよう，デボラ。どうしたの，大丈夫？ B：え？ ああ，ごめん，スタン。ちょっと機嫌が悪いの。 A：何があったの？ B：バクスター駅で乗り換えるときにまごついちゃって，いつもの電車に乗り遅れそうになったのよ。今，工事中で迷路みたいなの。 A：大改装中なんでしょう？ B：うん，それで乗客への案内もわかりづらいのよ。毎朝使っている駅で迷子になるとは思わなかったわ。 A：工事はいつまで続くの？ B：年末まで。慣れるしかないわね。

質問の訳 女性はなぜ機嫌が悪いのか。

選択肢の訳 **1** 駅の改装が予定より遅れている。 **2** 乗った列車がいつもより混んでいた。 **3** 乗り換えに苦労した。 **4** いつも使っている駅が閉鎖されていた。

解説　1往復目でA（＝Stan）から「どうしたの，大丈夫？」とたずねられたB（＝Deborah）は，「ちょっと機嫌が悪いの」と述べ，2往復目でAが「何があったの？」と言って，機嫌が悪い理由をたずねると，Bは「バクスター駅で乗り換えるときにまごついちゃって，いつもの電車に乗り遅れそうになったのよ」と述べている。よって，Bが機嫌が悪い理由は，駅で乗り換えに苦労したことだとわかるので，got confused while transferringを**had trouble changing trains**と言い換えた**3**が正解。

No.11　正解　1

放送文　***A:*** Have you finished that book already?　***B:*** Yes.　Since I turned 50, I've been trying to read more for mental stimulation.　I want to stay sharp and alert.　***A:*** That's great.　Lately, all I ever read are boring work-related documents and manuals.　***B:*** That does sound dull.　These days, I'm mostly reading historical fiction, although sometimes I try to read science books for general audiences.
A: Maybe I should start reading some fiction as well, before I forget how to enjoy a book.
Question: Why is the woman reading books?

訳　A：その本はもう読み終えたの？　B：うん。50歳を過ぎてから，精神的な刺激のためにより多く読書するようにしているの。いつまでも鋭敏でいたいわ。　A：すばらしいね。最近は，ぼくが読むものと言えば，仕事関係のつまらない書類やマニュアルばかりなんだ。　B：それはほんとに退屈そうね。私は最近は歴史小説を読むことが多いけど，たまに一般向けの科学書も読んでみているわ。　A：本の楽しみ方を忘れてしまう前に，ぼくも小説でも読み始めたほうがいいみたいだね。

質問の訳　女性はなぜ本を読んでいるのか。

選択肢の訳　**1**　心をアクティブに保つため。　**2**　仕事のスキルを向上させるため。　**3**　仕事を忘れるため。　**4**　小説のアイデアを得るため。

解説　1往復目でA（＝男性）から「その本はもう読み終えたの？」とたずねられたB（＝女性）は，「うん」と言ったあと，「精神的な刺激のためにより多く読書するようにしているの。いつまでも鋭敏でいたいわ」と述べているので，女性は精神的な刺激のためにより多く読書しようとしていることがわかる。よって，mental stimulationやstay sharp and alertを**keep her mind active**と言い換えた**1**が正解。

No.12　正解　2

放送文　***A:*** Which trail should we take, Jack?　***B:*** Trail A looks like the easiest one.　The cable car carries us halfway up the mountain, and then we hike for about an hour to the peak.　***A:*** How about something more challenging?　I think we could handle climbing the whole way.　***B:*** I don't know.　All the overtime I've been working recently has really cut into my workouts.　I'm not sure my legs will carry me all the way up.　***A:*** All right.　Trail A it is, then.
Question: What do we learn about the man?

訳　A：ジャック，どのコースに行こうかしら？　B：Aコースが一番簡単そうだね。ケーブルカーで山の中腹まで行って，そこから山頂まで1時間ほど歩くんだ。　A：もっと難しいコースはどう？　全行程を登っても大丈夫だと思うわ。　B：どうかな。最近，残業

続きで運動不足なんだ。この足で登りきれるかどうか自信がないよ。 A：わかったわ。じゃあ，Aコースにしましょう。

質問の訳 男性について何がわかるか。

選択肢の訳 **1** 経験豊富な登山家だ。 **2** 最近あまり運動していない。 **3** 難易度の高いコースを歩きたがっている。 **4** ケーブルカーに乗るのが嫌いだ。

解説 1往復目の対話から，A（＝女性）とB（＝Jack）が，登山道の入り口等で，どの登山コースを登るかについて話している場面であることがわかる。2往復目でA(＝女性)が「(Aコースより）もっと難しいコースはどう？ 全行程を登っても大丈夫だと思うわ」と述べると，Bは「最近，残業続きで運動不足なんだ。この足で登りきれるかどうか自信がないよ」と述べているので，Bは最近，運動不足であることがわかる。よって，recently has really cut into my workoutsをhas not gotten much exercise recentlyと言い換えた**2**が正解。

Part 2 一次試験・リスニング
(問題編pp.116～117)

指示文の訳 それでは，これからPart 2の指示を行います。このパートでは(A)から(F)までの6つの文章が放送されます。それぞれの文章に続いて，No.13からNo.24まで質問が2つずつ流れます。それぞれの質問に対して，最も適切な答えを選んで解答用紙にマークする時間が10秒あります。文章と質問は1度しか読まれません。それでは始めます。

(A)

放送文 *Annie Londonderry*

Annie Cohen Kopchovsky—commonly known as Annie Londonderry—was the first woman to ride a bicycle around the world. Some people say she did this in response to a bet that a woman could not make such a journey, though the truth of that story is debated. When she began her journey in 1894, she had only ridden a bicycle a few times. Still, she wanted to prove women had the mental and physical strength to meet such a challenge.

Londonderry believed women should be less restricted in their family and work lives and encouraged women to wear whatever clothing they wanted. In fact, she wore men's clothing for much of her journey. Along the way, Londonderry made money in various ways, including telling stories of her adventures and displaying companies' advertising posters on her bicycles. In fact, the nickname "Londonderry" comes from the name of a spring water company whose product she promoted.

Questions ***No.13*** What is one reason Annie Londonderry began her trip?

No.14 What is one way Londonderry earned money on her trip?

訳 アニー・ロンドンデリー

アニー・ロンドンデリーとして知られるアニー・コーエン・コプチョフスキーは，女性として初めて自転車で世界一周を果たした人物である。女性にはこのような旅はできないという賭けに応えてやったことだと言う人もいるが，その話の真偽については議論がある。1894年に旅を始めたとき，彼女はまだ数回しか自転車に乗ったことがなかった。それでも彼女は，女性にはこのような挑戦に見合う精神的肉体的な強靭さがあることを証明したかったのだ。

ロンドンデリーは，女性は家庭生活や仕事においてあまり制限されるべきではないと考え，女性が好きな服を着ることを奨励した。実際，彼女は旅の大半で男性用の服を着ていた。旅の道中，ロンドンデリーは冒険談を語ったり，自転車に企業の広告ポスターを貼ったりするなど，さまざまな方法でお金を稼いだ。実際，「ロンドンデリー」というニックネームは，彼女が宣伝した湧水会社の名前に由来している。

No.13 正解 **3**

質問の訳 アニー・ロンドンデリーが旅を始めた理由の1つは何か。

選択肢の訳 **1** 不調な体調を改善するため。 **2** サイクリングテクニックを披露するため。 **3** ジェンダーの固定観念に挑戦するため。 **4** 新しい種類の自転車をテストするため。

解説 アニー・ロンドンデリーが旅を始めた理由について，第1段落第2文では「女性にはこのような旅（＝自転車で世界一周）はできないという賭けに応えてやったことだと言う人もいる」と述べられ，第1段落最終文でも「彼女は，女性にはこのような挑戦に見合う精神的肉体的な強靭さがあることを証明したかったのだ」と述べられている。よって，ロンドンデリーが，男性・女性であることに基づいて定められた既成の社会的観念を打破するために旅を始めたことがわかるので，in response to a bet that a woman could not make such a journeyやprove women had the mental and physical strength to meet such a challengeを**challenge a gender stereotype**と言い換えた**3**が正解。

No.14 正解 **1**

質問の訳 ロンドンデリーが旅でお金を稼いだ方法の1つは何か。

選択肢の訳 **1** 企業の宣伝を手伝った。 **2** 婦人服を作って販売した。 **3** 湧水会社を設立した。 **4** 通常男性がする仕事を引き受けた。

解説 ロンドンデリーが旅でお金を稼いだ方法について，第2段落第3文では「旅の道中，ロンドンデリーは～自転車に企業の広告ポスターを貼ったりするなど，さまざまな方法でお金を稼いだ」と述べられ，さらに第2段落最終文で「『ロンドンデリー』というニックネームは，彼女が宣伝した湧水会社の名前に由来している」とも述べられている。よって，ロンドンデリーが，お金を稼ぐために企業の宣伝を手伝ったことがわかるので，displaying companies' advertising posters on her bicyclesを**helped companies to advertise their products**と言い換えた**1**が正解。

(B)

放送文 *Barn Quilts*

Quilting involves sewing layers of fabric into patterns to create a warm, attractive blanket known as a quilt. On farms in some parts of the US, however, quilt patterns are also used for a different purpose: to create artwork on the side of barns. The practice of painting symbols on barns was first brought to

the US in the 1800s by German immigrants, who believed the images would bring good fortune to their farms.

In 2001, one American woman decided to paint a quilt design on her barn to honor her mother, who had been a quilt maker. She encouraged other barn owners to decorate their barns with similar designs, now known as "barn quilts." This led to the creation of a "barn quilt trail" —a series of local barn quilts that visitors could view. Many communities now have such trails, and the boost to tourism has improved local economies.

Questions No.15 What does the speaker say about the paintings made by German immigrants?

No.16 What has been one effect of "barn quilts" in the US?

訳 バーン・キルト

キルティングでは，キルトと呼ばれる暖かくて魅力的な毛布を作るために，何層もの布を模様に縫い合わせる。しかし，アメリカのある地域の農場では，キルト模様が別の目的にも使われている。納屋の側面にアート作品を作るためである。納屋にシンボルを描く習慣は，1800年代にドイツからの移民によって初めてアメリカにもたらされたが，彼らはその描写が農場に幸運をもたらすと信じていたのだ。

2001年，一人のアメリカ人女性が，キルト職人だった母に敬意を表して，自分の納屋にキルトのデザインを描くことにした。彼女は他の納屋の所有者にも同様のデザインで納屋を飾ることを勧め，それは現在では「バーン・キルト」として知られている。これが，訪問者が一連の地域のバーン・キルトを見ることできる「バーン・キルト・トレイル」の創設につながった。現在では多くの地域でこのようなトレイルが整備され，観光客の増加によって地域経済が向上している。

No.15 正解 3

質問の訳 話者はドイツ系移民が描いた絵画についてどのように語っているか。

選択肢の訳 **1** その描写が彼らにドイツを思い出させた。 **2** その描写はプロの芸術家によって作られた。 **3** その描写が幸運をもたらすと信じられていた。 **4** その描写は短冊状の布に描かれていた。

解説 ドイツ系移民が描いた絵画について，第1段落最終文で「納屋にシンボルを描く習慣は，1800年代にドイツからの移民によって初めてアメリカにもたらされたが，彼らはその描写が農場に幸運をもたらすと信じていた」と述べられている。よって，believed the images would bring good fortuneをbelieved to bring good luckと言い換えた**3**が正解。

No.16 正解 2

質問の訳 アメリカにおける「バーン・キルト」の効果の1つは何か。

選択肢の訳 **1** 趣味として裁縫を始める人が増えた。 **2** いくつかの地域では観光客が増えた。 **3** 農場間の競争が激しくなった。 **4** 農場により多くの納屋が建てられた。

解説 アメリカにおける「バーン・キルト」の効果について，第2段落で，一人のアメリカ人女性が自分の納屋にキルトのデザインを描くことを始め，他の納屋の所有者にもこれを勧めたことが，「バーン・キルト・トレイル」の創設につながったことが述べられたあと，第２段落最終文で「現在では多くの地域でこのようなトレイルが整備され，観光客の増加によって地域経済が向上している」と述べられている。よって，the boost to tourismを**tourism has increased**と言い換えた**2**が正解。

(C)

放送文 *The Little Ice Age*

An era known as the Little Ice Age began in the fourteenth century and continued for around 500 years. Carbon dioxide levels in the atmosphere dropped considerably, which lowered air temperatures around the world. This resulted in reduced agricultural harvests worldwide. The traditional explanation is that this ice age came about due to erupting volcanoes and decreased solar activity.

However, according to more-recent research, farmland returning to forest may have been a major factor in the cooling of the planet. The native populations of North, Central, and South America had cleared large areas of forest for farming. When European colonists arrived in the late fifteenth century, they brought terrible illnesses. This caused the native populations to drop dramatically and left them unable to maintain the land. Researchers claim this resulted in a large increase in forest growth, which meant less carbon dioxide and a cooler planet.

Questions ***No.17*** What is true about the Little Ice Age?

No.18 According to more-recent research, what happened that led to the Little Ice Age?

訳 小氷期

小氷期と呼ばれる時代が14世紀に始まり, 約500年間続いた。大気中の二酸化炭素濃度が大幅に低下し，世界中の気温が低下した。その結果，世界中で農作物の収穫が減少した。従来の説明では, この氷河期は火山の噴火と太陽活動の低下によって起こったとされてきた。

しかし，より最近の研究によれば，農地が森林に戻ったことが地球を冷やした大きな要因であった可能性がある。北アメリカ，中央アメリカ，南アメリカの先住民は，農耕のために広大な森林を伐採していた。15世紀後半にヨーロッパから入植者がやってくると，彼らはひどい病気をもたらした。そのため先住民の人口が激減し，土地を維持することができなくなった。その結果，森林が大幅に増加し，二酸化炭素が減少して，地球がより寒冷化したのだと研究者たちは主張している。

No.17　正解　4

質問の訳 何が小氷期についての真実か。

選択肢の訳 **1**　１世紀弱続いた。　**2**　気象パターンに関する新しい発見につながった。　**3**　火山付近の人々に最も大きな影響を与えた。　**4**　農業に世界的な影響を与えた。

解説 小氷期について，第１段落第２文で「大気中の二酸化炭素濃度が大幅に低下し，世界中の気温が低下した」と述べられたあと，次の文で「その結果，世界中で農作物の収穫が減少した」と述べられている。よって，resulted in reduced agricultural harvests worldwideを**had a global impact on farming**と言い換えた**4**が正解。第１段落第１文で「小氷期と呼ばれる時代が～約500年間続いた」と述べられているので, **1**は不適切。

No.18 正解 2

質問の訳 より最近の研究によると，何が小氷期をもたらしたのか。

選択肢の訳 **1** 北アメリカのヨーロッパ人が大都市を建設し始めた。 **2** アメリカ大陸全域で森林が拡大した。 **3** 世界人口の増加により，公害が増加した。 **4** 病気がヨーロッパ中の多くの木を枯らした。

解説 最近の研究について，第２段落第１文では「より最近の研究によれば，農地が森林に戻ったことが地球を冷やした大きな要因であった可能性がある」と述べられ，そのあとの文で，ヨーロッパからの入植者がもたらした病気によって，北アメリカ，中央アメリカ，南アメリカで農耕のため広大な森林を伐採していた先住民の人口が激減したことで，「森林が大幅に増加し～地球がより寒冷化した」と述べられている。よって，farmland returning to forestを**forests expanded**と言い換えた**2**が正解。ヨーロッパからの入植者がもたらした病気によって先住民の人口が激減したという記述（第２段落第３，４文）はあるが，病気がヨーロッパ中の多くの木を枯らしたという記述はないので**4**は不適切。

(D)

放送文 *Disappearing Fireflies*

Fireflies are one of the most beloved insects because of their ability to create light, but firefly populations seem to be declining. The expansion of urban areas is a problem, not only because it destroys fireflies' habitats but also because of the constant artificial light in cities and suburbs. Fireflies attract mates by flashing their lights, so when these flashes become difficult to see, fireflies have trouble reproducing successfully.

Unfortunately, there have not been many studies of fireflies, in part because they are difficult to locate when they are not creating light. Scientists largely depend on information from amateurs, who report seeing fewer fireflies recently. Fireflies' light-flashing patterns vary by species, and scientists are requesting that more people count firefly flashes and report their observations. In this way, scientists will be able to better track the various species.

Questions ***No.19*** What is one thing the speaker says is putting fireflies in danger?

No.20 What have scientists asked people to do?

訳 消えゆくホタル

ホタルはその光を作り出す能力から，最も愛されている昆虫のひとつだが，ホタルの個体数は減少しているようだ。都市部の拡大は，ホタルの生息地を破壊するだけでなく，都市や郊外では人工的な光が絶えないこともホタルにとって問題となる。ホタルは光を点滅させることで交尾の相手を集めるので，その点滅が見えにくくなると繁殖がうまくいかなくなるのだ。

残念なことに，ホタルの研究はあまり行われてこなかったが，その理由のひとつは，ホタルが光を発していないときにその場所を特定するのが難しいからである。科学者たちは，最近ホタルを見かけることが少なくなったというアマチュアからの情報に大きく依存している。ホタルの発光パターンは種類によって異なるため，科学者たちはより多くの人々にホタルの発光を数え，観察結果を報告するよう求めている。こうすることで，科学者たちは様々な種をよりよく追跡できるようになるだろう。

No.19 正解 3

質問の訳 ホタルを危険な状態にしていると話者が述べていることの1つは何か。

選択肢の訳 **1** 都市の発展による騒音の増加。 **2** それらを捕まえようとする人々の試み。 **3** 都市部の明るさ。 **4** 他の昆虫との競争の激化。

解説 ホタルを危険な状態にしている要因について，第1段落第2文では「都市や郊外では人工的な光が絶えないこともホタルにとって問題となる」と述べ，次の文でその具体的な理由について「ホタルは光を点滅させることで交尾の相手を集めるので，その点滅が見えにくくなると繁殖がうまくいかなくなる」と述べられている。よって，the constant artificial light in cities and suburbsを**the brightness of urban areas**と言い換えた**3**が正解。「都市部の拡大は，ホタルの生息地を破壊する」という記述（第1段落第2文）はあるが，都市の発展による騒音の増加に関する記述はないので**1**は不適切。

No.20 正解 4

質問の訳 科学者たちは人々に何をするよう求めているか。

選択肢の訳 **1** 光を発していないホタルを探す。 **2** 彼らがより多くの研究資金を得られるように協力する。 **3** 家の周りに違うタイプの光を使う。 **4** 見たホタルについてレポートを作成する。

解説 科学者たちが人々に求めていることについて，第2段落第1文で，ホタルの研究があまり行われてこなかった理由として「ホタルが光を発していないときにその場所を特定するのが難しい」ことを述べたあと，第3文では「科学者たちはより多くの人々にホタルの発光を数え，観察結果を報告するよう求めている」と述べられている。よって，count firefly flashes and report their observationsを**make reports on any fireflies they see**と言い換えた**4**が正解。

(E)

放送文 *Smart Dogs*

Dogs can be taught to respond to many words. For example, they can obey commands to sit or roll over. But do dogs actually process and understand words in the same way humans do? One team of researchers attempted to investigate this question. The researchers wanted to gather data directly from dogs themselves rather than from their owners' reports, so they used an imaging machine to scan dogs' brains while the dogs heard different words.

Before the scan, the dogs, which were of various breeds, were taught certain words. While the dogs were in the machine, the words they had been taught and words they did not know were both spoken to them. Surprisingly, the dogs' brains showed more activity after they heard the unfamiliar words. This is the reverse of a human response—our brains are more active in response to words we know.

Questions ***No.21*** What was the purpose of the research?

No.22 What did the researchers discover about the dogs' brain activity?

訳 賢い犬

犬は多くの言葉に反応するように教えることができる。例えば，犬は，お座りや転がれという命令に従うことができる。しかし，犬は実際に人間と同じように言葉を処理し，理解しているのだろうか。ある研究チームがこの疑問を調査しようと試みた。研究者たちは，飼い主の報告からではなく，犬自身から直接データを集めたいと考え，画像処理装置を使って，犬がさまざまな言葉を聞いている間に犬の脳をスキャンした。

スキャンの前に，様々な犬種の犬たちが特定の言葉を教えられた。犬たちが装置の中にいる間，教えられた単語と知らない単語の両方が話しかけられた。驚いたことに，犬たちの脳は知らない言葉を聞いた後，より活発な活動を示した。これは人間の反応とは逆で，私たちの脳は知っている言葉に対してより活発に反応する。

No.21 正解 1

質問の訳 研究の目的は何だったか。

選択肢の訳 **1** 言葉についての犬の理解を調べる。 **2** いろいろな声に対する犬の反応を調べる。 **3** 犬のいろいろな訓練の仕方を研究する。 **4** 飼い主の感情に対する犬の反応の仕方を調べる。

解説 研究の目的について，第1段落第3文で「犬は実際に人間と同じように言葉を処理し，理解しているのだろうか」という疑問が述べられ，次の文で「研究チームがこの疑問（＝犬は実際に人間と同じように言葉を処理し，理解しているのか）を調査しようと試みた」と述べられている。よって，investigate を **study** に，また do dogs ～ understand words in the same way humans do を **dogs' understanding of words** に言い換えた **1** が正解。

No.22 正解 3

質問の訳 研究者は犬の脳の活動について何を発見したか。

選択肢の訳 **1** 飼い主の報告と一致した。 **2** 犬種によって異なった。 **3** 人間の脳のそれとは逆だった。 **4** 慣れた命令に反応すると増加した。

解説 犬の脳の活動に関する発見について，第2段落第3文で「犬たちの脳は知らない言葉を聞いた後，より活発な活動を示した」と述べられ，次の文で「これは人間の反応とは逆」と述べられている。よって，the reverse of a human response を **opposite to that of human brains** と言い換えた **3** が正解。

(F)

放送文 *Root Cellars*

Elliston is a village on the Canadian island of Newfoundland. Its long winters mean preserving and storing food has always been an important part of life there. Traditionally, local people accomplished this by using root cellars, which are tunnel-like structures in the sides of small hills. They are called root cellars because they commonly hold root vegetables, such as potatoes and carrots. The root cellars maintain the perfect temperature and moisture levels for preserving the vegetables.

Root cellars can be found in many places with long winters. However, Elliston is known as the "Root Cellar Capital of the World." For much of its history, the village was a fishing town. But when commercial fishing was banned after a decline in fish populations, Elliston's residents needed a new source of income. They decided to promote their root cellars as an attraction, and today, visitors come from all over to see them.

Questions ***No.23*** What is one thing the speaker says about root cellars?

No.24 What is one reason root cellars are important in Elliston today?

訳 ルートセラー

エリストンはカナダのニューファンドランド島にある村だ。冬が長いため，食料の保存と貯蔵が常に生活の重要な部分を占めてきた。伝統的に，地元の人々は小高い丘の側面にあるトンネルのような構造物であるルートセラーを使ってこれを実現してきた。ジャガイモやニンジンなどの根菜類を入れるのが一般的なので，ルートセラーと呼ばれている。ルートセラーは，野菜を保存するのに最適な温度と水分レベルを保つ。

ルートセラーは，冬が長い多くの場所で見られる。しかし，エリストンは「世界のルートセラーの首都」として知られている。村の歴史の大半は漁業の町だった。しかし，魚の数が減少して商業漁業が禁止されると，エリストンの住民は新たな収入源を必要とした。エリストンの人々は，ルートセラーを観光名所として宣伝することにし，今日では各地からルートセラーを見にやってくる観光客がいる。

No.23 正解 2

質問の訳 話者がルートセラーについて述べていることの１つは何か。

選択肢の訳 **1** 冬の保温に役立つ。 **2** 一部の野菜を保存するのに役立つ。 **3** 名前はその形に由来している。 **4** 一年中野菜を育てるのに使われる。

解説 ルートセラーについて，第１段落最終文に「ルートセラーは，野菜を保存するのに最適な温度と水分レベルを保つ」と述べられている。よって，ルートセラーが野菜を保存するのに役立っていることがわかるので，maintain the perfect temperature and moisture levels for preserving the vegetablesをuseful for storing some vegetablesと言い換えた**2**が正解。

No.24 正解 1

質問の訳 ルートセラーが今日のエリストンで重要である１つの理由は何か。

選択肢の訳 **1** 地域経済を支えるのに役立っている。 **2** 周辺の村の模範となっている。 **3** 漁業の存続に役立っている。 **4** 貴重な鉱物が含まれていることがわかった。

解説 今日のエリストンにおけるルートセラーの重要性については，第２段落第４文で「魚の数が減少して商業漁業が禁止されると，エリストンの住民は新たな収入源を必要とした」とエリストンの住民の経済状況について述べられたあと，第２段落最終文で「今日では各地からルートセラーを見にやってくる観光客がいる」と述べられている。よって，ルートセラーがそれを見に来る観光客の存在によって地域経済を支えるのに役立っていることがわかるので，visitors come from all over to see themをhelp to support the local economyと言い換えた**1**が正解。

Part 3 一次試験・リスニング

(問題編pp.118～119)

CD 赤-21 ～ CD 赤-26

指示文の訳 それでは最後に，Part 3の指示を行います。このパートでは(G)から(K)までの5つの文章が放送されます。英文は実生活における状況を述べたもので，効果音を含むものもあります。それぞれの文章には，No.25からNo.29まで，質問が1問ずつ用意されています。それぞれの文章が流れる前に，問題冊子に書かれている状況の説明と質問を読む時間が10秒あります。文章を聞いた後に，最も適切な答えを選んで解答用紙にマークする時間が10秒あります。文章は1度しか読まれません。それでは始めます。

No.25 正解 **2**

放送文 *(G)* You have 10 seconds to read the situation and Question No.25.

The bus downtown leaves every half hour, and you can take a taxi from the taxi stand at any time. However, all the streets going to the center of town are very busy at this time of day. It's likely to take more than 40 minutes. The subway leaves every 5 to 10 minutes from the underground station. It's a 15-minute ride from the airport to downtown. You can also take the light-rail train. It's slower than the subway but provides a nice view of the city.

Now mark your answer on your answer sheet.

訳 *(G)* 状況と質問25を読む時間が10秒あります。

ダウンタウンへのバスは30分おきに出ていますし，タクシー乗り場からはいつでもタクシーに乗車できます。ただ，この時間帯は中心街へ行く道はどこもとても混んでいます。40分以上はかかるでしょう。地下鉄は地下の駅から5分から10分おきに出ています。空港からダウンタウンまでは15分ほどです。ライトレールにお乗りになることもできます。地下鉄より遅いですが，街の景色をお楽しみいただけます。

それでは，解答用紙に答えをマークしなさい。

状況の訳 あなたは空港に着いたばかりだ。あなたはできるだけ早くダウンタウンに行く必要がある。あなたは案内所で次のように言われた。

質問の訳 あなたはどのようにダウンタウンに行くべきか。

選択肢の訳 **1** バスで。 **2** 地下鉄で。 **3** タクシーで。 **4** ライトレールで。

解説 Situationからわかるのは，①「あなた」は空港に着いたばかりであることと，②「あなた」はできるだけ早くダウンタウンに行く必要があること。案内所のスタッフの発言から，ダウンタウンへの交通手段として，バス（第1文），タクシー（第1文），地下鉄（第4文），ライトレール（第6文）の4つがあることがわかる。それぞれの交通手段に関して，案内所のスタッフは，バスは30分おきに出ていて，タクシーはタクシー乗り場からいつでも乗車できるが，いずれも「40分以上はかかる」と述べている。また，地下鉄については「駅から5分から10分おきに出ています」「空港からダウンタウンまでは15分ほど」と述べ，ライトレールは「地下鉄より遅い」と述べている。よって，できるだけ早くダウンタウンに行く必要がある「あなた」が選ぶべき交通手段としては，駅から5分から10分おきに出ていて，15分ほどでダウンタウンに行ける**2**の地下鉄が正解。

No.26 正解 4

放送文 *(H)* You have 10 seconds to read the situation and Question No.26.

We offer several courses. Giovanni's introductory course on Monday evenings is ideal if this will be your first experience learning Italian. Martina's course on Tuesdays is for businesspeople looking to develop their written fluency in Italian to an advanced level. It's not suitable for beginners. Alfredo's intermediate course on Thursdays is suitable for people who want to improve their language skills in just a few months. Finally, Teresa's course on Fridays is for people who want to learn Italian and Italian culture through operas. This is a popular course, so I recommend registering today if you are interested.

Now mark your answer on your answer sheet.

訳 *(H)* 状況と質問26を読む時間が10秒あります。

いくつかのコースをご用意しております。月曜夜のジョバンニの入門コースは，初めてイタリア語を学ばれるなら最適です。火曜日のマルティナのコースは，イタリア語の筆記能力を上級レベルまで伸ばしたいビジネスパーソンのためのコースです。 初心者の方には適していません。木曜日のアルフレッドの中級コースは，たった数か月でイタリア語の能力を向上させたい方に適しています。最後に，金曜日のテレサのコースは，オペラを通してイタリア語とイタリア文化を学びたい方のためのコースです。人気のコースなので，興味がおありなら，今すぐ申し込むことをお勧めします。

それでは，解答用紙に答えをマークしなさい。

状況の訳 あなたはイタリア語を少し話せるが，3か月後のイタリアでの休暇の前にブラッシュアップしたいと思っている。あなたは月曜日と木曜日は時間がある。語学学校の担当者があなたに次のように言った。

質問の訳 あなたはどのコースを選ぶべきか。

選択肢の訳 **1** マルティナのコース。 **2** ジョバンニのコース。 **3** テレサのコース。 **4** アルフレッドのコース。

解説 Situationからわかるのは，①「あなた」はイタリア語を少し話せること，②「あなた」は3か月後のイタリアでの休暇の前にイタリア語をブラッシュアップしたいと思っていること，③「あなた」は月曜日と木曜日に時間があることの3つ。語学学校の担当者の発言から，「月曜夜」（第2文），「火曜日」（第3文），「木曜日」（第5文），「金曜日」（第6文）の4つの曜日にコースが開講されていることがわかる。③から，「あなた」が通えるコースは，時間がある「月曜夜」か「木曜日」の2つのみ。「木曜日」のコースについて，語学学校の担当者は「中級コース」（第5文）と述べているところ，①から，「あなた」はイタリア語を少し話せるので「中級コース」は適切。また②から，「あなた」は3か月でブラッシュアップしたいと思っているところ，担当者は「たった数か月でイタリア語の能力を向上させたい方に適しています」（第5文）と述べており，この点からも「木曜日」のコースは適切と言える。よって，**4**が正解。「月曜夜」のコースは，担当者が「初めてイタリア語を学ばれるなら最適」（第2文）と述べているところ，①から，「あなた」はイタリア語を少し話せるので不適切。

No.27 正解 **4**

放送文 *(I)* You have 10 seconds to read the situation and Question No.27.

Good morning, shoppers. Today is the Mayfield Mall 15th Anniversary Sale. Check out the first-floor shops for huge discounts on kids' clothing and back-to-school items. All business wear on the second floor, including suits and shoes, is 50 percent off. And don't forget the sporting goods center on the third floor, where we're offering 25 percent off every item. Remember, discounts are only available for shoppers who have registered for the sale at the fourth-floor kiosk. By registering, you will receive a card that you can present at all participating shops.

Now mark your answer on your answer sheet.

訳 *(I)* 状況と質問27を読む時間が10秒あります。

お買い物の皆様，おはようございます。本日はメイフィールド・モール15周年記念セールです。1階のショップでは，子供服や新学期アイテムが大幅割引中です。スーツや靴など，2階のビジネスウェアはすべて50%オフです。3階のスポーツ用品センターでは，全品25%オフで販売しておりますので，お見逃しなく。割引は，4階のキオスクでセールにご登録いただいたお客様にのみ適用されることをお忘れなく。ご登録いただきますと，全参加店舗でご提示いただけるカードを差し上げます。

それでは，解答用紙に答えをマークしなさい。

状況の訳 あなたは新しいビジネススーツを買うためにショッピングモールに到着したところだ。あなたはできるだけお金を節約したい。あなたは次のようなアナウンスを聞いた。

質問の訳 あなたはどの階に最初に行くべきか。

選択肢の訳 **1** 1階。 **2** 2階。 **3** 3階。 **4** 4階。

解説 Situationからわかるのは，①「あなた」は新しいビジネススーツを買うためにショッピングモールに来たことと，②「あなた」はできるだけお金を節約したいこと。アナウンスの第4文では，「スーツや靴など，2階のビジネスウェアはすべて50%オフ」と述べられており，ビジネススーツは2階で販売されていることがわかる。しかし，最後の2文では，「割引は，4階のキオスクで～ご登録いただいたお客様にのみ適用」，「ご登録いただきますと，全参加店舗でご提示いただけるカードを差し上げます」と述べられている。②から，「あなた」はできるだけお金を節約したいと考えているので，「あなた」は割引の適用を受けるために，最初に4階のキオスクに行ってセールに登録する必要があるので，**4**が正解。

No.28 正解 **2**

放送文 *(J)* You have 10 seconds to read the situation and Question No.28.

Welcome to All Adventures Park. Unfortunately, due to repairs, the walk-through reptile attraction Lizard Encounter will be closed until further notice. Our space-themed roller coaster, Into the Sky, has also suspended operation today due to strong winds. We apologize for the inconvenience. Please note, however, that our ranger-guided drive-through safari, Discovery Drive, is operating as usual, and most of the animals will be outdoors and visible. Finally, don't forget to check out the park's newest addition, Dream Fields, where guests can use VR technology to experience the game of baseball like never before!

Now mark your answer on your answer sheet.

訳 *(J)* 状況と質問28を読む時間が10秒あります。

オール・アドベンチャーズ・パークへようこそ。あいにく修理のため，通り抜け型の爬虫類アトラクション「リザード・エンカウンター」は，追ってお知らせするまで閉鎖いたします。また，宇宙をテーマにしたジェットコースター「イントゥ・ザ・スカイ」も強風のため，本日は運転を見合わせます。ご不便をおかけして申し訳ございません。なお，森林警備隊員のガイドによるドライブスルー・サファリの「ディスカバリー・ドライブ」は通常通り営業しており，ほとんどの動物は屋外でご覧いただけます。最後に，VR技術を使って今までにない野球を体験できる，当パークの最新施設「ドリーム・フィールズ」のチェックもお忘れなく！

それでは，解答用紙に答えをマークしなさい。

状況の訳 あなたとあなたの家族はテーマパークにいる。あなたの子供たちは動物や自然にとても興味を持っている。あなたは次のようなアナウンスを聞いた。

質問の訳 あなたはどのアトラクションに行くべきか。

選択肢の訳 **1** リザード・エンカウンター。 **2** ディスカバリー・ドライブ。 **3** イントゥ・ザ・スカイ。 **4** ドリーム・フィールド。

解説 Situationからわかるのは，①「あなた」が家族とテーマパークにいることと，②「あなた」の子供たちは動物や自然にとても興味を持っていること。テーマパークのアナウンスから，「リザード・エンカウンター」は修理のため現在閉鎖されており（第2文），また「イントゥ・ザ・スカイ」も，強風のため今日は運転を見合わせている（第3文）ことがわかるので，「あなた」は，この2つのアトラクションには行くことができない。残りのアトラクションは，森林警備隊員のガイドによるドライブスルー・サファリの「ディスカバリー・ドライブ」と，VR技術を使って今までにない野球を体験できる「ドリーム・フィールズ」の2つだが，②から，「あなた」の子供たちは動物や自然にとても興味を持っているので，動物や自然に関するアトラクションである**2**の「ディスカバリー・ドライブ」に行くのが適切。

No.29 正解 1

放送文 *(K)* You have 10 seconds to read the situation and Question No.29.

Parents, I'd like to introduce the faculty members in charge of the new after-school activities. Mr. Gilbert will be teaching students table tennis once a week on Fridays. Ms. DeLuca is in charge of the swimming club, which will meet on Mondays and Thursdays. Mr. Roth will be sharing his expertise in music by giving clarinet lessons every Wednesday. And Ms. Santos will be available in the library for study group to help students with their homework on Tuesdays and Thursdays. Please speak to the appropriate faculty member for further details.

Now mark your answer on your answer sheet.

訳 *(K)* 状況と質問29を読む時間が10秒あります。

保護者の皆様，新しい放課後活動の担当教員をご紹介します。ギルバート先生は週1回，金曜日に生徒に卓球を指導します。デルーカ先生はスイミングクラブを担当し，月曜日と木曜日に開催します。ロス先生は毎週水曜日にクラリネットのレッスンを行い，音楽の専門知識を伝えます。また，サントス先生は，火曜日と木曜日に生徒の宿題を支援するため，図書館で勉強会を開きます。詳細は担当教員にお声がけください。

それでは，解答用紙に答えをマークしなさい。

状況の訳 あなたは息子に新しい技能を学ばせたいと思っている。息子はすでに 水曜日の放課後に水泳のレッスンを受けている。学校の管理者が次のようなアナウンスをした。

質問の訳 あなたは誰に声をかけるべきか。

選択肢の訳 **1** ギルバート先生。 **2** デルーカ先生。 **3** ロス先生。 **4** サントス先生。

解説 Situationからわかるのは，①「あなた」は息子に新しい技能を学ばせたいと思っていることと，②「あなた」の息子は水曜日の放課後に水泳のレッスンを受けていること。消去法で考える。①と②から，スイミングクラブを担当するデルーカ先生は不適切。同様に②から，「あなた」の息子は水曜日の放課後は水泳のレッスンがあるので，同じ時間帯である水曜日の放課後に行われるロス先生の活動も不適切。サントス先生は，活動内容が生徒の宿題を支援するための勉強会であり，新しい技能を学ぶとは言えないので，①に合わず不適切。ギルバート先生の活動内容は卓球の指導であり新しい技能を学ぶことができるので①の要請に合致し，また時間も金曜日の放課後なので，②の水泳のレッスンとも重ならない。よって，**1**が正解。

カードA 二次試験・面接

(問題編pp.120～121)

指示文の訳 1分間，準備する時間があります。

これは，小さな会社の社長についての話です。

ストーリーのナレーションを行うのに与えられる時間は２分間です。

ストーリーは以下の文で始めてください。

ある日，社長は会社を歩き回っていました。

ナレーションの解答例 **One day, a company president was walking around the office.** He passed the break room, where a couple of employees were drinking coffee and chatting. He heard one of them say, “I've been feeling tired lately.” The president was surprised to hear this. That afternoon, he was in his office reading an article. The article was saying that naps boost worker performance, and this gave the president an idea. A month later, the company president was checking on the company's new nap room. The president was happy to see that several employees were using the room to take a nap and become refreshed. The next day, the company president was in a meeting. An employee ran into the meeting room because he was late for the meeting. He looked like he had just woken up, and he said that he had forgotten to set an alarm.

解答例の訳 **ある日，社長はオフィスを歩き回っていました。**彼は休憩室を通り過ぎ，そこでは２人の従業員がコーヒーを飲みながら談笑していました。彼は彼らのうちの１人が，「私は最近，疲れを覚えているのです」と言うのを耳にしました。社長はこれを聞いて驚きました。その日の午後，彼は自分のオフィスで記事を読んでいました。その記事には仮眠が労働者の仕事ぶりを高めると書かれており，これが社長に着想を与えました。１カ月後，社長は会社の新しい仮眠室を確認していました。社長は，数人の従業員が仮眠を取ってリフレッシュするためにその部屋を利用しているのを見て満足でした。翌日，社長は会議に出ていました。１人の従業員が，会議に遅れていたため会議室に走って入って来ました。彼は目を覚ましたばかりの様子で，目覚ましをかけ忘れていたと言いました。

解説 ナレーションは，４コマのイラストの進行に沿ってまとめていく。２～４コマ目の左上方にある時間の経過を表す語句は，各コマの描写の冒頭部分で必ず使うこと。また，吹き出し内のせりふは，間接話法または直接話法を使ってストーリーに盛り込むが，間接話法を使う場合，主語や動詞などを適切な形に変える必要がある点に注意する。他，新聞，プレートなどに書かれた文字など，イラスト内の情報も適切な形でストーリーに取り入れること。なお，動詞の時制は，過去形および過去進行形を基本に，時間の経過がわかるよう描写する。

①１コマ目：社長が従業員たちの会話を耳にしている場面。休憩室では２人の従業員が休んでおり，コーヒーを飲みながら話をしている。そのうちのI've been feeling tired lately.「私は最近，疲れを覚えているのです」という男性による発言に対し，女性がうなずいている様子が描かれている。２人の表情から，彼らは最近疲れを覚えるという点について意見が一致しており，これを，たまたま休憩室のそばを通っていた社長が耳にして驚いている様子をナレーションに盛り込む。なお，解答例では男性のせりふは直接話法を用いてそのまま取り入れている。

②２コマ目：That afternoonで始める。社長が新聞記事を読んでいる場面。新聞内の見出しから，仮眠が労働者のパフォーマンスを向上させることについての記事だとわかる。明るい表情をした社長の吹き出しに豆電球が描かれていることから，社長はこの記事から仮眠に関連した何かしらの着想を得たと判断できるだろう。

③３コマ目：A month laterで始める。社長が，Nap Room「仮眠室」というプレートが掲示されている部屋を満足げに眺めている場面。ちょうど１人の従業員がリフレッシュした様子で部屋から出て来ているところであり，部屋の中では数名の従業員が仮眠を取っている様子が描かれている。これらのことから，この会社では最近，２コマ目の新聞記事にインスパイアされた社長によって仮眠室が設けられ，社長がその様子を確認しに来ているのだと推測できる。

④４コマ目：The next dayで始める。社長が従業員たちと会議に出ている場面。ドアを開けながら入って来ている男性の吹き出しにI forgot to set an alarm.「目覚ましをかけ忘れました」とある点，社長の隣に座る人物が眉をひそめている点，その男性が慌てている点などから，彼は仮眠室を利用していたものの，寝過ぎてしまい会議に遅刻してしまったのだと推測できる。解答例ではこの遅れた従業員の発言内容を間接話法で表している。

質問の訳 No.1　４番目の絵を見てください。あなたがその社長なら，どのようなことを考えているでしょうか。

では～さん（受験者の氏名），カードを裏返して置いてください。

No.2　給料は職業を選ぶ際の最も重要な要素だと思いますか。

No.3　人々の意見はメディアにあまりにも影響されやすいでしょうか。

No.4　政府は労働者の権利を保護するためにもっと多くのことをすべきでしょうか。

No.1 **解答例** I'd be thinking, "It's natural that people need some time to get used to using the nap room. It will improve our productivity in the long term. For now, I can just send out a reminder about not oversleeping.”

解答例の訳 「仮眠室の利用に慣れるのにはいくらかの時間が人々に必要であるというのは当然だ。それは長期的には私たちの生産性を高めてくれることだろう。差し当たりは，寝過ごさないようにという通知を出すことくらいしか私にできることはない」と私は思っているでしょう。

解説 質問の仮定法過去形に合わせて，直接話法で**I'd be thinking, “～.”** のように始めると良い。解答例では，It's natural that ～「～ということは当然である」を用いて，仮眠室に慣れるのに当然時間がかかるものだという一般論を述べてから，長期的に見れば生産性の向上につながるだろうというメリットを説明している。そして，差し当たりは自分には注意喚起することしかできないという点を述べ，発言を締め括っている。あるいは，解答例とは異なる観点で，後悔を表す〈should have＋過去分詞〉「～すべきだった」を使って，引用符内をI should have reminded my employees of not oversleeping. I need to take some measures in order to make sure that such a thing would never happen again.「私は従業員に，寝過ごさないように念押ししておくべきだった。私は，そのようなことが二度と起こらないよう，何らかの策を講じる必要がある」などとしても良いだろう。

No.2 **解答例** No. It's more important for people to find a career that interests them personally. Being interested makes people feel passion for their work, and this allows them to become much better workers.

解答例の訳 いいえ。人々にとっては，個人的に自分の興味をそそる職業を見つけることの方が大切です。興味が湧くことで人々は仕事への情熱を覚え，これによって彼らははるかに優秀な労働者になることができるのです。

解説 解答例では，Noの立場から，職業を選ぶ際には仕事への関心の方が給料よりも大切であるという観点から，関心を抱くことが仕事への情熱につながり，これにより優秀な労働者になれるという利点を中心に述べている。あるいは，Yesの立場で，Yes. There are many other important factors such as being interested and how challenging the job is. But nevertheless, how much money people get paid really counts when it comes to choosing a career. In my opinion, the higher the income is, the more motivated workers can get, this leading to enriching their lives.「はい。関心を持つことや仕事のやり甲斐といった別の大事な要素はたくさんあります。しかしそれでもやはり，どれくらいのお金をもらえるかという点は，職業を選択する際には極めて重要です。私の意見では，収入が高ければ高いほど，労働者はより意欲的になり，このことは彼らの人生の充実につながります」と，譲歩しつつも給料に力点を置く観点で答えても良いだろう。

No.3 **解答例** Definitely. People have gotten worse at thinking for themselves. These days, people tend to believe everything that is reported in the news. People need to think more critically about the truth of media reports.

解答例の訳 絶対にそうです。人々は自分の頭で考えることがますます苦手になっています。近頃では，人々はニュースで報道されていることを全部信じてしまう傾向にあります。人々は，メディア報道の真実についてもっと批判的に考える必要があります。

解説 解答例ではまず，Definitely「絶対にそうです」と自分がYesの立場にあることを強調してから，人々が自分の頭で考えることが不得手になってきている状況を説明し，あらゆるニュース報道を信じてしまう傾向にあるという問題点に言及している。そして，報道の真実についてもっと批判的に考える必要性を訴えている。あるいは，Noの立場から，No. Certainly, some people accept what is reported in the news without question, but others do not, including my friends and acquaintances. In addition, many experts point out the risk of being deceived by fake news these days, and as a result of this, I think public awareness about media literacy has steadily improved.「いいえ。確かに，ニュースで報道されることをうのみにする人々もいますが，私の友人や知人を含め，そうではない人々もいます。さらに，今日では多くの専門家がフェイクニュースにだまされることの危険性について指摘しており，この結果，メディアリテラシーについての人々の意識は着実に向上していると思います」などと答えても良いだろう。

No.4 **解答例** Yes. In recent years, many companies have been taking advantage of their workers. It's very difficult for many workers to protect themselves, so the government needs to make sure that companies follow the law.

解答例の訳 はい。近年では，多くの企業が従業員を都合よく利用し続けています。大勢の労働者にとっては自分を守ることはとても難しいので，政府は確実に会社が法を守るようにする必要があります。

解説 解答例ではYesの立場から，従業員を都合よく利用している企業が数多く存在する現状に触れた後，労働者側が自分自身を守ることが困難であるがゆえに，政府こそが会社に働きかけるべきだという意見を展開している。あるいは，3文目を，The government should closely monitor and punish such companies more severely so that workers' rights can be guaranteed, if necessary.「労働者の権利が保障されるよう，政府は必要に応じてそのような会社をしっかり監視してより厳しく罰するべきです」などとするのも良いだろう。

カードB 二次試験・面接

(問題編pp.122～123)

指示文の訳 1分間，準備する時間があります。
これは，スケートボードでの滑り方を習得したいと思った少女についての話です。
ストーリーのナレーションを行うのに与えられる時間は2分間です。
ストーリーは以下の文で始めてください。
ある日，少女は学校から歩いて家に帰っていました。

ナレーションの解答例 One day, a girl was walking home from school. She passed by a skate park and looked around. Some kids were skateboarding there. There was a boy doing a big jump on his skateboard, and the girl was quite impressed. She thought that skateboarding was really cool. The next day, the girl was at home talking with her parents. She told them that she wanted to start skateboarding. Her mother looked a little worried about it, but they decided to let her get a skateboard. A month later, the girl was skateboarding at the skate park. She was practicing hard to learn how to skateboard. One of the other kids at the park was cheering her on. A week later, though, the girl was in the hospital. She had injured herself, and a nurse was putting a bandage on her head. Her mother looked very upset and said that she wasn't allowed to skateboard anymore.

訳 **ある日，少女は学校から歩いて家に帰っていました。**彼女はスケートボード場のそばを通り，辺りを見回しました。そこでは数人の子どもがスケートボードで滑っていました。スケートボードで大きくジャンプしている少年がいて，少女はとても感銘を受けました。彼女は，スケートボードで滑ることがとてもかっこいいと思いました。翌日，少女は家で両親と話をしていました。彼女は彼らに，スケートボードを始めたいと伝えました。お母さんはそれについて少し心配そうでしたが，彼らは彼女にスケートボードを持たせてあげることにしました。1か月後，少女はスケートボード場でスケートボードで滑っていました。彼女は，スケートボードでの滑り方を習得するために熱心に練習していました。他の子どものうちの1人は，彼女に声援を送っていました。しかし，1週間後，少女は病院にいました。彼女はけがをしていて，看護師が彼女の頭に包帯を巻いていました。お母さんはとても動揺した様子で，彼女にはもうスケートボードで滑ることが許されないと言いました。

解説 ナレーションは，4コマのイラストの進行に沿ってまとめていく。2～4コマ目の左上方にある時間の経過を表す語句は，各コマの描写の冒頭部分で必ず使うこと。吹き出し内のせりふは，間接話法または直接話法を使ってストーリーに盛り込むが，間接話法を使う場合，主語や動詞などを適切な形に変える点に注意する。また，場所を表す看板のイラスト内にある文字情報も適切な形でストーリーに盛り込む。動詞の時制は，過去形および過去進行形を基本に，時間の経過がわかるように描写する。

①1コマ目：少女が，スケートボードで滑っている子どもたちを眺めている場面。Skate Park「スケートボード場」という看板がフェンスに取り付けられている場所で，2人の子どもがスケートボードで遊んでいる。この様子を見ている少女が明るい表情を浮かべていることから，彼女は彼らおよびスケートボードに肯定的な感情を抱いているのだと読み取れる。解答例のように，遊んでいる子どものうちの1人が大きく跳躍している様子をナレーションに盛り込むと効果的だろう。

②2コマ目：The next dayで始める。少女が自宅で両親と話をしている場面。少女の吹き出し内に，少女自身がスケートボードで滑っているさまが描かれていることから，彼女は両親に，自分もスケートボードを始めたいと伝えているのだと判断できる。なお，解答例では，少女の話を聞いて懸念を抱いている様子の母親についても，look「～のように見える」を使って描写している。

③3コマ目：A month laterで始める。少女が他の子どもたちとスケートボードで遊んでいる場面。一番右にいる少年が少女を見ながら片腕を上げていることから，彼は少女に声援を送っているのだと推察できる。解答例では少女が熱心に練習しているという設定にしているが，これとは違う観点で，すでに少女がかなり滑れるようになっており，これに少年が感銘を受けているという設定にしても良いだろう。

④4コマ目：A week laterで始める。少女が病院にいる場面。看護師に包帯を巻かれ

ている点，および取り乱している様子の母親とNo more skateboarding!「もうスケートボードは禁止！」というせりふの内容から，少女はスケートボードで遊んでいる最中にけがをしてしまったのだとわかる。解答例では，母親のNo more skateboarding!という発言を，be allowed to ～「～することが許されている」を否定文で用いた間接話法で表現している。

質問の訳 No.1　4番目の絵を見てください。あなたがその少女なら，どのようなことを考えているでしょうか。

では～さん（受験者の氏名），カードを裏返して置いてください。

No.2　親にとって，自分の子どもの学校生活に関与するのは大切ですか。

No.3　スポーツをするのは若者にとって，たくましい性格を育むのに良い方法でしょうか。

No.4　オリンピック大会のような国際的なイベントは国々の間の関係を向上させ得ると思いますか。

No.1 **解答例**　I'd be thinking that it isn't fair for my mom to stop me from skateboarding. My injury isn't so serious. It's more important that I stay active and make a lot of friends at the skate park.

解答例の訳　私は，スケートボードで滑るのをお母さんが禁止するのはフェアではないと思っているでしょう。私のけがはそんなに深刻なものではありません。私が活動的であり続けてスケートボード場でたくさんの友人を作る方が大切です。

解説　解答例では，質問の仮定法過去形に合わせて，間接話法の**I'd be thinking that ～.**の形で答えている。母によってスケートボードを禁止されることに納得がいかない点とけがが深刻ではない点に言及した上で，引き続き活動的にスケートボードで滑ることで得られるメリットを述べて解答を締め括っている。あるいは，I'd be thinking that I admit I should have been more careful not to be injured, but my mom's decision to forbid me to skateboard go too far. Since minor injuries are not rare in playing outside, I'll persuade her into letting me skateboard somehow after recovering from my injury.「けがをしないようにもっと気をつけるべきだったことは認めるけれども，自分にスケートボードで滑るのを禁止する母の決断は行き過ぎだと私は思っていることでしょう。外で遊ぶのにちょっとしたけがは珍しくないものなので，けがが回復したら，どうにかしてスケートボードをさせてもらえるよう母を説得するつもりです」などと，自身の注意不足を悔やみつつも，禁止の決断を下した母親を説得しようと試みる意思を表明する内容にしても良いだろう。

No.2 **解答例**　Yes, I think so. Children perform better in school with support from their parents. Parents can talk to their children about school, and they can give them good advice about their classes and social life.

解答例の訳　はい，そう思います。子どもは親からの支援があれば学校でもっとうまくやっていけるようになるものです。親は学校について子どもと話すことができ，子どもに，授業や社会生活についての良い助言を与えることができます。

解説　解答例では，Yesの立場で，子どもが学校生活を送る上では親からの支援がプラスに働くという意見を述べ，学校生活に関与することで親は子どもにとっての良き助言者になれることを主張している。あるいは，Noの立場から，No. I know parents are concerned about their children's school life, but I think they should interfere in it as little as they can. Rather, parents should encourage their children to think for themselves in order to solve problems they are facing.「いいえ。親が子どもの学校生活を心配するのはわかりますが，彼らは極力それに干渉すべきではないと思います。むしろ，親は子どもが直面している問題を解決するために自分の頭で考えるよう彼らに奨励すべきです」などとしても良いだろう。

No.3 **解答例** Definitely. Many sports help children to learn the value of teamwork, and they also teach the importance of hard work and practice. These lessons will help them to successfully achieve their goals in the future.

解答例の訳 絶対にそうです。多くのスポーツは子どもたちがチームワークの価値を学ぶのに役立ち，それらは勤勉さや練習の大切さを悟らせてくれもします。これらの教訓は，彼らが将来，目標を達成する上で役立つことでしょう。

解説 解答例ではまず，Definitely「絶対にそうです」と自分がYesの立場にあることを強調してから，多くのスポーツがチームワーク，勤勉さ，練習の大切さなどの価値を悟らせてくれるという点を述べ，さらに，これらの教訓が将来の目標達成において役立つだろうと付け加えている。あるいは，解答例とは違う観点から，I don't think it's always true. There are many other ways to achieve the same result. For instance, I have learned the value of persistence and teamwork through my guitar practice and my band's activity, so we should not limit the choice to sports.「いつもそうであるとは思いません。同様の結果を達成するのには別の方法もたくさんあります。例えば，私はギターの練習やバンド活動を通じて粘り強さやチームワークの価値を学んできましたので，選択肢をスポーツに限定すべきではありません」と，実体験に触れながら説明しても良いだろう。

No.4 **解答例** No. Many different nations have to work together to hold large events like the Olympics, but such relationships are only temporary. In the end, these events don't have a lasting effect on political relations.

解答例の訳 いいえ。オリンピック大会のような大規模なイベントを開催するにはさまざまな国が協力し合う必要がありますが，そのような関係性は一時的なものにすぎません。結局，この手のイベントは政治的関係には永続的な影響を及ぼしません。

解説 解答例では，Noの立場から，オリンピック大会のような大規模な国際的なイベントを通じて育まれる関係性が一時的なものにすぎないと述べ，開催に当たって必要とされる協力関係も結局は政治的関係には永続的な影響を及ぼさないと説明している。あるいは，3文目を，Giving financial support or cultural exchanges with each other will be a lot more effective in improving relations between nations.「経済的な支援や相互の文化的な交流の方が，国々の間の関係を向上させるにははるかに効果的でしょう」と，代替案を述べる形にしても良いだろう。

2022年度 第2回

筆記 解答欄

問題番号		1	2	3	4
1	(1)	①	❷	③	④
	(2)	①	②	③	❹
	(3)	①	❷	③	④
	(4)	①	❷	③	④
	(5)	①	②	③	❹
	(6)	①	❷	③	④
	(7)	①	❷	③	④
	(8)	①	②	③	❹
	(9)	①	②	❸	④
	(10)	①	❷	③	④
	(11)	❶	②	③	④
	(12)	❶	②	③	④
	(13)	❶	②	③	④
	(14)	①	②	❸	④
	(15)	❶	②	③	④
	(16)	①	②	③	❹
	(17)	①	②	③	❹
	(18)	①	②	③	❹
	(19)	①	②	③	❹
	(20)	①	②	❸	④
	(21)	①	②	③	❹
	(22)	❶	②	③	④
	(23)	①	②	❸	④
	(24)	❶	②	③	④
	(25)	①	②	❸	④

問題番号		1	2	3	4
2	(26)	①	❷	③	④
	(27)	①	②	③	❹
	(28)	❶	②	③	④
	(29)	①	❷	③	④
	(30)	①	②	❸	④
	(31)	①	❷	③	④

問題番号		1	2	3	4
3	(32)	①	②	③	❹
	(33)	❶	②	③	④
	(34)	①	❷	③	④
	(35)	①	②	③	❹
	(36)	①	②	③	❹
	(37)	❶	②	③	④
	(38)	①	②	③	❹
	(39)	❶	②	③	④
	(40)	①	②	❸	④
	(41)	①	②	❸	④

4の解答例はp.150をご覧ください。

リスニング 解答欄

問題番号			1	2	3	4
Part 1		No.1	①	②	③	❹
		No.2	①	②	③	❹
		No.3	①	❷	③	④
		No.4	①	❷	③	④
		No.5	①	②	❸	④
		No.6	❶	②	③	④
		No.7	①	❷	③	④
		No.8	❶	②	③	④
		No.9	①	②	❸	④
		No.10	①	❷	③	④
		No.11	①	❷	③	④
		No.12	①	②	③	❹
Part 2	A	No.13	①	②	❸	④
		No.14	❶	②	③	④
	B	No.15	①	②	③	❹
		No.16	①	②	❸	④
	C	No.17	❶	②	③	④
		No.18	①	②	③	❹
	D	No.19	①	②	❸	④
		No.20	①	❷	③	④
	E	No.21	❶	②	③	④
		No.22	❶	②	③	④
	F	No.23	①	❷	③	④
		No.24	①	②	③	❹
Part 3	G	No.25	①	②	❸	④
	H	No.26	①	②	③	❹
	I	No.27	①	❷	③	④
	J	No.28	①	②	❸	④
	K	No.29	①	❷	③	④

1 一次試験・筆記
(問題編pp.126～129)

指示文の訳 各英文を完成させるのに最も適切な単語または語句を４つの選択肢の中から選び，その番号を解答用紙の所定欄にマークしなさい。

(1) 正解 2

訳 ***A:*** お母さん，今夜の夕食にハンバーグを作ってもらえる？ ***B:*** いいわよ，でもまず冷凍庫からお肉を出して解凍しないといけないわね。

解説 A（＝子供）がB（＝母親）に対して夕食に食べたいものを伝えている場面。Bの発言のtake the meat out of the freezer「冷凍庫からお肉を出す」から，ハンバーグを作るために使う肉は冷凍された状態であるとわかる。したがって，空所には**2のthaw**「解凍する」を入れると状況に合う。reckon「数える，考える」，stray「道に迷う」，shatter「粉々になる」。

(2) 正解 4

訳 ジョスリンはいつも息子に嘘を言わないよう言い聞かせていた。彼女は彼に強い正直の観念を植え付けることが重要だと考えていた。

解説 空所直前にit was important to「～することが重要だ」とあるので，空所には直後のa strong sense of honesty「強い正直の観念」をどうするかを表す動詞が入る。**instill ～ in ...**で「…に～を教え込む，…に～を植え付ける」という意味を表すので，**4のinstill**が正解。remodel「～を作り変える」，stumble「つまづく」，overlap「～を重ね合わせる」。

(3) 正解 2

訳 ザラは彼氏にとても腹を立てていたが，彼の誠実な謝罪を聞いた後で彼を許した。彼女は彼が本当にすまなく思っていると確信した。

解説 空所直後にapology「謝罪」とあり，空所にはどのような謝罪かを表す形容詞が入る。第２文のShe was sure that he really was sorry.「彼女は彼が本当にすまなく思っていると確信した」から，ザラの彼氏は心から謝ったとわかるので，この様子を表すのに適切な語は，**2のearnest**「誠実な」。detectable「検知できる」，cumulative「次第に増加する」，underlying「根本的な，潜在する」。

(4) 正解 2

訳 最初，スミス一家は裏庭の水泳プールを楽しんでいたが，清潔に保つのが非常に面倒になってきたので，ほとんどの時間はふたをしたまま放っておいた。

解説 空所の後のthey left it(＝backyard swimming pool) covered most of the time「ほとんどの時間はふたをしたまま放っておいた」から，スミス一家はプールを使わなくなったとわかる。その理由はkeeping it clean「清潔に保つこと」が大変だったからだと考えられる。such ～ that ...で「非常に～なので…」という意味を表すので，空所には**2のnuisance**「面倒なもの［こと・人］」を入れると文脈に合う。bureau「事

※2024年度第１回から，試験形式の変更に伴い大問１の問題数は18問になります。

務局」，sequel「続き」，metaphor「隠喩」。

(5) 正解 4

訳 歴史を通じて，多くの偉大な思想家たちが最初はその考えのために嘲笑されたものの，結局は真剣に受け取られるようになった。

解説 空所直前にat first「最初は」とあることに注目。文の後半にeventually being taken seriously「結局は真剣に受け取られるようになった」とあるので，空所にはそれとは逆の言動を表す語が入る。ridiculeで「～を嘲笑する」という意味を表すので，その過去分詞である**4のridiculed**が正解。saturate「～を浸す」，flatter「～にお世辞を言う」，ingest「～を摂取する」。

(6) 正解 2

訳 最初，その小さな女の子はスピーチコンテストで大勢の聴衆を前に恥ずかしかったが，1分ぐらい経つと彼女はもっと自信が出てきた。

解説 文後半にbut after about a minute she began to feel more confident「だが，1分ぐらい経つと彼女はもっと自信が出てきた」とあるので，その前は女の子はあまり自信がなかったとわかる。この様子を表すには，**2のbashful**「内気な，恥ずかしがって」が適切。mortal「死を免れない」，pious「信心深い」，concise「簡潔な」。

(7) 正解 2

訳 タイプライターは過去の遺物である。それは会社や家庭にタイプライターが普通に見られた頃から，科学技術がどれだけ進歩したかを思い出させてくれる。

解説 第1文の主語Typewritersが現在ではほとんど使われていないという事実や，空所直後のof the past，さらに第2文のsince they(＝typewriters) were common in offices and homes「会社や家庭にタイプライターが普通に見られた頃から」から，空所には古いものについて表す語が入ると推測できる。したがって，**2のrelic**「遺物」が正解。「タイプライターというもの」という1つの種類として扱っているので，不定冠詞のaが付いていることに注意。jumble「寄せ集め，不用品」，fraud「詐欺」，treaty「条約」。

(8) 正解 4

訳 その男性がトラの檻に近づいたとき，その大きな動物は低くうなった。その男性は恐ろしい音におののいて後ずさりした。

解説 第1文前半にthe man approached the tiger's cage「その男性がトラの檻に近づいた」，第2文にin fear at the terrifying sound「恐ろしい音におののいて」とある。トラの出す恐ろしい音を表す語としては**4のgrowled**「うなった」が適切。sparkle「輝く」，leer「流し目で見る」，disprove「～の誤りを証明する」。

(9) 正解 3

訳 警察官は法律を擁護することを誓わなければならない。これにはもちろん，自分自身が法律に従うことも含まれる。

解説 空所に入る動詞の目的語がthe lawであり，第2文にfollowing the law

themselves「自分自身が法律に従うこと」とあるので，空所にもfollowに近い意味を表す語が入る。したがって，**3のuphold**「～を擁護する」が正解。gravitate「（重力によって）～を引きつける」，detach「～を引き離す」，eradicate「～を根絶する」。

(10) 正解 **2**

訳 全従業員が毎年必須の健康診断を受ける。会社はすべての労働者が必ずそうするよう法律によって義務づけられている。

解説 空所直後にmedical checkupとあるので，空所にはどのような健康診断かを表す形容詞が入る。第2文にCompanies are required by law to make sure all their workers do it.「会社はすべての労働者が必ずそうするよう法律によって義務づけられている」とあり，このitは「健康診断」を指すので，**2のcompulsory**「義務的な，必須の」が正解。gloomy「薄暗い，陰鬱な」，reminiscent「～を連想させる」，muddled「混乱した」。

(11) 正解 **1**

訳 生物学の学生は細胞分裂がどのように起こるかを学ばなければならないが，それは1つの細胞が2つに分かれるこの過程は自然界ではよく見られるからである。

解説 空所直前にcell「細胞」とあることに注目。文後半にthis process of a single cell splitting into two「1つの細胞が2つに分かれるこの過程」とあり，**cell division**で「細胞分裂」という意味なので，**1のdivision**「分裂，分割」が正解。appliance「器具」，imposition「賦課」，longitude「経度」。

(12) 正解 **1**

訳 その2つの会社が合併した後で，数人の上級従業員が不要となり，職を失った。

解説 空所直前のthe two companiesに注目。空所には2つの会社によって行われることを表す動詞が入る。したがって，**1のmerged**「合併した」が正解。pose「ポーズをとる」，conform「従う」，flock「群れをなす」。

(13) 正解 **1**

訳 運動中に脱水状態になるのを避けるために，常に十分な水を飲むべきである。トレーニングが長ければ長いほど，それだけ多くの水が必要である。

解説 空所直後にwhile exercising「運動中に」とあり，one should always drink enough water「常に十分な水を飲むべきである」と続いているので，空所には運動中に十分な水を飲まなかった場合に陥る状態を表す語が入る。したがって，**1のdehydrated**「脱水状態の」が正解。eternal「永遠の」，punctuated「中断させられた」，cautious「用心深い」。

(14) 正解 **3**

訳 ケンは家ではいつも行儀が良かったので，先生がケンはクラスで最も反抗的な生徒の1人だと言ったとき，母親はショックを受けた。

解説 文前半にKen was always well behaved at home「ケンは家ではいつも行儀が良かった」とあり，その後でhis mother was shocked「母親はショックを受けた」と続いているので，ケンは家での態度と学校での態度が大きく違っていたと考えられる。したがって，well behavedとは対照的な意味を表す，**3のdisobedient**「反抗的な」が正解。momentary「瞬間の」，miniature「小型の」，invincible「無敵の，不屈の」。

(15) 正解 1

訳 警察官は近くにいた人が何が起こったのかを目撃していたことを期待して，犯行現場で傍観者たちに質問をした。

解説 空所には警察官が質問をした相手に当たる目的語が入る。文後半にsomeone who had been nearby「近くにいた人」とあるので，この意味を1語で表す**1のbystanders**「傍観者」が適切。reformer「改革者」，mourner「会葬者」，pioneer「先駆者」。

(16) 正解 4

訳 数人の将官がその国の総理大臣を打倒しようと試みた。だが，彼らは失敗し，彼は権力を維持している。

解説 第2文にthey(＝several generals) were unsuccessful, and he(＝the country's prime minister) remains in power「彼らは失敗し，彼は権力を維持している」とあるので，軍がクーデターに失敗したのだとわかる。空所には総理大臣を辞めさせる行動を表す動詞が入るので，**4のoverthrow**「～を打倒する」が正解。irrigate「～を灌漑する」，harmonize「～を調和させる」，outpace「～より速い，～に勝る」。

(17) 正解 4

訳 ケイレブは提案の下書きを終えたので，部長にそれを評価するよう頼んだ。残念ながら，それにはまだ多くの改善が必要だと部長は思った。

解説 空所直後のitはa draft of his proposalを指し，ケイレブが「提案の下書き」について部長に何かをするように頼んだとわかる。第2文にshe(＝Caleb's manager) thought it still needed a lot of improvement「それにはまだ多くの改善が必要だと部長は思った」とあり，「提案の下書き」の感想を述べ評価している。したがって，**4のevaluate**「～を評価する」を入れると文脈に合う。scrub「～をごしごし洗う」，enchant「～を魅了する」，prune「～を切り取る」。

(18) 正解 4

訳 アメリカ大統領のトマス・ジェファソンとジョン・アダムズは50年以上に渡り，お互いに手紙をやりとりした。この文通はアメリカ史の重要な一部である。

解説 第1文にexchanged letters with each other「お互いに手紙をやりとりした」とある。この内容を1語で簡潔に言い換えた**4のcorrespondence**「文通」が正解。matrimony「結婚生活」，federation「連邦」，horizon「地平線，水平線」。

(19) 正解 4

訳 暴動の間，町は無秩序状態に陥った。人々は通りに出て争ったり，窓を壊したりし，多くの店は略奪された。

解説 第2文の内容から，町は統制の効かない大混乱に陥ったことがわかる。この状態を表す語としては，**4のanarchy**「無秩序，無政府状態」が適切。disclosure「暴露，開示」，admittance「入場（許可）」，attainment「到達，学識」。

(20)　正解　3

訳 いくつかの植物の花は実際に食べられ，サラダをもっとおいしく，見栄えも良くするために使うことができる。

解説 文後半にcan be used to make salads both more delicious ...「サラダをもっとおいしく…するために使うことができる」とあり，花をサラダに入れて食べるということなので，**3のedible**「食べられる，食用の」が正解。stationary「静止した」，candid「率直な」，hideous「恐ろしい，ぞっとする」。

(21)　正解　4

訳 その有名な科学者がスピーチの間中，多くの間違いをしてもだれも驚かなかった。彼は話し下手で悪評が高い。

解説 スピーチをした科学者は有名である一方，第２文にはhis poor speaking skills「話し下手」とある。**notorious for 〜**で「〜で悪評が高い」という意味を表すので，**4のnotorious**が正解。treacherous「不誠実な，裏切りの」，momentous「重大な」，flirtatious「誘惑するような」。

(22)　正解　1

訳 先月，上司がブラッドを昇進させたとき，ブラッドの厳しい労働と長時間の勤務はすべて報われた。

解説 文後半にhis boss gave him a promotion「上司がブラッドを昇進させた」とあるので，ブラッドの労力に見合う結果が得られたとわかる。**pay off**で「利益をもたらす，報われる」という意味を表すので，**1のpaid off**が正解。write back「返事を書く」，chop up 〜「〜を切り刻む」，make over 〜「〜を作り直す」。

(23)　正解　3

訳 最高経営責任者のスピーチが非常にあいまいだったので，会社が深刻な財政難に陥っているという事実をジーナが理解するのにしばらくかかった。

解説 空所直後にtoがあることに注目。文前半にthe CEO's speech was so vague「最高経営責任者のスピーチが非常にあいまいだった」とあるので，「会社が深刻な財政難に陥っているという事実」がジーナにはわかりづらかったと考えられる。**catch on to 〜**で「〜を理解する」という意味を表し文脈に合うので，**3のcatch on**が正解。fill in 〜「〜を満たす」，duck out「外に出る」，give up「あきらめる」。

(24)　正解　1

訳 チームのメンバーそれぞれに新しいプロジェクトのためにすべき仕事があるが，彼らの作業すべてを調整する責任は部長が負う。

解説 文後半の主語はthe responsibility for coordinating all of their efforts「彼らの作業すべてを調整する責任」であり，目的語がthe manager「部長」である。空所には責任が部長にどうなるかを表す語句が入る。**fall on 〜**で「〜の負担となる」という意味を表すので，**1のfalls on**が正解。square with ～「～と一致する」，drop by「立ち寄る」，stack up「積み重なる」。

(25) 正解 3

訳 その従業員は自分の罪を証明するファイルやその他の証拠を隠滅することによって，会社からの窃盗を隠そうとした。

解説 文後半にby destroying files and other evidence that proved his guilt「自分の罪を証明するファイルやその他の証拠を隠滅することによって」とあるので，空所には証拠隠滅によって「会社からの窃盗」をどうしようとしたかを表す語句が入る。**cover up ～**で「～を隠す」という意味を表すので，**3**が正解。tuck away ～「～をしまい込む」，latch onto ～「～をつかまえる，～を理解する」，doze off「うたた寝する」。

2 一次試験・筆記

ナブタプラヤのストーンサークル（問題編pp.130～131）
グッドロード運動（問題編pp.132～133）

指示文の訳 それぞれの文章を読んで，各空所に入れるのに最も適切な語句を４つの選択肢の中から選び，その番号を解答用紙の所定欄にマークしなさい。

ナブタプラヤのストーンサークル

Key to Reading 第１段落：導入（ナブタプラヤのストーンサークル）→第２段落：本論①（ナブタプラヤの発展）→第３段落：本論②（ストーンサークルの目的）という３段落構成の説明文。それぞれの段落のトピックセンテンスを意識し，ナブタプラヤのストーンサークルの特徴とその目的について，論理的に読み進めていく。

訳

多くの先史時代の社会は，ストーンサークルを造った。これらは，太陽の動きを追跡するなど，様々な理由で造られた。科学者に知られているそのような最古のサークルは，エジプトのナブタプラヤにある。このサークルは約7,000年前に造られたもので，恐らく世界で最も有名な先史時代のストーンサークルである，イギリスのストーンヘンジよりも1,000年以上も前のものである。今日のナブタプラヤの気候は非常に乾燥しているが，常にそうとは限らなかった。実際，サークルが造られた時期の激しい季節降雨により，一時的に湖が形成され，これらがウシを放牧する部族を，この地域に呼び込むことになった。

ナブタプラヤの最初の移住民は，約10,000年前にやって来た。考古学者は，これらの移住民が，１年中水を利用できるよう深井戸のシステムを構築し，家をまっすぐに並べて貯蔵スペースを備えつけたことを示す証拠を発見した。彼らはまた，彼らの生活の中心である，ウシの崇拝に焦点を当てた宗教を信仰した。これらの発見は，移住民が洗練された社会を発展させた証拠である。

研究結果によると，サークルの石の一部は，約7,000年前の１年で最も日が長い日に，太陽と並んでいた。これは，サークルが暦として使用されたことを示唆している。しかし，ある天体物理学者は，サークルには別の目的もあったと考えている。彼は，他の石の配置が，サークルが造られた当時のオリオン座の星の配置と一致していると指摘している。このため，彼はサークルが，夜空の星の位置を示す占星地図であったと提唱している。

(26) 正解　2

選択肢の訳　**1**　一方　**2**　実際　**3**　それなのに　**4**　同様に

解説　空所の前後の内容に注目する。前にNabta Playa's climate is extremely dry today, but this was not always the case.「今日のナブタプラヤの気候は非常に乾燥しているが，常にそうとは限らなかった」とあり，後でheavy seasonal rainfall during the period when the circle was built led to the formation of temporary lakes「サークルが造られた時期の激しい季節降雨により，一時的に湖が形成され」と，this was not always the caseの具体的内容を示していることから，**2のIn fact**「実際」が正解。not always the caseは「いつでも当てはまるというわけではない」という意味。

(27) 正解　4

選択肢の訳　**1**　宗教思想に疑問を抱いた　**2**　牧畜への興味を失った　**3**　深刻な内部抗争を経験した　**4**　洗練された社会を発展させた

解説　空所を含む文の前半の，「これらの発見」(These discoveries) が何の「証拠」(evidence) になっているのかを考える。These discoveriesは，直前の2文より，ナブタプラヤの移住民が，深井戸のシステムを構築し，宗教への信仰心を持っていたことを指す。つまり，ナブタプラヤでは技術や文化が発展していたと推測できることから，**4のdeveloped a sophisticated society**「洗練された社会を発展させた」を入れると意味がとおる。

(28) 正解　1

選択肢の訳　**1**　別の目的もあった　**2**　もっと以前に造られた　**3**　元々は別の場所に造られた　**4**　人々がその地域を避ける原因となった

解説　空所の前後の内容に注目する。サークルの目的として，前の1文がThis suggests the circle was used as a calendar.「これは，サークルが暦として使用されたことを示唆している」，2文後がhe proposes that the circle was an astrological map showing the positions of stars in the night sky.「彼はサークルが，夜空の星の位置を示す占星地図であったと提唱している」で，サークルの2つの異なる目的について示していることから，**1のalso had another purpose**「別の目的もあった」を入れると意味がとおる。

グッドロード運動

Key to Reading　第1段落：導入（グッドロード運動の起源）→第2段落：本論①（グッドロード運動と農民）→第3段落：本論②（グッドロード運動と自動車の普及）という3段落構成の説明文である。グッドロード運動について，ドライバー，サイクリスト，農民のそれぞれの立場から読み進めよう。

訳

19世紀後半に始まったグッドロード運動は，アメリカの景観を変え，国の道路と幹線道路のシステムを構築するのに役立った。この運動には驚くべき起源があった。今日，ほとんどの人は，道路システムがまず自動車ドライバーのニーズに応えて発達したと思い込んでいるが，これは誤った通説である。実はサイクリストを中心に要求が始まったのだ。近代の自転車の発明により，1890年代にサイクリングが流行し，何百万人ものアメリカ人がより良く，安全な自転車道を求めた。

サイクリストは，整備が不十分で危険なことが多かった道路の質を改善するよう，地方政府に圧力をかけ始めた。当初，この運動は，都市のサイクリストのレジャー活動を支援するために自分たちの税金が費やされることを望まない農民には，受け入れられなかった。しかし，次第に，農民たちは考えを変え始めた。この理由の1つは，「良い道路の真理：アメリカの農民たちへの手紙」と呼ばれる，影響力を持った論説集であった。これは，作物を市場に運ぶのが容易になるなど，道路の利点を強調することで，多くの農民を納得させた。

自動車が普及するにつれ，この動きは急速に勢いを増した。特に，1900年代初頭にフォード・モデルT が開発されたことで，より良い道路を切望する多くの新しいドライバーが現れた。こうした手頃な価格の車が何百万台も販売され，ドライバーが増加したことにより，より多くの道路を建設し，既存の道路の質を改善するよう，政府への圧力がかけられることになった。

(29) 正解 **2**

選択肢の訳 **1** 自動車メーカーによって始められた **2** 驚くべき起源があった **3** ドライバーの間で反対の声が生まれた **4** 多くのサイクリストを怒らせた

解説 空所を含む文の直後の文で，グッドロード運動が自動車ドライバー（automobile drivers）のニーズに応えたものであるという考え方を，「誤った通説」（a myth）と表している。さらに次の文で，Actually, the demand started mainly with cyclists.「実はサイクリストを中心に要求が始まった」と述べていることから，運動の始まりが意外なものであったことを示す，**2のhad a surprising origin**「驚くべき起源があった」を入れると意味がとおる。

(30) 正解 **3**

選択肢の訳 **1** 抗議の声を高めた **2** 別の道路を使い始めた **3** 考えを変え始めた **4** サイクリストと敵対した

解説 空所を含む文の直前にAt first, the movement was resisted by farmers「当初，この運動は，農民には，受け入れられなかった」とあり，Gradually, however, farmers (　　).「しかし，次第に，農民たちは（　　）」につながることから，**3のbegan to change their minds**「考えを変え始めた」を入れると意味がとおる。

(31) 正解 **2**

選択肢の訳 **1** 一方 **2** 特に **3** それにもかかわらず **4** したがって

解説 空所を含む文の直前のAs automobiles became common, the movement quickly gained momentum.「自動車が普及するにつれ，この動きは急速に勢いを増した」から，(　　), the invention of the Ford Model T in the early 1900s led to many new drivers, who were also eager for better roads.「(　　)，1900年代初頭にフォード・モデルTが開発されたことで，より良い道路を切望する多くの新しいドライバーが現れた」につながることから，強調したい事柄を表すときに使う，**2のIn particular**「特に」が正解。

3 一次試験・筆記

顔の認識（問題編pp.134～135）
ドリアンとオオコウモリ（問題編pp.136～137）
長距離砂漠挺身隊（問題編pp.138～140）

指示文の訳　それぞれの文章を読んで，各質問に対する最も適切な答えを４つの選択肢の中から選び，その番号を解答用紙の所定欄にマークしなさい。

顔の認識

Key to Reading　第１段落: 導入＋本論①（人間の顔認識能力）→第２段落: 本論②（オーストラリアの研究者の発見①）→第３段落: 本論③（オーストラリアの研究者の発見②）という３段落構成の説明文。人間の脳が，本物の顔と偽の顔をそれぞれどのように認識するかを考えながら読み進めよう。

訳

人間は一般的に，顔を認識し，その表情を素早く読み取ることにとても長けている。これは，顔の特徴の処理を専門とする脳の特定の領域があるために，なし得ることである。古代人は，例えば，周囲の人々が怒っているかどうか，そのため，潜在的に危険であるかどうかを判断する必要があったであろうことから，この能力の発達は，進化という観点においては理にかなっている。しかし，意図しない結果の１つが，人々がしばしば，周囲の物体に顔があると考えてしまうことである。人々は，雲や木の幹，食べ物やコンセントに至るまで，様々な物体に，こうしたいわゆる偽の顔を認識する。

オーストラリアの研究者は最近，脳が偽の顔をどのように処理するかについて詳しく知るための研究を行った。これまでの研究で，本物の顔の場合，その顔が表現している感情を判断するのに，見たばかりの顔の影響を受けることが明らかになった。例えば，幸せそうな顔を続けて見ると，人々は次に見た顔を，幸せを表現していると判断する傾向がある。オーストラリアの研究では，研究者が参加者に，特定の感情を表現する偽の顔を続けて見せた。本当の顔と同様に，参加者は偽の顔によって表現された感情を判断するのに，見せられたばかりの顔の影響を受けることを，彼らは発見した。この発見に基づいて，研究者は，脳は本物の顔を処理するのと同様の方法で，偽の顔を処理すると結論付けた。

研究者はまた，人間の顔の配置に大まかにでも似ている特徴―口の上の２つの目と鼻―を持つ物体は，脳に，これらの特徴を感情表現の判断に使わせることがあると述べた。つまり，顔を認識するための脳の基準は，細部ではなく全体なのだ。研究者たちは，これが，脳が顔の表情をとても素早く判断できる理由の１つであると述べている。

(32)　正解　4

質問の訳　第１段落で，なぜこの文章の著者は雲のような物体について言及したか。

選択肢の訳　**1**　周囲の環境が，他人の感情をどれだけうまく判断できるかに影響を与え得るという考えを支持するため。　**2**　顔を識別できない人は，他の特定の物体を識別するのにも，いかに苦労するかを説明するため。　**3**　周りにある日用品に対する私達の反応が，脳の様々な領域によって制御されていることを説明するのに役立てるため。
4　人々が，顔が見えると想像する，日常にある物の例を提供するため。

解説　第１段落では，人間がどのように顔を認識するかについて述べている。「意図しな

※2024年度第１回から，試験形式の変更に伴い大問３の１問目(32)～(34)が削除されます。

い結果の１つ」（one unintended consequence）として，最後から２文目でpeople often think they see faces on objects in their environment「周囲の物体に顔があると考えてしまう」ことを挙げている。次の文のa variety of objects, from clouds and tree trunks to pieces of food and electric sockets.「雲や木の幹，食べ物やコンセントに至るまで，様々な物体」はそれを示した日常にある物の例（examples of everyday things）なので，**4**が正解。

(33) 正解 1

質問の訳 過去の研究は，～ことを示している。

選択肢の訳 **1** 本物の顔が表現している感情に関する人々の判断は，直前に見た他の本物の顔の影響を受ける。 **2** 人々は本物の顔よりも偽の顔に，より早く感情的な意味付けをする。 **3** 人々は，本物の顔よりも偽の顔によって表現された感情を，より幸せでポジティブなものとして判断する傾向がある。 **4** 顔が感情を表していない場合, 人々は偽の顔を区別するのにより時間がかかる。

解説 顔の認識に関する過去の研究については，第２段落第２～３文を参照。for real faces, people's judgement of what emotion a face is expressing is affected by the faces they have just seen.「本物の顔の場合，その顔が表現している感情を判断するのに，見たばかりの顔の影響を受けることが明らかになった」とあり，次の文で具体的な例を挙げている。この内容をまとめた選択肢**1**が正解。

(34) 正解 2

質問の訳 オーストラリアの研究者は，顔によって表現される感情を判断する脳の能力について，何と言っているか。

選択肢の訳 **1** この能力は，生き延びるという点ではもはや人間への利点がないので，時間の経過と共に消滅する可能性がある。 **2** 脳が大まかな基準で顔を識別するという事実は，顔が表現する感情を人々が素早く判断することを可能にする。 **3** 脳は，顔が非常に明確な特徴を持っている場合にのみ，顔が表現する感情を正確に識別できる。
4 この能力は過去に，人間に利益だけでなく不利益をもたらしたにもかかわらず，進化した。

解説 脳の感情表現を判断する能力については，第３段落を参照。any object with features that even loosely resemble the layout of a human face ... can trigger the brain to assess those features for emotional expression「人間の顔の配置に大まかにでも似ている特徴を持つ物体は, 脳に, これらの特徴を感情表現の判断に使わせることがある」とあり, 最終文でこれを,「脳が顔の表情をとても素早く判断できる理由の１つ」と言っている。この内容と一致する選択肢**2**が正解。本文のtriggerは「～させる」という意味。

ドリアンとオオコウモリ

Key to Reading 第１段落：導入（ドリアンの人気の高まりと栽培状況）→第２段落：本論①（ドリアン栽培の困難さ）→第３段落：本論②＋結論（ドリアン栽培におけるオオコウモリの重要性）という３段落構成の説明文。選択肢を検討するときは, 本文中の語（句）の言い換えに注意しよう。

訳

フットボールサイズのドリアンの果実は，その不快な臭いとクリーミーで甘い果肉でよく知られている。「果物の王様」として知られるドリアンは，ボルネオ島が原産と考えられているが，現在ではより広く栽培されており，世界中で消費されるドリアンの半分以上がタイで栽培されている。ドリアンは長い間，東南アジア全体で人気があったが，その人気は現在，世界の他の地域に広がっている。ドリアンには何百もの種類があるが，ほぼマレーシアのみで栽培されているムサンキングは，最も高く評価されている品種の1つである。ドリアンには高レベルのビタミンが含まれているため，その健康効果で売り込まれることが多く，輸出の増加につながっている。実際，専門家は，今後10年間でマレーシアから中国への出荷だけで，50%増加すると予測している。この状況を生かすべく，多くのマレーシアの農家は，ドリアンの生産を優先し，パーム油などの作物の生産をやめた。

しかし，ドリアンの木を育てるのは簡単ではない。定期的な水やりと肥料を与える必要があり，温度に非常に敏感である。さらに，木立状に自生することはなく，他の樹木や低木の間で育つことでよく茂るため，果樹園で単一の作物として育てることは困難である。果実をたくさん収穫するために，樹木の花を確実に十分受粉させることは，農家にとってさらに困難である。ドリアンの木の特徴の1つは，花が夜にしか花粉を放出しないことであり，そのため，日中に採餌するミツバチなどの昆虫は，ドリアンに授粉しない。夜に活動する動物が授粉の役目を果たすが，自然に授粉されるのは，ドリアンの木の花の約25%のみである。このため，多くの農家は手作業で授粉するという，多くの労働力を要する方法に頼っている。

研究によると，オオコウモリがドリアンの花の主な自然花粉媒介者であることが示されている。しかし，多くの農家はこれらのコウモリを，果実を食べて農家に損害を与え，利益を減らす単なる害獣と見なしているため，コウモリは追い払われたり，殺されたりしている。東南アジアの一部の文化では，コウモリの肉を食べると呼吸疾患が治ると信じられているため，コウモリは捕えられ，食料として売られ，その結果，絶滅の危機にさらされてもいる。オオコウモリの利点について人々に教えなければ，コウモリの数はさらに減少し，ドリアン農業に深刻な影響を与える可能性がある。

(35) 正解 4

質問の訳 第1段落によると，ドリアンの生産について正しいのはどれか。

選択肢の訳 **1** ドリアンは現在，主にマレーシアで栽培されているが，これは，他の東南アジア諸国ではドリアンを栽培するのに十分な土地がもうないためである。 **2** ドリアンは，従来栽培されていた場所ではよく売れているものの，他の国ではまだ人気がない。 **3** 高級品種のドリアンは，安価な品種よりも栄養価が高くないため，消費者から批判されている。 **4** ドリアンの需要が高まっているため，マレーシアの農家は他の作物の栽培からドリアンの栽培に切り替えている。

解説 第1段落最後の3文を参照。最初の2文より，ドリアンの輸出が増加しており，今後もその傾向が続くことがわかる。さらに最終文で，In order to take advantage of this situation, many Malaysian farmers have stopped producing crops such as palm oil in favor of producing durians.「この状況を生かすべく，多くのマレーシアの農家は，ドリアンの生産を優先し，パーム油などの作物の生産をやめた」と述べている。この内容をまとめた選択肢**4**が正解。

(36) 正解 4

質問の訳 ドリアン農家が考慮する必要がある要素の1つは,

選択肢の訳 **1** ドリアンの木はほぼ全ての温暖な気候で栽培できるが，他の植物がほとんど生育していない地域で最もよく育つ。 **2** ドリアンの木が他の植物を追い出す傾向があるため，在来植物の数が急激に減少している。 **3** ドリアンの木は，ミツバチや他の昼間の花粉媒介者が簡単に見つけられる場所で栽培する必要がある。 **4** ドリアンの木は，自然に受粉するために放っておかれると，木が大量の果実を付ける可能性は低くなる。

解説 ドリアンの栽培の難しさについては，第2段落を参照。夜にのみ花粉を出すというドリアンの受粉について，最後から2文目で，Animals that are active at night take over the role of pollination, but only about 25 percent of a durian tree's flowers ever get pollinated naturally.「夜に活動する動物が授粉の役目を果たすが，自然に授粉されるのは，ドリアンの木の花の約25%のみである」と述べている。この内容を言い換えた選択肢**4**が正解。授粉の可能性の低さを，unlikely to produce a large amount of fruitと言い換えている。

(37) 正解 1

質問の訳 この文章の筆者がオオコウモリについて述べていることの1つは何か。

選択肢の訳 **1** ドリアンの花の受粉において，オオコウモリが果たす重要な役割についての認識が高まらなければ，ドリアンの生産は厳しいかもしれない。 **2** 東南アジアでは，一部の市場で違法に販売されたコウモリの肉を食べた結果，多くの人が病気になった。 **3** 一部のドリアン農家は，捕まえて肉を売ることができるように，オオコウモリを意図的に果樹園に誘い込んでいる。 **4** 多くのオオコウモリが呼吸障害で死んだため，ドリアンの花の自然受粉媒介者が大幅に減少している。

解説 オオコウモリについて述べているのは，第3段落。前半より，オオコウモリがドリアンの花にとって，重要な受粉媒介者であるとわかる。しかし，害獣として，また食肉のために殺され，絶滅の危機に瀕している。この現実を受け，最終文で，Without educating people about the benefits of giant fruit bats, the bats' numbers may decline further, which could have serious consequences for durian farming.「オオコウモリの利点について人々に教えなければ，コウモリの数はさらに減少し，ドリアン農業に深刻な影響を与える可能性がある」と結論づけている。この内容と一致する**1**が正解。本文のthe benefits of giant fruit batsを，the important role giant fruit bats play in durian flower pollinationと言い換えている。

長距離砂漠挺身隊

Key to Reading 第1段落: 導入(第二次世界大戦中の砂漠戦)→第2段落: 本論①(LRDGの結成）→第3段落: 本論②（LRDGの特徴）→第4段落: 本論③（LRDGとSAS）→第5段落: 結論（LRDGの最大の功績）という5段落構成の説明文。設問に先に目を通し，読み取るべきポイントを押さえてから，本文を読み進めよう。

訳

第二次世界大戦中，イギリスは北アフリカの砂漠でドイツとイタリアと戦った。砂漠戦は，広く分散した部隊間の小規模な戦闘が特徴であり，敵からの発見と危険な日中の暑さの両方を回避するために，夜間に迅速に移動する必要があった。この地域は広大な砂地であるため，物資の輸送が困難であり，水不足により軍事行動は大幅に制限されていた。

しかし，イギリス陸軍将校のラルフ・バグノルド少佐に，これらの過酷な状況は戦略上のチャンスをもたらした。戦争前に北アフリカの砂漠を何年も探索してきたバグノルドは，地形をよく知っており，敵軍を監視および追跡できる小型で機動性の高い車両部隊が非常に有益であると確信していた。当初，イギリスの司令官は，そのような長距離の情報収集には飛行機の方が適していると考え，そのような部隊を編成するという彼の提案を却下した。しかし，バグノルドは，地上で情報を収集することが有利であると主張し，彼の粘り強さが1940年6月のバグノルドを指揮官とする長距離砂漠挺身隊（LRDG）の結成につながった。

LRDGは当初から型破りな部隊であった。階級間の通常の区別は適用されず，将校と正規兵はファーストネームで呼び合い，全員が同じ任務を遂行するものとされた。バグノルドは，戦場で勇敢に戦う者を求めるのではなく，例えば飲み水が限られているにもかかわらず，モチベーションを維持し，長時間でも注意を怠らないというような，並はずれたスタミナがあり，機知に富み，精神的な強さを備えた者を求めていた。LRDGの哨戒隊は，砂漠の状況に適応した特殊なトラックを使って約3週間，1,600キロメートル以上の範囲を単独で活動できるように装備されていた。燃料，弾薬，食料などの必要な物資はすべて部隊によって運ばれたため，念入りな補給計画が大変重要であった。

LRDGの任務は主に，敵陣の背後深くに潜り，その動きを監視することであった。部隊は様々な武器を入手でき，隊員は主に情報を収集するように訓練されていたものの，地雷を設置したり，敵の飛行場や燃料貯蔵所への攻撃も展開したりした。敵陣の背後で攻撃を行うために1941年に編成されたイギリス軍の特殊空挺部隊（SAS）が，最初の任務で敵の領土にパラシュート降下した後，多くの死傷者を出した時には，LRDGは生存者を連れ戻す任務を負った。救助作戦は成功し，その隊員は砂漠に関する幅広い知識を持っていたため，LRDGはSASをすべての将来的標的まで陸上で運ぶ，または標的から連れ戻す任務を与えられ，移動と案内に携わった。これはほぼ確実に，SASが襲撃を成功させ，死傷者を減らすのに役立った。

LRDGの最大の功績は1943年に達成されたが，この時，部隊は防御の固い敵の前線を見つかることなく回避するルートを見つけ，これにより敵の防御の弱点を攻撃できた。これは北アフリカ戦線における重要な転換点であり，そこでのイギリスの勝利に大きく貢献した。LRDGは，1945年までヨーロッパでの戦争遂行に多大な貢献を続けた。

(38) 正解　4

質問の訳 ラルフ・バグノルド少佐は，イギリス軍司令官に～ということを納得させることができた。

選択肢の訳 **1**　兵士達は，適切な物資が供給されていなかったため，砂漠での任務において，ある程度の成功しか収められていない。　**2**　敵陣上を飛行し，砂漠で偵察を行うために使用された飛行機は，大幅な改良が必要である。　**3**　自身がそのような環境での経験がほとんどないという事実にもかかわらず，砂漠での任務で部隊を率いることができる。　**4**　砂漠での敵の活動に関する情報を収集するために，地上部隊を使用することは効果的な戦略である。

解説 ラルフ・バグノルド少佐の主張として，第2段落最終文にgathering information on the ground would be advantageous「地上で情報を収集することが有利である」とある。当初，イギリスの司令官は，砂漠での情報収集には飛行機の方が適していると考えていたが，少佐の説得により，LRDG結成が実現した。よって選択肢**4**が正解。選択肢は地上での情報収集について，an effective strategy「効果的な戦略」と表している。

(39) 正解 1

質問の訳 長距離砂漠挺身隊（LRDG）について正しいのはどれか。

選択肢の訳 **1** 選ばれた隊員の特性とその行動方法は，従来の軍隊のそれとは異なっていた。 **2** 予算が限られていたため，他の部隊よりも少ない物資と古い武器で間に合わせなければならなかった。 **3** 巡回には多数の隊員がいたため，将校は管理手法に関する特別な訓練を受けなければならなかった。 **4** その任務の成功は，部隊が定期的に敵陣の背後に物資を送ってもらえるかどうかに大きく依存していた。

解説 LRDGの特徴については，第3段落を参照。1文目にThe LRDG was an unconventional unit from the outset.「LRDGは当初から型破りな部隊であった」とあり，その後の文で，階級間の通常の区別が適用されない，将校と正規兵はファーストネームで呼び合う，全員が同じ任務を遂行するなど，LRDG独自の特徴を述べている。この内容を1文で表した選択肢**1**が正解。本文のunconventional unit（型破りな部隊）をdifferent from those of traditional military units（従来の軍隊のそれとは異なる）と表している。

(40) 正解 3

質問の訳 次のうち，LRDGと特殊空挺部隊（SAS）の関係を最もよく表しているのはどれか。

選択肢の訳 **1** 2つの部隊を組み合わせて，陸からと空からの襲撃を同時にできるようにした。 **2** 作戦の性質が似ていたため，2つの部隊は競合し，力を貸し合うことを望まなかった。 **3** LRDGは砂漠に関する知識を利用して，SASが任務の有効性と安全性の両方を改善するのを支援した。 **4** SASがLRDGの任務に関与したことで，LRDGは長期間にわたり，敵陣の背後にとどまることがより困難になった。

解説 LRDGとSASの関係については，第4段落3文目以降を参照。LRDGはSASの隊員救助作戦（the rescue mission）を行い，砂漠に関する知識を生かし，移動や案内（transportation and navigation）に携わった。その結果として，最終文でThis almost certainly helped the SAS accomplish its raids with greater success and fewer casualties.「これはほぼ確実に，SASが襲撃を成功させ，死傷者を減らすのに役立った」と述べている。この内容とほぼ一致する選択肢**3**が正解。

(41) 正解 3

質問の訳 この文章の筆者によると，1943年に何が起こったか。

選択肢の訳 **1** LRDGが犯した失敗により，敵軍は，イギリスが獲得を望んでいた領土の支配を強化することができた。 **2** LRDGのヨーロッパへの移管は，SASがLRDGの支援なしに，防御の固い地域で敵軍を攻撃する以外に，選択の余地がなかったことを意味した。 **3** LRDGの活動により，イギリス軍は大きな強みを得ることができ，その地域の敵軍を破ることができた。 **4** イギリス軍司令官は，LRDGは敵の活動を監視するよりも，イギリス領土を守るために役立てた方がよいと判断した。

解説 1943年の出来事については，第5段落を参照。1文目より，LRDGのおかげでイギリス軍が敵の防御の弱点を攻撃したとわかり，次の文で，This was a crucial turning point in the campaign in North Africa and contributed greatly to the British victory there.「これは北アフリカ戦線における重要な転換点であり，そこでのイギリスの勝利に大きく貢献した」と述べている。この内容と一致する選択肢**3**が正解。

4 一次試験・英作文

（問題編p.141）

指示文の訳
●次のトピックについてエッセイを書きなさい。
●答えの裏付けに，以下に挙げたポイントのうちの2つを使いなさい。
●構成：導入，本論，結論
●長さ：120～150語
●エッセイは解答用紙のB面に用意されたスペースに書きなさい。
スペースの外側に書かれた内容は，採点の対象とはなりません。

トピックの訳 人々はインターネット上の情報を信頼すべきですか。

ポイントの訳 ●学習 ●ニュース ●オンラインショッピング
●ソーシャルメディア

解答例

In my opinion, people should trust information on the Internet. I have two reasons to support this based on news and learning.

Firstly, Internet news sites are a fantastic source of trustworthy information. The demand for up-to-date news has led to more people submitting videos and photos of events as they happen, such as natural disasters. This information is easy to verify because it comes directly from people experiencing such events, making it easier to trust this information.

Secondly, there are many online learning courses on the Internet with content that can be trusted. To ensure their courses are reliable, educational institutions rigorously check the content of their online resources. Moreover, these courses are widely recognized, adding to their authenticity.

In conclusion, due to the increasing amount of news generated directly from the source and the high quality of learning resources online, we should trust information on the Internet.

解答例の訳

私の意見では，人々はインターネット上の情報を信頼すべきだ。私には，ニュースと学習に基づいてこのことを裏付ける理由が2つある。

第一に，インターネット上のニュースサイトは，信頼できる素晴らしい情報源だ。最新のニュースに対する需要の結果，より多くの人々が自然災害のような出来事の動画や写真

※2024年度第1回から，大問4に文章の要約を書く問題が加わります。

をその発生時に投稿している。この情報はその類の出来事を経験している人々に直接由来するため正しいと確認することは容易であり，それがこの情報を信頼しやすいものにしている。

第二に，インターネット上には信頼できるコンテンツを有しているオンライン上の学習講座がたくさんある。これらの講座が信頼できるものであることを保証するため，教育機関は，そのオンライン教材の中身を厳密に確認している。その上，これらの講座は広く認知されており，このことがその信頼性を高めている。

結論として，情報源から直接作り出されるニュースの量がどんどん増えていること，並びにオンライン上の学習教材の質の高さにより，私たちはインターネット上の情報を信頼すべきだ。

解説 TOPIC文について，「信頼すべきである／信頼すべきではない」のどちらかの立場に立って，自分の意見とその根拠をエッセイの形でまとめる形式。まとめる際には，POINTSとして示されたキーワードのうち２つを選んで使用する必要がある。なお，キーワードに挙げられている語句については，必要に応じて形を変えて表現したり類義語で置き換えたりしても良い。

段落構成に関する，導入（introduction）→本論（main body）→結論（conclusion）という基本的な指定は必ず守ること。解答例のように本論を２つに分ける場合は，論点の重複がないように注意する。また，結論をまとめる際には第１段落の単純な繰り返しにならないよう，表現を若干でも工夫すると良いだろう。ただし，どうしても時間が足りない場合はエッセイの完成を優先する。

TOPIC文 「人々はインターネット上の情報を信頼すべきですか」という質問について意見を求める内容。

語句 trust「～を信頼する」

第１段落（導入） まずエッセイの冒頭で，自分がTOPIC文のテーマを正しく理解していることと，「信頼すべきである／信頼すべきではない」のいずれの立場に立っているのかを明示する必要がある。解答例は，文をIn my opinion「私の考えでは」から始め，自分が前者の立場にあることを，つまりインターネット上の情報を信頼すべきだと考えている立場にあることを表明している。これに続けて，２つの理由があると前置きし，POINTSのNews「ニュース」とLearning「学習」を観点として取り上げている。

語句 reason「理由」/ support「～を裏付ける」/ based on ～「～に基づいて」

第２段落（本論①） 第１段落第２文で示した２つの理由のうち１つ目の観点である「ニュース」についての段落。この段落をFirstly「第一に」で，次の段落をSecondly「第二に」という，列挙を表す談話標識でそれぞれ始めることで，各段落の論点を明確にしている。第２段落では，第１文で「インターネット上のニュースサイトは信頼できる素晴らしい情報源だ」という意見を提示した後，より大勢の人々が自然災害時に情報発信をしている現状について触れ，そのような情報が出来事をじかに体験している人々による一次情報であるという点こそが信頼性の向上につながっているという持論を展開している。

語句 site「サイト」/ fantastic「素晴らしい」/ source「源」/ trustworthy「信頼できる」/ demand「需要」/ up-to-date「最新の」/ lead to ～「～につながる」/ submit「～を投稿する」/ video「動画」/ happen「発生する」/ such as ～「～のような」/ natural disaster「自然災害」/ verify「～を正しいと確認する」/ come from ～「～に由来する」/ directly「直接」/ experience「～を経験する」/ make it easy to ～「～

することを容易にする」

第３段落（本論②） 第１段落で示した２つの理由のうち２つ目の観点である「学習」についての段落。この段落では，まず「インターネット上には信頼できるコンテンツを有しているオンライン上の学習講座がたくさんある」と意見を述べた後，これらの講座の信頼性の高さの理由について２点補足することで，意見に説得力を持たせている。この際，①教育機関による厳密な確認作業，②認知度の高さ，という２点を，追加を表すMoreover「その上」を用いて簡潔にまとめている。

語句 course「講座」/ content「コンテンツ，中身」/ ensure (that) ～「～だと保証する」/ reliable「信頼できる」/ educational「教育の」/ institution「機関」/ rigorously「厳密に」/ check「～を確認する」/ resource「教材，資源」/ widely「広く」/ recognize「～を認識する」/ add to ～「～を増す」/ authenticity「信頼性」

第４段落（結論） 最終段落では，文章を締め括る際に用いるIn conclusion「結論として」という談話標識から文を始め，理由・原因を表すdue to ～「～のために」によって導かれる前置詞句で２つの論点を簡潔にまとめ上げた後，第１段落で述べた意見を再度提示することでエッセイを結んでいる。

語句 increasing「ますます増加する」/ amount「量」/ generate「～を生み出す」/ quality「品質」

Part 1 一次試験・リスニング

(問題編pp.142～143)

CD 赤-27 ～ CD 赤-39

指示文の訳 準１級の試験のリスニングテストが始まります。指示を注意して聞いてください。テスト中に質問をすることは許されていません。

このテストは３つのパートに分かれています。これら３つのパートの質問は全て選択肢の中から正解を選ぶ問題です。それぞれの質問について，問題冊子に書かれている４つの選択肢の中から最も適切な答えを選び，解答用紙の該当箇所にその答えをマークしなさい。このリスニングテストの全てのパートで，メモを取ってもかまいません。

それでは，これからPart 1の指示を行います。このパートではNo. 1からNo. 12まで12の会話が放送されます。それぞれの会話に続いて，質問が１つ流れます。各質問に対して，最も適切な答えを選んで解答用紙にマークする時間が10秒あります。会話と質問は１度しか読まれません。それでは，準１級のリスニングテストを始めます。

No. 1 正解 4

放送文 ***A:*** Leaving for lunch already, Noah? ***B:*** Actually, I'm on my way upstairs. We have our company medical checkups today, remember? ***A:*** No, I completely forgot about them. ***B:*** You can still go. You don't need an appointment. ***A:*** Yeah, but I had a big breakfast this morning. You're not supposed to eat before the blood test, right? ***B:*** Right. In fact, I'm starving. Anyway, you'll have another chance next week. They'll be back again on Wednesday. ***A:*** Really? I'll make sure to remember.

Question: What will the woman probably do?

訳 *A:* もう昼食に行くの，ノア？ *B:* 実は，今2階に行くところなんだ。今日は会社の健康診断があるんだよ，覚えてる？ *A:* いいえ，そのことはすっかり忘れてたわ。*B:* まだ行けるよ。予約はいらないんだ。 *A:* うん，でも今朝は朝食をたくさん食べたの。血液検査の前に食べちゃいけないんでしょ？ *B:* そうだね。実は，お腹が空いているんだ。いずれにせよ，来週もう一度チャンスがあるよ。水曜日にまたやってくれるんだ。
A: そうなの？ 必ず覚えておくね。

質問の訳 女性はおそらくどうするか。

選択肢の訳 **1** 今日，血液検査を受ける。 **2** 朝食を少なくするようにする。
3 ノアとランチに行く。 **4** 来週，健康診断を受ける。

解説 1往復目でB（＝Noah）から，「今日は会社の健康診断があるんだよ，覚えてる？」と言われたA（＝女性）は「そのことはすっかり忘れてたわ」と述べ，さらにBに，(今日)まだ健康診断に行けると言われても，「今朝は朝食をたくさん食べたの。血液検査の前に食べちゃいけないんでしょ」と述べていることから，Aが今日は健康診断を受けないことがわかる。3往復目でBが「来週もう一度（健康診断の）チャンスがあるよ」(you'll have another chance next week) と述べると，Aは「必ず覚えておくね」と答えているので，女性が来週，健康診断を受けるつもりであることがわかる。よって，have another chanceを**have a medical checkup**と言い換えた**4**が正解。

No. 2 正解 **4**

放送文 *A:* Looks like I'll be putting in another 60-hour week. Seems like I live here at the office these days. *B:* You do live at the office these days, and they don't pay you nearly enough. Why don't you drop a hint that you'd like to review your compensation? *A:* But I've only been working here a year. *B:* In which time they've doubled your responsibilities. Come on, Laurie! You need to stand up for yourself. *A:* Well, maybe you're right.
Question: How does the man feel about the woman's situation?

訳 *A:* また週60時間労働になりそうなの。最近，私はこのオフィスに住んでいるようなものよ。 *B:* 君はここのところ，まさにオフィスに住んでいるみたいだけど，会社は君に十分な報酬を支払っていないよね。報酬を見直したいとほのめかしてみたらどうかな？ *A:* でも，ここで働き始めてからまだ1年しか経ってないのよ。 *B:* その間に，君の責任は2倍になったよね。さあ，ローリー！ 自分のために立ち上がるべきだよ。
A: うーん，あなたの言う通りかもしれないね。

質問の訳 男性は女性の状況をどのように感じているか。

選択肢の訳 **1** 彼女はもっと休みを取るべきだ。 **2** 彼女はお金についてあまり気にするべきではない。 **3** 彼女はそれほどまでの責任を負う準備ができていない。
4 彼女はもっと給料をもらっていいはずだ。

解説 1往復目で，週60時間労働になりそうだと長時間労働を嘆いているA（＝Laurie）に対し，B（＝男性）は「会社は君に十分な報酬を支払っていないよね。報酬を見直したいとほのめかしてみたらどうかな？」と述べ，2往復目でも「君の責任は2倍になったよね」と，Aの仕事の大変さを述べているので，Aの過大な労働量に比べて，Aが受け取る報酬が十分でないとBが考えていることがわかる。よって，don't pay you nearly enoughを**deserves more pay**とAの立場で言い換えた**4**が正解。

No. 3 正解 **2**

放送文 ***A:*** Doctor, how were the test results? ***B:*** Not bad. It's just a sprain. Nevertheless, I still think you should avoid strenuous exercise for at least a couple of weeks after you leave the hospital today. ***A:*** But my softball team's got a big game this Thursday. ***B:*** I'm afraid you're going to have to sit that one out. You should wait till you fully recover or you may make it worse.

Question: What does the doctor tell the man?

訳 ***A:*** 先生，検査結果はどうでしたか。 ***B:*** 悪くないですね。ただの捻挫です。でも，今日退院してから少なくとも２週間は激しい運動は避けたほうがいいと思います。 ***A:*** でも，今度の木曜日にソフトボールチームの大事な試合があります。 ***B:*** 残念ながら，その試合は見送るしかないでしょう。完全に回復してからにすべきで，さもないと悪化するかもしれませんよ。

質問の訳 医者は男性に何と言っているか。

選択肢の訳 **1** 彼はさらなる検査を受ける必要がある。 **2** 彼は試合に出ることができないだろう。 **3** 彼は別の形の運動を見つける必要がある。 **4** 彼は病院にいなければならない。

解説 1往復目でB（＝医師）はA（＝男性）に，「今日退院してから少なくとも2週間は激しい運動は避けたほうがいい」と言い，2往復目で「今度の木曜日にソフトボールチームの大事な試合があります」と言ったAに対して，Bは「残念ながら，その試合は見送るしかないでしょう」(I'm afraid you're going to have to sit that one out.) と述べている。sit outで「参加しない，加わらない」の意味。よって，have to sit that one outをnot be able to play in the gameと言い換えた**2**が正解。

No. 4 正解 **2**

放送文 ***A:*** Hi, Phil. I'm sorry to bother you on your day off, but I'm not feeling well. Could you cover my shift this afternoon? ***B:*** Unfortunately, I've already got plans. ***A:*** I see. Do you know who might be able to change shifts with me? ***B:*** I'm not sure. ***A:*** Maybe the new guy can cover it. ***B:*** I'd just get in touch with the manager. It's her responsibility to deal with these issues. ***A:*** I know, but I hate bothering her. Maybe I should just work the shift. ***B:*** No, don't do that. You might make everyone else sick.

Question: What does the man imply the woman should do?

訳 ***A:*** こんにちは，フィル。お休みのところ申し訳ないんだけど，体調がよくないの。今日の午後のシフトを代わってもらえる？ ***B:*** あいにく，もう予定があるんだ。 ***A:*** そうなんだ。誰か私とシフトを代わってくれそうな人を知ってる？ ***B:*** わからないな。 ***A:*** もしかしたら，あの新入社員がカバーしてくれるかもしれないよね。 ***B:*** 店長に連絡すればいいんじゃない。こういうことに対処するのは彼女の責任だよ。 ***A:*** わかってるけど，彼女に迷惑をかけるのは嫌なの。私がシフトに入ればいいだけだよね。 ***B:*** だめだよ，そんなことしちゃ。他のみんなを病気にしてしまうかもしれないよ。

質問の訳 男性は女性が何をすべきと示唆しているか。

選択肢の訳 **1** 新入社員に連絡する。 **2** 店長に相談する。 **3** 自分でシフトに入る。

4 彼とシフトを変わる。

解説 1往復目で，A（＝女性）がB（＝Phil）に「体調がよくないの。今日の午後のシフトを代わってもらえる？」と述べたのに対し，Bは「あいにく，もう予定があるんだ」と述べてシフト交代の求めを断ったあと，3往復目で「店長に連絡すればいいんじゃない。こういうことに対処するのは彼女の責任だよ」と述べているので，Bは，Aが店長に相談するべきだと考えていることがわかる。よって，get in touch with the managerを**speak to the manager**と言い換えた**2**が正解。

No. 5 正解 **3**

放送文 ***A:*** I'm looking forward to our business trip next week. ***B:*** Me, too. I'll double-check the flight schedule tomorrow. ***A:*** Thanks. ***B:*** Have you finished putting together the presentation for our meeting? ***A:*** Not yet. I was planning to get it done tomorrow. ***B:*** That's a good idea. I remember trying to finish one at a hotel last year, and I couldn't connect to the Internet. ***A:*** Our hotel is supposed to have good Wi-Fi, but don't worry. It'll be done before we go.

Question: What will the woman do before leaving for the trip?

訳 ***A:*** 来週の出張が楽しみね。 ***B:*** 僕もだよ。明日，フライトスケジュールを再確認しておくよ。 ***A:*** ありがとう。 ***B:*** 会議で使うプレゼン資料の作成は終わったの？ ***A:*** まだよ。明日には完成させようと思っていたの。 ***B:*** それはいい考えだね。去年，ホテルでプレゼン資料を仕上げようとしたら，インターネットに接続できなかったのを覚えているよ。 ***A:*** 私たちのホテルはWi-Fiが充実しているはずだけど，心配しないで。私たちが行く前に終わらせておくから。

質問の訳 女性は出張に出発する前に何をするか。

選択肢の訳 **1** ホテルにインターネット接続について問い合わせる。 **2** 会議のスケジュールを確認する。 **3** プレゼンテーションの準備を終える。 **4** 飛行機のチケットを購入する。

解説 1往復目でA（＝女性）が「来週の出張が楽しみね」と述べているので，出張に出発するのは来週だとわかる。2往復目でB（＝男性）から「会議で使うプレゼン資料の作成は終わったの？」とたずねられたAは「まだよ。明日には完成させようと思っていたの」と述べ，4往復目でも「私たちが行く前に終わらせておくから」（It'll be done before we go.）と述べているので，Aは出張に出発する前にプレゼン資料の作成を終えるつもりだとわかる。よって，it'll be doneを**finish preparing the presentation**と具体的に言い換えた**3**が正解。

No. 6 正解 **1**

放送文 ***A:*** Shall we order some more wine? ***B:*** I'd love to, but we should probably catch the bus home soon. It's already eleven. ***A:*** Eleven? Oh, dear. The last one will have left by the time we get to the bus stop. ***B:*** We can still catch the last train. ***A:*** That train doesn't come for another hour. I say we treat ourselves to a taxi. ***B:*** Works for me. ***A:*** Great. Let's head over to the main street. We can probably catch one there.

Question: What does the couple decide to do?

訳 ***A:*** ワインをもう少し頼みましょうか。 ***B:*** そうしたいけど，そろそろバスで帰らないとね。もう11時だよ。 ***A:*** 11時？ あら，そう。バス停に着くまでに，最終バスが出発してしまうわ。 ***B:*** まだ最終の電車に乗れるよ。 ***A:*** 電車は，あと1時間は来ないわ。タクシーに乗りましょうよ。 ***B:*** ぼくはそれで構わないよ。 ***A:*** よかった。大通りに行ってみましょう。たぶんそこでタクシーが捕まえられるわ。

質問の訳 夫婦はどうすることにするか。

選択肢の訳 **1** タクシーで帰宅する。 **2** さらにワインを注文する。 **3** 終電で帰宅する。 **4** 最寄りのバス停まで歩く。

解説 1往復目から，飲食店での対話で，現在の時刻は（夜の）11時という設定。2往復目でA（＝女性）が「バス停に着くまでに，最終バスが出発してしまうわ」と述べているのでバスでは帰宅できないことがわかる。2往復目でB（＝男性）が「まだ最終の電車に乗れるよ」と言っているが，Aが「電車は，あと1時間は来ないわ。タクシーに乗りましょうよ」と言うと，Bも「ぼくはそれで構わないよ」と同意し，さらにAが「大通りに行ってみましょう。たぶんそこでタクシーが捕まえられるわ」と述べているので，夫婦はタクシーで帰宅するつもりだとわかる。よって，treat ourselves to a taxiやcatch oneをtake a taxi homeと言い換えた**1**が正解。

No. 7 正解 **2**

放送文 ***A:*** Honey, did you see that the new restaurant down the block finally opened? ***B:*** I'm sorry, I can't chat right now. I need to start making dinner so it'll be ready by the time the kids get home from school. ***A:*** Leave dinner to me. ***B:*** Really? But you don't cook. You aren't planning to order takeout, are you? We just bought groceries. ***A:*** No. I know I'm not a good chef, but I found a cooking website for beginners. I saw a great recipe for a pasta dish I think I can make. ***B:*** Oh, that would be lovely!

Question: What does the man offer to do?

訳 ***A:*** ねえ，1ブロック行ったところにある新しいレストランがついにオープンしたのを知ってる？ ***B:*** ごめん，今おしゃべりできないわ。子供たちが学校から帰ってくるまでに準備できるように，夕食を作り始めなくちゃいけないの。 ***A:*** 夕食はぼくに任せて。 ***B:*** そうなの？ でも，あなたは料理をしないわよね。テイクアウトを頼むつもりじゃないよね？ ちょうど食料品を買ってきたばかりなのよ。 ***A:*** いいや。ぼくが料理が下手なのはわかっているけど，初心者向けの料理のウェブサイトを見つけたんだ。ぼくにも作れそうなパスタのすごいレシピを見たんだ。 ***B:*** ああ，それは素敵ね！

質問の訳 男性は何を申し出ているか。

選択肢の訳 **1** 学校帰りの子どもたちを迎えに行く。 **2** 家族のために夕食を作る。 **3** 今夜の夕食の材料を買う。 **4** 新しいレストランに料理を注文する。

解説 子供たちが学校から帰ってくるまでに夕食の準備をしなければならないと言ったB（＝女性）に対し，2往復目でA（＝男性）は「夕食はぼくに任せて」(Leave dinner to me.）と言い，3往復目でも「初心者向けの料理のウェブサイトを見つけたんだ。ぼくにも作れそうなパスタのすごいレシピを見たんだ」と述べているので，Aは妻や子供たちのために夕食を作ることを申し出たことがわかる。よって，leave dinner to meを

cook dinner for his familyと言い換えた**2**が正解。「テイクアウトを頼むつもりじゃないよね？」とBに言われたAは「いいや」(No) と答えているので，**4**は不適。

No. 8 正解 1

放送文 ***A:*** AFP Automotive. ***B:*** Hi. I'm on Highway 5. My engine overheated, and it won't start. I need my car towed, and I could use a ride downtown. I have to be at a meeting in an hour. ***A:*** Could you tell me your policy number? ***B:*** It's A735. ***A:*** I'm sorry. A car will arrive in about 10 minutes to take you downtown, but the system says you don't have towing coverage. ***B:*** Really? I thought my plan included towing. ***A:*** Unfortunately, you'll have to pay out of pocket this time, but we can add it to your insurance policy in the future.

Question: What is one problem the man has?

訳 ***A:*** AFPオートモーティブです。 ***B:*** こんにちは，ハイウェイ5号線にいます。エンジンがオーバーヒートしてしまって，かからないんです。車を牽引して，ダウンタウンまで送ってもらえませんか。1時間後に会議に出なければならないんです。 ***A:*** 保険証券番号を教えていただけますか。 ***B:*** A735です。 ***A:*** 申し訳ございません。10分ほどで車が到着し，ダウンタウンまでお送りいたしますが，システム上，お客様はレッカー移動の補償を受けられないことになっています。 ***B:*** そうなんですか。私のプランにはレッカー移動が含まれていると思ったのですが。 ***A:*** 残念ながら，今回は自己負担になりますが，将来的に保険に追加していただくことは可能でございます。

質問の訳 男性が抱えている問題は何か。

選択肢の訳 **1** 予想外の料金を支払わなければならない。 **2** 保険契約をキャンセルした。 **3** 会議に遅刻している。 **4** 保険会社が保険番号を見つけることができない。

解説 1往復目から，車のエンジンがオーバーヒートしてしまったB（＝男性）が，車を牽引して，ダウンタウンまで送ってもらうことをA（＝AFPオートモーティブの担当者の女性）に依頼している場面。3往復目でAは「システム上，お客様はレッカー移動の補償を受けられないことになっています」と述べ，4往復目で「残念ながら，今回は自己負担になります」と述べているから，Bはレッカー移動の費用を自己負担しなければならないことがわかる。また，3往復目でBは「私のプランにはレッカー移動が含まれていると思ったのですが」と述べているので，Bがレッカー移動の費用が保険で賄われると誤解していたこともわかる。よって，don't have towing coverageをhas to pay an unexpected feeとBの立場で表した**1**が正解。

No. 9 正解 3

放送文 ***A:*** Excuse me, Professor Garcia. Could I ask you for some advice? ***B:*** Of course. Is it about our art classes? ***A:*** Sort of. I'm thinking about changing my major from communications to graphic design, but I'm not sure if it's a good idea. ***B:*** Why are you considering the change? ***A:*** It gives me career options. I could do advertising, marketing, or even web design. ***B:*** Those are good careers. What's your concern? ***A:*** Well, I'm not confident that my artistic skills are good enough. ***B:*** I've seen your work. If you make the effort, I think you could be quite successful.

Question: What does the woman imply?

訳 ***A:*** すみません，ガルシア教授。アドバイスをいただいてもよろしいでしょうか。 ***B:*** もちろんです。美術の授業のことですか。 ***A:*** そんなところです。専攻をコミュニケーションからグラフィックデザインに変えようと思っているのですが，いいのかどうかわからないんです。 ***B:*** なぜ変更を考えているのですか。 ***A:*** 職業の選択肢が増えるからです。広告やマーケティング，あるいはウェブデザインもできるかもしれません。 ***B:*** それらはすばらしい職業ですね。何が心配なんですか。 ***A:*** そうですね，自分の絵の技能が十分なものか自信がないんです。 ***B:*** あなたの作品を見たことがあります。努力すれば，かなり成功すると思いますよ。

質問の訳 女性は何をほのめかしているか。

選択肢の訳 **1** その男性は専攻を変えるべきではない。 **2** コミュニケーション関係の仕事の方がその男性には合っているかもしれない。 **3** グラフィックデザインはその男性にとって良い選択だ。 **4** その男性は授業で成績がよくない。

解説 1～2往復目から，A（＝男性）が，B（＝Professor Garcia）に，専攻をコミュニケーションからグラフィックデザインに変えることについてアドバイスを求めている場面だとわかる。4往復目でAが「自分の絵の技能が十分なものか自信がないんです」と述べたのに対し，Bは「努力すれば，かなり成功すると思いますよ」と述べているので，女性は，Aが専攻をグラフィックデザインに変えることをよい選択だと思っていることがわかる。よって，you could be quite successfulを**a good choice for the man**と言い換えた**3**が正解。

No. 10 正解 2

放送文 ***A:*** Alicia, can I talk to you about that online meeting software we're using? ***B:*** Sure, Ben. What is it? ***A:*** We've been using the free version, but I think we should consider paying to upgrade to the full version. The free version can be inconvenient at times. ***B:*** The participant limit has been a problem. Sometimes we'd like to have more than eight people in a meeting at once. Could you submit an official request with the cost? ***A:*** Does that mean there's room in the budget for an upgrade? ***B:*** I'll see what I can do.

Question: What will the man do next?

訳 ***A:*** アリシア，今使っているオンラインミーティング・ソフトウェアのことで相談してもいい？ ***B:*** もちろん，ベン。何？ ***A:*** 今までは無料版を使ってきたけど，お金を払ってフルバージョンにアップグレードすることを検討した方がいいと思うんだ。無料版ではときどき不便なことがあるんだ。 ***B:*** 参加者数の制限がいつも問題になるよね。一度に8人以上で会議に参加したいときがあるものね。費用といっしょに正式な要望書を出してもらえる？ ***A:*** それって，アップグレードのための予算の余地があるということ？ ***B:*** 何とか考えてみるわね。

質問の訳 男性は次に何をするか。

選択肢の訳 **1** 他のオンラインチャットツールを探す。 **2** ソフトウェアのアップグレードのための要望書を準備する。 **3** オンラインミーティングにもっと多くの人に参加してもらう。 **4** 会社の予算を増やすように依頼する。

解説 1～2往復目から，A（＝Ben）が，今使っている無料版のオンラインミーティング・ソフトウェアを有料のフルバージョンにアップグレードすることについてB（＝Alicia）に相談している場面。２往復目でBは「参加者数の制限がいつも問題になるよね」と述べアップグレードする必要性に同意し，「費用といっしょに正式な要望書を出してもらえる？」とAに依頼しているので，ベンはそれに応じて，これから正式な要望書を作成することがわかる。よって，submit an official requestを**prepare a request**と言い換えた**2**が正解。

No. 11　正解　**2**

放送文 ***A:*** Carol, I have a favor to ask you. ***B:*** What is it? ***A:*** Inspectors from Mexico are coming to our plant tomorrow, and our regular interpreter is on vacation. I remember you majored in Spanish in college. Do you think you could substitute? ***B:*** Well, I did study Spanish, but I'm not sure I can handle all the technical terms. ***A:*** What if we asked Barbara to do your regular work today, and you spent the rest of the afternoon brushing up on vocabulary? ***B:*** OK. I'll do my best.

Question: What will the woman do for the rest of the day?

訳 ***A:*** キャロル，お願いがあるんだけど。 ***B:*** 何ですか？ ***A:*** 明日，メキシコの検査官がうちの工場に来るんだけど，いつもの通訳が休暇中なんだ。君は大学でスペイン語を専攻していたよね。代わってもらえないかな？ ***B:*** ええ，確かにスペイン語は勉強しましたけど，専門用語のすべてに対応できるか自信がありません。 ***A:*** 今日は，バーバラに君の通常の業務を頼んで，君は午後の残りの時間で語彙のブラッシュアップをしたらどうかな？ ***B:*** わかりました。がんばります。

質問の訳 女性は今日このあとどうするか。

選択肢の訳 **1**　工場へ行く。　**2**　スペイン語を勉強する。　**3**　バーバラと会う。　**4**　通訳を探す。

解説 １～２往復目から，A（＝男性）が，明日，メキシコの検査官が来るが通訳が休暇中なので，大学でスペイン語を専攻していたB（＝Carol）に通訳をしてもらえないかと依頼している場面。２往復目でBが「専門用語のすべてに対応できるか自信がありません」と述べたのに対し，Aが「君は午後の残りの時間で語彙のブラッシュアップをしたらどうかな？」（you spent the rest of the afternoon brushing up on vocabulary）と提案すると，Bは「わかりました。がんばります」（OK. I'll do my best.）と答えているので，Bはこのあとスペイン語の語彙のブラッシュアップをすることがわかる。よって，brushing up on vocabularyを**study Spanish**と言い換えた**2**が正解。

No. 12　正解　**4**

放送文 ***A:*** Excuse me, ma'am, this is a no-parking zone. ***B:*** I'm sorry, officer. I felt ill while I was driving, so I stopped my car here to take a short rest. ***A:*** Are you OK? I can call an ambulance for you. ***B:*** No, thanks. I'm feeling much better now, but can I rest here for another 10 minutes or so? ***A:*** No problem. I'll stand by in the police car until you feel well enough to leave. Honk your horn if you need help. ***B:*** I will. Thanks.

Question: What is the police officer going to do?

訳 *A:* すみません，奥様，ここは駐車禁止区域です。　*B:* すみません，お巡りさん。運転中に気分が悪くなったので，ここで少し休むために車を停めました。　*A:* 大丈夫ですか。救急車を呼びましょうか。　*B:* いいえ，結構です。もうだいぶ良くなったんですが，あと10分くらいここで休んでもいいですか。　*A:* 大丈夫です。あなたが帰れるくらい元気になるまで，パトカーで待機しています。何かあったらクラクションを鳴らしてください。　*B:* そうします。ありがとうございます。

質問の訳 警察官は何をするつもりか。

選択肢の訳 **1**　無線で救急車を呼ぶ。　**2**　女性の車を動かしてあげる。　**3**　女性に駐車違反の切符を切る。　**4**　パトカーで待つ。

解説 1往復目から，運転中に気分が悪くなり，少し休むために駐車禁止区域に車を停めていたB（＝女性）に，A（＝警察官）が声をかけた場面。2～3往復目で「あと10分くらいここで休んでもいいですか」と述べたBに，Aは「大丈夫です。あなたが帰れるくらい元気になるまで，パトカーで待機しています」と述べているので，AはBが元気になるまでパトカーで待つつもりだとわかる。よって，stand by in the police carをwait in his police carと言い換えた**4**が正解。

Part 2 一次試験・リスニング

(問題編pp.144～145)

CD 赤-40 ～ CD 赤-46

指示文の訳 それでは，これからPart 2の指示を行います。このパートでは(A)から(F)までの6つの文章が放送されます。それぞれの文章に続いて，No. 13からNo. 24まで質問が2つずつ流れます。それぞれの質問に対して，最も適切な答えを選んで解答用紙にマークする時間が10秒あります。文章と質問は1度しか読まれません。それでは始めます。

(A)

放送文 *The P-47　Thunderbolt*

When the P-47 Thunderbolt first appeared in World War II, American pilots worried that this extremely heavy fighter plane would be at a disadvantage against smaller, lighter German planes. The P-47 was indeed slower at low altitudes, but when it was flying high, it could outrun almost any other plane. One serious weakness early on was its limited fuel supply. Eventually, however, extra tanks were fitted onto the P-47 so that it could go on longer missions.

The P-47 had eight powerful machine guns and was able to carry an impressive selection of bombs and rockets. The real reason that pilots came to love it, though, is that it was one of the most durable planes of the war and survived many hits that would have destroyed other planes. In one extreme case, a pilot was able to land his P-47 after it was shot over 100 times.

Questions ***No. 13*** What problem did the P-47 Thunderbolt have at first?

No. 14 What did pilots like most about flying the P-47 Thunderbolt?

訳 P-47　サンダーボルト

第二次世界大戦でP-47サンダーボルトが初めて登場したとき，アメリカのパイロットたちは，この非常に重い戦闘機が小さくて軽いドイツ機に対して不利になるのではないかと心配した。確かにP-47は低空飛行では遅かったが，高い高度を飛行しているときは，他のほとんどの飛行機を凌駕することができた。初期の深刻な弱点は，燃料の供給が限られていたことだった。しかし，やがてP-47に追加タンクが装着され，より長時間の任務に対応できるようになった。

P-47は8門の強力な機関銃を持ち，優れた種類の爆弾とロケット弾を搭載することができた。しかし，パイロットがP-47を愛するようになった本当の理由は，それが戦時中最も耐久性のある飛行機の1つであり，他の飛行機なら破壊されていたような多くの被弾に耐えたことである。極端な例を挙げれば，あるパイロットは，100回以上も被弾したP-47を着陸させることができた。

No.13 正解 3

質問の訳 P-47サンダーボルトには最初どんな問題があったのか。

選択肢の訳 **1** あまり高く飛べなかった。 **2** 小さくて軽すぎた。 **3** 短い距離しか飛べなかった。 **4** 珍しい種類の燃料を使った。

解説 第1段落第3文で「初期の深刻な弱点は，燃料の供給が限られていたことだった」(One serious weakness early on was its limited fuel supply.) と述べられている。燃料の供給が限られているとは，長い距離を飛ぶことができない，すなわち短い距離しか飛べないということ。よって，limited fuel supplyによる結果を**could only fly short distances**と表した**3**が正解。

No.14 正解 1

質問の訳 P-47サンダーボルトの操縦について，パイロットは何が最も気に入ったか。

選択肢の訳 **1** 他の飛行機より丈夫だった。 **2** 新しい種類の武器を持っていた。 **3** とても速く着陸することができた。 **4** 正確に爆弾を落とすことができた。

解説 第2段落第2文で「パイロットがP-47を愛するようになった本当の理由は，それが戦時中最も耐久性のある飛行機の1つであり，他の飛行機なら破壊されていたような多くの被弾に耐えたことである」(The real reason that pilots came to love it, though, is that it was one of the most durable planes of the war and survived many hits that would have destroyed other planes.) と述べられている。「他の飛行機なら破壊されていたような多くの被弾に耐えた」とは他の飛行機より丈夫だということ。よって，survived many hits that would have destroyed other planesを**tougher than other planes**と言い換えた**1**が正解。

(B)

放送文 *Ascension Island*

Ascension Island lies in the middle of the Atlantic Ocean. Originally, it was nearly treeless, and fresh water was scarce, which made for tough living conditions for the first settlers. However, in the 1840s, a British scientist named Sir Joseph Hooker started a program to transform the desert island. He started importing trees and other plants that were able to survive in the island's dry environment by absorbing water from mist in the air. His program eventually

resulted in an entire mountain being covered in forest. However, Hooker's plants have been so successful that several native plant species have gone extinct.

There is now a debate about the island's future. Some people say efforts must be made to preserve the plants that were originally found on the island. Others, though, want the new ecosystem to be left as is, since it has had benefits, such as increasing available water and creating the potential for agriculture.

Questions ***No. 15*** What was one result of Sir Joseph Hooker's program for Ascension Island?

No. 16 What do people disagree about regarding Ascension Island?

訳 アセンション島

アセンション島は，大西洋の真ん中に浮かんでいる。もともとは樹木がほとんどなく，淡水も乏しかったため，最初の入植者にとっては厳しい生活環境だった。しかし，1840年代，イギリスの科学者ジョセフ・フッカー卿が，この無人島を改造するプログラムに着手した。彼は，空気中の霧から水分を吸収し，乾燥した環境で生き抜くことができる樹木や植物の輸入を始めた。彼のプログラムの結果，山全体が森に覆われるようになった。しかしながら，フッカーの植物があまりにうまく生育したため，いくつかの在来種の植物が絶滅してしまった。

今，この島の将来について議論が起きている。元々この島にあった植物を保護する努力をしなければならないという人々がいる。しかし他方では，新しい生態系は，利用できる水を増やし，農業を可能にするなどの利点があるため，このまま残したいという人々もいる。

No.15 正解 4

質問の訳 アセンション島に対するジョセフ・フッカー卿のプログラムの一つの結果は何だったか。

選択肢の訳 **1** 水の供給量が減った。 **2** 大気汚染が少なくなった。 **3** 多くの人が島を離れなければならなくなった。 **4** 木の本数が増えた。

解説 第１段落第５文で「彼のプログラムの結果，山全体が森に覆われるようになった」(His program eventually resulted in an entire mountain being covered in forest.) と述べられている。山全体が森に覆われるようになったとは，木の本数が増えたということ。よって，resulted in an entire mountain being covered in forestをthe number of trees increasedと言い換えた**4**が正解。

No.16 正解 3

質問の訳 アセンション島について，人々は何の意見が合わないか。

選択肢の訳 **1** 新しい生態系をどう分類するか。 **2** 給水を何に使うか。 **3** 在来植物が保護されるべきかどうか。 **4** 農業がどこで許可されるべきか。

解説 第２段落第２文で一方の人々の意見として「元々この島にあった植物を保護する努力をしなければならない」(efforts must be made to preserve the plants that were originally found on the island) と述べられ，第２段落第３文で他方の意見として「(新しい生態系を) このまま残したい」(want the new ecosystem to be left as is) と述べられている。2つの意見の対立点は，利点があるフッカーの植物によって駆逐されつつある在来植物を保護すべきかどうかということ。よって，preserve the plants that were originally found on the islandを**native plants should be protected**と言い換えた**3**が正解。

(C)

放送文 *Vivian Maier*

One of the twentieth century's greatest street photographers, Vivian Maier is known for her fascinating images of people in cities like Chicago and New York. Maier worked in childcare, but her true passion was photography. She always had her camera with her, and this habit allowed her to capture unique and unusual shots of people going about their daily lives. Her photos depict everything from strangely dressed tourists to emergency workers caring for accident victims.

Despite the incredible number of photos she took, Maier was an intensely private person. Unlike most photographers, she refused to allow others to see her work. Nevertheless, a collection of her photos was purchased at an auction in 2007, and the buyers began exhibiting her unusual work. It was not until after her death in 2009, however, that she was recognized as an artistic genius.

Questions ***No. 17*** What is one thing we learn about Vivian Maier?

No. 18 How was Maier different from other photographers?

訳 ヴィヴィアン・マイヤー

20世紀のもっとも偉大なストリート・フォトグラファーの一人であるヴィヴィアン・マイヤーは，シカゴやニューヨークなどの都市の人々を魅力的に撮影した写真で知られている。マイヤーは保育士として働いていたが，彼女が本当に情熱を注いだのは写真だった。彼女は常にカメラを持ち歩いたので，日常生活を送る人々のユニークで珍しい場面を撮影することができた。奇妙な服装をした観光客から，事故の被害者を介抱する救急隊員まで，彼女の写真にはあらゆるものが写っていた。

彼女は膨大な数の写真を撮ったが，マイヤーは極めて引っ込み思案の人間だった。他のたいていの写真家とは異なり，彼女は自分の作品を他人が見ることを拒んでいた。それでも2007年にオークションで彼女の写真集が落札されると，その買い主は彼女の珍しい作品を展示し始めた。しかしながら，彼女が天才写真家として認められるようになったのは，2009年に彼女が亡くなってからのことだった。

No.17 正解 **1**

質問の訳 ヴィヴィアン・マイヤーについてわかることの1つは何か。

選択肢の訳 **1** どこにでもカメラを持ち歩いていた。 **2** 救急隊員と友達になった。 **3** 世話をしている子供たちにカメラを貸した。 **4** 旅行者としていろいろな場所に行った。

解説 第1段落第3文で「彼女は常にカメラを持ち歩いたので～」(She always had her camera with her) と述べられている。常にカメラを持ち歩いたとは，どこにでもカメラを持ち歩いていたということ。よって，always had her camera with herをcarried her camera everywhereと言い換えた**1**が正解。

No.18 正解 4

質問の訳 マイヤーは他の写真家とどう違ったか。

選択肢の訳 **1** 早くから有名になった。 **2** 主にオークションで写真を撮っていた。 **3** とても大きな展覧会を開いた。 **4** 自分の写真を人に見せなかった。

解説 第２段落第２文で「彼女は自分の作品を他人が見ることを拒んでいた」(she refused to allow others to see her work) と述べられている。自分の作品を他人が見ることを拒むとは，自分の写真を人に見せなかったということ。よって，refused to allow others to see her workをdid not show people her photosと言い換えた**4**が正解。

(D)

放送文 *The Impact of Cats*

Cats are one of the most popular pets today, but like many other pets, they affect the environment through their eating habits. As carnivores, cats primarily eat meat, the production of which releases substantial amounts of carbon dioxide gas into the atmosphere and often creates air and water pollution. According to a recent study, however, the management of cats' waste may be more harmful to the environment than their diet is.

Cat owners commonly prepare boxes for their cats that contain cat litter, a material that traps the cats' waste. However, the clay that is used in most litter is usually acquired through surface mining, a process that requires oil-powered heavy machinery and can destroy large natural areas. Recently, more manufacturers have begun producing litter made from environmentally friendly materials like wood and seeds. Nevertheless, clay-based litter is still the most used type due to its low cost and exceptional odor absorption.

Questions ***No. 19*** What is one thing the speaker says about cat-food production?

No. 20 What do we learn about the process of collecting clay?

訳 猫が与える影響

猫は，現在最も人気のあるペットの一つだが，他の多くのペットと同様に，その食習慣を通じて環境に影響を与えている。肉食動物として，猫は主に肉を食べるが，その生産過程で大量の炭酸ガスが大気中に放出され，大気汚染や水質汚染を引き起こすことがよくある。しかし，最近の研究によると，猫の食事よりも排泄物の処理の方が環境に対してより有害である可能性がある。

猫を飼っている人は，猫の排泄物を閉じ込めるための猫砂を入れた箱を用意するのが一般的だ。しかし，たいていの猫砂に使用される粘土は，石油を動力源とする重機が必要な地表採掘で入手されるのが一般的であり，広大な自然を破壊してしまうことがある。最近では，木材や種子など，より環境に配慮した素材を使って猫砂を製造し始めるメーカーも増えてきた。それでも，安価で優れた臭いの吸着力があることから，粘土質の猫砂が現在でも最も多く使用されている。

No.19 正解 3

質問の訳 キャットフードの製造について，話し手が言っていることの1つは何か。

選択肢の訳 **1** 真水を使う必要はない。 **2** 特定の気候でのみ可能だ。 **3** 大量のガスを発生させる。 **4** 昔より肉の使用量が減っている。

解説 第1段落第2文で「猫は主に肉を食べるが，その生産過程で大量の炭酸ガスが大気中に放出され〜」(cats primarily eat meat, the production of which releases substantial amounts of carbon dioxide gas into the atmosphere 〜）と述べられている。よって，releases substantial amounts of carbon dioxide gasをproduces a large amount of gasと言い換えた**3**が正解。

No.20 正解 2

質問の訳 粘土の採取過程について何がわかるか。

選択肢の訳 **1** 使用する機械が非常に高価だ。 **2** 広範囲の土地にダメージを与えている。 **3** 近隣の農地に化学物質を放出する。 **4** 作業員にとって高頻度で危険だ。

解説 第2段落第2文で「たいていの猫砂に使用される粘土は〜広大な自然を破壊してしまうことがある」(the clay that is used in most litter 〜 can destroy large natural areas）と述べられている。よって，destroy large natural areasをdamaging to wide areas of landと言い換えた**2**が正解。

(E)

放送文 *Profitable Experiences*

For many young people today, experiences have become more important than material things. This has created money-making opportunities for businesses that can provide memorable and exciting experiences. One recent example is "axe-throwing bars." While axes would normally be associated with chopping wood in a forest, now people in many cities can go to special bars and throw axes like darts. Some worry about the possible dangers of this activity, but fans argue that it is a fun way to release stress.

Such businesses that sell experiences have spread across the US, but critics argue these businesses may negatively affect communities in the long run. They say the businesses are probably a short-term trend whose popularity will not last. And, when the businesses close, their employees are left without a source of income. The critics recommend that cities encourage the development of businesses that will be popular for decades, not just a few years.

Questions ***No. 21*** What is one reason for the popularity of "axe-throwing bars"?

No. 22 What is one criticism of businesses that sell experiences?

訳 有益な経験

現代の多くの若者にとって，モノよりも体験がより重要なものとなっている。このこと

は，記憶に残るようなエキサイティングな体験を提供できる企業に，お金儲けの機会を生み出している。最近の例では，「斧投げバー」がある。斧といえば，ふつう森で薪を割ることが連想されるが，今では多くの都市では，特別なバーに行って斧をダーツのように投げることができる。この活動の危険性を心配する人もいるが，ストレス発散のための楽しいやり方だと言うファンもいる。

体験を販売するこのようなビジネスは全米に広がっているが，批評家たちは，これらのビジネスは長期的には地域社会に悪影響を与える可能性があると主張する。このビジネスは人気が長続きしない，おそらく短期的な流行だろうと言うのだ。そして，ビジネスが終了すると，その従業員は収入源を失うことになる。批評家たちは，数年ではなく，何十年にもわたって人気を博すようなビジネスの開発を都市が奨励するよう提言している。

No.21　正解　1

質問の訳「斧投げバー」の人気の理由のひとつは何か。

選択肢の訳　**1**　若者の興味の変化。　**2**　若者の運動ニーズの高まり。　**3**　若者の経済状況。　**4**　若者の自然に対する情熱。

解説　第1段落第1文で「現代の多くの若者にとって，モノよりも体験がより重要なものとなっている」(For many young people today, experiences have become more important than material things.) と述べられている。モノよりも体験がより重要なものとなっているとは，若者の興味がモノから体験へと変化しているということ。よって，experiences have become more important than material thingsをchanging interestsと抽象的に表した**1**が正解。

No.22　正解　1

質問の訳　体験を売りにしたビジネスに対する批判の一つは何か。

選択肢の訳　**1**　長く生き残る可能性が低い。　**2**　都市部以外ではうまくいかない。　**3**　地元の人をほとんど雇っていない。　**4**　場所をとりすぎる。

解説　第2段落第2文で，批評家の意見として「このビジネスは人気が長続きしない，おそらく短期的な流行だろう」(the businesses are probably a short-term trend whose popularity will not last) と述べられている。よって，a short-term trendやwill not lastをunlikely to survive longと言い換えた**1**が正解。

(F)

放送文　*T. rex Skulls*

T. rex had two large holes at the top of its skull, which scientists used to believe held muscles that aided jaw movement. Recently, however, researchers realized that this would not have been an efficient location for jaw muscles, so they began searching for another explanation. They looked at a modern animal descended from dinosaurs: the alligator.

The researchers found that alligator skulls have similar holes. They are filled with blood vessels that help alligators control the amount of heat in their bodies. When alligators need to warm themselves, these areas absorb external heat, and they release heat when alligators need to cool down. Since large meat-eating dinosaurs such as *T. rex* likely tended to overheat, these holes and blood vessels could have functioned as a sort of internal air-conditioning system. Of course, we cannot observe living dinosaurs, but studies like this provide interesting clues as to what these prehistoric giants were like.

Questions ***No. 23*** Why did the researchers decide to analyze alligators?

No. 24 What do the researchers now think the holes in *T. rex* skulls were used for?

訳 Tレックス（ティラノサウルス・レックス）の頭骨

Tレックスの頭骨の上部には2つの大きな穴があったが，そこには顎を動かすための筋肉があると科学者たちは考えていた。しかし，最近になって，この穴は顎の筋肉にとって効率的な場所ではないことがわかり，研究者たちは別の説明を探し始めた。そこで彼らは，恐竜の子孫である現代の動物，ワニに注目した。

研究者たちは，ワニの頭骨にも同じような穴があることを発見した。この穴には，ワニが体内の熱量をコントロールするのに役立っている血管が通っていた。ワニが体を温める必要があるときには，この部分が外部の熱を吸収し，冷やす必要があるときには，熱を放出するのだ。Tレックスのような大型の肉食恐竜は体温が高くなりやすいので，この穴と血管が，体内エアコンのような役割を担っていたのかもしれない。もちろん，生きている恐竜を観察することはできないが，このような研究は，先史時代の巨大な恐竜がどのようなものだったかを知る上で興味深い手がかりを与えてくれる。

No.23 正解 2

質問の訳 なぜ研究者たちはワニを分析することにしたか。

選択肢の訳 **1** ワニは効率的な顎を持っている。 **2** ワニは恐竜と同族だ。 **3** ワニは変わった場所に筋肉がある。 **4** ワニはTレックスと同じ時期に進化した。

解説 第1段落最終文で「恐竜の子孫である現代の動物，ワニ」(a modern animal descended from dinosaurs: the alligator) と述べられている。子孫であるとは，ワニとTレックスが同族であるということ。よって，descended from dinosaursを**related to dinosaurs**と言い換えた**2**が正解。

No.24 正解 4

質問の訳 今，研究者は，Tレックスの頭骨の穴が何に使われていたと考えているか。

選択肢の訳 **1** 食べ物の消化を助けるため。 **2** 他の動物の気配を察知するため。 **3** 新しい血管を作るため。 **4** 体温を調節するため。

解説 第2段落第4文で「この穴と血管が，体内エアコンのような役割を担っていたのかもしれない」(these holes and blood vessels could have functioned as a sort of internal air-conditioning system) と述べられている。体内エアコンのような役割とは体温を調節する役割ということ。よって，internal air-conditioning systemを**control their body temperature**と言い換えた**4**が正解。

Part 3 一次試験・リスニング

(問題編pp.146〜147)

CD 赤-47 〜 CD 赤-52

指示文の訳 それでは最後に，Part 3の指示を行います。このパートでは(G)から(K)までの5つの文章が放送されます。英文は実生活における状況を述べたもので，効果音を含むものもあります。それぞれの文章には，No. 25からNo. 29まで，質問が1問ずつ用意されています。それぞれの文章が流れる前に，問題冊子に書かれている状況の説明と質問を読む時間が10秒あります。文章を聞いた後に，最も適切な答えを選んで解答用紙にマークする時間が10秒あります。文章は1度しか読まれません。それでは始めます。

No. 25 正解 3

放送文 *(G)* You have 10 seconds to read the situation and Question No. 25.

Welcome to Greenville. As we approach the gate, please remain in your seats with your seat belts fastened. We realize many of you have connecting flights, so we have gate agents standing by who can direct you to your connecting gates once you exit the plane. Please have your boarding passes ready to show them. If this is your final destination, you can find your luggage on the carousels in the main terminal. If you need to arrange ground transportation, look for the bus service just past the baggage claim. Customer service representatives are available throughout the airport if you need assistance.

Now mark your answer on your answer sheet.

訳 *(G)* 状況と質問25を読む時間が10秒あります。

グリーンヴィルへようこそ。ゲートに近づく間，シートベルトを締めたまま着席していてください。乗り継ぎ便がある方も多いと思いますので，飛行機を降りると，乗り継ぎゲートまでご案内する係員が待機しています。搭乗券をお手元にご用意の上，ご提示ください。こちらが最終目的地の場合は，メインターミナルのコンベヤーでお荷物をお探しいただけます。地上交通機関の手配が必要な場合は，手荷物受取所を過ぎたところにあるバスサービスをお探しください。サポートが必要な場合は，空港内のカスタマー・サービス担当者が対応いたします。

それでは，解答用紙に答えをマークしなさい。

状況の訳 あなたは今，着陸したばかりの飛行機に乗っていて，乗り継ぎ便に乗らなければならない。客室乗務員がアナウンスしている。

質問の訳 飛行機を降りたら，あなたはまず何をすべきか。

選択肢の訳 **1** 荷物を受け取る。 **2** バスに乗って別のターミナルに移動する。 **3** ゲートの係員を探す。 **4** 新しい搭乗券を印刷してもらう。

解説 Situationからわかるのは，①「あなた」は着陸したばかりの飛行機に乗っていることと，②「あなた」は乗り継ぎ便に乗らなければならないこと。客室乗務員は，乗り継ぎに関して，第3文で「乗り継ぎ便がある方も多いと思いますので〜乗り継ぎゲートまでご案内する係員が待機しています」(We realize many of you have connecting flights, so we have gate agents standing by who can direct you to your connecting gates）と述べている。よって,「あなた」がまずすべきことは, 乗り継ぎゲートまで案内してくれる係員のところに行くことなので, **3**が適切。

No. 26 正解 **4**

放送文 *(H)* You have 10 seconds to read the situation and Question No. 26.

We sell four original incense brands. Bouquet Himalaya is a paper-type incense that features the scents of flowers from India. It has a deep, calming effect and helps relieve stress and anxiety. Next, Magnolia's Sanctuary is a stick-type incense that contains sweet-smelling substances. This incense will immediately lift your spirits and is perfect for creating an energizing mood. Akebono is a cone-type purifying incense made with sage, and it's popular among meditation practitioners. Finally, Shirley's Gift is a stick-type incense that was also developed specifically for releasing tension. The aroma calms the mind, creating a tranquil atmosphere.

Now mark your answer on your answer sheet.

訳 *(H)* 状況と質問26を読む時間が10秒あります。

当社では，4つのオリジナルのお香ブランドを販売しています。ブーケ・ヒマラヤは，インドの花の香りをモチーフにしたペーパータイプのお香です。鎮静作用がありストレスや不安の解消に役立ちます。次にマグノリアズ・サンクチュアリは，甘い香りの物質を含んだスティックタイプのお香です。このお香は，すぐに気分が高揚するので元気なムード作りに最適です。アケボノは，セージを使用した円錐形の浄化作用のあるお香で，瞑想をする人たちに人気があります。最後に，シャーリーズ・ギフトは，同じく緊張をほぐすことに特化して開発されたスティックタイプのお香です。香りは心を落ち着かせ，静寂な空間を創出します。

それでは，解答用紙に答えをマークしなさい。

状況の訳 あなたは，リラックスするために焚くスティックタイプのお香を買いたいと考えている。店員はあなたに次のように言う。

質問の訳 あなたはどのブランドのお香を買うべきか。

選択肢の訳 **1** ブーケ・ヒマラヤ。 **2** マグノリアズ・サンクチュアリ。 **3** アケボノ。 **4** シャーリーズ・ギフト。

解説 Situationからわかるのは，①「あなた」がお香を買う目的は，リラックスするためであることと，②「あなた」が買いたいのは，スティックタイプのお香であるということ。①に関しては，第3文に「鎮静作用がありストレスや不安の解消に役立ちます」とあるのでブーケ・ヒマラヤが適する。また，第7文に「緊張をほぐすことに特化して開発された」とあるのでシャーリーズ・ギフトも①に適する。しかし，②に関して，第2文に「ブーケ・ヒマラヤは～ペーパータイプのお香です」とありスティックタイプではないのでブーケ・ヒマラヤは不適。第7文に「シャーリーズ・ギフトは～スティックタイプのお香です」とあるのでシャーリーズ・ギフトは②にも適する。よって，「あなた」が買うべきお香は**4のシャーリーズ・ギフト**。

No. 27 正解 **2**

放送文 *(I)* You have 10 seconds to read the situation and Question No. 27.

I'm calling to confirm your appointment to set up your new Internet service. It's scheduled for this Thursday. Our technician will arrive sometime between noon and 3 p.m. If this time slot is OK, no action is necessary. However, if it's not, please contact us to reschedule. Please note that we're currently experiencing high demand, so our only available appointment times would be next week. Also, our technicians are only available Monday through Friday between 9 a.m. and 6 p.m. Remember that our offices are closed on weekends. Thank you.

Now mark your answer on your answer sheet.

訳 *(I)* 状況と質問27を読む時間が10秒あります。

新しいインターネットサービス設定の予約の確認のお電話をさせていただきました。今週の木曜日に予約されています。弊社の技術者が，正午から午後3時の間にお伺いいたします。この時間帯でご都合がよろしければ，何もしていただく必要はありません。しかし，もしご都合が悪い場合は，予定を変更するよう私どもにご連絡ください。現在，予約が殺到しているため，予約可能な時間帯は来週のみとなりますのでご了承ください。また，技術者は月曜から金曜の午前9時から午後6時までの間のみ対応しております。週末は休業となりますのでご注意ください。ありがとうございました。

それでは，解答用紙に答えをマークしなさい。

状況の訳 今日は月曜日で，あなたは新しいインターネット・プロバイダーの担当者から音声メール［留守電］のメッセージを受け取る。あなたは今週の木曜日，正午から午後8時まで仕事をしなければならない。

質問の訳 あなたは何をすべきか。

選択肢の訳 **1** 今週末にスケジュールを変更する。 **2** 来週の平日にスケジュールを変更する。 **3** 今週の木曜日の午前中にスケジュールを変更する。 **4** 今週の金曜日の午後6時以降にスケジュールを変更する。

解説 Situationからわかるのは，①今日が月曜日であることと，②「あなた」は今週の木曜日，正午から午後8時まで仕事をしなければならないこと。第2～3文から，当初の予約では，インターネットサービス設定のために技術者が来るのは，今週の木曜日の正午から午後3時の間。しかし，Situationの②から，「あなた」は今週の木曜日の正午から午後8時まで仕事がある。したがって，第5文から，「あなた」は予約変更の連絡を入れなければならない。第6文から予約可能な時間帯は「来週のみ」で，しかも第7文から技術者が対応するのは「月曜から金曜」，すなわち「平日のみ」。よって，「あなた」が予約すべき日程は「来週の平日」となるので，Monday through Fridayをa weekdayと言い換えた**2**が正解。なお，第6文から予約可能な時間帯は来週のみなので，**1**，**3**，**4**は不適。

No. 28 正解 **3**

放送文 *(J)* You have 10 seconds to read the situation and Question No. 28.

I've checked your application, and it appears that you've submitted all of the required forms that were on our website. It looks like you also paid your application fee when you submitted those documents. And we've been contacted by your high school regarding your transcripts, which should be arriving shortly. If you aren't sure what you want to major in yet, please consider attending our open-campus event next week. Otherwise, all that's left for you to do is submit a letter from a teacher or employer recommending you. Once we receive that, we can start processing your application.

Now mark your answer on your answer sheet.

訳 *(J)* 状況と質問28を読む時間が10秒あります。

あなたの出願書類を確認したところ，ウェブサイトに掲載されている必要書類はすべて提出されたようですね。書類提出時に入学検定料もお支払いいただいているようです。また，あなたの高校から成績証明書について連絡がありましたので，まもなく到着するはずです。まだ何を専攻したいかが決まっていないのであれば，来週のオープンキャンパス・イベントへの参加も検討してみてください。そうでなければ，あとは先生や雇用主からの推薦状を提出するだけです。それを受領しましたら，あなたの出願手続きを開始します。

それでは，解答用紙に答えをマークしなさい。

状況の訳 あなたは心理学を学ぶために大学に入学しようとしている。入学担当者があなたの出願書類について話している。

質問の訳 あなたは何をすべきか。

選択肢の訳 **1** 出願料を払う。 **2** 来週，キャンパスイベントに行く。 **3** 推薦状をもらう。 **4** 高校の成績表を提出する。

解説 Situationからわかるのは，「あなた」は心理学を学ぶために大学に入学しようとしているということ。第４文で入学担当者は「まだ何を専攻したいかが決まっていないのであれば，来週のオープンキャンパス・イベントへの参加も検討してみてください」と述べているが，Situationから「あなた」は心理学を専攻することに決めているので，2は不適。続く第５文で入学担当者は「そうでなければ（＝すでに専攻が決まっているのなら），あとは先生や雇用主からの推薦状を提出するだけです」と述べているので，「あなた」がすることは推薦状をもらうこと。よって，a letter from a teacher or employer recommending youを**a letter of recommendation**と言い換えた**3**が正解。

No. 29 正解 **2**

放送文 *(K)* You have 10 seconds to read the situation and Question No. 29.

There are four local tours today. Our bus tour starting at 1 p.m. takes passengers to major sites all over the city, and it costs nothing. Next, a walking tour starts at 2:30. Local volunteer guides will escort you around the downtown area, and there's no charge. If you enjoy bike riding, join the tour starting at three. It costs $35, which includes bike rental fees and refreshments. Finally, if you take our tour starting at five, you can try various kinds of local cuisine. The participation fee is just a few dollars, but you'll have to pay for what you eat and drink at food stands or restaurants.

Now mark your answer on your answer sheet.

訳 *(K)* 状況と質問29を読む時間が10秒あります。

今日は4つの現地ツアーがあります。午後1時からのバスツアーは，お客様を市内各地の主要スポットにご案内するもので，参加費無料です。次に，2時30分からウォーキングツアーがあります。地元のボランティアガイドが繁華街を案内してくれるもので，料金は無料です。自転車に乗るのをお楽しみになるのなら，3時からのツアーに参加してくだ

さい。料金は35ドルで，自転車のレンタル料と軽食が含まれています。最後に，5時からのツアーに参加されれば，いろいろな種類の郷土料理が味わえます。参加費はほんの数ドルですが，屋台やレストランで食べたり飲んだりした分はお支払いいただく必要があります。

それでは，解答用紙に答えをマークしなさい。

状況の訳 あなたは海外旅行中で，現地の無料ツアーに参加したいと思っている。あなたは車酔いしやすい。あなたはホテルのインフォメーションで次のように言われる。

質問の訳 あなたにとってどのツアーが最適か。

選択肢の訳 **1** 午後1時からのツアー。 **2** 午後2時30分からのツアー。 **3** 午後3時からのツアー。 **4** 午後5時からのツアー。

解説 Situationからわかるのは，①「あなた」は海外旅行中であること，②「あなた」は現地の無料ツアーに参加したいと思っていること，③「あなた」は車酔いしやすいこと。Situationの②に関して，無料のツアーは，第2文にある「午後1時からのバスツアー」と，第3～4文にある「2時30分からウォーキングツアー」の2つ。Situationの③から「あなた」は車酔いしやすいので，「午後1時からのバスツアー」は不適。したがって，「あなた」に最適なツアーは**2**の「**2時30分からのウォーキングツアー**」となる。

カードA 二次試験・面接

（問題編pp.148～149）

指示文の訳 1分間，準備する時間があります。

これは，貯金したいと思っていた夫婦についての話です。

ストーリーのナレーションを行うのに与えられる時間は2分間です。

ストーリーは以下の文で始めてください。

ある日，女性は彼女の夫と話をしていました。

ナレーションの解答例 **One day, a woman was talking with her husband.** They were sitting at the dining room table, and they both looked concerned. The woman was looking at a lot of bills they needed to pay, and she said that living in the city was very expensive. That night, her husband was using the computer. He had found a website inviting people to come to ABC Village. It said that housing was cheap there, and the couple thought it looked like a nice place to live. A few months later, the woman's family was moving into a traditional Japanese house in the countryside. It was surrounded by beautiful nature. Two old farmers were happily working in the field nearby, and they looked up to see the family. A few weeks later, however, the family members were sitting inside their house, and the children were complaining that they missed their friends in the city.

解答例の訳 **ある日，女性は彼女の夫と話をしていました。**彼らはダイニングルームのテーブルの前に座っており，彼らは二人とも心配そうな様子でした。女性は彼らが支払う必要のある何枚もの請求書を眺めており，彼女は，都会暮らしがとても費用のかかるものだと言いました。その晩，彼女の夫はコンピュータを使っていました。彼は，ABC村へ来ることを人々に勧めているウェブサイトを見つけました。それには，現地では住宅が安価であると書かれており，夫婦は，そこが住みやすそうな場所だと思いました。数か月後，女性の家族は，地方の伝統的な日本家屋へと引っ越しました。そこは美しい自然に囲まれていました。近くの畑では２名の高齢の農業従事者が満足げに働いており，彼らは目線を上げて一家を見ました。しかし，数週間後，一家は自宅の中で座っており，子どもたちは，都会にいる友だちと会えなくて寂しいと不満を漏らしていました。

解説 ナレーションは，４コマのイラストの進行に沿ってまとめていく。２～４コマ目の左上方にある時間の経過を表す語句は，各コマの描写の冒頭部分で必ず使うこと。吹き出し内のせりふはもちろん，紙に書かれている文字情報，パソコンの画面に映っている文字情報なども適切な形でストーリーに取り入れること。動詞の時制は，過去形および過去進行形を基本に，時間の経過がわかるように描写する。

①１コマ目：夫婦で会話している場面。複数枚あるBill「請求書」と書かれた紙のうちの１枚を手にしている女性が，Living in the city is very expensive.「都会暮らしはとても費用がかかる」と発言している様子を，解答例ではshe said that living in the city was very expensiveと，間接話法で表している。ダイニングテーブルの椅子に腰掛けている夫婦が共に困っている表情を浮かべていることから，彼らは金銭面での懸念を抱いているのだと判断できるだろう。

②２コマ目：That nightで始める。夫がパソコンを使用しており，その画面を夫婦で一緒に見ている場面。解答例では，画面に映っているCome to ABC Village「ABC村にお越しください」という文字情報から，a website inviting people to come to ABC Village「ABC村へ来ることを人々に勧めているウェブサイト」と，現在分詞を使って簡潔に表現している。Cheap Housing「安価な住宅」という文字情報についても，It said that housing was cheap thereと間接話法で表している。二人の表情から，彼らはABC村に転居するという考えを肯定的にとらえていると推察できるだろう。

③３コマ目：A few months laterで始める。夫婦一家が新居へと引っ越して来た場面。直前までのコマの流れから，この伝統的な外観を持つ日本家屋はABC村の家屋だと推測できる。また，解答例のように，新居が豊かな自然に囲まれている点，および２名の高齢男女が楽しそうに畑仕事をしている点についての描写もナレーションに盛り込むとよい。

④４コマ目：A few weeks laterで始め，解答例ではその直後に逆接を表すhowever「しかし」を続けることで，物語の展開の仕方が直前のコマまでとは異なることを明確に示している。一家で話し合いをしている場面。困った表情を浮かべている２人の子どもが，We miss our friends in the city.「都会にいる友だちと会えなくて寂しい」と発言している様子を，解答例では動詞complain that ～「～と不満を漏らす」を間接話法で用いて表現している。

質問の訳 No. 1　４番目の絵を見てください。あなたがその女性なら，どのようなことを考えているでしょうか。
では～さん（受験者の氏名），カードを裏返して置いてください。
No. 2　住む場所を賃借するよりも家を買った方がよいと思いますか。
No. 3　日本は都市部の緑地の数を増やすべきですか。
No. 4　近頃の人々は私生活と仕事のバランスを上手に保っていますか。

No. 1 **解答例** I'd be thinking that I should have considered my children's needs more before moving. It's natural for them to feel lonely in a village with few friends. Perhaps we can take the children to the city on the weekends.

解答例の訳 引っ越し前に，子どもたちのニーズをもっとよく考えるべきだったと私は思っているでしょう。彼らが友人のほとんどいない村で寂しく感じるのは当然です。おそらく，私たちは週末に子どもたちを都会へ連れて行くことができるでしょう。

解説 解答例では，質問の仮定法過去形に合わせて，間接話法で**I'd be thinking that ～.**の形で答えている。また，後悔を表す〈should have＋過去分詞〉を用いて，子どもたちが必要とするものを事前に熟慮すべきだったと悔やみ，続けて彼らが孤独感を覚えるのも無理はないと言った上で，最後に今後の対応策の一案を述べている。あるいは，基本的には解答例と同じ路線でありながらも，２文目以降を，But I'm sure my children will adapt to life in the countryside as time goes by, and find new friends here. Until then, maybe we should take them to the city sometimes.「でも，子どもたちはきっと，時が経過するにつれて地方での生活に順応し，ここで新しい友だちを見つけるでしょう。それまで，私たちは彼らをたまには都会へ連れて行くべきかもしれません」などとしても良いだろう。

No. 2 **解答例** No, renting is better. Homeowners can't easily move to a different city to change jobs, for example. This means they might miss out on some big opportunities. Also, it's a lot of work to take care of a house.

解答例の訳 いいえ，賃貸の方が良いです。例えば，マイホームを持っていると，転職するために別の市へ容易には引っ越せません。この結果，彼らは絶好のチャンスを見逃してしまう可能性があります。また，家を管理するのは大変な負担でもあります。

解説 解答例では，Noの立場から，賃貸の方が良いと思う理由を，賃貸のメリットを直接的に述べるのではなく，自宅所有者が抱えると思われる２つのデメリット（①転職のために転居するのが容易ではないこと，②持ち家の管理が大変であること）を述べることで，賃貸という選択肢の方が望ましいという考えを間接的に伝えている。あるいは，解答例と同様にNoの立場から，２文目以降をGiven natural disasters such as big earthquakes, I think buying a home is a great risk, since they might be severely damaged or destroyed unexpectedly. As long as we rent a place to live, we can move elsewhere if necessary.「巨大地震のような自然災害を考慮に入れると，家を買うのは大きなリスクだと思います，というのもそれらは不意にひどく損傷を受けたり破壊されたりしかねないからです。住むための場所を賃借している限りは，私たちは必要に応じて別の場所に引っ越すことができます」などと答えるのも良いだろう。

No. 3 **解答例** Yes. It's clearly important to have nature in our surroundings. It gives people a place where they can relax and relieve their stress. Having large parks full of trees and other plants also helps to keep the air clean.

解答例の訳 はい。環境中に自然があることが重要なのは明らかです。それは人々に，くつろいだりストレスを軽減したりできる場を提供します。また，木や他の植物であふれた広い公園の存在は，空気をきれいにし続けることにも寄与します。

解説 解答例では，Yesの立場から，質問文のgreen spaceをnatureやlarge parks full of trees and other plantsなどと言い換えながら，それらが持つ２点のメリット（①くつろいだりストレスを軽減したりできる場の提供，②空気の浄化作用）を軸に，国は都市部の緑地の数を増やすべきだという意見を補強している。もしくは，解答例と同じ路線をたどりつつ，３文目で，In addition, since trees and plants are known to absorb carbon dioxide in the atmosphere, increasing the amount of green space itself will lead to reducing global warming.「加えて，木や植物は大気中の二酸化炭素を吸収することで知られているため，緑地の数を増やすこと自体は地球温暖化の低減につながるでしょう」などと，別のメリットを答えても良いだろう。

No. 4 **解答例** Not at all. These days, workplace culture is very competitive, so most people are under huge pressure to work hard. That leaves them with very little time to spend on hobbies or with family.

解答例の訳 まったくそうではありません。近頃では，職場文化はとても競争的なので，大半の人は熱心に働くよう非常に強く迫られています。その結果，彼らには趣味に費やす時間や家族と過ごす時間がほとんど残りません。

解説 解答例では，まずNot at all.「まったくそうではありません」と，自分がNoの立場にあることを強調してから，競争的な仕事文化のせいで大半の人は私生活とキャリアのバランスを上手に取ることができていない状況にあることを伝えている。あるいは，YesとNoを折衷した立場から，It depends. Certainly, some people work too hard, resulting in making a sacrifice of their private lives. However, not a few people, including an acquaintance of mine, seem to enjoy both their hobbies and work.「人によります。確かに，働きすぎにより私生活を犠牲にしている人もいます。しかし，私の知人を含めて，趣味と仕事の両方を楽しんでいるように見受けられる人も少なくありません」などとしても良いだろう。

カードB 二次試験・面接

（問題編pp.150～151）

指示文の訳 １分間，準備する時間があります。

これは，海の近くに住んでいた夫婦についての話です。

ストーリーのナレーションを行うのに与えられる時間は２分間です。

ストーリーは以下の文で始めてください。

ある日，夫婦は海辺を散歩していました。

ナレーションの解答例 One day, a couple was taking a walk by the beach.

They passed by a fenced area, where a construction worker was putting up a sign that said a new airport was being constructed by ABC Construction. The couple was shocked to learn about the plan. A few days later, the couple joined a protest against the construction project. The husband was holding a sign that said "protect ocean life," and the wife was collecting signatures from people who opposed the construction of the airport. Six months later, the couple was at the construction site with a group of people. A sign said that the construction had been canceled, and the couple and the supporters of the protest were very pleased. A year later, the couple was looking at a newspaper at home. The wife was surprised to see an article that said ABC Construction had gone bankrupt.

訳 **ある日，夫婦は海辺を散歩していました。**彼らはフェンスで囲まれた区域のそばを通りましたが，そこでは建設作業員が，ABC建設会社によって新しい空港が建設中であると書かれている看板を立てていました。夫婦はその計画を知り，ショックを受けました。数日後，夫婦は建設計画に反対する抗議運動に参加しました。夫は，「海洋生物を守れ」と書かれたプラカードを手に持っており，妻は，空港の建設に反対する人々の署名を集めていました。6か月後，夫婦は人々の集団と共に建設現場にいました。看板には建設作業が中止されたと書かれており，夫婦と抗議運動の支持者たちはとても喜ばしく思っていました。1年後，夫婦は自宅で新聞を見ていました。妻は，ABC建設会社が倒産したと書かれている記事を見て驚きました。

解説 ナレーションは，4コマのイラストの進行に沿ってまとめていく。2～4コマ目の左上方にある時間の経過を表す語句は，各コマの描写の冒頭部分で必ず使うこと。また，看板や新聞に書かれている文字情報を動詞say「～と書いてある」などの表現を用いて間接話法でストーリーに盛り込む際，時制の一致に注意する。他，登場人物たちの表情などにも留意して彼らの感情をストーリーに取り入れながら，動詞の時制は過去形および過去進行形を基本に，時間の経過がわかるように描写すること。

①1コマ目: 夫婦が看板を見ている場面。建設作業員がフェンスで囲まれた区域の前に立てている看板にAirport Construction Site「空港建設現場」と書かれており，その下に社名があることから，ABC建設会社によって新空港が建設中であることを知らせる看板であるとわかる。また，夫婦が浮かべている表情から，彼らはそのことにショックを受けていると判断できるだろう。

②2コマ目: A few days laterで始める。夫婦が他の人々と抗議運動に参加している場面。男性が持っているプラカードにあるProtect Ocean Life!「海洋生物を守れ！」という文字情報，および女性が集めている署名の吹き出しにあるイラストから，彼らは1コマ目に登場した空港建設計画に反対しているのだと考えられる。

③3コマ目: Six months laterで始める。夫婦が他の人々と看板を見ている場面。彼らは1コマ目で登場した建設現場にいると考えられ，看板にConstruction Canceled「建設作業中止」とあることから，新空港建設の計画は中止になったのだとわかる。夫婦を含め複数の人々が看板を見ながらうれしそうな表情を浮かべており，拍手をしていることから，彼らは2コマ目で描かれている抗議運動の参加者なのだと推察可能。

④4コマ目: A year laterで始める。夫婦が新聞記事を見ている場面。夫が広げている

新聞にはABC Construction Goes Bankrupt「ABC建設会社，倒産」とあり，妻はその記事を見て驚いている。ここでのABC建設会社とはもちろん，新空港の建設計画を立てていた企業である。なお，会社の倒産は妻が新聞を見ている時点よりも前に起きた出来事であると考えられるため，解答例では最終文のthat節で過去完了形〈had＋過去分詞〉を用いて，時系列を明確にしている。

質問の訳 No. 1　4番目の絵を見てください。あなたがその夫なら，どのようなことを考えているでしょうか。

では～さん（受験者の氏名），カードを裏返して置いてください。

No. 2　日本人はもっと自分の政治的意見を表明すべきだと思いますか。

No. 3　企業は社会に役立つためにもっと多くのことをすべきだと思いますか。

No. 4　個人の行動が地球温暖化の低減に寄与することはあり得ますか。

No. 1 **解答例** I'd be thinking that it was partially my fault that the company went bankrupt. However, it's extremely important to protect the ocean environment, so I still think that we did the right thing by protesting the airport's construction.

解答例の訳 その会社が倒産したのは，部分的には自分のせいだったと私は思っているでしょう。しかし，海洋環境を保護することは肝要なので，私たちは空港建設に抗議することで正しい行いをしたと私は依然として考えています。

解説 解答例では，質問の仮定法過去形に合わせて，間接話法で**I'd be thinking that ～.**と表現している。ABC建設会社が倒産してしまったのは抗議運動に参加していた自分のせいでもあることを述べながらも，2文目は逆接を表すHoweverから始め，海洋環境保護の重要性に言及し，自分たちが正しいことをしたと締め括っている。あるいは，ABC建設会社の倒産はあくまで企業側の責任であるという立場で，**I'd be thinking that they should have listened to people living near the ocean before going forward with the construction project. I'm sorry that employees working for the company lost their jobs, but in these days when environmental protection is considered important, it is quite natural to care about the environment first.**「彼らは建設計画を推し進める前に，海の近くに暮らす人々の意見に耳を傾けるべきだったと私は思っているでしょう。その会社に勤めていた従業員が職を失ったことについては気の毒に思いますが，環境保護が重要視される昨今，まず環境を気にかけることはごく当たり前のことです」などとしても良いだろう。

No. 2 **解答例** Yes. There are many big problems in our society, so it's essential for Japanese people to feel more comfortable discussing political issues. It's the only way for us to begin solving these problems.

解答例の訳 はい。私たちの社会には大きな問題がたくさんあるので，日本人にはもっと気楽に政治問題を議論することが必要です。それは私たちにとって，これらの問題を解決し始めるための唯一の手段です。

解説 解答例では，Yesの立場から，自分たちの社会が大きな問題を多数抱えている点を指摘してから，政治議論こそ諸問題の唯一の解決手段であると述べている。あるいは，解答例と同じ路線でありながらも，３文目を，具体例を表すFor example「例えば」で始め，For example, it is important that each of us talk with our friends about politics in our daily lives, as well as about our favorite subjects like music, sports, etc.「例えば，私たち一人一人が日常生活において，音楽やスポーツといった好きな話題についてと同様に，政治についても友人と話すことが大切です」でも良いだろう。

No. 3 **解答例** No. Businesses already provide their communities with employment opportunities, and they contribute to society by developing new products. They shouldn't be expected to do more than that.

解答例の訳 いいえ。企業はすでにその地域社会に雇用機会を提供しており，新製品を開発することで社会に寄与しています。彼らはそれ以上のことをするよう求められるべきではありません。

解説 解答例では，Noの立場から，企業はすでに雇用機会の提供，および新製品の開発によって社会貢献しているのだから，それ以上のことが求められるべきではないと主張している。あるいは，Yesの立場から，Yes. Since each company is a part of society where it is doing business, they should never stop making efforts to help it in their own ways so that the whole society can develop more. In my opinion, that's also a part of their duties.「はい。各企業はそれが事業を行っている社会の一部なのだから，彼らは，社会全体がもっと発展できるよう，自分たちなりにその力になろうとする努力をやめるべきではありません。私の意見では，それも彼らの職務のうちの一つです」などとしても良いだろう。

No. 4 **解答例** Absolutely. Reducing the amount of electricity people use at home would reduce the amount of fossil fuels burned. Things like air conditioners use a lot of energy, so limiting their use would definitely reduce global warming.

解答例の訳 もちろんです。家庭で人々が使用する電力量を減らせば，燃やされる化石燃料の量も減るでしょう。エアコンのような物はたくさんのエネルギーを使用するため，その使用を制限すれば地球温暖化が低減するということは間違いありません。

解説 解答例では，Absolutely.「もちろんです」と，自分がYesの立場にあることを強調してから，電力量の削減が燃やされる化石燃料の量の削減につながる点を伝えている。そして，具体例としてエアコンを挙げた上で，多くのエネルギーを使用するその手の機器の使用の制限が地球温暖化の低減につながると，確信を持って述べている。あるいは，同じくYesの立場で，Yes. But global warming is a global issue, so I admit the actions of individuals alone will not solve the problem easily. Nonetheless, I'm certain each individual's effort will lead to reducing global warming however small it is.「はい。しかし，地球温暖化は地球規模の問題なので，確かに個人の行動だけでは問題をたやすく解決することはないだろうという点は認めます。しかしそれでも，各個人の努力はそれがどんなに小さなものであっても地球温暖化の低減につながると私は確信しています」などでも良いだろう。

2022年度 第1回

筆記 解答欄

問題番号		1	2	3	4
1	(1)	①	②	❸	④
	(2)	❶	②	③	④
	(3)	①	②	③	❹
	(4)	①	②	③	❹
	(5)	①	②	❸	④
	(6)	①	②	❸	④
	(7)	①	❷	③	④
	(8)	①	②	③	❹
	(9)	❶	②	③	④
	(10)	①	②	❸	④
	(11)	❶	②	③	④
	(12)	❶	②	③	④
	(13)	①	❷	③	④
	(14)	①	②	③	❹
	(15)	①	②	③	❹
	(16)	❶	②	③	④
	(17)	❶	②	③	④
	(18)	❶	②	③	④
	(19)	①	❷	③	④
	(20)	①	②	❸	④
	(21)	❶	②	③	④
	(22)	①	❷	③	④
	(23)	❶	②	③	④
	(24)	❶	②	③	④
	(25)	①	②	③	❹

問題番号		1	2	3	4
2	(26)	①	②	③	❹
	(27)	❶	②	③	④
	(28)	①	❷	③	④
	(29)	❶	②	③	④
	(30)	①	②	❸	④
	(31)	①	②	③	❹

問題番号		1	2	3	4
3	(32)	①	②	③	❹
	(33)	①	❷	③	④
	(34)	❶	②	③	④
	(35)	①	②	❸	④
	(36)	①	❷	③	④
	(37)	①	②	③	❹
	(38)	①	❷	③	④
	(39)	❶	②	③	④
	(40)	①	②	❸	④
	(41)	①	②	❸	④

4 の解答例は p.194をご覧ください。

リスニング 解答欄

問題番号			1	2	3	4
Part 1		No.1	❶	②	③	④
		No.2	①	②	❸	④
		No.3	①	②	③	❹
		No.4	①	②	③	❹
		No.5	①	❷	③	④
		No.6	❶	②	③	④
		No.7	❶	②	③	④
		No.8	①	②	❸	④
		No.9	①	❷	③	④
		No.10	①	②	③	❹
		No.11	①	②	❸	④
		No.12	①	❷	③	④
Part 2	A	No.13	①	②	❸	④
		No.14	①	②	③	❹
	B	No.15	①	②	❸	④
		No.16	①	②	③	❹
	C	No.17	①	❷	③	④
		No.18	❶	②	③	④
	D	No.19	❶	②	③	④
		No.20	①	②	❸	④
	E	No.21	①	②	③	❹
		No.22	①	❷	③	④
	F	No.23	①	❷	③	④
		No.24	❶	②	③	④
Part 3	G	No.25	①	②	❸	④
	H	No.26	❶	②	③	④
	I	No.27	❶	②	③	④
	J	No.28	①	②	③	❹
	K	No.29	①	②	③	❹

1 一次試験・筆記
(問題編pp.154〜157)

指示文の訳 各英文を完成させるのに最も適切な単語または語句を４つの選択肢の中から選び，その番号を解答用紙の所定欄にマークしなさい。

(1) 正解 3

訳 その訴訟を審理した後で，裁判官は情状酌量することに決め，その男に警告を与えただけであった。彼女は，彼が自分の罪をとても後悔しているのは明らかだと言った。

解説 空所の後のonly gave the man a warning「その男に警告を与えただけであった」から，裁判官はその男の刑を軽くしたことがわかる。**show mercy**で「情けをかける」という意味を表し，状況に合うので，**3のmercy**「情け，慈悲」が正解。disgrace「不名誉」，closure「閉鎖」，seclusion「隔離」。

(2) 正解 1

訳 リサは双子の姉にそっくりだが，気質は全く違う。彼女は姉と違ってとても穏やかで，めったに腹を立てない。

解説 第２文のShe（＝Lisa）is very calm and rarely gets angry, unlike her sister.「彼女は姉と違ってとても穏やかで，めったに腹を立てない」はリサの性格を表している。したがって，**1のtemperament**「気質」が正解。accumulation「蓄積」，veneer「化粧板」，glossary「用語集」。

(3) 正解 4

訳 A：アナベル，宿題を終えたかどうか聞いているのにただ肩をすくめたりしないの。はっきりと答えなさい。 B：ごめんなさい，お母さん。もうすぐ終わるわ。

解説 A（＝Mom）がB（＝Annabel）の態度を叱っている場面。母親のAがGive me a clear answer.「はっきりと答えなさい」と言っていることから，娘のアナベルはあいまいな答え方をしたとわかる。**shrug one's shoulders**で「肩をすくめる」という意味を表し，宿題を終えたかどうかがはっきりわからない動作と言えるので，**4のshrug**が正解。echo「〜を反響させる，〜をおうむ返しに言う」，bow「〜を曲げる，おじぎをする」，dump「〜を捨てる」。

(4) 正解 4

訳 町で大きなビジネス会議があるとき，空室のあるホテルを見つけることはほぼ不可能である。たいていのホテルはすぐに予約でいっぱいになってしまう。

解説 第２文Most hotels quickly get fully booked.「たいていのホテルはすぐに予約でいっぱいになってしまう」から，会議期間中はホテルの予約が取れないことがわかる。この状況を表すのに適切なのは**4のvacancy**「空室」。sprain「ねんざ」，segment「区分」，transition「推移」。

※2024年度第１回から，試験形式の変更に伴い大問１の問題数は18問になります。

(5) 正解 3

訳 刑事は何時間もそのギャングの一員を尋問したが，だれが犯罪に手を貸したのか言おうとしなかった。結局，刑事は彼から情報を得るのをあきらめた。

解説 第1文のhe（＝the gang member）would not say who had helped him commit the crime「だれが犯罪に手を貸したのか言おうとしなかった」から，刑事は取り調べをしていることがわかる。**interrogate**で「～を尋問する」という意味を表すので，**3のinterrogated**が正解。discharge「～を解放する」，convert「～を変換する」，affiliate「～を会員にする」。

(6) 正解 3

訳 怪我をした足首を治療するために，医者は圧迫を勧める。これは傷の周りに包帯をきつく巻くことによって行うことができる。

解説 第2文のwrapping a bandage tightly around the injury「傷の周りに包帯をきつく巻くこと」が，空所に当てはまる治療法の具体的なやり方を説明している。したがって，**3のcompression**「圧迫」が正解。depression「不況，憂鬱」，progression「進歩」，suspicion「疑惑」。

(7) 正解 2

訳 A：家に帰る途中で突然激しい雨が降り出して，ずぶ濡れになったよ。 B：私の助言に従って，傘を持って行くべきだったね。

解説 Aの発言のI got completely wet.「ずぶ濡れになったよ」から，Aは傘を持っていなかったことがわかる。BはYou should have ... taken an umbrella with you.「傘を持って行くべきだったね」と言っており，空所の後にはmy adviceとあるので，Bの助言にAが従わなかったと考えられる。**heed someone's advice**で「～の助言に従う」という意味を表すので，**2のheeded**が正解。mold「～を形成する」，twist「～をより合わせる，～をねじる」，yield「～を生み出す」。

(8) 正解 4

訳 もっと裕福な顧客を引きつける方法として，その香水会社は主に富裕層の人々に読まれている雑誌で製品の宣伝を始めた。

解説 空所直後にcustomersとあるので，空所にはどのような顧客かを表す形容詞が入る。文末にby wealthy people「富裕層の人々に」とあるので，この会社がターゲットにしている顧客層は裕福な人々だとわかる。したがって，**4のaffluent**「裕福な」が正解。theatrical「演劇の」，brutal「残酷な」，frantic「取り乱した，熱狂した」。

(9) 正解 1

訳 先生は，いくつかのささいな誤りを除けば，その生徒の小論文は完璧だと言った。彼は可能な限りの高得点を与えた。

解説 空所直後にerrorsとあるので，空所にはどのような誤りかを表す形容詞が入る。第1文後半にthe student's essay was perfect「その生徒の小論文は完璧だった」，さらに第2文にHe（＝The teacher）gave it（＝the student's essay）the highest score possible.「彼は可能な限りの高得点を与えた」とあるので，大きな誤りではなく，取るに足らないものだったとわかる。したがって，**1のtrivial**「ささいな」が正解。conclusive「決定的な」，palatial「宮殿のような」，offensive「侮辱的な」。

(10) 正解 3

訳 その怪我をしたサッカー選手は，決勝戦で自分の代わりの選手がプレーするのをうらやましそうに見た。彼は本当はプレーし続けたかった。

解説 空所にはこのサッカー選手が決勝戦をどのような気持ちで見ていたのかを表す副詞が入る。第２文にHe had really wanted to continue playing.「彼は本当はプレーし続けたかった」とあるので，この気持ちを表すには，**3のenviously**「うらやましそうに」が適切。substantially「実質的に，かなり」，previously「以前に」，relevantly「関連して」。

(11) 正解 1

訳 エイブラハムのアパートの前にある新しいホテルは，町の向こうに見える山の景色を遮るほどには高くない。彼は今でも山々をはっきりと見ることができる。

解説 第２文にHe can still see them（＝the mountains）clearly.「彼は今でも山々をはっきりと見ることができる」とあるので，ホテルは低いため，景色を遮っていないことがわかる。したがって，**1のobstruct**「～を遮る，～を妨害する」が正解。delegate「～を委任する」，entangle「～をからませる」，boost「～を引き上げる，～を増加させる」。

(12) 正解 1

訳 白いカーペットの上に赤ワインをこぼしたので，マーサは石鹸と水で染みを落とそうとした。だが，それを完全に取り去ることはできなかった。

解説 第１文前半にHaving spilled red wine on the white carpet「白いカーペットの上に赤ワインをこぼしたので」とあり，カーペットに染みがついたとわかる。空所の語はremoveの目的語に当たり，空所直後にwith soap and waterとあるので，マーサは染みを取ろうとしたと考えられる。したがって，**1のstain**「染み」が正解。slit「切り込み」，bump「こぶ」，blaze「炎」。

(13) 正解 2

訳 戦争は１年間続いたが，どちらの側も優勢となることができなかった。どうやら勝利は不可能と思われたので，その２つの国は停戦することで合意した。

解説 空所に入る動詞の主語がneither side「どちら側も～ない」であり，第２文にWith victory seemingly impossible「どうやら勝利は不可能と思われたので」とあるので，空所を含む節は戦争当事国のうちのどちら側も優位に立てなかったという意味を表すと考えられる。したがって，**2のprevail**「優勢である，勝つ」を入れると状況に合う。devise「～を考案する」，evolve「進化する」，reconstruct「～を再建する」。

(14) 正解 4

訳 その指導者は自国の政情不安を，自分の支配に対するいかなる反対をも阻止することを目的とした厳格な新法を導入するための口実として利用した。

解説 空所直後にfor introducing strict new laws aimed at preventing any opposition to his rule「自分の支配に対するいかなる反対をも阻止することを目的とした厳格な新法を導入するための」と，空所の語に説明を加えている。この説明に適するのは，**4のpretext**「口実」。trance「恍惚」，downfall「失墜」，rampage「大暴れ」。

(15) 正解 4

訳 その容疑者は警察に無実を主張し続けた。彼は犯罪の起こった場所の近くにはいなかったと繰り返し言った。

解説 第2文にhe（＝the suspect）had been nowhere near the place where the crime had occurred「彼は犯罪の起こった場所の近くにはいなかった」とあるので，容疑者は自分は無実だと訴えていると考えられる。空所に入る動詞の目的語がhis innocenceなので，**4のassert**「～を主張する」を入れると意味が通る。conceal「～を隠す」，counter「～に反論する」，expire「期限が切れる」。

(16) 正解 1

訳 良い著者は自分の作品から間違いを取り除くためにあらゆる努力をするが，しかし時には誤りを見逃し，後から訂正しなければならないこともある。

解説 文の後半がbutで始まり，occasionally they（＝good writers）miss some errors「時には誤りを見逃す」とあるので，前半はそれとは対照的な内容となる。空所の直後がerrorsと同義語のmistakesであり，空所に入る動詞の目的語に当たるので，**1のeliminate**「～を取り除く」を入れ，make every effort to eliminate mistakes「間違いを取り除くためにあらゆる努力をする」とすると文脈に合う。expend「～を費やす」，stabilize「～を安定させる」，oppress「～を虐げる」。

(17) 正解 1

訳 誘拐犯たちは多額の身代金と引き換えに子供を両親に返した後で，その金を持って逃亡しようとした。だが，警察は間もなく彼らを捕まえ，その金を夫婦に返した。

解説 第1文前半にthe kidnappers returned the child to its parents「誘拐犯たちは…子供を両親に返した」とあり，空所の前にin exchange for「～と引き換えに」とあるので，誘拐された子供と引き換えに犯人が要求するものである**1のransom**「身代金」が正解。applause「拍手喝采」，monopoly「独占」，prank「いたずら」。

(18) 正解 1

訳 ギャスパーは名門大学に出願した。残念ながら，彼の成績では不十分だったため，あまり知られていない大学に行かなければならなかった。

解説 残念ながらあまり知られていない大学に行かなくてはならなかったという第2文の内容から，1文目にあるギャスパーが出願した大学は，合格した大学と違い，より知名度が高いと考えられる。したがって，**1のprestigious**「名声のある」が適切。spontaneous「自発的な」，cordial「友好的な」，petty「ささいな」。

(19) 正解 2

訳 スパイたちは気づかれずに軍事基地に侵入しようとして陸軍将校に変装した。

解説 文の後半にin an attempt to enter the military base without being noticed「気づかれずに軍事基地に侵入しようとして」とあり，軍人に変装すれば目立たないため，空所には**2のdisguised**を入れると状況に合う。**disguise *oneself* as ～**で「～に変装する」という意味を表す。chronicle「年代順に記録する」，render「～を与える」，revitalize「～を生き返らせる」。

(20) 正解 3

訳 ティモシーはとても献身的な従業員である。彼は頼りがいがあり，役に立ちたがっており，常に自分の会社と同僚に忠誠を示している。

解説 空所直後にemployeeが続くので，空所にはティモシーがどのような従業員なのかを表す形容詞が入る。第2文後半のhe always shows loyalty to his company and coworkers「常に自分の会社と同僚に忠誠を示している」から，会社にとても忠実な社員だとわかるので，**3のdevoted**「献身的な」が適切。grotesque「奇怪な」，defiant「反抗的な」，feeble「弱い」。

(21) 正解 1

訳 ポールが減量するのを手助けするために，主治医は食事を変えるよう勧めた。具体的には，彼女は彼に脂肪の多い食べ物を減らし，食物繊維をもっと摂るよう提案した。

解説 空所直後にhis dietとあるので，空所にはポールが食事をどうすべきかを表す動詞が入る。第2文に，she（＝his doctor）suggested that he eat fewer fatty foods and more fiber「彼女は彼に脂肪の多い食べ物を減らし，食物繊維をもっと摂るよう提案した」と具体的な指示があるので，空所に入るのは**1のmodify**「～を（部分的に）変える，～を修正する」が適切。pluck「～を引き抜く」，exclaim「～と叫ぶ」，distill「～を蒸留する」。

(22) 正解 2

訳 A：仕事がすごく忙しい上に，今度は新入社員の研修に対処しないといけないんだ。
B：それは荷が重すぎるね。だれかほかの人が代わりにできないか，上司に聞いたほうがいいよ。

解説 AはI've been so busy at work「仕事がすごく忙しい」と言っており，すでにたくさんの仕事を抱えていることがわかる。また，空所直前にI have toとあり，直後にtraining our newest employeeと続くので，Aは自分の仕事に加え，新人研修に関しても何かする必要があると考えられる。したがって，空所には**2のcontend with**「～に対処する」を入れると状況に合う。turn over「～をひっくり返す」，prop up「～を支える」，count off「番号を唱える」。

(23) 正解 1

訳 その幼い男の子は花瓶が割れたのを犬のせいにしようとした。けれども，母親はうそにはだまされず，彼を自分の部屋に行かせた。

解説 空所の直後のthe lie「うそ」とは，具体的には第1文のto blame his dog for the broken vase「花瓶が割れたのを犬のせいにすること」である。第2文がHoweverで始まり，空所直前にはdid notとあるので，母親は男の子の言い分を信じなかったと考えられる。したがって，**1のfall for**「～にだまされる」が正解。hang on「～にしがみつく」，see out「～を玄関まで見送る」，flag down「～を停止させる」。

(24) 正解　1

訳 スピーチの中で，最高経営責任者は今後５年間の会社の発展計画を打ち出した。彼はこれが会社の成長に伴い皆の仕事に指針を示すのに役立つよう望んだ。

解説 空所直後にhis planとあり，**map out a plan**で「計画を立てる」という意味を表すので，**1のmapped out**が正解。leap in「飛びつく」，rack up「～を積み重ねる」，space out「～を一定の間隔で置く」。

(25) 正解　4

訳 昨年，ハロルドは全財産を費やして様々な会社の株を買った。彼は今後数年にわたって株式市場が好調に動くと見込んでいたのである。

解説 第１文のspent all his money buying shares in various companies「全財産を費やして様々な会社の株を買った」から，ハロルドが全財産をつぎ込んでも損はしないと見込んでいたと推測できる。**bet on ～ *doing***で「～が…することに賭ける，～が…することを見込む」という意味を表すので，**4のbetting on**を入れると状況に合う。cast away「～を捨てる」，put down「～を置く」，step up「～を高める」。

2　一次試験・筆記

ピーターの法則（問題編pp.158～159）
近視（問題編pp.160～161）

指示文の訳 それぞれの文章を読んで，各空所に入れるのに最も適切な語句を４つの選択肢の中から選び，その番号を解答用紙の所定欄にマークしなさい。

ピーターの法則

Key to Reading 第１段落：導入（昇進とピーターの法則）→第２段落：本論①（ピーターの法則に関する研究内容）→第３段落：本論②（研究結果より推測できること）という３段落構成の説明文。それぞれの段落のトピックセンテンスを意識して論理的に読み進めていく。ピーターの法則がどのようなものか，その影響を軽減させるためにどのようなことをすべきかを中心に読み取ろう。

訳

ピーターの法則として知られる理論は，管理職に仕事ぶりが良くない人が多い理由を明らかにするかもしれない。この理論によると，下の職務で活躍できる社員は，準備ができないまま，いずれ昇進する。その理由は，社員は通常，現在の職務での実績に基づいて昇進するためである。この種の昇進方法は論理的に思えるかもしれないが，社員の長所と短所を十分に考慮していないので，最終的に能力に適さない役職に就くことになってしまう。

ある研究では，管理職に昇進した営業担当者のキャリアを調査した。予想通り，この調査では，最も優れた営業担当者が昇進する可能性が最も高いことがわかったが，管理職での実績は最も低かったこともわかった。この研究では，現在の実績のみに基づいて従業員を昇進させることには，２つのデメリットがあることが示された。企業は最終的に駄目な管理職を生むだけでなく，下の職務で最も優秀な社員を失うことにもなる。

この研究を行った研究者は，問題の１つは，企業が，優秀な社員は当然優れた管理職になると単純に推測するという過ちを犯していることであると述べている。ほとんどの企業では，新入社員は仕事の仕方について専門研修を受ける。一方，新しい管理職はたいてい，ほとんど，またはまったく研修を受けない。これは，新しい管理職に適切な研修を受けさせることが，ピーターの法則の影響を軽減する１つの方法であることを示唆しているように思われる。

(26) 正解 4

選択肢の訳 **1** 平均以下の給料を稼ぐ **2** 自分の仕事を愛する **3** 複数の会社で働いたことがある **4** 仕事ぶりがよくない

解説 空所を含む文の直後の文を参照。通常，会社では，employees who perform well in lower-level positions will eventually rise to positions they are not prepared for「下の職務で活躍できる社員は，準備ができないまま，いずれ昇進する」。新しい職務に就く準備が不十分なので，管理職に昇進しても活躍できないと考えられることから，**4のperform poorly**「仕事ぶりがよくない」が正解。第２，３段落からも，ピーターの法則が，優秀な社員が昇進によって活躍できなくなる現象を表すことがわかる。

(27) 正解 1

選択肢の訳 **1** ２つのデメリットがある **2** 避けることができない **3** 出る価値のある賭けである **4** 創造的な思考を妨げる

解説 空所を含む文の直後の文で，Not only do companies end up with poor managers but they also lose their best workers in lower-level positions.「企業は最終的に駄目な管理職を生むだけでなく，下の職務で最も優秀な社員を失うことにもなる」と述べている。すなわち，優秀な社員を昇進させることにより，会社は二重のダメージを受けることから，**1のhas two disadvantages**「２つのデメリットがある」が正解。

(28) 正解 2

選択肢の訳 **1** もちろん **2** 一方 **3** さらには **4** 同様の理由で

解説 空所の前後の内容に注目する。前がnew employees receive specialized training in how to do their jobs「新入社員は仕事の仕方について専門研修を受ける」，後がnew managers are often given little or no training「新しい管理職はたいてい，ほとんど，またはまったく研修を受けない」で反対の内容を述べていることから，**2のOn the other hand**「一方」が正解。

近視

Key to Reading 第１段落：導入（近視とデジタル画面使用の関係）→第２段落：本論①（近視の本当の原因）→第３段落：本論②（近視の予防）という３段落構成の説明文である。近視の原因と予防法を整理しながら読み進めていくことを心がけよう。

訳

近視は世界中で急速に増加している。これを患う人は，近くにあるものははっきりと見えるが，遠くにあるものはぼやけて見える。多くの人が，この傾向をデジタル画面使用のせいにしている。彼らは，コンピュータやスマートフォンなどのデバイスを使用することは眼精疲労につながり，さらに，デジタル画面から発せられるブルーライトは眼底の感光性細胞にダメージを与えると主張している。しかし，デジタル画面が視力に長期的な影響を与えるという明確な証拠はない。

実際，近視の増加は，デジタル画面が広く使用される以前に始まった。いくつかの研究は，本当の問題は，人々が屋内で過ごす時間が長すぎることにあると示唆している。これにより，自然光を十分に浴びられなくなる。近視は，眼の水晶体が伸び，光を焦点に集める力が低下することによって引き起こされる。しかし，脳によって生成される化学物質であるドーパミンが分泌されることで，これが起こるのを防ぐことができ，自然光を浴びることで，ドーパミンの分泌が増える。

一部の専門家は，1日約3時間屋外にいることが，近視の予防に役立つと述べている。しかし，多くの人にとって，学校や仕事のスケジュールのために，これを行うことは不可能である。代わりに，人々が自宅で使用する照明の種類を変える方が，より実用的かもしれない。自然光と同じような効果を得られる照明はすでに市販されており，将来的には研究によってさらに多くの代替手段が提供されると見込まれる。

(29) 正解　1

選択肢の訳　**1**　視力に長期的な影響を与える　**2**　問題を解決するのに役立つ　**3**　すべての機器に使用し得る　**4**　将来より良くなる

解説　空所を含む文がHowever（しかし）で始まっていることから，これより前の文を否定する内容が入ると推測できる。2文前で近視の人が増加している現状について，Many people blame this trend on the use of digital screens.「多くの人が，この傾向をデジタル画面使用のせいにしている」と述べていることから，**1のhave long-term effects on eyesight**「視力に長期的な影響を与える」を入れ，デジタル画面が近視の原因である明確な証拠はないという内容にすると意味がとおる。

(30) 正解　3

選択肢の訳　**1**　画面に近すぎる　**2**　視覚に頼りすぎている　**3**　屋内で過ごす時間が長すぎる　**4**　体を十分に動かせていない

解説　空所を含む文の直後の文，This results in a lack of exposure to natural light.のThisの内容を考える。a lack of exposure to natural light「自然光を十分に浴びられない」状況を生み出すのは，**3のspend too much time indoors**「屋内で過ごす時間が長すぎる」。

(31) 正解　4

選択肢の訳　**1**　同じように　**2**　例えば　**3**　それなのに　**4**　代わりに

解説　近視の予防策として専門家の意見として，第3段落第1文でbeing outdoors for about three hours a day「1日約3時間屋外にいること」を挙げているが，第2文ではそれについてimpossible（不可能な）と述べている。ここから，(　　), it may be more practical for people to change the kind of lighting they use in their homes「(　　)，人々が自宅で使用する照明の種類を変える方が，より実用的かもしれない」と代わりとなる事柄を挙げているので**4のInstead**「代わりに」が正解。

3	一次試験・筆記	ハチミツ菌（問題編pp.162～163） インテンショナル・コミュニティ（問題編pp.164～165） インドのイギリス人（問題編pp.166～168）

指示文の訳 それぞれの文章を読んで，各質問に対する最も適切な答えを４つの選択肢の中から選び，その番号を解答用紙の所定欄にマークしなさい。

ハチミツ菌

Key to Reading 第１段落：導入＋本論①（オレゴン州のハチミツ菌）→第２段落：本論②（ハチミツ菌がもたらす問題）→第３段落：本論③（ハチミツ菌問題の解決策）という３段落構成の説明文。ハチミツ菌（ナラタケ）の性質と生態系に与える影響について読み取ろう。

訳

地球上で最大の生物は，クジラやその他の大型動物ではない。むしろ，キノコや毒キノコを含む生物群に属している。それはハチミツ菌（ナラタケ）として一般に知られている菌類の一種で，根のようなその菌糸は，米国オレゴン州の広大な森林地帯全体の地下に広がっている。 DNA検査により，この地域の全てのハチミツ菌の起源が同じ生物であることが確認されており，その年間成長率に基づき，それが8000年以上前のものである可能性があると，科学者達は推定している。また，それらは全て合わせると，約3万5000トンの重量になると計算している。

このハチミツ菌は見事ではあるものの，森の多くの樹木に問題を引き起こす。その菌は樹木に感染し，根や幹から養分を吸収し，最終的には枯死させることもよくある。残念ながら，菌は樹皮の下に隠れており，その菌糸は樹皮を取り除いた場合にのみ見えるため，通常，影響を受けた木を見分けるのは困難である。晩秋になると，キノコの子実体が樹木の外側に現れるが，それは冬の前の数週間のみである。樹木は菌に抵抗しようとするものの，菌は根にダメージを与え，水と栄養素が上部に達するのを妨げるため，大抵は結局，その戦いに負けてしまう。

オレゴン州のハチミツ菌を完全に除去することも検討されているが，費用と時間がかかりすぎることが分かっている。現在研究されている別の解決策は，菌に耐えられる樹種を植えることだ。しかし，一部の専門家は，見方を変える必要があるかもしれないと示唆している。ハチミツ菌の影響を否定的に見るのではなく，人々はそれを自然の成り行きの一例と考えるべきである。枯れ木は最終的に土に還され，地域の生態系に利益をもたらす。

(32) 正解 4

質問の訳 この文章によれば，オレゴン州のハチミツ菌について正しいことの１つは何か。

選択肢の訳 **1** 異なるキノコの種が組み合わさったもので，長い時間をかけて混生するようになった。 **2** 最初はゆっくりと生長したが，ここ1000年でより急速に拡大している。 **3** 集めた栄養を，寄生している樹木や他の植物と共有している。
4 樹木に寄生して育つことで，広い範囲に広がった単一生物である。

解説 第１段落では，オレゴン州の森林地帯に生育するハチミツ菌について述べている。ハチミツ菌について，第３文でits rootlike filaments spread underground

※2024年度第１回から，試験形式の変更に伴い大問３の１問目(32)～(34)が削除されます。

throughout a huge area of forest in the US state of Oregon「根のようなその菌糸は，米国オレゴン州の広大な森林地帯全体の地下に広がっている」と述べており，第4文ではDNA検査の結果，それらがthe same organism「同じ生物」であることもわかっている。また，第2段落第2文から，この菌が樹木に感染し，根や幹から養分を吸収することがわかる。つまり，ハチミツ菌は樹木に寄生して広範囲に生息している単一生物なので，この文とほぼ同じ内容を述べている**4**が正解。

(33) 正解 **2**

質問の訳 ハチミツ菌は～ので，見つけるのが難しい。

選択肢の訳 **1** そこからできるキノコが，寄生する樹木の種類によって色を変える。 **2** 毎年，子実体ができる短い間以外，通常目に見えない。 **3** 地下に育つだけでなく，樹木の根のような見た目をしている。 **4** 生長に必要な特定の気象条件を持つ地域でしか生き残ることができない。

解説 ハチミツ菌が寄生した樹木を見分けにくい理由については，第2段落第3～4文を参照。通常樹皮（bark）の下に隠れている菌を見ることができるのは，晩秋（the late fall）のみであり，しかも，the fruiting bodies of the fungus appear on the outside of the trees, but only for a few weeks before winter「キノコの子実体が樹木の外側に現れるが，それは冬の前の数週間のみである」とある。これらの内容をまとめた選択肢**2**が正解。except「～ということを除いて。」

(34) 正解 **1**

質問の訳 専門家の一部はどのように考えているか。

選択肢の訳 **1** 人々は，ハチミツ菌が樹木に与える影響を，自然で有益なプロセスと見なすべきである。 **2** ハチミツ菌に対処する唯一の実際的な方法は，それを取り除く試みに，より多くの時間とお金を投資することである。 **3** ハチミツ菌に感染した樹木を，それがさらに広がるのを防ぐために利用できる。 **4** ハチミツ菌は，人々に優れた栄養源を提供するために収穫してもよい。

解説 一部の専門家の意見については，第3段落第3～4文を参照。ハチミツ菌の害について，a change of perspective may be necessary「見方を変える必要があるかもしれない」とし，具体的に，people should consider it an example of nature taking its course「人々はそれを自然の成り行きの一例と考えるべきである」と言っている。この内容と一致する選択肢**1**が正解。本文のnature taking its courseを，a natural and beneficial processと言い換えている。

インテンショナル・コミュニティ

Key to Reading 第1段落：導入（インテンショナル・コミュニティの歴史）→第2段落：本論①（インテンショナル・コミュニティの課題）→第3段落：本論②（インテンショナル・コミュニティの成功例：ダマヌール）→第4段落：本論③＋結論（インテンショナル・コミュニティの成功条件）という4段落構成の説明文。選択肢を検討するときは，本文中の語（句）の言い換えに注意しよう。

訳

何百年もの間，人々は自立したコミュニティを形成してきたが，これはしばしばインテンショナル・コミュニティ（意図的共同体）と呼ばれ，理想の共有，共同所有，および財産の共用によって特徴付けられる。知られている最初のインテンショナル・コミュニティは，紀元前6世紀にギリシャの哲学者によって構築された。その後の何世紀にもわたって，社会の本流から離れて暮らすことを望む宗教団体によって，そのようなコミュニティが数多く作られた。キリスト教の修道院やイスラエルのキブツと呼ばれる農業共同体など，これらのいくつかは何世代にもわたって成功を収めてきたが，他のものは数年しか続かなかった。

20世紀には，1960年代と1970年代の帰農運動に見られるような哲学的理想主義も，人々にインテンショナル・コミュニティを形成する動機を与えた。1970年代初頭までに，米国だけでそのようなコミュニティは数千あったと推定されているが，その多くは後に解散した。インテンショナル・コミュニティ協会は現在，多くとも米国で800，その他の地域で250をわずかに下回る数のコミュニティをリストアップしている。失敗したインテンショナル・コミュニティは，一般的に同様の課題に直面した。滞在するようになった人の中には，仕事を分け合い，自分の食べ物を育て，集団で生活するという理想実現のために尽力する人もいたが，それほど真剣ではない人もいた。あるコミュニティの共同創設者は，「私たちは，非現実的ではあるが崇高なビジョンを持っていたが，それは，ただ遊びで来た人々によって，絶えず揺るがされてきた」と思い返す。

しかし，全てのインテンショナル・コミュニティが崩壊する運命にあるわけではない。イタリアのトリノ近郊にあるスピリチュアルで芸術的な共同体，ダマヌールが現在も成功しているのは，開かれたコミュニケーションと実践的なアプローチによるものである。ダマヌールは，メンバーを15人から20人の家族のようなグループに編成する。そのコミュニティは，「家族」が25人を超える場合，親密さを築くことが難しくなることに気付いた。対照的に，「家族」の人数が少なすぎると，効果的な意思決定を行うための十分な集合的知性がなくなる。ダマヌールの理念はその憲法で述べられており，選出された指導者によって遵守され，またコミュニティ内における緊張関係は，人々が塗料の入ったおもちゃの銃で戦う，遊びの模擬戦を行うことによって処理される。

成功しているインテンショナル・コミュニティは全て，共通の特徴を共有しているようである。それは，常に先を考える能力である。ダマヌールのメンバーの1人がそれを，「うまく行かない時ではなく，うまく行く時に，物事を変えるべきだ」と言ったように。問題が生じる前に変えるというこの戦略は，ダマヌールやその他の成功したコミュニティでうまく機能しており，インテンショナル・コミュニティがメンバーのニーズを長期的に満たすための効果的な方法であることを示唆している。

(35) 正解 3

質問の訳 失敗したインテンショナル・コミュニティが直面した共通の問題は，

選択肢の訳 **1** コミュニティの大多数はある人が参加することに賛成したが，少数の個人がそれに反対したこと。 **2** 人々は純粋な興味を持ってコミュニティに参加したが，効果的に貢献するためのスキルや知識が不足していたこと。 **3** コミュニティの理想に従うために一生懸命努力したメンバーがいた一方で，他のメンバーは共同生活に対してもっとカジュアルな取り組み方をしたこと。 **4** コミュニティは大掛かりなプロジェクトを完成させることを目指したが，知識と財源の不足のためにそれを完成させられなかったこと。

解説 第2段落第4文に，Intentional communities that failed generally faced a similar challenge.「失敗したインテンショナル・コミュニティは，一般的に同様の課題に直面した」とあり，次の文でその内容について，Some people who came to stay were committed to ideals of shared work, growing their own food, and living collectively, but others were less serious.「滞在するようになった人の中には，仕事を分け合い，自分の食べ物を育て，集団で生活するという理想実現のために尽力する人もいたが，それほど真剣ではない人もいた」と述べている。この内容をまとめた選択肢**3**が正解。

(36) 正解 2

質問の訳 ダマヌールの社会構造について正しいことは何か。

選択肢の訳 **1** 「家族」は自由に独自のルールを作ることができ，必ずしもコミュニティの憲法に含まれるルールに従う必要はない。 **2** グループの問題を解決し，良好な関係を維持するための最良の条件を作り出すために，「家族」の人数は調整される。
3 意見の相違を解消するための模擬戦は時に深刻化し，一部のメンバーが「家族」を離れることもある。 **4** コミュニティには様々な規模の「家族」が含まれているため，メンバーは大集団で生活するか，小集団で生活するかを選択できる。

解説 ダマヌールの社会構造については，第3段落を参照。第4～5文で「家族」の人数について，25人を超えると親密さを築くこと（creating intimacy）が難しくなり，逆に人数が少なすぎると，効果的な意思決定（effective decision-making）が難しくなると述べている。つまり，コミュニティを維持できるかは「家族」の人数によって決まるということ。この内容を言い換えた選択肢**2**が正解。2文の内容を，The number of people in a “family” is controlledと言い換えている。

(37) 正解 4

質問の訳 この文章によると，ダマヌールは他の成功しているインテンショナル・コミュニティとどのように類似しているか。

選択肢の訳 **1** コミュニティのメンバーは，疲れ果ててしまわないよう，時々責任を取り替えることができる。 **2** 収入を得るためにコミュニティが行う仕事の種類は，メンバーが新しいスキルを習得できるよう定期的に変わる。 **3** コミュニティのメンバーは，共同で所有している建物や設備のメンテナンスを交替で行う。 **4** コミュニティは，単に問題が発生した時に対応するよりはむしろ，メンバーのニーズを満たす方法を絶えず探し出している。

解説 第4段落最終文で，成功しているインテンショナル・コミュニティに共通する特徴（trait）として，strategy of making changes before problems occur「問題が生じる前に変えるという戦略」を挙げており，これがan effective way for intentional communities to fulfill the needs of their members in the long term「インテンショナル・コミュニティがメンバーのニーズを長期的に満たすための効果的な方法である」と述べている。この内容と一致する**4**が正解。本文のfulfill the needs of their membersを，satisfy the needs of its membersと言い換えている。

インドのイギリス人

Key to Reading 第１段落：導入＋本論①（東インド会社とその影響力の拡大）→第２段落：本論②（イギリスのインド直接統治の過程）→第３段落：本論③（イギリスのインド支配の影響と結末）→第４段落：結論（東インド会社の現代経済への影響）という４段落構成の説明文。設問に先に目を通し，読み取るべきポイントを押さえてから，本文を読み進めよう。

訳

1600年に設立されたイギリス所有の東インド会社は，２世紀以上にわたり，世界最大の企業の１つであった。インドや中国など様々な国と海外貿易を行うことで，これらの国から高級品をイギリスに輸入することができた。イギリス政府は会社の莫大な利益の一部を受け取っていたため，政治的支援を行うことをいとわなかった。その規模，力，そして何十万人ものインド人兵士から成る私軍を含む資源によって，会社はインドに圧力をかけ，概して会社にのみ利益をもたらす貿易契約を受け入れさせた。1750年代に現地の支配者との戦いに勝利した後，会社はインドで最も裕福な州の１つを掌握した。その結果，東インド会社は企業としてだけでなく，政治機関としても機能するようになり，インド国民に納税を強いるようになった。

東インド会社は，取引先の国の間で信頼できないとの悪評を得ていた。また，同社の不正な取引習慣が中国との外交関係を損なったため，イギリス議会内での人気も低下し始めた。その後，1850年代に，扱われ方に腹を立てた東インド会社の兵士一団が，反乱を起こした。彼らはインド皇帝を権力の座に戻すためにデリーに向かって行進し，彼らの行動はイギリスに対する反乱をインドの他の地域にまで広げた。反乱は約２年後，ついに鎮圧されたが，それは東インド会社終焉の引き金となった。東インド会社が反乱を許したことを非難したイギリス政府はインドを支配し，イギリスの直接統治の時代が始まった。イギリスは東インド会社を解散し，インド皇帝を権力の座から排除し，ほぼ１世紀にわたってインドを支配し続けた。

一般的には鉄道の建設を例として挙げ，インドがイギリスの支配により恩恵を受けたと主張する人もいるが，多くの歴史家は，同国が悪影響を受けたと異議を唱えている。イギリス文化が優れているという意識を強化するために，インド人はイギリス人と同じ意見，道徳，社会的嗜好を持つように教育された。イギリスはまた，「分割統治」として知られる政策を実施し，異なる宗教的背景を持つインド人を互いに敵対させた。これらの宗教の信者らは先の反乱時に互いに協力し合ったため，イギリス政府はこの戦略を利用して，インドに対する支配を維持した。しかし，1900年代初頭からインド人のナショナリズム感情が高まり，1940年代後半に，インドは最終的に独立を果たした。

東インド会社は１世紀以上前に活動を停止したが，その影響力は継続している。一部の専門家は，それが多国籍企業という概念の先駆けとなり，最終的に今日広く普及している資本主義の経済システムをもたらしたと述べている。さらに，イギリス政府と東インド会社との関係は，ビジネス目標の達成を促すために政治力を利用する前例を作った。

(38)　正解　2

質問の訳 インドが東インド会社と取引を行ったことにより得られた結果の１つは何か。

選択肢の訳 **1**　インドは他国と貿易協定を結ぶことができたので，軍隊の規模を拡大する余裕ができた。　**2**　インドに不利な取引契約に同意する以外の選択肢がほとんどなくなった。　**3** インド政府は，貿易契約締結失敗による損失を補うために，増税しなければならなくなった。　**4** インド政府と中国との関係が悪化し，両国間の貿易はほぼ途絶えることになった。

解説 インドとの貿易を始めた東インド会社について，第1段落第4文後半でthe company pressured India into accepting trade contracts that, in general, were only of benefit to the company「会社はインドに圧力をかけ，概して会社にのみ利益をもたらす貿易契約を受け入れさせた」と述べている。これに一致する選択肢**2**が正解。選択肢は主語をインドにし，had little choice but to agree to ～「～に同意する以外の選択肢はほとんどなかった」と言い換えている。

(39) 正解 1

質問の訳 イギリス政府は何によってインドの支配権を握ったか。

選択肢の訳 **1** イギリス政府は，発生した暴動の責任を東インド会社に押し付けた。
2 インド国民は，国を実質的に統治するインド皇帝の能力に対する信頼を失った後，イギリスの統治に賛成票を投じた。　**3** インドの人々は，インドと中国の間の戦争を回避するために，イギリスの助けを求めた。　**4** インドの皇帝は，インドの支配を維持するための政治戦略として，イギリスと協力関係を築くことに決めた。

解説 イギリスがインドを統治するまでの過程については，第2段落を参照。東インド会社の兵士の反乱が起こった後の出来事として，第6文でThe British government, which blamed the East India Company for allowing the rebellion to happen, took control of India「東インド会社が反乱を許したことを非難したイギリス政府はインドを支配した」と述べている。この内容と一致する選択肢**1**が正解。

(40) 正解 3

質問の訳 イギリス統治がインドに与えた影響の1つは，

選択肢の訳 **1** インド人は，彼らの経済的および社会的ニーズを反映した政府を構築するプロセスに参加することができた。　**2** 学校は，インドとイギリスの両方の文化への認識を深めるよう生徒を教育することに努めた。　**3** インド人がイギリス統治に異議を唱えるのを防ぐために，インド人の様々なグループの間に分裂を生じさせた。
4 インド政府によって建設された鉄道やその他の輸送システムの多くが破壊された。

解説 イギリス統治のインドへの影響については，第3段落を参照。良い影響として，鉄道の建設（第1文），悪い影響として，イギリス寄りの教育（第2文），分割統治（第3～4文）を挙げている。中でも分割統治（divide and rule）については，turned Indians from different religious backgrounds against each other「異なる宗教的背景を持つインド人を互いに敵対させた」，The British government used this strategy to maintain its control over India「イギリス政府はこの戦略を利用して，インドに対する支配を維持した」と述べているので，この内容とほぼ一致する選択肢**3**が正解。

(41) 正解 3

質問の訳 この文章の筆者は，東インド会社について何と言っているか。

選択肢の訳 **1** その会社は，イギリス政府がその統治をアジアの他の国に拡大するという目的を達成するのを妨げた。　**2** その会社は，当時は成功を収めていたかもしれないが，その事業モデルは今日の経済においては効果的ではないだろう。　**3**　会社はもう存在しないものの，現在の世界経済の展望に大きな影響を与えてきた。　**4**　会社が設立されていなかったとしたら，別の会社が同様の政治的および経済的影響力を持つことになった可能性がある。

解説　第４段落第１文より，東インド会社は既に活動を停止しているとわかる。また第２文に，東インド会社についての専門家の意見として，pioneered the concept of multinational corporations and ultimately led to the economic system of capitalism that is widespread today「多国籍企業という概念の先駆けとなり，最終的に今日広く普及している資本主義の経済システムをもたらした」とある。この内容と一致する選択肢**3**が正解。

4　一次試験・英作文

（問題編p.169）

指示文の訳　●次のトピックについてエッセイを書きなさい。
●答えの裏付けに，以下に挙げたポイントのうちの２つを使いなさい。
●構成：導入，本論，結論
●長さ：120～150語
●エッセイは解答用紙のＢ面に用意されたスペースに書きなさい。
スペースの外側に書かれた内容は，採点の対象とはなりません。

トピックの訳　人の給料は本人の業務実績に基づいたものであるべきですか。

ポイントの訳　●年齢　●会社の利益　●意欲　●技能

解答例

In my opinion, from the perspectives of motivation and company profits, people's salaries should definitely be related to their job performance.

To begin with, while standardized salaries for workers in companies today are common, the level of motivation among employees can vary greatly. Rewarding enthusiastic employees who produce better work with higher salaries is not only fair but would also have the wider benefit of motivating other employees.

Additionally, the efforts that employees put into performing their work duties well ultimately benefit companies by increasing their profits. One of the responsibilities of a business is said to be the distribution of profits to those who contribute to its growth. Therefore, to fulfill this responsibility, companies must make sure that salaries match workers' job performance.

To conclude, when considering the importance of employee motivation and sharing company profits, I feel that people's salaries should be based on their job performance.

解答例の訳

私の意見では，意欲および会社の利益という観点から，人の給料は絶対に本人の業務実

※2024年度第１回から，大問４に文章の要約を書く問題が加わります。

績と結びついたものであるべきだ。

第一に，昨今は企業内の労働者向けに給料が標準化されているのが一般的ではあるが，従業員間における意欲の度合いは大きく異なり得る。より好成績を上げる熱心な従業員に高めの給料で報いるのは公正なことであるのみならず，それには，他の従業員に意欲を起こさせるというより広範なメリットがあるだろう。

さらに，従業員が自らの業務で好成績を上げることに注ぐ努力は，帰するところ，利益を増加させることにより企業のためにもなる。事業の責務の一つは，その成長に貢献を果たす人々への利益の分配であると言われている。したがって，この責務を全うすべく，企業は必ず，給料が労働者の業務実績に対応するよう取り計らう必要がある。

結論として，従業員の意欲並びに会社の利益の共有の重要性を考慮すると，私は，人の給料は本人の業務実績に基づいたものであるべきだと思う。

解説 TOPIC文について，「基づいたものであるべきである／基づいたものであるべきではない」のどちらかの立場に立って，自分の意見とその根拠をエッセイの形でまとめる形式である。エッセイをまとめる際には，POINTSとして示されたキーワードのうち2つを選んで使用する必要がある。なお，キーワードに挙げられている語句については，必要に応じて形を変えて表現したり類義語で置き換えたりしても良い。

段落構成に関する，導入（introduction）→本論（main body）→結論（conclusion）という基本的な指定は必ず守ること。解答例のように本論を2つに分ける場合は，論点の重複がないように注意する。また，結論をまとめる際には第1段落の単純な繰り返しにならないよう，表現を若干でも工夫すると良いだろう。ただし，どうしても時間が足りない場合はエッセイの完成を優先する。

TOPIC文 「人の給料は本人の業務実績に基づいたものであるべきですか」という質問について意見を求める内容。

語句 salary「給料」/ be based on ～「～に基づいている」/ performance「業績」

第1段落（導入） まずエッセイの冒頭で，TOPIC文のテーマを正しく理解していることと，自分が「基づいたものであるべきである／基づいたものであるべきではない」のいずれの立場かを示す必要がある。解答例は，文をIn my opinion「私の考えでは」から始め，自分が前者の立場に，つまり給料は業績に基づいたものであるべきだという立場にいることを示している。その際，副詞definitely「絶対に」を用いることで，自分の主張を強調している。また，POINTSのMotivation「意欲」とCompany profits「会社の利益」を観点として取り上げている。

語句 perspective「観点」/ profit「利益，収益」/ be related to ～「～に関連している」

第2段落（本論①） 第1段落で示した1つ目の観点である「意欲」についての段落。接続詞while「～ではあるが」を用いて給料の標準化が一般的である点について譲歩しつつも，従業員の意欲向上のために，高給をもってして優秀な従業員に報いることの重要性について述べている。

語句 to begin with「第一に」/ standardize「～を標準化する」/ vary「異なる」/ greatly「著しく」/ reward ～ with ...「…で～に報いる」/ enthusiastic「熱心な」/ produce「～をもたらす」/ benefit「メリット」/ motivate「～に意欲を起こさせる」

第3段落（本論②） 第1段落で示した2つ目の観点である「会社の利益」についての段落。この段落では，追加を表す談話標識であるAdditionally「さらに」から始めることで文章の構成をより論理的なものにしている。「事業の責務の一つは，その成長に貢献を果たす人々への利益の分配である」という世間一般に流布している言説を述べた後，帰結を表すTherefore「したがって」を用いて，給料が労働者の業務実績に対応する必要性について説明している。

語句 put effort into ～「～に努力を注ぐ」/ perform「～を成し遂げる」/ duties「職務」/ ultimately「結局，最終的には」/ benefit「～の利益になる」/ increase「～を増やす」/ responsibility「責務，責任」/ business「事業，企業」/ distribution「分配」/ those who ～「～する人々」/ contribute to ～「～に貢献する」/ growth「成長」/ fulfill「～を果たす」/ make sure that ～「必ず～であるようにする」/ match「～と対応する，～と釣り合う」

第４段落（結論） 最終段落では，To conclude「結論として」という談話標識から文を始め，第１段落でも述べた内容を，表現を若干変えつつも結論として再度述べ，エッセイを締め括っている。

語句 consider「～を考慮する」/ importance「重要性」/ share「～を共有する」

Part 1 一次試験・リスニング

（問題編pp.170～171）

指示文の訳 準１級の試験のリスニングテストが始まります。指示を注意して聞いてください。テスト中に質問をすることは許されていません。

このテストは３つのパートに分かれています。これら３つのパートの質問は全て選択肢の中から正解を選ぶ問題です。それぞれの質問について，問題冊子に書かれている４つの選択肢の中から最も適切な答えを選び，解答用紙の該当箇所にその答えをマークしなさい。このリスニングテストの全てのパートで，メモを取ってもかまいません。

それでは，これからPart １の指示を行います。このパートではNo. １からNo. 12まで12の会話が放送されます。それぞれの会話に続いて，質問が１つ流れます。各質問に対して，最も適切な答えを選んで解答用紙にマークする時間が10秒あります。会話と質問は１度しか読まれません。それでは，準１級のリスニングテストを始めます。

No.1 正解 1

放送文 ***A:*** Hi, Vince. Nice day for a walk, huh? ***B:*** Yeah, it is. Actually, I'm on my way to work. ***A:*** I thought you drove to work. Is something wrong with your car? ***B:*** No, I've just been putting on a bit of weight recently. ***A:*** I guess you have to get up pretty early now, though. ***B:*** I don't mind that. And I feel a lot healthier. ***A:*** Great! And I bet walking is easier on your wallet, too. ***B:*** Definitely! I'm planning to use the gas savings to buy a new bike.

Question: What do we learn about Vince?

訳 A：こんにちは，ヴィンス。散歩にいい天気だね。　B：ああ，そうだね。実は，仕事に行く途中なんだ。　A：あなたは車で通勤しているんだと思ってた。車の調子が悪いの？　B：いいや，最近ちょっと太ってきたんで。　A：でも，今は結構早起きしないといけないんじゃない。　B：それは気にしてないよ。それにずいぶん健康になった気がするんだ。　A：すごいね！　それに, 歩くとお財布にも優しいでしょ。　B：その通り！

ガソリン代が浮いた分を，新しい自転車を買うために使おうと思っているんだ。

質問の訳 ヴィンスについて何がわかるか。

選択肢の訳 **1** 彼はもう車で通勤していない。 **2** 彼の車は修理中だ。 **3** 彼はガソリンを買う余裕がない。 **4** 彼の新しい自転車が盗まれた。

解説 A（＝女性）が，1往復目で「散歩にいい天気だね」と述べ，2往復目では「あなたは車で通勤しているんだと思ってた」，4往復目では「歩くとお財布にも優しいでしょ」と述べていることから，この会話をしているとき，ヴィンスは歩いていることがわかる。また，B（＝Vince）が2往復目で「最近ちょっと太ってきたんで」と歩いて仕事に行っている理由を述べ，4往復目では「ガソリン代が浮いた分を～」と述べていることから，ヴィンスは，以前は車で通勤していたが，今は車ではなく歩いて通勤していることがわかる。よって，walking（4往復目のAの発言）を**no longer drives**と言い換えた**1**が正解。

No.2 正解 3

放送文 ***A:*** Fernando, how are you getting along with your dorm roommate? ***B:*** Oh, he's all right, Mom, I guess. He's pretty tidy, but he's not very communicative. I never know what's on his mind. ***A:*** Do you ever do things together? ***B:*** Almost never. I spend more time with the other guys on my floor. They're a little crazy, but they're fun. ***A:*** Well, I'm glad you're enjoying yourself, but don't forget to spend enough time on your studies.

Question: What does Fernando suggest about his roommate?

訳 A：フェルナンド，寮のルームメイトとはうまくいってるの？ B：ああ，彼は大丈夫だよ，母さん，たぶんね。彼はかなりきれい好きだけど，あまり話し好きではないんだ。何を考えているのかわからないんだ。 A：いっしょに何かをすることはあるの？ B：ほとんどないね。同じフロアの他の人たちといっしょにいることの方が多いよ。彼らはちょっとクレイジーだけど，楽しいんだ。 A：楽しんでいるみたいで嬉しいけど，勉強に十分な時間を割くことを忘れないでね。

質問の訳 フェルナンドはルームメイトについてどう考えているか。

選択肢の訳 **1** 彼は引っ越したいと思っている。 **2** 彼はパーティーをするのが好きだ。 **3** 彼はあまり気さくではない。 **4** 彼はとてもだらしない。

解説 1往復目でA（＝母親）から「寮のルームメイトとはうまくいってるの？」とたずねられたB（＝Fernando）は，ルームメイトについて「あまり話し好きではないんだ。何を考えているのかわからないんだ」(he's not very communicative. I never know what's on his mind.) と述べており，フェルナンドが，寮のルームメイトはあまり気さくではないと考えていることがわかる。よって，not very communicativeを**not very open**と言い換えた**3**が正解。

No.3 正解 4

放送文 ***A:*** How are things going, Matt? ***B:*** Not so good. I was supposed to have a job interview yesterday, but all the trains were stopped due to an accident, so I couldn't make it. ***A:*** But they'll give you another chance, won't they? ***B:*** No. I called the manager as soon as I got home. He said they'd already seen enough people. Looks like I'm out of luck. ***A:*** That's awful. ***B:***

Yeah, well, I guess they have a lot of good candidates to choose from.
Question: Why did Matt not get the job?

訳 A：調子はどう，マット？　B：あまりよくないよ。昨日面接を受けることになっていたんだけど，事故で電車が全部止まってしまって，間に合わなかったんだ。　A：でも，またチャンスをくれるんでしょう？　B：ううん，家に帰ってからすぐに店長に電話したんだ。もう十分な人数と会ったって言ってた。ぼくはもうダメみたいだね。　A：それはひどいね。　B：うん，でも，きっといい候補者がたくさんいるんだろうね。

質問の訳 なぜマットは仕事を得られなかったのか。

選択肢の訳 **1**　他の候補者たちの方が優秀だった。　**2**　彼は昨日店長に電話するのを忘れた。　**3**　店長は彼のことが好きではなかった。　**4**　彼は面接に欠席した。

解説 1往復目でB（＝Matt）は「昨日面接を受けることになっていたんだけど，～間に合わなかったんだ」（I was supposed to have a job interview yesterday, ～ I couldn't make it.）と述べているので，Bは面接の時間に間に合わず，面接を受けられなかったことがわかる。さらに，2往復目でBは「（店長に電話したら）もう十分な人数と会ったって言ってた。ぼくはもうダメみたいだね」と述べているので，Bは面接を欠席したことで，仕事を得られなかったことがわかる。よって，couldn't make itをmissed the interviewと具体的に言い換えた**4**が正解。

No.4　正解　4

放送文 ***A:*** Professor Cranfield, can I ask you something?　***B:*** Sure, Lucinda.　***A:*** It's about your intensive Spanish writing course.　I feel like I'm already busy with my other classes.　Doing the writing course might be too much.　***B:*** I understand.　I think you certainly have the ability, but I don't want to push you.　It's not a mandatory course, but future employers would be impressed if you passed it.　***A:*** Thanks for your advice.　I'll think it over a little more.
Question: What does the man imply about the writing course?

訳 A：クランフィールド教授，ちょっとお伺いしてもいいですか。　B：もちろんだよ，ルシンダ。　A：スペイン語のライティング集中講座のことなんです。私は他の授業ですでにいっぱいのような気がします。ライティング講座をやるのはやりすぎかもしれません。　B：わかるよ。君は確かに能力があると思うけど，無理強いはしないよ。それは必修科目ではないけれど，合格すれば，将来の雇用主は感心するだろうね。　A：アドバイスありがとうございます。もう少し考えてみます。

質問の訳 男性はライティング講座についてどんなことをほのめかしているか。

選択肢の訳 **1**　その女性が卒業するためには合格する必要がある。　**2**　その女性の目標には合致していない。　**3**　その女性には高度すぎる。　**4**　それに合格すれば，その女性が就職するのに役立つかもしれない。

解説 1，2往復目から，学生のA（＝Lucinda）と，ルシンダのスペイン語の講師であるクランフィールド教授との対話だとわかる。スペイン語のライティング集中講座について，「ライティング講座をやるのはやりすぎかもしれません」と述べたルシンダに対し，クランフィールド教授は「合格すれば，将来の雇用主は感心するだろうね」（future employers would be impressed if you passed it）と言い，スペイン語のライティング集中講座に合格することが，ルシンダの将来の就職活動に役立つだろうと述べている。よって，future employers would be impressedを**could help the woman find a job**と言い換えた**4**が正解。

No.5 正解 **2**

放送文 ***A:*** Amy, I heard you're looking for a part-time job. ***B:*** I'm thinking about working at a restaurant as a server. I could use the money to help pay for school fees. ***A:*** Well, I hope you like standing for long periods of time. ***B:*** I would get breaks, you know. I doubt it would be that bad. ***A:*** Well, I think you should buy some comfortable shoes, just in case. ***B:*** I need to get the job first.
Question: What does the man imply?

訳 A：エイミー，アルバイトを探してるって聞いたよ。 B：レストランで給仕の仕事をしようと思っているの。学費を払うのに給料が役立つからね。 A：ええと，君が長時間立っているのが好きならいいんだけど。 B：休憩も取れるしね。そんなに悪くないと思うわ。 A：じゃあ，念のため履き心地がいい靴を買っておいたほうがいいよ。 B：まずは仕事をゲットしないとね。

質問の訳 男性は何をほのめかしているか。

選択肢の訳 **1** 女性は学校を休んだほうがいい。 **2** 給仕の仕事は肉体的にきつい。 **3** レストランの店員はあまり稼げない。 **4** 学生はアルバイトをしないほうがいい。

解説 1往復目でB（＝Amy）から「レストランで給仕の仕事をしようと思っているの」と言われたA（＝男性）は，2往復目で「ええと，君が長時間立っているのが好きならいいんだけど」と述べ，給仕の仕事が長時間の立ち仕事であることに関してエイミーを心配する発言をしている。Aは，さらに3往復目で「念のため（長く立っていても疲れないように）履き心地がいい靴を買っておいたほうがいいよ」ともアドバイスしている。したがって，Aは，レストランでの給仕は立ち仕事で肉体的にきついものだと考えていることがわかる。よって，standing for long periods of timeを**physically demanding**と言い換えた**2**が正解。

No.6 正解 **1**

放送文 ***A:*** We still need to buy a present for Carla and Antonio's wedding. Have you checked out the gift registry yet? ***B:*** Yes, but the only things left on the list are really expensive items, like the silver dining set. ***A:*** I warned you that if we didn't choose something quickly, the affordable stuff would all be gone. ***B:*** Sorry. You were right. What should we do? Get them something cheaper that's not on the list? ***A:*** No. I'd rather not take any chances. We don't want to give them something they might not want.
Question: What will these people probably do?

訳 A：カルラとアントニオの結婚式のプレゼントを買わなきゃ。もうギフトレジストリーをチェックした？ B：うん，でもリストに残っているのは銀のダイニングセットとか，すごく高いものばかりなんだ。 A：早く選ばないと，手頃なものが全部なくなっちゃうよって注意したわよね。 B：ごめん。君の言うとおりだったよ。どうしたらいいんだろう？リストにないもっと安いものを買って贈ろうか？ A：ううん，なるべくなら冒険はしたくないわ。彼らが欲しがらないようなものを贈りたくないのよ。

質問の訳 この人たちは，おそらく何をするか。

選択肢の訳 **1** リストの中からギフトを購入する。 **2** 結婚式の招待を断る。 **3** カルラとアントニオに相談する。 **4** 銀のダイニングセットを返す。

解説 1往復目のA（＝女性）の発言から，結婚式のプレゼントに何を贈るかについての対話だとわかる。同発言内にある「ギフトレジストリー」とは，お祝いをもらう側（＝Carla と Antonio）が，お祝いをくれる人たち（＝AとBなど）に案内状などといっしょに送るリストで，自分たちの欲しいものが掲載されているリスト。お祝いを贈る人たちは，通常，そのリストの中から贈るものを選ぶ。1往復目でBは「リストに残っているのは～すごく高いものばかりなんだ」と述べ，2往復目では「リストにないもっと安いものを買って贈ろうか？」と提案しているが，Aは「ううん」とBの提案を否定した後，「彼らが欲しがらないようなものを贈りたくないのよ」とも述べている。したがって，Aは「ギフトレジストリー」の中からギフトを購入すべきだと考えていることがわかる。よって，don't want to give them something they might not wantを**buy a gift from the list**と言い換えた**1**が正解。

No.7 正解 1

放送文 ***A:*** Would you mind picking up some takeout on your way home? ***B:*** No problem. How about burgers? ***A:*** Too greasy. I was thinking about that Korean restaurant we went to last week. ***B:*** That's not exactly on my way home, and it's a little pricey. ***A:*** I know, but the servings are huge. We'd have enough for lunch tomorrow, too. Korean food is just as good the next day. ***B:*** All right. They're usually pretty quick with orders, so I should be home by around six.

Question: What is one reason the woman suggests the Korean restaurant?

訳 A：帰りにテイクアウトを買ってきてくれる？ B：いいよ。ハンバーガーはどう？ A：油っこすぎるわ。先週行った韓国料理店のことを考えていたんだけど。 B：あそこは帰り道にあるわけじゃないし，値段もちょっと高いんだよね。 A：そうなんだけど，量はすごく多いわ。明日の昼ご飯にも十分よ。韓国料理は翌日もおいしいわよ。 B：そうだね。いつも素早く注文を取ってくるので，6時ごろまでには帰れると思うよ。

質問の訳 女性が韓国料理店を勧める理由の1つは何か。

選択肢の訳 **1** 料理の量が多い。 **2** 家から車ですぐのところにある。 **3** 他の店より安い。 **4** 評判がいい。

解説 1往復目から，A（＝女性）がB（＝男性）に，帰りに夕食用のテイクアウトを買ってきてくれるように頼んでいる場面だとわかる。2往復目でAが韓国料理店でのテイクアウトを提案したのに対し，Bが「あそこ（＝韓国料理店）は帰り道にあるわけじゃないし，値段もちょっと高いんだよね」と否定的な意見を述べると，Aは「（料理の）量はすごく多いわ」（the servings are huge）と，韓国料理店を勧める理由の1つとして，（料理の）量が多いことを挙げている。よって，the servings are hugeを**large portions**と言い換えた**1**が正解。

No.8 正解 3

放送文 ***A:*** We should start planning our vacation for this year. ***B:*** How about

escaping the cold weather and going somewhere tropical with a nice beach? ***A:*** I was hoping we could go skiing. ***B:*** Well, what did we do on our last vacation? ***A:*** We went camping. You caught that giant fish at the lake, remember? ***B:*** Oh, right. And you wanted to go sightseeing in town, but the kids and I outvoted you. ***A:*** That's right. ***B:*** OK. Let's do what you want this time. I'll tell the kids we're headed for the mountains.
Question: What are these people going to do for their vacation?

訳 A：そろそろ今年の休暇の計画を立てないとね。 B：寒さから逃れて，すてきなビーチのある南国のどこかに行くのはどうかな？ A：私はスキーに行けたらいいなと思ってたの。 B：そういえば，この前の休暇は何をしたんだっけ？ A：キャンプに行ったわ。あなたが湖であの大きな魚を釣ったの，覚えてる？ B：ああ，そうだった。君は街を観光したかったみたいだけど，ぼくと子どもたちが反対したんだったよね。 A：そうだったわね。 B：わかった。今回は君のやりたいことをしよう。子どもたちには山へ行くと言っておくよ。

質問の訳 この人たちは休暇に何をするつもりか。

選択肢の訳 **1** ハイキングをして過ごす。 **2** 湖に釣りに行く。 **3** スキー旅行に行く。 **4** 観光に行く。

解説 1往復目でB（＝男性）が「すてきなビーチのある南国のどこかに行くのはどうかな？」と述べたのに対し，A（＝女性）は「私はスキーに行けたらいいなと思ってたの」と述べている。3往復目でBは「（この前の休暇は）君（＝A）は街を観光したかったみたいだけど，ぼくと子どもたちが反対したんだったよね」と述べ，これを受けて4往復目で「（この前の休暇は君の希望を叶えられなかったので）今回は君のやりたいこと（＝スキー旅行）をしよう」（Let's do what you want this time.）と述べ，今回の休暇ではAの希望の通りにすると述べている。よって，do what you wantを**take a ski trip**と言い換えた**3**が正解。

No.9 正解 **2**

放送文 ***A:*** Hey, Kenneth. I was looking at the latest post on our company's blog. The one about the release of our new earphones. The release date is wrong. It should be May 15th, not the 5th as stated in the post. ***B:*** Really? That post was added by Jason last night. ***A:*** Well, we need to take care of it immediately so we don't mislead our customers. Ask Jason to do that right away. ***B:*** I'm afraid he has the day off today. I'll handle it instead. ***A:*** Thanks.
Question: What does the woman say about the company's blog?

訳 A：こんにちは，ケネス。会社のブログの最新記事を見ていたところです。新しいイヤホンの発売に関するものです。発売日が間違っていますよ。投稿に記されている5月5日ではなく，5月15日のはずです。 B：そうなんですか？ その記事は昨夜ジェイソンが追加したんです。 A：ええと，お客様に誤解を与えないよう，すぐそれに対処する必要がありますね。ジェイソンにすぐにやるように言ってください。 B：あいにく，彼は今日は休みです。私が代わりにやっておきます。 A：ありがとう。

質問の訳 女性は会社のブログについて何と言っているか。

選択肢の訳 **1** 一部の客がそれについてクレームを言った。 **2** 投稿の1つを修正す

る必要がある。　**3**　ケネスは最新の投稿を編集すべきではない。　**4**　もっと頻繁に更新されるべきだ。

解説　1往復目でA（＝女性）は，会社のブログの最新記事について「(新しいイヤホンの)発売日が間違っていますよ」と述べている。さらにAは2往復目で「お客様に誤解を与えないよう，すぐそれ（＝イヤホンの発売日が間違っていること）に対処する必要がありますね」(we need to take care of it immediately so we don't mislead our customers)と述べ，イヤホンの発売日を修正する必要があるとケネスに伝えている。よって，take care of itを**needs to be revised**と言い換えた**2**が正解。

No.10　正解　4

放送文　***A:*** Excuse me, sir. Has anyone turned in a train pass today? ***B:*** I'm afraid not. Have you lost yours? ***A:*** Yeah. When I used mine this morning, I was certain I put it back in my wallet, but I guess I didn't. ***B:*** I can give you the form to purchase another one. ***A:*** Looks like I have no choice. It makes me so frustrated, though. I had just put $50 on it. Now, I've lost it all. ***B:*** I'm sorry. Here's the form. It should only take a couple of minutes to fill out. ***A:*** Thanks. I'll do that now.

Question: Why is the woman upset?

訳　A：すみません。今日，電車の定期券を届けてくれた方はいますか。　B：残念ながら，いらっしゃいません。定期券を失くされたのですか。　A：はい。今朝使ったとき，確かに財布に戻したと思ったのですが，戻さなかったようです。　B：もう一枚購入するための用紙をお渡しします。　A：仕方ないですね。でも，すごくイライラします。せっかく50ドル出したばかりなのに。今，全部なくなっちゃいました。　B：お察し申し上げます。これがその書類です。記入には数分しかかからないと思います。　A：ありがとうございます。今，記入します。

質問の訳　なぜその女性は動揺しているのか。

選択肢の訳　**1**　財布が見当たらない。　**2**　電車の定期券の期限が切れている。　**3**　電車に乗り遅れた。　**4**　お金を浪費した。

解説　1～2往復目のやりとりから，定期券を紛失したA（＝女性）とB（＝駅員）の対話だとわかる。2往復目で，駅員に「もう一枚（定期券を）購入するための用紙をお渡しします」と言われたAは，「でも，すごくイライラします。せっかく50ドル出したばかりなのに。今，全部なくなっちゃいました」(It makes me so frustrated, though. I had just put $50 on it. Now, I've lost it all.)とお金を無駄にしたことにいら立ちを感じている。よって，(have) lost it allを**wasted her money**と言い換えた**4**が正解。

No.11　正解　3

放送文　***A:*** Michelle, I'm sorry I couldn't make it to the piano concert last Sunday. ***B:*** No problem. I sold your ticket to Jasmine, so it wasn't wasted. ***A:*** I'm relieved to hear that. Did you enjoy the concert? ***B:*** Well, the pianist was superb. Unfortunately, we were bothered by another audience member, though. ***A:*** What happened? ***B:*** He was continuously whispering to the person next to him and playing with his smartphone. It was hard to concentrate. ***A:***

Oh, that's a shame.
Question: What was the woman's problem?
訳 A：ミッシェル, 先週の日曜日のピアノコンサートに行けなくて悪かったね。 B：大丈夫よ。あなたのチケットはジャスミンに売ったから, 無駄にはならなかったし。 A：それを聞いて安心したよ。コンサートは楽しめた？ B：そうね, ピアニストの演奏は素晴らしかった。残念ながら, 他の観客に迷惑をかけられちゃったけど。 A：どうしたの？ B：その人は, ずっと隣の人とヒソヒソ話をしたり, スマートフォンをいじったりしていたのよ。なかなか集中できなかったわ。 A：ああ, それは残念だったね。
質問の訳 その女性の問題は何だったか。
選択肢の訳 **1** ピアニストの演奏が好きではなかった。 **2** コンサートに遅れて到着した。 **3** コンサートに集中することができなかった。 **4** チケットを見つけることができなかった。
解説 2往復目でA（＝男性）から「(先週の日曜日のピアノ）コンサートは楽しめた？」と感想をたずねられたB（＝Michelle）は, ピアニストの演奏は素晴らしかったと言いつつ,「残念ながら, 他の観客に迷惑をかけられちゃったけど」と述べ, 続く3往復目では,「その人は, ずっと隣の人とヒソヒソ話をしたり, スマートフォンをいじったりしていたのよ」と言った後,「なかなか集中できなかったわ」(It was hard to concentrate.）とコンサートの問題点を述べている。よって, hard to concentrateを**could not focus on the concert**と言い換えた**3**が正解。

No.12 正解 2

放送文 ***A:*** Hello, Jenny Williams speaking. ***B:*** Hello. I'm calling about a package I'm supposed to deliver to your house. ***A:*** Oh, I see. Is there something wrong? ***B:*** When you selected your delivery option online, you asked us to use the delivery box. ***A:*** Yes, I won't be home until seven tonight. ***B:*** Unfortunately, the package won't fit in the box. Could I leave it in another location instead? ***A:*** Sure. If you can take it around to the side of the house, there's a bicycle shelter. You can leave it there.
Question: What does the man ask the woman to do?
訳 A：はい, ジェニー・ウィリアムズです。 B：こんにちは。お客様のお宅に届けることになっている荷物のことでお電話を差し上げています。 A：ああ, そうですか。何かあったんですか。 B：インターネットで配送方法を選択されたとき, お客様は宅配ボックスを使うようにご用命されました。 A：はい, 今夜は7時まで家にいないんです。 B：あいにく, 荷物がボックスに入りません。別の場所に置いていってもよろしいですか。 A：もちろんです。家の横まで持って行っていただければ, 自転車置き場があります。そこに置いてください。
質問の訳 男性は女性に何をすることを頼んでいるか。
選択肢の訳 **1** 夕方, 彼に折り返し電話をする。 **2** 彼に新しい配達の指示を出す。 **3** ネットで配達方法を変更する。 **4** 何時に帰宅するかを伝える。
解説 1往復目から, B（＝男性配達員）が, A（＝Jenny Williams）に配達する荷物に関することで電話をかけている場面とわかる。また, 2～3往復目から, 当初, Aは宅配ボックスへの配達を指示していたが, 荷物が宅配ボックスに入らない状況だとわかる。

3往復目で配達員が「別の場所に置いていってもよろしいですか」(Could I leave it in another location instead?) と，荷物の置き場所について，当初の指示（＝宅配ボックス）とは別の新しい指示を出すようにAに求めている。よって，leave it in another location insteadを**new delivery instructions**と言い換えた**2**が正解。

Part 2 一次試験・リスニング

(問題編pp.172〜173)

CD 緑-14 〜 CD 緑-20

指示文の訳 それでは，これからPart 2の指示を行います。このパートでは(A)から(F)までの6つの文章が放送されます。それぞれの文章に続いて，No. 13からNo. 24まで質問が2つずつ流れます。それぞれの質問に対して，最も適切な答えを選んで解答用紙にマークする時間が10秒あります。文章と質問は1度しか読まれません。それでは始めます。

(A)

放送文 *International Rivers*

Many of the world's rivers are not contained within the borders of a single country. Because of the importance of water, international laws about how neighboring countries share these rivers are essential. Typically, all countries have equal rights to use a river that flows through their lands. Also, all countries are legally forbidden from doing anything to a river that would considerably decrease its flow of water into other countries.

However, sharing a river is not always simple. For example, the Nile River runs through a number of countries, including Ethiopia and Egypt. Ethiopia has requested international loans to build a dam on its section of the river to generate electricity. However, Egypt has used its political influence to block the loans, complaining that a dam would reduce the Nile's water flow into Egypt. At the same time, Ethiopia points out that Egypt currently uses the river for power generation, so it is unfair if Ethiopia cannot.

Questions ***No. 13*** What is one thing the speaker says about rivers?

No. 14 Why is the Nile River discussed?

訳 国際河川

世界の河川の多くは，1つの国の国境の中には収まっていない。水の重要性ゆえに，近隣諸国がこれらの河川をどのように共有するかについての国際法が不可欠となる。通常は，すべての国が自国を流れる河川を利用する平等な権利を有している。また，すべての国は，他国への水の流れを著しく減少させるような行為を河川に対してすることが一切，法的に禁じられている。

しかしながら，川を共有するということは，必ずしも単純なことではない。例えば，ナイル川はエチオピアやエジプトなど多くの国々を流れている。エチオピアは，発電を目的として自国内のナイル川にダムを建設するために国際借款を要請している。しかし，エジプトは，ダムができるとエジプトに流れるナイル川の水量が減るとして，政治的な影響力を行使して融資を阻止している。一方，エチオピアは，エジプトは現在，ナイル川を発電に利用しており，エチオピアが利用できないのは不公平だと指摘している。

No.13 正解 3

質問の訳 話者が河川について言っていることの１つは何か。

選択肢の訳 **1** 多くの河川で水量が減少している。 **2** 河川を保護するための法律をもっと厳しくする必要がある。 **3** 河川を共有している国々は，通常，同じ使用権を持っている。 **4** 河川があると国境を守ることが難しくなることが多い。

解説 第１段落第３文で「通常は，すべての国が自国を流れる河川を利用する平等な権利を有している」(Typically, all countries have equal rights to use a river that flows through their lands.) と述べられている。よって，equal rights to use a river をthe same usage rightsと言い換えた**3**が正解。

No.14 正解 4

質問の訳 なぜナイル川について論じられているのか。

選択肢の訳 **1** 国境問題の解決策を提案するため。 **2** 貧しい国が電力のために川を必要とすることを示唆するため。 **3** ダムはしばしばコストがかかりすぎることを示すため。 **4** 河川使用権がいかに複雑になりうるかを示すため。

解説 第２段落第１文で「川を共有するということは，必ずしも単純なことではない」(sharing a river is not always simple) と述べた後，「例えば」(For example) に続けて，発電目的でのナイル川の利用に関するエチオピアとエジプトの間の紛争の例を挙げている。したがって，話者がナイル川について論じたのは，国際河川の河川使用権の問題が単純ではない（＝複雑になりうる）ことの事例を挙げるためだと考えられる。よって，sharing a riverをriver usage rightsと，not always simpleをcan be complicatedと言い換えた**4**が正解。

(B)

放送文 *Theriac*

For thousands of years, people believed that a substance known as theriac was a wonder drug. According to legend, it was created by an ancient king who lived in fear of being poisoned. He was said to have taken theriac daily to protect himself from all forms of poison. The use of theriac gradually spread around the ancient world, and people began to believe that it was also effective against all kinds of illnesses. Making it, however, required time and effort, as some theriac recipes contained over a hundred ingredients, some of which came from poisonous snakes.

By the fifteenth century, there were regulations in many places about how theriac could be manufactured, and in some cities, such as Venice, it had to be made in a public ceremony. Though the scientific community now believes that theriac is ineffective, the regulations on the manufacture of theriac marked an important milestone in the development of modern medicine.

Questions ***No. 15*** What is one thing that we learn about theriac?

No. 16 What is one thing the speaker says about theriac in Venice?

訳 テリアック

何千年もの間，人々はテリアックという物質が不思議な薬であると信じていた。伝説によると，この薬は毒殺を恐れて生きていた古代の王によって作られたと言われている。彼は，あらゆる毒から身を守るために，毎日テリアックを飲んでいたと言われている。テリアックの使用は次第に古代世界に広まり，万病にも効くと信じられていった。しかしながら，テリアックの製法の中には，毒ヘビから採取したものなど，100種類以上の材料を含むものもあったので，その製造には時間と手間がかかった。

15世紀までには，テリアックの製造方法について各地で規制が行われるようになり，ヴェネツィアなどいくつかの都市では，公開される儀式の場で作らなければならなかった。現在，科学界ではテリアックは効果がないと考えられているが，テリアックの製造に関する規制は，近代医学の発展における重要な一里塚となった。

No.15 正解 **3**

質問の訳 テリアックについてわかることの1つは何か。

選択肢の訳 **1** 毒として使える可能性がある。 **2** ヘビで実験された。 **3** 作るのが困難だった。 **4** 最初の医療用薬品だった。

解説 第1段落最終文で「しかしながら，テリアックの製法の中には，毒ヘビから採取したものなど，100種類以上の材料を含むものもあったので，その製造には時間と手間がかかった」(Making it, however, required time and effort, as some theriac recipes contained over a hundred ingredients, some of which came from poisonous snakes.) と述べられている。よって，required time and effortを**difficult**と言い換えた**3**が正解。

No.16 正解 **4**

質問の訳 ヴェネツィアのテリアックについて，話者が言っていることの1つは何か。

選択肢の訳 **1** 作るのに何日もかかった。 **2** 毎日，少量しか作れなかった。 **3** 製造の規制は非常に緩やかだった。 **4** そこの人々はそれが作られるのを見ることができた。

解説 第2段落第1文で「ヴェネツィアなどいくつかの都市では，テリアックは公開される儀式の場で作らなければならなかった」(in some cities, such as Venice, it had to be made in a public ceremony) と述べられている。公開されるということは一定の人々の面前でということなので，ヴェネツィアなどいくつかの都市の一定の人々は，テリアックが作られるのを見ることができたということ。よって，made in a public ceremonyを**people ～ watch it being made**と言い換えた**4**が正解。

(C)

放送文 *Spirit Bears*

Found only in parts of Canada, spirit bears are black bears that are born with white fur due to a rare gene. Scientists estimate there may be as few as a hundred of these beautiful animals in the wild. For years, native peoples did their best to prevent the bears' existence from becoming known to the outside world. Because the bears' fur is so unusual, native peoples feared it would become a great prize for hunters and collectors.

Spirit bears' bright fur also provides them with a unique advantage when hunting salmon. Unlike the fur of ordinary black bears, spirit bears' fur is difficult for fish to see, so the fish are less able to avoid the bears. Unfortunately, however, spirit bear numbers may decrease even further. Recent research has revealed the gene that results in spirit bears' white fur is rarer than once thought. Additionally, many spirit bears live outside the areas where they are protected.

Questions ***No. 17*** What does the speaker say about native peoples?

No. 18 What advantage do spirit bears have over ordinary black bears?

訳 シロアメリカグマ

カナダの一部にのみ生息するシロアメリカグマは，まれな遺伝子により，生まれつき白い毛をもつアメリカグマである。科学者たちは，この美しい動物は野生では100頭ほどしかいないと推測している。長年，先住民はこのクマの存在が外部に知られないよう，最善を尽くしてきた。そのクマの毛皮は非常に珍しいため，ハンターやコレクターの格好の獲物となることを恐れたのだ。

また，シロアメリカグマの鮮やかな毛皮は，サケを捕獲する際にも特有の利点となる。普通のアメリカグマと違って，シロアメリカグマの毛皮は魚に見えにくいので，魚がそのクマを避けることができなくなるのだ。しかし，残念なことに，シロアメリカグマの数はさらに減少する可能性がある。シロアメリカグマの白い毛皮をつくる遺伝子は，かつて考えられていたよりも希少であることが，最近の研究によって明らかになったからだ。また，多くのシロアメリカグマは保護されている地域の外に生息しているからでもある。

No.17 正解 2

質問の訳 話者は先住民についてどのように言っているか。

選択肢の訳 **1** 黒い毛皮を持つシロアメリカグマだけを狩った。 **2** シロアメリカグマを秘密にしておこうとした。 **3** シロアメリカグマを危険だと考えていた。 **4** シロアメリカグマが自分たちを守ってくれていると信じていた。

解説 第1段落第3文で「長年，先住民はこのクマ（＝シロアメリカグマ）の存在が外部に知られないよう，最善を尽くしてきた」(For years, native peoples did their best to prevent the bears' existence from becoming known to the outside world.) と述べられている。よって，did their bestを**tried to**と，prevent the bears' existence from becoming known to the outside worldを**keep spirit bears a secret**と言い換えた**2**が正解。

No.18 正解 1

質問の訳 普通のアメリカグマと比べて，シロアメリカグマにはどんな利点があるか。

選択肢の訳 **1** エサを捕るのがより簡単である。 **2** 日光にあまり敏感ではない。 **3** 猟師が見つけにくい。 **4** 生息地はすべて保護されている。

解説 第2段落第1文で「シロアメリカグマの鮮やかな毛皮は，サケを捕獲する際にも特有の利点となる」(Spirit bears' bright fur also provides them with a unique advantage when hunting salmon.) と述べられ，続く文で「普通のアメリカグマと違っ

て，シロアメリカグマの毛皮は魚に見えにくいので，魚がそのクマを避けることができなくなる」とも述べている。普通のアメリカグマよりもエサであるサケを捕らえやすいということなので，**1**が正解。

(D)

放送文 *Distributed Generation*

In many parts of the United States, the electric power industry has been shifting away from the traditional system of centralized generation to a newer system known as distributed generation. With centralized generation, electricity is generated in one central location and then delivered to homes and businesses. Distributed generation is a network of smaller energy sources, such as solar panels or wind turbines, that produce electricity close to where it is needed. This can make the distributed-generation system more cost-effective.

Distributed generation has some disadvantages, however. The required infrastructure takes up space in communities, and residents generally consider it unattractive. In fact, homes close to large solar-energy facilities often sell for less than homes that are farther away. In addition, some distributed-generation systems require water to run, which is a limitation in areas that experience water shortages.

Questions ***No. 19*** What is true about distributed-generation systems?

No. 20 What is one downside of distributed generation?

訳 分散型発電

アメリカ合衆国の多くの地域では，電力業界が，従来のシステムである集中型発電から分散型発電という新しいシステムへの移行を進めている。集中型発電では，電力は一箇所で集中的に発電され，その後，家庭や企業に配電されている。分散型発電とは，電気が必要とされる場所の近くで発電する太陽光パネルや風力発電機などのより小型のエネルギー源をネットワーク化したものだ。そのため，分散型発電システムの費用対効果はより高くなることがある。

しかし，分散型発電にはいくつかのデメリットもある。必要とされるインフラが地域社会のスペースを占有し，住民は一般的にそのことをやっかいなことだと考えている。実際，大規模な太陽光発電施設に近い住宅は，遠い住宅よりも安く売られることが多い。また，分散型発電システムの中には水を必要とするものがあり，そのことは水不足に見舞われる地域では制約となる。

No.19 正解 1

質問の訳 分散型発電システムについて何が本当か。

選択肢の訳 **1** 電気が使われる場所の近くで発電する。 **2** 小規模事業者により好まれる。 **3** 太陽エネルギーを利用しない。 **4** 維持費が非常に高い。

解説 第1段落第3文で「分散型発電とは，電気が必要とされる場所の近くで発電する～より小型のエネルギー源をネットワーク化したものだ」(Distributed generation is a network of smaller energy sources ～ that produce electricity close to where it is needed.）と述べられている。よって，produce electricityを**generate power**と，close to where it is neededを**near where the power is used**と言い換えた**1**が正解。

No.20 正解 3

質問の訳 分散型発電のデメリットの１つは何か。

選択肢の訳 **1** 政府は通常，その開発に反対する。 **2** エネルギー会社が通常，そこから利益を得ることはない。 **3** 資産価値に悪影響を及ぼす可能性がある。 **4** しばしば地域の水源を汚染する。

解説 分散型発電のデメリットは第２段落で述べられている。第１段落から，分散型発電は，太陽光パネルなど小型のエネルギー源をネットワーク化したものだが，第２段落第３文には，「（分散型発電で使われる）大規模な太陽光発電施設に近い住宅は，遠い住宅よりも安く売られることが多い」（homes close to large solar-energy facilities often sell for less than homes that are farther away）と書かれている。よって，homes ～ sell for lessを**negatively affect property values**と言い換えた**3**が正解。

(E)

放送文 *What Zoos Can't Do*

In recent decades, zoos have been essential to efforts to save endangered animals. Several species of frogs, birds, and turtles have been saved from extinction by conservation programs that breed endangered animals in the safe environment of zoos. Unfortunately, certain species, such as tarsiers, which are animals that look like tiny monkeys, and great white sharks, cannot survive in captivity. These animals usually die quickly after being captured, making it impossible to breed them.

For this reason, the survival of tarsiers and great white sharks depends on the conservation of their natural environments. Though many of their habitats are already legally protected, the current laws are often ignored. Governments must try harder to stop the illegal destruction of the forests where tarsiers live and breed. They must also reduce illegal fishing activities that threaten great white sharks.

Questions ***No. 21*** Why are zoos unable to breed some endangered animals?

No. 22 What does the speaker say about saving tarsiers and great white sharks?

訳 動物園にできないこと

ここ数十年，動物園は，絶滅の危機に瀕した動物を救う取り組みに不可欠な存在となっている。動物園という安全な環境で絶滅危惧種を繁殖させる保護プログラムによって，カエル，鳥，カメのいくつかの種が絶滅の危機から救われている。残念ながら，小さなサルのような動物であるメガネザルや，ホホジロザメなど，飼育下では生きられない種もいる。これらの動物はたいてい捕獲後すぐに死んでしまうため，繁殖させるのが不可能なのだ。

そのため，メガネザルやホホジロザメが生き残るかは，彼らの自然環境の保護にかかっている。それらの生息地の多くはすでに法律で保護されているが，現行法が無視されるこ

とも頻繁にある。各国政府は，メガネザルが生息や繁殖をする場である森林の違法な破壊を食い止めるために，より努力する必要がある。また，各国政府は，ホホジロザメを脅かす違法な漁業をも減らさなければならない。

No.21 正解 **4**

質問の訳 なぜ動物園はいくつかの絶滅危惧種を繁殖させることができないのか。

選択肢の訳 **1** 世話をするのにお金がかかりすぎる。 **2** 捕獲することがあまりに難しい。 **3** 重い病気にかかる。 **4** 捕獲された後，長生きすることが少ない。

解説 第1段落第3文で，メガネザルや，ホホジロザメなど，動物園での飼育下では生きられない種がいることを述べた後，第4文で「これらの動物はたいてい捕獲後すぐに死んでしまうため，繁殖させるのが不可能なのだ」(These animals usually die quickly after being captured, making it impossible to breed them.)と述べられている。よって，usually die quicklyを**rarely live long**と，being capturedを**being caught**と言い換えた**4**が正解。

No.22 正解 **2**

質問の訳 話者は，メガネザルやホホジロザメを保護することについて何と言っているか。

選択肢の訳 **1** 動物園は繁殖の仕方を学ぶ必要がある。 **2** 政府は法律が守られるようにしなければならない。 **3** 新しい生息地に移動させなければならない。 **4** 野生で保護することは不可能だ。

解説 第2段落で，メガネザルやホホジロザメの保護に関して各国政府がやるべきこととして，「メガネザルが生息や繁殖をする場である森林の違法な破壊を食い止めるために，より努力する必要がある」(最後から2文目)，「ホホジロザメを脅かす違法な漁業をも減らさなければならない」(最後の文) と述べ，話者は，政府は違法行為が行われないよう尽力すべきだと主張している。よって，stop the illegal destruction of the forestsやreduce illegal fishing activitiesを**make sure laws are followed**と言い換えた**2**が正解。

(F)

放送文 *Written in Stone*

Petroglyphs are ancient drawings or carvings on rock surfaces. For researchers in the Americas, they are an important source of information about the Native Americans who lived there before the arrival of Europeans. Some of the most famous petroglyphs are those at Castle Rock Pueblo in Colorado. These images were not drawn in the style typical of the area, but in a way that was common in another settlement hundreds of kilometers away. There are also drawings of human conflict. This suggests that there may have been contact, and likely fighting, between these two communities.

Another interesting feature of the carvings is their use of light. On the longest and shortest days of the year, the carvings create specific patterns of light and shadow. This has led researchers to conclude that they were used as a type of solar calendar.

Questions ***No. 23*** What is one thing we learn about the Castle Rock Pueblo petroglyphs?

No. 24 How do researchers think the Castle Rock Pueblo petroglyphs were used?

訳 石に書かれたもの

ペトログリフとは，岩肌に描かれた古代の絵や彫刻のことだ。アメリカ大陸の研究者にとって，ペトログリフはヨーロッパ人が到着する前に住んでいたネイティブアメリカンについての重要な情報源になっている。最も有名なペトログリフのいくつかは，コロラド州のキャッスル・ロック・プエブロにあるものだ。これらの描写は，その地域に典型的なスタイルで描かれているのではなく，何百キロも離れた別の集落で一般的だった方法で描かれている。また，人間の争いの絵もある。このことは，この２つの集落の間に接触，そしておそらく戦闘があったことを示唆している。

その彫刻についてもうひとつ興味深いのは，それらの光の使い方である。一年のうちで日が最も長い日と最も短い日に，この彫刻は光と影の特定のパターンを作り出す。このことから，研究者たちは，この彫刻は一種の太陽暦として使われていたのではないかと考えている。

No.23 正解 2

質問の訳 キャッスル・ロック・プエブロのペトログリフについてわかることの１つは何か。

選択肢の訳 **1** 典型的なものよりも数が多い。 **2** 遠くの地域のものと似ている。 **3** その地域で最も大きい。 **4** ヨーロッパ人の描写が含まれている。

解説 キャッスル・ロック・プエブロのペトログリフについては，第１段落第３文以降で書かれており，第１段落第４文では「これらの描写（＝キャッスル・ロック・プエブロのペトログリフ）は～何百キロも離れた別の集落で一般的だった方法で描かれている」(These images were ～, but (drawn) in a way that was common in another settlement hundreds of kilometers away.）と述べられている。よって，another settlement hundreds of kilometers awayを**a distant area**と言い換えた**2**が正解。

No.24 正解 1

質問の訳 研究者たちは，キャッスル・ロック・プエブロのペトログリフがどのように使われていたと考えているか。

選択肢の訳 **1** 一年のうちのある時期を示すため。 **2** 敵に，近づかないように警告するため。 **3** 他の集落への道を示すため。 **4** 光源を供給するため。

解説 第２段落第２，３文で「一年のうちで日が最も長い日と最も短い日（＝一年のうちのある時期）に，この彫刻は光と影の特定のパターンを作り出す」，「研究者たちは，この彫刻は一種の太陽暦として使われていたのではないかと考えている」と述べられている。よって，On the longest and shortest days of the year ～ create specific patterns of light and shadowやa type of solar calendarを，**indicate certain times of the year**と言い換えた**1**が正解。

Part 3 一次試験・リスニング

(問題編pp.174～175)

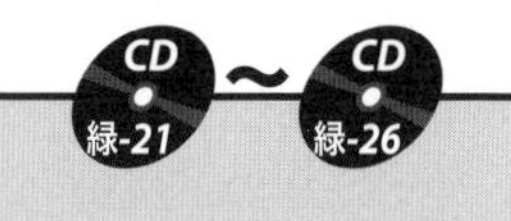

指示文の訳 それでは最後に，Part 3の指示を行います。このパートでは(G)から(K)までの5つの文章が放送されます。英文は実生活における状況を述べたもので，効果音を含むものもあります。それぞれの文章には，No. 25からNo. 29まで，質問が1問ずつ用意されています。それぞれの文章が流れる前に，問題冊子に書かれている状況の説明と質問を読む時間が10秒あります。文章を聞いた後に，最も適切な答えを選んで解答用紙にマークする時間が10秒あります。文章は1度しか読まれません。それでは始めます。

No. 25 正解 3

放送文 *(G)* You have 10 seconds to read the situation and Question No. 25.

Hi, dear. I'm sorry, I was in a rush this morning and wasn't able to do a few things. Could you take care of them? The living room is a mess. Miranda's toys are all over the place, so could you put them away? Also, Toby's new bird food arrived this morning. I know we usually store it in that box near the kitchen shelves, but when the package was delivered, I left it at the front door. Sorry. It should still be sitting there. And can you change one of the light bulbs in the garage? When I got home last night, I saw that one was flickering.

Now mark your answer on your answer sheet.

訳 *(G)* 状況と質問25を読む時間が10秒あります。

ああ，あなた。ごめんなさい。今朝は急いでいて，いくつかのことができなかったの。お願いできるかしら？ リビングが散らかってるの。ミランダのおもちゃがあちこちにあるから，片付けてくれる？ あと，トビーの新しい鳥の餌が今朝届いたの。いつもは台所の棚の近くにある箱に入れてあるんだけど，荷物が届いたとき，玄関に置いてきちゃったのよ。ごめんね。まだそこに置いてあるはずなの。それと，車庫の電球を一つ替えてくれる？ 昨夜帰宅したとき，1つだけチカチカしていたわ。

それでは，解答用紙に答えをマークしなさい。

状況の訳 あなたはオウムのトビーに餌をやりたいが，ペットフードが見つからない。携帯電話を見て，妻からの留守電が入っているのを知る。

質問の訳 トビーの餌を見つけるのに，どこに行けばよいか。

選択肢の訳 **1** 台所へ。 **2** リビングルームへ。 **3** 玄関へ。 **4** 車庫へ。

解説 Situationからわかるのは，①「あなた」はトビーに餌をやりたいが，ペットフードが見つからないことと，②携帯電話に妻からの留守電が入っていること。「あなた」の妻は留守電の第7文で，トビーの餌について，いつもは台所の棚の近くにある箱に入れておくが，今朝は，荷物（＝トビーの新しい鳥の餌）が届いたとき「玄関に置いてきちゃったのよ」(I left it at the front door) と述べ，さらに第9文で「(トビーの新しい鳥の餌は) まだそこ（＝玄関）に置いてあるはずなの」と言っている。したがって，トビーの新しい餌は今も玄関にあるはずなので，**3**が正解。

No. 26 正解 1

放送文 *(H)* You have 10 seconds to read the situation and Question No. 26.

Greta Bakken has written in various genres over her long career. I would recommend four books to a first-time reader. First, *The Moon in Budapest* is considered to be a masterpiece of romance, and it has the biggest fan base. *Along That Tree-Lined Road* is a beautifully crafted fantasy novel with a touch of mystery. If you're a travel fan, I recommend you try *Mixed Metaphors*. It's a travel journal documenting her trip to Siberia, with a number of stunning photographs she snapped along the way. Lastly, *Trishaws* is her latest book, and it has been getting great reviews from science fiction enthusiasts.

Now mark your answer on your answer sheet.

訳 *(H)* 状況と質問26を読む時間が10秒あります。

グレタ・バッケンは長いキャリアの中で様々なジャンルの作品を書いてきました。初めてお読みになる方には4冊の本をお勧めしたいです。まず，『ブダペストの月』はロマンスの傑作と言われ，最も多くのファンがいます。『あの並木道で』は，ミステリータッチの美しいファンタジー小説です。もし旅行がお好きなら，『ミックストゥ・メタファー』をお読みになることをお勧めします。シベリアへの旅を記録した旅行記で，道中で撮った見事な写真が多数掲載されています。最後に，『トライショウズ』は彼女の最新作で，熱心なSFファンから絶賛されています。

それでは，解答用紙に答えをマークしなさい。

状況の訳 あなたは作家のグレタ・バッケンの書いた本を読みたいと思っている。あなたは彼女の最も人気のある本を読みたい。本屋の店員があなたに次のように言う。

質問の訳 あなたはどの本を買うべきか。

選択肢の訳 **1** 『ブダペストの月』。 **2** 『あの並木道で』。 **3** 『ミックストゥ・メタファー』。 **4** 『トライショウズ』。

解説 Situationからわかるのは，①「あなた」はグレタ・バッケンの本を読みたいことと，②「あなた」が読みたいのは彼女の最も人気のある本だということ。本屋の店員は4冊勧めているが，第3文で「『ブダペストの月』はロマンスの傑作と言われ，最も多くのファンがいます」（*The Moon in Budapest* is considered to be a masterpiece of romance, and it has the biggest fan base）と述べている。最も多くのファンがいる本である『ブダペストの月』が，グレタ・バッケンの最も人気のある本なので，**1**が正解。Situationのher most popular bookが**has the biggest fan base**と言い換えられていることに注意。

No. 27 正解 1

放送文 *(I)* You have 10 seconds to read the situation and Question No. 27.

The company has decided to outsource the personnel department's services to ABC Resource Systems. There will be two main changes. First, we'll be using a new website to handle all scheduling, requests for time off, and complaints. More importantly, time-off requests will now need to be submitted two weeks in advance. These changes will apply at the end of next month, so

please submit requests on the website at that time. Until then, please direct all personnel issues to the manager of your department. Thank you for your cooperation.

Now mark your answer on your answer sheet.

訳 *(I)* 状況と質問27を読む時間が10秒あります。

当社は，人事部の業務をABCリソース・システムズ社にアウトソーシングすることを決定しました。主な変更点は2つあります。まず，スケジュール管理，休暇申請，クレーム処理などは，すべて新しいウェブサイトを利用することになります。さらに重要なこととしては，休暇の申請は2週間前に提出する必要があることです。この変更は来月末に適用されますので，その時点でウェブサイトから申請してください。それまでは，人事に関することはすべて所属部署のマネージャーに直接お伝えください。皆様のご協力をお願いいたします。

それでは，解答用紙に答えをマークしなさい。

状況の訳 あなたの会社の社長が，事務手続きの変更について発表しています。あなたは来週，休暇を取りたいと考えています。

質問の訳 あなたは何をすべきか。

選択肢の訳 **1** マネージャーに相談する。 **2** 新しいウェブサイトから申請する。
3 自分の部署のメンバーにメールする。 **4** ABCリソース・システムズに連絡する。

解説 Situationからわかるのは，①「あなた」の会社で事務手続きの変更についての発表がなされていることと，②「あなた」は来週，休暇を取りたいということ。社長は発表の第4文で「休暇の申請は2週間前に提出する必要がある」と述べている。しかし，続く第5文では「この変更は来月末に適用されます」と述べ，第6文で「それまで（＝来月末より前）は，人事に関することはすべて所属部署のマネージャーに直接お伝えください」(Until then, please direct all personnel issues to the manager of your department.）と述べている。したがって，現在，「あなた」が休暇を申請する場合は，所属部署のマネージャーに直接伝えることとなる。よって，direct ～ to the manager of your departmentをspeak to your managerと言い換えた**1**が正解。

No. 28 正解 **4**

放送文 *(J)* You have 10 seconds to read the situation and Question No. 28.

The course website is now accessible. On the left side, you'll see the menu. At the top of the menu, there's a news section where I'll post event reminders and assignment due dates. I've already posted a notification about a guest lecture that you can attend for additional credit. You can click on the icon to reserve a seat. Below the news section, there's a link to a page where you can check on your weekly reading assignments. Finally, in the resources section, I put some links that might help you when working on your final research project.

Now mark your answer on your answer sheet.

訳 *(J)* 状況と質問28を読む時間が10秒あります。

講座のウェブサイトにアクセスできるようになりました。左側には，メニューが表示されます。メニューの一番上にはニュース欄があり，イベントのお知らせや課題の提出期限を掲載します。すでに，追加単位取得のために参加できる客員の講義のお知らせを掲載しました。アイコンをクリックして，席を予約することができます。ニュース欄の下には，毎週のリーディング課題を確認できるページへのリンクがあります。最後に，リソースセクションに，最終研究プロジェクトに取り組む際に役立ちそうなリンクをいくつか載せてあります。

それでは，解答用紙に答えをマークしなさい。

状況の訳 教授がクラスのみんなに講座のウェブサイトを見せている。あなたは成績を上げるために追加単位を取得したいと思っている。

質問の訳 あなたは何をすべきか。

選択肢の訳 **1** ウェブサイトから追加の研究論文を提出する。 **2** 追加の読書課題を完了する。 **3** 授業のためのオンライン資料を作成する。 **4** ニュース欄から受講を申し込む。

解説 Situationからわかるのは，①教授が講座のウェブサイトを見せていることと，②「あなた」は追加単位を取得したいということ。第3文で，教授はメニューの一番上にはニュース欄があると述べ，続く第4文で「(ニュース欄に) すでに，追加単位取得のために参加できる客員の講義のお知らせを掲載しました」と述べている。「あなた」は追加単位を取得したいので，この客員の講義を受講すべきであり，受講の申し込みについて教授は，第5文で「(ニュース欄の) アイコンをクリックして，(講義の) 席を予約することができます」(You can click on the icon to reserve a seat.) と述べているので，ニュース欄から客員の講義の受講を申し込めることがわかる。よって，click on the iconを**via the news section**と，reserve a seatを**sign up for a lecture**と言い換えた**4**が正解。

No. 29 正解 **4**

放送文 *(K)* You have 10 seconds to read the situation and Question No. 29.

Hi, this is Bill. As you know, today's the deadline for your column. How is it coming along? If you've already finished it, please send the column directly to my office e-mail address. If you're likely to finish it by tomorrow morning, send the file to Paula. I'll be out all day tomorrow. However, if you're not likely to make it by tomorrow morning, could you call me on my office phone tonight? I'll be here until eight. Otherwise, you can reach me on my smartphone after eight. If necessary, I can give you another few days to finish it. Thanks.

Now mark your answer on your answer sheet.

訳 *(K)* 状況と質問29を読む時間が10秒あります。

やあ，ビルです。ご存知のように，今日はあなたのコラムの締め切り日です。どうなっていますか。もう完成しているなら，コラムを直接私のオフィスのメールアドレスに送ってください。明日の朝までに完成しそうな場合は，ポーラにファイルを送ってください。私は明日は一日中外出しています。でも，明日の朝までに間に合いそうになかったら，今夜，私のオフィスの電話に電話してくれませんか。8時までここにいます。そうでなければ，8時以降に私のスマートフォンに連絡を取ってくれてもいいです。必要であれば，終わらせるためのあと数日の猶予をあげることもできます。よろしく。

それでは，解答用紙に答えをマークしなさい。

状況の訳 あなたは，ある新聞社の記者です。あなたは午後8時半に帰宅し，編集者からの次のような留守電を聞きます。あなたはコラムを書き上げるのに，あと2日必要です。

質問の訳 あなたは何をすべきか。

選択肢の訳 **1** ファイルをビルに送る。 **2** ファイルをポーラに送る。 **3** ビルのオフィスに電話をする。 **4** ビルのスマートフォンに電話をする。

解説 Situationからわかるのは，①「あなた」は午後8時半以降に，編集者からの留守電を聞いていることと，②「あなた」はコラムをまだ書き上げておらず，書き上げるのにあと2日必要だということ。「あなた」は明日の朝までには間に合わないが，この点について，編集者のビルは第7，8文で「明日の朝までに間に合いそうになかったら，今夜，私のオフィスの電話に電話してくれませんか。8時までここにいます」と述べ，続く第9文で「そうでなければ，8時以降に私のスマートフォンに連絡を取ってくれてもいいです」(Otherwise, you can reach me on my smartphone after eight.) と言っている。「あなた」がこの留守電を聞いたのは午後8時半以降なので，あなたがすべきことは，ビルのスマートフォンに連絡すること。よって，reach me on my smartphoneをcall Bill on his smartphoneと言い換えた**4**が正解。

カードA 二次試験・面接

(問題編pp.176～177)

指示文の訳 1分間，準備する時間があります。

これは，自分の町の力になりたいと思った町長についての話です。

ストーリーのナレーションを行うのに与えられる時間は2分間です。

ストーリーは以下の文で始めてください。

ある日，町長は会議を行っていました。

ナレーションの解答例 **One day, a mayor was having a meeting.** The meeting was about the decreasing number of tourists. This was a problem, and the mayor asked if her staff members had any ideas. They all looked worried. That weekend, the mayor was drinking coffee and watching TV at home. The TV show was saying that camping was popular, and this gave the mayor an idea. Six months later, the mayor and one of her staff members were visiting the new ABC Town campsite. They were happy to see that there were a lot of campers using the campsite. A few months later, the mayor and the staff member were watching TV in her office. The staff member was shocked to see breaking news that a bear had entered the campsite because there was a lot of food garbage.

解答例の訳 **ある日，町長は会議を行っていました。**会議は観光客数の減少についてのものでした。これは問題であり，町長は，何かアイデアがあるか職員たちに尋ねました。彼らは皆，懸念を抱いている様子でした。その週末，町長は自宅でコーヒーを飲みながらテレビを見ていました。テレビ番組はキャンプが人気であると伝えており，これにより町長はアイデアが浮かびました。6カ月後，町長と職員の一人は，新設されたABC町営キャンプ場を訪れていました。そのキャンプ場を使ってキャンプをする人がたくさんいるのを目にし，彼らは喜ばしく思いました。数カ月後，町長とその職員は彼女のオフィスでテレビを見ていました。職員は，食べ物のごみがたくさんあったせいでクマがキャンプ場に侵入していたというニュース速報を見て，衝撃を受けていました。

解説 ナレーションは，4コマのイラストの進行に沿ってまとめていく。2～4コマ目の左上方にある時間の経過を表す語句は，各コマの最初で必ず使うこと。吹き出し内のせりふはもちろん，ホワイトボード，テレビなどに書かれた文字情報やイラスト内の情報も適切な形でストーリーに取り入れること。動詞の時制は，過去形および過去進行形を基本に，時間の経過がわかるように描写する。

①1コマ目：町長が職員らと会議を行っている場面。町長がAny ideas?「何かアイデアはありますか」と尋ねている様子を，解答例ではthe mayor asked if her staff members had any ideasとask if ～「～かどうか尋ねる」の形で表現している。町長を含め，イラスト内の人物たちが困った表情を浮かべている点もナレーションに盛り込むと効果的。

②2コマ目：That weekendで始める。町長が自宅でテレビを見ている場面。解答例では，テレビにあるCamping is popular now「今，キャンプが流行している」という文字情報を，間接話法を用いて盛り込んでいる。また，町長の吹き出しに豆電球が描かれていることから，町長は今見ているテレビをきっかけに何かしらの着想を得たことがわかるので，その点もしっかりと盛り込む。なお，テレビ番組内でレポーターと思しき女性が男性にインタビューしている様子について描写しても良い。

③3コマ目：Six months laterで始める。町長と職員がABC Town Campsite「ABC町営キャンプ場」を訪れている場面。直前までのコマの流れから，このキャンプ場は町長がひらめいたアイデアを基に新しく作られたものだと推測できる。また，キャンプ場が人々で賑わっている様子，2人が頷いている様子から，町に観光客を取り込むためのこのアイデアは目下，うまくいっているのだとわかる。

④4コマ目：A few months laterで始める。町長と職員がテレビを見ている場面。ニュース番組には3コマ目にあるキャンプ場が映っているが，そこには，1匹のクマと地面に散乱している食べ物と思しきものも映っている。これは，ごみのせいで野生のクマがキャンプ場に侵入してしまっている状況をとらえている映像だと判断できるだろう。職員がこのニュースを見て驚いている点もナレーションに含めると良い。

質問の訳 No. 1　4番目の絵を見てください。あなたがその町長なら，どのようなことを考えているでしょうか。
では～さん（受験者の氏名），カードを裏返して置いてください。
No. 2　人々は自然について学ぶためにもっと屋外で時間を過ごすべきだと思いますか。
No. 3　企業は従業員にもっと多くの休暇日数を付与すべきですか。
No. 4　政府は絶滅の危機に瀕した動物を保護するためにもっと多くのことをすべきですか。

No. 1 **解答例** **I'd be thinking that I should've planned the campsite more carefully. It was a good way to increase the number of tourists who come to our town, but I should've asked experts for advice about how to avoid problems with wildlife.**

解答例の訳 もっと入念にキャンプ場を計画すべきだったと私は思っているでしょう。

それは，私たちの町を訪れてくれる観光客の数を増やすのに効果的な方法でしたが，私は，野生動物に関する問題を回避する方法について専門家に助言を求めるべきでした。

解説 解答例では，質問の仮定法過去形に合わせて，間接話法で**I'd be thinking that ～.**の形で答えている。また，1文目では，後悔を表す〈should've＋過去分詞〉を用いて，キャンプ場の計画をもっとしっかり行うべきだったと悔やんでいる。あるいは，解答例と同じ路線でありながらもややポジティブな観点で，2文目をBut our attempt to increase the number of tourists itself was a success, so this is a chance to learn from our failures, and we only have to come up with an effective strategy for the disposal of garbage at the campsite.「しかし，観光客の数を増やすという私たちの試み自体は成功だったので，これは失敗から学ぶチャンスであり，キャンプ場のごみ処分の効果的な戦略を思いつきさえすれば良いのです」などと述べても良いだろう。

No. 2 **解答例** **Yes. These days, people spend a lot of time inside using computers and tablets. People should learn about the natural world, and personal experiences can be more effective for learning than the Internet or books.**

解答例の訳 はい。近頃，人々はコンピュータやタブレットを使用しながら屋内でたくさんの時間を過ごしています。人々は自然界について学ぶべきですし，個人的な体験はインターネットや書物よりも学習にはより効果的であり得ます。

解説 解答例では，Yesの立場から，人が屋内で過ごすことが多いという昨今の傾向を挙げつつ，人は自然界について学ぶためにもっと屋外で時間を過ごすべきだと主張している。あるいは，YesとNoを折衷した立場から，It depends. Certainly, spending a lot of time indoors could lead people away from nature, but people can also learn precious information about nature online these days. So, I believe trying to keep the balance between being indoors and outdoors leads to a better understanding about nature.「状況によります。確かに，屋内で多くの時間を過ごすことは人々を自然から遠ざけてしまう可能性はありますが，昨今はオンライン上で自然についての貴重な情報を学ぶこともできます。そのため，私は，屋内にいることと屋外にいることのバランスを保とうと努めることが，自然についてのより良い理解につながると思います」などとしても良いだろう。

No. 3 **解答例** **Yes, I think so. These days, many people damage their health by working too hard, so it's important for people to relax and take care of themselves. By doing so, their performance at work will naturally improve, too.**

解答例の訳 はい，そう思います。近頃，熱心に働きすぎることで健康を損なっている人々がたくさんいるので，人々にとってはリラックスして体を大切にすることは重要です。そうすることで，彼らの仕事での業績も当然の帰結として向上するでしょう。

解説 解答例では，Yesの立場から，従業員にもっと多くの休暇日数を付与することで得られるメリットを軸に，企業が彼らにもっと多くの休暇日数を与えるべきだと述べている。もしくは，Noの立場から，I don't think so. Of course, there are some companies which do not give their employees enough vacation days, and this is a serious problem to be solved. However, I think some companies are sensible, and they already provide workers enough vacation days, so we should not treat those two types of companies equally.「そうは思いません。もちろん，従業員に十分な休暇日数を与えていない企業もあり，これは解決されるべき深刻な問題です。しかし，中には思慮分別のある企業もあり，彼らはすでに従業員に十分な休暇日数を与えているので，私たちはその２種類の企業を同列に語るべきではありません」などと答えても良いだろう。

No. 4 **解答例 I don't think so. Unfortunately, the government has more important responsibilities. Taking care of people's problems should be the priority. Besides, the government already spends a lot of money protecting endangered animals.**

解答例の訳 そうは思いません。残念ながら，政府にはもっと重要な責務があります。国民が抱えている問題を処理することが優先事項であるべきです。加えて，政府はすでに，絶滅の危機に瀕している動物の保護に多額の資金を費やしています。

解説 解答例では，Noの立場から，政府は国民の問題解決を優先するべきであることに加え，絶滅の危機に瀕している動物の保護にはすでに多額の資金を充てていると主張している。あるいは，Yesの立場から，Yes. I think the government should put more efforts into protecting various animal species from going extinct. The fact that many animals are currently endangered means such efforts are still not enough, in my opinion.「はい。政府はさまざまな動物種が絶滅してしまうのを防ぐことにもっと力を注ぐべきです。現在，多くの動物が絶滅の危機に瀕しているという事実は，そのような努力がいまだ十分なものではないということを物語っていると思います」などとしても良いだろう。

カードB 二次試験・面接

(問題編pp.178～179)

指示文の訳 1分間，準備する時間があります。
これは，自分のキャリアをアップさせたいと思った女性についての話です。
ストーリーのナレーションを行うのに与えられる時間は２分間です。
ストーリーは以下の文で始めてください。
ある日，女性はオフィスで，自分の会社の最高経営責任者と話をしていました。

ナレーションの解答例 **One day, a woman was talking with her company's CEO in the office.** He was telling her that she was promoted to manager, and she looked happy to hear that. That evening, she was at home with her husband and baby. She showed her husband that she had gotten a promotion. He said that he could pick up their baby from the day care center instead. A month later, the woman was working in her new position as manager. She got a message from her husband at 7 p.m. saying that he had picked up their baby from day care, and she was glad that she could continue working. A few days later, she was working on a project, and her husband called her at seven. He seemed very busy, and he told her that he could not pick up the baby that day.

訳 **ある日，女性はオフィスで，自分の会社の最高経営責任者と話をしていました。**彼は彼女に，彼女がマネージャーに昇進すると伝えており，彼女はそれを聞いてうれしそうでした。その晩，彼女は夫と赤ん坊と一緒に自宅にいました。彼女は夫に，自分が昇進を受けたことを教えました。彼は，自分が彼女の代わりに保育所に赤ん坊を迎えに行くことができると言いました。１カ月後，女性はマネージャーとしての新しい職位で働いていました。彼女は午後７時に夫からメッセージを受信し，それには彼が保育所に赤ん坊を迎えに行ったと書かれており，彼女は自分が働き続けられることを喜ばしく思いました。数日後，彼女はあるプロジェクトに取り組んでおり，７時に夫が彼女に電話しました。彼は多忙な様子であり，彼女に，自分はその日に赤ん坊を迎えに行くことができないと伝えました。

解説 ナレーションは，４コマのイラストの進行に沿ってまとめていく。２～４コマ目の左上方にある時間の経過を表す語句は，各コマの描写の冒頭部分で必ず使うこと。また，吹き出し内のせりふは，間接話法または直接話法を使ってストーリーに盛り込むが，間接話法を使う場合，主語や（助）動詞などを適切な形に変える点に注意。職位を表すプレート，用紙，看板などに書かれた文字情報なども適切な形でストーリーに取り入れる。動詞の時制は，過去形および過去進行形を基本に，時間の経過がわかるように描写すること。

①１コマ目：女性がCEO「最高経営責任者」と話をしている場面。CEOの吹き出し内にYou're promoted to manager.「あなたはマネージャーに昇進です」とあることから，CEOが女性に昇進を伝えている状況だとわかる。ナレーションには女性のうれしそうな表情も盛り込む。

②２コマ目：That eveningで始める。女性が夫と赤ん坊と在宅している場面。女性が夫にPROMOTION「昇進」と書かれた紙を見せており，これを受けて，夫はI can pick up our baby instead.「自分が（女性の）代わりに赤ん坊を迎えに行くことができる」と申し出ているのだと考えられる。なお，解答例ではHe said that ～.と，間接話法を用いてこの夫の発言を表現している。

③３コマ目：A month laterで始める。女性がマネージャーとして働いている場面。女性の持っているコンピュータ機器の吹き出し内に，Day Care「保育所」の看板のある建物と，赤ん坊を抱きかかえている夫が描かれている。このイラストから，夫は保育所に赤ん坊を迎えに行き，そのことを女性にメッセージなどで伝えているのだと考えられる。背景には７時を指している時計があるので，これもナレーションに盛り込むとより効果的な描写になる。

④４コマ目：A few days laterで始める。女性と夫が電話をしている場面。夫は忙しそうな様子であり，I can't pick her up today.「私は今日，彼女を迎えに行くことができない」と話している。また，女性の傍にABC PROJECT「ABCプロジェクト」と書かれた用紙が積み上がっていることから，女性はプロジェクトに携わっているのだと推測可能。なお，ナレーションをする際には，３コマ目同様，時刻が７時であることを盛り込むと良い。

質問の訳 No. 1　４番目の絵を見てください。あなたがその女性なら，どのようなことを考えているでしょうか。
では～さん（受験者の氏名），カードを裏返して置いてください。
No. 2　近頃，親は子どもに対して過保護だと思いますか。
No. 3　現代生活のめまぐるしさは人々に否定的な影響を及ぼしますか。
No. 4　日本の出生率は今後，低下しなくなると思いますか。

No. 1　解答例　I'd be thinking, "Neither of us can go to pick up our baby from the day care center. The same problem is probably going to happen again. Maybe I shouldn't have accepted the promotion to manager."

解答例の訳　「私たちのうちどちらも，保育所に赤ん坊を迎えに行くことができない。同様の問題はおそらく，再び発生することだろう。私はマネージャーへの昇進を受け入れるべきではなかったのかもしれない」と私は思っているでしょう。

解説　解答例では，質問の仮定法過去形に合わせて，直接話法で**I'd be thinking, "～."**のように始めている。解答例では，保育所に赤ん坊を迎えに行くことができないという問題が今後も発生するだろうと推測し，後悔を表す〈shouldn't have＋過去分詞〉を用いて，昇進を受け入れるべきではなかったかもしれないと悔やんでいる。あるいは，別の観点から，３文目を，It is absolutely necessary for either of us to pick up our baby, so both of us should consult with our coworkers about the matter to make sure it happens.「私たちのうちどちらかが赤ん坊を迎えに行くことは絶対に必要なので，これを必ず実現するために，私たちは二人ともこの件について同僚と相談すべきだ」などとしても良いだろう。

No. 2　解答例　I think so. Parents these days try to control every part of their children's lives, so children never get a chance to make their own decisions. As a result, the younger generation is becoming less independent.

解答例の訳　そう思います。近頃の親は子どもの人生のあらゆる側面を管理しようとしているので，子どもたちは自分で決断を下す機会をまったく持ちません。その結果，若い世代は自主的でなくなってきています。

解説　解答例では，Yesの立場から，近頃の親は子どもに対して過保護だと思う点，並びにその結果子どもの自主性が損なわれているという点を述べている。あるいは，Noの立場で，I don't think so. Although some parents are too protective of their children, others are not. It goes without saying that the former should change their way of educating their children so they can have an independent mind, but for example, I have known many parents who do not interfere with their children's lives too much, putting an emphasis on their independence.「そうは思いません。子どもに対して過保護な親もいますが，そうでない親もいます。子どもが自主的な精神を持てるよう，前者のグループは子どもの教育の仕方を改めるべきなのは言うまでもありませんが，例えば，私は，子どもの自主性を重要視して彼らの生活にあまり干渉しない親もたくさん知っています」などと，自分の身の回りにいる人物を引き合いに出しながら答えても良いだろう。

No. 3 **解答例** **Yes. Especially in big cities, it seems like people never have time to relax. I think that the biggest reason is the work culture. This definitely has a negative effect on people's mental and physical health.**

解答例の訳 はい。とりわけ大都会では，人々はリラックスする時間をまったく持たないように思われます。最大の理由は仕事の文化にあると私は思います。これは確実に，人の心身の健康に悪影響を及ぼしています。

解説 解答例では，Yesの立場から，人々がくつろぐ時間を持てない最大の理由は仕事の文化にあると私見を述べ，これが心身の健康に悪影響を及ぼすと主張している。あるいは，Noの立場から，No. In my humble opinion, the fast pace of modern society itself is neither good nor bad. It depends on each person whether they can lead a good life, adapting to it. Therefore, developing skills to deal with it is important in modern times, I guess.「いいえ。私見では，現代社会のあわただしさそれ自体は良くも悪くもありません。自分がそれに適応して良い人生を送ることができるかどうかは一人一人次第です。そのため，それに対処するスキルを育むことが現代では重要なことだと思います」などとしても良いだろう。

No. 4 **解答例** **I think so. The government realizes the decreasing birth rate is a problem, and it's spending money to encourage people to have more children. Also, companies provide more childcare leave these days.**

解答例の訳 そう思います。政府は出生率の低下が問題であるということに思い至り，もっと子どもをつくることを人々に奨励するためにお金を費やしています。また，近頃，企業はより多くの育児休暇を提供しています。

解説 解答例では，Yesの立場から，政府や企業の努力ゆえに，日本の出生率が今後低下しなくなると思うと述べている。あるいは，Noの立場から，I don't think so. Despite the governments' efforts to stop the decreasing birth rate, it seems things have not improved yet. It is highly likely that this trend will persist unless something miraculous happens.「そうは思いません。出生率の低下を止めようとする政府の試みにもかかわらず，状況はまだ改善していないように思われます。何か奇跡的なことでも起こらない限り，この傾向が続く可能性は非常に高いです」などでも良いだろう。

2021年度 第3回

筆記 解答欄

問題番号		1	2	3	4
1	(1)	①	❷	③	④
	(2)	①	❷	③	④
	(3)	①	②	❸	④
	(4)	①	❷	③	④
	(5)	①	❷	③	④
	(6)	①	❷	③	④
	(7)	①	②	❸	④
	(8)	❶	②	③	④
	(9)	①	❷	③	④
	(10)	①	②	③	❹
	(11)	❶	②	③	④
	(12)	❶	②	③	④
	(13)	①	②	❸	④
	(14)	①	②	❸	④
	(15)	①	②	③	❹
	(16)	①	②	③	❹
	(17)	①	②	❸	④
	(18)	①	❷	③	④
	(19)	❶	②	③	④
	(20)	①	②	③	❹
	(21)	❶	②	③	④
	(22)	❶	②	③	④
	(23)	①	❷	③	④
	(24)	❶	②	③	④
	(25)	①	❷	③	④

問題番号		1	2	3	4
2	(26)	①	❷	③	④
	(27)	①	②	③	❹
	(28)	❶	②	③	④
	(29)	①	②	❸	④
	(30)	❶	②	③	④
	(31)	①	②	❸	④

問題番号		1	2	3	4
3	(32)	❶	②	③	④
	(33)	①	❷	③	④
	(34)	①	❷	③	④
	(35)	①	②	③	❹
	(36)	①	❷	③	④
	(37)	❶	②	③	④
	(38)	①	②	❸	④
	(39)	①	②	③	❹
	(40)	❶	②	③	④
	(41)	①	❷	③	④

4の解答例はp.238をご覧ください。

リスニング 解答欄

問題番号			1	2	3	4
Part 1		No.1	①	②	③	❹
		No.2	❶	②	③	④
		No.3	❶	②	③	④
		No.4	❶	②	③	④
		No.5	①	②	❸	④
		No.6	❶	②	③	④
		No.7	①	②	❸	④
		No.8	①	②	③	❹
		No.9	❶	②	③	④
		No.10	①	❷	③	④
		No.11	❶	②	③	④
		No.12	①	②	③	❹
Part 2	A	No.13	①	②	❸	④
		No.14	❶	②	③	④
	B	No.15	❶	②	③	④
		No.16	①	②	③	❹
	C	No.17	❶	②	③	④
		No.18	①	❷	③	④
	D	No.19	①	❷	③	④
		No.20	❶	②	③	④
	E	No.21	①	②	❸	④
		No.22	①	②	❸	④
	F	No.23	①	❷	③	④
		No.24	❶	②	③	④
Part 3	G	No.25	①	②	❸	④
	H	No.26	①	②	③	❹
	I	No.27	❶	②	③	④
	J	No.28	①	②	③	❹
	K	No.29	①	❷	③	④

1 一次試験・筆記
(問題編pp.182〜185)

指示文の訳 各英文を完成させるのに最も適切な単語または語句を4つの選択肢の中から選び，その番号を解答用紙の所定欄にマークしなさい。

(1) 正解 2

訳 ロベルトは真の愛国者だったので，自国が隣国から攻撃されたとき，直ちに軍隊に加わることを志願した。

解説 空所にはロベルトがどのような人物だったかを表す名詞が入る。文後半のhe immediately volunteered to join the army when his country was attacked by its neighbor「自国が隣国から攻撃されたとき，直ちに軍隊に加わることを志願した」から，ロベルトは愛国心が強かったことがわかる。したがって，**2のpatriot**「愛国者」が正解。villain「悪役」，spectator「観客」，beggar「乞食」。

(2) 正解 2

訳 「では休憩しましょう」と議長は言った。「次の協議事項を話し合うために，会議はおよそ15分後に再開します。」

解説 第1文のLet's take a break now「では休憩しましょう」と空所直後のthe meetingから，会議はいったん中断されることがわかる。第2文の後半にto talk about the next item on the agenda「次の協議事項を話し合うために」とあるので，休憩後に会議が再び行われるとわかる。したがって，**2のresume**「〜を再開する」を入れると状況に合う。parody「〜をもじる」，impede「〜を遅らせる」，erect「〜を建てる」。

(3) 正解 3

訳 ダンは初めてスキーをしてみたときは難しいと思ったが，その後スキー旅行に行くたびに上達した。今では彼はスキーの達人だ。

解説 第2文のNow he (＝Dan) is an expert skier.「今では彼はスキーの達人だ」から，最初は難しいと思ったが，徐々に上達したことがわかる。**3のsubsequent**「その後の」を入れるとon each subsequent ski trip「その後スキー旅行に行くたびに」となり，文脈に合う。sufficient「十分な」，arrogant「傲慢な」，prominent「卓越した」。

(4) 正解 2

訳 その教授はその分野の専門家だが，奇抜な行動は同僚にとっては困惑の種である。「彼はいつも奇妙なことをやっているか言っている」と同僚の1人は言った。

解説 空所直前にhis，直後にbehavior「行動」とあるので，空所には教授がどのような行動をとるのかを表す語が入る。第2文の同僚の発言He's always doing or saying strange things「彼はいつも奇妙なことをやっているか言っている」から，**2のeccentric**「奇抜な」が適切。secular「非宗教的な」，vigilant「油断のない」，apparent「明らかな」。

※2024年度第1回から，試験形式の変更に伴い大問1の問題数は18問になります。

(5) 正解 2

訳 その八百屋は売っている野菜が有機栽培だと証明することができなかったので，エディーは野菜を買うのを断った。有機食品だけを食べることが彼の厳格な方針であった。

解説 第２文のIt was his strict policy to eat only organic foods.「有機食品だけを食べることが彼の厳格な方針であった」から，エディーは有機栽培かどうかわからない野菜は買いたくなかったと考えられる。したがって，**2のcertify**「～を証明する」を入れると，was unable to certify that ～「～だと証明することができなかった」となり，文脈に合う。diverge「分岐する」，evade「～を避ける」，glorify「～を賛美する」。

(6) 正解 2

訳 進路指導員として，ペレイラ先生は生徒たちが適職を見つける手助けを専門としている。彼女は，人は性格や技能に適した職業を持つべきだと考えている。

解説 第２文のpeople should have careers that fit their personality and skills「人は性格や技能に適した職業を持つべきだ」から，ペレイラ先生はそれぞれの生徒に合った職業が見つかるよう手助けをしているとわかる。したがって，careers that fit their personality and skills「性格や技能に適した職業」を１語で表す，**2のvocation**「適職」が正解。boredom「退屈」，insult「侮辱」，publicity「評判，広報」。

(7) 正解 3

訳 そのマラソンランナーはレース後にとても喉が渇いていたので，大きなスポーツドリンクをほんの数口で飲んでしまい，すぐにもう１本要求した。

解説 空所の前にshe drank a large sports drink「大きなスポーツドリンクを飲んだ」とあることから，空所には飲み物を飲む様子を表す語が入る。**gulp**で「ごくりと（ひと口）飲むこと」という意味を表すので，**3のgulps**を入れ，in just a few gulps「ほんの数口で」とすると状況に合う。herd「群れ」，lump「かたまり」，sack「袋」。

(8) 正解 1

訳 その眠っていた赤ちゃんは，兄の部屋から聞こえてくる騒々しい音楽に驚いた。彼女は泣きながら目覚め，再び寝付くまでに長い時間がかかった。

解説 第２文にShe（＝The sleeping baby）woke up crying「彼女は泣きながら目覚め」とあり，その原因が第１文にあるthe loud music coming from her brother's room「兄の部屋から聞こえてくる騒々しい音楽」だったと考えられる。**be startled**で「驚く」という意味を表すので，**1のstartled**が正解。improvise「～を即興で作る」，prolong「～を延長する」，tolerate「～を許容する」。

(9) 正解 2

訳 A：私はこのアパートにもう１年住んでいて，賃貸借契約がもうすぐ終わります。住み続けるか引っ越すかを決めないといけないんです。 B：家賃が同じなら，契約を更新して住み続けることをお勧めします。

解説 BがIf your rent will be the same「家賃が同じなら」と言っていることから，Aはアパートを借りて住んでいることがわかる。したがって，**2のlease**「賃貸借契約」

を入れるとthe lease is about to end「賃貸借契約がもうすぐ終わる」となり，状況に合う。token「しるし，代用硬貨」，vicinity「付近」，dialect「方言」。

(10) 正解 4

訳 その大統領候補は不況を現大統領のせいにした。彼は当選したら経済を改善すると約束した。

解説 空所直後にeconomy「経済」とあるので，空所には経済状況を表す形容詞が入る。また，第2文にhe（＝the presidential candidate）would improve it（＝economy）「経済を改善する」とあることから，現在の経済状況は良くないとわかる。したがって，**4のsluggish**「停滞した，不振な」が正解。bulky「かさばった」，functional「機能上の」，ethnic「民族の」。

(11) 正解 1

訳 A：アニー，どうしてた？ 去年，イタリアへの旅行は楽しかった？ B：楽しかったわよ，パブロ。実は，とても気に入ったので移住しようと考えてるくらいなの。息子が高校を卒業するまで待たないといけないでしょうけどね。

解説 B（＝Annie）の発言第2文I loved it（＝Italy）so muchから，アニーはイタリアのことがとても気に入ったことがわかる。空所直後にmoving there（＝to Italy）とあり，**contemplate *doing***で「～しようと考える」という意味を表すので，**1のcontemplating**が適切。emphasize「～を強調する」，vandalize「～を破壊する」，illustrate「～を説明する」。

(12) 正解 1

訳 すべての上院議員がその新法を支持すると言ったので，満場一致で可決されたのも驚きではなかった。

解説 文の前半にAll the senators said they supported the new law「すべての上院議員がその新法を支持すると言った」とあるので，全員が賛成に投票したと考えられる。したがって，**1のunanimously**「満場一致で」が正解。abnormally「異常に」，mockingly「あざけって」，savagely「獰猛（どうもう）に」。

(13) 正解 3

訳 A：マーカム教授の講義に行ったの？ B：行ったけど，すごくつまらなくて15分しか耐えられなかった。その後は抜け出してカフェに行ったよ。

解説 Bの発言第1文のit was so boring「すごくつまらなくて」や，第2文のI left and went to a café「抜け出してカフェに行ったよ」から，Bは講義を聴くのを途中でやめてしまったことがわかる。空所直後のitはProfessor Markham's lecture「マーカム教授の講義」を指すので，**3のendure**「～に耐える」を入れると状況に合う。execute「～を実行する」，discern「～を見分ける」，relay「～を中継する」。

(14) 正解 3

訳 寒い地域に建てられた家屋は冬の間，驚くほど居心地が良いことがある。暖炉，木製の家具，すてきなカーペットが家庭に暖かく，心地良い雰囲気を与えてくれる。

解説 第1文のHouses built in cold regions「寒い地域に建てられた家屋」の室内の様子を，第2文が具体的に説明している。この内容を1語で表す形容詞としては，**3のcozy**「居心地が良い」が適切。rigid「厳格な」，rash「軽率な」，clumsy「不器用な」。

(15) 正解 4

訳 息子が窓を割ったときウィルソンさんは怒ったが，だれか他の人がやったと言って彼女をだまそうとしたのでむしろがっかりした。

解説 空所の後にby telling her that someone else had done it「だれか他の人がやったと言って」とあり，息子が正直に言わず，母親にうそをついたことがわかる。したがって，**4のdeceive**「～をだます」が正解。pinpoint「～を正確に示す」，suppress「～を鎮圧する」，reroute「～を迂回させる」。

(16) 正解 4

訳 ワンダがひと月に3回目の遅刻をした後で，責任者は時間厳守の重要性について彼女と長い話し合いをした。

解説 文前半にWanda was late for the third time in one month「ワンダがひと月に3回目の遅刻をした」，空所直前にthe importance of ～「～の重要性」とあるので，責任者がワンダと話し合うべき重要な話題としては**4のpunctuality**「時間厳守」が適切。congestion「混雑」，drainage「排水」，optimism「楽観主義」。

(17) 正解 3

訳 その若い作家は慣習的な物語のルールには従わないことに決め，独自の作風で小説を書いた。

解説 文後半にwrote his novel in a unique style「独自の作風で小説を書いた」とあり，小説を書く際の従来の決まりごとには従わなかったとわかる。したがって，空所には**3のconventional**「慣習的な」を入れると状況に合う。vulnerable「脆弱な」，clueless「無知な」，phonetic「音声の」。

(18) 正解 2

訳 箱の中の商品は壊れやすかったので丁寧に梱包されていたが，それでもそのいくつかは配送中に破損した。

解説 文の後半にsome of them were still damaged when they were being delivered「それでもそのいくつかは配送中に破損した」とあるので，箱の中の商品は壊れやすいものだったとわかる。したがって，**2のfragile**「壊れやすい」が正解。coarse「きめの粗い」，immovable「動かせない」，glossy「光沢のある」。

(19) 正解 1

訳 女王は宮殿に顧問を呼び付けたが，到着に時間がかかって彼女は激怒した。

解説 文の後半にwhen he（＝her adviser）took a long time to arrive「到着に時間がかかって」とあるので，女王は顧問が来るのを待っていたとわかる。**1のsummoned**「呼び付けた」を入れると，空所の後のto the palace「宮殿に」につながり文意が通る。hammer「～をハンマーでたたく」，mingle「～を混ぜる」，tremble「～を震えさせる」。

(20) 正解　4

訳 将軍は自分の部隊が戦いに負けていることを知っていたので，退却するよう命じた。いったん彼らが無事に戦場から離れると，彼は敵を倒すための新たな作戦作りに取りかかった。

解説 第2文にOnce they were safely away from the battlefield「いったん彼らが無事に戦場から離れると」とあるので，将軍が部隊に命じたのは退却することだと考えられる。したがって，**4のretreat**「退却する」が正解。entrust「～を任せる」，discard「～を捨てる」，strangle「～を窒息させる」。

(21) 正解　1

訳 ビルは大学に通い始めてすぐに自分には高等数学を勉強する能力がないことに気づいたので，専攻を地理学に変えた。

解説 空所直後にto study advanced math「高等数学を勉強する」と空所内の名詞を修飾する語句が続いている。文の後半にhe changed his major to geography「専攻を地理学に変えた」とあり，高等数学の勉強をやめたことがわかるので，**1のcapacity**「能力」が文脈に合う。novelty「目新しさ」，bait「(釣りなどの) 餌」，chunk「大きな塊」。

(22) 正解　1

訳 その警察官は，金を盗んだことを認めさせるために容疑者を痛めつけようと相棒が提案したときに衝撃を受けた。このように暴力を使うことは許されていなかった。

解説 第2文にUsing violence in this way「このように暴力を使うこと」とあるので，同僚の警察官が提案したのは，暴力を使うことだったと考えられる。したがって，**1のrough up**「～を痛めつける」が正解。give out「～を発表する」，break up「～を解体する」，take over「～を引き継ぐ」。

(23) 正解　2

訳 ジュリアスは初めてバードウォッチングをした日に運良く珍しいワシを見た。けれども，もう1羽を見るまでにそれから20年が過ぎた。

解説 空所直前に20 years，直後にbefore ～とあるので，空所には年月の経過を表す語句が入る。**go by**で「(時が) 過ぎる」という意味を表すので，**2のwent by**が正解。hold out「持ちこたえる」，lay off「～を一時解雇する」，cut off「～を切り離す」。

(24) 正解　1

訳 A：週末の海辺への旅行は中止するつもり？　台風が近づいてきてるよ。　B：まだ行くことは除外していないよ。台風がどの方向に進むかによるね。

解説 Bの発言の第2文It depends on which direction the typhoon moves in.「台風がどの方向に進むかによるね」から，Bはまだ海辺への旅行に行ける可能性があると思っていることがわかる。空所の直前がhaven'tなので，**rule out**「～を除外する」の過去分詞形である**1のruled out**を入れ，We haven't ruled out going yet.「まだ行くことは除外していない」とすると，文脈に合う。stand down「辞任する」，drag into「～に引きずり込む」，scoop up「～をすくい上げる」。

(25) 正解 2

訳 ジュンは職を失っても何か頼れるだけのものがあるように，いつもできるだけたくさんお金を貯めていた。

解説 空所の後にif he lost his job「職を失っても」とあるので，ジュンがお金を貯めていた理由は，万一失業しても生活していけるようにするためだとわかる。したがって，空所には**2のfall back on**「〜に頼る」を入れ，something to fall back on「何か頼れるだけのもの」とする。look up to「〜を尊敬する」，come down with「(病気に) かかる」，do away with「〜を廃止する」。

2 一次試験・筆記

寄付者への返礼品（問題編pp.186〜187）
政府の政策と交通安全（問題編pp.188〜189）

指示文の訳 それぞれの文章を読んで，各空所に入れるのに最も適切な語句を４つの選択肢の中から選び，その番号を解答用紙の所定欄にマークしなさい。

寄付者への返礼品

Key to Reading 第１段落：導入（返礼品が寄付者に与える影響）→第２段落：本論①（返礼品の有無を知らせるタイミングと寄付額の関係）→第３段落：本論②（寄付者への返礼品の間接的なメリット）という３段落構成の説明文。それぞれの段落のトピックセンテンスを意識して論理的に読み進めていく。寄付者への返礼品について，現状，研究結果，考察を中心に，読み進めていこう。

訳

近年，慈善団体がお金を寄付した人々に対し，返礼品，すなわちコーヒーマグなどのささやかな贈り物を返すことが一般的になっている。多くの慈善団体がそれを提供しており，返礼品を受け取ると，人々はより多くの寄付をすると広く信じられている。しかし，研究者らによると，返礼品は寄付者の態度を変えてしまう傾向があるという。ほとんどの人は，始めのうちは，世界をより良い場所にしたい，または恵まれない人々を助けたいという理由で，お金を寄付する。しかし，贈り物を受け取ると，人々は利己心や欲望に駆られるようになることがある。実際，彼らはその後あまり寄付しなくなる可能性が高いようだ。

しかし，この問題を回避する方法はあるかもしれない。研究では，寄付をすれば贈り物をもらえることを人々に伝えるのは，その後確実に寄付をしてもらうための最良の方法ではないことが示されている。ある研究では，贈り物を期待していなかった時の方が，寄付者は贈り物を受け取ることに対する反応は良かった。さらに，そうした人々からのその後の寄付は，最大75%増加した。一方，寄付後に贈り物を受け取ることを知っていた寄付者は，それが何であれ，贈り物を重んじなかった。

寄付者への返礼品には，間接的なメリットもあるかもしれない。専門家は，贈り物は慈善事業の推進に役立ちうると述べている。たとえば，慈善団体のロゴが入ったしゃれたショッピングバッグなどのアイテムは，寄付者が上流階級の一員であることを示す。このような贈り物は，寄付者を満足させるだけでなく，慈善事業に対する一般の人々の意識も高めることになる。

(26) 正解 2

選択肢の訳 **1** 慈善団体の資金を使い果たす **2** 寄付者の態度を変える **3** 人々により多く寄付をするよう促す **4** 市民の慈善活動に対するイメージを良くする

解説 空所を含む文の直後3文を参照。人々は始めのうちは世界や人のために寄付をするが，返礼品を受け取ることによって，people can start to become motivated by selfishness and desire. In fact, they may become less likely to donate in the future.「人々は利己心や欲望に駆られるようになることがある。実際，彼らはその後あまり寄付しなくなる可能性が高いようだ」と述べていることから，**2のchange donors' attitudes**「寄付者の態度を変える」が正解。

(27) 正解 4

選択肢の訳 **1** その代わりに **2** それにもかかわらず **3** その一方 **4** さらに

解説 空所を含む文の1文前でIn one study, donors responded better to receiving gifts when they did not expect them.「ある研究では，贈り物を期待していなかった時の方が，寄付者は贈り物を受け取ることに対する反応は良かった」と述べている。ここから，( ), future donations from such people increased by up to 75 percent.「( )，そうした人々からのその後の寄付は，最大75%増加した」とつながることから，情報を追加する意味を持つ**4のFurthermore**「さらに」が正解。

(28) 正解 1

選択肢の訳 **1** 慈善事業の推進に役立つ **2** 容易に真似される **3** 望ましくない効果がある **4** 寄付者の間に混乱を引き起こす

解説 空所を含む文の2文後で返礼品について，not only keep donors satisfied but also increase the general public's awareness of charities.「寄付者を満足させるだけでなく，慈善事業に対する一般の人々の意識も高めることになる」と述べていることから，**1のhelp promote charities**「慈善事業の推進に役立つ」が正解。

政府の政策と交通安全

Key to Reading 第1段落：導入（速度制限に関する米国政府の政策の問題点）→第2段落：本論①（車両安全規制に関する米国政府の政策の問題点）→第3段落：本論②（信号機カメラと普及の現状）という3段落構成の説明文である。米国政府による交通安全政策の現状や問題点を整理しながら読み進めていくことを心がけよう。

訳

米国では，シートベルトなどの安全対策の実施により，交通関連の死亡が減少している。しかし，政府の政策を批判する多くの人々は，政府の規制をより強化すれば，死亡者数をさらに減らすことができると主張している。実際，速度制限に関する現在の政府の政策は，危険な運転を助長する可能性があると言う人もいる。これは，速度制限が「運転速度方式」を用いて設定されることが多いためである。この方式では，道路を利用する車両が実際に走行する速度に基づいて制限速度が設定され，危険性を高める道路の特徴が軽視されている。残念ながら，これは，制限が安全でないレベルに設定される時もあるということである。

批評家たちはまた，車両安全規制に関して，米国は他の国に遅れをとっていると指摘している。米国では，安全規制は車内の人々を守ることを意図している。一部の車両は大型化し，形状も変わっているにもかかわらず，歩行者にもたらす危険の高まりを反映した法律改正がなされていない。批評家たちは，車に乗っている人の安全だけを規制するのは無責任であり，歩行者の死亡を防ぐために講じることができる簡単な方策があるにもかかわらず，歩行者の死亡が増加していると述べている。

道路の安全性を高めるための1つの方法は，信号機のカメラを使って，赤信号で停止しないドライバーを検出することである。そのようなカメラの多くは1990年代に設置され，命を救えることを示してきた。それなのに，そのようなカメラの数は近年減少している。その理由の1つは，プライバシーに関する懸念から，一般市民から反対の声が出ることが多いためである。

(29) 正解 3

選択肢の訳 **1** この傾向をさらに後押しする　**2** シートベルトの使用が減る　**3** 危険な運転を助長する　**4** 代替となる解決策を提供する

解説 第1段落最後の2文を参照。現在の速度制限の設定法について，speed limits are decided based on the speeds at which vehicles that use the road actually travel, and little attention is paid to road features that could increase danger「道路を利用する車両が実際に走行する速度に基づいて制限速度が設定され，危険性を高める道路の特徴が軽視されている」，またそれにより，limits are sometimes set at unsafe levels「制限が安全でないレベルに設定される時もある」と述べていることから，**3**の**encourage dangerous driving**「危険な運転を助長する」が正解。

(30) 正解 1

選択肢の訳 **1** 車内の人々を守ることを意図している　**2** 多くのドライバーの反対を受けている　**3** 実際は縮小されている　**4** 大型車両に対してより厳しい

解説 空所を含む文の直後2文を参照。米国の車両安全規制について，laws have not changed to reflect the increased danger they pose to pedestrians「歩行者にもたらす危険の高まりを反映した法律改正がなされていない」と述べている。また批評家からも，regulating only the safety of vehicle occupants is irresponsible「車に乗っている人の安全だけを規制するのは無責任である」，pedestrian deaths have increased「歩行者の死亡が増加している」という意見が上がっていることから，**1**の**designed to protect those inside vehicles**「車内の人々を守ることを意図している」が正解。

(31) 正解 3

選択肢の訳 **1** 例えば　**2** 同様に　**3** それなのに　**4** それゆえに

解説 空所を含む文の1文前で信号機のカメラについて，Many such cameras were installed in the 1990s and have been shown to save lives.「そのようなカメラの多くは1990年代に設置され，命を救えることを示してきた」と述べている。ここから，(　　), the number of such cameras has declined in recent years.「(　　)，そのようなカメラの数は近年減少している」とつながることから，期待とは異なる状況を示す時に使う**3**の**Despite this**「それなのに」が正解。

3 一次試験・筆記

カリグラ（問題編pp.190～191）
エディ・コイルの友人たち（問題編pp.192～193）
マミー・ブラウン（問題編pp.194～196）

指示文の訳 それぞれの文章を読んで，各質問に対する最も適切な答えを4つの選択肢の中から選び，その番号を解答用紙の所定欄にマークしなさい。

カリグラ

Key to Reading 第1段落：導入＋本論①（カリグラと脳炎）→第2段落：本論②（カリグラの異常行動の考えられる理由①）→第3段落：本論③（カリグラの異常行動の考えられる理由②）という3段落構成の説明文。カリグラが狂気の皇帝と呼ばれる理由と，それを否定するいくつかの説について読み取ろう。

訳

「狂気の皇帝」としても知られるローマ皇帝カリグラは，あまりにも悪名高くなったため，彼の生涯について事実と伝説を区別するのが難しい。その治世中，カリグラは「脳炎」とされるものを患った。この病気が原因で彼は精神に異常をきたしたのだとよく言われるが，この主張は彼の病気後の一見非理性的な行動によって裏付けられている。しかし，今日，一部の歴史家は，彼の行動は，巧妙で恐ろしく暴力的な政治戦略の意図的な部分であった可能性があると主張している。

病気後，カリグラは膨大な数の市民を，たとえ軽犯罪を犯しただけでも，拷問し，殺害し始めた。彼はまた，生ける神であると主張した。こうした行動は精神的不安定さを示唆している可能性があるものの，別の説明では，自らの地位を確保することを意図していたという。カリグラの病気中，彼に生き延びる見込みがなかったため，代わりを立てることが計画され，結果として彼はおそらく，裏切られ，脅かされたと感じた。同様に，神であると主張することは確かに精神異常の兆候のように聞こえるが，多くのローマ皇帝は死ぬと神になると考えられており，カリグラは敵が彼を暗殺するのを阻止するために，そう主張したのかもしれない。

カリグラが，彼の馬のインキタトゥスを政府の権力ある地位に任命しようとしたとされる話もまた，彼の精神病の証拠として挙げられることがある。しかし，カリグラはしばしばローマ元老院の議員に屈辱を与え，着心地の悪い服を着させたり，自分の馬車の前を走らせたりしたと言われている。自分の馬を彼らよりも高い地位に昇進させることは，元老院の議員に価値がないと感じさせる別の方法だったのだろう。しかし結局，カリグラの行動は行き過ぎ，彼は殺された。彼を歴史から消し去ろうとする試みがなされたため，現代の歴史家が研究すべき，信頼できる情報源はほとんど残っていない。その結果，彼が本当に狂気の皇帝であったかどうかは，決して明らかにならないのかもしれない。

(32) 正解 1

質問の訳 一部の現代の歴史家は，～と主張している。

選択肢の訳 **1** カリグラの一見狂った行動は，実際には綿密に考え抜かれた計画の一部であるかもしれない。 **2** カリグラが患った「脳炎」は，当初考えられていたよりも深刻なものだった。 **3** カリグラは，精神病を患っていた時期を元に評価されるべきではない。 **4** カリグラが行ったと伝えられる暴力行為の多くは，別のローマ皇帝

※2024年度第1回から，試験形式の変更に伴い大問3の1問目(32)～(34)が削除されます。

が行ったものである。

解説 第1段落では，カリグラが「狂気の皇帝」と呼ばれるようになったのは，「脳炎」(brain fever) が原因であるという従来の説について述べている。これに反する現代の歴史家の主張については，第1段落最終文にhis actions may have been a deliberate part of a clever, and horribly violent, political strategy「彼の行動は，巧妙で恐ろしく暴力的な政治戦略の意図的な部分であった可能性がある」とある。この文とほぼ同じ内容を述べている**1**が正解。thought-out plan「考え抜かれた計画」。

(33) 正解　2

質問の訳 カリグラの病気の結果であったかもしれないことの1つは何か。

選択肢の訳 **1** 死にかけたという事実は，彼に神と宗教以外に興味を持たせなくなった。　**2** 彼はもはやだれも信用できないと感じ，統治方法を変えることになった。　**3** ローマ市民は彼がまだ死ぬ可能性が高いと考えていたので，彼は，神々が自分を守ってくれることを彼らに示そうとした。　**4** 彼がローマ皇帝についての古い信念を疑い始めたため，政府の他の議員たちとの深刻な対立につながった。

解説 病気後のカリグラについては，第2段落第1～2文で，Caligula began torturing and putting to death huge numbers of citizens for even minor offenses. He also claimed to be a living god.「カリグラは膨大な数の市民を，たとえ軽犯罪を犯しただけでも，拷問し，殺害し始めた。彼はまた，生ける神であると主張した」と述べており，その統治に大きな変化があったことがわかる。その原因として挙げられているのが，第4文のWhile Caligula was ill, plans were made to replace him, since he had not been expected to survive, and he likely felt betrayed and threatened as a result.「カリグラの病気中，彼に生き延びる見込みがなかったため，代わりを立てることが計画され，結果として彼はおそらく，裏切られ，脅かされたと感じた」こと。これらの内容をまとめた選択肢**2**が正解。no longer「もはや～でない」。

(34) 正解　2

質問の訳 この文章によれば，カリグラはローマ元老院の議員たちについてどのように感じていたか。

選択肢の訳 **1** 彼らは彼を敵から守るために何でもするので，人々は彼らにもっと敬意を払うべきだと感じた。　**2** 彼らに対する自分の力を示したかったので，彼らに価値がないと感じさせる方法をしばしば探した。　**3** 彼らは体が弱く，ファッションセンスが悪いと感じたので，彼らを嫌った。　**4** 彼らの支援に感謝し，彼らを称えるために馬車レースなどのイベントを行った。

解説 第3段落第2文より，カリグラはローマ元老院の議員に屈辱を与えており，その一例として，第3文でElevating his horse to a position higher than theirs would have been another way to make the Senate members feel worthless.「自分の馬を彼らよりも高い地位に昇進させることは，元老院の議員に価値がないと感じさせる別の方法だったのだろう」と述べている。この内容と一致する選択肢**2**が正解。

エディ・コイルの友人たち

Key to Reading 第1段落：導入＋本論①（「エディ・コイルの友人たち」が生まれるまで）

→第2段落：本論②（「エディ・コイルの友人たち」の独自性）→第3段落：本論③＋結論（ヒギンズのその後の作品と人生）という3段落構成の説明文。設問に先に目を通し，読み取るべきポイントを押さえてから，本文を読み進めよう。

訳

1970年，アメリカの作家ジョージ・V・ヒギンズは，自身初の小説，『エディ・コイルの友人たち』を出版した。この犯罪小説は，ヒギンズが弁護士として働いていた頃から発想を得ているが，その頃，彼は自分が関わった事件に関連する何時間もの警察の監視カメラのビデオテープと記録を調べていた。彼は普通の犯罪者の日常の言葉を聞いたり読んだりしたが，それは，当時のテレビの犯罪ドラマのセリフのようなものでは全くなかった。ヒギンズは本物の犯罪者がどのように話すかを知り，そして彼らの独特で，しばしば乱雑でもある言葉遣いが，『エディ・コイルの友人たち』のベースとなった。この小説のざらついた臨場感は，当時ベストセラーリストを独占していた，洗練された犯罪小説とはかけ離れていた。ヒギンズは犯罪者の人生を美化することも，警察や連邦捜査官を英雄的に描写することもしなかった。

『エディ・コイルの友人たち』が他の犯罪小説と異なる点の1つは，ほぼ完全にセリフで書かれていることである。犯罪小説が，サスペンスを作り上げる慎重に練られたストーリーに頼っていることを考えると，これは非常に独創的なアプローチであった。重要な出来事は直接描写されるのではなく，小説の登場人物同士の会話を通じて挿入されるのだ。そのため読者は，エディ・コイルと彼の犯罪仲間との会話を密かに聞いているという感覚を与えられる。アクションシーンでさえセリフで描かれ，ナレーションが必要な場合は，ヒギンズは控えめに書き，読者が筋書きを追うのに必要な情報だけを提供する。登場人物，彼らが住む世界，彼らが従う行動規範に，主に焦点を当てている。

ヒギンズの最初の小説はすぐに大当たりしたが，すべての読者が，筆者が後の作品でも用いたその文体を気に入ったわけではなかった。多くの人は，彼の後の小説には明確な筋書きがなく，アクションが少なすぎると不満を漏らした。それでもヒギンズは，読者をセリフに注目させ続けられるからと，物語を語る最も魅力的な方法は，登場人物の会話を通してである，という自分の信念を守り続けた。多くの小説を書いたにもかかわらず，ヒギンズはデビュー作の成功を再現することはできなかった。人生の終わりに向かって，彼は自分の本への関心や評価が足りないことに落胆し，失望した。それにもかかわらず，『エディ・コイルの友人たち』は，これまでに書かれた最も優れた犯罪小説の1つであると，多くの人に考えられている。

(35)　正解　4

質問の訳　この一節によると，ジョージ・V・ヒギンズは，～『エディ・コイルの友人たち』を書いた。

選択肢の訳　**1**　この小説がベストセラーになり，法律の専門家を辞めてフルタイムで執筆できるようになると信じていたので。　**2**　米国での犯罪活動の広がりに対する一般のアメリカ人の意識の欠如に不満を感じて。　**3**　犯罪の犠牲者を守るために弁護士がどれほど懸命に働いたかを読者に示したかったので。　**4**　弁護士時代に行った調査の間に気づいたことから発想を得て。

解説　第1段落第2文に，This crime novel was inspired by the time Higgins spent working as a lawyer「この犯罪小説は，ヒギンズが弁護士として働いていた頃

から発想を得ている」とあるので，この内容と一致する選択肢**4**が正解。

(36)　正解　2

質問の訳　第2段落で，『エディ・コイルの友人たち』について何がわかるか。
選択肢の訳　**1**　ヒギンズは，犯罪フィクションの伝統的なルールが現代にも当てはまることを証明する小説を書きたいと考えた。　**2**　ヒギンズは，特定の出来事を詳細に描写するのではなく，登場人物間のやりとりを通じて物語を語っているため，この小説は他とは異なっている。　**3**　ヒギンズは，長いナレーションを書く自信がなかったため，小説全体を通して会話に頼るところが大きかった。　**4**　この小説は犯罪の世界を確実に描写しているが，ヒギンズはそれが真の犯罪小説であるとは考えていなかった。
解説　『エディ・コイルの友人たち』の特徴として，第2段落第1文でit is written almost entirely in dialogue「ほぼ完全にセリフで書かれている」と述べている。これは，当時の犯罪小説特有の，慎重に練られたストーリー（carefully plotted stories）とは大きく異なる。この内容と一致する選択肢**2**が正解。

(37)　正解　1

質問の訳　次の意見のうち，この文章の著者が同意する可能性が最も高いのはどれか。
選択肢の訳　**1**　ヒギンズは自分の文体を変えることでより多くの読者を惹きつけることができた可能性があるにもかかわらず，彼は自分の創造的なビジョンに忠実であり続けた。　**2**　ヒギンズが最初に書いた本は下手だったが，彼の作品の質はその後数年で着実に向上した。　**3**　犯罪小説の作家が，他のジャンルの作家と同じレベルの名声と称賛を得ることは決してないだろう。　**4**　犯罪小説の作家が，自分の作品が最初に出版されてから数十年後に読者の共感を得ることを期待するのは，非現実的である。
解説　第3段落第1～3文で，ヒギンズの2作目以降の作品は，その独特の文体から必ずしも好評ではなかったが，彼は，remained committed to his belief that the most engaging way to tell a story is through the conversations of its characters「物語を語る最も魅力的な方法は，登場人物の会話を通してである，という自分の信念を守り続けた」と述べている。この内容と一致する**1**が正解。

マミー・ブラウン

Key to Reading　第1段落：導入＋本論①（ミイラを巡る古代の考え）→第2段落：本論②（ヨーロッパでのミイラ人気）→第3段落：本論③（ミイラから生まれた顔料，マミー・ブラウン）→第4段落：結論（マミー・ブラウンの真実）という4段落構成の説明文。選択肢を検討するときは，本文中の語（句）の言い換えに注意しよう。

訳

何千年も前に，古代エジプト人は，死体を乾燥させ，様々な物質で処理し，それらを包んで保存するというプロセス，すなわちミイラ化を実践し始めた。これにより，死者の魂が死後の世界に入ることができると信じられていた。しかし，12世紀始め，ミイラの一部を使って作られた医薬品の市場がヨーロッパに出現したため，多くの古代のミイラが奇妙な運命を辿った。人々は，ミイラの黒い色は，中東で自然に発生し，古代社会で病気を治療するために使用された，黒い石油ベースの物質である瀝青（れきせい）で処理されたためだと考えていた。しかし，古代エジプト人はミイラを瀝青でコーティングして保存することもあったが，この方法はヨーロッパに持ち込まれたミイラの多くには使用されていなかった。さらに，アラビア語の文書が誤って訳されたことにより，ミイラの処理に使用された瀝青が，実際にミイラの体内に入っていたという誤った考えが生まれた。

18世紀までに，医学知識の進歩により，ヨーロッパ人はミイラから作られた薬の使用をやめた。それにもかかわらず，フランスの指導者，ナポレオン・ボナパルトがエジプトでの軍事作戦を主導した時，ミイラに対するヨーロッパの大衆の関心は，新たな高みに達した。これは大規模な研究遠征も兼ねており，重要な考古学的発見と古代遺物の文書化につながった。個人のコレクションとして古代遺物を手に入れるために，裕福な観光客はエジプトを訪れることまでした。実際，個人のパーティーでミイラを開封したり飾ったりするのが，人気のアクティビティとなった。ミイラは，作物の肥料や鉄道エンジンの燃料など，様々な方法でも利用された。

ミイラの特に珍しい用途の1つは，茶色の絵の具を作るための顔料として使用されたことである。すりつぶしたミイラを用いて作られた顔料は，マミー・ブラウンとして知られるようになり，16世紀には早くも使用されていたが，その需要はナポレオンのエジプトでの軍事作戦の頃に増加した。その色はヨーロッパの一部の芸術家によって称賛され，彼らは今日美術館で見ることができる作品にそれを使用した。それでも，その顔料にはファンよりも，批判する人の方が多かった。多くの芸術家は，乾燥性の低さやその他のマイナス面について不満を漏らした。さらに，亡くなった人々から作られた顔料で絵を描くことは，次第に冒涜であると考えられるようになった。マミー・ブラウンを使用した有名な英国の画家は，それを作るのに本物のミイラが使用されていることを知った時，すぐに絵の具のチューブを地面に埋めた。

マミー・ブラウンに嫌悪感を持たなかった芸術家でさえ，死んだ動物の一部がミイラの一部として販売されることもあったため，その原料が本物であると必ずしも確信できるわけではなかった。また，様々なメーカーがミイラの様々な部分を使用して顔料を作ったという事実は，市場に出回っている様々な仕様の間に，ほとんど均一性がないことを意味していた。さらに，遺体を保存するために使用される物質を含む，ミイラ化のプロセス自体も，時間の経過とともに変化した。これら同様な要因により，今日の研究者が特定の絵画にマミー・ブラウンを見つけるのは，ほとんど不可能になっている。しかし，顔料の起源が物議を醸していることを考えると，芸術愛好家は，賞賛する絵画のいずれかにそれが使用されていることを発見した場合，恐らく衝撃を受けるだろう。

(38) 正解 3

質問の訳 この文章の著者によると，古代エジプトのミイラがヨーロッパで薬を作るために使われたのはなぜか。

選択肢の訳 **1** 当時のヨーロッパでは病気が蔓延していたので，ヨーロッパ人は効果的な薬を作るためにあらゆることを試みるのを厭わなかった。 **2** ミイラが経過年数にかかわらず黒くなっていなかったため，ヨーロッパ人はミイラが健康に良いと考えていた。 **3** ヨーロッパ人は，薬効があると考えられていた物質がすべてのミイラに存在すると誤って信じていた。 **4** ミイラが古代エジプト人にとって宗教的な意味を持っていたという事実により，ヨーロッパ人はミイラに特別な力があると信じていた。

解説 ミイラが薬を作るために使われた理由は，第1段落第4文で，病気の治療に使われていた瀝青（bitumen）が，ミイラの処理に使われていたと考えられていたためであると述べている。しかし第5文にあるように，実際は，this method had not been used on many of the mummies that were taken to Europe「この方法はヨーロッパに持ち込まれたミイラの多くには使用されていなかった」。つまり，ヨーロッパ人は瀝青を使っていないミイラもあることを認識していなかったということなので，これに一致する選択肢**3**が正解。

(39) 正解 4

質問の訳 ナポレオン・ボナパルトのエジプトでの軍事作戦について，わかることの1つは何か。

選択肢の訳 **1** 多くの指導者は，それをエジプトにも侵攻する理由と見なし，多くの古代遺物の破壊につながった。 **2** それは，ミイラから作られた薬に対するヨーロッパ人の意見を変えることにつながった，古代エジプトの文化に関する情報を明らかにした。 **3** 裕福なヨーロッパ人は，それにより自分たちの古代遺物のコレクションが破壊されると考え，反対した。 **4** ミイラへの関心を高め，ヨーロッパ人をミイラを様々な目的に使用する気にさせた。

解説 ナポレオンのエジプトでの軍事作戦については第2段落で，the European public's fascination with mummies reached new heights「ミイラに対するヨーロッパの大衆の関心は，新たな高みに達した」と述べており，その具体例として，富裕層がパーティーでミイラを開封したり飾ったりしたこと（the unwrapping and displaying of mummies）を挙げている。この内容と一致する選択肢**4**が正解。inspire … to ～「…を～する気にさせる。」

(40) 正解 1

質問の訳 この文章の著者は～ために，英国の画家について言及している。

選択肢の訳 **1** 死者への敬意が欠けているために，マミー・ブラウンの使用が一部の人々によってどう反対されたかの例を示す。 **2** その技術性能が低いにもかかわらず，マミー・ブラウンが有名な芸術家の間で人気を保ち続けた理由を説明する。 **3** マミー・ブラウンは，その特有の成分から，他の塗料顔料よりも優れていたという見解を支持する。 **4** 一部の芸術家が，最初マミー・ブラウンの使用を拒否した後，それに対して肯定的な意見を展開した理由の1つを説明する。

解説 英国の画家について言及しているのは，第3段落最終文。painting with a pigment made from deceased people increasingly came to be thought of as disrespectful「亡くなった人々から作られた顔料で絵を描くことは，次第に冒涜であると考えられるようになった」と述べた後で，マミー・ブラウンにミイラが使用されていることを知って絵の具を埋めた英国の画家について言及している。この内容と一致する選択肢**1**が正解。本文のdisrespectfulをa lack of respectで言い換えている。

(41) 正解 2

質問の訳 絵画にマミー・ブラウンが含まれているかどうかを判断するのを難しくしていることの1つは何か。

選択肢の訳 **1** 色を良くするために顔料に加えられた物質が，検査で検出できた可能性のある生物学的証拠をすべて消し去ってしまった。 **2** 古代エジプト人がミイラを作る方法が変化したため，顔料の中身に均一性がなかった。　**3**　芸術家が，絵画に用いる前に顔料を他の種類の塗料と混ぜたため，それがごく少量しか存在しなかった。
4　美術業界が，結果が絵画の価値に影響を与える可能性があるという懸念から，研究者が絵画の検査を行うのを阻止しようとしてきた。

解説　マミー・ブラウンが絵画に使用されているかどうかを見極めるのが困難であることは，第４段落第４文で述べている。文頭のThese same factorsは，その前の３文の内容（①本物のミイラが使われていない可能性がある，②ミイラの様々な部分が使われているので製品に均一性がない，③ミイラ化のプロセスが変化した）を指している。これらのうち③の内容と一致する選択肢**2**が正解。

4　一次試験・英作文
（問題編p.197）

指示文の訳　●次のトピックについてエッセイを書きなさい。
●答えの裏付けに，以下に挙げたポイントのうちの２つを使いなさい。
●構成：導入，本論，結論
●長さ：120～150語
●エッセイは解答用紙のＢ面に用意されたスペースに書きなさい。
スペースの外側に書かれた内容は，採点の対象とはなりません。

トピックの訳　人は動物から作られた商品の使用をやめるべきですか。

ポイントの訳　●動物の権利　●絶滅危惧種　●商品の品質　●伝統

解答例

I believe that the quality of alternative products and respecting animal rights are reasons why people should not use goods made from animals.

Many products made from animals are being replaced by artificial goods, and technological advancements have greatly improved the quality of these man-made goods. For example, the quality of fake fur is almost the same as that of real fur. Such high-quality alternative goods mean that using animal products is unnecessary.

Furthermore, some animal products come from animals living in conditions that restrict their freedom. However, animals deserve the right to live freely, and this right should not be ignored for the sake of commercial gain. Therefore, stopping the use of animal-based goods is an effective way to protect animal rights.

In conclusion, the high quality of other types of products and the importance of protecting animal rights mean that people should stop using goods made from animals.

解答例の訳

私は，代替商品の品質と動物の権利の尊重こそが，人が動物から作られた商品を使用すべきではない理由だと思う。

動物から作られた多数の商品は人工的な商品に置き換えられつつあり，技術の発達はこ

※2024年度第１回から，大問４に文章の要約を書く問題が加わります。

れらの人工の商品の品質を著しく向上させている。例えば，人工毛皮の品質は本物の毛皮の品質とほぼ同じである。そのような高品質の代替商品は，動物性商品の使用が不要なものであるということを物語っている。

さらに，動物性商品の中には，自由が束縛された状況下で生きる動物に由来するものもある。しかし，動物には束縛されずに生きる権利があり，この権利は営利目的でないがしろにされるべきではない。そのため，動物を主材料とした商品の使用をやめることは動物の権利を保護するための効果的な手段である。

結論として，他の種類の商品の品質の高さおよび動物の権利の保護の重要性は，人が動物から作られる商品の使用をやめるべきだということを指し示している。

解説 TOPIC文について，「使用をやめるべきである／使用をやめるべきではない」のどちらかの立場に立って，自分の意見とその根拠をエッセイの形でまとめる形式。エッセイをまとめる際には，POINTSとして示されたキーワードのうち２つを選んで使用する必要がある。これらのキーワードに挙げられている語句については，例えば，Endangered speciesはspecies in danger of extinction「絶滅の危機に瀕している種」などと，Animal rightsはAnimal welfare「動物愛護」などと，必要に応じて形を変えて表現したり類義語で置き換えたりしても良い。

段落構成に関する，導入（introduction）→本論（main body）→結論（conclusion）という基本的な指定は必ず守ること。解答例のように本論を２つに分ける場合は，論点の重複がないように，それぞれの段落を別の視点からまとめる。その際，各段落の論点が明確になるように，談話標識（discourse markers）を使うと論理的にまとまりのある文章となり，効果的である。また，結論をまとめるときは，第１段落の単純な繰り返しにならないよう，表現を若干でも工夫することが好ましい。

TOPIC文 「人は動物から作られた商品の使用をやめるべきですか」という質問について意見を求める内容。

語句 goods「商品」/ be made from ～「～から作られた」

第１段落（導入） まずエッセイの冒頭で，TOPIC文のテーマを正しく理解していることと，自分が「使用をやめるべきである／使用をやめるべきではない」のどちらの立場に立っているかを明示する必要がある。解答例は，文をI believe that ～「私は～と思う」から始め，自分が前者の立場にいることを示している。また，POINTSの中からProduct quality「商品の品質」とAnimal rights「動物の権利」の２つを取り上げている。

語句 quality「品質」/ alternative「代替の」/ product「商品」

第２段落（本論①） 第２段落では，第１段落で示した１つ目の観点である「商品の品質」について述べている。また，第２文では，第１文で言及した高品質の人工的な商品の具体例を，For example「例えば」という談話標識を用いて挙げている。

語句 replace「～を置き換える」/ artificial「人工の」/ technological「技術的な」

第３段落（本論②） 第３段落では，第１段落で示した２つ目の観点である「動物の権利」について意見を展開している。この段落では，追加を表すFurthermore「さらに」，逆接を表すHowever「しかし」，帰結を表すTherefore「そのため」という３つの談話標識を駆使しながら，動物の権利の保護の重要性について論理的に説明することで，意見の説得力を高めている。

語句 condition「状況，状態」/ restrict「～を制限する」/ freedom「自由」/ deserve「～に値する」/ freely「制約なく，自由に」/ ignore「～を無視する」/ for the sake of ～「～のために」/ commercial「商業的な」/ gain「利益」/ animal-based「動物を主材料とした」/ effective「効果的な」/ protect「～を保護する」

第４段落（結論） 最終段落では，in conclusion「結論として」という談話標識から文を始めて，人々は動物から作られた商品を使用すべきではないという結論を再度述べ，文章を締め括っている。

語句 type「種類」/ importance「重要性」

Part 1 一次試験・リスニング

CD 緑-27 ～ CD 緑-39

（問題編pp.198～199）

指示文の訳 準１級の試験のリスニングテストが始まります。指示を注意して聞いてください。テスト中に質問をすることは許されていません。

このテストは３つのパートに分かれています。これら３つのパートの質問は全て選択肢の中から正解を選ぶ問題です。それぞれの質問について，問題冊子に書かれている４つの選択肢の中から最も適切な答えを選び，解答用紙の該当箇所にその答えをマークしなさい。このリスニングテストの全てのパートで，メモを取ってもかまいません。

それでは，これからPart 1の指示を行います。このパートではNo. 1からNo. 12まで12の会話が放送されます。それぞれの会話に続いて，質問が１つ流れます。各質問に対して，最も適切な答えを選んで解答用紙にマークする時間が10秒あります。会話と質問は１度しか読まれません。それでは，準１級のリスニングテストを始めます。

No.1 正解 4

放送文 ***A:*** Dr. Jenkins, could I speak with you for a moment? ***B:*** Sure, Eric. What's on your mind? ***A:*** I'm embarrassed to say this, but I'm having a hard time keeping my eyes open in class. I have to work two part-time jobs to make ends meet, and your class is so early in the morning. ***B:*** So are you thinking about dropping the class? That would be a shame, considering that your test scores have been pretty good. ***A:*** No, not that. I need this class in order to graduate next year. Actually, I was wondering if you could arrange your seating chart so I'm sitting right up in front. That should help me pay better attention in class. ***B:*** I think I can probably do that.

Question: What is the student concerned about?

訳 A：ジェンキンス博士，ちょっとお話できますか。　B：もちろんです，エリック。何か気になることがあるのですか？　A：お恥ずかしい話なんですが，授業中，目を開けているのが辛いんです。生活のためにアルバイトを２つ掛け持ちしているのですが，先生の授業は朝とても早いので。　B：それで，授業をやめようと思っているのですか。テストの点数がかなりよいのに，それは残念ですね。　A：いいえ，そうではありません。来年卒業するためにこの授業が必要です。実は，私が一番前に座れるように座席表をアレンジしていただけないかと思っているんです。そうすれば，もっと授業に集中できると思います。　B：たぶんできると思いますよ。

質問の訳 学生は何を心配しているか。

選択肢の訳 **1** 彼の最近のテストの点数。 **2** 授業をやめなければならないこと。 **3** 仕事を見つけること。 **4** 授業中に起きていること。

解説 1往復目でA（＝Eric）は「ジェンキンス博士，ちょっとお話できますか」と述べているので，学生であるAが，先生であるジェンキンス博士に相談している場面だとわかる。2往復目でAは「授業中，目を開けているのが辛いんです」(I'm having a hard time keeping my eyes open in class）と述べているので，Aが心配していることは，授業中に起きているのが大変であること。よって，having a hard time keeping my eyes open in classを**staying awake in class**と言い換えた**4**が正解。

No.2 正解 1

放送文 ***A:*** You're not sending a personal e-mail from your office computer, are you, Allen? ***B:*** It's just a quick note to my mom—it's her birthday tomorrow. ***A:*** Didn't you read the memo from the CEO? Using office computers for private communications could get you fired. I heard they're looking for excuses to cut staff. ***B:*** I doubt if they'd take a birthday message that seriously, but thanks for the warning. ***A:*** Better safe than sorry.

Question: Why is the woman concerned?

訳 A：まさか，会社のパソコンから個人的なメールを送ろうとしているんじゃないでしょうね，アレン？ B：母へのちょっとした手紙だよ，明日は母の誕生日なんだ。 A：CEOからのメモを読んでないの？ 会社のコンピュータを私的な通信に使うと，解雇されるかもしれないよ。会社は，従業員を減らす口実を探していると聞いたよ。 B：誕生日のメッセージをそんなに真剣に受け取るとは思えないけど，警告してくれてありがとう。A：用心するに越したことはないからね。

質問の訳 なぜ女性は心配しているのか。

選択肢の訳 **1** 男性が仕事を失うかもしれない。 **2** 男性は母親の誕生日を忘れていた。 **3** 男性は彼女の電子メールに返信しなかった。 **4** 男性は社長に好かれていない。

解説 1往復目から，B（＝Allen）が会社のパソコンから個人的なメールを送ろうとしているところを，A（＝女性）が目撃した場面であることがわかる。2往復目で女性は，「会社のコンピュータを私的な通信に使うと，解雇されるかもしれないよ」(Using office computers for private communications could get you fired.）と述べているので，女性は，Bが仕事を失うかもしれないことを心配していることがわかる。よって，could get you firedを**could lose his job**と言い換えた**1**が正解。

No.3 正解 1

放送文 ***A:*** Sam, next week, it's my turn to drive us to work, but my car's in the shop. ***B:*** What's wrong with it? ***A:*** Oh, I had an accident over the weekend. ***B:*** Nothing too serious, I hope. ***A:*** No. Just a fender bender. ***B:*** OK. Well, why don't I do the driving next week, and you can take your turn once your car's fixed? ***A:*** That would be great. Thanks a lot.

Question: What do we learn about these people?

訳 A：サム，来週は私が車で職場まで運転する番だけど，私の車は修理に出しているの。 B：どうしたの？ A：ああ，週末に事故に遭ったのよ。 B：大したことないといいね。 A：ええ，ちょっとぶつけただけよ。 B：わかった。じゃあ，来週はぼくが運転して，君の車が直ったら君が運転するのはどう？ A：そうしてもらえると助かるわ。どうもありがとうね。

質問の訳 この人たちについてわかることは何か。

選択肢の訳 **1** 彼らは交代で運転している。 **2** 彼らは重大な事故に遭った。
3 彼らは車の修理工場で働いている。 **4** 二人とも来週は運転できない。

解説 1往復目でA（＝女性）は，「来週は私が車で職場まで運転する番だけど〜」（next week, it's my turn to drive us to work）と述べているので，AとB（＝Sam）は，職場まで通勤するときの車の運転を当番制で交代で行っていることがわかる。このturnは「順番，番」という意味。よって，it's my turn to drive us to workを**take turns driving**と言い換えた**1**が正解。fender benderで「軽度の衝突事故」。

No.4 正解 1

放送文 ***A:*** I'm sorry, sir, but your credit card was declined. ***B:*** I don't understand why. It was fine yesterday. ***A:*** Perhaps you've reached your limit. It happens quite often. ***B:*** I don't know. That's certainly possible, I suppose.
A: Anyway, I suggest you call your card issuer. Do you have a debit card or a personal check you'd like to use for today's purchases? ***B:*** No, I'll just pay with cash.
Question: What's the man's problem?

訳 A：申し訳ございませんが，お客様のクレジットカードは使用できませんでした。 B：なぜだかわかりません。昨日は大丈夫だったのですが。 A：おそらく限度額に達しているのでしょう。よくあることなんです。 B：どうでしょう。確かにその可能性はありますね。 A：いずれにせよ，カード発行会社に電話することをお勧めします。今日のお買い物にご使用なさりたいデビットカードか個人用小切手をお持ちですか。 B：いいえ，現金で払います。

質問の訳 男性の問題は何か。

選択肢の訳 **1** クレジットカードが使えない。 **2** カード発行会社に連絡するのを忘れた。 **3** 今日，現金が不足している。 **4** デビットカードを紛失した。

解説 買い物での会計時の客と店員の会話。1往復目でA（＝店員）は，B（＝客）に「申し訳ございませんが，お客様のクレジットカードは使用できませんでした」（I'm sorry, sir, but your credit card was declined.）と述べているので，Bのクレジットカードが使えない状況であることがわかる。よって，your credit card was declinedを**cannot use his credit card**と言い換えた**1**が正解。

No.5 正解 3

放送文 ***A:*** How's the job-hunting going, Tyler? You know your dad and I can't support you forever. ***B:*** Actually, I've been offered a second interview for a call-center job. I'm not sure it's my thing, though. ***A:*** It doesn't have to be. The more jobs you try your hand at, the more you'll learn about the working world. ***B:*** But what if I take it and end up missing out on my dream job? ***A:*** You can keep applying to other places while you work. ***B:*** Fair enough. I'll call

them back and schedule the second interview.
Question: What is the woman's opinion about her son?

訳 A：タイラー, 就職活動はどうなの？ お父さんも私も, いつまでもあなたをサポートすることはできないわよ。 B：実は, コールセンターの仕事の二次面接を受けることになったんだ。僕に向いているかどうかわからないけどね。 A：そんなことないわ。多くの仕事に挑戦すればするほど, 実社会というものを知ることができるんだから。 B：でも, もしそれを受けてみて, 自分の理想の仕事を逃してしまったらどうしよう？ A：働きながら, 他のところに応募し続ければいいのよ。 B：その通りだね。電話をかけ直して, 二次面接の日程を決めるよ。

質問の訳 息子についての女性の意見は何か。

選択肢の訳 **1** 息子はコールセンターの仕事には向いていない。 **2** 息子は間違った面接のテクニックを学んでいる。 **3** 息子は, 機会を提供された面接に行くべきだ。 **4** 息子は夢の仕事を見つけることを優先させるべきだ。

解説 1往復目のA（＝女性）の発言から, 職探しをしているB（＝Tyler）との会話だとわかる。1往復目でBは, コールセンターの仕事の二次面接を受けることになったが, 自分に向いているかどうかわからないと述べており, 面接を受けることを迷っていることがわかる。それに対しAは2, 3往復目で「多くの仕事に挑戦すればするほど, 実社会というものを知ることができる」「働きながら, 他のところに応募し続ければいい」と述べているので, AはBが面接を受けるべきだと考えていることがわかる。よって, the more jobs you try your hand atをgo to the interviewと言い換えた**3**が正解。try one's hand at ～「～をやってみる［～に挑戦する］」。working world「実社会」。Fair enough.「あなたの言う通りですね」。

No.6 正解 1

放送文 ***A:*** Hello, Sergio. What brings you to the clinic today? ***B:*** My energy's been really low recently, so I thought I should have a checkup. ***A:*** Any major changes since your last appointment? ***B:*** I got promoted to a new position that's pretty stressful and requires a lot of business trips. I've been eating unhealthy food, too. ***A:*** I see. Getting adequate nutrition can be a challenge when you're traveling. ***B:*** What should I do? ***A:*** Let's get a few tests done, and then we'll look at your options once the results come in.
Question: What is the doctor going to do next?

訳 A：セルジオさん, こんにちは。今日はどのような症状でクリニックにいらっしゃいましたか。 B：最近本当に元気がないので, 健康診断を受けた方がいいと思いまして。A：前回の診察から何か大きな変化はありましたか。 B：新しいポジションに昇進したのですが, 出張が多くてストレスがたまります。ずっと不健康な食事もしています。 A：そうなんですね。出張先で十分な栄養を摂るのは大変ですよね。 B：どうしたらいいんでしょうか。 A：いくつか検査をして, 結果が出たら, どうするかを検討しましょう。

質問の訳 医師は次に何をするつもりか。

選択肢の訳 **1** 男性にいくつかの検査を受けさせる。 **2** 男性にもっと運動するよう勧める。 **3** 男性に仕事に関するストレスについて助言する。 **4** 男性に専門医を勧める。

解説 1往復目の会話から，クリニックでのA（＝医者）とB（＝患者のSergio）との会話とわかる。3往復目でBが「どうしたらいいんでしょうか」とたずねたのに対し，Aは「いくつか検査をして，結果が出たら，どうするかを検討しましょう」（Let's get a few tests done, and then we'll look at your options once the results come in.）と述べている。よって，get a few tests doneを**take some tests**と言い換えた**1**が正解。

No.7　正解　3

放送文 ***A:*** Jasper? I thought you were on vacation this week. ***B:*** Officially, I am. My manager was planning to take some time off, so I thought I'd do the same. Unfortunately, she's still working, which means she's asking me to do stuff. ***A:*** She's making you work during your vacation? You should complain to the personnel department. ***B:*** But I've only been here a year. I want to prove I'm committed to the company. ***A:*** Well, be sure to set aside a little time for yourself this week. You are technically on vacation. ***B:*** I will. Thanks.
Question: What is one thing we learn about the man?

訳 A：ジャスパー？　今週は休暇中じゃなかったの。　B：公式にはそうなんだけどね。部長が休暇を取る予定だったので，僕もそうしようと思ったんだ。でも残念ながら，彼女はまだ働いていて，僕にいろいろ頼んでくるんだ。　A：休暇中に上司に仕事をさせられているの？　人事部に文句を言うべきだよ。　B：でも僕は，入社してたった1年なんだ。会社に貢献してるって証明したいよ。　A：じゃあ，今週は必ず少しは自分の時間を作ってね。表向きは休暇なんだから。　B：そうするよ。ありがとう。

質問の訳 男性についてわかることの1つは何か。

選択肢の訳 **1**　彼は年内に休暇を取るだろう。　**2**　彼は人事部長と会うだろう。
3　彼は部長が彼に頼むことをやるだろう。　**4**　彼は女性に手伝ってくれるように頼むだろう。

解説 1往復目からB（＝Jasper）が，休暇の予定を返上して仕事をしている場面であることがわかる。1往復目の最後でBは「彼女（＝部長）はまだ働いていて，僕にいろいろ頼んでくるんだ」と述べ，2往復目では「会社に貢献してるって証明したい」と述べているので，Bは部長の仕事を手伝うつもりであることがわかる。she's asking me to do stuffを**do what his manager asks him to do**と言い換えた**3**が正解。

No.8　正解　4

放送文 ***A:*** What do you think of the proposed design for our new company logo? ***B:*** I quite like the style of the lettering, but the logo doesn't have enough impact. How about you? ***A:*** The colors are appealing, but I think the shape of our current logo represents our company better. ***B:*** I heard there's a trend toward simplicity these days, but the designers have gone too far in that direction. ***A:*** Agreed. We should talk to them again.
Question: What do these people think about the proposed logo?

訳 A：会社の新しいロゴのデザイン案について，どう思う？　B：文字のスタイルはかなり好きだけど，ロゴのインパクトが十分じゃないよ。あなたはどう思う？　A：色は魅力的だけど，今のロゴの形の方が，うちの会社をうまく表現していると思うな。　B：

最近，シンプルなものが流行っているそうだけど，デザイナーはその方向に行き過ぎたね。 A：そうだね。もう一度彼らと相談してみるべきだね。

質問の訳 この人たちは，提案されたロゴについてどう考えているか。

選択肢の訳 **1** もっと明るい色にする必要がある。 **2** 会社のイメージに合っている。 **3** 現在のものと類似しすぎている。 **4** デザインを変える必要がある。

解説 1往復目でB（＝女性）は「ロゴのインパクトが十分じゃない」と述べ，2往復目でA（＝男性）は「今のロゴの形の方が，うちの会社をうまく表現していると思う」と述べているので，A，Bともに，提案されたロゴに不満を感じていることがわかる。また，2往復目でBが「デザイナーはその方向に行き過ぎた」と述べたのに対し，Aは「そうだね」と同意した後，「もう一度彼らと相談してみるべきだ」（We should talk to them again.）と述べている。よって，talk to them（＝the designers）againを**needs to be redesigned**と言い換えた**4**が正解。

No.9 正解 1

放送文 ***A:*** Sheena, are you going to Alice's book-launch party on Wednesday? ***B:*** Of course. It's taken her a decade to write, but the book turned out great! ***A:*** You've already read it? That's not fair! But I suppose you two have been friends since kindergarten. ***B:*** And I helped with research for one of the chapters. ***A:*** I guess I'll just have to read it when it's available to the general public. ***B:*** You only have to wait a few days.

Question: What is one thing we learn about the man?

訳 A：シーナ，水曜日のアリスの出版記念パーティーに行くつもり？ B：もちろんよ。彼女は書くのに10年もかかったけど，素晴らしいでき栄えよ！ A：もう読んじゃったの？ そんなのずるいよ。でも，二人は幼稚園の頃からの友達なんだよね。 B：それに，ある章では私もリサーチを手伝ったの。 A：ぼくは，一般公開されてから読むしかないね。 B：数日待たなくちゃいけないだけよ。

質問の訳 男性についてわかることの1つは何か。

選択肢の訳 **1** まだアリスの本を読んでいない。 **2** アリスのパーティーに参加できない。 **3** もうアリスと友達ではない。 **4** アリスの本を読んでがっかりした。

解説 1往復目でB（＝Sheena）が「彼女（＝Alice）は書くのに10年もかかったけど，（出版される本は）素晴らしいでき栄えよ！」と述べているので，Bはすでにアリスが出版する本を読んでいることがわかる。一方，これを聞いたA（＝男性）は，「もう読んじゃったの？ そんなのずるいよ」と述べ，3往復目でも「ぼくは，一般公開されてから読むしかないね」と述べ，シーナも「（あなたが読めるようになるまで）数日待たなくちゃいけないだけよ」と述べているので，Aはアリスの本をまだ読んでいないことがわかる。よって**1**が正解。

No.10 正解 2

放送文 ***A:*** Morning. Sorry to be late. ***B:*** No problem. Was your train delayed again? ***A:*** Yes, for the third time this month. I take an early train, but there are always big delays on weekdays during rush hour. ***B:*** Isn't there another train line in your area? ***A:*** Yes, but the station on that line is a 45-minute walk from my house. ***B:*** Perhaps you could ride your bicycle there. ***A:*** That's an idea. If I did that, I could catch a later train than I do now. ***B:*** Cycling would be good exercise, too. ***A:*** Good point. I think I'll give it a try.

Question: What will the woman probably do in the future?

訳 A：おはよう。遅れてごめんね。 B：大丈夫だよ。また電車が遅れたの？ A：うん，今月3回目よ。私は早い時間の電車に乗るんだけど，平日のラッシュアワーにはいつも大きな遅れが出るの。 B：君のところには別の路線はないの？ A：あるけど，その路線の駅は家から歩いて45分もかかるのよ。 B：自転車で行けばいいんじゃない？ A：それはいい考えね。そうすれば，今より遅い電車に乗れるかもしれないし。 B：自転車もいい運動になるよ。 A：いいこと言うわね。試してみようかしら。

質問の訳 女性はおそらく将来何をするだろうか。

選択肢の訳 **1** 確実にもっと早い電車に乗るようにする。 **2** 別の路線を使う。
3 自転車で会社に行く。 **4** 週末に出社する。

解説 1～2往復目の会話から，A（＝女性）が，ふだん利用している電車によく遅れが出るので困っている状況であることがわかる。2往復目でB（＝男性）が「別の路線はないの？」とたずねたのに対し，Aは最初，「その（別の）路線の駅は家から歩いて45分もかかる」と述べ，別の路線を使うことに消極的な意見を述べたが，Bから自転車の利用を促されると，「それはいい考えね」(4往復目)，「いいこと言うわね。試してみようかしら」（最後の発言）と述べ，Aが自転車で別の路線の駅に行き，よく遅れが出る今の路線とは別の路線を使うことを肯定的に考えるようになったことがわかる。よって，give it a tryをuse a different train lineと言い換えた**2**が正解。

No.11 正解 **1**

放送文 ***A:*** What're you doing with those garbage bags, Ronan? ***B:*** I was just about to put them outside. Wednesday is collection day, right? ***A:*** Actually, they've switched over to a 14-day schedule. There was an announcement in the local paper last month. ***B:*** They're only collecting every two weeks now? I sometimes wonder what we pay our taxes for. ***A:*** I know what you mean, but I guess the city needs to reduce spending. They're also talking about lowering the number of bags you can put out.

Question: What is one thing we learn from the conversation?

訳 A：そのゴミ袋をどうするつもりなの，ローナン？ B：外に置こうと思ってただけだよ。水曜日が収集日だよね？ A：実は，14日制に切り替わったの。先月，地元新聞に告知があったのよ。 B：2週間に1回しか収集しないの？ ときどきぼくたちは，何のために税金を払っているんだろうって思うよね。 A：言いたいことはわかるけど，市は支出を減らす必要があるんでしょう。市では，出せる袋の数を減らすことについても話し合っているみたいよ。

質問の訳 この会話からわかることの1つは何か。

選択肢の訳 **1** ゴミの収集頻度が少なくなった。 **2** ゴミ袋が高くなりそうだ。
3 もうすぐ地方税が上がりそうだ。 **4** 新聞の配達スケジュールが変わった。

解説 1往復目でB（＝Ronan）が「水曜日が（ゴミの）収集日だよね？」と述べたのに対し，A（＝女性）は「実は，14日制に切り替わったの」(Actually, they've switched over to a 14-day schedule.）と述べている。「水曜日がゴミの収集日」とは，週に1回のごみの収集日があるということなので，それが「14日制（＝2週間に1回）に切り替わった」ということは，「ゴミの収集頻度が少なくなった」ということ。よって，(have) switched over to a 14-day schedule を **has become less frequent** と言い換えた**1**が正解。

No.12 正解 4

放送文 ***A:*** Hey, Sharon. Are you OK? You look exhausted. ***B:*** Hi, Ranjit. Yeah, I can't sleep because of my upstairs neighbors. They're awake at all hours of the night. Even earplugs haven't worked, so I'm going to complain to the landlord. ***A:*** Have you thought about writing a polite note to them first? They might get upset if you go directly to the landlord. ***B:*** I hadn't thought about that. Have you ever tried something like that? ***A:*** No, but I've read online that it can be quite effective. ***B:*** Thanks. I think I'll do that.
Question: What will the woman most likely do?

訳 A：やあ，シャロン。大丈夫？ 疲れてるみたいだね。 B：こんにちは，ランジット。ええ，上の階の住人のせいで眠れないの。彼らは夜中ずっと，起きているのよ。耳栓も役立たないし，大家さんに文句を言おうと思ってるの。 A：まずは丁寧な手紙を書くことを考えてみたら？ 大家さんに直接言ったら，その人たちは怒るかもしれないよ。 B：それは考えもしなかったわ。そういうことを試したことがあるの？ A：ないけど，ネットで結構効果があるって読んだことがあるよ。 B：ありがとう。そうしてみるわ。

質問の訳 その女性は何をする可能性が最も高いか。

選択肢の訳 **1** 耳栓をしてみる。 **2** ランジットに近所の人と話をしてもらう。
3 大家さんについて文句を言う。 **4** 隣人にメッセージを書く。

解説 1往復目の発言から，B（＝Sharon）が，夜中も起きている上の階の住人のせいで眠れなくて悩んでいる場面だとわかる。A（＝Ranjit）が2往復目で「まずは丁寧な手紙を書くことを考えてみたら？」と提案し，さらに3往復目で「ネットで結構効果があるって読んだことがあるんだ」と述べたのに対して，Bは「そうしてみるわ」（I think I'll do that.）と述べている。よって，writing a polite note to them を **write a message to her neighbors** と言い換えた**4**が正解。

Part 2 一次試験・リスニング

(問題編pp.200〜201) CD 緑-40 〜 CD 緑-46

指示文の訳 それでは，これからPart 2の指示を行います。このパートでは(A)から(F)までの6つの文章が放送されます。それぞれの文章に続いて，No. 13からNo. 24まで質問が2つずつ流れます。それぞれの質問に対して，最も適切な答えを選んで解答用紙にマークする時間が10秒あります。文章と質問は1度しか読まれません。それでは始めます。

(A)

放送文 *Picky Eaters*

Some children are picky eaters. They will only eat a few foods and refuse to eat anything else, and this is generally considered unhealthy. Researchers have found that genetics may be one cause of this behavior, but the environment in which children are raised may also be important. Parents, for example, serve as role models for their children, so it can be damaging if their children see them following limited, unhealthy diets.

Once children form such eating habits, how can they be changed? Parents often use rewards. For example, they will tell their children they can have ice cream if they eat their vegetables. However, some experts warn against doing this. They say it does little to change children's negative attitudes toward foods they dislike. Instead, these experts recommend involving children in the growing, purchasing, and preparation of these foods. This may help children develop a positive relationship with healthy meals.

Questions ***No. 13*** What may be one reason children become picky eaters?

No.14 What is one thing that some experts recommend?

訳 偏食の人

子どもの中には，好き嫌いの激しい子がいる。一部の食べ物しか食べず，他のものは一切食べないという子どももいて，これは一般的には不健康だと考えられている。研究者は，遺伝がこの行動の原因の一つかもしれないことを発見したが，子どもが育つ環境もまた，重要かもしれない。例えば，両親は子どものお手本となる存在なので，親が制限された不健康な食生活を送っているのを子どもが見てしまうと，悪影響を与える可能性がある。

そのような食習慣を子どもたちがいったん身につけてしまった場合，どうすれば変えることができるだろうか。親がよく使うのはご褒美を与えることだ。例えば，野菜を食べたらアイスクリームを食べさせてあげると子どもたちに言ったりする。しかし，専門家の中には，このような方法をとることに警告を発する人もいる。専門家らは，子どもの嫌いな食べ物に対する態度は，ご褒美ではほとんど変わらないと言っている。それよりも，これらの専門家は，これらの食品を育てたり，買ったり，調理したりすることに子どもたちを参加させることを勧めている。そうすることが，子どもたちが健康的な食事とポジティブな関係を築くことに役立つかもしれないからだ。

No.13 正解 3

質問の訳 子供が偏食になる理由の1つは何かもしれないか。

選択肢の訳 **1** 食事の選択肢が多すぎる。 **2** 学校がおもしろみのない料理をよく作る。 **3** 彼らは親の食習慣を真似している。 **4** 彼らには痩せたいという願望がある。

解説 第1段落第3文で「遺伝がこの行動（＝子どもの偏食）の原因の一つかもしれない」と述べた後，第4文で「両親は子どものお手本となる存在なので，親が制限された不健康な食生活を送っているのを子どもが見てしまうと，悪影響を与える可能性がある」と述べている。「お手本となる存在」とは，「真似すべき存在」ということで，「悪影響を与える」とは，親を真似して親と同じように「制限された不健康な食生活を送ること」なので，if their children see them following limited, unhealthy dietsを**copy their parents' eating habits**と言い換えた**3**が正解。

No.14 正解 1

質問の訳 専門家が勧めていることの１つは何か。

選択肢の訳 **1** 子どもに自分自身の食事を作るのを手伝わせること。 **2** 子どもにもっとスポーツをするように勧めること。 **3** ときどき子どもが不健康な食べ物を食べるのを許すこと。 **4** 野菜を食べたらご褒美をあげること。

解説 第２段落第６文で「これらの専門家は，これらの食品を育てたり，買ったり，調理したりすることに子どもたちを参加させることを勧めている」と述べられている。よって，involving children in the growing, purchasing, and preparation of these foodsを**getting children to help make their own meals**と言い換えた**1**が正解。

(B)

放送文 *Ching Shih the Pirate*

It is sometimes said that a Chinese woman named Ching Shih was one of history's most successful pirates. Her husband was also a pirate. Following his death in 1807, Ching Shih took control of their pirate operations, which grew rapidly. The Chinese government then ordered its navy to capture her. The sea battle that followed, however, went badly for the government. Ching Shih's pirates captured several naval vessels, which increased Ching Shih's power.

However, it is thought that Ching Shih began having difficulty controlling her huge forces. In 1810, therefore, she came to an agreement with government officials in which she promised to end her operations. In exchange, she was allowed to keep her wealth, and she and most of her followers were given their freedom. While many pirates throughout history died violently, Ching Shih avoided that fate.

Questions ***No. 15*** What was one result of the sea battle?

No. 16 What did Ching Shih do in 1810?

訳 海賊のチン・シー

中国のチン・シーという女性は，歴史上最も成功した海賊の一人であると言われることがある。彼女の夫もまた海賊であった。1807年の夫の死後，チン・シーが彼らの海賊業を管理し，それは急速に成長した。すると，中国政府は海軍に彼女を捕らえるように命じた。しかし，その後の海戦は中国政府にとって形勢不利なものとなった。チン・シーの海賊たちはいくつかの海軍の船を拿捕し，それによってチン・シーの勢力は拡大した。

しかし，チン・シーはその巨大な軍勢を制御することが難しくなり始めたと考えられている。それゆえ，1810年，彼女は政府高官と協定を結び，作戦を終了することを約束した。代わりに，チン・シーは財産をそのまま保持し，チン・シーとその仲間たちのほとんどは自由を与えられた。歴史上，多くの海賊が非業の死を遂げる中，チン・シーはそのような運命をたどらなかった。

No.15 正解 1

質問の訳 海戦の結果の1つは何だったか。

選択肢の訳 **1** チン・シーの海賊は多くの船を獲得した。 **2** 多くの海賊の指揮官が捕らえられた。 **3** 大部分の海賊が殺された。 **4** チン・シーは中国海軍を援助することに同意した。

解説 海戦の様子は，第1段落第5文以降で述べられており，第1段落最終文では「チン・シーの海賊たちはいくつかの海軍の船を拿捕し～」(Ching Shih's pirates captured several naval vessels ～）と述べられている。よって，captured several naval vesselsを**gained a number of ships**と言い換えた**1**が正解。

No.16 正解 4

質問の訳 1810年，チン・シーは何をしたか。

選択肢の訳 **1** 罰から逃れるために中国を離れた。 **2** 自分の財産を手放した。 **3** 新しい海賊の組織を結成した。 **4** 海賊行為を止めることに同意した。

解説 第2段落第2文で「それゆえ，1810年，彼女（＝チン・シー）は政府高官と協定を結び，作戦を終了することを約束した」(In 1810, therefore, she came to an agreement with government officials in which she promised to end her operations.）と述べられている。よって，came to an agreement ～ in which she promised to end her operationsを**agreed to stop her pirate operations**と言い換えた**4**が正解。

(C)

放送文 *The Canada Lynx*

The Canada lynx is a type of wildcat found mainly in Canada and the northern United States. The animals are skilled at avoiding humans, so they are rarely seen in the wild. However, lynx sightings increase roughly every 10 years. This is because the population of animals called snowshoe hares rises and falls in a roughly 10-year cycle. Lynx hunt snowshoe hares, and when there are more hares to hunt, the lynx population tends to grow.

It was long believed that Canada lynx live their whole lives in one particular area. However, scientists have discovered that lynx can journey thousands of kilometers to establish new territories. Some scientists think it is likely that these animals are following hares. However, lynx have also been observed making long journeys at other times, so there may be another reason why they travel.

Questions ***No. 17*** What does the speaker say about Canada lynx?

No. 18 What did scientists discover about Canada lynx?

訳 カナダオオヤマネコ

カナダオオヤマネコは，主にカナダとアメリカ合衆国北部に生息するヤマネコの一種である。この動物は人間を避けるのが得意なため，野生ではめったに見ることができない。しかし，オオヤマネコの目撃情報は，およそ10年ごとに増えている。これは，カンジキウサギという動物の生息数が，ほぼ10年周期で増減しているためだ。オオヤマネコはカンジキウサギを狩るので，狩りの対象となるノウサギが増えるとオオヤマネコの個体数も増える傾向にあるのだ。

カナダオオヤマネコは，ある特定の場所で一生を過ごすと長い間信じられてきた。しかし，科学者は，オオヤマネコが新しい縄張りを作るために何千キロも移動することがあることを発見した。科学者の中には，この動物がノウサギを追いかけているのだろうと考える人もいる。しかし，オオヤマネコが長旅をするのは他の時期にも観察されており，移動するのには別の理由があるのかもしれない。

No.17 正解 1

質問の訳 カナダオオヤマネコについて，話者は何と言っているか。

選択肢の訳 **1** ある時期に生息数が増える。 **2** 人間によって狩られている。 **3** 最近，生息地が狭くなってきた。 **4** カンジキウサギを食べることが少なくなっている。

解説 第1段落第3文で「オオヤマネコの目撃情報は，およそ10年ごとに増えている」と述べられ，続けて「カンジキウサギ～の生息数が，ほぼ10年周期で増減している」としたうえで「狩りの対象となるノウサギが増えるとオオヤマネコの個体数も増える傾向」と述べられている。よって，increase roughly every 10 yearsをincrease at certain timesと言い換えた**1**が正解。

No.18 正解 2

質問の訳 カナダオオヤマネコについて，科学者は何を発見したか。

選択肢の訳 **1** 食べ物を探しているときにだけ移動する。 **2** ときには長距離を移動することもある。 **3** 他のヤマネコよりもずっと長生きする。 **4** いつも元の縄張りに戻ってくる。

解説 第2段落第2文で「科学者は，オオヤマネコが新しい縄張りを作るために何千キロも移動することがあることを発見した」（scientists have discovered that lynx can journey thousands of kilometers to establish new territories）と述べられている。よって，can journey thousands of kilometersをsometimes travel long distancesと言い換えた**2**が正解。

(D)

放送文 *The Catacombs of Priscilla*

In Rome, there are networks of tunnels that were built around the beginning of the second century AD. These tunnels were used as burial places for people of many religions. However, the tunnels became especially important for Christians. Their religion was not officially recognized at the time, so Christians used the tunnels to hold religious ceremonies.

One famous section of tunnels is called the Catacombs of Priscilla. In this section, there are some early Christian paintings. One of the paintings seems to show a woman dressed in a priest's robe, and others show women performing religious ceremonies. Some people believe the paintings are proof of female priests in the church in ancient times. This is significant because some Christian churches today do not allow women to become priests. Other observers, however, say that we cannot be sure exactly what the paintings show.

Questions ***No. 19*** What is one thing we learn about the tunnels?

No. 20 What do some people believe the paintings show?

訳 プリシラのカタコンベ

ローマには，紀元2世紀初頭ごろに作られたトンネル網がある。このトンネルは，さまざまな宗教の人々の埋葬場所として利用されていた。しかし，このトンネルはキリスト教徒にとって特に重要なものとなった。当時，キリスト教は公的に認められていなかったので，キリスト教徒は宗教的な儀式を行うためにそのトンネルを利用したのだった。

トンネルの中で有名な区画の１つは，プリシラのカタコンベと呼ばれている。この区画には，初期キリスト教の絵画がいくつか残されている。その絵画の中には，司祭の式服をまとった女性を表しているように見えるものや，宗教的な儀式を行う女性たちを表しているように見えるものがある。これらの絵は，古代の教会に女性の司祭がいたことの証明だと考える人もいる。現在，キリスト教の教会の中には，女性が司祭になることを認めていないところもあるので，このことの意義は深い。しかし，これらの絵が何を示しているのか正確にはわからないと言う人もいる。

No.19 正解 2

質問の訳 そのトンネルについてわかることの１つは何か。

選択肢の訳 **1** 現代の埋葬地は，そのトンネルの設計がベースになっている。 **2** そのトンネルは，宗教的な目的のために使われた。 **3** そのトンネルは，非キリスト教徒のみによって使用されていた。 **4** （そのトンネルの）入り口は最近になって発見された。

解説 第１段落最終文で「キリスト教徒は宗教的な儀式を行うためにそのトンネルを利用した」(Christians used the tunnels to hold religious ceremonies) と述べられている。よって，used the tunnels to hold religious ceremoniesを**were used for religious purposes**と言い換えた**2**が正解。

No.20 正解 1

質問の訳 何人かの人々は，その絵画が何を表すと考えているか。

選択肢の訳 **1** 大昔は女性が司祭であった。 **2** トンネルは教会としては使われなかった。 **3** 初期のキリスト教徒に女性はほとんどいなかった。 **4** かつて司祭は絵画を制作していた。

解説 第２段落で，プリシラのカタコンベの絵画について，司祭の式服をまとった女性や宗教的な儀式を行う女性を表しているように見えるものがあると述べられた後，「これらの絵は，古代の教会に女性の司祭がいたことの証明だと考える人もいる」と述べられている。よって，female priests in the church in ancient timesを**women used to be priests long ago**と言い換えた**1**が正解。

(E)

放送文 *Happiness and Success*

Many people believe that only by working hard and having a successful career can they find happiness. However, trying to make a lot of money or get promoted at work may not make people truly happy. People who focus on such success often prioritize work over other activities. Consequently, they may lose opportunities to enjoy the things that make life truly enjoyable, such as simple, relaxing times with their families.

After reviewing many studies, researchers recently concluded that success may actually follow happiness. They believe that happy people are more energetic and confident because they experience frequent positive moods, and that this leads to success. Of course, success also depends on factors such as intelligence and social support. More research is needed, but it may be that those whose happiness leads them to success are more likely to stay happy.

Questions ***No. 21*** What does the speaker say about people who focus on success?

No. 22 What did researchers recently conclude about happy people?

訳 幸せと成功

多くの人は，一生懸命に働いて職業で成功することでしか，幸せを見つけることができないと信じている。しかし，お金をたくさん稼ごうとしたり，職場で昇進しようとしたりすることが，人を本当に幸せにするとは限らないかもしれない。そのような成功を重視する人は，他の活動よりも仕事を優先させることが多い。その結果，家族とのささやかなやすらぎのひとときなど，人生を真に楽しむべきものにしてくれるものを享受する機会を失ってしまうかもしれない。

多くの研究を検討した結果，研究者たちは最近，成功は，実は幸せの後にやってくるのかもしれないという結論に達した。研究者たちは，幸せな人は前向きな気分を頻繁に経験するので，より精力的で自信に満ちており，それが成功につながると考えているのだ。もちろん，成功は知性や社会的なサポートなどの要因にも依存している。さらなる研究が必要だが，幸せが成功につながる人は，幸せであり続ける可能性が高いのかもしれない。

No.21 正解 **3**

質問の訳 成功を重視する人について，話者は何と言っているか。

選択肢の訳 **1** 家族に成功者がいることが多い。 **2** ストレスのレベルが低いことが多い。 **3** ささやかな楽しみを味わうチャンスを逃すかもしれない。 **4** 周囲の人を幸せにするかもしれない。

解説 第1段落第3文で「成功を重視する人は，他の活動よりも仕事を優先させることが多い」と述べられた後，次の文で「その結果，家族とのささやかなやすらぎのひとときなど，人生を真に楽しむべきものにしてくれるものを享受する機会を失ってしまうかもしれない」(Consequently, they may lose opportunities to enjoy the things that make life truly enjoyable, such as simple, relaxing times with their families）と述べられている。よって，lose opportunities to enjoy the things ～, such as simple, relaxing times with their familiesをmiss chances to enjoy simple pleasuresと言い換えた**3**が正解。

No.22　正解　3

質問の訳　幸せな人々について，研究者たちは最近どのような結論を出したか。

選択肢の訳　**1**　幸せでいるために，家族のサポートを必要としない。　**2**　収入が多いとは言えない。　**3**　前向きな気分を持っていることでより活動的である。　**4**　不幸せな人よりも知的である。

解説　第2段落第1文で「研究者たちは最近，成功は，実は幸せの後にやってくるのかもしれないという結論に達した」と述べられた後，次の文で「幸せな人は前向きな気分を頻繁に経験するので，より精力的で自信に満ちており～」と述べられている。よって，more energetic and confident because they experience frequent positive moods を**positive moods make them more active**と言い換えた**3**が正解。

(F)

放送文　*Ancient Oysters*

For thousands of years, Native Americans along what is now called the US East Coast used oysters as a food source. Today, however, oyster stocks have been greatly reduced. Overharvesting, pollution, and disease have caused oyster populations to fall, especially since the late 1800s, when European settlers introduced new harvesting methods. These methods included dredging, which involves removing huge numbers of oysters from the seabed. This process also damages the ecosystem in which the oysters live.

In recent years, archaeologists have studied Native American harvesting practices. The archaeologists found that Native Americans did not harvest young oysters. Instead, Native Americans waited for oysters to grow and reproduce before they harvested them. The archaeologists also discovered that average shell size increased until the 1800s, which indicates that Native American practices helped ancient oysters to become larger. This finding surprised the archaeologists, who expected oyster shells to gradually get smaller in response to being harvested.

Questions ***No. 23*** What do we learn about oysters along the US East Coast today?

No. 24 What is one thing the archaeologists discovered?

訳　太古の牡蠣（かき）

現在のアメリカ東海岸沿いのアメリカ先住民は，数千年もの間，牡蠣を食料として利用していた。しかし，現在，牡蠣の資源は大幅に減少している。特に1800年代後半，ヨーロッパからの入植者が新しい漁法を導入して以来，乱獲，汚染，病気などが原因で牡蠣の個体数が減少してしまった。これらの漁法には浚渫（しゅんせつ）が含まれるが，それは海底から大量の牡蠣を掘り起こすことだ。この行為も，牡蠣が生息する生態系に損傷を与えている。

近年，考古学者たちがアメリカ先住民の漁獲慣習を研究している。考古学者たちは，アメリカ先住民が若い牡蠣を収穫していないことを発見した。その代わりに，アメリカ先住民は牡蠣が成長し，繁殖するのを待ってから収穫していたのだ。また考古学者たちは，平均的な殻の大きさは1800年代まで増大していたことを発見した。それはアメリカ先住民の（漁獲）慣習が古代の牡蠣を大きくするのに役立ったことを示唆している。この発見は考古学者たちを驚かせた，というのは，彼らは，牡蠣の殻は収穫されることによって徐々に小さくなると考えていたからだ。

No.23　正解　2

質問の訳　現在のアメリカ東海岸沿いの牡蠣について，どのようなことがわかるか。

選択肢の訳　**1**　病気との闘い方が巧妙になってきている。　**2**　数がかつてより減っている。　**3**　それらの多くは食用として獲られることはない。　**4**　それらの生息水域がきれいになってきている。

解説　現在のアメリカ東海岸沿いの牡蠣の状況については，第1段落第2文以降で述べられており，第1段落第2文では「現在，牡蠣の資源は大幅に減少している」，続く第3文では「乱獲，汚染，病気などが原因で牡蠣の個体数が減少してしまった」(Overharvesting, pollution, and disease have caused oyster populations to fall）と述べられている。よって，oyster populations to fallを**their numbers are lower**と言い換えた**2**が正解。

No.24　正解　1

質問の訳　考古学者が発見したことの1つは何か。

選択肢の訳　**1**　アメリカ先住民の漁獲慣習が，牡蠣の成長に役立った。　**2**　アメリカ先住民の収穫方法には，浚渫が含まれていた。　**3**　アメリカ先住民は今でも牡蠣を獲っている。　**4**　アメリカ先住民は若い牡蠣だけを獲っていた。

解説　第2段落第2文以降で，考古学者たちが，アメリカ先住民が若い牡蠣を収穫せず，牡蠣が成長し繁殖するのを待ってから収穫していたことを発見したことが述べられた後，第2段落の最後から2文目では「考古学者たちは，平均的な殻の大きさは1800年代まで増大していたことを発見した。それはアメリカ先住民の（漁獲）慣習（＝牡蠣が成長し繁殖するのを待ってから収穫すること）が，古代の牡蠣を大きくするのに役立ったことを示唆している」と述べられている。よって，helped ancient oysters to become largerを**helped oysters grow**と言い換えた**1**が正解。

Part 3　一次試験・リスニング

(問題編pp.202〜203)

指示文の訳　それでは最後に，Part 3の指示を行います。このパートでは*(G)*から*(K)*までの5つの文章が放送されます。英文は実生活における状況を述べたもので，効果音を含むものもあります。それぞれの文章には，No. 25からNo. 29まで，質問が1問ずつ用意されています。それぞれの文章が流れる前に，問題冊子に書かれている状況の説明と質問を読む時間が10秒あります。文章を聞いた後に，最も適切な答えを選んで解答用紙にマークする時間が10秒あります。文章は1度しか読まれません。それでは始めます。

No.25　正解　3

放送文　*(G)*　You have 10 seconds to read the situation and Question No. 25.

This bus goes around town all day, so you can just hop on and off anytime.

The castle can be accessed from stop 4, and the medieval library is also just a five-minute walk away from that stop. If you're interested in the San Giovanni church, stop 7 is the nearest. It's also normally the meeting place for our 30-minute guided walking tour, but please note that due to an ongoing construction project, that tour will begin from stop 9, just in front of Montalto Gardens. Stop 13 offers access to famous sights like the Gravina Bridge and the town fountain.

Now mark your answer on your answer sheet.

訳 *(G)* 状況と質問25を読む時間が10秒あります。

このバスは一日中街を回っているので，いつでも乗り降りが可能です。城へは4番のバス停からアクセスでき，中世の図書館もそのバス停からたった徒歩5分です。サン・ジョバンニ教会に興味がおありなら，7番のバス停が最寄りです。そのバス停は，通常は30分のガイド付きウォーキングツアーの集合場所でもありますが，現在工事中のため，ツアーはモンタルトガーデンのすぐ前の9番のバス停からとなりますので，ご注意ください。13番のバス停からは，グラヴィーナ橋や街の噴水などの有名な観光スポットへ行くことができます。

それでは，解答用紙に答えをマークしなさい。

状況の訳 あなたはこれからツアーバスでイタリアの街を回ろうとしている。あなたはガイド付きのウォーキングツアーに参加したいと思っている。次のようなアナウンスが聞こえてきた。

質問の訳 あなたはどのバス停で降りるべきか。

選択肢の訳 **1** 4番のバス停。 **2** 7番のバス停。 **3** 9番のバス停。 **4** 13番のバス停。

解説 Situationからわかるのは，①「あなた」はツアーバスでイタリアの街を回ろうとしていることと，②「あなた」はガイド付きのウォーキングツアーへの参加を希望していること。アナウンスでは，第4文で「そのバス停（＝7番のバス停）は，通常は30分のガイド付きウォーキングツアーの集合場所でもありますが，現在工事中のため，ツアーはモンタルトガーデンのすぐ前の9番のバス停からとなります」と述べられている。よって，ガイド付きのウォーキングツアーに参加するためには，通常であれば7番のバス停で降りるべきだが，現在は工事中のため9番のバス停で降りるべきだとわかるので，**3**が正解。

No.26 正解 **4**

放送文 *(H)* You have 10 seconds to read the situation and Question No. 26.

You can apply online to renew your working-holiday visa. However, there are some things you should prepare before you apply. You'll need to provide proof that you've had a medical examination by a qualified doctor and have no serious health issues. Once you've done that, you'll also have to present evidence of your employment until now. You mentioned you had all of your salary statements, so those should be sufficient. Since you're applying from within the country, proof that you've saved enough to cover your living costs will not be required this time around.

Now mark your answer on your answer sheet.

訳 *(H)* 状況と質問26を読む時間が10秒あります。

ワーキングホリデービザの更新は，オンラインで申請できます。ただし，申請前に準備しておくことがいくつかあります。資格のある医師による健康診断を受け，健康に重大な問題がないことを証明する必要があります。それができたら，これまでの就労歴を証明する書類を提出する必要があります。給与明細がすべてあるとのことですので，それで十分でしょう。今回は国内からの申請なので，生活費をまかなえるだけの貯蓄があることの証明は必要ないでしょう。

それでは，解答用紙に答えをマークしなさい。

状況の訳 あなたはワーキングホリデープログラムで海外に滞在している。ビザの更新について入国管理局に電話したところ，次のように言われた。

質問の訳 あなたはまず何をすべきか。

選択肢の訳 **1** オンラインで申請書を作成する。 **2** 勤務先から給与明細を取り寄せる。 **3** 貯蓄を証明するものを提示する。 **4** 健康診断書を取得する。

解説 Situationからわかるのは，①「あなた」はワーキングホリデープログラムで海外に滞在中であることと，②「あなた」がビザの更新について入国管理局に電話している場面であること。入国管理局の担当者は，ワーキングホリデービザの更新はオンラインで申請できると述べた後，「(オンラインでの) 申請前に (まず) 準備しておくこと」として，第3文で「資格のある医師による健康診断を受け，健康に重大な問題がないことを証明する必要」があると述べている。よって，「あなた」がまずすべきこととしては，proof that you've had a medical examination by a qualified doctorを**obtain a medical examination certificate**と言い換えた**4**が正解。

No.27 正解 1

放送文 *(I)* You have 10 seconds to read the situation and Question No. 27.

The new security cameras, warning signs, and staff training have all worked. Shoplifting of most products is much lower than in the last quarter. However, stock records for low-cost fruit items like bananas and oranges and expensive things like avocados and mangoes don't match the sales records. This usually means some customers at the self-checkout registers are entering false information to get costly items at a cheaper price. I recommend extra guidance for staff observing the self-checkout stations. If this doesn't work, you may have to think about checking customers' receipts at the exit.

Now mark your answer on your answer sheet.

訳 *(I)* 状況と質問27を読む時間が10秒あります。

新しい防犯カメラ，警告標識，スタッフへのトレーニングのすべてが功を奏しています。ほとんどの商品の万引きは，前四半期に比べてかなり減少しています。しかし，バナナやオレンジのような低価格の果物や，アボカドやマンゴーのような高価なものの在庫記録が，販売記録と一致しません。これは通常，セルフレジで偽の情報を入力し，高価な商品をより安く手に入れているお客様がいることを意味します。私は，セルフレジを監視しているスタッフに，さらなる指導をすることをお勧めします。それでもうまくいかなければ，出口でお客様のレシートをチェックすることについても考えなければならないかもしれません。

それでは，解答用紙に答えをマークしなさい。

状況の訳 あなたはスーパーマーケットの店長である。あなたは，盗難による損失を減らしたいと思っている。警備のアナリストが次のように言っている。

質問の訳 あなたはまず何をすべきか。

選択肢の訳 **1** 一部のスタッフをさらにトレーニングする。 **2** より多くの防犯カメラを設置する。 **3** 出口で客のレシートを確認する。 **4** 果物の価格を明確に表示する。

解説 Situationからわかるのは，①「あなた」はスーパーマーケットの店長であることと，②「あなた」は盗難による損失を減らしたいと思っていること。警備のアナリストは，第3文で，低価格の果物と高価格のものの在庫記録が販売記録と一致しないことに触れ，それはセルフレジで偽の情報を入力する客がいることを意味すると指摘した上で，盗難による損失を減らすために，「セルフレジを監視しているスタッフに，さらなる指導をすることをお勧めします」と提案している。よって，extra guidanceを**more training**と，staff observing the self-checkout stationsを**some staff members**と，それぞれ言い換えた**1**が正解。

No. 28 正解 **4**

放送文 *(J)* You have 10 seconds to read the situation and Question No. 28.

Welcome to our summer sale. We're offering great discounts on all brands, including Rannexe and Duplanne. Interested in a new vacuum cleaner? Use the coupon available on our smartphone app to get $50 off any brand. How about a new washing machine? This month, exchange your used Rannexe washing machine for a $100 credit toward any new Rannexe product. During the month of August, exchange any old Duplanne appliance and get $150 off a new one. Finally, we are offering $75 cash back on any new dishwasher until the end of August.

Now mark your answer on your answer sheet.

訳 *(J)* 状況と質問28を読む時間が10秒あります。

サマーセールへようこそ。ラネックス，デュプランを含む全ブランドを大幅割引でご提供中です。新しい掃除機にご興味がおありですか。スマートフォンのアプリで入手できるクーポンを使えば，どのブランドでも50ドル引きになります。新しい洗濯機はいかがでしょうか。今月は，ご使用済みのラネックス製洗濯機を，どの新しいラネックス製品にも使える100ドル分のクーポンと交換します。8月中は，古いデュプラン製品を交換すると，新しい製品が150ドル割引になります。最後に，8月末まで，新しい食器洗い機を購入すると，75ドルのキャッシュバックをご提供します。

それでは，解答用紙に答えをマークしなさい。

状況の訳 あなたは新しい洗濯機が欲しいと思っている。あなたは現在，デュプランの洗濯機を所有している。あなたは7月にある電器店を訪れ，次のようなアナウンスを聞く。

質問の訳 お金を最も節約するためにあなたは何をすべきか。

選択肢の訳 **1** その店のスマートフォンアプリをダウンロードする。 **2** キャッシュバック取引を申し込む。 **3** 今月，洗濯機を交換する。 **4** 8月に新しいデュプランの洗濯機を購入する。

解説 Situationからわかるのは，①「あなた」が欲しいものは新しい洗濯機であること，②「あなた」は現在デュプランの洗濯機を所有していること，③アナウンスは，「あなた」

が7月にある電器店を訪れているときのものであること。アナウンスでは，新しい掃除機，新しい洗濯機，新しい食器洗い機の3つについて述べられているが，「あなた」がほしいのは「新しい洗濯機」なので，「新しい洗濯機」についての発言に注目する。アナウンスでは，「新しい洗濯機」について，使用済みのラネックス製洗濯機を，どの新しいラネックス製品にも使える100ドル分のクーポンと交換することと，8月中は，古いデュプラン製品を交換すると新しい製品が150ドル割引になるという，2つのキャンペーンについて述べている。「あなた」は7月現在でデュプランの洗濯機を所有しているというSituationから，8月に行われる2つ目のキャンペーンを利用して「あなた」の所有しているデュプランの洗濯機と交換で新しいデュプランの洗濯機を買えば，150ドル割引になって，お金を最も節約できることになる。よって，「8月に」と「新しい洗濯機を買う」という2つの条件を満たしている**4**が正解。

No. 29 正解 **2**

放送文 *(K)* You have 10 seconds to read the situation and Question No. 29.

This suit is a clearance item, so we only have what's here on the shelves. Our other location may still have one in your size, though. If you'd like, I can check online for you. If our other store has one, you could go there, if you don't mind driving out of town. The other option would be to reserve one for you and have it sent over to this store at no extra cost. That might take a few days, but if you give me your number, I can call you when it arrives.

Now mark your answer on your answer sheet.

訳 *(K)* 状況と質問29を読む時間が10秒あります。

このスーツは在庫処分品ですので，この棚にあるものしかありません。他の店舗ならまだあなたのサイズのものがあるかもしれませんが。よろしければ，ネットでお調べいたします。もし，他の店舗にある場合，車で市外にお出かけになっても構わないのであれば，そちらへ行かれるのもいいと思います。もうひとつの方法は，予約しておいて，追加料金なしでこの店に送ってもらうことです。その場合，数日かかるかもしれませんが，電話番号を教えていただければ，商品が到着した際に電話いたします。

それでは，解答用紙に答えをマークしなさい。

状況の訳 あなたは地元の店で欲しいスーツを見つけたが，あなたのサイズのスーツがない。あなたは市外には出かけたくない。店員はあなたに次のように言う。

質問の訳 あなたは何をすべきか。

選択肢の訳 **1** その店舗に新しい在庫が入るまで待つ。 **2** 店員に他の店舗を調べてもらう。 **3** オンラインショップでスーツを注文する。 **4** スーツを自宅まで配送してもらう。

解説 Situationからわかるのは，①「あなた」は地元の店で欲しいスーツを見つけたこと，②しかし，その地元の店には「あなた」に合うサイズのスーツがないこと，③「あなた」は市外には出かけたくないということ，の3つ。店員は，他の店舗に「あなた」のサイズのスーツがあるかについて，ネットで調べると述べ，他の店舗に「あなた」のサイズのスーツがあった場合に「あなた」が取るべき手段として，市外のその店舗に車で行くこと，または，在庫があるその店舗で予約し，地元のその店舗に送ってもらうこと，という2つの方法を提案している。Situationから，「あなた」は市外には出かけたくないのだか

ら「あなた」のとるべき手段は2つ目の方法となるが，いずれにせよ，店員に他の店舗に「あなた」のサイズのスーツがあるかを調べてもらうことが必要となる。よって，I can check online for youをhave the clerk check the other storeと言い換えた**2**が正解。

カードA 二次試験・面接

（問題編pp.204～205）

指示文の訳 1分間，準備する時間があります。
これは，自分たちの地域社会に参加したいと思った夫婦についての話です。
ストーリーのナレーションを行うのに与えられる時間は２分間です。
ストーリーは以下の文で始めてください。
ある日，夫と妻は一緒に散歩をしていました。

ナレーションの解答例 **One day, a husband and wife were going on a walk together.** They saw a group of volunteers picking up garbage in the park. The husband and wife looked pleased to see them cleaning up the area. The next day, the couple was walking around their neighborhood again, and they saw a poster. It said that volunteers were wanted to help at the city marathon. The couple thought it was a good opportunity for them, so they decided to volunteer. At a volunteer staff meeting, the couple was listening to an explanation about their duties at the marathon. A man was explaining that volunteers would help with tasks like working at water stations and at the information booth. The couple seemed to be looking forward to volunteering at the marathon. The day before the marathon, however, the wife was speaking with her manager at work. He told her that she needed to meet a client the next day.

解答例の訳 **ある日，夫と妻は一緒に散歩をしていました。**彼らは，ボランティアの集団が公園内のごみ拾いをしているのを目にしました。夫と妻は，彼らが地域の清掃をしているのを見て喜ばしく思っている様子でした。翌日，夫婦は再び彼らの近所をぶらぶら歩いていて，彼らは１枚のポスターを目にしました。それには，市のマラソン大会での手伝いのボランティアが募集中であると書かれていました。夫婦はそれが彼らにとっての良い機会だと思い，ボランティアをすることに決めました。ボランティアスタッフの会議で，夫婦はマラソン大会での自分たちの務めに関する説明を聞いていました。男性が，ボランティアは例えば給水所や案内所での作業といった務めを手伝うことになると説明していました。夫婦は，マラソン大会でボランティアをするのを心待ちにしている様子でした。しかし，マラソン大会の前日に，妻は職場でマネージャーと話をしていました。彼は彼女に，彼女が翌日に顧客と会う必要があると伝えました。

解説 ナレーションは，４コマのイラストの進行に沿ってまとめていく。２～４コマ目の左上方にある時間の経過や場所を表す語句は，各コマの描写の冒頭部分で必ず使うこと。また，吹き出し内のせりふは，間接話法または直接話法を使ってストーリーに盛り込むが，間接話法を使う場合，主語や動詞などを適切な形に変える必要がある点に注意する。他，ポスター，ホワイトボードなどに書かれた文字など，イラスト内の情報も適切な形でストーリーに取り入れること。なお，動詞の時制は，過去形および過去進行形を基本に，時間の経過がわかるよう描写する。

①1コマ目：夫婦が公園のそばを歩いている場面。ごみ拾いをしている3名の人物が描かれているが，そのうちの手前の人物の背中にVolunteer「ボランティア」と書かれていることから，彼らは園内の清掃ボランティアなのだと判断できる。夫婦の表情から，彼らはボランティアたちが作業している様子を見て，肯定的な感情を抱いているのだと考えられるため，その点をナレーションに盛り込む。

②2コマ目：The next dayで始める。夫婦がポスターを見ている場面。ポスター内の文字情報とイラストから，市主催のマラソンイベントにおけるボランティアを募集することを目的としたポスターだとわかる。女性が明るい表情を浮かべていること，および夫が頷いていることから，夫婦はそのボランティア募集に応募することに乗り気なのだと推測できるだろう。

③3コマ目：At a volunteer staff meetingで始める。夫婦が，ボランティアスタッフ向けの会議に参加している場面。ホワイトボード内の最上部にABC City Marathonとあり，その下にはDuties「務め」に続けてWater Stations「給水所」およびInformation Booth「案内所」と示されている。これらのことから，マラソンイベントにおけるボランティアスタッフとしての務めを出席者に説明することを目的とした会議なのだと判断できる。二人の表情・仕草から，夫婦はやる気に満ちているのだと推測可能。

④4コマ目：The day before the marathonで始める。女性がマネージャーと話をしている場面。マネージャーの吹き出しにYou need to meet a client tomorrow.「あなたは明日，顧客と会う必要があります」と書かれているので，解答例のように，その発言内容をHe told her that ～.「彼は彼女に，～と伝えた」と間接話法で表すと良い。その際，吹き出し内のtomorrow「明日」はthe next day「翌日」とすべき点に注意。なお，デスクの上に置かれているカレンダーから，マラソンの開催日は11月13日の土曜日だとわかるので，その正確な日付をナレーションに盛り込んでも良いだろう。

質問の訳 No. 1　4番目の絵を見てください。あなたがその妻なら，どのようなことを考えているでしょうか。

では～さん（受験者の氏名），カードを裏返して置いてください。

No. 2　親は体育祭のような学校行事に参加すべきだと思いますか。

No. 3　公共図書館は今なお地域社会において重要な役割を果たしていますか。

No. 4　もっと多くの企業が従業員に，時間の融通がきく仕事のスケジュールを提供すべきですか。

No.1 **解答例 I'd be thinking that I should have talked about becoming a volunteer with my boss first. Now I can't fulfill my responsibilities to both my work and the marathon. I should be more careful about my schedule in the future.**

解答例の訳 まずはボランティアになることについて上司と相談すべきだったと私は思っているでしょう。今や，私は仕事とマラソンの両方の務めを果たすことはできません。私は先々のスケジュールについてもっと気をつけるべきです。

解説 解答例では，質問の仮定法過去形に合わせて，間接話法でI'd be thinking that ～.の形で答えている。また，もはや仕事とボランティアへの参加の両立が困難な状況に置かれてしまっているため，後悔を表す〈should have＋過去分詞〉「～すべきだった」を用いて，ボランティアへの参加の決定前に上司と相談すべきだったと反省している。あるいは，解答例の1文目のthat以降を，I should have told my boss about my decision to take part in the volunteer work「ボランティア活動への参加について，上司に伝えておくべきだった」などとして，ボランティアへの参加を決定事項として上司に伝えておくべきだったと悔やむ内容にしても良いだろう。

No.2 **解答例** Yes. It's a chance for parents to better understand their children's relationships with their classmates. This is good for building strong family relationships. It also gives parents and teachers an opportunity to communicate.

解答例の訳 はい。それは，親にとっては我が子がクラスメートと育んでいる関係についての理解を深める機会です。これは濃密な家族関係を築くのに役立ちます。また，それは，親と教師にコミュニケーションする機会を与えます。

解説 解答例では，Yesの立場から，子どもが友人と築いている関係についての理解が濃密な家族関係の構築につながるというメリットを述べてから，親と教師の間のコミュニケーションの機会も生まれるという別のメリットにも言及している。あるいは，Noの立場で，I don't think so. Many parents are busy, and they have a lot of things to do such as working and housework. Also, in the first place, I think it is important whether their children want their parents to participate in school events, so parents should not decide to participate without having a talk with their children about it in advance.「私はそうは思いません。多くの親は忙しく，彼らには仕事や家事をはじめ，すべきことがたくさんあります。それから，そもそも，子どもが親に学校の行事への参加をしてほしいと思っているかが重要だと思うので，親はそれについて前もって子どもと話をすることなしに参加を決定すべきではありません」のように答えても良いだろう。

No.3 **解答例** No. The purpose of public libraries is to give people access to information, but I think we can achieve the same goal using digital libraries online. That way, we don't need to spend a lot of money maintaining library buildings.

解答例の訳 いいえ。公共図書館の目的は人々に情報へのアクセスを与えることですが，私たちはオンライン上の電子図書館を利用して同じ目標を達成することができると思います。それなら，私たちは図書館の建物の維持管理に大金を費やす必要がありません。

解説 解答例では，Noの立場から，公共図書館の代替的な存在としてオンライン上の電子図書館に言及し，後者で同じことができる上に，それには建物の維持管理に金を使う必要がないという利点があることを伝えている。あるいは，Yesの立場から実体験を交えて，Yes. There are many public libraries which hold various fruitful events for communities. I have participated in some of those events before, and came to know a lot of people there, some of whom became close friends later.「はい。地域社会のためにさまざまな有益なイベントを開催している公共図書館はたくさんあります。私はこれまでにそのようなイベントのうちいくつかに参加したことがあり，そこでたくさんの人々と知り合いました。彼らの中にはのちに親友になった人もいます」などと答えても良いだろう。

No.4 **解答例** **Definitely. It might not be realistic for some companies, but I think in many cases having a more flexible schedule is an easy way to increase employee satisfaction. This will especially help employees who have young children.**

解答例の訳 絶対にそうです。それは一部の企業にとっては現実的ではないかもしれませんが，多くの場合，より融通がきくスケジュールにすることは手っ取り早く従業員の満足度を向上させることのできる手段です。これは，とりわけ幼い子どもを持つ従業員の助けとなるでしょう。

解説 解答例ではまず，Definitely.「絶対にそうです」と自分がYesの立場にあることを強調してから，より融通がきくスケジュールを従業員に提供するのが現実的な選択肢ではない企業があるかもしれないと譲歩しながらも，それが従業員の満足度を向上させるのに手軽な手段であり，特に幼児を持つ人々にとって有益だろうと述べている。あるいは，No. If companies introduce flexible work schedules, the time management of their employees would be more difficult and tiring. Additionally, some companies allow their employees to work remotely nowadays. In that case, the difficulty of managing people's time would be much greater.「いいえ。融通がきくスケジュールを企業が導入すれば，従業員の時間管理はもっと困難で疲れさせるものとなるでしょう。さらに，近頃では，従業員の遠隔勤務を認めている企業もあります。その場合，人々の時間を管理する困難さははるかに大きくなるでしょう」などと答えることもできるだろう。

カードB 二次試験・面接

(問題編pp.206〜207)

指示文の訳 1分間，準備する時間があります。
これは，旅行に出かけたいと思った女性についての話です。
ストーリーのナレーションを行うのに与えられる時間は2分間です。
ストーリーは以下の文で始めてください。
ある日，女性は友人と話をしていました。

ナレーションの解答例 **One day, a woman was talking with her friend.** They were sitting at a table, and her friend was holding a brochure for a beach resort. The woman's friend suggested they go together, but the woman looked worried about the price. Later that evening, the woman was looking at her computer, and she saw that she could earn money by doing some part-time work before the trip. According to the calendar, the woman's trip was just a few weeks away. Two weeks later, the woman was working at a restaurant. She was taking an order while her manager looked on. A few days later, the woman's suitcase was almost packed, and she was nearly ready for her trip. She was talking on the phone with her manager. The manager had an injured leg and was telling her that the restaurant would need her help the next day.

訳 **ある日，女性は友人と話をしていました。**彼らはテーブル席に座っていて，彼女の友人は海辺のリゾート地のパンフレットを手に持っていました。女性の友人は2人で一緒に行くことを提案しましたが，女性は料金について心配そうな様子でした。その日の夜，女性はコンピュータを見ていて，旅行前にアルバイトの仕事をすることでお金を稼ぐことができると知りました。カレンダーによると，女性の旅行はほんの数週間後でした。2週間後，女性はレストランで働いていました。彼女は，彼女のマネージャーに見守られながらオーダーを取っていました。数日後，女性のスーツケースはほぼ荷造りができている状態で，彼女はもう少しで旅行の準備が整うところでした。彼女は電話でマネージャーと話をしていました。マネージャーは脚をけがしており，翌日に彼女の助けがレストランに必要であると伝えていました。

解説 ナレーションは，4コマのイラストの進行に沿ってまとめていく。2～4コマ目の左上方にある時間の経過を表す語句は，各コマの描写の冒頭部分で必ず使うこと。吹き出し内のせりふは，間接話法または直接話法を使ってストーリーに盛り込むが，間接話法を使う場合，主語や動詞などを適切な形に変える点に注意する。また，雑誌，パソコンの画面，カレンダーなどのイラスト内にある文字情報も適切な形でストーリーに盛り込む。動詞の時制は，過去形および過去進行形を基本に，時間の経過がわかるように描写する。

①1コマ目：カフェのような場所で友人と話をしている場面。女性の友人はBeach Resort「海辺のリゾート地」と書かれた冊子を指さしており，その吹き出し内にはLet's go together!「一緒に行こう！」とある。このことから，友人は海辺のリゾート地に一緒に行くことを女性に提案しているのだと考えられる。しかし，女性は困った表情を浮かべており，その吹き出し内には¥と書かれた札束に×印がついているので，女性は友人の提案に対し，金銭面で不安を抱えているのだと推測できる。

②2コマ目：Later that eveningで始める。女性が自分の部屋でパソコンを見ている場面。背景のカレンダーより，女性は旅行に出かけることにし，日程も確定済みなのだとわかる。また，パソコンの画面にはPart-time job　Earn extra money!「アルバイトの職。追加のお金を稼ごう！」とあるので，女性は旅行資金の不足という問題を解決するために，求人情報を見ているところだと判断できる。

③3コマ目：Two weeks laterで始める。女性がレストランで働いている場面。女性はテーブル席についている家族客のオーダーを取っており，背後にはManager「マネージャー」というプレートをつけた男性がその様子を見守っている。マネージャーが飲み物を運んでいる点や，女性が家族客に対応している点にふれても良い。

④4コマ目：A few days laterで始める。女性とマネージャーが電話している場面。困った表情を浮かべているマネージャーの左脚には包帯が巻かれており，ベッドの背景には松葉杖が確認できることから，マネージャーは左脚をけがしてしまったのだとわかる。彼は

We need your help tomorrow.「明日，あなたの助けが必要です」と女性に伝えている。ところが一方，女性はといえば，背景のカレンダーより，旅行の日程は差し迫っているところであり，スーツケースはほぼ荷造りができている状態にあることがわかる。解答では，この不運さやタイミングの悪さなどに言及することで臨場感を出しても良いだろう。

質問の訳 No. 1　4番目の絵を見てください。あなたがその女性なら，どのようなことを考えているでしょうか。
では～さん（受験者の氏名），カードを裏返して置いてください。
No. 2　大学生にとってアルバイトの仕事をすることは良いと思いますか。
No. 3　個人情報をオンライン事業者に渡すのは安全だと思いますか。
No. 4　政府は日本の雇用率を上げるためにもっと多くのことをすべきですか。

No.1 解答例 I'd be thinking, "I'm sorry to hear that my manager hurt his leg, but it's impossible for me to work tomorrow. I've already booked everything for the trip, including the plane ticket and hotel reservation."

解答例の訳 「マネージャーが脚をけがしたと聞いて気の毒ではあるが，私は明日働くことが不可能だ。飛行機のチケットやホテルの予約をはじめ，私はすでに旅行に向けて何もかも手配済みだ」と私は思っているでしょう。

解説 質問の仮定法過去形に合わせて，直接話法でI'd be thinking, "～." のように始めると良い。解答例では，マネージャーのことを気の毒に思うものの，すでに旅行に出かける準備ができている状況なので，自分は力にはなれないという立場で述べている。あるいは，解答例とは違う観点で，I'd be thinking, "In the first place, I decided to apply for the job to earn money for the trip. Since the trip is much more important to me than working, I should put the trip before my job. Unfortunately, the manager will need to find someone else."「『そもそも，私は旅行の資金を稼ぐために仕事に応募することを決心した。私にとっては旅行の方が仕事よりもはるかに重要なのだから，私は仕事よりも旅行を優先すべきだ。あいにく，マネージャーは誰か別の人を見つける必要があるだろう』と私は思っているでしょう」などと答えても良いだろう。

No.2 解答例 It depends. Classwork should always come first. However, some university students have a lot of free time. In such cases, getting a part-time job is a good way to earn extra money and learn responsibility.

解答例の訳 状況によります。教室での学習が常に最優先であるべきです。とはいえ，自由時間がたくさんある大学生もいます。そのような場合，アルバイトの仕事を得ることは，追加のお金を稼いだり責任感を身につけたりする上で効果的な手段です。

解説 解答例では，まずIt depends.「状況による」と，人や状況次第であることを述べ，最優先すべきなのは教室での学習だが，自由時間を多く持つ者にとっては，アルバイトはお金を稼いだり責任感を身につけたりする上での良い手段であると主張している。あるいは，Yesの立場から，Yes. Through working part-time, they can learn many things such as the importance of money. Moreover, they'll have an opportunity to meet new people at workplace.「はい。アルバイトをすることを通じて，彼らはお金の大切さのような多くのことを学ぶことができます。その上，彼らは職場で新しい人と出会う機会が得られるでしょう」などとしても良いだろう。

No.3 **解答例** **No. These days, there are many different types of theft on the Internet. Even large online businesses have had their information stolen by hackers. Traditional, face-to-face businesses are safer.**

解答例の訳 いいえ。近頃では，インターネット上には多種多様な窃盗が存在します。大手のオンライン事業者でさえ，ハッカーによってその情報を盗まれています。従来の対面型の事業者の方が安全です。

解説 解答例では，Noの立場から，個人情報を含めたオンライン上の情報はハッカーに盗まれ得るので，従来の対面型の事業者とのやり取りの方がオンライン事業者よりも安全である点を述べている。解答例とは別に，It depends. Some online businesses are proficient in information management, and generally, they can prevent hackers from stealing their information. However, it is true that there are online businesses which are careless about managing information, so we should always judge whether we can give our personal information to a particular online business.「状況によります。オンライン事業者の中には情報管理に熟達しているところもあり，概して，彼らはハッカーが情報を盗むのを防ぐことができます。しかし，情報管理がずさんなオンライン事業者が存在していることは確かなので，私たちは，個人情報を特定のオンライン事業者に渡すことができるかどうか絶えず判断すべきです」なども可。

No.4 **解答例** **I don't think so. Companies should only hire as many employees as they need. Hiring too many workers would mean the companies become less efficient. In addition, the unemployment rate in Japan is not so bad.**

解答例の訳 そうは思いません。企業は，自分たちに必要なだけの数の従業員しか雇用すべきではありません。従業員を雇用しすぎると，その結果，企業は能率が落ちることになります。さらに，日本の失業率はそんなに悪くありません。

解説 解答例では，Noの立場から，雇用しすぎるとかえって企業の能率が落ちてしまうというデメリットを述べてから，日本の失業率の現状がそれほど悪くはないと述べている。あるいは，Yesの立場で，Yes. Although some people say the unemployment rate in Japan is low, I hear that there are as many as over one million people who cannot work currently. I think this number is high, and the situation has to be improved by the government.「はい。日本の失業率は低いという人もいますが，現在働くことができていない人は100万人を超えると聞いています。私はこの数が高いと思いますし，この状況は政府によって改善されるべきだと思います」と，数字などを引き合いに出しながら答えることもできるだろう。

●準1級　解答用紙●

A面…………マークシート用

B面…………ライティング用

英検®準1級　解答用紙（A面）

【注意事項】

◎HBの黒鉛筆またはシャープペンシル以外の筆記具でのマークは、解答が無効となるので、注意してください。

キリトリ

筆記 解答欄

問題番号		1	2	3	4
1	(1)	①	②	③	④
	(2)	①	②	③	④
	(3)	①	②	③	④
	(4)	①	②	③	④
	(5)	①	②	③	④
	(6)	①	②	③	④
	(7)	①	②	③	④
	(8)	①	②	③	④
	(9)	①	②	③	④
	(10)	①	②	③	④
	(11)	①	②	③	④
	(12)	①	②	③	④
	(13)	①	②	③	④
	(14)	①	②	③	④
	(15)	①	②	③	④
	(16)	①	②	③	④
	(17)	①	②	③	④
	(18)	①	②	③	④
	(19)	①	②	③	④
	(20)	①	②	③	④
	(21)	①	②	③	④
	(22)	①	②	③	④
	(23)	①	②	③	④
	(24)	①	②	③	④
	(25)	①	②	③	④

問題番号		1	2	3	4
2	(26)	①	②	③	④
	(27)	①	②	③	④
	(28)	①	②	③	④
	(29)	①	②	③	④
	(30)	①	②	③	④
	(31)	①	②	③	④

問題番号		1	2	3	4
3	(32)	①	②	③	④
	(33)	①	②	③	④
	(34)	①	②	③	④
	(35)	①	②	③	④
	(36)	①	②	③	④
	(37)	①	②	③	④
	(38)	①	②	③	④
	(39)	①	②	③	④
	(40)	①	②	③	④
	(41)	①	②	③	④

4の解答欄はB面（裏面）にあります。

リスニング 解答欄

問題番号			1	2	3	4
Part 1		No.1	①	②	③	④
		No.2	①	②	③	④
		No.3	①	②	③	④
		No.4	①	②	③	④
		No.5	①	②	③	④
		No.6	①	②	③	④
		No.7	①	②	③	④
		No.8	①	②	③	④
		No.9	①	②	③	④
		No.10	①	②	③	④
		No.11	①	②	③	④
		No.12	①	②	③	④
Part 2	A	No.13	①	②	③	④
		No.14	①	②	③	④
	B	No.15	①	②	③	④
		No.16	①	②	③	④
	C	No.17	①	②	③	④
		No.18	①	②	③	④
	D	No.19	①	②	③	④
		No.20	①	②	③	④
	E	No.21	①	②	③	④
		No.22	①	②	③	④
	F	No.23	①	②	③	④
		No.24	①	②	③	④
Part 3	G	No.25	①	②	③	④
	H	No.26	①	②	③	④
	I	No.27	①	②	③	④
	J	No.28	①	②	③	④
	K	No.29	①	②	③	④

くり返し解く場合は、コピーをとってご利用ください。

英検®準1級　解答用紙(B面)

・指示事項を守り、文字は、はっきり分かりやすく書いてください。
・太枠に囲まれた部分のみが採点の対象です。

4 English Composition

Write your English Composition in the space below.

キリトリ

英検®準1級　解答用紙（A面）

【注意事項】

◎HBの黒鉛筆またはシャープペンシル以外の筆記具でのマークは、解答が無効となるので、注意してください。

筆記 解答欄

問題番号		1	2	3	4
1	(1)	①	②	③	④
	(2)	①	②	③	④
	(3)	①	②	③	④
	(4)	①	②	③	④
	(5)	①	②	③	④
	(6)	①	②	③	④
	(7)	①	②	③	④
	(8)	①	②	③	④
	(9)	①	②	③	④
	(10)	①	②	③	④
	(11)	①	②	③	④
	(12)	①	②	③	④
	(13)	①	②	③	④
	(14)	①	②	③	④
	(15)	①	②	③	④
	(16)	①	②	③	④
	(17)	①	②	③	④
	(18)	①	②	③	④
	(19)	①	②	③	④
	(20)	①	②	③	④
	(21)	①	②	③	④
	(22)	①	②	③	④
	(23)	①	②	③	④
	(24)	①	②	③	④
	(25)	①	②	③	④

問題番号		1	2	3	4
2	(26)	①	②	③	④
	(27)	①	②	③	④
	(28)	①	②	③	④
	(29)	①	②	③	④
	(30)	①	②	③	④
	(31)	①	②	③	④

問題番号		1	2	3	4
3	(32)	①	②	③	④
	(33)	①	②	③	④
	(34)	①	②	③	④
	(35)	①	②	③	④
	(36)	①	②	③	④
	(37)	①	②	③	④
	(38)	①	②	③	④
	(39)	①	②	③	④
	(40)	①	②	③	④
	(41)	①	②	③	④

4の解答欄はB面（裏面）にあります。

リスニング 解答欄

問題番号			1	2	3	4
Part 1		No.1	①	②	③	④
		No.2	①	②	③	④
		No.3	①	②	③	④
		No.4	①	②	③	④
		No.5	①	②	③	④
		No.6	①	②	③	④
		No.7	①	②	③	④
		No.8	①	②	③	④
		No.9	①	②	③	④
		No.10	①	②	③	④
		No.11	①	②	③	④
		No.12	①	②	③	④
Part 2	A	No.13	①	②	③	④
		No.14	①	②	③	④
	B	No.15	①	②	③	④
		No.16	①	②	③	④
	C	No.17	①	②	③	④
		No.18	①	②	③	④
	D	No.19	①	②	③	④
		No.20	①	②	③	④
	E	No.21	①	②	③	④
		No.22	①	②	③	④
	F	No.23	①	②	③	④
		No.24	①	②	③	④
Part 3	G	No.25	①	②	③	④
	H	No.26	①	②	③	④
	I	No.27	①	②	③	④
	J	No.28	①	②	③	④
	K	No.29	①	②	③	④

キリトリ

くり返し解く場合は、コピーをとってご利用ください。

英検®準1級　解答用紙(B面)

・指示事項を守り、文字は、はっきり分かりやすく書いてください。
・太枠に囲まれた部分のみが採点の対象です。

4 English Composition

Write your English Composition in the space below.

キリトリ

英検®準1級　解答用紙(A面)

【注意事項】

◎HBの黒鉛筆またはシャープペンシル以外の筆記具でのマークは、解答が無効となるので、注意してください。

筆記 解答欄

問題番号		1	2	3	4
1	(1)	①	②	③	④
	(2)	①	②	③	④
	(3)	①	②	③	④
	(4)	①	②	③	④
	(5)	①	②	③	④
	(6)	①	②	③	④
	(7)	①	②	③	④
	(8)	①	②	③	④
	(9)	①	②	③	④
	(10)	①	②	③	④
	(11)	①	②	③	④
	(12)	①	②	③	④
	(13)	①	②	③	④
	(14)	①	②	③	④
	(15)	①	②	③	④
	(16)	①	②	③	④
	(17)	①	②	③	④
	(18)	①	②	③	④
	(19)	①	②	③	④
	(20)	①	②	③	④
	(21)	①	②	③	④
	(22)	①	②	③	④
	(23)	①	②	③	④
	(24)	①	②	③	④
	(25)	①	②	③	④

問題番号		1	2	3	4
2	(26)	①	②	③	④
	(27)	①	②	③	④
	(28)	①	②	③	④
	(29)	①	②	③	④
	(30)	①	②	③	④
	(31)	①	②	③	④

問題番号		1	2	3	4
3	(32)	①	②	③	④
	(33)	①	②	③	④
	(34)	①	②	③	④
	(35)	①	②	③	④
	(36)	①	②	③	④
	(37)	①	②	③	④
	(38)	①	②	③	④
	(39)	①	②	③	④
	(40)	①	②	③	④
	(41)	①	②	③	④

4の解答欄はB面(裏面)にあります。

リスニング 解答欄

問題番号			1	2	3	4
Part 1		No.1	①	②	③	④
		No.2	①	②	③	④
		No.3	①	②	③	④
		No.4	①	②	③	④
		No.5	①	②	③	④
		No.6	①	②	③	④
		No.7	①	②	③	④
		No.8	①	②	③	④
		No.9	①	②	③	④
		No.10	①	②	③	④
		No.11	①	②	③	④
		No.12	①	②	③	④
Part 2	A	No.13	①	②	③	④
		No.14	①	②	③	④
	B	No.15	①	②	③	④
		No.16	①	②	③	④
	C	No.17	①	②	③	④
		No.18	①	②	③	④
	D	No.19	①	②	③	④
		No.20	①	②	③	④
	E	No.21	①	②	③	④
		No.22	①	②	③	④
	F	No.23	①	②	③	④
		No.24	①	②	③	④
Part 3	G	No.25	①	②	③	④
	H	No.26	①	②	③	④
	I	No.27	①	②	③	④
	J	No.28	①	②	③	④
	K	No.29	①	②	③	④

キリトリ

くり返し解く場合は、コピーをとってご利用ください。

英検®準1級　解答用紙(B面)

・指示事項を守り、文字は、はっきり分かりやすく書いてください。
・太枠に囲まれた部分のみが採点の対象です。

4 English Composition

Write your English Composition in the space below.

キリトリ

英検®準1級　解答用紙(A面)

【注意事項】

◎HBの黒鉛筆またはシャープペンシル以外の筆記具でのマークは、解答が無効となるので、注意してください。

キリトリ

筆記 解答欄		

問題番号		1	2	3	4
1	(1)	①	②	③	④
	(2)	①	②	③	④
	(3)	①	②	③	④
	(4)	①	②	③	④
	(5)	①	②	③	④
	(6)	①	②	③	④
	(7)	①	②	③	④
	(8)	①	②	③	④
	(9)	①	②	③	④
	(10)	①	②	③	④
	(11)	①	②	③	④
	(12)	①	②	③	④
	(13)	①	②	③	④
	(14)	①	②	③	④
	(15)	①	②	③	④
	(16)	①	②	③	④
	(17)	①	②	③	④
	(18)	①	②	③	④
	(19)	①	②	③	④
	(20)	①	②	③	④
	(21)	①	②	③	④
	(22)	①	②	③	④
	(23)	①	②	③	④
	(24)	①	②	③	④
	(25)	①	②	③	④

問題番号		1	2	3	4
2	(26)	①	②	③	④
	(27)	①	②	③	④
	(28)	①	②	③	④
	(29)	①	②	③	④
	(30)	①	②	③	④
	(31)	①	②	③	④

問題番号		1	2	3	4
3	(32)	①	②	③	④
	(33)	①	②	③	④
	(34)	①	②	③	④
	(35)	①	②	③	④
	(36)	①	②	③	④
	(37)	①	②	③	④
	(38)	①	②	③	④
	(39)	①	②	③	④
	(40)	①	②	③	④
	(41)	①	②	③	④

4の解答欄はB面(裏面)にあります。

リスニング 解答欄

問題番号			1	2	3	4
Part 1		No.1	①	②	③	④
		No.2	①	②	③	④
		No.3	①	②	③	④
		No.4	①	②	③	④
		No.5	①	②	③	④
		No.6	①	②	③	④
		No.7	①	②	③	④
		No.8	①	②	③	④
		No.9	①	②	③	④
		No.10	①	②	③	④
		No.11	①	②	③	④
		No.12	①	②	③	④
Part 2	A	No.13	①	②	③	④
		No.14	①	②	③	④
	B	No.15	①	②	③	④
		No.16	①	②	③	④
	C	No.17	①	②	③	④
		No.18	①	②	③	④
	D	No.19	①	②	③	④
		No.20	①	②	③	④
	E	No.21	①	②	③	④
		No.22	①	②	③	④
	F	No.23	①	②	③	④
		No.24	①	②	③	④
Part 3	G	No.25	①	②	③	④
	H	No.26	①	②	③	④
	I	No.27	①	②	③	④
	J	No.28	①	②	③	④
	K	No.29	①	②	③	④

くり返し解く場合は、コピーをとってご利用ください。

英検®準1級　解答用紙(B面)

・指示事項を守り、文字は、はっきり分かりやすく書いてください。
・太枠に囲まれた部分のみが採点の対象です。

4 English Composition

Write your English Composition in the space below.

キリトリ

英検®準1級　解答用紙(A面)

【注意事項】

◎HBの黒鉛筆またはシャープペンシル以外の筆記具でのマークは、解答が無効となるので、注意してください。

キリトリ

筆記 解答欄

問題番号		1	2	3	4
1	(1)	①	②	③	④
	(2)	①	②	③	④
	(3)	①	②	③	④
	(4)	①	②	③	④
	(5)	①	②	③	④
	(6)	①	②	③	④
	(7)	①	②	③	④
	(8)	①	②	③	④
	(9)	①	②	③	④
	(10)	①	②	③	④
	(11)	①	②	③	④
	(12)	①	②	③	④
	(13)	①	②	③	④
	(14)	①	②	③	④
	(15)	①	②	③	④
	(16)	①	②	③	④
	(17)	①	②	③	④
	(18)	①	②	③	④
	(19)	①	②	③	④
	(20)	①	②	③	④
	(21)	①	②	③	④
	(22)	①	②	③	④
	(23)	①	②	③	④
	(24)	①	②	③	④
	(25)	①	②	③	④

問題番号		1	2	3	4
2	(26)	①	②	③	④
	(27)	①	②	③	④
	(28)	①	②	③	④
	(29)	①	②	③	④
	(30)	①	②	③	④
	(31)	①	②	③	④

問題番号		1	2	3	4
3	(32)	①	②	③	④
	(33)	①	②	③	④
	(34)	①	②	③	④
	(35)	①	②	③	④
	(36)	①	②	③	④
	(37)	①	②	③	④
	(38)	①	②	③	④
	(39)	①	②	③	④
	(40)	①	②	③	④
	(41)	①	②	③	④

4の解答欄はB面(裏面)にあります。

リスニング 解答欄

問題番号			1	2	3	4
Part 1		No.1	①	②	③	④
		No.2	①	②	③	④
		No.3	①	②	③	④
		No.4	①	②	③	④
		No.5	①	②	③	④
		No.6	①	②	③	④
		No.7	①	②	③	④
		No.8	①	②	③	④
		No.9	①	②	③	④
		No.10	①	②	③	④
		No.11	①	②	③	④
		No.12	①	②	③	④
Part 2	A	No.13	①	②	③	④
		No.14	①	②	③	④
	B	No.15	①	②	③	④
		No.16	①	②	③	④
	C	No.17	①	②	③	④
		No.18	①	②	③	④
	D	No.19	①	②	③	④
		No.20	①	②	③	④
	E	No.21	①	②	③	④
		No.22	①	②	③	④
	F	No.23	①	②	③	④
		No.24	①	②	③	④
Part 3	G	No.25	①	②	③	④
	H	No.26	①	②	③	④
	I	No.27	①	②	③	④
	J	No.28	①	②	③	④
	K	No.29	①	②	③	④

くり返し解く場合は、コピーをとってご利用ください。

英検®準1級　解答用紙(B面)

・指示事項を守り、文字は、はっきり分かりやすく書いてください。
・太枠に囲まれた部分のみが採点の対象です。

4 English Composition

Write your English Composition in the space below.

キリトリ

英検®準1級　解答用紙（A面）

【注意事項】

◎HBの黒鉛筆またはシャープペンシル以外の筆記具でのマークは、解答が無効となるので、注意してください。

キリトリ

筆記 解答欄

問題番号		1	2	3	4
1	(1)	①	②	③	④
	(2)	①	②	③	④
	(3)	①	②	③	④
	(4)	①	②	③	④
	(5)	①	②	③	④
	(6)	①	②	③	④
	(7)	①	②	③	④
	(8)	①	②	③	④
	(9)	①	②	③	④
	(10)	①	②	③	④
	(11)	①	②	③	④
	(12)	①	②	③	④
	(13)	①	②	③	④
	(14)	①	②	③	④
	(15)	①	②	③	④
	(16)	①	②	③	④
	(17)	①	②	③	④
	(18)	①	②	③	④
	(19)	①	②	③	④
	(20)	①	②	③	④
	(21)	①	②	③	④
	(22)	①	②	③	④
	(23)	①	②	③	④
	(24)	①	②	③	④
	(25)	①	②	③	④

問題番号		1	2	3	4
2	(26)	①	②	③	④
	(27)	①	②	③	④
	(28)	①	②	③	④
	(29)	①	②	③	④
	(30)	①	②	③	④
	(31)	①	②	③	④

問題番号		1	2	3	4
3	(32)	①	②	③	④
	(33)	①	②	③	④
	(34)	①	②	③	④
	(35)	①	②	③	④
	(36)	①	②	③	④
	(37)	①	②	③	④
	(38)	①	②	③	④
	(39)	①	②	③	④
	(40)	①	②	③	④
	(41)	①	②	③	④

4の解答欄はB面（裏面）にあります。

リスニング 解答欄

問題番号			1	2	3	4
Part 1		No.1	①	②	③	④
		No.2	①	②	③	④
		No.3	①	②	③	④
		No.4	①	②	③	④
		No.5	①	②	③	④
		No.6	①	②	③	④
		No.7	①	②	③	④
		No.8	①	②	③	④
		No.9	①	②	③	④
		No.10	①	②	③	④
		No.11	①	②	③	④
		No.12	①	②	③	④
Part 2	A	No.13	①	②	③	④
		No.14	①	②	③	④
	B	No.15	①	②	③	④
		No.16	①	②	③	④
	C	No.17	①	②	③	④
		No.18	①	②	③	④
	D	No.19	①	②	③	④
		No.20	①	②	③	④
	E	No.21	①	②	③	④
		No.22	①	②	③	④
	F	No.23	①	②	③	④
		No.24	①	②	③	④
Part 3	G	No.25	①	②	③	④
	H	No.26	①	②	③	④
	I	No.27	①	②	③	④
	J	No.28	①	②	③	④
	K	No.29	①	②	③	④

くり返し解く場合は、コピーをとってご利用ください。

英検® 準1級　解答用紙（B面）

・指示事項を守り、文字は、はっきり分かりやすく書いてください。
・太枠に囲まれた部分のみが採点の対象です。

4 English Composition

Write your English Composition in the space below.

キリトリ

矢印の方向に引くと切り離せます。